# LOCAL EXPLORER

# WILTSHIRE

## & SWINDON

www.philips-maps.co.uk

Published by Philip's, a division of
Octopus Publishing Group Ltd
www.octopusbooks.co.uk
Carmelite House, 50 Victoria Embankment,
London EC4Y 0DZ
An Hachette UK Company
www.hachette.co.uk

First edition 2024
First impression 2024
WILDA

ISBN 978-1-84907-640-1

© Philip's 2024

This product includes mapping data licensed from Ordnance Survey® with the permission of the Controller of His Majesty's Stationery Office. © Crown copyright 2024. All rights reserved. Licence number 100011710.

*All streets named in the source Ordnance Survey dataset at the time of going to press are included in this Philip's Street Atlas.

Photographic acknowledgements:
*Alamy Stock Photo:* /David Askham III top left; /robertharding II top; /Donald Slack II bottom; /Anna Stowe Landscapes UK III top right; /Paul Strawson III bottom.
*Shutterstock:* /Steffen.E front cover.

Printed in China

# CONTENTS

| II | **Best places to visit** |
| IV | **Key to map pages** |
| VI | **Route planning** |
| X | **Key to map symbols** |

| 1 | **Street maps** at 3½ inches to 1 mile |
| 163 | **Street maps** at 1¾ inches to 1 mile |
| 213 | **Street maps** at 3½ inches to 1 mile |
| 218 | **Town maps** of Andover and Frome |

| 219 | **Index** of towns, villages, streets, hospitals, industrial estates, railway stations, schools, shopping centres, universities and places of interest |

# Best places to visit

## Outdoors

**Avebury** Internationally significant collection of Neolithic and Bronze Age monuments. The circular bank and ditch of **Avebury Henge** enclose a large stone circle, within which are the remains of two smaller circles as well as Avebury village. The other nearby sites are West Kennet Avenue, the Sanctuary, Silbury Hill, West Kennet Long Barrow and Windmill Hill. Within the village is **Avebury Manor**, a 16th-century manor house with rooms furnished and decorated as they would have been at various points in the house's history. Alexander Keiller, the main archaeologist on the Avebury sites, lived here in the 1920s and 30s. Important finds from his local excavations are displayed in the **Alexander Keiller Museum**.
💻 www.nationaltrust.org.uk
💻 www.english-heritage.org.uk **173 C8**

**Bratton Camp and Westbury White Horse** Iron Age hillfort and Neolithic long barrow. Visitors can walk among the earth banks and ditches and see the large white horse, a local landmark believed to have been cut into the hillside in the late 17th century. The expanse of chalk grassland is an important habitat for some rare butterflies. *Westbury* 💻 www.english-heritage.org.uk **186 A6 & 109 F3**

**Cherhill Down and White Horse** Area of chalk downland, an important habitat for rare butterflies and wildflowers. A steep path leads up to the striking white horse, which was carved into the chalk hillside in the 18th century. Also on Cherhill Down is the Lansdowne Monument, a Victorian obelisk visible for miles around. On top of the hill, earth banks and ditches indicate the location of the Iron Age hillfort Oldbury Castle. *Calne* 💻 www.nationaltrust.org.uk **172 D8**

**Iford Manor Garden** Grade 1-listed garden designed by renowned Edwardian garden designer Harold Peto, who lived in the house from 1899 to 1933. The garden is noted for its architectural features, such as statues, ponds and terraces. There are walks in the wider estate, a café and a restaurant. *Bradford on Avon* 💻 www.ifordmanor.co.uk **99 E3**

**Larmer Tree Gardens** Gardens created by the ethnologist and archae-

ologist General Pitt Rivers in the late 19th century and restored in the late 20th century. Some of the original garden buildings remain and there is a children's trail. *Shaftesbury* 💻 www.larmertree.co.uk **207 B3**

**Ludgershall Castle** Remains of a castle begun in the 11th century and developed by King John and Henry III in the 13th. Some ruined walls and a tower remain, as well as the foundations of the royal apartments; also visible are the earthwork banks and ditches surrounding the site. *Ludgershall* 💻 www.english-heritage.org.uk **192 A6**

**Old Sarum** Well-preserved earthworks marking the site of an Iron Age hillfort, within which are the ruins of a 12th-century castle and cathedral. It was an important centre in the 11th and 12th centuries, and the original site of Salisbury Cathedral. The ruins of a gatehouse, keep and courtyard house can be seen. Little of the cathedral remains, but its footprint is marked in cement. There are footpaths in the surrounding grounds.
💻 www.english-heritage.org.uk **145 F6**

**Stonehenge** Prehistoric monument believed to be about 4,500 years old, comprising a circle of huge standing stones, with some horizontal lintel stones connecting them. The purpose of the circle is unclear, but its alignment with the sun on solstices is believed to be significant. Visitors can walk around the outside of the stone circle. At the visitor centre is an exhibition with henge artefacts and recreated Neolithic houses.
💻 www.english-heritage.org.uk **197 E5**

**Stourhead** Gardens surrounding a grand Palladian mansion. The gardens were designed in the early 18th century and are dotted with the architectural features fashionable at the time, including lakeside Roman-style temples, a grotto, obelisk and ornamental bridge. The house contains important collections of furniture and fine art. There are walking trails and family activities. Within the wider estate are **King Alfred's Tower**, a Victorian folly, and White Sheet Hill, the site of Neolithic, Bronze Age and Iron Age settlements. *Warminster* 💻 www.nationaltrust.org.uk **123 F1**

▲ **Salisbury Cathedral**

▶ **Stonehenge**

**Woodhenge** Neolithic monument, near to Stonehenge and part of the same World Heritage Site. It is made up of a series of concentric ovals of timber posts, now marked with concrete pillars, surrounded by an earth bank and ditch. The posts are aligned with midsummer sunrise. Nearby are the earthworks of Durrington Walls.
💻 www.english-heritage.org.uk
💻 www.nationaltrust.org.uk **217 A7**

## Towns & villages

**Amesbury** Small market town near Stonehenge and Woodhenge, known for the early Bronze Age grave of the Amesbury Archer. Its contents are now on display in the Salisbury Museum. The small Amesbury History Centre relates the long history of the town. There are walks in the surrounding historic landscape, and from here to Stonehenge. **217 C4**

**Bradford on Avon** Historic town on the River Avon and the Kennet and Avon Canal, an important settlement in Saxon times and later a centre for the wool, weaving and rubber industries. The medieval town centre clusters around the 14th-century town bridge and The Shambles, a street of historic buildings. Nearby, **St Laurence's Church** is an unusually complete Saxon building which may date back as far as the 8th century. **Bradford on Avon Museum** tells the history of the town. Abbey Mill, a former 19th-century cloth factory, is a reminder of the town's industrial past, as is the Iron Duke, a large calender machine from the rubber industry. **The Hall**, a manor house built in the 1500s and remodelled in the early 1600s, was owned by wealthy industrialists. From the **Bradford on Avon wharf**, with its traditional canal heritage architecture, the towpath passes the **Tithe Barn**, one of the largest medieval barns in England, and through Barton Farm Country Park towards the Avoncliff Aqueduct, which carries the canal over the River Avon. 💻 www.bradfordonavonmuseum.co.uk **100 E6**

**Cricklade** Small Saxon town, site of a royal mint in the 11th century. It is the first town downstream on the River Thames. St Sampson's and St Mary's are 12th-century churches with Saxon roots. The small **Cricklade Museum**, housed in an 1850s Baptist Chapel, has items from the 19th and 20th centuries, including some Cricklade Pottery. On the outskirts of town is the **North Meadow Nature Reserve**, on the flood plain of the rivers Thames and Churn. Rare wildflowers, insects and birds flourish in this rare lowland hay meadow. 💻 www.cricklademuseum.co.uk **19 E7**

**Devizes** Medieval market town, an important trading centre for textiles and corn, and later brewing and tobacco. Among the elegant 18th- and 19th-century buildings are the Victorian Corn Exchange, which dominates the Market Place, the Georgian town hall and the Bear Hotel, a 16th-century coaching inn. The **Wiltshire Museum** houses an important collection of archaeological artefacts, including from nearby Avebury. There are interactive displays and activities. Also in

the centre are two 12th-century churches, St John's and St Mary's. On the outskirts are the famous **Caen Hill Locks**. Here, the Kennet and Avon Canal rises nearly 240 feet thanks to a ladder of 29 locks. There are walks along the towpath, boat rides and a small museum.
💻 www.wiltshiremuseum.org.uk **214 A3**

**Malmesbury** Historic market town on the River Avon, with the beautiful 12th-century **Malmesbury Abbey** at its heart. Much of the building has been lost, but the nave remains. Of particular interest are the tomb of King Athelstan and a 15th-century illuminated bible. Nearby is an elaborately carved 15th-century Market Cross and a 16th-century manor house, **Abbey House** (private), with five acres of gardens that can be visited. The **Athelstan Museum** has a varied collection that includes Iron Age artefacts, local agricultural heritage and social history. There are talks and family activities.
💻 www.malmesburyabbey.com **28 B3**

**Marlborough** Attractive market town on the River Kennet. Notable among the many historic buildings on the High Street is the 17th-century **Merchant's House**, which belonged to a wealthy silk merchant. The house and garden are full of period features and artefacts and provide an insight into middle-class life at the time. Also on the High Street is **St Peter's Church**, built in the 15th century and restored in Victorian times. Visitors can climb the tower to see the Priest's Room and the belfry. The **Stonebridge Wild River Reserve** encompasses a large area of water meadow on the edge of town. Visitors might be able to spot water voles, herons and kingfishers.
💻 www.themerchantshouse.co.uk **213 F3**

**Salisbury** Medieval city at the confluence of the rivers Avon, Bourne and Nadder, with a beautiful 13th-century cathedral at its core. Early English Gothic in style, the **cathedral** houses one of the four original copies of the Magna Carta and has the world's oldest working mechanical clock. Its spire is the tallest in the country, and visitors can climb within it for a fascinating view over the nave and out over the city. The cathedral is noted for its contemporary stained glass and spacious cloisters. The large Cathedral Close is filled with historic buildings, including **Arundells**, home of former prime minister Edward Heath, and **Mompesson House**, a grand Queen Anne townhouse. Arundells displays Heath's collection of artworks, including unusual gifts from world leaders. Mompesson House is noted for its elaborate stucco decoration. The **Salisbury Museum** has an important archaeology collection, with significant artefacts from Stonehenge and Old Sarum among others, as well as galleries devoted to ceramics and glass, textiles and social history. The **Rifles Berkshire and Wiltshire Museum** relates the regiments' involvement in wars from the 19th century up to the present day. Salisbury's imposing Guildhall (built 1795) looks over the market place, which is lined with historic buildings. A weekly market

has been held here for 800 years. Beside the River Avon, Queen Elizabeth Gardens has spacious lawns, a playground and a sensory garden. Churchill Gardens is a large activity-filled riverside park with playgrounds, a skatepark, a sports area and paths for walking and cycling. On the outskirts of the city, the **River Bourne Community Farm** has farm animals, birds and small animals, many of which can be fed. There are nature trails round the farm and the adjoining water meadows. 🖳 www.salisburycathedral.org.uk **152 C7**

**Swindon** Wiltshire's largest town, a hub for business and shopping. It was a small market town until the arrival of the Great Western Railway in the 1840s. The **STEAM museum** relates the railway's history with interactive displays, films and artefacts as well as original locomotives and rolling stock. It is housed in what was the GWR's Swindon Works. There are events and activities. The **Museum of Computing** tells the history of computing and digital development, with hands-on activities and exhibits. On the outskirts of Swindon, the **Coate Water Park** is a large country park with a reservoir, lake, nature reserve and woodland areas, where waterfowl and woodland birds flourish. There are walking routes and a cafe. 🖳 www.museumofcomputing.org.uk 🖳 www.steam-museum.org.uk **50 E4**

## Buildings

**Bowood House** Georgian country house within gardens and parkland designed by Capability Brown in the 1760s. The state rooms display an interesting collection of artworks and books, as well as more unusual items, such as Napoleon's death mask. Visitors can see the room where Joseph Priestley discovered oxygen in 1774. There are Italianate terraced gardens and colourful herbaceous borders, as well as spacious lawns and woodlands leading to an ornamental lake. There is an adventure playground and children's activities. *Calne* 🖳 www.bowood.org **88 C8**

**Corsham Court** Elizabethan country house built on the site of a 10th-century royal manor house and substantially remodelled in the mid 18th century. Its Picture Gallery houses an important collection of paintings, notably works by Antony van Dyck, Fra Filippo Lippi and Joshua Reynolds. The grounds, designed by Capability Brown, include formal gardens, a lake and parkland. Also in Corsham are 17th-century almshouses and a school room built by the then owners of Corsham Court. 🖳 www.corsham-court.co.uk **77 A2**

**Crofton Beam Engines** Two early 19th-century steam engines which pumped water to the highest point of the Kennet and Avon Canal. They have been restored to working order and operate on steaming days. *Burbage* 🖳 www.croftonbeamengines.org **176 A1**

**Great Chalfield Manor** 15th-century manor house and gardens, restored in the early 20th century. Visitors can tour its atmospheric, medieval rooms; the hall, at the heart of the house, is noted for its oriel windows. The gardens are Arts and Crafts in style, with ponds, terraces, colourful borders and topiary 'rooms'. *Melksham.* 🖳 www.nationaltrust.org.uk **92 D3**

**Lacock Abbey** Country house, once owned by the Victorian photography pioneer William Henry Fox Talbot. The house was founded as a nunnery in the 13th century, converted into a private house in the 16th century, and remodelled in the early 18th. The interior reflects its varied history and retains its medieval stone cloister and Gothic-style Great Hall. Within the grounds are a woodland garden, rose garden, orchard and a wildflower meadow. The **Fox Talbot Museum**, in a 16th-century barn, relates the history of photography and hosts changing exhibitions. *Chippenham* 🖳 www.nationaltrust.org.uk **86 D5**

**Longleat** See under family activities

**Lydiard Park** Grand country house and parkland. The house dates from the medieval period but was remodelled in the 1740s in Palladian style, with typical pediment, symmetry and classical details. The state rooms are noted for their elaborate plasterwork and fireplaces. Visitors can also explore St Mary's Church (12th century) and the Georgian walled garden. Paths lead around the wider estate, encompassing lawns, woodlands and lakes. There are children's trails in the house, a playground and events. *Swindon* 🖳 www.lydiardpark.org.uk **48 E6**

**Old Wardour Castle** Ruins of a fortified manor house in a picturesque lake-side setting. It was built in the 14th century to an unusual hexagonal design, but severely damaged in the 1640s during the Civil War. The ruins were later reimagined as the focal point of a pleasure park. Still visible are fireplaces, stone carvings and bread ovens, and it is possible to climb the East Tower for far-reaching views. There is an 18th-century banqueting house beside the lake. www.english-heritage.org.uk **203 D5**

**Westwood Manor** Small stone manor house, dating from the 15th century with Tudor and Jacobean alterations. The decorative plasterwork, wall panelling and ceilings have been carefully restored, and there is some interesting period furniture. Particularly noteworthy are two early keyboard instruments – a virginal from 1537 and an early 18th-century spinet, both in working order. The garden has modern topiary and ponds. *Bradford on Avon* 🖳 www.nationaltrust.org.uk **100 A3**

**Wilton House** Imposing country house, with a significant art collection. Of the original house, only a Tudor tower remains; the rest was remodelled by Inigo Jones in the 17th century and James Wyatt

in the 19th. The most impressive features are the Palladian South Front and the state rooms, which are lavishly decorated and furnished. Paintings and statuary are on display throughout. Garden highlights are the Palladian Bridge, a water garden and a rose garden. There is an adventure playground and special events. 🖳 www.wiltonhouse.co.uk **144 D2**

## Museums & galleries

**Atwell-Wilson Motor Museum** Small museum with an interesting collection of cars and motorbikes, as well as a reconstructed 1930s garage. The exhibits range from classic vehicles to rare models, including some from the USA. There is also a display of motoring memorabilia. *Calne* 🖳 https://atwellwilson.org.uk **89 D7**

**Boscombe Down Aviation Collection** Collection of aircraft, cockpits and weapons associated with Boscombe Down airfield, a centre for the development of military flight since 1917. Visitors can sit in many of the cockpits and see aircraft being restored. There are talks and occasional special events. *Salisbury* 🖳 www.boscombedownaviation collection.co.uk **198 E3**

**REME Museum** Museum of the Royal Electrical and Mechanical Engineers from their formation during World War 2 up to the present day. There are family activities and workshops, changing exhibitions and hands-on displays. *Lyneham* 🖳 www.rememuseum.org.uk **60 A1**

**Trowbridge Museum** Museum in a former woollen cloth mill, Trowbridge's largest and last working mill. It relates the history of the town from its development in medieval times to its role as a centre in the West Country wool trade. Its collection encompasses rare machinery and artefacts from the textile trade, as well as costumes, paintings and photographs relating the social history of the town and surrounding area. There are hands-on activities and workshops for all ages. 🖳 https://trowbridgemuseum.co.uk **105 D8**

▲ Caen Hill Locks near Devizes
◄ STEAM museum at Swindon

## Family activities

**Cholderton Rare Breeds Farm** Farm park which focuses on rare breeds of farm animals. Visitors can see goats, ponies, donkeys and alpacas among others, with opportunities to interact with the animals. Smaller animals can be handled, and alpaca walking can be organised. There are woodland play areas and a café. Tours and tastings can be arranged at the adjoining vineyard. *Amesbury* 🖳 https://choldertonrarebreedsfarm.com **199 A5**

**Longleat** Animal park in the grounds of an Elizabeth manor house. The drive-through safari passes through enclosures with lions, tigers, wolves and monkeys among others. There is a boat ride, along-side sea lions, and an on-foot area with koalas, red pandas, meerkats, crocodiles and more. The imposing house can also be visited. It is noted for its Elizabethan Great Hall, ornate state rooms and ceilings, and its important collection of paintings, tapestries and historic documents. There are formal gardens, and extensive parkland designed by Capability Brown. *Warminster* 🖳 www.longleat.co.uk **115 B4**

**Roves Farm** Working livestock farm and family farm park. Visitors can see and interact with goats, sheep, donkeys and alpacas among others, and there are often piglets in the barn. There is also a pets' corner, with handling and feeding activities. Sheep, pigs and cows are reared on the wider farm, which can be toured on tractor rides. There are indoor and outdoor play areas and an activity trail. *Swindon* 🖳 https://rovesfarm.co.uk **37 B6**

**Studley Grange** Butterfly house, zoo and farm park. Visitors can walk among hundreds of species of butterfly within the tropical butterfly house. Animals in the small zoo area include meerkats, wallabies and reptiles. The farm park has traditional farm animals – cows, pigs, sheep – as well as pets that can be handled, and there are trailer rides. Also on site are a soft play area and a garden centre. *Swindon* 🖳 www.studleygrange.co.uk **48 F1**

**Swindon & Cricklade Railway** Heritage railway which runs between Hayes Knoll station, where there is a locomotive shed and restoration centre, and Taw Valley Halt, with access to Mouldon Hill Country Park. The main visitor centre is at Blunsdon, where there is a small museum of railway memorabilia and a wartime museum, with a collection relating to the wartime history of the line. The railway runs steam and diesel trains. There are special events. 🖳 https://swindon-cricklade-railway.org **33 F8**

◄ Lacock Abbey

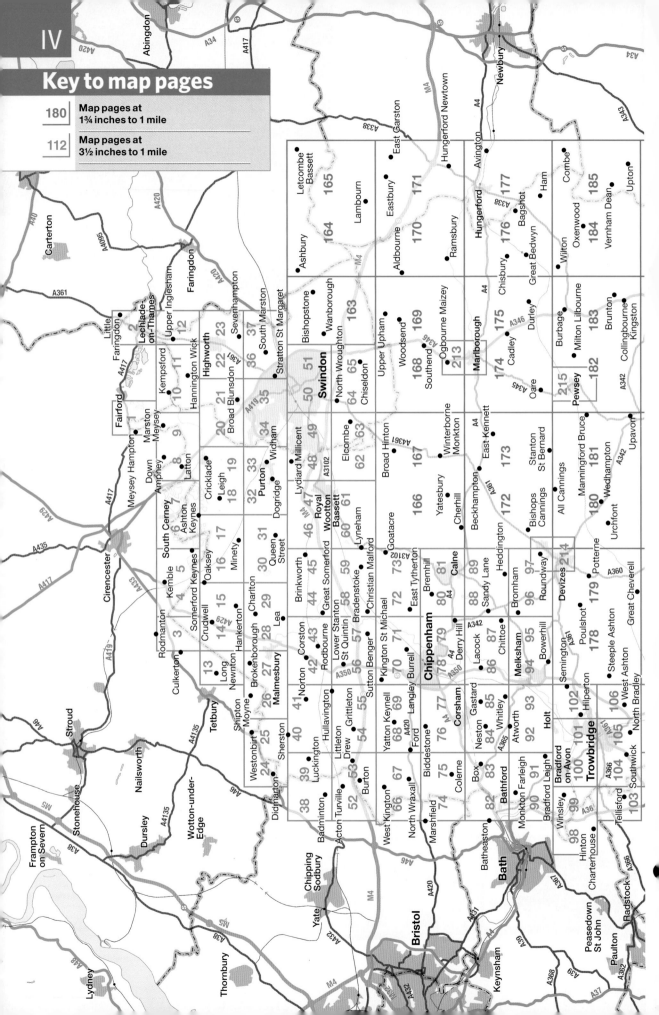

# IV

## Key to map pages

| | |
|---|---|
| **180** | Map pages at 1¾ inches to 1 mile |
| **112** | Map pages at 3½ inches to 1 mile |

V

Whitchurch · Whitchurch · Winchester · Twyford · Bishopstoke · Eastleigh · Netley · Fawley · Hythe · Holbury · Blackfield · Southampton · Totton · Dibden Purlieu · Romsey · Lyndhurst · Brockenhurst

Wildhern **193** · Penton Mewsey · Andover **218** · Ludgershall **192** · Kimpton · Everleigh · North Tidworth **216** **191** · Coombe **190** · Ablington · Fittleton · Bulford Camp · Durrington **198 217** · Amesbury · Boscombe · Newton Tony · Idmiston **134** · Lopcombe Corner **135** · Middle Winterslow · Pitton **148** · Farley · West Grimstead **155 154** · West Dean · Plaitford **212** · Nomansland · Bramshaw

West Chisenbury · Larkhill · **189 188** · Tilshead · Orcheston **196 197** · Winterbourne Stoke · Berwick St James · Stapleford—Upper Woodford **130 131** · Lake · South Newton **145** · Winterbourne **146 147** Dauntsey · **Salisbury 152 153** Whaddon · Milford · Nunton **159 158** · Homington · Charlton-All-Saints **157** · Downton **211 210** · Breamore · Woodgreen · Godshill · **Fordingbridge** · Ringwood

West Lavington · Edington · Bratton **186** · Chitterne **187 195** · Heytesbury · Tytherington **194** · Codford St Mary · Hanging Langford **201 200** · Chilmark · Baverstock **142 143** · Barford St Martin · Compton Chamberlayne **150 151** · Fovant · Coombe Bissett · Harnham · **Wilton 144** · Great Wishford **128 129** · Martin **208 209** · Pentridge · Damerham · Woodyates · Sixpenny Handley · Farnham **207** · Ashmore **206** · Cann Common · Berwick St John · Tisbury · Semley **202 203** · Shaftesbury · Sedgehill · Motcombe · Gillingham · Wincanton

Westbury **108 109** · Dilton Marsh **112 113** · Upton Scudamore · **Warminster 116 117** · Crockerton · Sutton Veny · Longbridge Deverill · Brixton Deverill **120 121** · Kingston Deverill **126 127** · Higher Pertwood · West Knoyle · East Knoyle **140 141** · Lower Rudge **107** · Corsley Heath **110 111 114 115** · Chapmanslade · Horningsham **118 119** · Maiden Bradley · Kilmington **124 125** · **Mere 138 139** · Zeals · Stourton **137** · Bourton **136** · North Brewham **122 123** · Frome **218** · Bruton · Castle Cary · Shepton Mallet · Evercreech

Scale 0 5 10 15 20 km · 5 10 miles

Blandford Forum · Verwood · Ferndown · Wimborne Minster · Stalbridge · Sturminster Newton · Milborne Port · Sherborne

# Route planning

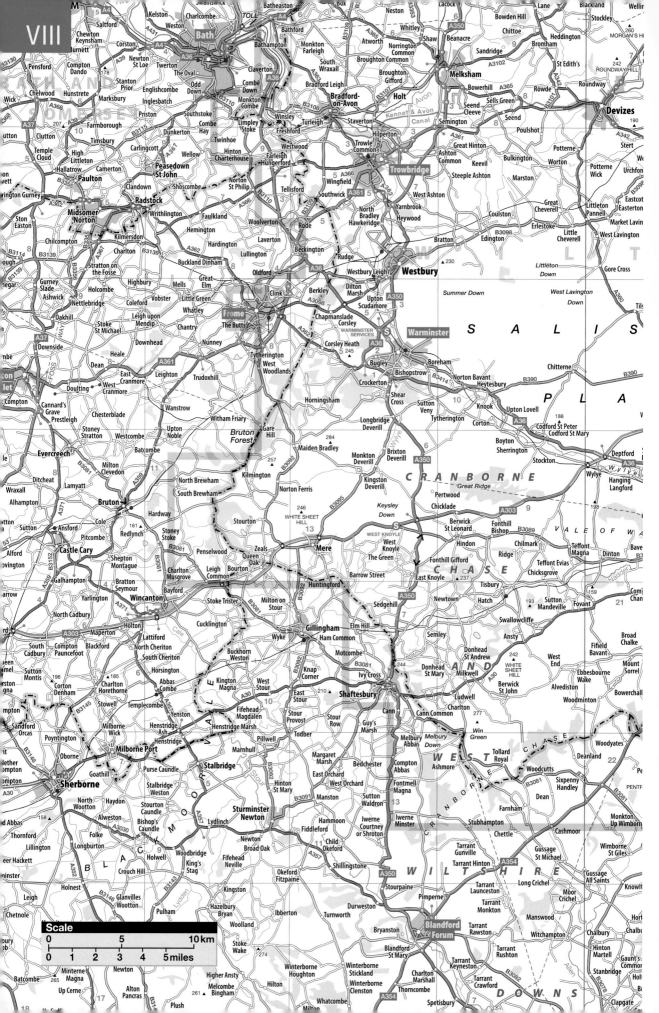

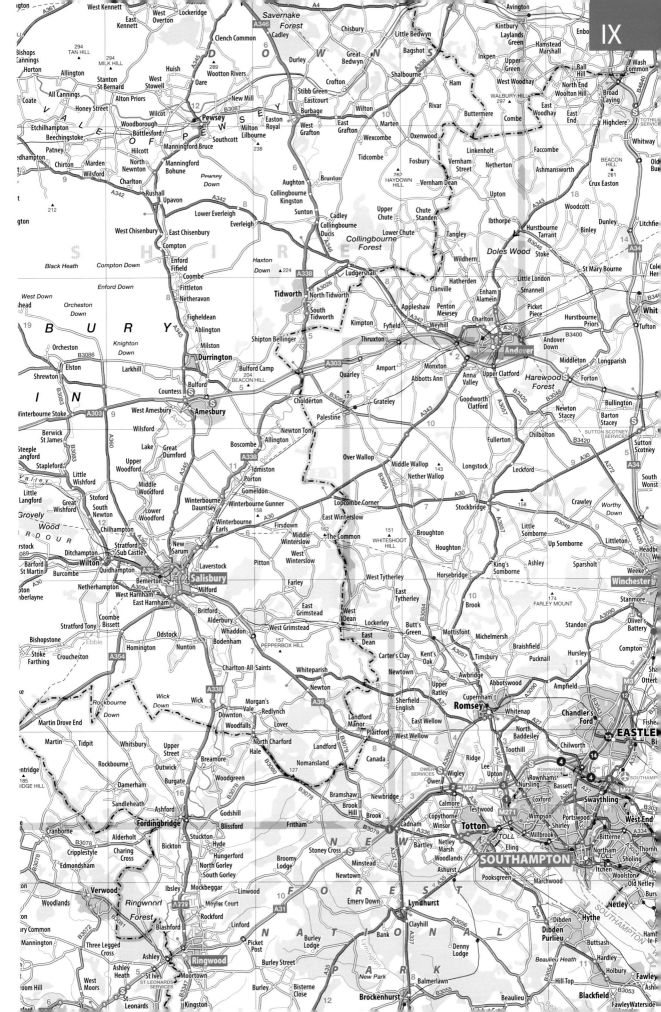

X

# Key to map symbols

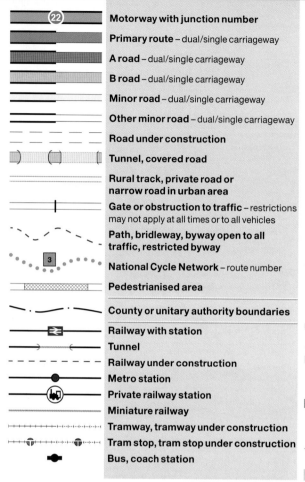

| | |
|---|---|
| **Motorway with junction number** | |
| **Primary route** – dual/single carriageway | |
| **A road** – dual/single carriageway | |
| **B road** – dual/single carriageway | |
| **Minor road** – dual/single carriageway | |
| **Other minor road** – dual/single carriageway | |
| **Road under construction** | |
| **Tunnel, covered road** | |
| **Rural track, private road or narrow road in urban area** | |
| **Gate or obstruction to traffic** – restrictions may not apply at all times or to all vehicles | |
| **Path, bridleway, byway open to all traffic, restricted byway** | |
| **National Cycle Network** – route number | |
| **Pedestrianised area** | |
| **County or unitary authority boundaries** | |
| **Railway with station** | |
| **Tunnel** | |
| **Railway under construction** | |
| **Metro station** | |
| **Private railway station** | |
| **Miniature railway** | |
| **Tramway, tramway under construction** | |
| **Tram stop, tram stop under construction** | |
| **Bus, coach station** | |

**Ambulance station**
**Coastguard station**
**Fire station**
**Police station**
**Accident and Emergency entrance to hospital**
**H** **Hospital**
**+** **Place of worship**
**i** **Information centre**
**P** **Shopping centre, parking**
**P&R** **Park and Ride, Post Office**
**Camping site, caravan site**
**Golf course, picnic site**
*Church* ROMAN FORT **Non-Roman antiquity, Roman antiquity**
Univ **Important buildings, schools, colleges, universities and hospitals**
**Woods, built-up area**
River Medway **Water name**
**River, weir**
**Stream**
**Canal, lock, tunnel**
**Water**
**Tidal water**

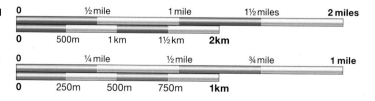

**58** **87** **Adjoining page indicators and overlap bands** – the colour of the arrow and band indicates the scale of the adjoining or overlapping page (see scales below)

The dark grey border on the inside edge of some pages indicates that the mapping does not continue onto the adjacent page

The small numbers around the edges of the maps identify the 1-kilometre National Grid lines

## Abbreviations

| | | | |
|---|---|---|---|
| Acad | Academy | Meml | Memorial |
| Allot Gdns | Allotments | Mon | Monument |
| Cemy | Cemetery | Mus | Museum |
| C Ctr | Civic centre | Obsy | Observatory |
| CH | Club house | Pal | Royal palace |
| Coll | College | PH | Public house |
| Crem | Crematorium | Recn Gd | Recreation ground |
| Ent | Enterprise | Resr | Reservoir |
| Ex H | Exhibition hall | Ret Pk | Retail park |
| Ind Est | Industrial Estate | Sch | School |
| IRB Sta | Inshore rescue boat station | Sh Ctr | Shopping centre |
| Inst | Institute | TH | Town hall / house |
| Ct | Law court | Trad Est | Trading estate |
| L Ctr | Leisure centre | Univ | University |
| LC | Level crossing | W Twr | Water tower |
| Liby | Library | Wks | Works |
| Mkt | Market | YH | Youth hostel |

## Enlarged maps only

**Railway or bus station building**
**Place of interest**
**Parkland**

**The map scale on the pages numbered in green is 1¾ inches to 1 mile**
2.76 cm to 1 km • 1:36 206

0   ½ mile   1 mile   1½ miles   2 miles
0   500m   1 km   1½ km   2km

**The map scale on the pages numbered in blue is 3½ inches to 1 mile**
5.52 cm to 1 km • 1:18 103

0   ¼ mile   ½ mile   ¾ mile   1 mile
0   250m   500m   750m   1km

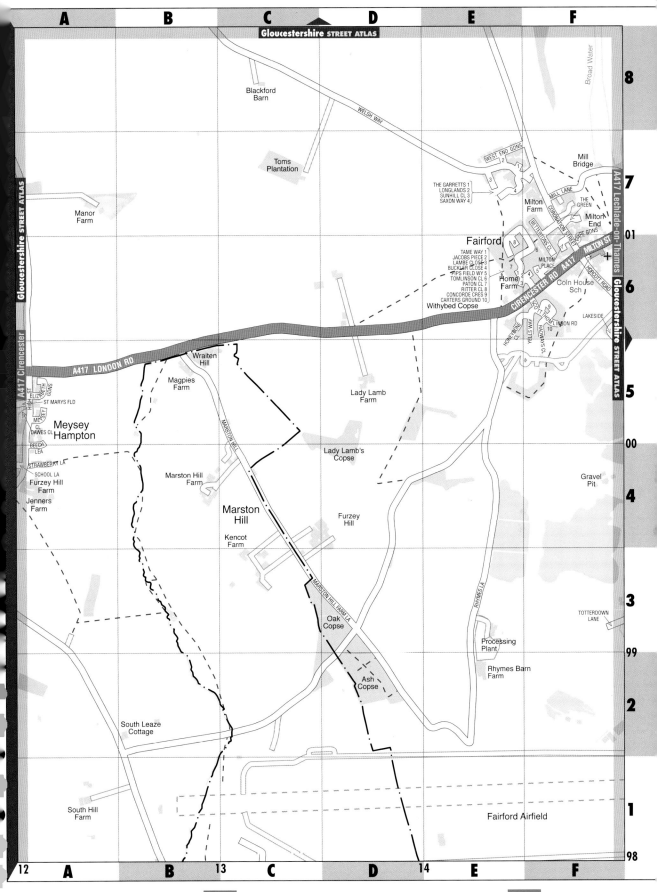

Gloucestershire STREET ATLAS

8

Blackford Barn

WELSH WAY

Broad Water

7

01

Mill Bridge

WEST END GDNS

Manor Farm

Toms Plantation

THE GARRETTS 1
LONGLANDS 2
SUNHILL CL 3
SAXON WAY 4

Milton Farm

MILL LANE

THE GREEN

Milton End

6

Fairford

TAME WAY 1
JACOBS PIECE 2
LAMBE CLOSE 3
BUCKLER CLOSE 4
TIPS FIELD WY 5
TOMLINSON CL 6
PATON CL 7
RITTER CL 8
CONCORDE CRES 9
CARTERS GROUND 10

Home Farm

MILTON PLACE

Coln House Sch

LAKESIDE

Withybed Copse

CIRENCESTER RD

HORCOTT ROAD

TOMLINSON RD

RADWAYS CL

5

A417 LONDON RD

Wraiten Hill

Magpies Farm

Lady Lamb Farm

00

ST MARYS FLD

Meysey Hampton

MARSTON HILL

Marston Hill Farm

Lady Lamb's Copse

Gravel Pit

4

STRAWBERRY LA

SCHOOL LA

Furzey Hill Farm

Jenners Farm

Furzey Hill

Kencot Farm

Marston Hill

3

RHYMES LA

TOTTERDOWN LANE

MARSTON HILL FARM LA

Oak Copse

Processing Plant

99

Ash Copse

Rhymes Barn Farm

2

South Leaze Cottage

South Hill Farm

Fairford Airfield

1

98

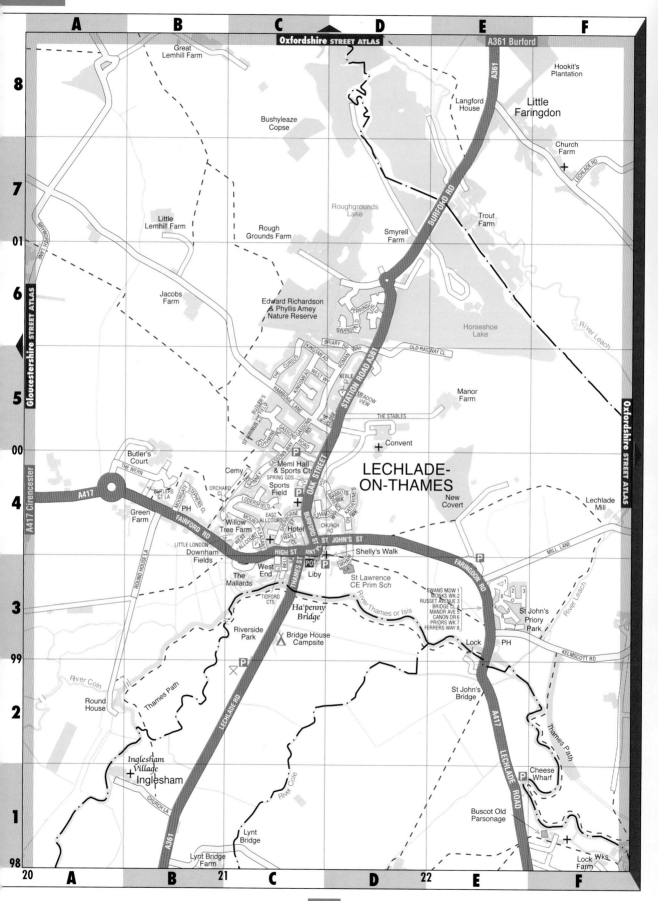

A361 Burford

Great Lemhill Farm

Hookit's Plantation

Bushyleaze Copse

Langford House

Little Faringdon

Church Farm

Little Lemhill Farm

Roughgrounds Lake

Rough Grounds Farm

Smyrell Farm

Trout Farm

Jacobs Farm

Edward Richardson & Phyllis Amey Nature Reserve

Horseshoe Lake

River Leach

BURFORD RD

PERRINSFIELD

SWANSFIELD

BRIARY RD    ROMAN WAY    OLD RAILWAY CL

KINGSMEAD

THE CURSUS    KINGSMEAD WEST WY

HAMBIDGE LANE

STATION ROAD A361

KEBLE CL

MEADOW VIEW

Manor Farm

ST PIRINAS CT FIELD    BUTLER'S CLOSE

GASSONS WAY    GASSONS ROAD    HIL CLOSE

THE STABLES

Butler's Court

Convent

THE WERN

BUTLERS CT LA

Cemy

THE SPINNEY

Meml Hall & Sports Ctr

Sports Field

SPRING GDS

OAK STREET

LECHLADE-ON-THAMES

New Covert

Lechlade Mill

A417 Cirencester

A417

MOORGATE    STEPHENS CL

ORCHARD CL

LODERSFIELD

EAST ALLCOURT

ABBOTS WK

ST LAWRENCE

New Covert

PH

Green Farm

FAIRFORD RD

MOUNT PLEASANT

Willow Tree Farm

WEST ALLCOURT

SHERBORNE

BURFORD ST

SWAN    CHAPEL    CHURCH RD

ST JOHN'S ST

OLD ST KATHERINE'S WK

FARINGDON RD

MILL LANE

LITTLE LONDON LA

ROUND HOUSE LA

Downham Fields

BELL LA

West End

THAMES ST

Hotel

HIGH ST    MKT PL    PO

Liby    WHARF

Shelly's Walk

St Lawrence CE Prim Sch

SWANS MDW 1
MONKS WK 2
RUSSET AVENUE 3
BRIDGE CL 4
MANOR AVE 5
CANON DR 6
PRIORS WK 7
FERRERS WAY 8

St John's Priory Park

River Leach

The Mallards

TIDFORD CTS

Ha'penny Bridge

River Thames or Isis

Lock

PH

KELMSCOTT RD

River Coln

Riverside Park

Bridge House Campsite

St John's Bridge

A417

LECHLADE RD

Round House

Thames Path

Thames Path

Inglesham Village    Inglesham

Cheese Wharf

River Cole

LECHLADE ROAD

CHURCH LA

Buscot Old Parsonage

A361

Lynt Bridge

Lynt Bridge Farm

Lock Wks

Lock Farm

A    B    C    D    E    F

8    7    01    6    5    00    4    3    99    2    1    98

20    21    22

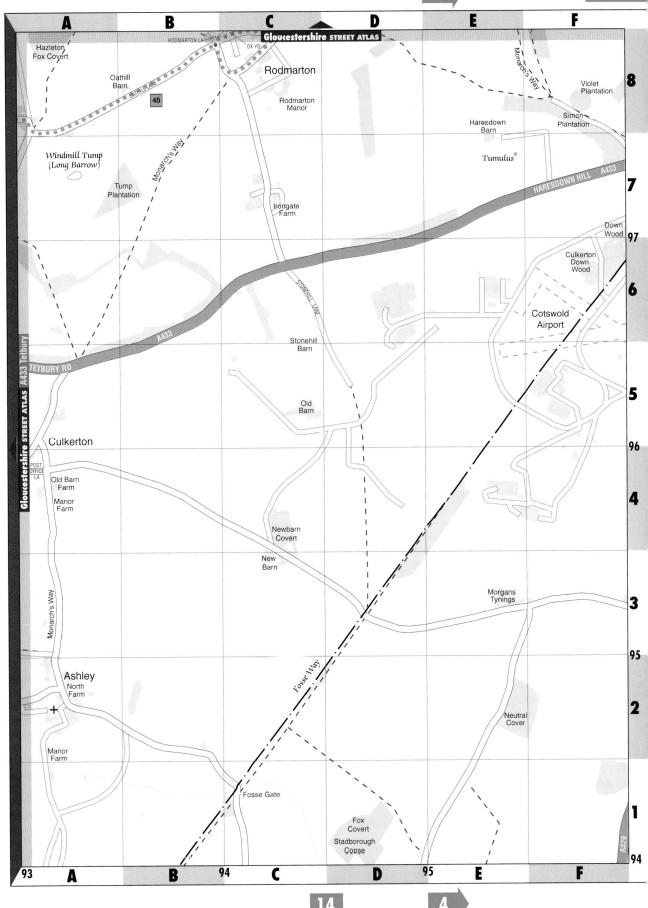

**Gloucestershire STREET ATLAS**

A B C D E F

Hazleton
Fox Covert

Oathill
Barn

OATHILL LANE

45

RODMARTON LA

OX YD

Rodmarton

Rodmarton
Manor

Monarch's Way

Violet
Plantation

Haresdown
Barn

Simon
Plantation

8

Windmill Tump
(Long Barrow)

Monarch's Way

Tumulus

Tump
Plantation

Irongate
Farm

HARESDOWN HILL A433

7

Down
Wood

97

STONEHILL LANE

Culkerton
Down
Wood

6

A433

Stonehill
Barn

Cotswold
Airport

TETBURY RD

A433 Tetbury

Old
Barn

5

96

Culkerton

POST
OFFICE
LA

Old Barn
Farm

Manor
Farm

4

Newbarn
Covert

New
Barn

Morgans
Tynings

3

Monarch's Way

Fosse Way

95

Ashley

North
Farm

Neutral
Cover

2

+

Manor
Farm

Fosse Gate

Fox
Covert

Stadborough
Copse

1

A429

94

93 A 94 B C 95 D E F

**Gloucestershire STREET ATLAS**

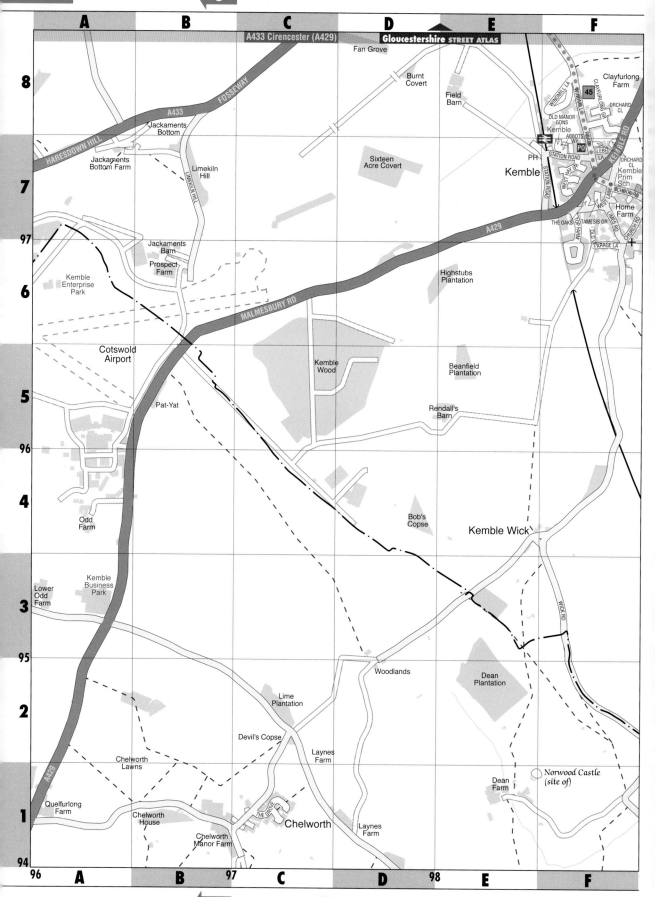

A433 Cirencester (A429)

**Gloucestershire** STREET ATLAS

Fan Grove

Burnt Covert

Field Barn

FOSSEWAY

A433

Jackaments Bottom

Limekiln Hill

LIMEKILN HILL

HARESDOWN HILL

Jackaments Bottom Farm

Sixteen Acre Covert

Clayfurlong Farm

WINDMILL LA

45

CLAYFURLONG GR

ORCHARD CL

OLD MANOR GDNS

Kemble

ABBOTS WY

PO

STATION ROAD

GLEBE LA

ORCHARD CL

Kemble Prim Sch

PH

Kemble

STATION ROAD

WEST WAY GR

WEST LANE

SCHOOL RD

CHURCH RD

KEMBLE RD

Home Farm

Jackaments Barn

Prospect Farm

Kemble Enterprise Park

THE OAKS

TAMESIS DR

TOP FARM

LIMES RD

OLD Y

GARAGE LA

A429

Highstubs Plantation

Kemble Wood

Beanfield Plantation

Cotswold Airport

MALMESBURY RD

Pat-Yat

Rendall's Barn

Odd Farm

Bob's Copse

Kemble Wick

Kemble Business Park

Lower Odd Farm

A429

Woodlands

Dean Plantation

WICK RD

Lime Plantation

Devil's Copse

Laynes Farm

Norwood Castle (site of)

Quelfurlong Farm

Chelworth Lawns

THE GROVE

Chelworth

Dean Farm

Chelworth House

Laynes Farm

Chelworth Manor Farm

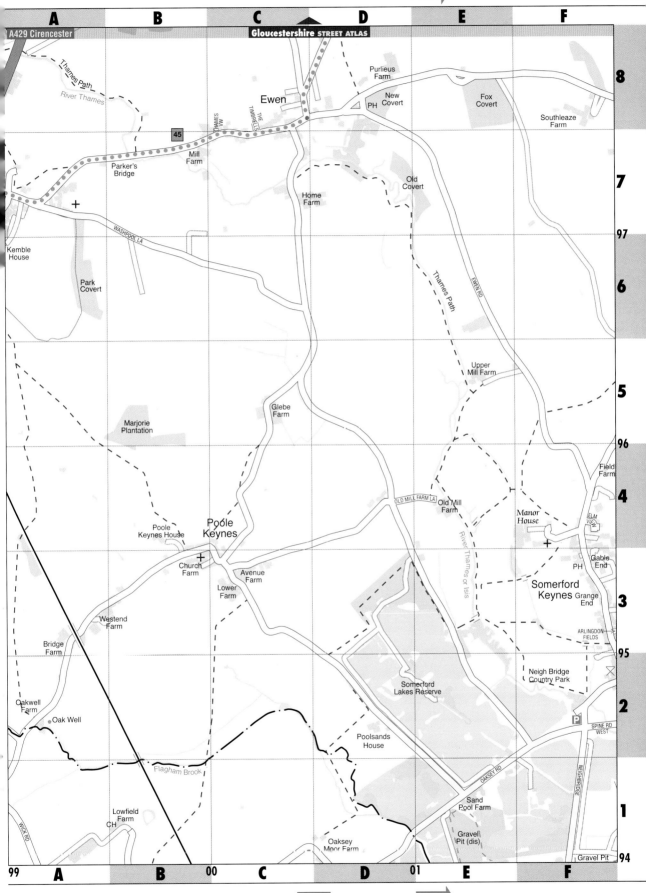

A   B   C   D   E   F

8   7   97   6   5   96   4   3   95   2   1   94

Thames Path

River Thames

Ewen

PH

Purlieus Farm

New Covert

Fox Covert

Southleaze Farm

THAMES W

THE TIMBRELLS

45

Mill Farm

Parker's Bridge

Home Farm

Old Covert

Thames Path

EWEN RD

Kemble House

WASHPOOL LA

Park Covert

Upper Mill Farm

Marjorie Plantation

Glebe Farm

Field Farm

OLD MILL FARM LA

Old Mill Farm

Manor House

ELM VIEW

Poole Keynes House

Poole Keynes

Church Farm

Avenue Farm

Lower Farm

River Thames or Isis

PH

Gable End

Somerford Keynes

Grange End

ARLINGTON FIELDS

Westend Farm

Bridge Farm

Neigh Bridge Country Park

Oakwell Farm

Oak Well

Somerford Lakes Reserve

P

SPINE RD WEST

NEIGHBRIDGE

Flagham Brook

Poolsands House

OAKSEY RD

Lowfield Farm

CH

WICK RD

Oaksey Moor Farm

Sand Pool Farm

Gravel Pit (dis)

Gravel Pit

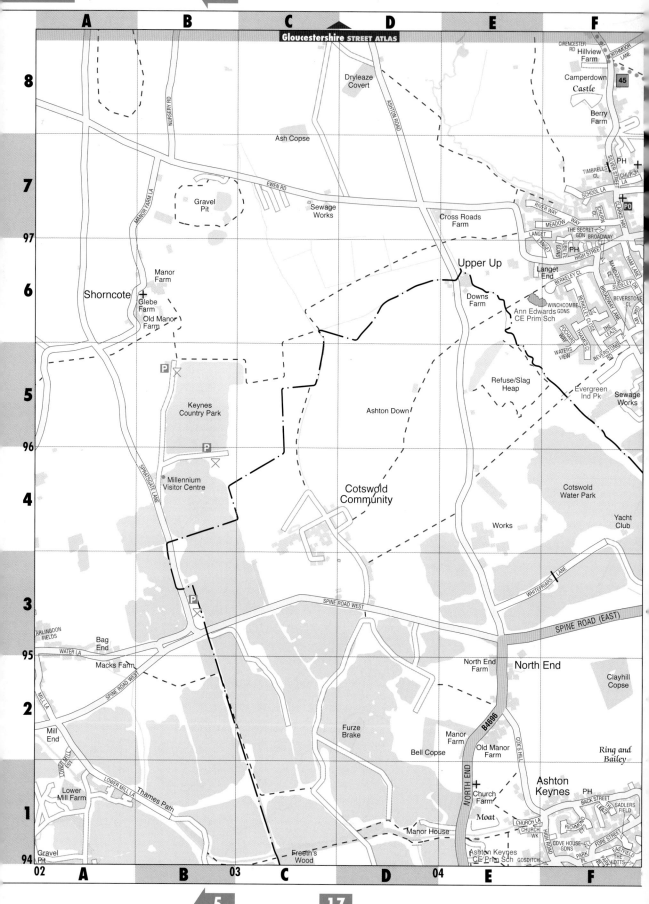

Gloucestershire STREET ATLAS

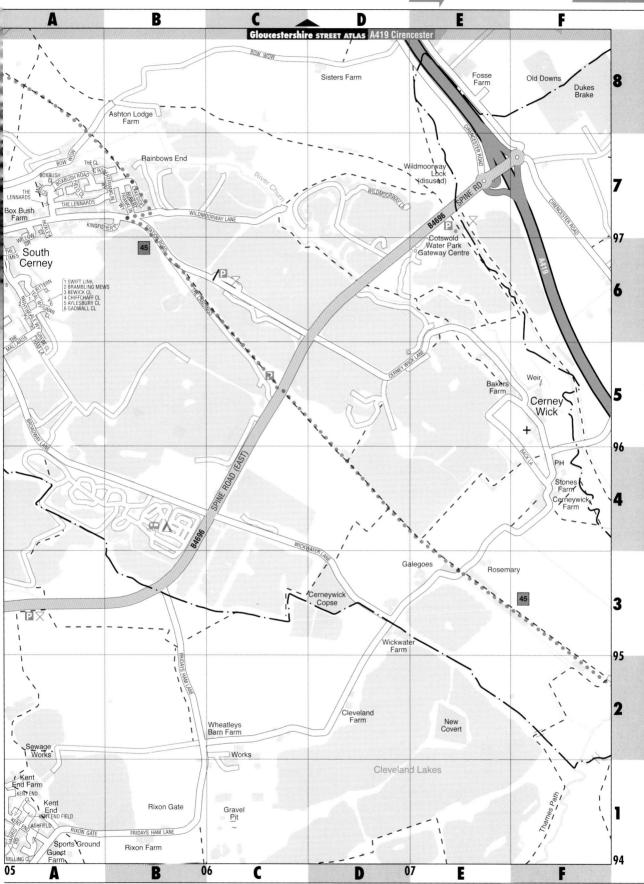

**Gloucestershire STREET ATLAS** A419 Cirencester

8

7

97

6

5

96

4

3

95

2

1

94

A    B    C    D    E    F

BOW WOW

Sisters Farm

Fosse Farm

Old Downs

Dukes Brake

Ashton Lodge Farm

Rainbows End

Wildmoorway Lock (disused)

River Churn

WILDMOORWAY LA

SPINE RD

CIRENCESTER ROAD

CIRENCESTER ROAD

A419

BOW WOW

THE CL

ROBERT FRANKLIN WY

BOXBUSH CL

Boxbush Road

FIELD CL

THE LENNARDS

THE LENNARDS

ROBERT FRANKLIN WY

KINGFISHER'S

STATION RD

WILDMOORWAY LANE

B4696

P

Cotswold Water Park Gateway Centre

Box Bush Farm

BOX BUSH

WILLOW DR

HUXLEY CL

THE LIMES

South Cerney

45

1 SWIFT LINK
2 BRAMBLING MEWS
3 BEWICK CL
4 CHIFFCHAFF CL
5 AYLESBURY CL
6 GADWALL CL

BITTERN CL

TEAL WY

SWAN CL

GREBE CL

BRANT CL

NUTHATCH WY

THE MALLARDS

THE MEWS

P

P

Cerney Wick Lane

CERNEY WICK LANE

Bakers Farm

Weir

Cerney Wick

BACK LA

PH

Stones Farm

Cerneywick Farm

BROADWAY LANE

SPINE ROAD (EAST)

B4696

WO

Galegoes

Rosemary

45

WICKWATER LANE

Cerneywick Copse

Wickwater Farm

P

FRIDAYS HAM LANE

Wheatleys Barn Farm

Works

Cleveland Farm

New Covert

Cleveland Lakes

Thames Path

Sewage Works

Kent End Farm

KENT END

Kent End

KENT END FIELD

ASHFIELD

KENT END RD

HARRIS CL

MILLING CL

RIXON GATE

Rixon Gate

FRIDAYS HAM LANE

Gravel Pit

Sports Ground

Guest Farm

Rixon Farm

05    A    B    06    C    D    07    E    F

7

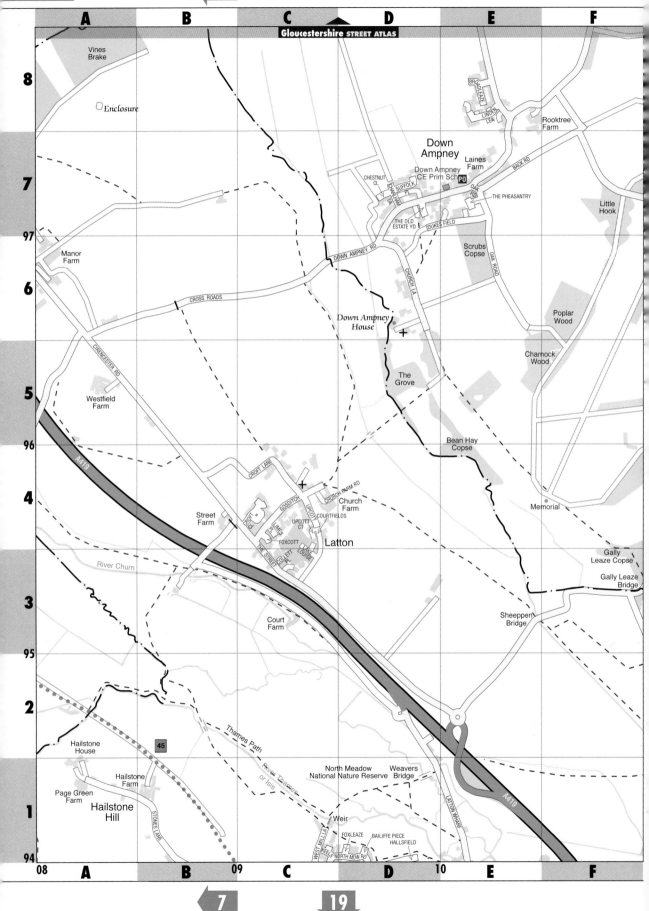

Gloucestershire STREET ATLAS

Vines Brake

Enclosure

Down Ampney

BROOMLEAZE

LINDEN LEA

Rooktree Farm

Laines Farm

CHESTNUT CL

Down Ampney CE Prim Sch

SUFFOLK PL

PO

BACK RD

Little Hook

THE PHEASANTRY

OAK RD

THE OLD ESTATE YD

DUKES FIELD

DOWN AMPNEY RD

Manor Farm

CROSS ROADS

CHURCH LA

Scrubs Copse

OAK ROAD

Poplar Wood

Down Ampney House

Charnock Wood

CIRENCESTER RD

Westfield Farm

The Grove

Bean Hay Copse

A419

Memorial

CROFT LANE

CHURCH FARM RD

Church Farm

GOSDITCH

UPCOTT CT

COURTFIELDS

Gally Leaze Copse

CROFT

Street Farm

LIMES

UPCOTT

Gally Leaze Bridge

THE STREET

FOXCOTT

Latton

River Churn

COLLETT

LAKE LOUISE

Sheeppen Bridge

Court Farm

A419

Thames Path

45

LATTON WHARF

Hailstone House

River Thames or Isis

North Meadow National Nature Reserve

Weavers Bridge

A419

Hailstone Farm

STONEY LANE

Page Green Farm

Hailstone Hill

Weir

WEST MILL LA

FOXLEAZE

BAILIFFE PIECE

HALLSFIELD

KEELS

NORTH MDW RD

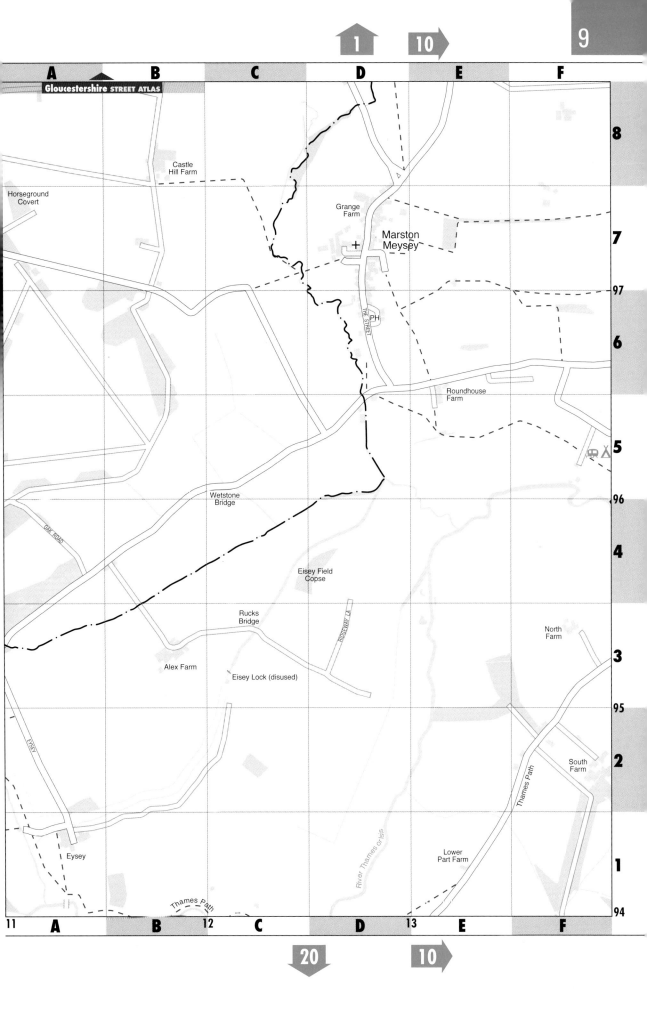

Gloucestershire STREET ATLAS

Castle
Hill Farm

Horseground
Covert

Grange
Farm

Marston
Meysey

PH

THE STREET

Roundhouse
Farm

OAK ROAD

Wetstone
Bridge

Eisey Field
Copse

Rucks
Bridge

RIDGEWAY LA

North
Farm

Alex Farm

Eisey Lock (disused)

EYSEY

Thames Path

South
Farm

River Thames or Isis

Eysey

Lower
Part Farm

Thames Path

A  B  C  D  E  F

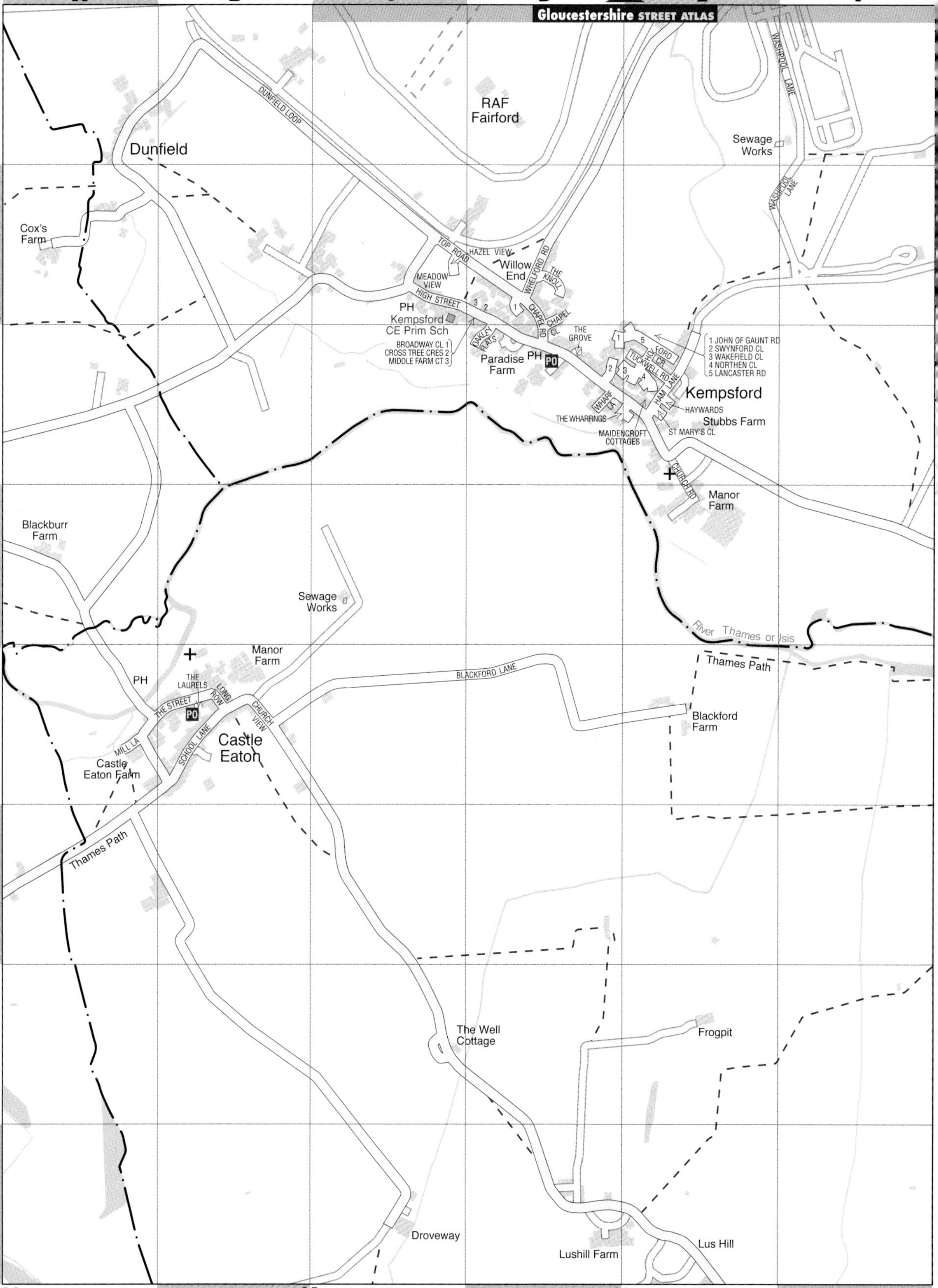

Gloucestershire STREET ATLAS

8

RAF
Fairford

Dunfield

DUNFIELD LOOP

Sewage
Works

WASHPOOL LANE

Cox's
Farm

7

TOP ROAD  HAZEL VIEW

Willow
End

WHELFORD RD

THE KNOLL

WASHPOOL LANE

MEADOW
VIEW

HIGH STREET

PH
Kempsford
CE Prim Sch

97

BROADWAY CL 1
CROSS TREE CRES 2
MIDDLE FARM CT 3

CHAPEL RD  CHAPEL

THE GROVE

1 JOHN OF GAUNT RD
2 SWYNFORD CL
3 WAKEFIELD CL
4 NORTHEN CL
5 LANCASTER RD

Paradise
Farm

PH PO

Kempsford

6

THE WHARFINGS

HAYWARDS

Stubbs Farm

MAIDENCROFT
COTTAGES

ST MARY'S CL

Manor
Farm

Blackburr
Farm

5

Sewage
Works

River Thames or Isis

96

Manor
Farm

BLACKFORD LANE

Thames Path

PH

THE
LAURELS

LONG ROW

PO

Blackford
Farm

CHURCH VIEW

4

MILL LA

THE STREET

SCHOOL LANE

Castle
Eaton

Castle
Eaton Farm

Thames Path

3

95

The Well
Cottage

Frogpit

2

1

Droveway

Lushill Farm

Lus Hill

94

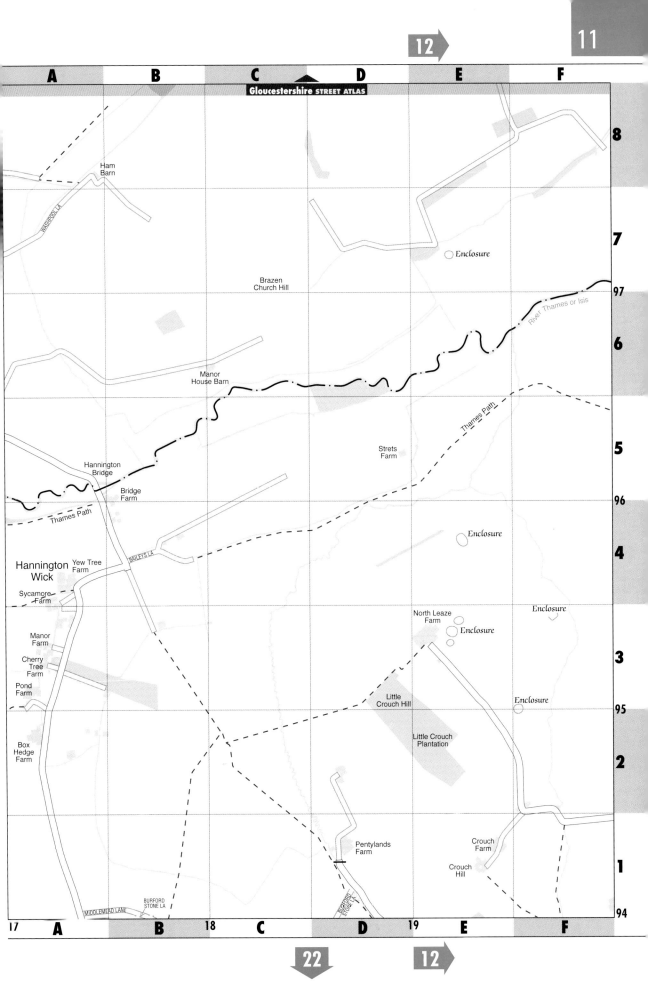

Gloucestershire STREET ATLAS

A   B   C   D   E   F

8

Ham
Barn

WASHPOOL LA

7

Enclosure

Brazen
Church Hill

97

River Thames or Isis

6

Manor
House Barn

Thames Path

Strets
Farm

5

Hannington
Bridge

96

Bridge
Farm

Thames Path

Enclosure

BAILEYS LA

4

Hannington   Yew Tree
Wick          Farm

Sycamore
Farm

Enclosure

North Leaze
Farm

Enclosure

Enclosure

Manor
Farm

3

Cherry
Tree
Farm

Pond
Farm

Little
Crouch Hill

Enclosure

95

Little Crouch
Plantation

Box
Hedge
Farm

2

Pentylands
Farm

Crouch
Farm

1

BURFORD STONE LA

Crouch
Hill

MIDDLEMEAD LANE

BURFORD
STONE LA

94

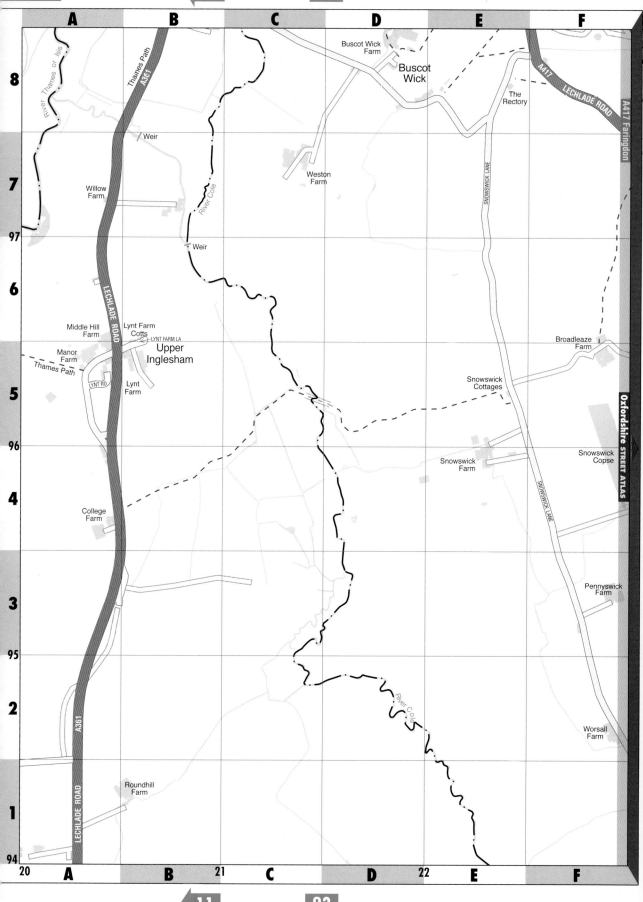

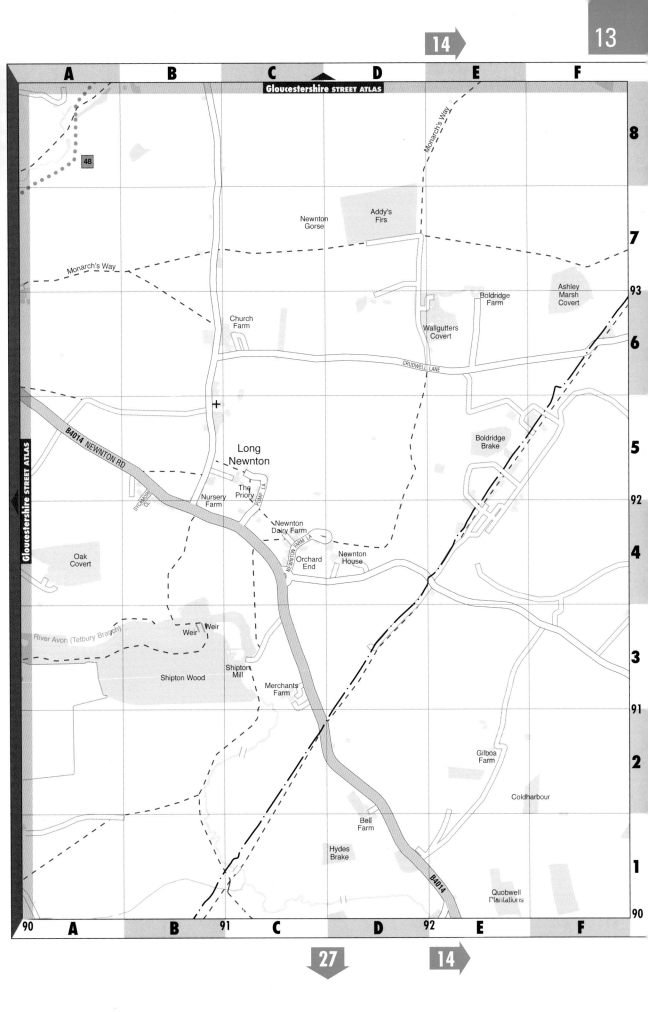

Gloucestershire STREET ATLAS

Gloucestershire STREET ATLAS

Monarch's Way

Newnton Gorse

Addy's Firs

Monarch's Way

Ashley Marsh Covert

Boldridge Farm

Church Farm

Wallgutters Covert

CRUDWELL LANE

B4014 NEWNTON RD

Long Newnton

Boldridge Brake

The Priory

PUMP LA

Nursery Farm

SYCAMORE CL

Newnton Dairy Farm

NEWNTON FARM LA

Oak Covert

Orchard End

Newnton House

River Avon (Tetbury Branch)

Weir Weir

Shipton Wood

Shipton Mill

Merchants Farm

Gilboa Farm

Coldharbour

Bell Farm

Hydes Brake

B4014

Quobwell Plantations

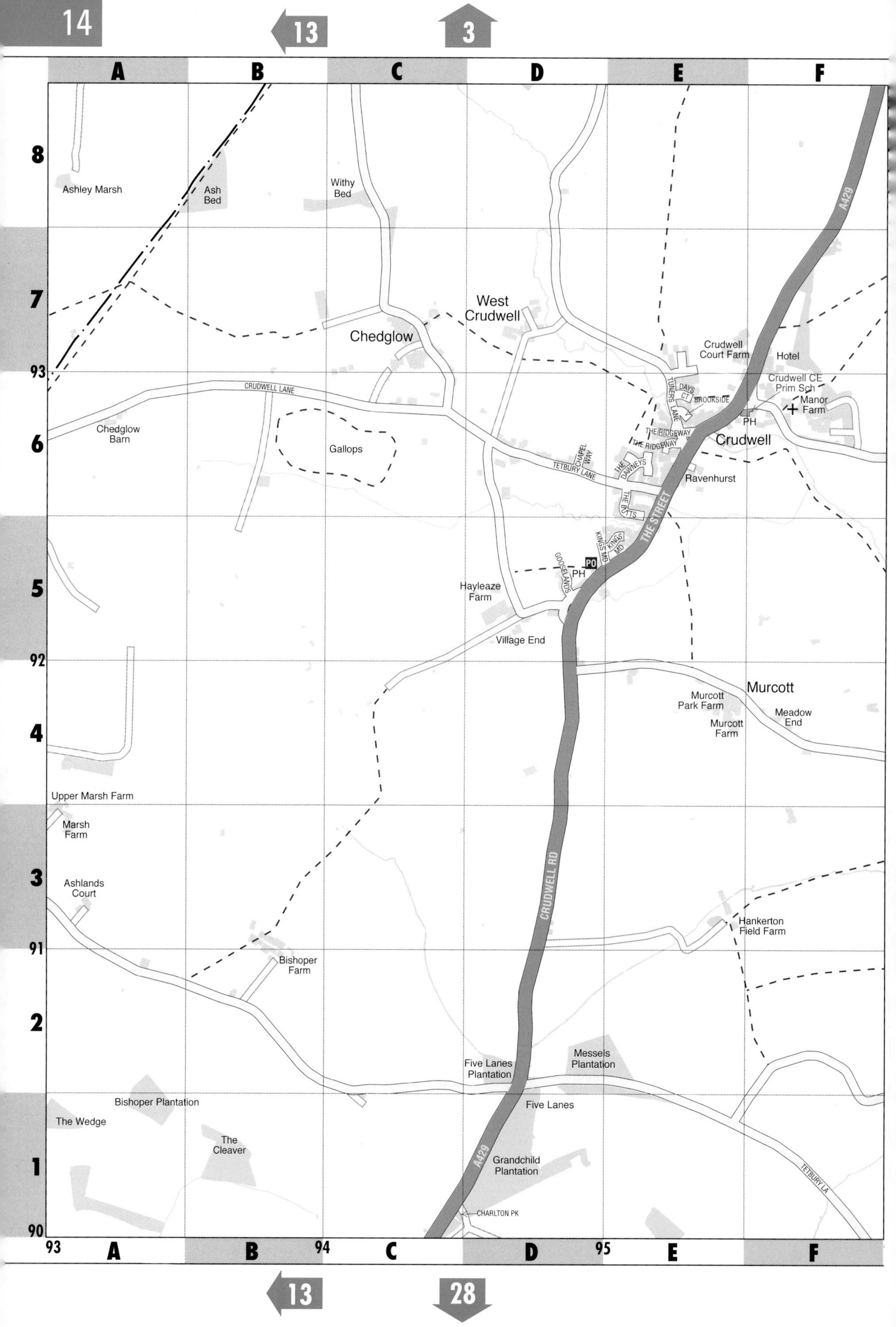

13
3

A B C D E F

8

Ashley Marsh

Ash Bed

Withy Bed

7

West Crudwell

Chedglow

Crudwell Court Farm

Hotel

93

Crudwell CE Prim Sch

CRUDWELL LANE

DAYS CT
BROOKSIDE

TOWERS LANE

Manor Farm

6

Chedglow Barn

Gallops

THE RIDGEWAY
THE RIDGEWAY

PH

Crudwell

CHAPEL WAY

TETBURY LANE

THE DAWNEYS

Ravenhurst

THE BUTTS

KINGS RD
KINGS MD

THE STREET

5

Hayleaze Farm

GOSPELANDS

PO
PH

92

Village End

Murcott Park Farm

Murcott

Meadow End

4

Murcott Farm

Upper Marsh Farm

Marsh Farm

CRUDWELL RD

3

Ashlands Court

Hankerton Field Farm

91

Bishoper Farm

2

Messels Plantation

Five Lanes Plantation

Bishoper Plantation

Five Lanes

The Wedge

TETBURY LA

The Cleaver

1

A429

Grandchild Plantation

90

CHARLTON PK

93 A 94 C B 95 E F

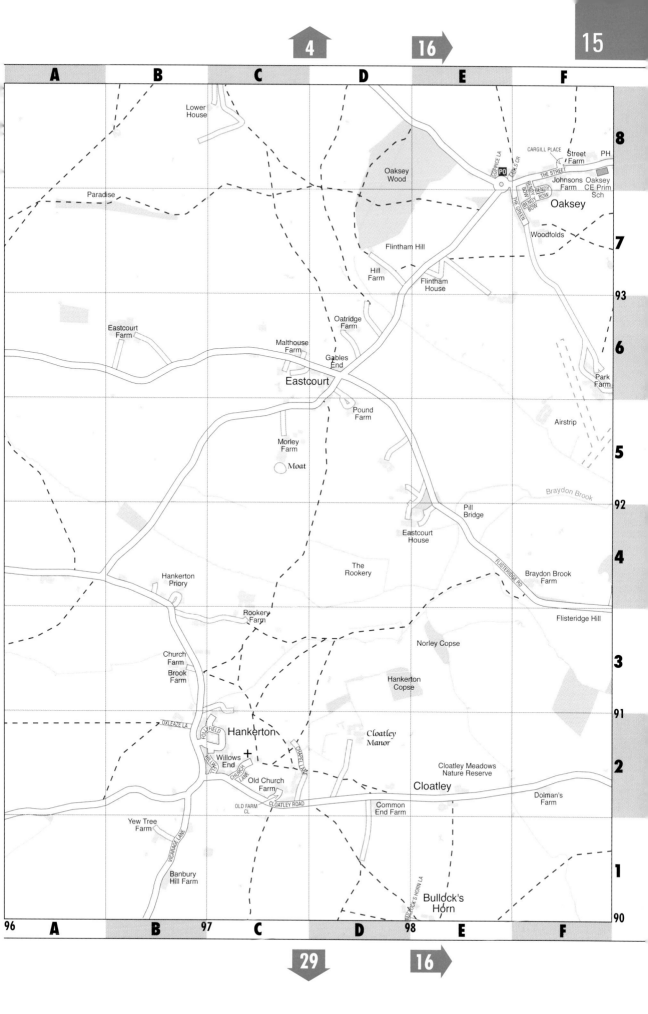

**A** · **B** · **C** · **D** · **E** · **F**

8
7
93
6
5
92
4
3
91
2
1
90

Lower House

Paradise

Oaksey Wood

CARGILL PLACE
Street Farm
PH
COPPICE LA
CAR'S CR
PO
THE STREET
BENDY BOW
BENDY BOW
BENDY BOW
Johnsons Farm
Oaksey CE Prim Sch
THE GREEN
Oaksey

Woodfolds

Flintham Hill

Hill Farm

Flintham House

Eastcourt Farm

Oatridge Farm

Malthouse Farm

Gables End

Eastcourt

Park Farm

Pound Farm

Airstrip

Morley Farm

Moat

Braydon Brook

Pill Bridge

Eastcourt House

FLISTERIDGE RD

Braydon Brook Farm

The Rookery

Hankerton Priory

Flisteridge Hill

Rookery Farm

Norley Copse

Church Farm
Brook Farm

Hankerton Copse

OXLEAZE LA

FOLLYFIELD

Hankerton

Cloatley Manor

HILL ST
CHURCH LANE
Willows End

CHAPEL LANE

Old Church Farm

Cloatley Meadows Nature Reserve

Cloatley

Dolman's Farm

OLD FARM CL
CLOATLEY ROAD

Common End Farm

Yew Tree Farm

VICARAGE LANE

Banbury Hill Farm

BULLOCK'S HORN LA

Bullock's Horn

96 **A** · **B** 97 **C** · **D** 98 **E** · **F**

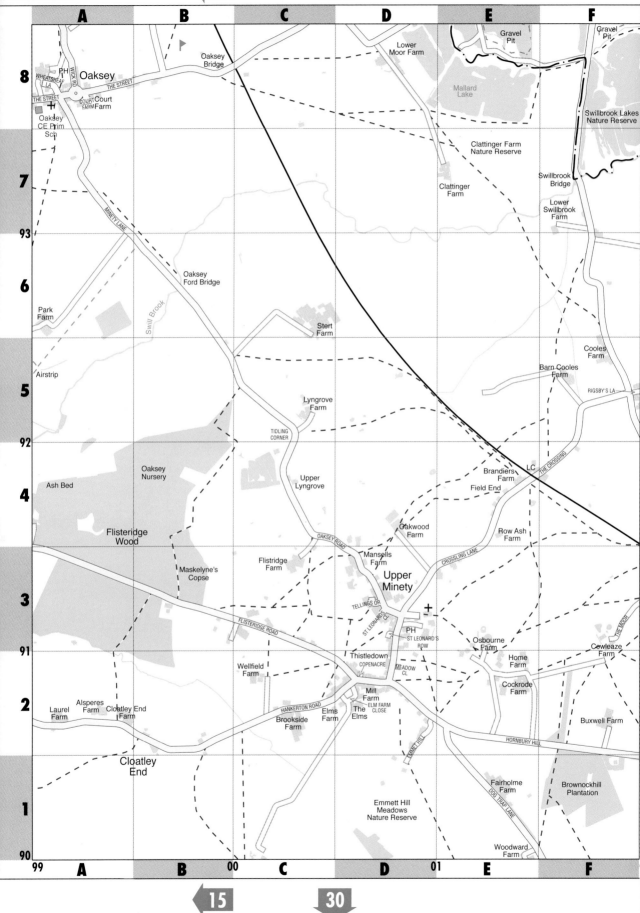

A B C D E F

8

7

93

6

5

92

4

3

91

2

1

90

Oaksey
Oaksey Bridge
Lower Moor Farm
Gravel Pit
Gravel Pit
PH
WHEATSHEAF LA
WICK RD
THE STREET
THE STREET
COURT FARM
Court Farm
Oaksey CE Prim Sch
Mallard Lake
Swillbrook Lakes Nature Reserve
Clattinger Farm Nature Reserve
Clattinger Farm
Swillbrook Bridge
MINETY LANE
Oaksey Ford Bridge
Lower Swillbrook Farm
Swill Brook
Park Farm
Stert Farm
Cooles Farm
Airstrip
Barn Cooles Farm
RIGSBY'S LA
Lyngrove Farm
Oaksey Nursery
TIDLING CORNER
Upper Lyngrove
Brandiers Farm
Field End
LC
THE CROSSING
Ash Bed
Flisteridge Wood
Oakwood Farm
Row Ash Farm
OAKSEY ROAD
Maskelyne's Copse
Flistridge Farm
Mansells Farm
Upper Minety
CROSSLING LANE
THE MOOR
FLISTERIDGE ROAD
TELLINGS OR
ST LEONARD'S CE
PH
ST LEONARD'S ROW
Osbourne Farm
Cewleaze Farm
Wellfield Farm
Thistledown
COPENACRE
MEADOW CL
Home Farm
Cockrode Farm
Buxwell Farm
Laurel Farm
Alsperes Farm
Cloatley End Farm
HANKERTON ROAD
Brookside Farm
Elms Farm
Mill Farm
ELM FARM CLOSE
The Elms
HORNBURY HILL
Cloatley End
EMMETT HILL
Emmett Hill Meadows Nature Reserve
DOG TRAP LANE
Fairholme Farm
Brownockhill Plantation
Woodward Farm

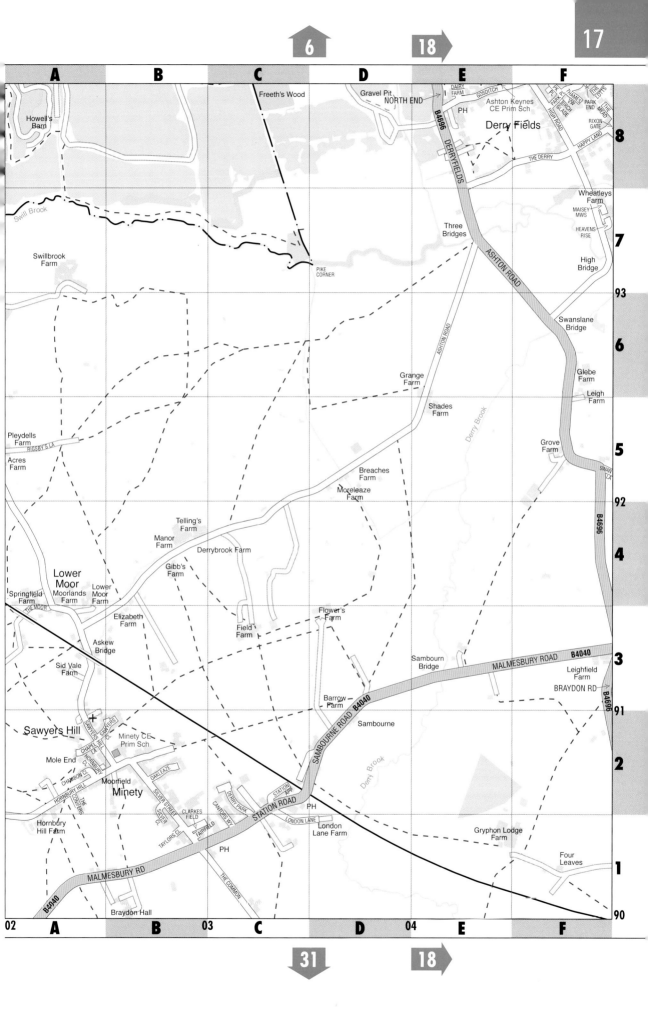

**A** **B** **C** **D** **E** **F**

Howell's Barn

Freeth's Wood

Gravel Pit
NORTH END

Dairy Farm

Ashton Keynes CE Prim Sch

GOSDITCH

PH

Derry Fields

RIXON GATE

THE MEAD

FIVE LOTS

PARK END

HIGH ROAD

HAPPY LAND

**8**

Swill Brook

Swillbrook Farm

PIKE CORNER

Three Bridges

DERRYFIELDS

ASHTON ROAD

Wheatleys Farm

MAISEY MWS

HEAVENS RISE

High Bridge

**7**

**93**

Pleydells Farm

Acres Farm

RIGSBY'S LA

Grange Farm

ASHTON ROAD

Shades Farm

Derry Brook

Swanslane Bridge

Glebe Farm

Leigh Farm

**6**

**5**

Telling's Farm

Manor Farm

Derrybrook Farm

Gibb's Farm

Breaches Farm

Moreleaze Farm

Grove Farm

SWAN LA

B4696

**92**

Lower Moor

Springfield Farm

THE MOOR

Moorlands Farm

Lower Moor Farm

Elizabeth Farm

Askew Bridge

Derrybrook Farm

Field Farm

Flower's Farm

Sambourn Bridge

MALMESBURY ROAD

B4040

Leighfield Farm

BRAYDON RD

B4696

**4**

**3**

Sid Vale Farm

Sawyers Hill

Mole End

Hornbury Hill Farm

CHAPEL HILL LA

HORNBURY HILL

THE CORNERS

SANTERS HILL

SAWYERS CL

Minety CE Prim Sch

Moorfield

Minety

OAKLEAZE

SILVER STREET

SILVER CL

CLARKES FIELD

FAIRFIELD

TAYLORS CL

DERRY PARK

CANTORS WAY

STATION RD

Barrow Farm

SAMBOURNE ROAD

B4040

Sambourne

Derry Brook

STATION ROAD

PH

LONDON LANE

London Lane Farm

Gryphon Lodge Farm

Four Leaves

**91**

**2**

**1**

MALMESBURY RD

B4040

THE COMMON

PH

Braydon Hall

**90**

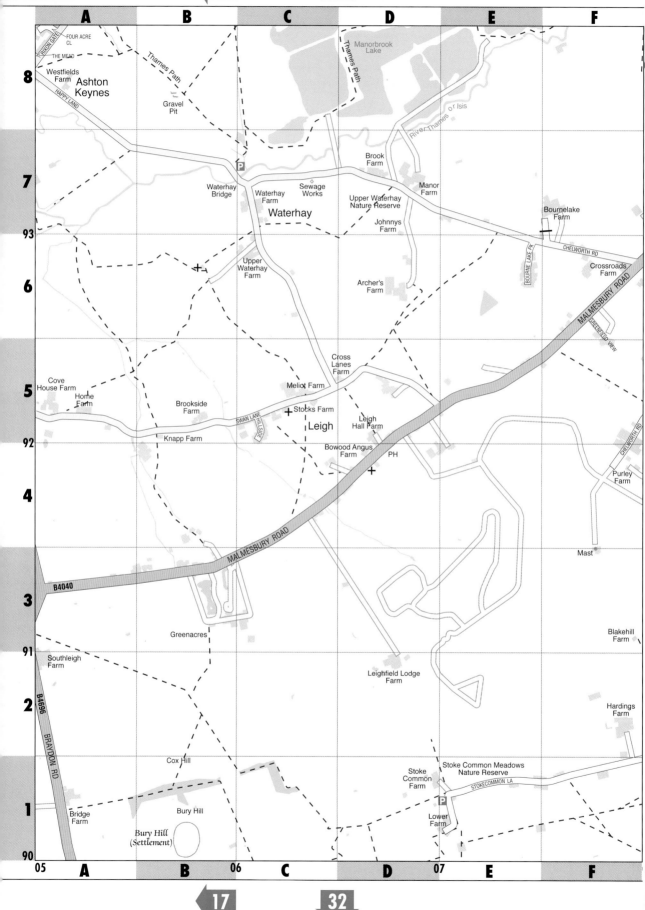

A B C D E F

8

Ashton
Keynes
FOUR ACRE
CL
THE MEAD
NIXON GATE
Westfields
Farm
HAPPY LAND
Thames Path
Gravel
Pit

Manorbrook
Lake
Thames Path

River Thames or Isis

7

P
Waterhay
Bridge
Waterhay
Farm
Sewage
Works
Waterhay
Brook
Farm
Upper Waterhay
Nature Reserve
Manor
Farm
Bournelake
Farm
BOURNE LAKE PK
CHELWORTH RD

93

Upper
Waterhay
Farm
Johnnys
Farm
Archer's
Farm
Crossroads
Farm
MALMESBURY ROAD
GREENFIELD VIEW

6

Cross
Lanes
Farm

5

Cove
House Farm
Home
Farm
Brookside
Farm
Meliot Farm
Stocks Farm
Leigh
Leigh
Hall Farm
CHELWORTH RD

92

Knapp Farm
SWAN LANE
HILLSIDE
Bowood Angus
Farm
PH
Purley
Farm

4

MALMESBURY ROAD
Mast

B4040

3

Greenacres
Blakehill
Farm

91

Southleigh
Farm
Leighfield Lodge
Farm

2

B4696
Hardings
Farm

BRAYDON RD
Cox Hill
Stoke
Common
Farm
Stoke Common Meadows
Nature Reserve
STOKECOMMON LA

1

Bridge
Farm
Bury Hill
P
Lower
Farm

Bury Hill
(Settlement)

90

05 A B 06 C D 07 E F

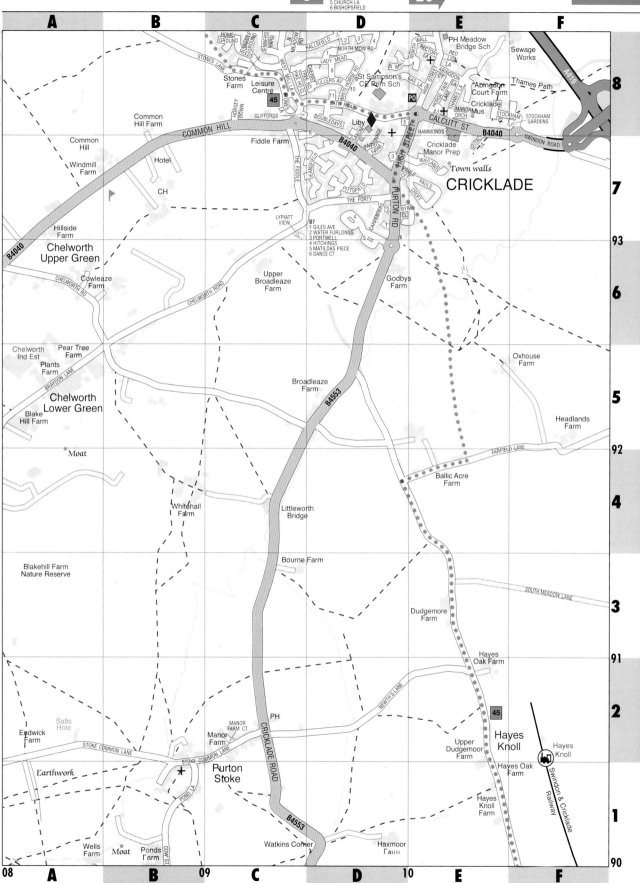

**D8**
1 FAIRFIELD
2 KITEFIELD
3 PLEYDELLS
4 BRANDERS
5 CHURCH LA
6 BISHOPSFIELD
7 BRAMBLE CT
8 CLOVER LA
9 WILLOW GRO
10 BLYTHE CL
11 SKYLARK RISE

**D7**
1 GILES AVE
2 WATER FURLONGS
3 PORTWELL
4 HITCHINGS
5 MATILDAS PIECE
6 DANCE CT

CRICKLADE

Cricklade
Mus

Chelworth
Upper Green

Chelworth
Lower Green

Purton
Stoke

Hayes
Knoll

A B C D E F

8 SWINDON RD

Thames Path

River Thames or Isis

Thames Path

Water Eaton House

Manor Farm

Calcutt

7 Calcutt Ct Farm

A419

Calcutt Farm

Manor Farm Cottages

Port Farm

93

Enclosures

6 Mast

Seven Bridges Bridge

Seven Bridges Farm

Great Rose La

Kingshill Farm

ROMAN BUILDING (site of)

Little Rose Lane

5 Farfield Farm

FARFIELD LA

92

4 Lower Widhill Farm

Newlands Farm

3 SOUTH MEADOW LANE

Weir

Chapel Farm

Blunsdon Hill

BLUNSDONHILL

91 River Ray

Blunsdonhill Copse

William Morris Prim Sch

Blunsdon Hill

2 Gravel Pit

Churchward Sch

Upper Widhill Farm

SOUTHALL CL 1
MERCER CL 2
BAYES CL 3
ARMFIELD RD 4
FAULKNER RD 5
SELWYN RD 6
LUMB CL 7
ARTISANS LA 8
WOOLNER RD 9
MILLAIS CL 10
TRELLIS ST 11
BALLIE CL 12
Tadpole Farm CE Prim Acad 13

Shepherd's Copse

Great Western Acad

Upper Widhill Copse

SHERRER LA

A419

1 HANKER CL
2 NEWLYN CL
3 JEFFREYCL
4 FELSTEAD
5 JOHN RUSKIN RD
6 DEMORGANCRES
7 SIDDAL ST
8 BURDEN RD
9 BEARDSLEY LA
10 NEWILL CL
11 KEMPE LA
12 DEARLE RD
13 JEBB CL
14 EGLANTYNE AVE
15 BURNE JONES AVE

PARSONS PL

BLANCHARD RD

COOPER

STICKLEY CL

SHAPLAND

IMAGE RD

KEOHLER

DRESSER CL

CHERWELL

IRVINE CL

HORTA CL

MUCHA CL

LALIQUE CL

STEINLEN CL

HEYGATE

EASTLAKE

PEARSON RD

HORNE TIFFANY

MACLAU RD

CRESWICK

Grove Farm

Abbey Farm Prim Sch

1 RODMARTON CL
ESCETON
BARNSLEY RD
VAN ERP CL
MATHEWS PL
JEKYLL

HIGH GROUND

STONEYWELL

THE LEASOWES

DANEWAY

GIMSON CRES

MACKAY CRES

GREENE ST

BRANTWOOD CL

TOYMBEE AVE

MAIZEY RD

CHATFIELD

MALORY CL

CITRINE CL

JASPER CL

DIAMOND CRES

RUBY CL

FLETT CRES

BLACKWELL CL

13

10

12

11

9

8

7

6

5

4

3

2

1

15

14

13

90

05 A 06 B C 07 D E F

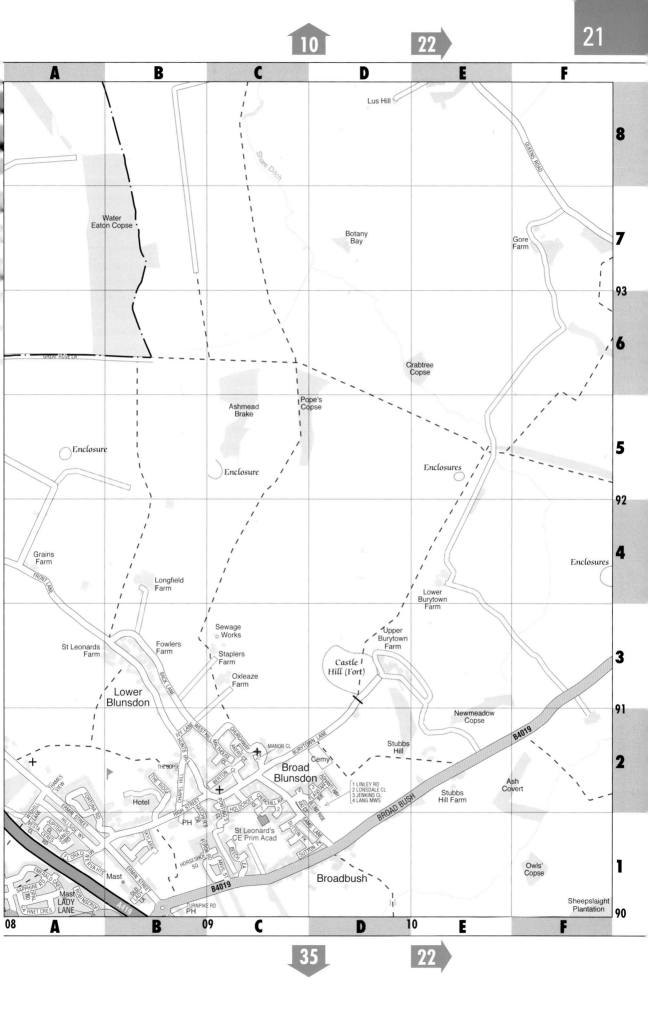

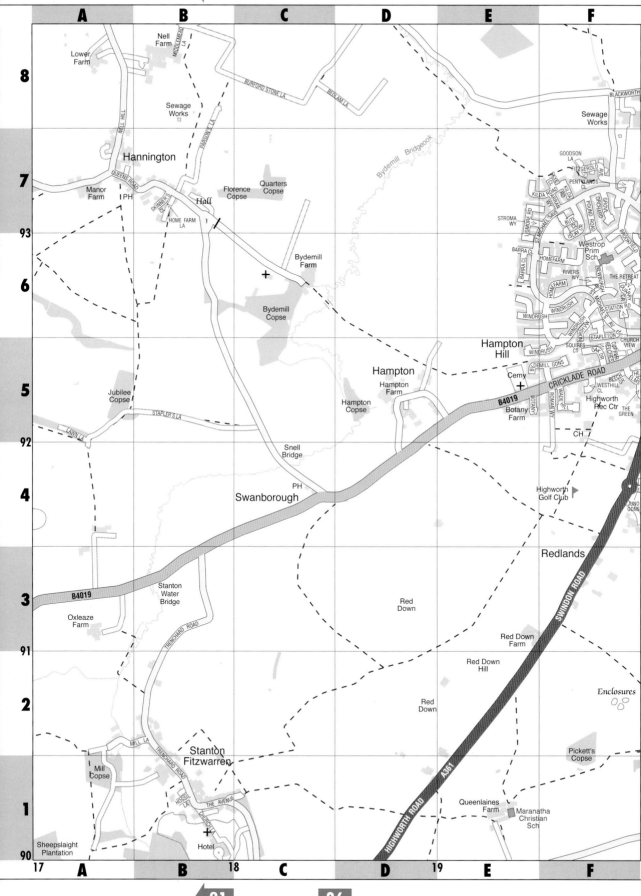

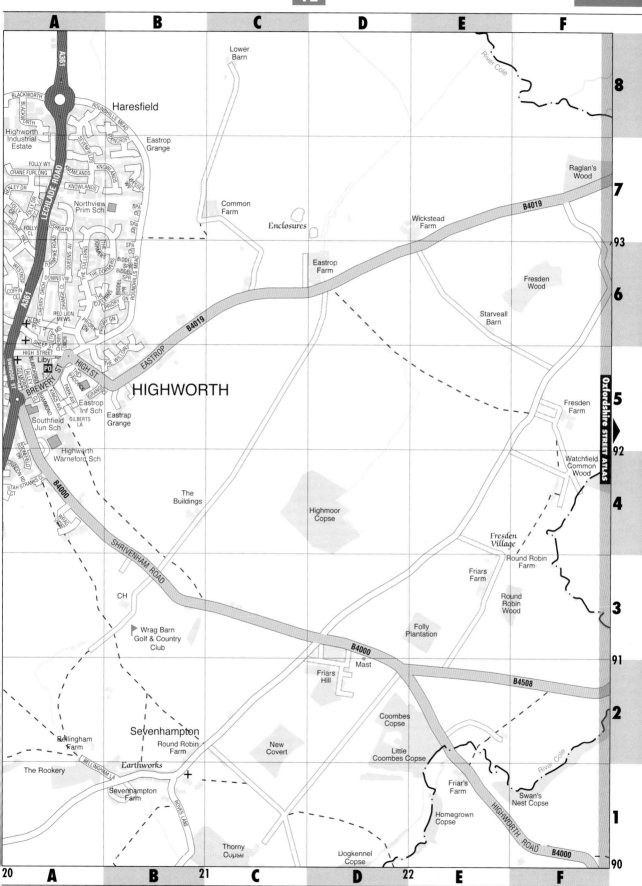

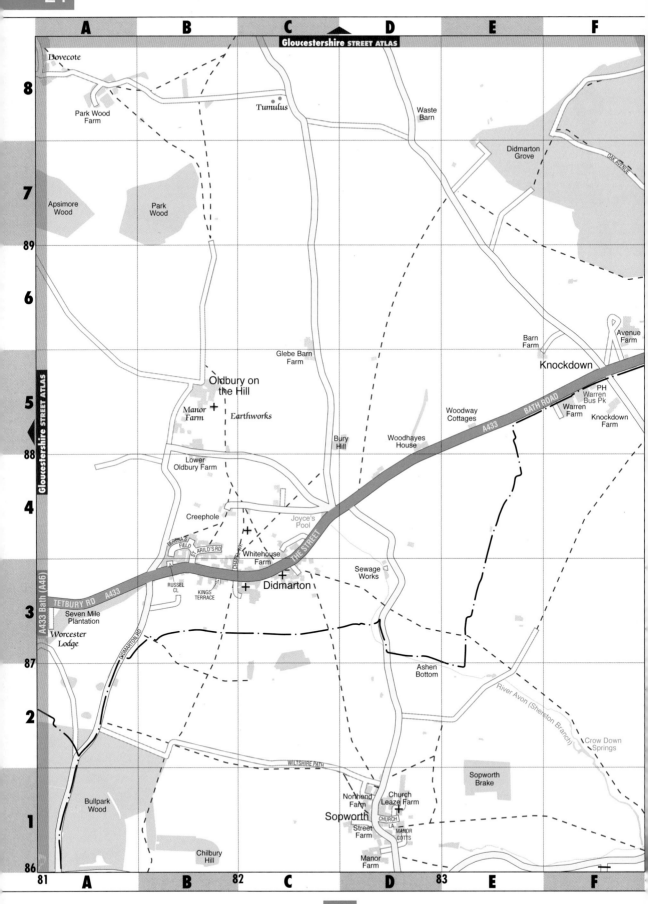

A B C D E F

8

Dovecote

Park Wood
Farm

Tumulus

Waste
Barn

Didmarton
Grove

OAK AVENUE

7

Apsimore
Wood

Park
Wood

89

6

Barn
Farm

Avenue
Farm

Knockdown

Glebe Barn
Farm

Oldbury on
the Hill

BATH ROAD

A433

PH
Warren
Bus Pk

Warren
Farm

Knockdown
Farm

5

Manor
Farm

Earthworks

Bury
Hill

Woodway
Cottages

Woodhayes
House

88

Lower
Oldbury Farm

4

Creephole

Joyce's
Pool

Sewage
Works

BERTHA'S
FIELD

ST ARILD'S RD

CHURCH LA

THE STREET

Whitehouse
Farm

Ashen
Bottom

River Avon (Sherston Branch)

Gloucestershire STREET ATLAS

A433 Bath (A46)

TETBURY RD    A433

RUSSEL
CL

KINGS
TERRACE

Didmarton

3

Seven Mile
Plantation

Worcester
Lodge

DIDMARTON RD

87

Crow Down
Springs

2

WILTSHIRE PATH

Sopworth
Brake

Bullpark
Wood

Nonhend
Farm

Church
Leaze Farm

1

Sopworth

Street
Farm

CHURCH
LA

MANOR
COTTS

Chilbury
Hill

Manor
Farm

86

81    A    82    B    C    82    C    D    83    E    F

26

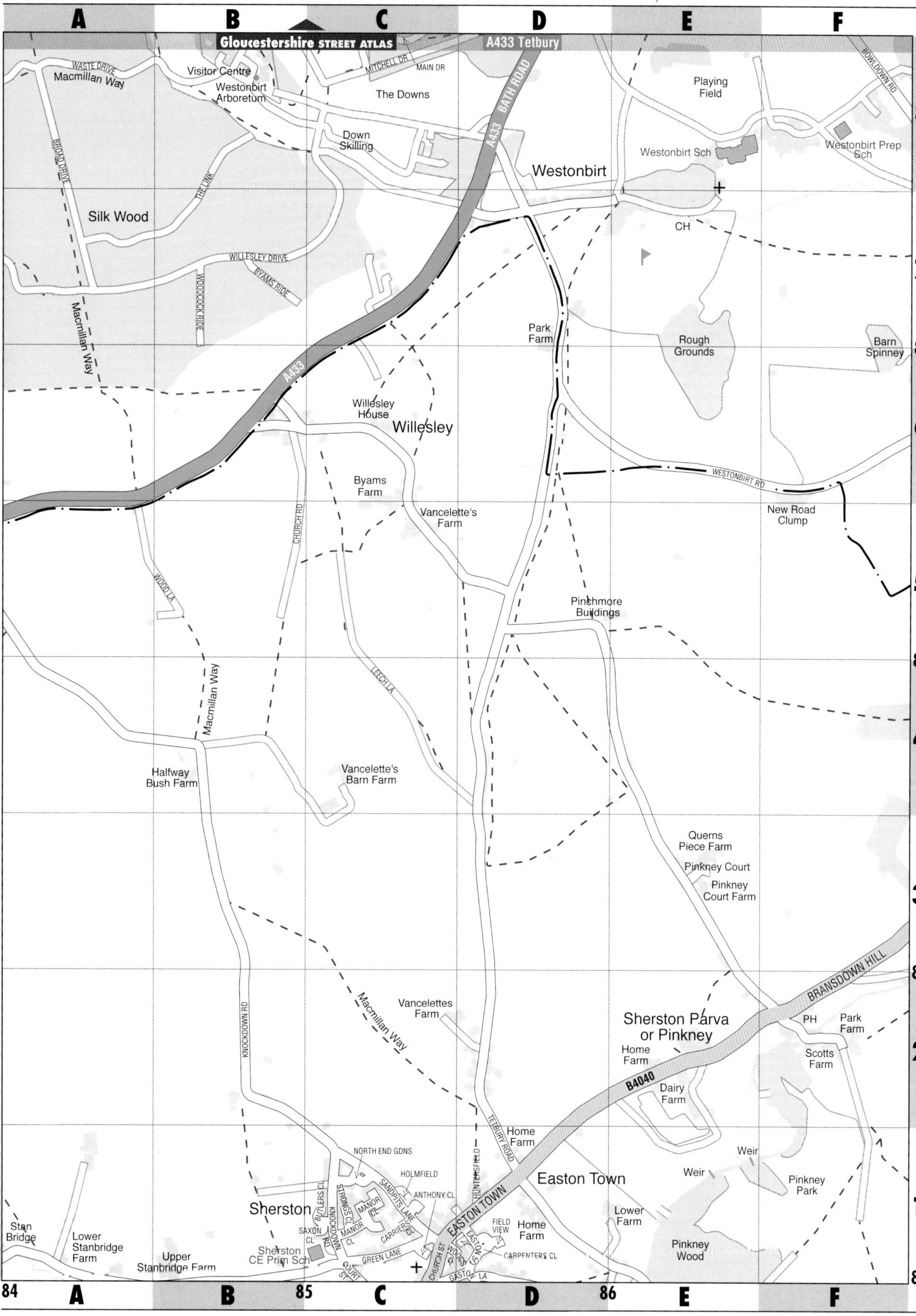
Gloucestershire STREET ATLAS
A433 Tetbury
A
B
C
D
E
F
8
7
89
6
5
88
4
3
87
2
1
86
84
85
86
WASTE DRIVE
Macmillan Way
Visitor Centre
Westonbirt Arboretum
MITCHELL DR
MAIN DR
The Downs
BATH ROAD
A433
Playing Field
BOWLDOWN RD
Down Skilling
Westonbirt
Westonbirt Sch
Westonbirt Prep Sch
BROAD DRIVE
THE LINK
Silk Wood
CH
WILLESLEY DRIVE
BYAMS RIDE
WOODCOCK RIDE
Macmillan Way
Park Farm
Rough Grounds
Barn Spinney
A433
Willesley House
Willesley
Byams Farm
WESTONBIRT RD
Vancelette's Farm
New Road Clump
CHURCH RD
WOOD LA
Pinchmore Buildings
LEECH LA
Macmillan Way
Halfway Bush Farm
Vancelette's Barn Farm
Querns Piece Farm
Pinkney Court
Pinkney Court Farm
BRANSDOWN HILL
Vancelettes Farm
Sherston Parva or Pinkney
PH
Park Farm
KNOCKDOWN RD
Macmillan Way
Home Farm
Scotts Farm
B4040
Dairy Farm
TETBURY ROAD
Home Farm
NORTH END GDNS
HUNTERSFIELD
Weir
Weir
HOLMFIELD
Easton Town
SANDPITS LANE
ANTHONY CL
BUTLERS CL
STRONGS CL
MANOR CL
Pinkney Park
Sherston
EASTON TOWN
Lower Farm
Stan Bridge
SAXON CL
KNOCKDOWN RD
MANOR CL
CARRIERS CL
FIELD VIEW
Home Farm
Lower Stanbridge Farm
Pinkney Wood
GREEN LANE
CARPENTERS CL
Upper Stanbridge Farm
Sherston CE Prim Sch
COURT ST
CHURCH ST
EASTON LA

40

26

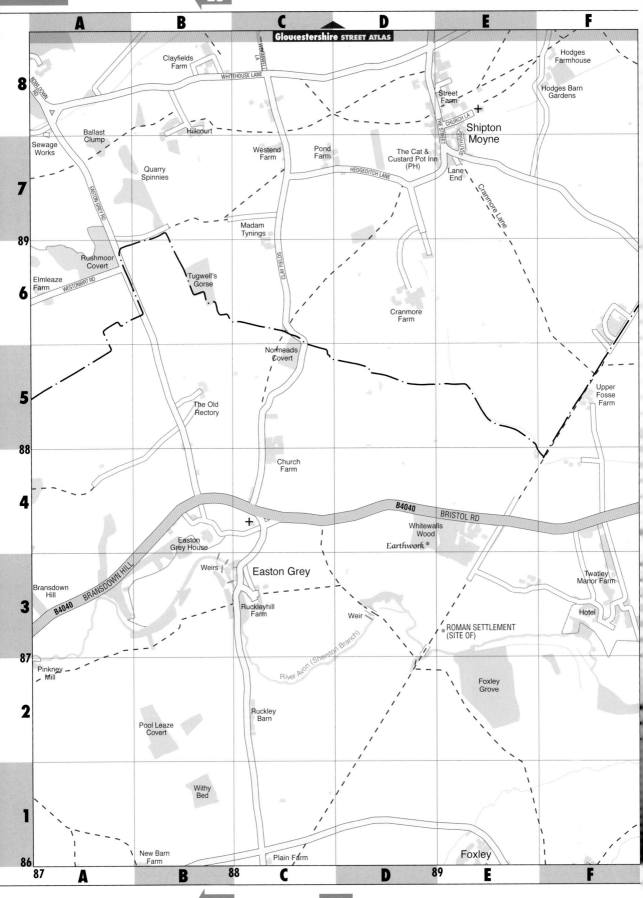

Gloucestershire STREET ATLAS

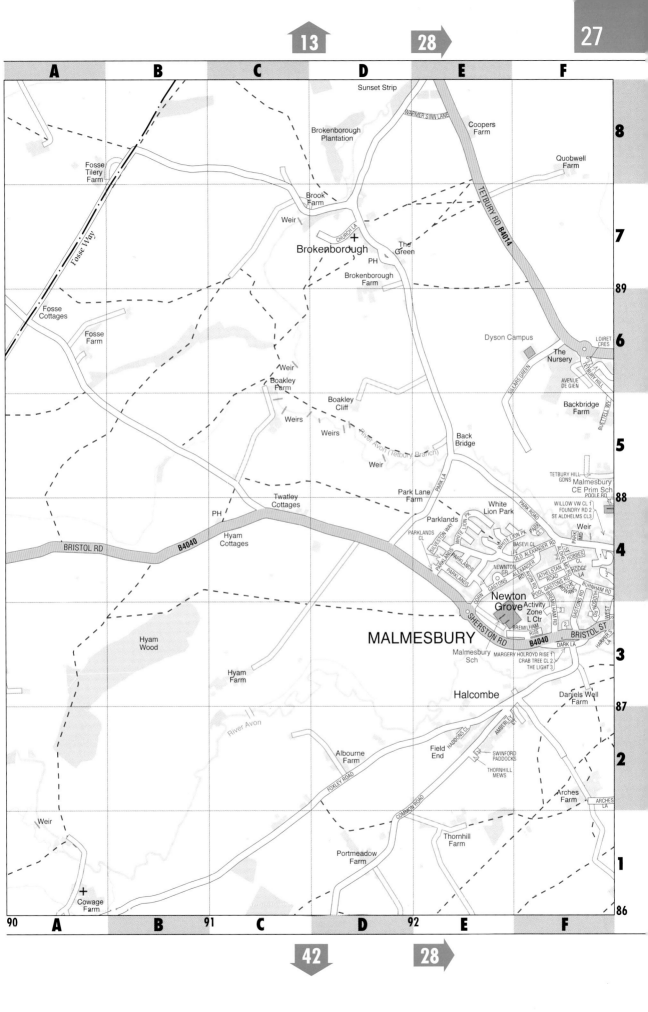

A  B  C  D  E  F

8

Sunset Strip
Brokenborough
Plantation
WARMER'S INN LANE
Coopers
Farm
Fosse
Tilery
Farm
TETBURY RD B4014
Quobwell
Farm

7

Brook
Farm
Weir
CHURCH LA
Brokenborough
The
Green
PH
Brokenborough
Farm

89

Fosse
Cottages
Dyson Campus
LOIRET
CRES
The
Nursery
Fosse
Farm
TETBURY HILL
AVENUE
DE GIEN
SILCARS GREEN
BLUEBELL WY

6

Weir
Boakley
Farm
Backbridge
Farm
Weirs
Boakley
Cliff
Weirs
River Avon (Tetbury Branch)
Back
Bridge

5

Weir
TETBURY HILL
GDNS
Malmesbury
CE Prim Sch
POOLE RD
Park Lane
Farm
PARK LA
White
Lion Park
Parklands
WILLOW VW CL 1
FOUNDRY RD 2
ST ALDHELMS CL3
Weir

88

Twatley
Cottages
PH
PARKLANDS
CL
SILVESTON WAN
WHITE LION PK
WHITE LION PK
PARK RD
PARK CL
BASEVI CL
OLD ALEXANDER RD
ST ALDHELMS RD
PARK MD
Hyam
Cottages
B4040
NEWTON
GR
ALEXANDER
AVON RD
ATHELSTAN
ROAD
ST HOBBES
HODGE
LA
1
BURNHAM RD

4

BRISTOL RD
PARKLANDS
PARKLANDS
NEWTON
GR
POOL GASTONS RD
BREMILHAM RD
TOWNS
GASTONS RD
WEST
Newton
Grove
Hyam
Wood
SHERSTON RD
Activity
Zone
L Ctr
BREMILHAM
RISE
BRISTOL ST
HARPER'S LA

Hyam
Farm
MALMESBURY
B4040
DARK LA

3

Malmesbury
Sch
MARGERY HOLROYD RISE 1
CRAB TREE CL 2
THE LIGHT 3
Halcombe
Daniels Well
Farm

87

River Avon
HADDONS CL
AMBERLEY CL
SWINFORD
PADDOCKS
THORNHILL
MEWS
Arches
Farm
ARCHES
LA

2

Albourne
Farm
Field
End
Weir
FOXLEY ROAD
COMMON ROAD
Thornhill
Farm

1

Cowage
Farm
Portmeadow
Farm

86

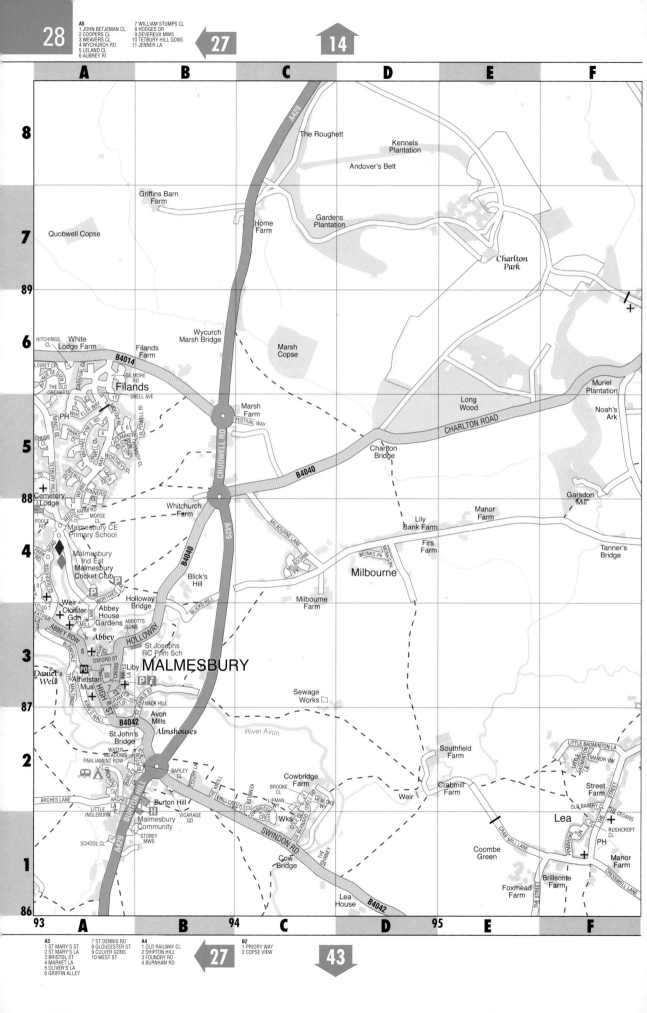

28

A5
1 JOHN BETJEMAN CL
2 COOPERS CL
3 WEAVERS CL
4 WYCHURCH RD
5 LELAND CL
6 AUBREY RI

7 WILLIAM STUMPS CL
8 HODGES DR
9 DEVEREUX MWS
10 TETBURY HILL GDNS
11 JENNER LA

27

14

A3
1 ST MARY'S ST
2 ST MARY'S LA
3 BRISTOL ST
4 MARKET LA
5 OLIVER'S LA
6 GRIFFIN ALLEY

7 ST DENNIS RD
8 GLOUCESTER ST
9 CULVER GDNS
10 WEST ST

A4
1 OLD RAILWAY CL
2 SHIPTON HILL
3 FOUNDRY RD
4 BURNHAM RD

B2
1 PRIORY WAY
2 COPSE VIEW

27

43

The Roughett

Kennels Plantation

Andover's Belt

Griffins Barn Farm

Quobwell Copse

Home Farm

Gardens Plantation

Charlton Park

Wycurch Marsh Bridge

Marsh Copse

Muriel Plantation

Noah's Ark

HITCHINGS CL
White Lodge Farm

Filands Farm

Marsh Farm

FESTIVAL WAY

Long Wood

CHARLTON ROAD

B4014

LOIRET CR
AVENUE DE GEN
THE OLD ORCHARD
Filands

GILMORE RD
SNELL AVE

Charlton Bridge

Garsdon Mill

CRUDWELL RD

B4040

Whitchurch Farm

MILBOURNE LANE

Manor Farm

Lily Bank Farm

Firs Farm

Tanner's Bridge

Malmesbury CE Primary School

Malmesbury Ind Est
Malmesbury Cricket Club

Blick's Hill

MILBOURNE PK

MONKS PK

Milbourne

MONKS PK

Weir

Cloister Gdn

Abbey House Gardens

Holloway Bridge

BLICKS HILL

ABBOTTS GDNS

Milbourne Farm

Abbey

HOLLOWAY

St Josephs RC Prim Sch

MALMESBURY

Sewage Works

Daniel's Well

Athelstan Mus

HIGH ST

B4042

Avon Mills

Almshouses

River Avon

Southfield Farm

LITTLE BADMINTON LA

MANOR VW

St John's Bridge

WATER MEADOWS
PARLIAMENT ROW

BARLEY CL

PRIORY LA

THE KNOLL

Cowbridge Farm

Crabmill Farm

Weir

Street Farm

OLD BAKERY CL

Lea

RUSHCROFT CL

PH

ARCHES LANE

Burton Hill

Malmesbury Community

VICARAGE GD

MILL CRES

BROOKE CL

LIPMAN WY

CONBRIDGE CRES

Wks

HEMLOCK WY

CRAB MILL LANE

Coombe Green

Manor Farm

CRESSWELL LANE

SCHOOL CL

STOREY MWS

SWINDON RD

Cow Bridge

THE SPINNEY

Foxmead Farm

Brillscote Farm

Lea House

B4042

93    A    94    B    C    94    D    95    E    F

86

1

2

87

3

88

4

5

89

6

7

8

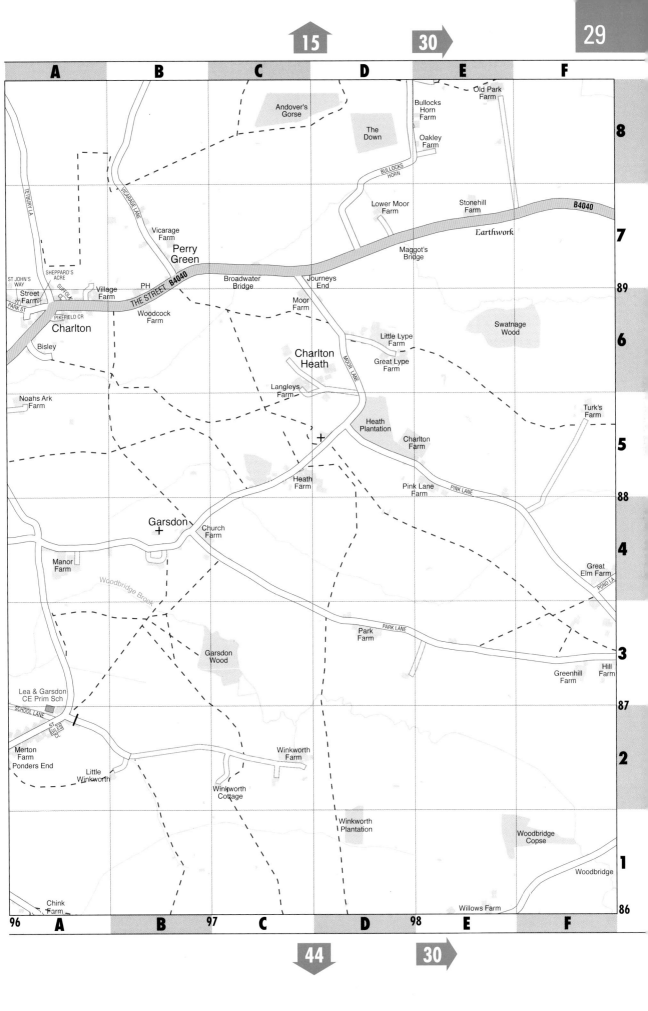

29
16

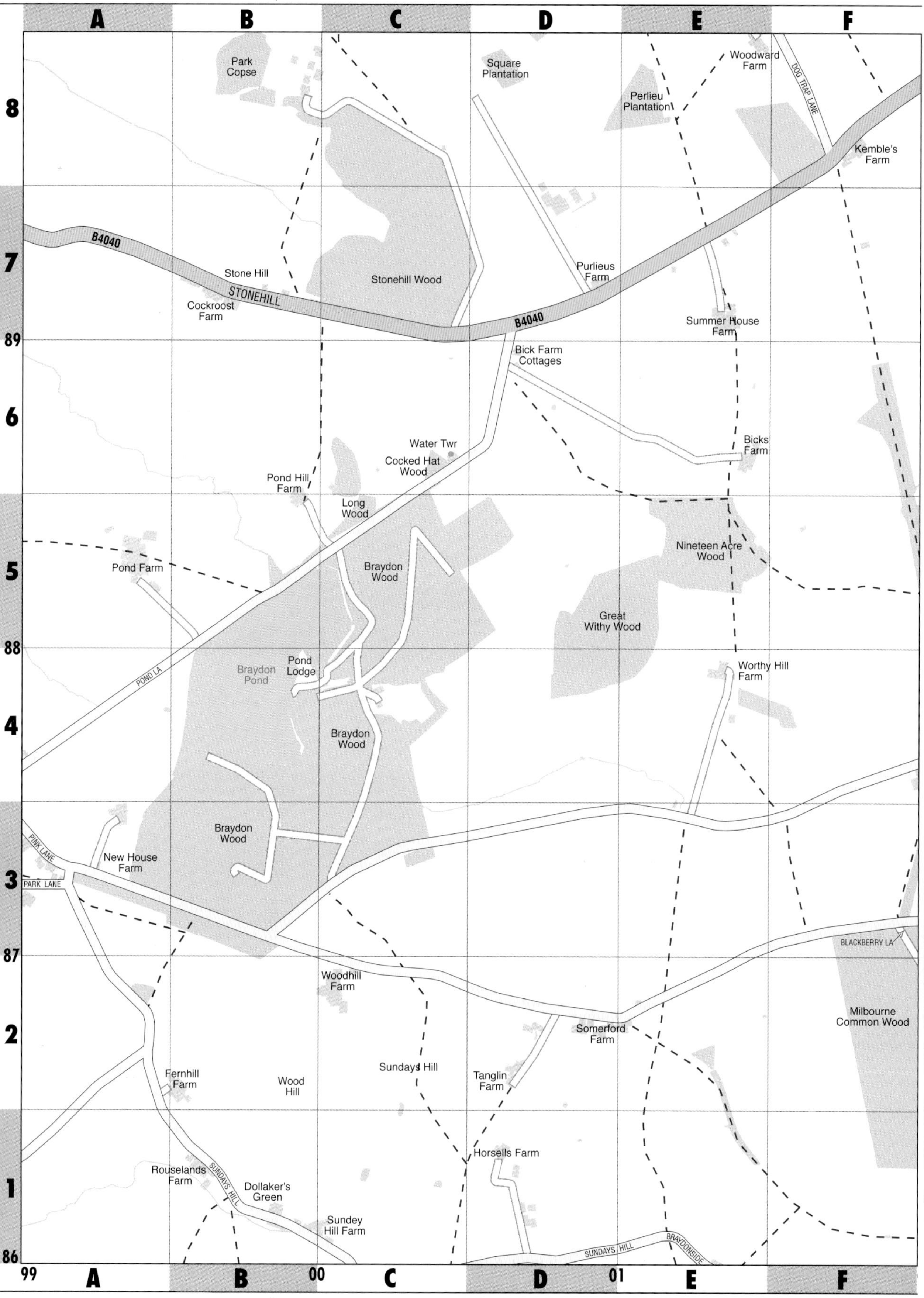

A B C D E F

8

7

89

6

5

88

4

3

87

2

1

86

Park Copse

Square Plantation

Woodward Farm

Perlieu Plantation

DOG TRAP LANE

Kemble's Farm

B4040

Stone Hill

STONEHILL

Stonehill Wood

Purlieus Farm

B4040

Cockroost Farm

Summer House Farm

Bick Farm Cottages

Bicks Farm

Water Twr

Cocked Hat Wood

Pond Hill Farm

Long Wood

Braydon Wood

Nineteen Acre Wood

Pond Farm

POND LA

Braydon Pond

Pond Lodge

Braydon Wood

Great Withy Wood

Worthy Hill Farm

Braydon Wood

PINK LANE

New House Farm

PARK LANE

PARK LANE

BLACKBERRY LA

Woodhill Farm

Milbourne Common Wood

Somerford Farm

Sundays Hill

Tanglin Farm

Fernhill Farm

Wood Hill

Horsells Farm

Rouselands Farm

SUNDAYS HILL

Dollaker's Green

Sundey Hill Farm

SUNDAYS HILL

BRAYDONSIDE

99 A B 00 C D 01 E F

29
45

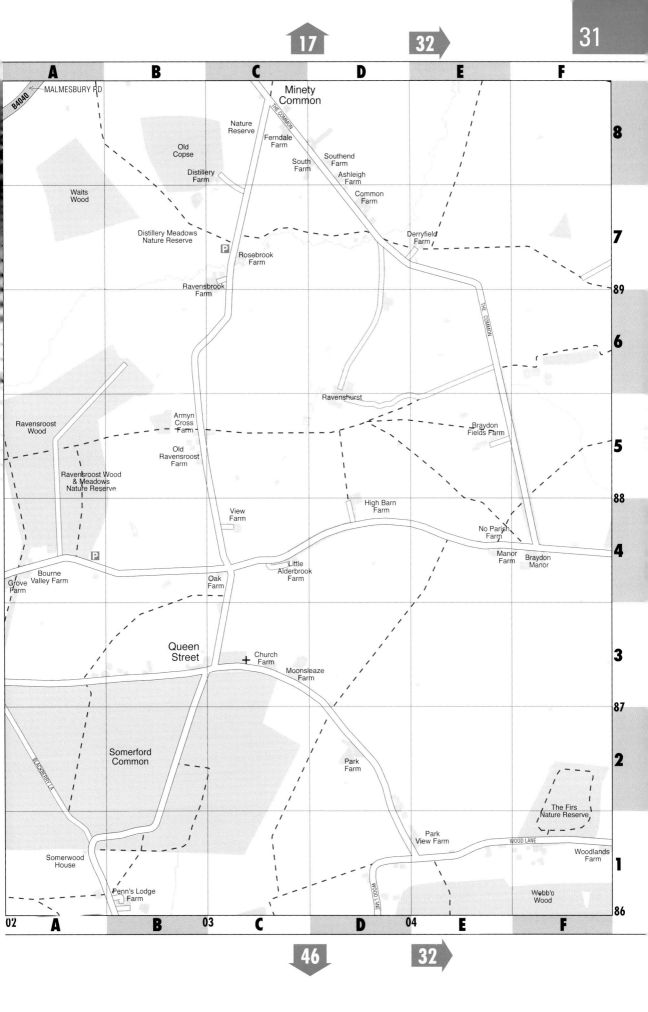

A  B  C  D  E  F

MALMESBURY RD
B4040

8

Minety
Common

Nature
Reserve

Old
Copse

Ferndale
Farm

Southend
Farm

South
Farm

Ashleigh
Farm

Distillery
Farm

THE COMMON

Common
Farm

Waits
Wood

7

Distillery Meadows
Nature Reserve

Derryfield
Farm

89

Rosebrook
Farm

Ravensbrook
Farm

6

THE COMMON

Ravenshurst

Ravensroost
Wood

Armyn
Cross
Farm

Braydon
Fields Farm

5

Old
Ravensroost
Farm

Ravensroost Wood
& Meadows
Nature Reserve

88

View
Farm

High Barn
Farm

No Parish
Farm

4

Grove
Farm

Bourne
Valley Farm

Oak
Farm

Little
Alderbrook
Farm

Manor
Farm

Braydon
Manor

Queen
Street

Church
Farm

Moonsleaze
Farm

3

87

Somerford
Common

Park
Farm

2

BLACKBERRY LN

The Firs
Nature Reserve

Park
View Farm

WOOD LANE

Woodlands
Farm

Somerwood
House

1

Penn's Lodge
Farm

WOOD LANE

Webb's
Wood

86

02        03        04

A  B  C  D  E  F

A   B   C   D   E   F

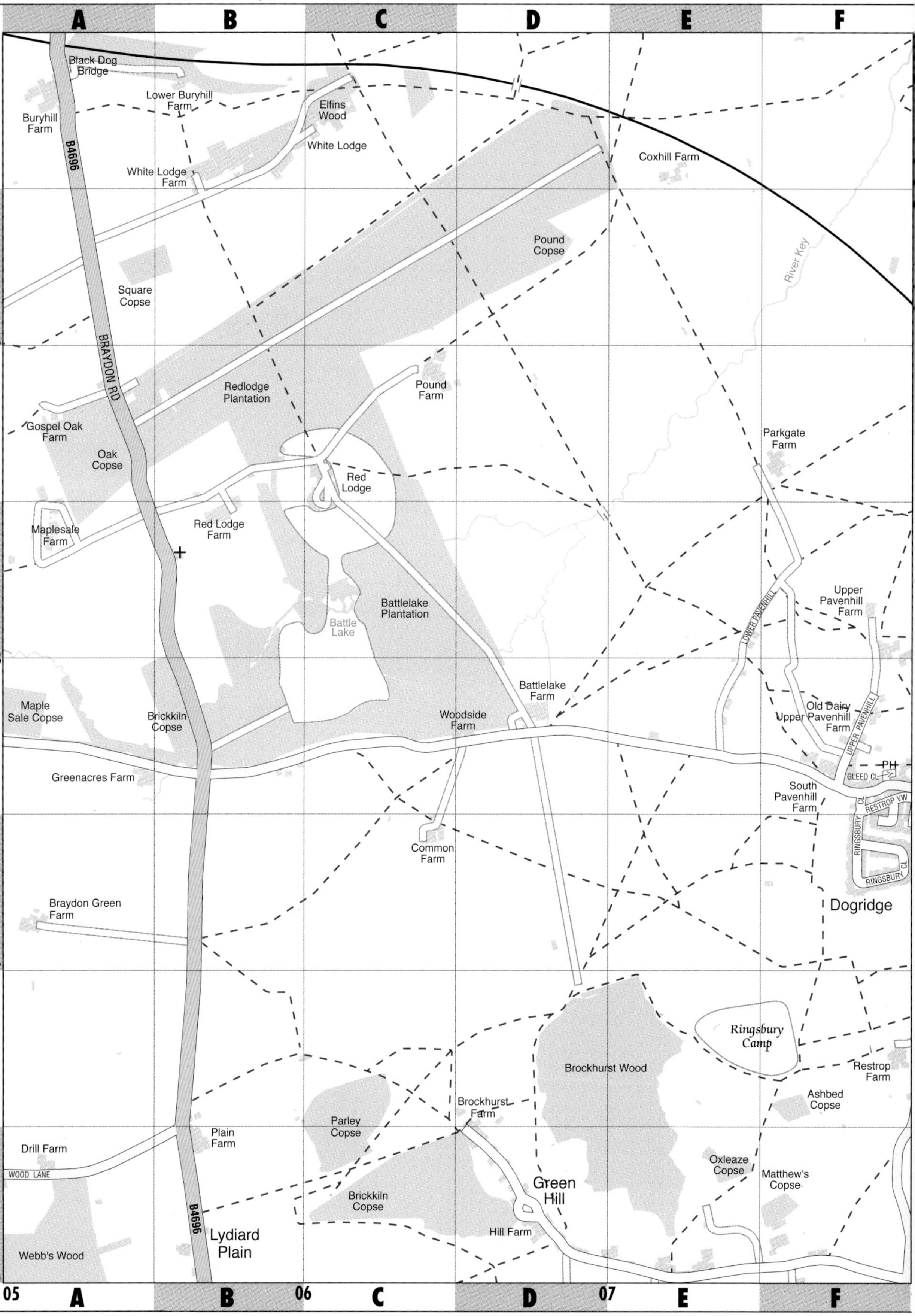

8

Black Dog Bridge

Buryhill Farm

Lower Buryhill Farm

Elfins Wood

White Lodge

B4696

White Lodge Farm

7

Square Copse

BRAYDON RD

Pound Copse

Coxhill Farm

River Key

89

Redlodge Plantation

Pound Farm

6

Gospel Oak Farm

Oak Copse

Red Lodge

Parkgate Farm

Maplesale Farm

Red Lodge Farm

+

Upper Pavenhill Farm

5

Battlelake Plantation

Battle Lake

LOWER PAVENHILL

88

Maple Sale Copse

Brickkiln Copse

Woodside Farm

Battlelake Farm

Old Dairy
Upper Pavenhill Farm

UPPER PAVENHILL

4

Greenacres Farm

PH
GLEED CL

South Pavenhill Farm

RESTROP VW

Common Farm

RINGSBURY CL

RINGSBURY CL

3

Braydon Green Farm

Dogridge

87

Ringsbury Camp

2

Brockhurst Wood

Restrop Farm

Brockhurst Farm

Ashbed Copse

Parley Copse

Oxleaze Copse

Matthew's Copse

Drill Farm

Plain Farm

WOOD LANE

Green Hill

Brickkiln Copse

1

B4696

Lydiard Plain

Hill Farm

Webb's Wood

86

05   A   B   06   C   D   07   E   F

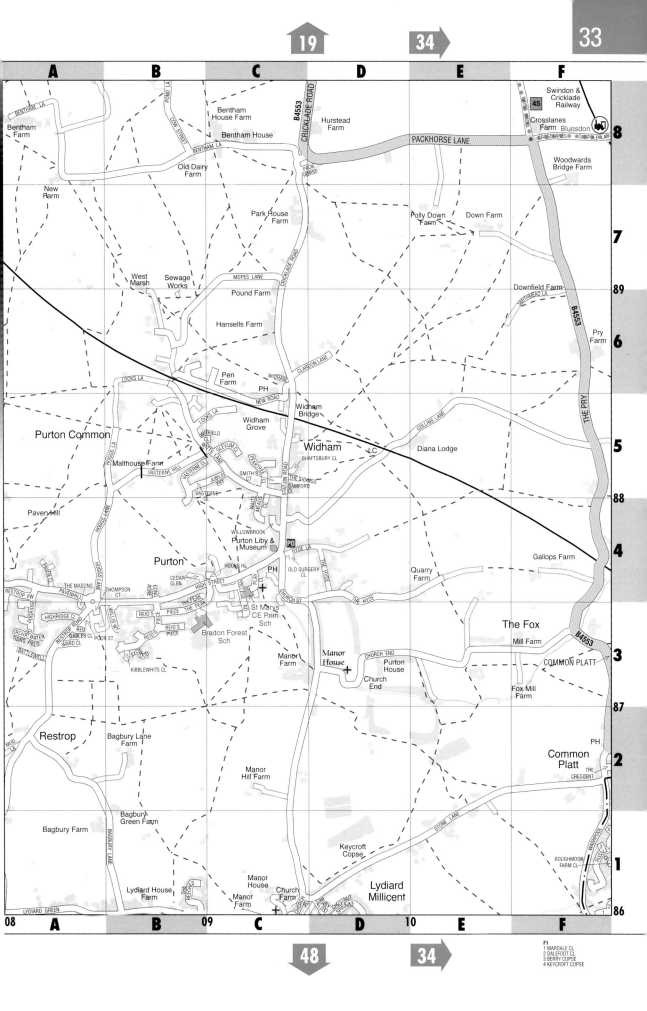

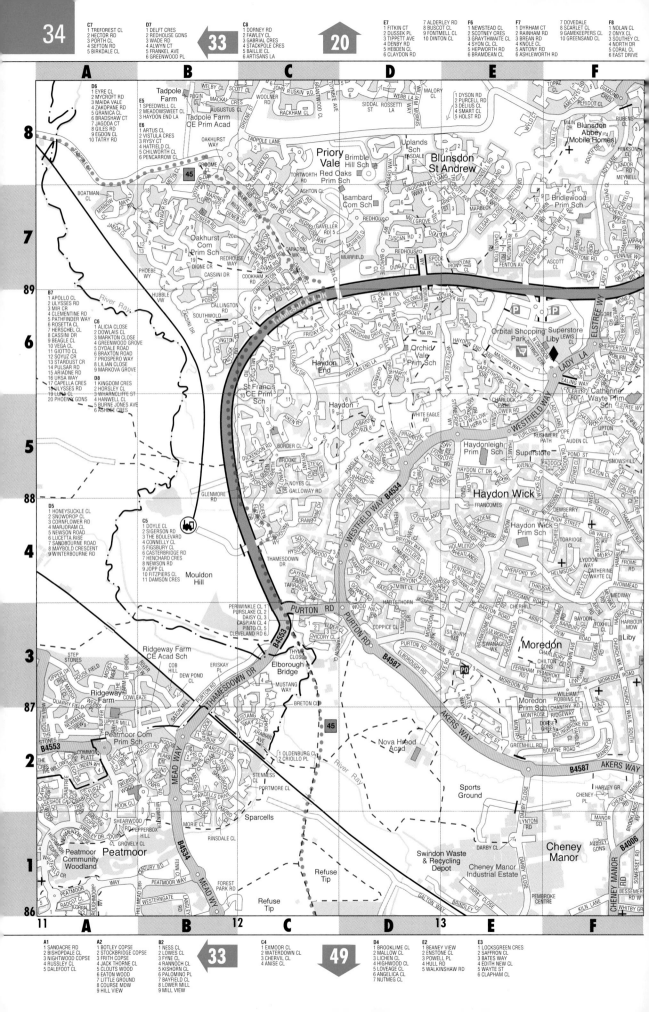

Priory Vale
Tadpole Farm
Tadpole Farm CE Prim Acad
Brimble Hill Sch
Red Oaks Prim Sch
Blunsdon St Andrew
Blunsdon Abbey (Mobile Homes)
Bridlewood Prim Sch
Oakhurst Com Sch
Isambard Com Sch
Uplands Sch
Orbital Shopping Park
Superstore
Orchid Vale Prim Sch
Haydon End
St Francis CE Prim Sch
Haydon
Catherine Wayte Prim Sch
Haydonleigh Prim Sch
Superstore
Haydon Wick
Haydon Wick Prim Sch
Mouldon Hill
Thamesdown Dr
Purton Rd
Moredon
Elborough Bridge
Ridgeway Farm CE Acad Sch
Ridgeway Farm
Peatmoor Com Prim Sch
Moredon Prim Sch
Nova Hreod Acad
Sports Ground
Cheney Manor
Swindon Waste & Recycling Depot
Cheney Manor Industrial Estate
Peatmoor Community Woodland
Peatmoor
Sparcells
Refuse Tip

| A6 | A8 | | B6 | C5 | | C6 | | 35 |
| 1 TIMANDRA CL | 1 DOBSON CL | 5 MILLARD RD | 1 GARSON RD | 1 HILMARTON AVE | | 1 TISBURY CL |
| 2 EXBURY CL | 2 RENOIR CL | 6 THE ARC | 2 PICKFORD WAY | 2 WARMINSTER AVE | | 2 STAVERTON WY |
| 3 HONEYLIGHT VW | 3 NASH CL | 7 LONGFELLOW CL | 3 STEWART CL | 3 POTTERDOWN RD | | 3 WOODFORD CL |
| | 4 ST ANDREWS | 8 BATSFORD CRES | 4 CHIPPENHAM CL | 4 FARNDALE CL | | 4 AMESBURY CL |
| | RIDGE | 9 WRIGHT CL | | | | 5 KENCOT CT |

**21** ▲    **36** ▶

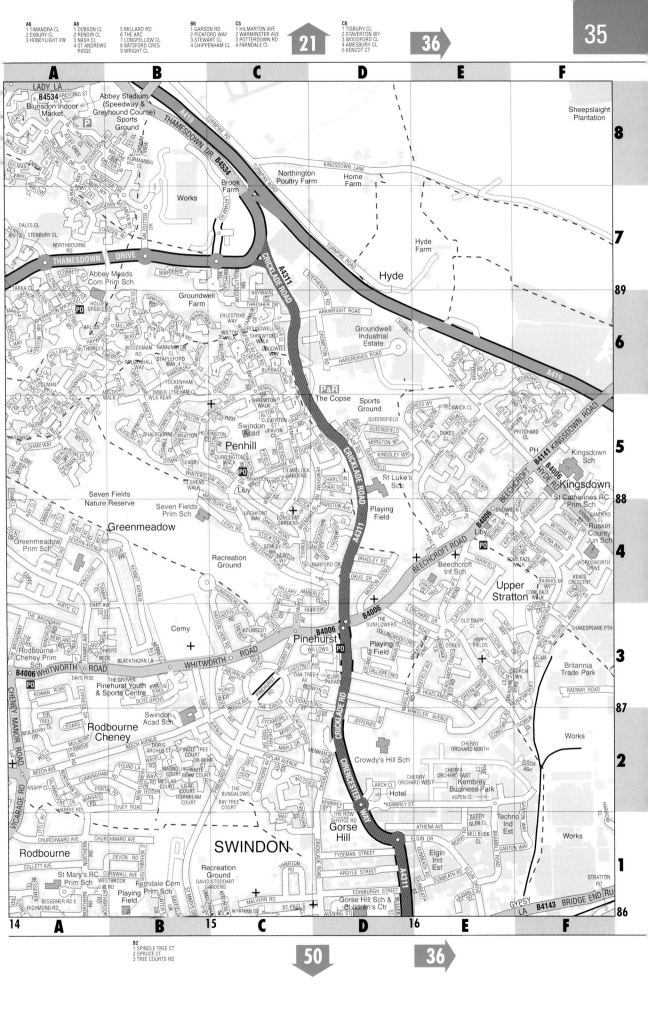

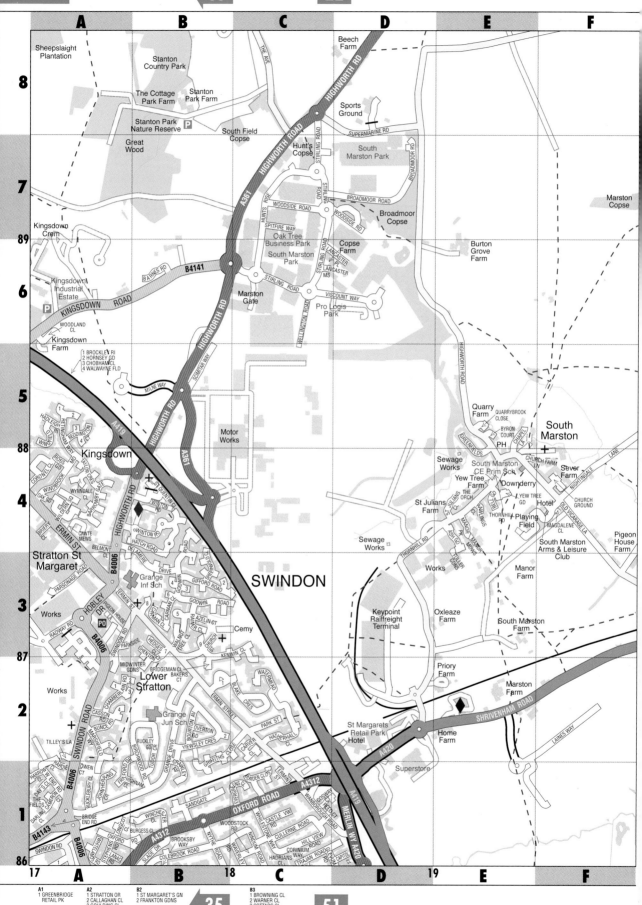

A1
1 GREENBRIDGE
RETAIL PK

A2
1 STRATTON OR
2 CALLAGHAN CL
3 GOULDING CL
4 SHAPLANDS
5 THE PADDOCKS

B2
1 ST MARGARET'S GN
2 FRANKTON GDNS

B3
1 BROWNING CL
2 WARNER CL
3 COTTARS CL
4 BARON CL
5 BOWMAN CL
6 CRISPIN CL
7 CHURCH WAY
8 FRANK WARMAN CT
9 CHURCH FARM

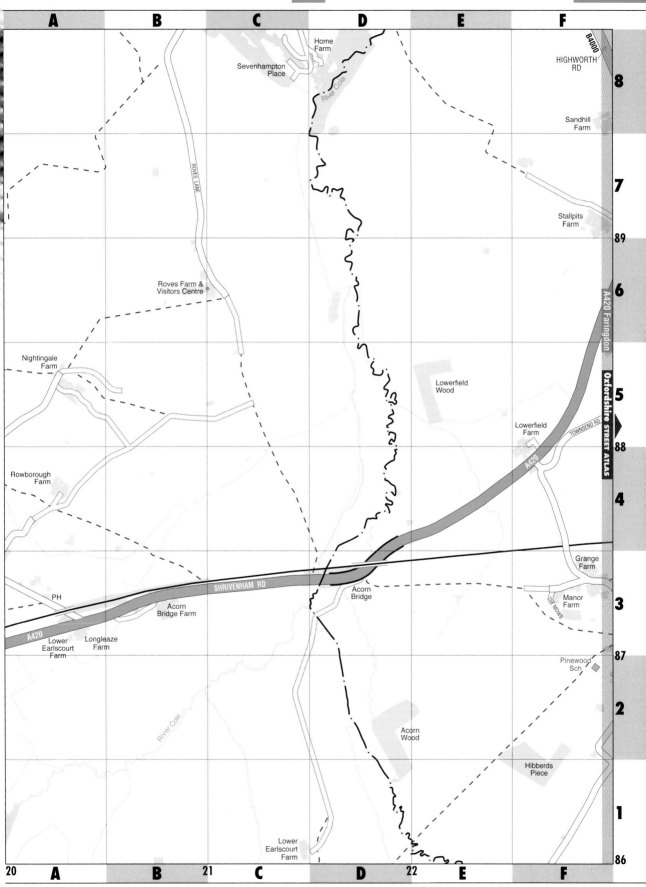

A B C D E F

**8**

HIGHWORTH RD

B4000

Home Farm

Sevenhampton Place

River Cole

Sandhill Farm

**7**

Stallpits Farm

**89**

Roves Farm & Visitors Centre

ROVES LANE

**6**

A420 Faringdon

Lowerfield Wood

Oxfordshire STREET ATLAS

Nightingale Farm

**5**

Lowerfield Farm

TOWNSEND RD

**88**

A420

Rowborough Farm

**4**

Grange Farm

Manor Farm

SHRIVENHAM RD

THE MDWS

PH

Acorn Bridge

Acorn Bridge Farm

**3**

A420

Lower Earlscourt Farm

Longleaze Farm

Pinewood Sch

**87**

River Cole

**2**

Acorn Wood

Hibberds Piece

**1**

Lower Earlscourt Farm

**86**

20 A B 21 C D 22 E F

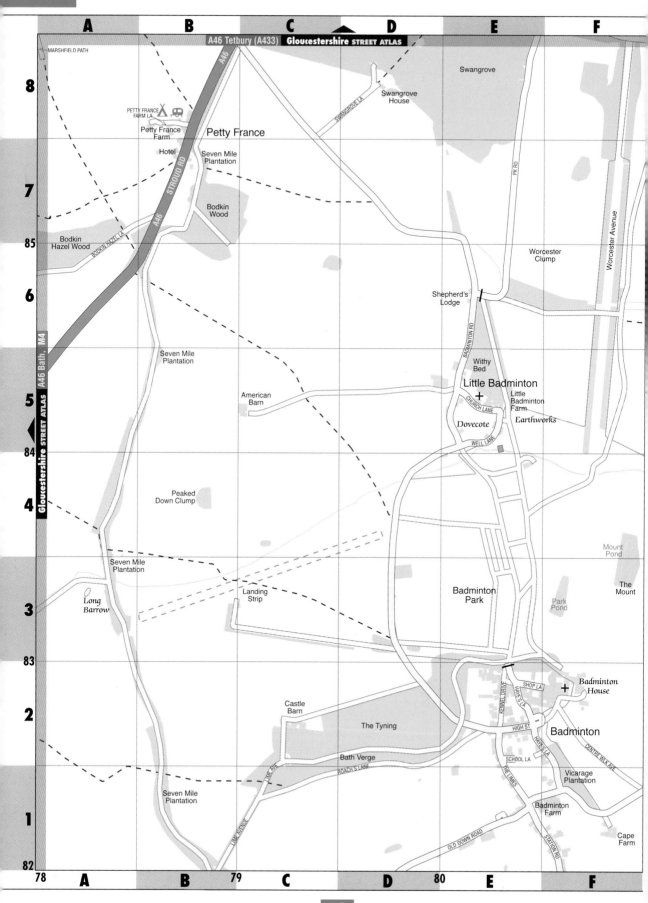

MARSHFIELD PATH

Swangrove

Swangrove House

SWANGROVE LA

Petty France

PETTY FRANCE FARM LA.

Petty France Farm

Hotel

Seven Mile Plantation

Bodkin Wood

Bodkin Hazel Wood

BODKIN HAZEL LA

STROUD RD

A46

PK RD

Worcester Avenue

Worcester Clump

Shepherd's Lodge

BADMINTON RD

Withy Bed

Little Badminton

Little Badminton Farm

Earthworks

Dovecote

CHURCH LANE

WELL LANE

Seven Mile Plantation

American Barn

Peaked Down Clump

Seven Mile Plantation

Long Barrow

Landing Strip

Mount Pond

The Mount

Badminton Park

Park Pond

Castle Barn

The Tyning

LIME AVE

Bath Verge

ROACH'S LANE

Seven Mile Plantation

LIME AVENUE

SHOP LA

KENNEL DRIVE

HAYE'S LA

HIGH ST

HAYES LA

SCHOOL LA

THE LIMES

CENTRE WLK AVE

Badminton House

Badminton

Vicarage Plantation

Badminton Farm

STATION RD

OLD DOWN ROAD

Cape Farm

A46 Bath, M4

78    79    80

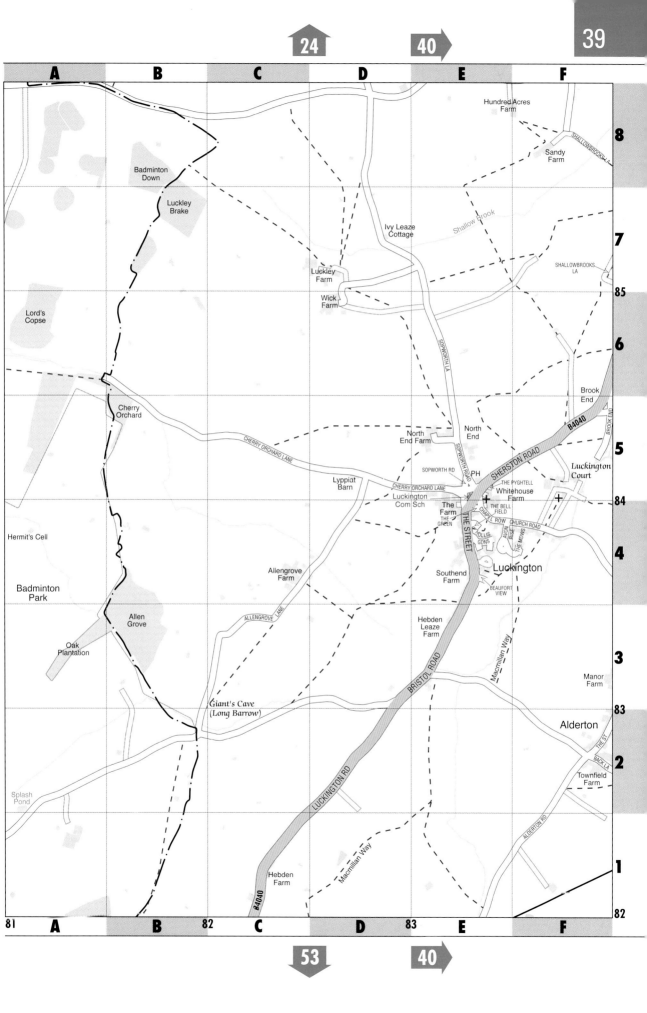

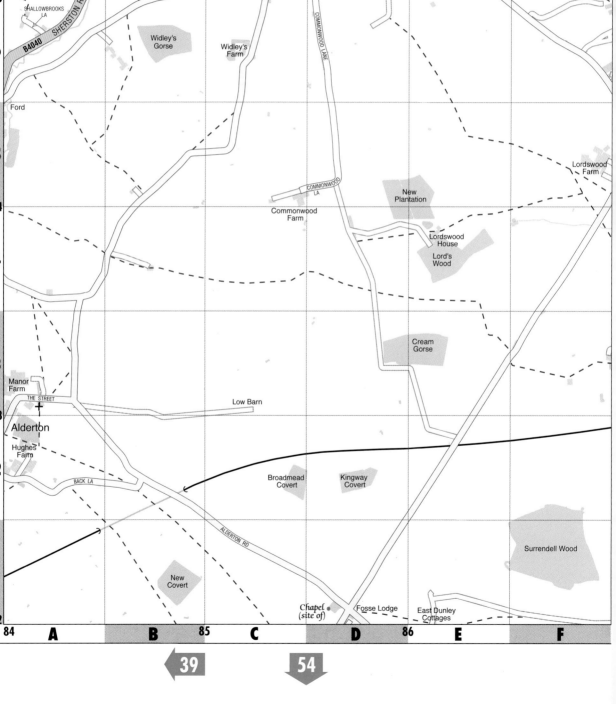

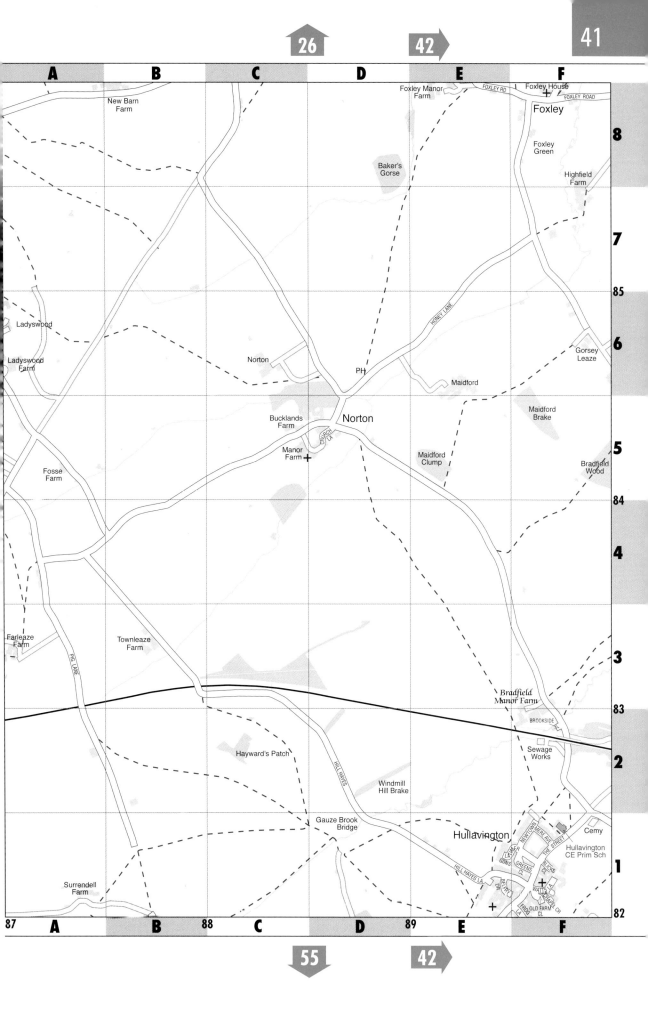

A    B    C    D    E    F

8

7

85

6

5

84

4

3

83

2

1

82

Foxley Manor Farm
FOXLEY RD
Foxley House
FOXLEY ROAD
Foxley
Foxley Green
Highfield Farm

New Barn Farm

Baker's Gorse

HONEY LANE

Ladyswood

Ladyswood Farm

Norton

PH

Maidford

Gorsey Leaze

Maidford Brake

Norton

Bucklands Farm

Manor Farm

Maidford Clump

Bradfield Wood

Fosse Farm

Farleaze Farm

PIG LANE

Townleaze Farm

Bradfield Manor Farm

BROOKSIDE

Hayward's Patch

HILL HAYES

Windmill Hill Brake

Sewage Works

Gauze Brook Bridge

Hullavington

NEWTOWN
MERE AVE
THE STREET
Cemy

Hullavington CE Prim Sch

BELFRY GDNS
GREENS CL
BELFRY CL
BELFRY DR
WATTS
OLD FARM CL
FROG LA
SHAPE CR

Surrendell Farm

87    A    B    88    C    D    89    E    F    82

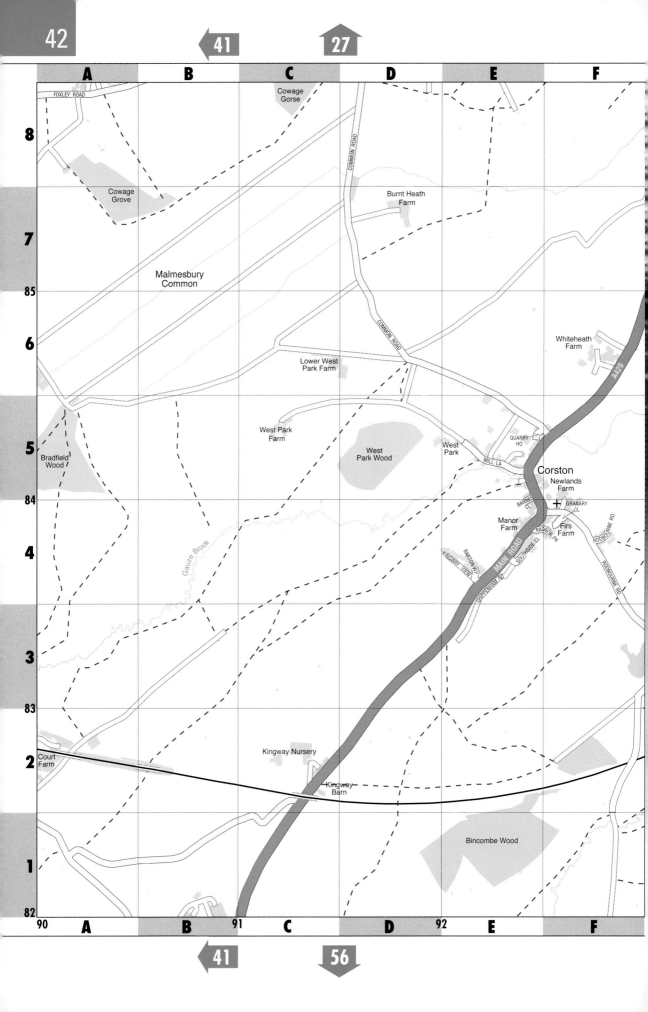

A B C D E F

8 7 85 6 5 84 4 3 83 2 1 82

FOXLEY ROAD

Cowage Gorse

Cowage Grove

Malmesbury Common

COMMON ROAD

Burnt Heath Farm

COMMON ROAD

Whiteheath Farm

A429

Lower West Park Farm

West Park Farm

West Park Wood

West Park

QUARRY HO

MILL LA

Corston

Newlands Farm

Bradfield Wood

GRANARY CL

BARNES CL

Manor Farm

Firs Farm

RODBOURNE RD

RADNOR PK

MAIN ROAD

KINGWAY VIEW

BARTON WY

CHIPPENHAM RD

SOUTHSIDE CL

RODBOURNE RD

Gauze Brook

Kingway Nursery

Court Farm

Kingway Barn

Bincombe Wood

90 A B 91 C D 92 E F

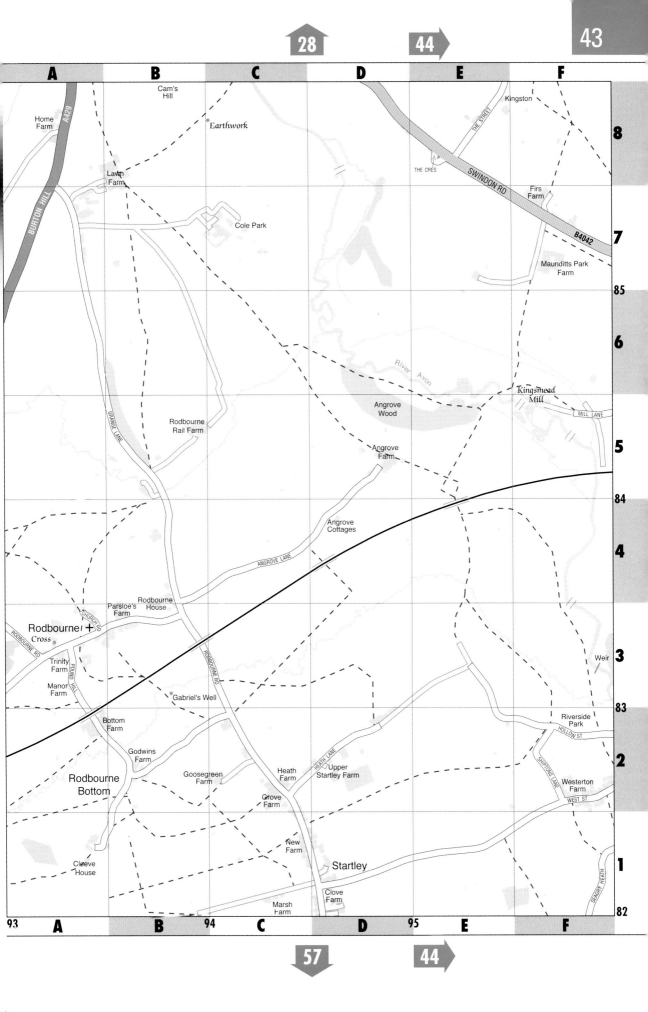

A  B  C  D  E  F

8
85
7
6
5
84
4
3
83
2
82
1

Cam's
Hill

Home
Farm

A429

BURTON HILL

Earthwork

Lawn
Farm

Cole Park

Kingston

THE STREET

THE CRES

SWINDON RD

B4042

Firs
Farm

Maunditts Park
Farm

River Avon

Kingsmead
Mill

MILL LANE

GRANGE LANE

Rodbourne
Rail Farm

Angrove
Wood

Angrove
Farm

Angrove
Cottages

ANGROVE LANE

Parsloe's
Farm

Rodbourne
House

CHURCH RD

RODBOURNE RD

Rodbourne
Cross

Trinity
Farm

POUND HILL

RODBOURNE RD

Manor
Farm

Gabriel's Well

Weir

Riverside
Park

HOLLOW ST

Bottom
Farm

Godwins
Farm

Goosegreen
Farm

Heath
Farm

HEATH LANE

Upper
Startley Farm

SHIPTONS LANE

Westerton
Farm

WEST ST

Rodbourne
Bottom

Grove
Farm

New
Farm

Startley

Cleeve
House

Clove
Farm

Marsh
Farm

SEAGRY HEATH

← 43
↑ 29

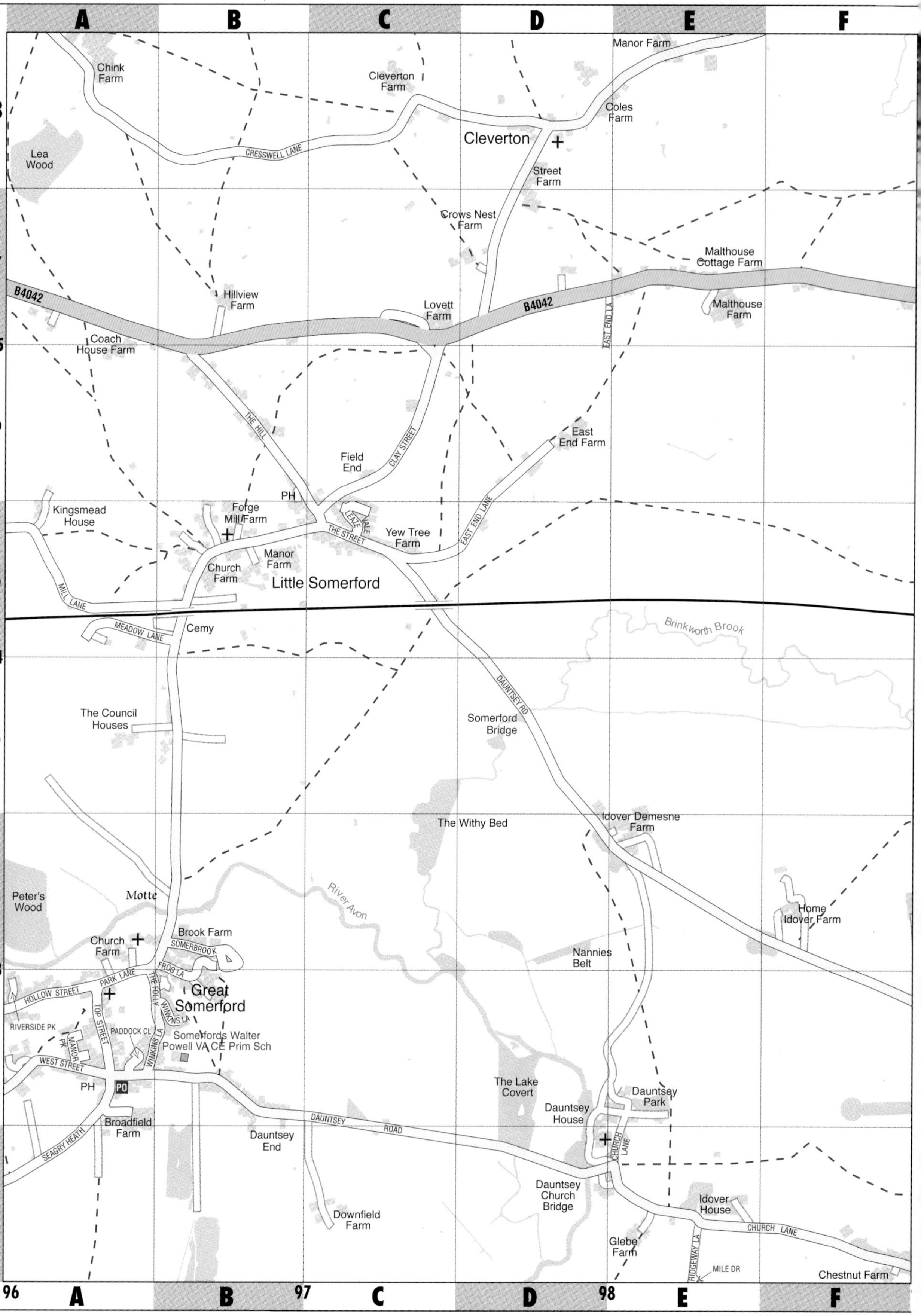

**A** **B** **C** **D** **E** **F**

**8**

Chink
Farm

Cleverton
Farm

Manor Farm

Coles
Farm

Cleverton

Lea
Wood

CRESSWELL LANE

Street
Farm

Crows Nest
Farm

**7**

Malthouse
Cottage Farm

B4042

Hillview
Farm

Lovett
Farm

B4042

Malthouse
Farm

**85**

Coach
House Farm

THE HILL

CLAY STREET

EAST END LA

**6**

Field
End

East
End Farm

PH

Kingsmead
House

Forge
Mill Farm

THE STREET

FOLLY LANE

Yew Tree
Farm

EAST END LANE

**5**

MILL LANE

Church
Farm

Manor
Farm

**Little Somerford**

MEADOW LANE

Cemy

Brinkworth Brook

**84**

DAUNTSEY RD

**4**

The Council
Houses

Somerford
Bridge

The Withy Bed

Idover Demesne
Farm

**3**

Peter's
Wood

Motte

River Avon

Home
Idover Farm

Church
Farm

Brook Farm

SOMERBROOK

Nannies
Belt

**83**

HOLLOW STREET

PARK LANE

FROG LA

THE FOLLY

**Great
Somerford**

TOP STREET

PADDOCK CL

NINE'S LA

**2**

RIVERSIDE PK

MANOR PK

WEST STREET

WINDMILL

Somerfords Walter
Powell VA CE Prim Sch

The Lake
Covert

Dauntsey
Park

Dauntsey
House

PH

PO

DAUNTSEY    ROAD

Dauntsey
End

CHURCH LANE

**1**

SEAGRY HEATH

Broadfield
Farm

Downfield
Farm

Dauntsey
Church Bridge

Idover
House

Church Lane

Glebe
Farm

RIDGEWAY LA

MILE DR

Chestnut Farm

**82**

96 **A** 97 **B** **C** 98 **D** **E** **F**

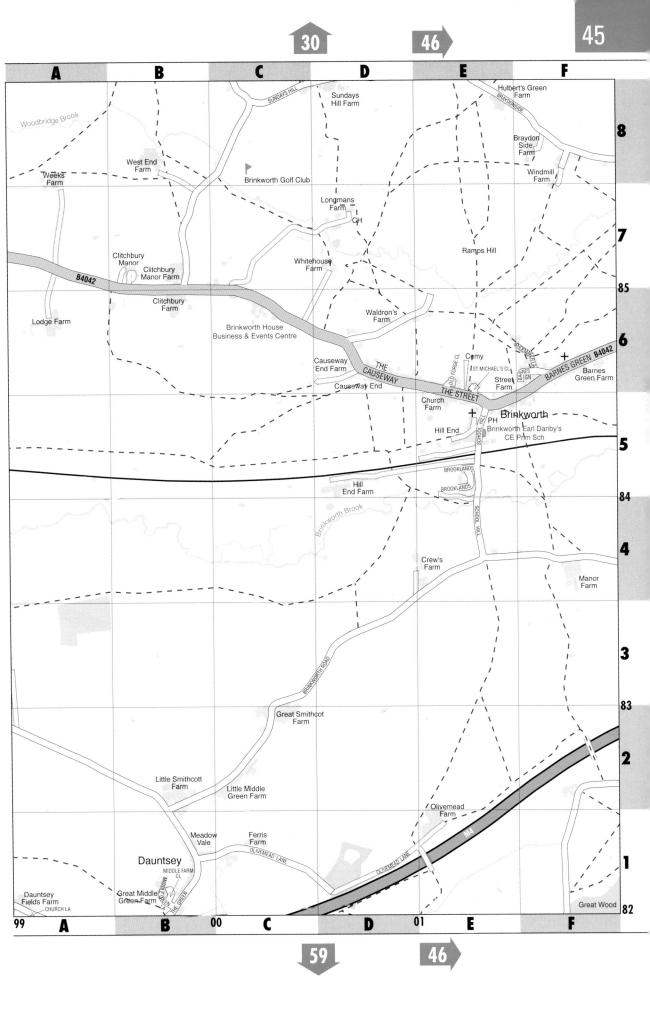

A B C D E F

8

Woodbridge Brook

Home Farm

Echo Lodge Farm

Webb's Wood

Braydonside

WASHPOOL

STOPPERS HILL

Woodside Farm

Wood Lane Farm

P

Seven Island Pond

Echo Lodge Meadows Nature Reserve

7

Stoppers Hill Farm

Yorks Farm

CUTTS CL

Bellamys Farm

Mill House Farm

WOOD LANE

THE STREET

YORK LANE

Fritterswell Farm

The Common

PH
SHEPPARDS RI

East End

85

Box Bush Farm

East Side

East End Farm

Highgate Farm

Lower Box Bush Farm

BARNES GREEN

B4042

CALLOWS CROSS

CROSSWAYS

EAST END

BRINKWORTH RD

B4042

6

Poplar Farm

Callow Hill

Highgate Cottage

5

Pittsland Farm

Callow Hill Farm

Highgate Cottage

Withy Bed

84

Hillside Farm

4

Brinkworth Brook

Dovey's Farm

Dovey's Bridge

3

Whites Farm

M4

Hooker's Gate Farm

83

Lukers Farm

Vines Farm

2

Goddards Farm

Pinnells Farm

Grittenham

Ivy House Farm

Grove Farm

CHESELEY HILL

1

Great Wood

Old Park Farm

82

02 A B 03 C D 04 E F

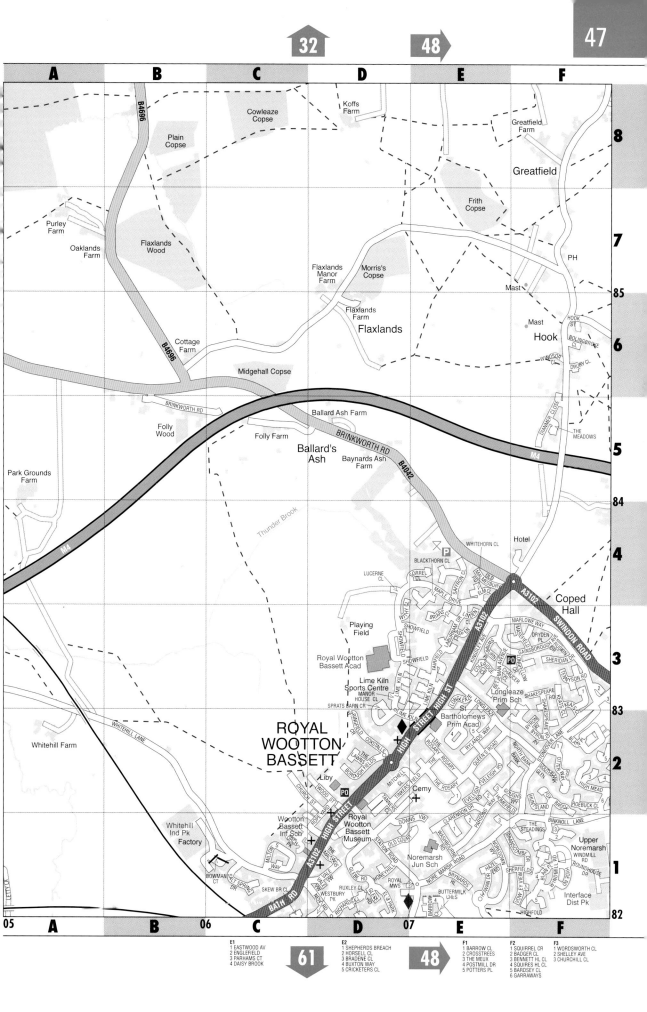

A B C D E F

Koffs Farm

Cowleaze Copse

Plain Copse

B4696

Greatfield Farm

Greatfield

Frith Copse

Purley Farm

Oaklands Farm

Flaxlands Wood

PH

Flaxlands Manor Farm

Morris's Copse

Mast

Hook ST

B4696

Cottage Farm

Flaxlands Farm

Flaxlands

Mast

Hook

HOOK ST

BOLINGBROKE CL

DRURY CL

WINDSOR CL

Midgehall Copse

Folly Wood

BRINKWORTH RD

Ballard Ash Farm

DIAMMER CLOSE

THE MEADOWS

Folly Farm

Ballard's Ash

BRINKWORTH RD

Baynards Ash Farm

B4042

M4

Park Grounds Farm

Thunder Brook

M4

Hotel

WHITEHORN CL

BLACKTHORN CL

OLD MALMESBURY

A3102

Coped Hall

SWINDON ROAD

LUCERNE CL

SORREL CL

MAPLE DRIVE

ELM CL

MARLOWE WAY

DRYDEN PL

RUSKIN DR

SHERIDAN DR

Playing Field

BRIARS CL

SHOWFIELD

WYCH CL

UBURNUM WAY

FAIRFIELD

LINZRIS

SAFFRON CL

KINGSLEY AVE

FREEMAN AVENUE

GAINSBOROUGH DR

CONSTABLE

CHAUCER

Longleaze Prim Sch

TENNYSON RD

Royal Wootton Bassett Acad

SHOWFIELD

SHOWFIELD

LIME KILN

LONGLEAZE

SHAKESPEARE RD

KEATS CL

KEATS

Lime Kiln Sports Centre

MANOR HOUSE CL

LIME KILN

LIME KILN

LONGLEAZE

BYRON

SHAKESPEARE RD

BYRON CL

GROSVENOR LANE

BLAY

SPRATS BARN CR

LIME KILN

Bartholomews Prim Acad

83

ROYAL WOOTTON BASSETT

SPRINGFIELD

COXSTALLS

HIGH STREET HIGH ST

RYLANDS WAY

RYLANDS WAY

NORTH BANK

OTTERLEY WAY

SOUTHBANK

HIGH MEAD

THE LAWNS

THE ROSARY

LIME

QUEEN'S ROAD

EVELEIGH RD

BARN CL

BOROUGHFIELDS

MITCHELL

TINKERS FIELD

THE ROSARY

GOUGHS

FOX BROOK

ROEBUCK CL

Liby

WOOD LANE

CHURCH ST

PO

Cemy

EVELGH

PARSONS WAY

CLARENDON DR

BINKNOLL LANE

ROPE YARD

ROYAL MWS

DOWNS VW

WASHBOURNE

HONEYFIELD RD

THE STEADINGS

Whitehill Ind Pk Factory

MILTON CL

THE MALTHAST

Royal Wootton Bassett Museum

STATION ROAD

OLD COURT

MOREMEAD

Upper Noremarsh

WINDMILL RD

ROUNDHOUSE DR

Wootton Bassett Inf Sch

ROPE YARD

GLEBE RD

HONEYFIELD RD

Noremarsh Jun Sch

NORE MARSH ROAD

BRYNARDS

BRANSCOMBE DR

HAZEL END

WINDMILL PL

BLAN PL

Interface Dist Pk

BOWMAN CT

GLT SPRING DR

SKEW BR CL

MILTON CL

WAY

WESTBURY PK

RUXLEY CL

RICHARDS CL

GLEBE RD

ELM PARK

BARROW

BUTTERMILK CRES

SHERFIELDS

OPWMAN DR

VW EV VIEW

HIGHFOLD

Whitehill Farm

WHITEHILL LANE

BATH RD

A3102

HIGH STREET

VALE

A    B    C    D    E    F

8

7

85

6

5

84

4

3

83

2

1

82

08   A    B    09   C    D    10   E    F

Godwins Farm
Lydiard Green
THE BUTTS
Lydiard Millicent CE Prim Sch
Cemy
CHURCH PL
Lydiard Farm
Lydiard Millicent
CHESTNUT SPRINGS
CHERRY BRCH CL
THE CLOSE
THE ST
THE MEWS
THE ORCH
PH
FORGE FIELDS
PARK LA
PARROW DR
WALNUT TREE GD
MEADOW SPRINGS
HOLBORN
WASHPOOL
NINE ELMS LA
THE OLD SHAW LA
MILLER DR
GARTONS RD
MIDDLELEAZE DR
KILPERT DR
CANTON CL
GARTONS RD
DANESTONE CL
WINCHCOMBE CL
TEWKESBURY WAY
TEWKESBURY WAY
SPENCER CLOSE
VILLIERS CL
WATERY LA
WHITMORE

Parkside Farm

Alder Plantation

Park Copse

Ash Plantation

Lydiard Tregoze

Lydiard House +

OLIVER CL
TREGOZE WAY
HAY LANE
WHITGIFT CL 1
CHANCELLOR CL 2
WILMOT

Cemy
Lower Hook Farm

HAMPTON DR

Lydiard Park

CARD CL
DARCEY CL

Hook Farm
Hook Street

Elm Plantation

BANCROFT CL

CAMPION GATE

Letterage Copse

P ×

Quarr Plantation

Lydiard Park Academy

GRANGE PK
ORMOND DR

M4

Midge Hall

HAMPTON CT

Park Farm

Grange Park

MULCASTER AVE
POTTERNE WY
KING HENRY DR
THURLOW CL
LINEACRE CL
HOOK ST

OTFORD CL
ELTHAM CL
OATLANDS
CLAXTON CL
DARCEY CL

Church Hill Farm

Lydiard Fields Business Park

Chiseldon Windmill

Windmill Hill Business Park

WHITEHILL WAY
B4534

STONEOVER LA
A3102
SWINDON ROAD

CHURCHILL
ROBBINS
GARRAWAYS
FARRE WK
RAVENS
BAILEYS
GARRAWAYS HSE
GARRAWAYS
BINKNOLL LA

Spittleborough Farm

PH

SWINDON ROAD    A3102

SWINDON RD

16

GREAT WESTERN WY

Hotel

Hagbourne Copse Nat Res
EURO WAY
FRANKLAND RD

Hotel

M4

Blagrove Employment Area

Woodshaw

Wickfield Farm

B4005

Upper Studley Farm

BINKNOLL LA
EVENING STAR
BINKNOLL

Lower Woodshaw Farm

Harris Croft Farm

HAY LA

Studley Grange Butterfly World

BASSET DOWN

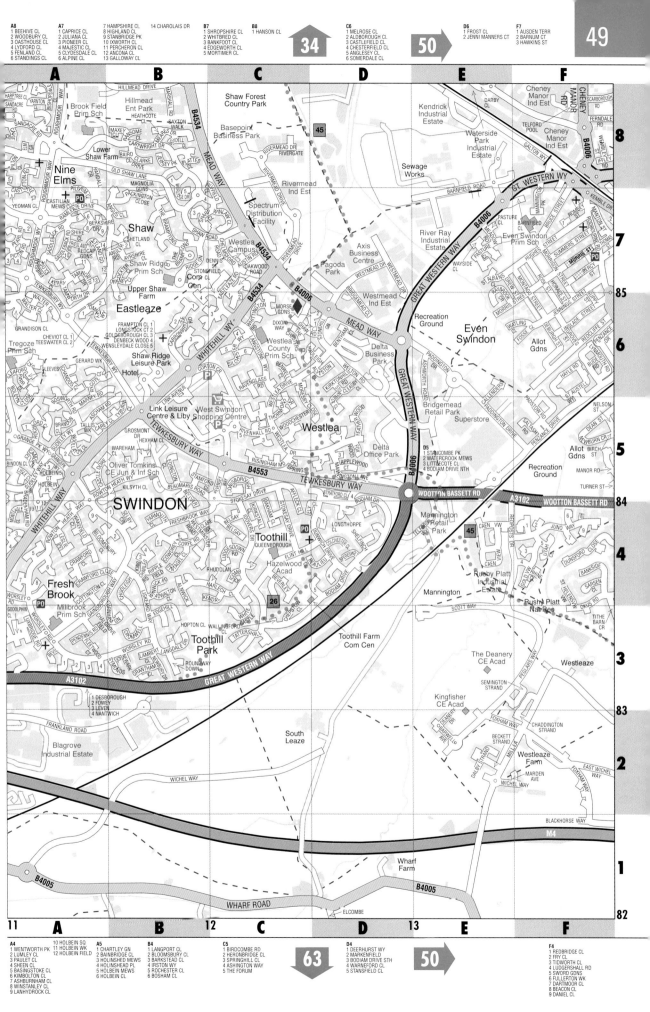

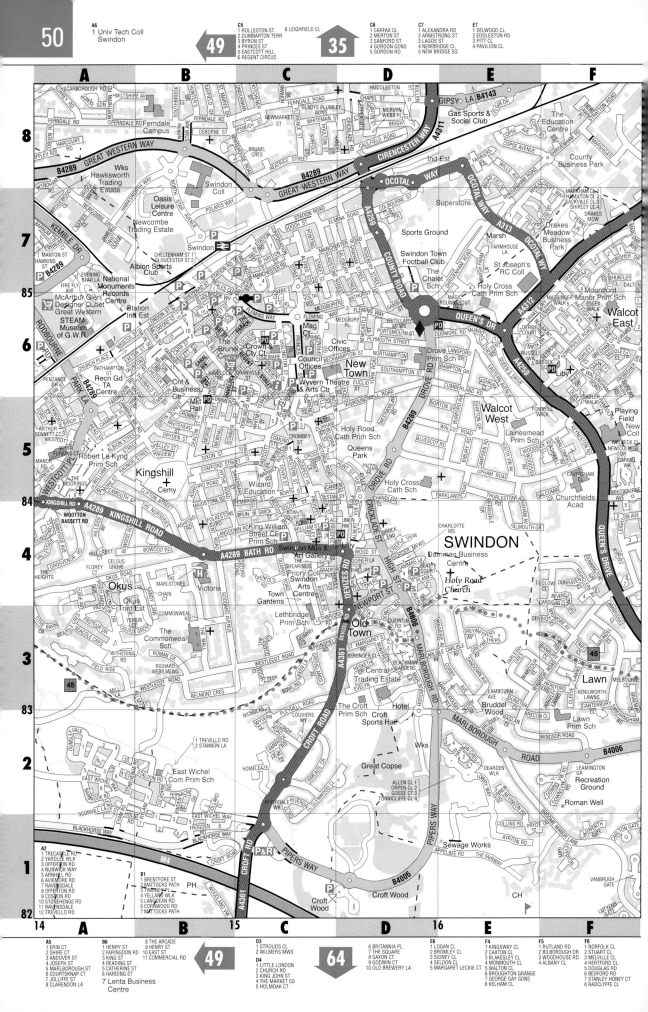

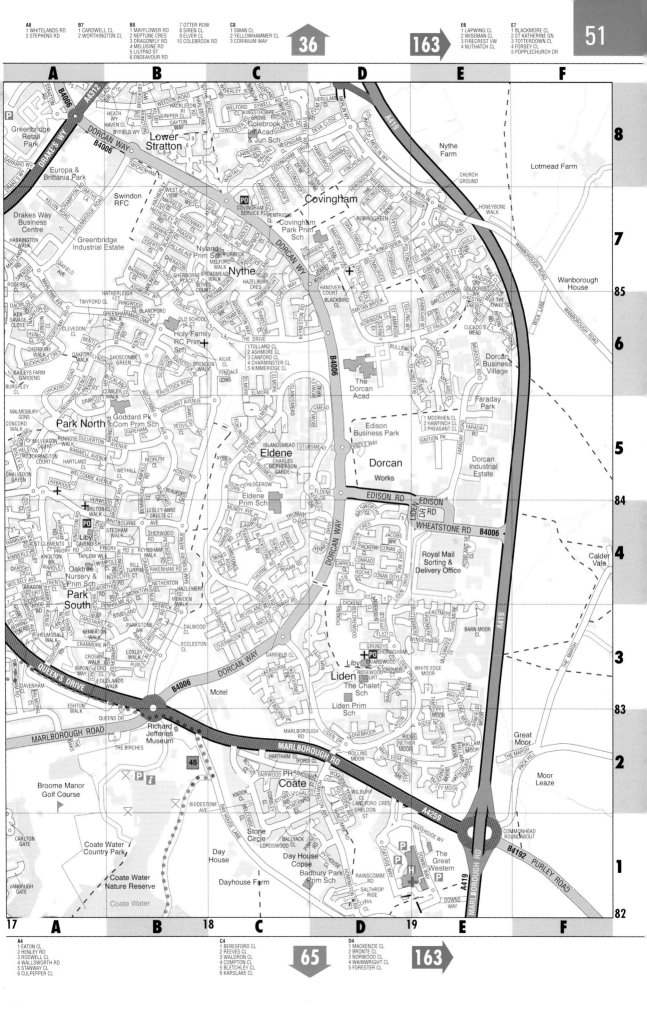

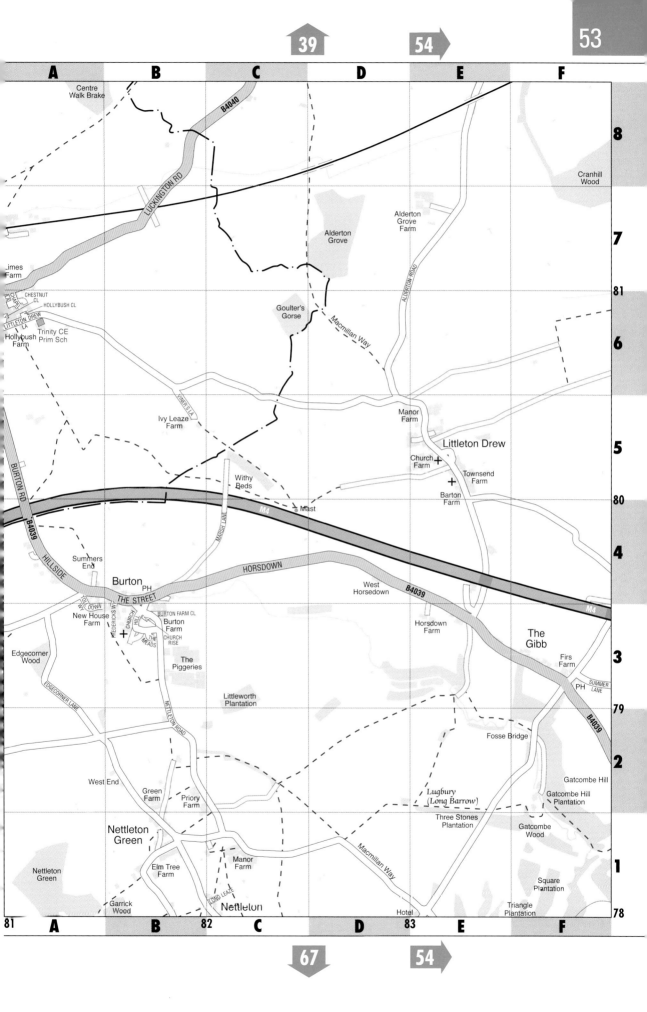

53 40

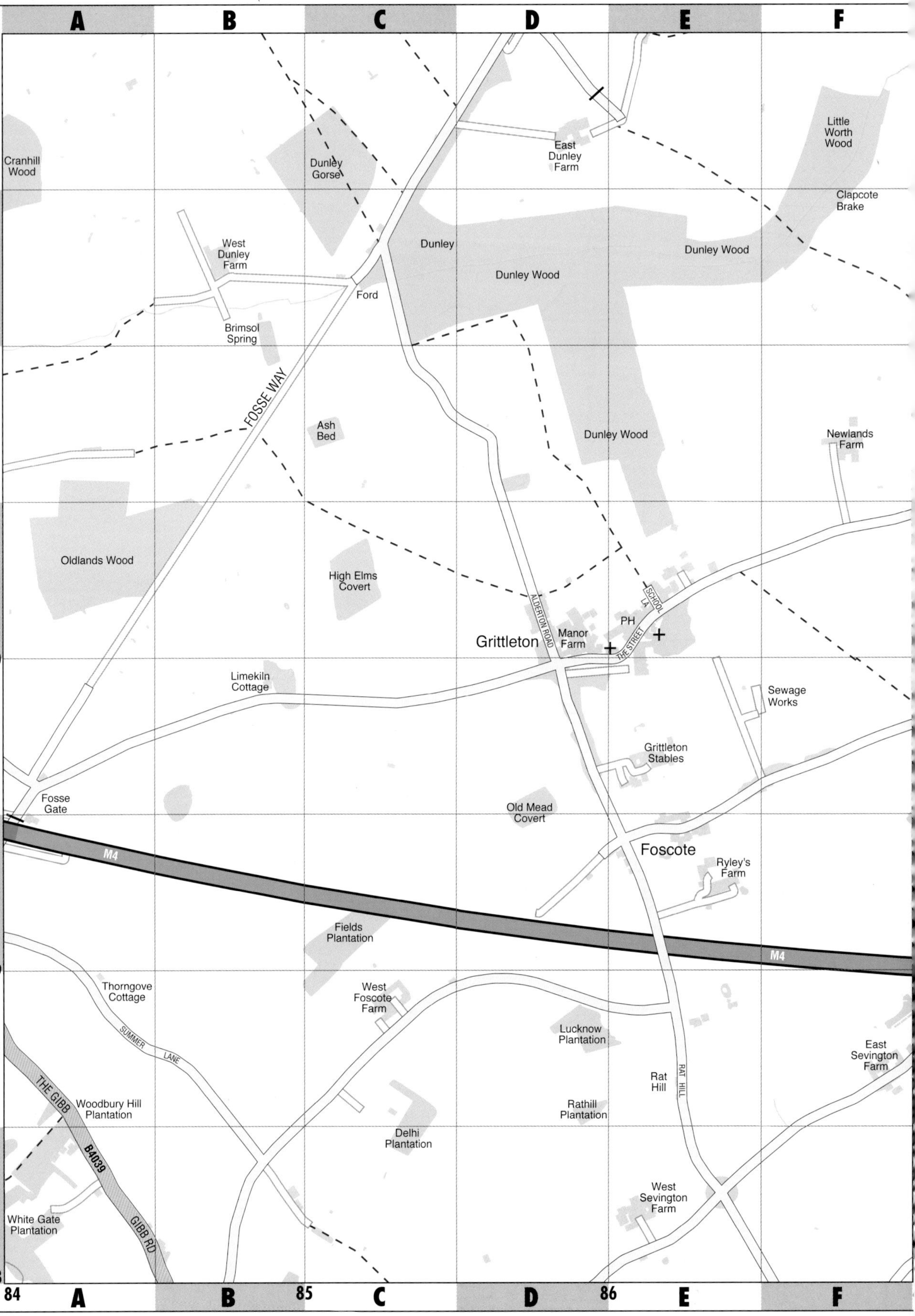

A B C D E F

8

Cranhill Wood

Dunley Gorse

East Dunley Farm

Little Worth Wood

Clapcote Brake

West Dunley Farm

Dunley

Dunley Wood

7

Ford

Dunley Wood

Dunley Wood

Brimsol Spring

81

FOSSE WAY

Ash Bed

6

Dunley Wood

Newlands Farm

Oldlands Wood

High Elms Covert

5

ALDERTON ROAD

SCHOOL LA

Grittleton

Manor Farm

PH

THE STREET

80

Limekiln Cottage

Sewage Works

4

Grittleton Stables

Fosse Gate

Old Mead Covert

Foscote

Ryley's Farm

M4

M4

3

Fields Plantation

79

Thorngove Cottage

West Foscote Farm

Lucknow Plantation

East Sevington Farm

SUMMER LANE

2

THE GIBB

Woodbury Hill Plantation

Rat Hill

RAT HILL

Rathill Plantation

Delhi Plantation

B4039

GIBB RD

White Gate Plantation

West Sevington Farm

1

78

84 A 85 B C 86 D E F

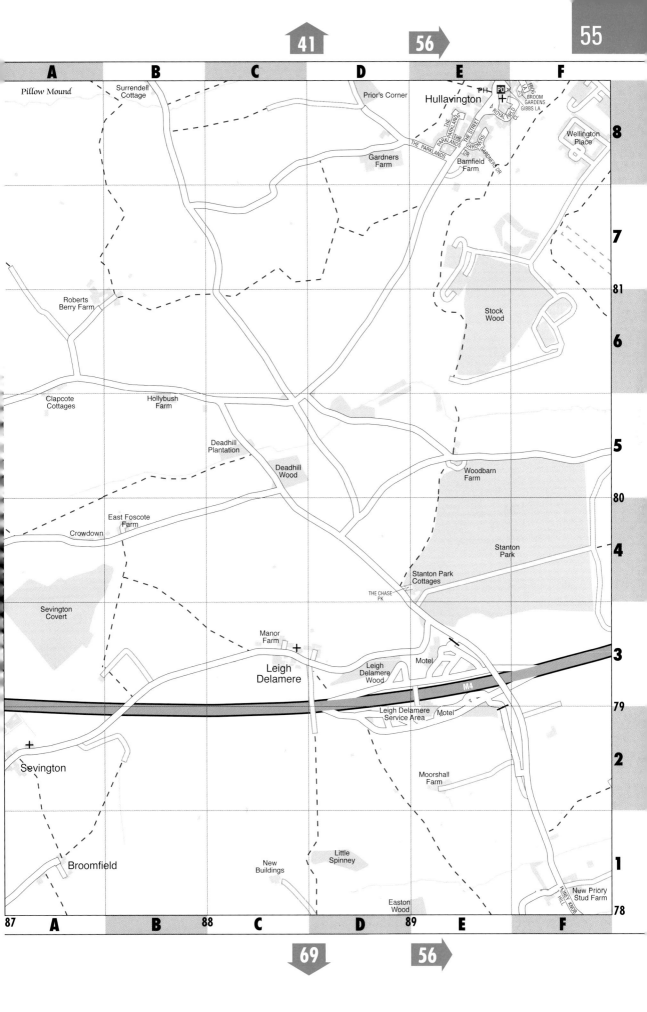

Pillow Mound

Surrendell Cottage

Prior's Corner

Hullavington

PH
PO
BROOM GARDENS
GIBBS LA

Wellington Place

THE PARKLANDS
THE PARKLANDS
THE STREET
GARDNERS DR
THE GARDENS
GARDNERS CR
ROYAL FIELD

Gardners Farm

Barnfield Farm

**8**

**7**

81

Roberts Berry Farm

Stock Wood

**6**

Clapcote Cottages

Hollybush Farm

Deadhill Plantation

Deadhill Wood

Woodbarn Farm

**5**

80

East Foscote Farm

Crowdown

Stanton Park

**4**

Stanton Park Cottages

THE CHASE PK

Sevington Covert

Manor Farm

Leigh Delamere

Leigh Delamere Wood

Motel

M4

**3**

79

Leigh Delamere Service Area

Motel

Sevington

Moorshall Farm

**2**

Broomfield

New Buildings

Little Spinney

New Priory Stud Farm

KINGTON HILL

**1**

Easton Wood

78

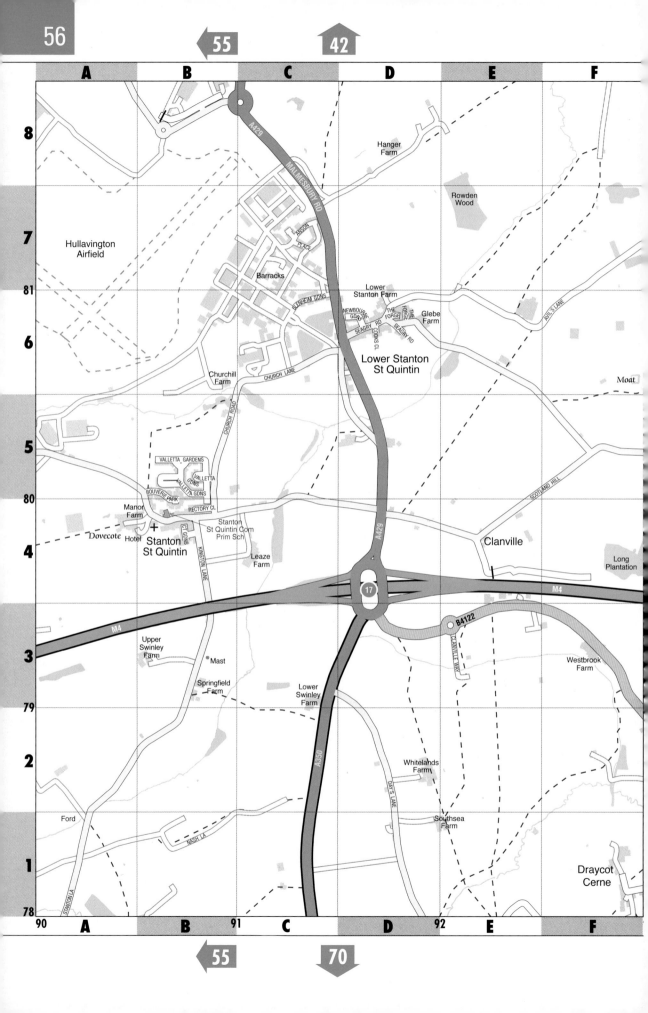

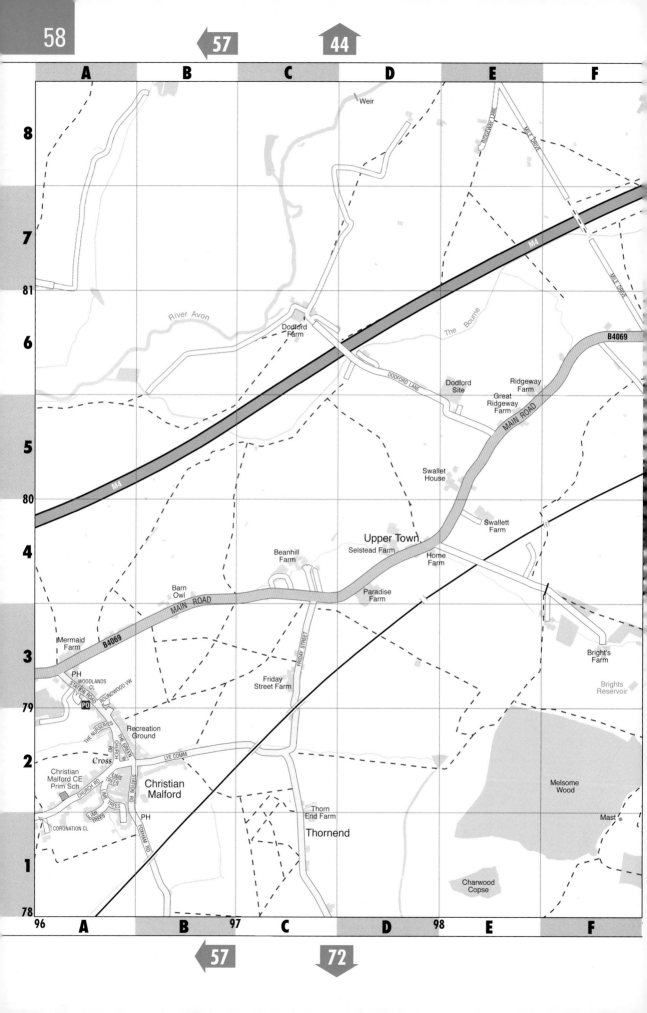

A B C D E F

8

7

81

6

5

80

4

3

79

2

1

78

Weir

M4

RIDGEWAY LANE

MILE DRIVE

MILE DRIVE

B4069

River Avon

Dodford Farm

The Bourne

DODFORD LANE

Dodford Site

Dodford Farm

Ridgeway Farm

Great Ridgeway Farm

MAIN ROAD

Swallet House

Swallett Farm

Upper Town

Selstead Farm

Home Farm

Beanhill Farm

Paradise Farm

Barn Owl

MAIN ROAD

FRIDAY STREET

Bright's Farm

Brights Reservoir

Mermaid Farm

B4069

PH

WOODLANDS CL

STATION ROAD

ROUNDWOOD VW

PO

THE NURSERIES

THE GREEN

CHURCH RD

Recreation Ground

Cross

Friday Street Farm

LYE COMM

Christian Malford CE Prim Sch

LIME TREES

STATION RD

LIME TREES

Christian Malford

FOXHAM RD

PH

LIME TREES

Melsome Wood

CORONATION CL

Thorn End Farm

Thornend

Mast

Charwood Copse

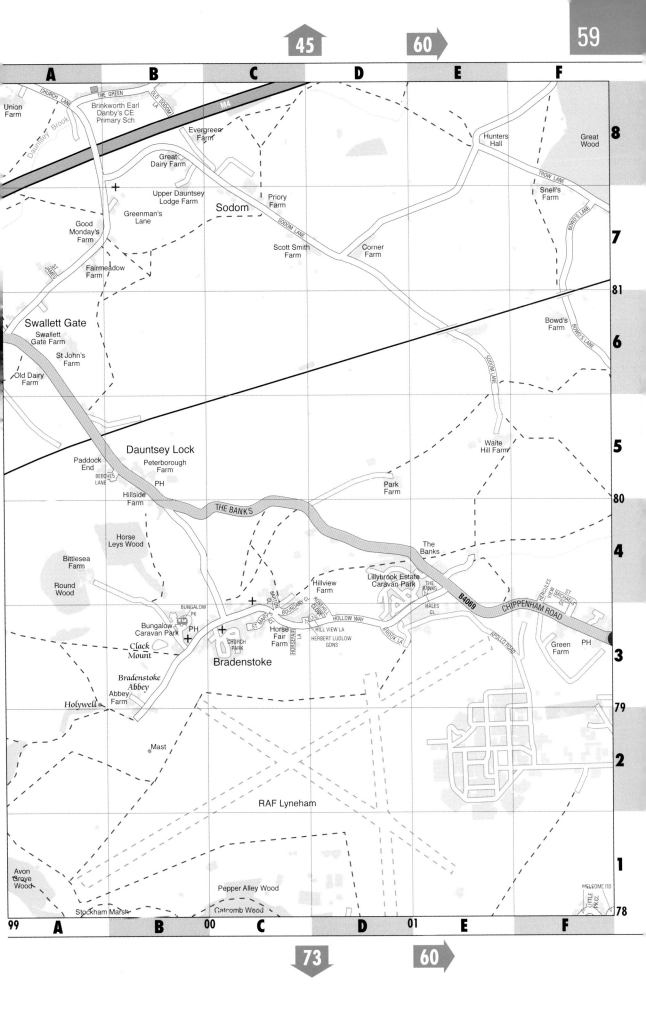

**A** **B** **C** **D** **E** **F**

Union Farm

CHURCH LANE

Dauntsey Brook

THE GREEN

Brinkworth Earl Danby's CE Primary Sch

OLD SODOM LA

M4

Evergreen Farm

Hunters Hall

Great Wood

**8**

Great Dairy Farm

TROW LANE

Snell's Farm

Upper Dauntsey Lodge Farm

Priory Farm

Sodom

BOWD'S LANE

Greenman's Lane

SODOM LANE

Good Monday's Farm

Scott Smith Farm

Corner Farm

**7**

ST JAMES

Fairmeadow Farm

**81**

Swallett Gate

Bowd's Farm

**6**

Swallett Gate Farm

St John's Farm

BOWD'S LANE

Old Dairy Farm

SODOM LANE

Waite Hill Farm

**5**

Dauntsey Lock

Paddock End

Peterborough Farm

Park Farm

**80**

BEECHES LANE

PH

Hillside Farm

THE BANKS

Horse Leys Wood

The Banks

**4**

Bittlesea Farm

Hillview Farm

Lillybrook Estate Caravan Park

THE BANKS

HERCULES VIEW

ST MICHAELS CL

Round Wood

BUNGALOW PK

BARTON CL

BOUNDARY CL

ROSEHILL CLOSE

Hollow Way

HALES CL

B4069

CHIPPENHAM ROAD

PH

Bungalow Caravan Park

PH

ST MARY'S CL

Horse Fair Farm

HILL VIEW LA

HERBERT LUDLOW GDNS

BROOK LA

APOLLO ROAD

Green Farm

PH

**3**

Clack Mount

CHURCH PARK

HORSEFAIR LA

Bradenstoke

Bradenstoke Abbey

Holywell

Abbey Farm

**79**

Mast

**2**

RAF Lyneham

Avon Grove Wood

**1**

MELSOME RD

Pepper Alley Wood

LITTLE PK CL

Stockham Marsh

Gatcomb Wood

**78**

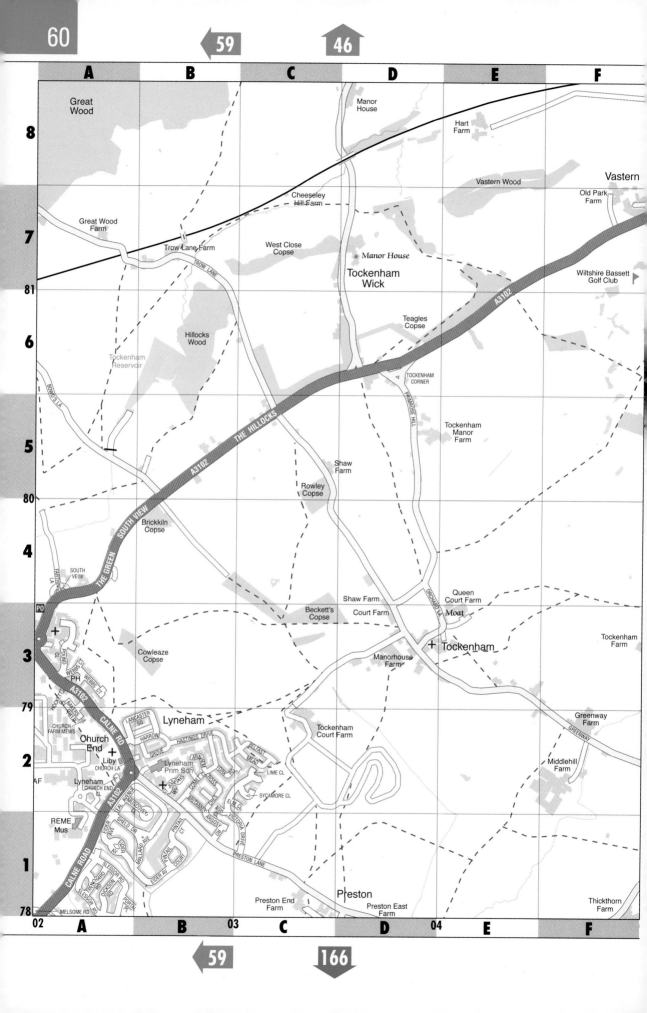

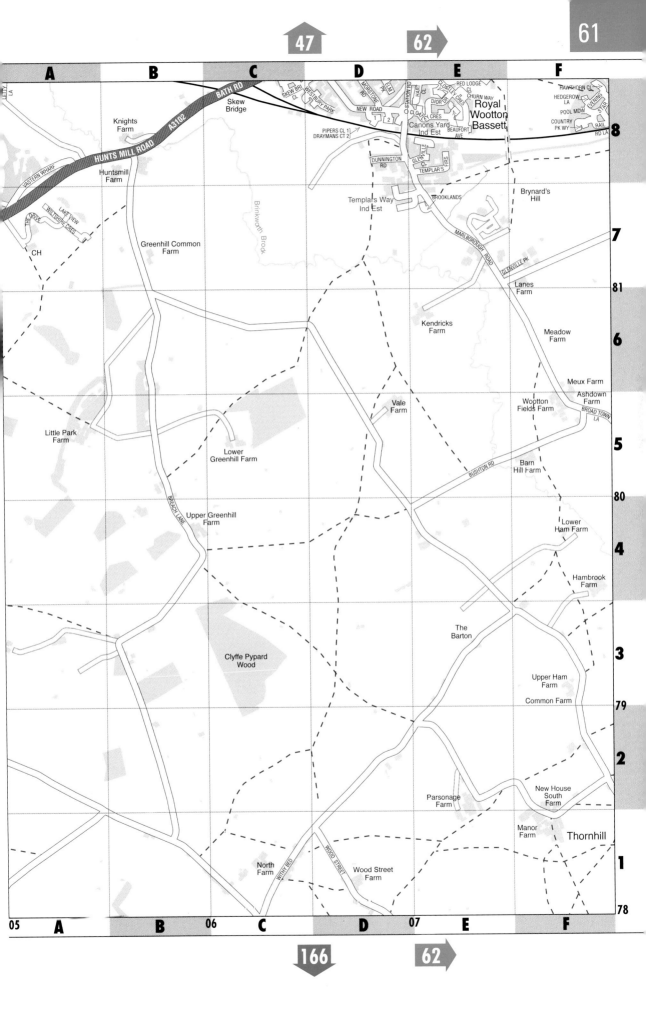

A  B  C  D  E  F

BATH RD
A3102

Skew Bridge

Knights Farm

HUNTS MILL ROAD

Huntsmill Farm

VASTERN WHARF

THE SPUR

LAKE VIEW
WILTSHIRE CRES

CH

Greenhill Common Farm

Brinkworth Brook

SKEW BRI
VESTBURY PARK

NEW ROAD

PIPERS CL 1
DRAYMANS CT 2

MORSTONE RD
ELM PK

STATION RD
CLOATL HART CL
DIOR DR
CLOATLEY CRES

RED LODGE CL
CHURN WAY
BEAUFORT AVE

HAWTHORN CL
HEDGEROW LA
POOL MDW
COUNTRY PK WY

Royal Wootton Bassett

EVENING STAR
RAIL
RD LA

Canons Yard Ind Est

DUNNINGTON RD

GLENVILLE CL
TEMPLAR'S FIRS

Templars Way Ind Est

Brooklands

Brynard's Hill

MARLBOROUGH ROAD
GLENVILLE PK

8

7

81

Lanes Farm

Meadow Farm

Kendricks Farm

6

Meux Farm

Ashdown Farm

Wootton Fields Farm

BROAD TOWN LA

Vale Farm

Little Park Farm

Lower Greenhill Farm

5

80

BREACH LANE

Upper Greenhill Farm

BUSHTON RD

Barn Hill Farm

Lower Ham Farm

4

Hambrook Farm

Clyffe Pypard Wood

The Barton

3

Upper Ham Farm

Common Farm

79

2

Parsonage Farm

New House South Farm

Manor Farm

Thornhill

North Farm

WITH BED

WOOD STREET

Wood Street Farm

1

78

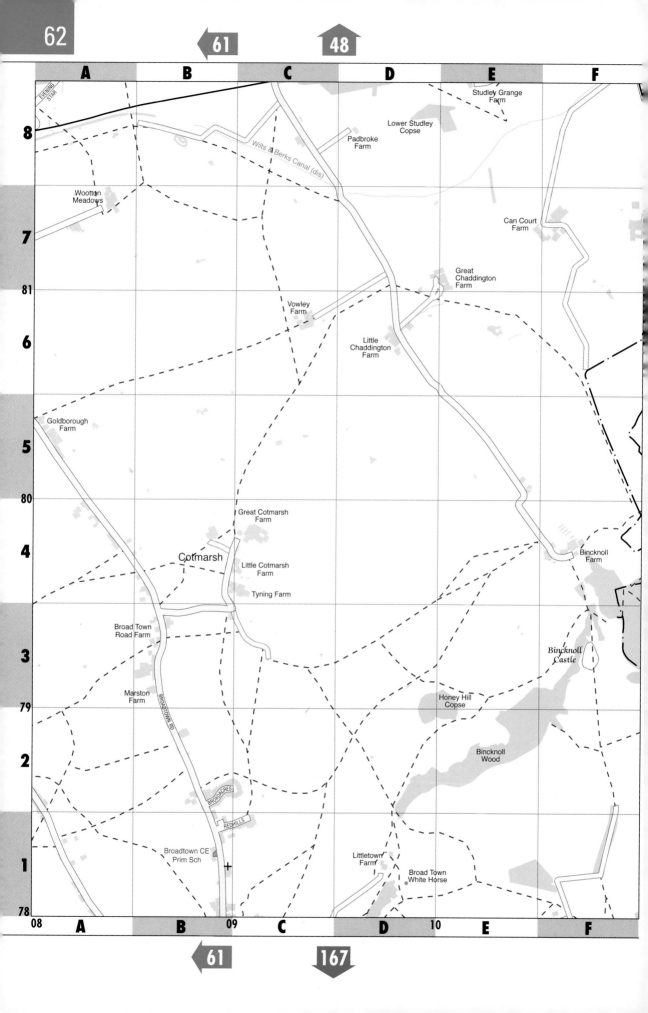

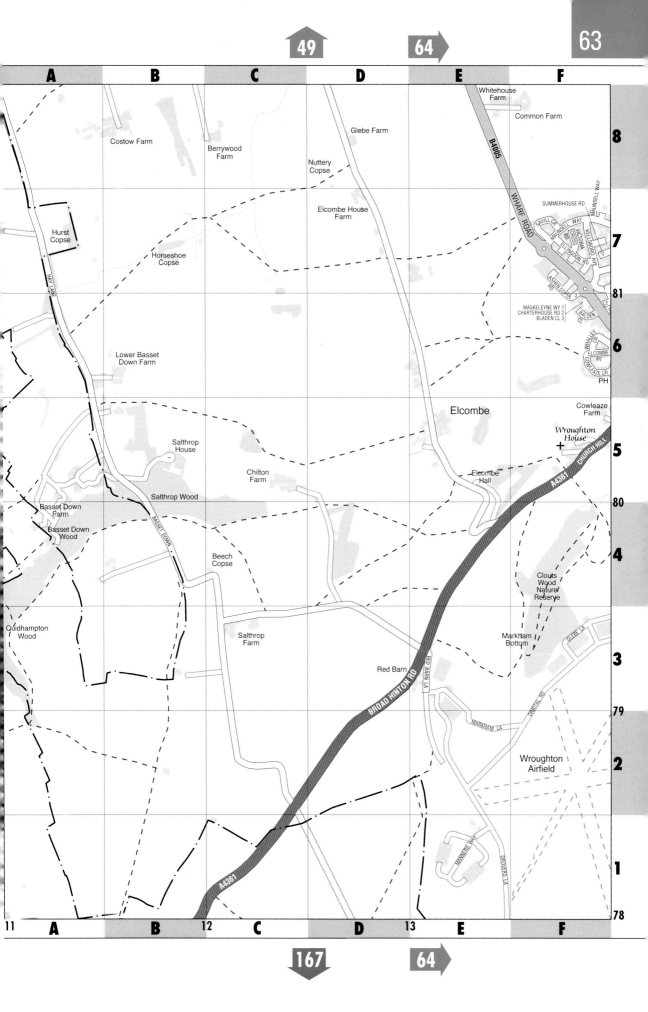

64

A6
1 EDGAR ROW CL
2 WHALLEY CR
3 ELCOMBE AVE
4 COWLEAZE CR
5 CHARTERHOUSE RD
6 MARKHAM PL
7 HALL CL
8 ELLENDUNE CTR

63

50

A B C D E F

8

WOODLAND VIEW

Wroughton Covert

Croft Wood

BRETTINGHAM GATE

Refuse Tip
North Wroughton

BURDEROP CL

MOORE CL

Nightingale Farm

Sewage Works

THE MOUNTINGS

M4

Wroughton Jun Sch

Sports Centre

The Ridgeway Sch

FREEMAN CRES

Summerhouse Rd

BEDFORD ST

Burderop Wood

7

MARINE CL

Berkeley Farm

KINGS CL

WAYTES CL

LOWER CL

81

Wood Farm

Hotel

6

MOORMEAD RD

BMI The Ridgeway

Lodge Farm

Wroughton Inf Sch

TALL CONIFERS

OLD BAKERY RD

Ladder Hill

Burderop Park

THREE TUNS ROUNDABOUT

PH

MARLBOROUGH ROAD

HIGH STREET

DEVIZES RD

A4361

B4005 WHARF ROAD

MANSION DR

5

Wroughton

Brook Meadow

BADGERS BROOK

FAIRWATER CT

B4005 BRIMBLE HILL

Burderop Barns

SNAPPS CL

80

PRIOR'S HILL

DAIRY ROAD

4

ORBITAL RD

Coombe Bottom

Overtown House

Moorleaze Farm

Great Moorleaze Farm

Overtown

GILBERT LA

Coombe Bottom

NOCTON ROAD

COSFORD

BURDEROP

3

THORNEY PARK

THORNEY PARK

LANGTON PK

Overtown Farm

CANBERRA RD
PARSLOES CL

THORNEY PARK

COMET WAY

79

BERANBURH FIELD

2

ORBITAL RD

BABURY LA

HACKPEN LA

1

Burderop Hackpen

78

Science Museum Wroughton

14 A 15 B C 16 D E F

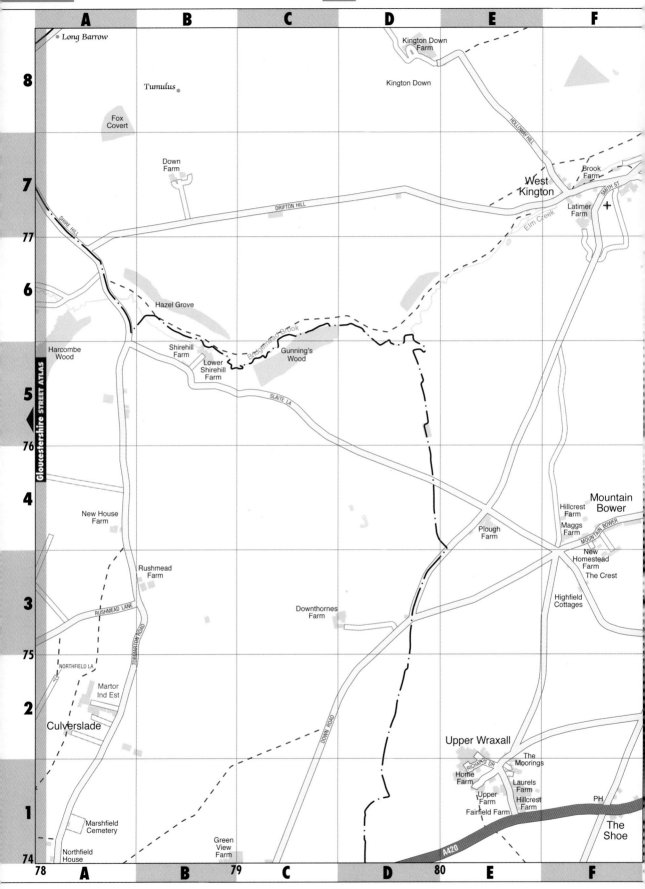

Long Barrow

Tumulus

Fox Covert

Kington Down Farm

Kington Down

Down Farm

HOLLOWAY HILL

SHIRE HILL

DRIFTON HILL

West Kington

Brook Farm

SMITH ST

Latimer Farm

Elm Creek

Hazel Grove

Harcombe Wood

Shirehill Farm

Lower Shirehill Farm

Bridgemead Brook

Gunning's Wood

SLAITE LA

Gloucestershire STREET ATLAS

New House Farm

Mountain Bower

Hillcrest Farm

Maggs Farm

MOUNTAIN BOWER

Plough Farm

New Homestead Farm

The Crest

Rushmead Farm

RUSHMEAD LANE

Downthornes Farm

Highfield Cottages

NORTHFIELD LA

TORMARTON ROAD

Martor Ind Est

Culverslade

DOWN ROAD

Upper Wraxall

RICHARDS DR

The Moorings

Home Farm

Laurels Farm

Hillcrest Farm

Upper Farm

Fairfield Farm

PH

The Shoe

Marshfield Cemetery

Northfield House

Green View Farm

A420

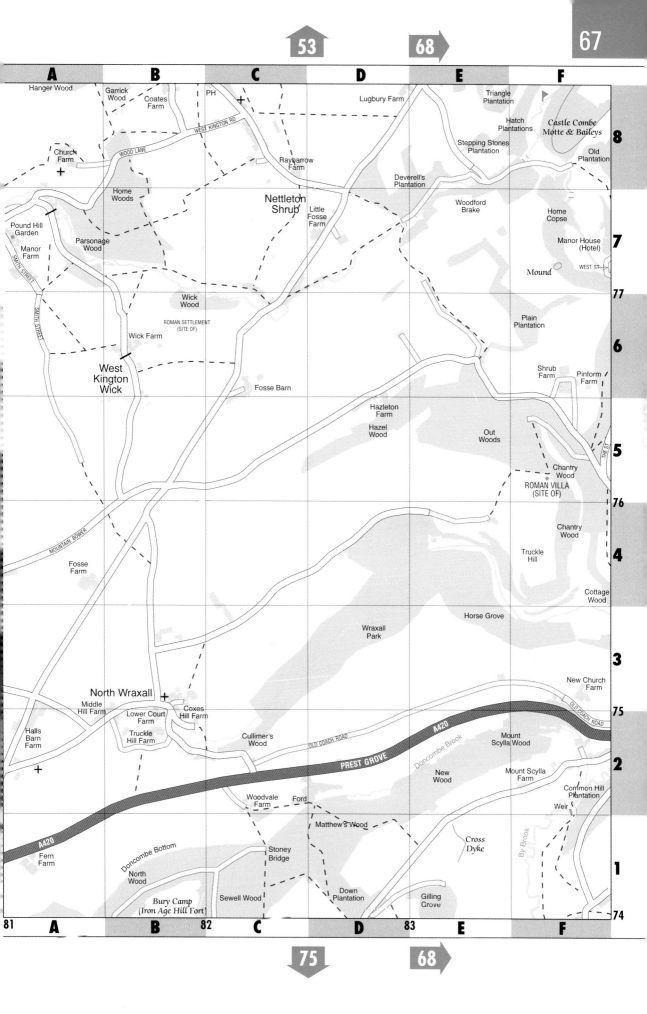

A      B      C      D      E      F

Hanger Wood

Garrick Wood

Coates Farm

PH

Lugbury Farm

Triangle Plantation

Hatch Plantations

Castle Combe Motte & Baileys

8

WEST KINGTON RD

Church Farm

WOOD LANE

Raybarrow Farm

Stepping Stones Plantation

Old Plantation

Home Woods

Nettleton Shrub

Deverell's Plantation

Woodford Brake

Home Copse

7

Pound Hill Garden

Parsonage Wood

Little Fosse Farm

Manor House (Hotel)

WEST ST

Manor Farm

Mound

77

SMITH STREET

Wick Wood

Plain Plantation

ROMAN SETTLEMENT (SITE OF)

6

Wick Farm

Shrub Farm

Pinform Farm

West Kington Wick

THE ST

Fosse Barn

Hazleton Farm

Hazel Wood

Out Woods

5

Chantry Wood

ROMAN VILLA (SITE OF)

76

Chantry Wood

MOUNTAIN BOWER

Truckle Hill

4

Fosse Farm

Cottage Wood

Horse Grove

Wraxall Park

3

New Church Farm

North Wraxall

Middle Hill Farm

Coxes Hill Farm

OLD COACH ROAD

75

Halls Barn Farm

Lower Court Farm

Cullimer's Wood

OLD COACH ROAD

A420

Doncombe Brook

Mount Scylla Wood

Truckle Hill Farm

PREST GROVE

New Wood

Mount Scylla Farm

2

Common Hill Plantation

Weir

Woodvale Farm

Ford

Matthew's Wood

Cross Dyke

By Brook

A420

Fern Farm

Doncombe Bottom

Stoney Bridge

Gilling Grove

1

North Wood

Bury Camp (Iron Age Hill Fort)

Sewell Wood

Down Plantation

74

81   A     B  82  C     D  83  E     F

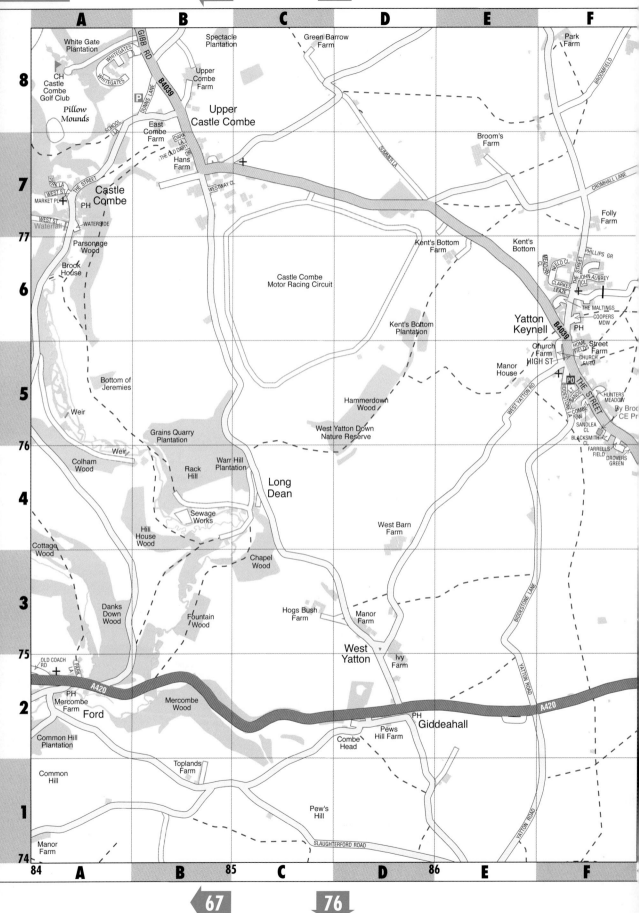

| | A | B | C | D | E | F |
|---|---|---|---|---|---|---|

**8**

Kington St Michael

Tradewinds Farm

Hillside Farm

Lypgate Farm · Westbrook Farm

Bowldown

Kington St Michael CE Prim Sch

PADDOCK END

Manor Farm
*Almshouses*

PH

Newlands Cl

Wayside Cl

Coles Terrace

**7**

STUBBS LANE

Tor Hill

Courtfield Farm

Kington Langley
PH

Ashes La

Church La

Silver St

Fairleigh
Fairleigh Rise

FAIRLEIGH RISE

Lower Common

Swindon Rd

**77**

Tor Farm

Bright Side

Langley Fitzurse CE Prim Sch

Church Farm

Middle Common

Upper Common

**6**

Kington St Michael Rd

The Moors

PARKERS LA

Limetree Farm

B4069

PLOUGH CNR

PLOUGH LA

PLOUGH LANE

Steinbrook Farm

Swindon Road

PH

A350

Lodge Farm

P

Nature Reserve

**5**

Hey Wood

Malmesbury Rd

**76**

White Wood

JACKSOM'S LANE

Marsh Farm

Langley House

Jacksom's Farm

**4**

Chippenham Golf Club

CH

Bird's Marsh

Dog Kennel Plantation

A350

**3**

HONEYSUCKLE CL

West Cepen Way

Superstore

PH

PAR DR

West Cepen Way

MALMESBURY ROAD

HOLLOWAY GR

Clutterbuck Cl

GAINEY GDNS

TYDDYMAN Cl

Barrow Farm

THE COMMON

BUTTERCUP CL 1
SORREL DR 2
BLUEBELL DR 3
PRIMROSE WY 4
HARES PATCH 5
PARTRIDGE CL 6
ROBINS CL 7
WOODPECKER MEWS 8
HARNISH WY 9

A350

Argyle Drive

CONSLIP WY

TRINITY GDNS

SCOTT CR

EDDOLLS LA

HARVEY DR

HATHERALL DR

B4069

Chippenham Rd

**75**

SANDPIPER GDNS

B4528

HARDENHUISH LA

Wiltshire Ambulance Service NHS Trust HQ

BELLINGER

VINES CL

BULL LA

SCOTT-ASHE

CLARK DR

FILBERT ST

HAZEL CRES

HICKORY WAY

CHIPPENHAM

**2**

STAINERS WY

Church La

B4528

THE GDNS

BROOKNELL

LONG RIDINGS

WITTS GR

COUZENS CL

ELMS RD

OAKLANDS

The Oaks

St Paul's Prim Sch

HILL CORNER RD

GREENWAY LA

MARSH VW

Maud Heath's Cw

VAN NUT DR

BRYANT

PEW HILL

Maud Heath's Cw

PARSONAGE WAY

Parsonage Way Industrial Estate

HOLLYBUSH CL

A420

Hardenhuish School

BROOMFIELD

OAKLANDS

DEANSWAY

Greenway Lane

MAPLE

HILL RISE

MOORLANDS

HEATHFIELD

HEATHFIELD

Upper Cocklebury Lane

PARSONAGE WAY

**1**

Bristol Road A420

MOUNT PLEASANT

Bumpers Farm Ind Est

JASMINE CL

ACACIA CL

MULBERRY

THE POPLARS

FOXGROVE

Sheldon School

Hardenhuish Park

PORTAL CLOSE

EAST TENSTOCK

Greenway Rd

ASHFIELD

HAMLET CT

LANGLEY RD

B4069

CEDAR

CLIFT AV

JUBILEE DR

GALILEO DR

O'DONNELL CL

EASTLANDS

WESTINGHOUSE WAY

Langley Park

Westpoint Business Park

BUMPERS WY

VINCIENTS RD

GREENFIELDS

BYTHEBROOK

Old Hardenhuish La

HUNGERDOWN

Bristol Rd

St Nicholas School

Hardenhuish School

Sports Ground

WEDMORE AV

PARKLANDS GDNS

ROWLANDS WAY

TUGELA RD

HAWTHORN RD

FOUNDRY LA

COWLEAZE

**74**

| 90 | A | | B | 91 | | C | | D | 92 | | E | | F |
|---|---|---|---|---|---|---|---|---|---|---|---|---|---|

**A1**
1 LONGSTONE RD
2 ALLINGTON WY
3 THE BATTENS
4 BARKEN RD
5 PIPSMORE RD
6 LOWER FIELD
7 CORNFIELDS
8 MIDDLELEAZE
9 BARLEY LEAZE

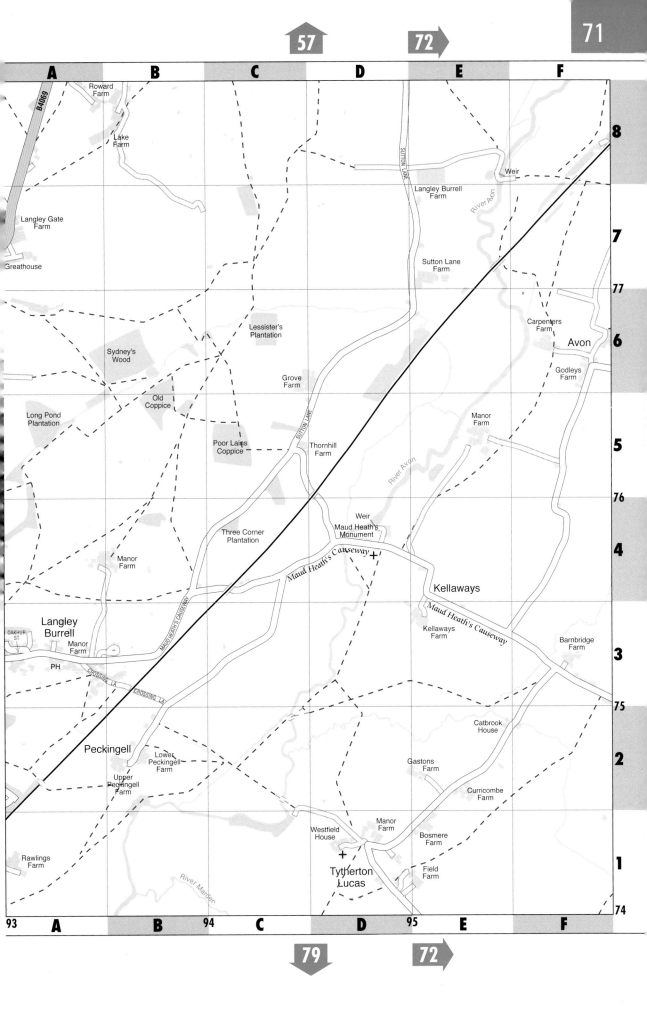

**A** | **B** | **C** | **D** | **E** | **F**

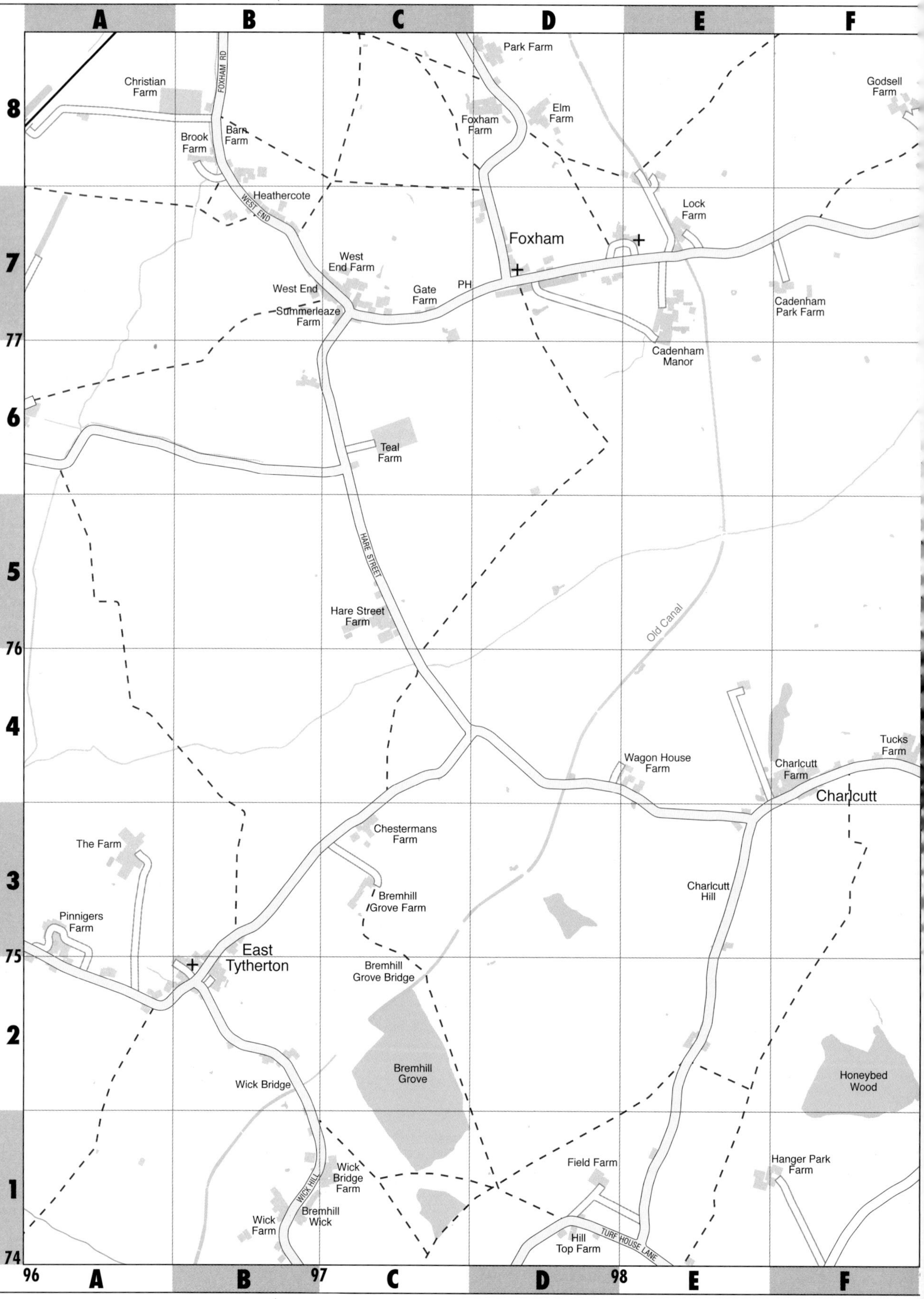

8

Christian Farm

FOXHAM RD

Brook Farm

Barn Farm

Park Farm

Foxham Farm

Elm Farm

Godsell Farm

Heathercote

WEST END

Lock Farm

West End Farm

7

Foxham

PH

Cadenham Park Farm

West End

Summerleaze Farm

Gate Farm

77

Cadenham Manor

6

Teal Farm

HARE STREET

Old Canal

5

Hare Street Farm

76

4

Wagon House Farm

Charlcutt Farm

Tucks Farm

Charlcutt

The Farm

Chestermans Farm

Charlcutt Hill

3

Pinnigers Farm

Bremhill Grove Farm

75

East Tytherton

Bremhill Grove Bridge

2

Wick Bridge

Bremhill Grove

Honeybed Wood

WICK HILL

Wick Bridge Farm

Field Farm

Hanger Park Farm

1

Wick Farm

Bremhill Wick

TURF HOUSE LANE

Hill Top Farm

74

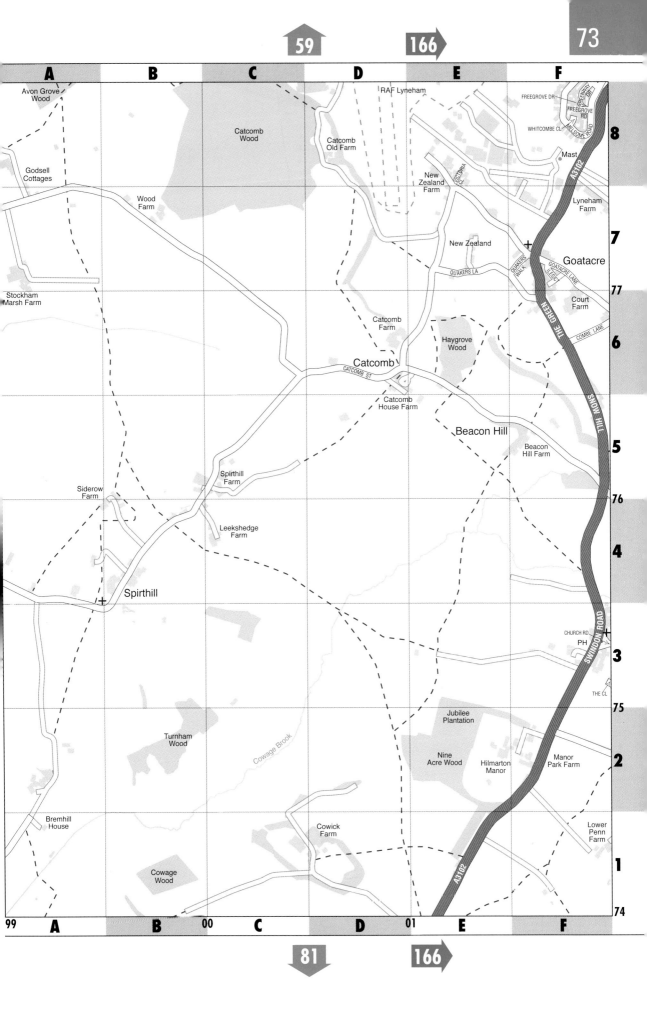

**A   B   C   D   E   F**

Avon Grove
Wood

Catcomb
Wood

RAF Lyneham

FREEGROVE DR
FREEGROVE
RD
WHITCOMBE CL

8

Godsell
Cottages

Catcomb
Old Farm

New Zealand
Farm

Mast

Wood
Farm

VICTORIA CL

Lyneham
Farm

A3102

New Zealand

7

Goatacre

QUAKERS LA

GOATACRE LANE
LEES CT

77

Stockham
Marsh Farm

Catcomb
Farm

Court
Farm

COMBE LANE

6

Catcomb

Haygrove
Wood

CATCOMB ST

THE GREEN

Catcomb
House Farm

Beacon Hill

SNOW HILL

Beacon
Hill Farm

5

Spirthill
Farm

76

Siderow
Farm

4

Leekshedge
Farm

Spirthill

SWINDON ROAD

CHURCH RD.
PH

3

THE CL

75

Jubilee
Plantation

Turnham
Wood

Cowage Brook

Nine
Acre Wood

Hilmarton
Manor

Manor
Park Farm

2

Bremhill
House

Cowick
Farm

Lower
Penn
Farm

Cowage
Wood

A3102

1

74

**Gloucestershire STREET ATLAS**

Marshfield

CHIPPENHAM RD

DOWN ROAD

A420

A420 Bristol

PO
HAYFIELD
BELL SQ
HAY STREET
HAYFIELD
CHIPPENHAM ROAD
FAIRFIELD CL
BACK LA
HIGH ST
MARKET PL
WEIR LA
TURNPIKE RD
WITHYMEAD
BARN END
WITHYMEAD RD
CHURCH LA
LITTLE END
PLACE
OLD SCHOOL CT
Marshfield
Prim Sch

East End

Pitt
Farm

Star
Farm

STAR LA

Bond's
Wood

Garston
Farm

Newleaze
Wood

Woodlands
Farm

Ringswell

Sewage
Works

Cloud
Wood

DONCOMBE HILL

Doncombe
Scrubs

PINEWOOD WAY
PINEWOOD WAY
PINEWOOD WAY

Northwood
Farm

Henleyhill
Barn

Henley
Hill

Henleyhill
Plantation

Marshfield
Wood

WALNUT DR
CYPRESS WLK
THE LUCERN
HOLLY DR
LARCH RD
LAUREL DRIVE
ASPEN CL
OAK WAY
POPLAR WAY

Raizes
Wood

FOSS WAY

Ashwicke
Grange

ASHWICKE RD

West
Lodge

Raizes
Plantation

The
Raizes

Grange
Plantation

Barracks

DUKWICK LA

Motcombe
Farm

Ashwicke
Home Farm

Centre
Plantation

East
Lodge

Colerne
Airfield

Clift Wood

ASHWICKE ROAD

Diamond
Wood

Colerne Rugby
Football Club

Cherry
Wood

BATH ROAD

Ranch
House Farm

Longley
Wood

Motcombe Wood

OAKFORD LANE

Bandywell
Wood

Lictum
Spring

Dicknick
Wood

Rocky
Wood

The
Rocks

Hunters
Hall

Breach
Wood

Orchard
Wood

Abbotscombe
Wood

Ryder's
Wood

Fewells
Wood

Moonshine
Wood

Draught
Wood

Brokenboro
Wood

RODE HILL

Westwood
Farm

West Wood

ST CATHERINE

Oakford
Farm

Rodney
Wood

Three Shire
Stones

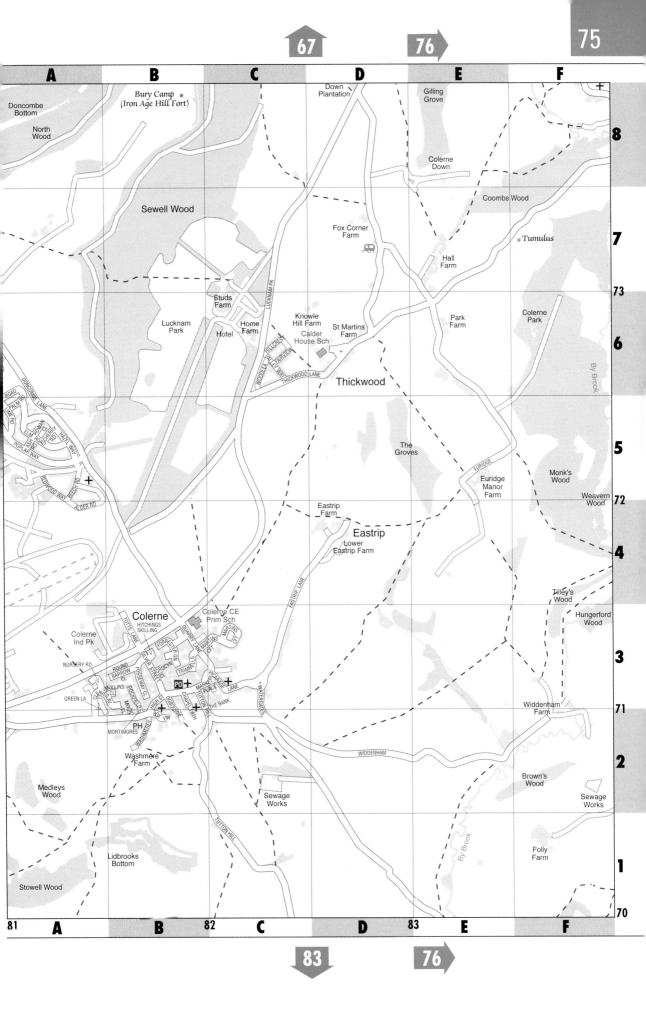

75 68

**A B C D E F**

Slaughterford

Backpath Wood

Germain's Lane

Weir

By Brook

Honeybrook Farm

Weavern Lane

Macmillan Way

White Cliff Wood

Ham Lane

Challows La

Little Glebe

The Chpy Town

Cemy

The Things

The Butts

Butts Cl

Field Farm

Mountjoy Farm

Church Road

Slaughterford Rd

Cuttle Lane

Yatton Road

Field Farm

The Green

Harts

Pool Farm

PH

Biddestone

Home Farm

Biddestone Manor

Chippenham Rd

Cross Keys

Field Barn Farm

Weavern Lane

Jubilee Wood

Husseyhill Wood

Erkwell Wood

Mound

The Grove

Square Covert

Tyning Wood

Home Farm

Hartham Farm

Leigh Wood

Weavern Lane

Weavern Farm

Tyning Wood

Hartham Park

Hartham Lane

Tyning Wood

Hungerford Wood

The Larches

Prestley Wood

Middlewick Lane

Church Farm

Long Plantation

Middlewick

Pickwick Lodge Farm

Upper Pickwick

Broad Wood

Churchill Way

Pickwick

Queens Avenue

Chippenham Rd

Rudloe Wood

Bybrook View

RAF Rudloe Manor

Gutters Lane

Academy Dr

Academy Drive

Bath Rd

A4

Corsham Regis Prim Sch

Arnolds Mead

Pickwick Road

B3353

Albion Cres

Copenacre Way

Travellers' Rest

Chestnut Grange

Bath Road

A4

Bradford Road

Springfield Sports Centre

Sports Ground

The Corsham Sch

Lower Rudloe Farm

Box Hill

Rudloe

Hotel

Half Way Firs

Underground Quarry

B3109

Halfway Firs

Groundstone Way

Corsham

Peel Circus

**A B C D E F**

69

78

77

F5
1 TOWCESTER PL
2 TAUNTON CL
3 GOODWOOD WY
4 HAYDOCK CL
5 METHUEN PK
6 LINGFIELD CL

F6
1 FARLEIGH CL
2 HAZEL COPSE
3 DERRIADS LA
4 HEXHAM CL
5 DEVON CL
6 NEWTON ABBOT CL

7 CATTERICK CL
8 PHEASANT CL
9 NEWMARKET CL
10 KEMPTON PK CT

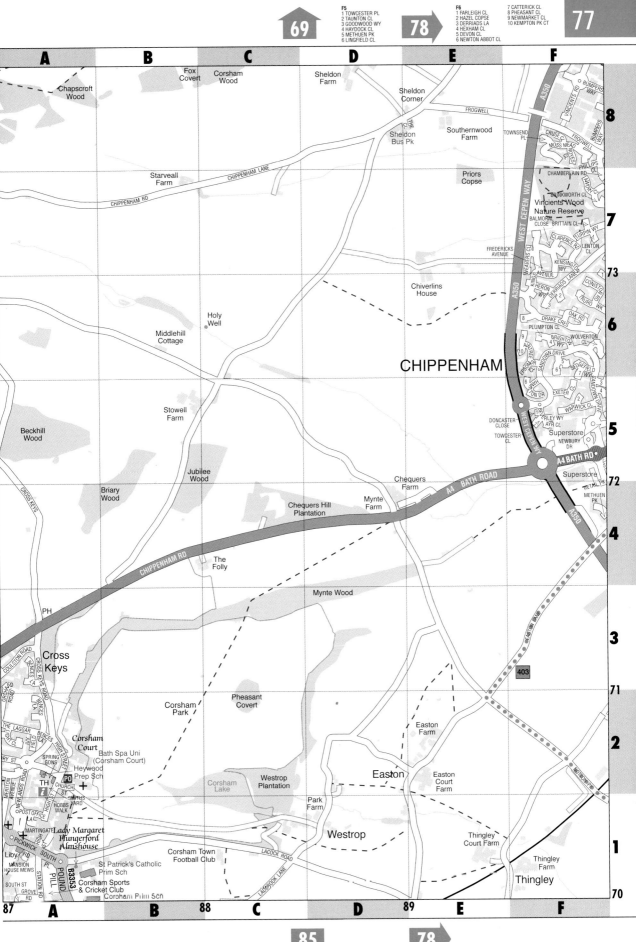

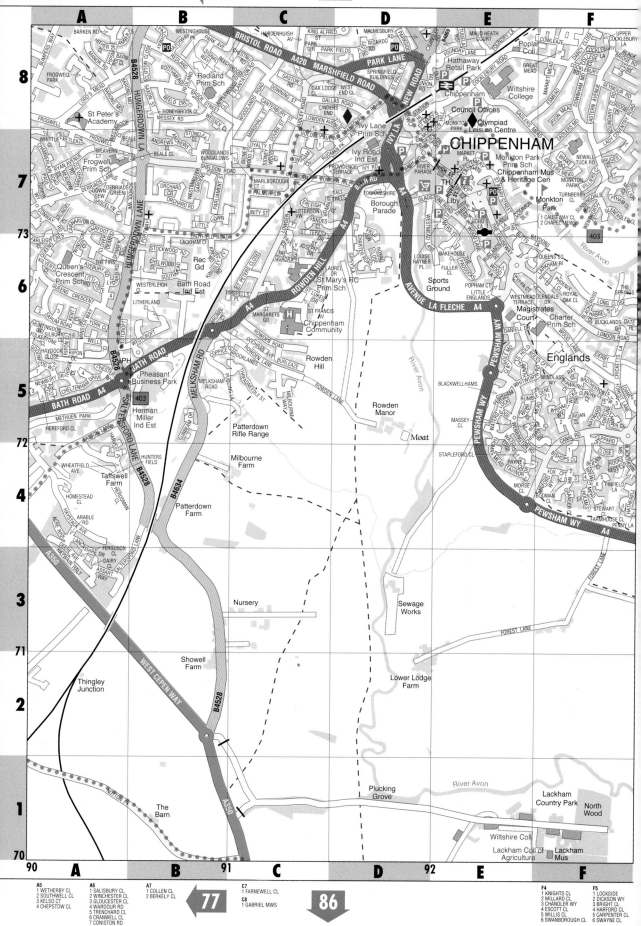

**A5**
1 WETHERBY CL
2 SOUTHWELL CL
3 KELSO CT
4 CHEPSTOW CL

**A6**
1 SALISBURY CL
2 WINCHESTER CL
3 GLOUCESTER CL
4 WARDOUR RD
5 TRENCHARD CL
6 CRANWELL CL
7 CONISTON RD

**A7**
1 COLLEN CL
2 BERKELY CL

**C7**
1 FARNEWELL CL

**C8**
1 GABRIEL MWS

**F4**
1 KNIGHTS CL
2 MILLARD CL
3 CHANDLER WY
4 ESCOTT CL
5 WILLIS CL
6 SWANBOROUGH CL

**F5**
1 LOCKSIDE
2 DICKSON WY
3 BRIGHT CL
4 HARFORD CL
5 CARPENTER CL
6 SWAYNE CL

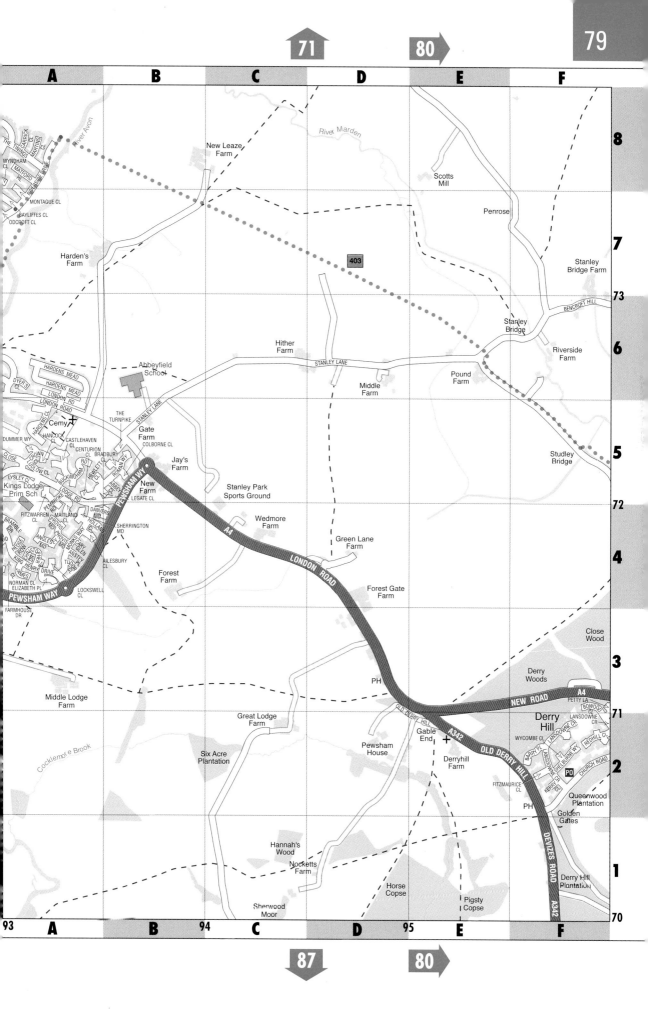

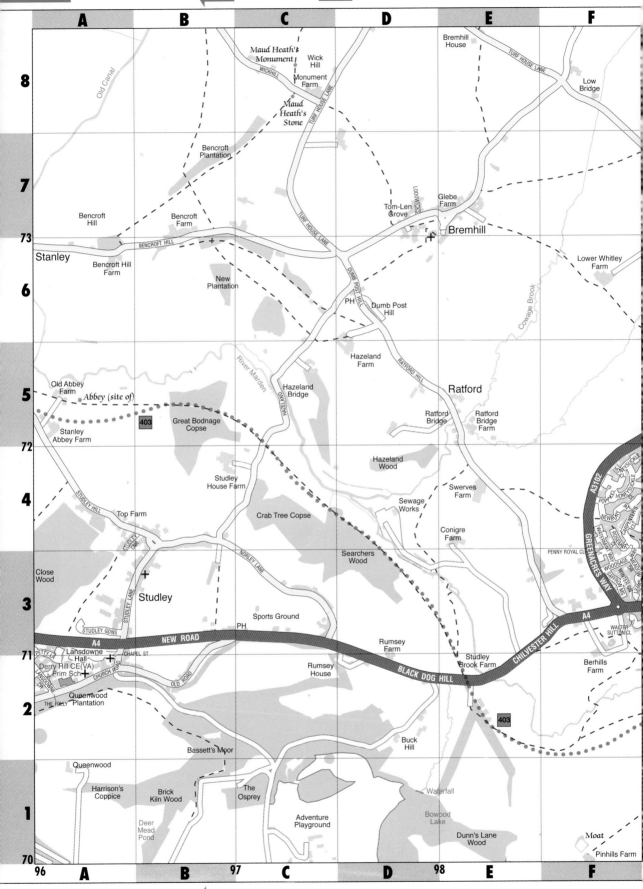

A    B    C    D    E    F

8

7

73

Stanley

6

5

72

4

3

71

2

1

70

Old Canal

Maud Heath's Monument
WICKHILL
Wick Hill
Monument Farm

Maud Heath's Stone

Bencroft Plantation

Bremhill House

TURF HOUSE LANE

Low Bridge

Bencroft Hill

Bencroft Farm

LODOWICKS
Tom-Len Grove
Glebe Farm

Bremhill

Bencroft Hill Farm

BENCROFT HILL

TURF HOUSE LANE

Lower Whitley Farm

New Plantation

DUMB POST HILL

PH
Dumb Post Hill

Cowage Brook

River Marden

Hazeland Farm

RATFORD HILL

Ratford

Old Abbey Farm
Abbey (site of)

Hazeland Bridge

403

Great Bodnage Copse

HAZELAND

Ratford Bridge

Ratford Bridge Farm

Stanley Abbey Farm

Studley House Farm

Hazeland Wood

STUDLEY HILL

Top Farm

Crab Tree Copse

Swerves Farm

A3102
HONEYSUCKLE
POPPY CL
HONEYSUCKLE
NEWBY
CARPENTER'S
GREENACRES WAY

STUDLEY LANE

MORLEY LANE

Sewage Works

Conigire Farm

PENNY ROYAL CL

WALTER SUTTON CL

Close Wood

Searchers Wood

Studley

Sports Ground
PH

Rumsey Farm

CHILVESTER HILL

A4

Berhills Farm

A4    NEW ROAD

STUDLEY GDNS

Lansdowne Hall
PETTY LA    CHAPEL ST
Derry Hill CE(VA) Prim Sch    CHURCH ROAD
LANSDOWNE CR
THE FOLLY
Queenwood Plantation

OLD ROAD

Rumsey House

BLACK DOG HILL

Studley Brook Farm

403

Buck Hill

Queenwood

Harrison's Coppice

Bassett's Moor

Brick Kiln Wood

The Osprey

Waterfall

Bowod Lake

Dunn's Lane Wood

Moat

Deer Mead Pond

Adventure Playground

Pinhills Farm

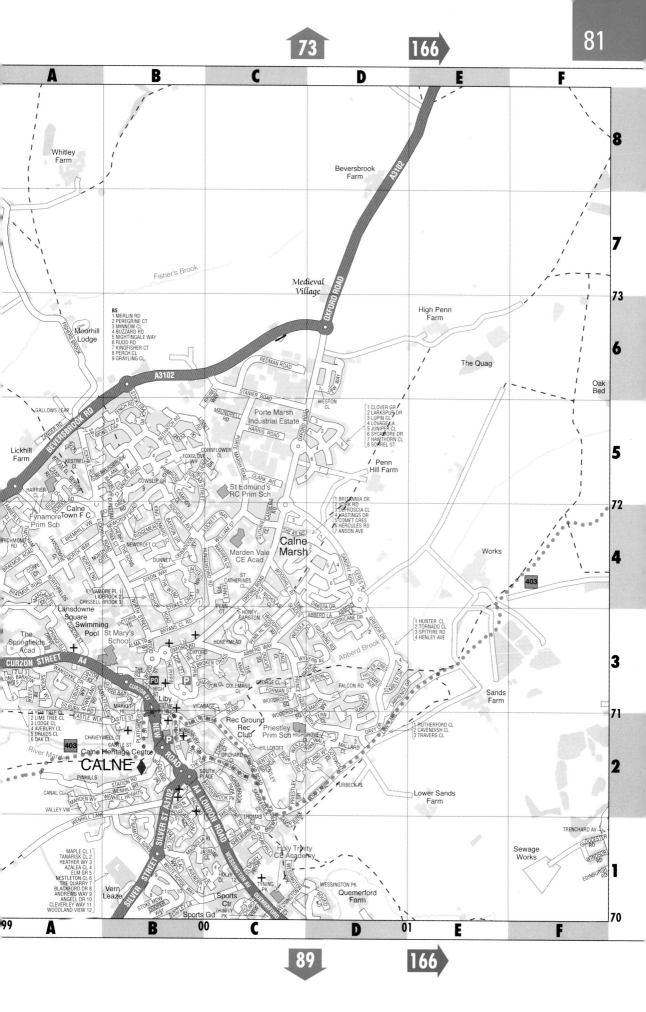

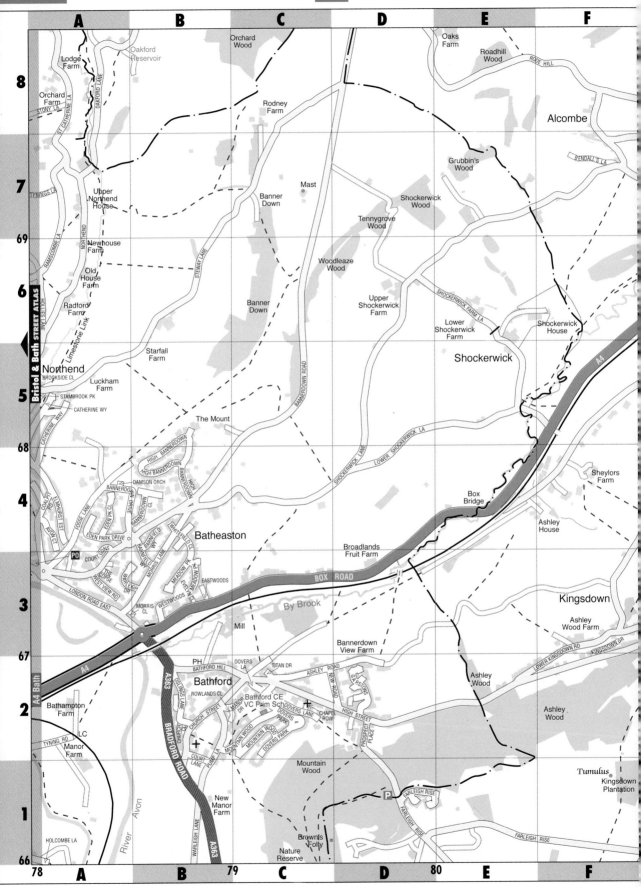

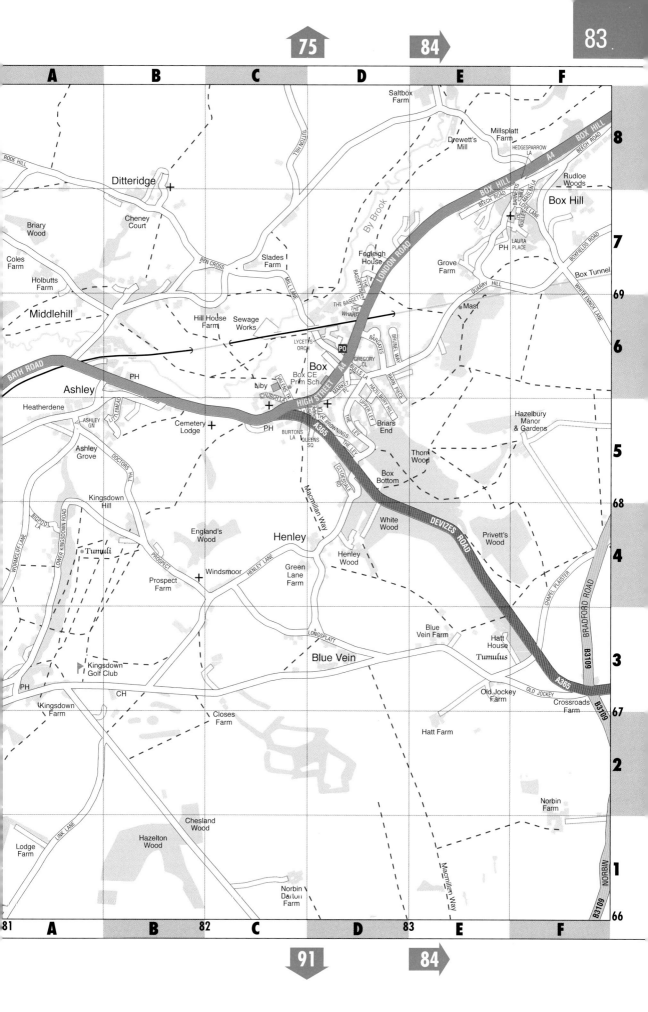

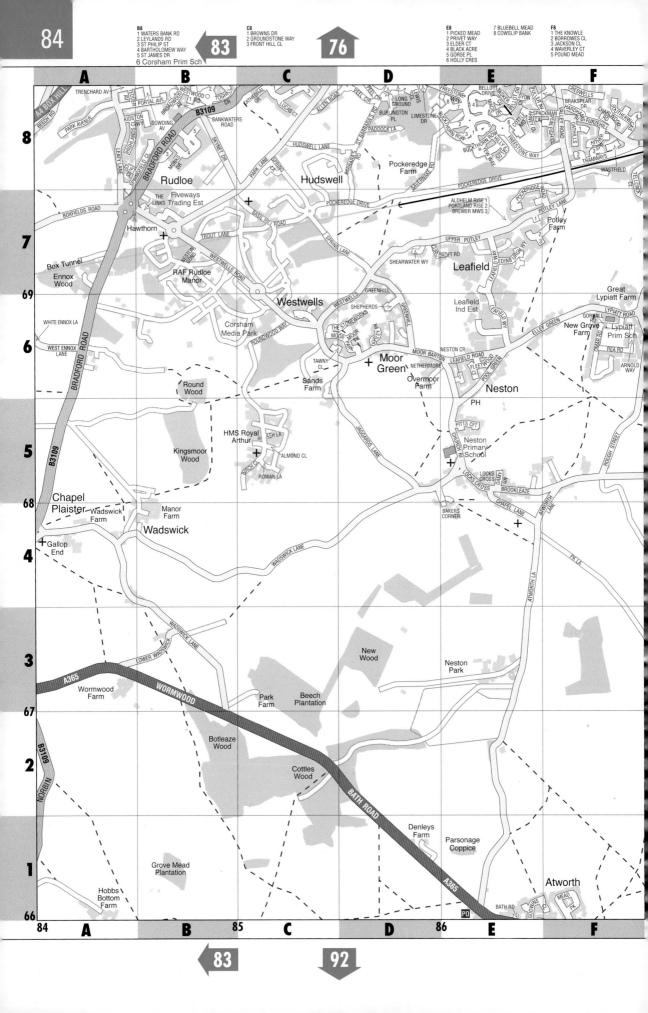

83
76

B8
1 WATERS BANK RD
2 LEYLANDS RD
3 ST PHILIP ST
4 BARTHOLOMEW WAY
5 ST JAMES DR
6 Corsham Prim Sch

C8
1 BROWNS DR
2 GROUNDSTONE WAY
3 FRONT HILL CL

E8
1 PICKED MEAD
2 PRIVET WAY
3 ELDER CT
4 BLACK ACRE
5 GORSE PL
6 HOLLY CRES

7 BLUEBELL MEAD
8 COWSLIP BANK

F8
1 THE KNOWLE
2 BORROWES CL
3 JACKSON CL
4 WAVERLEY CT
5 POUND MEAD

A   B   C   D   E   F

8
7
69
6
5
68
4
3
67
2
1
66

Rudloe
Hudswell
Pockeredge Farm
Leafield
Potley Farm
Great Lypiatt Farm
New Grove Farm
Lypiatt Prim Sch

Box Tunnel
Ennox Wood
RAF Rudloe Manor
Hawthorn
Westwells
Moor Green
Neston

Chapel Plaister
Wadswick Farm
Manor Farm
Wadswick
Gallop End

Kingsmoor Wood
HMS Royal Arthur
Sands Farm
Overmoor Farm
Neston Primary School
Bakers Corner
Brookleaze

Round Wood

New Wood
Neston Park

Wormwood Farm
Park Farm
Beech Plantation

Botleaze Wood
Cottles Wood

Grove Mead Plantation
Hobbs Bottom Farm

Denleys Farm
Parsonage Coppice
Atworth

BRADFORD ROAD
BATH ROAD
WORMWOOD
A365

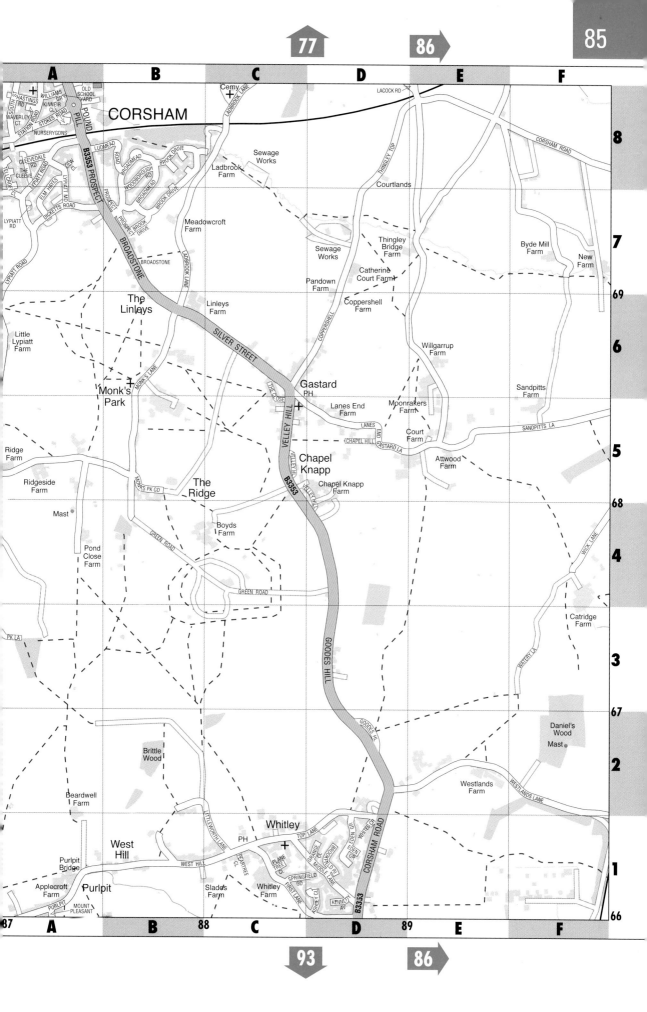

**A** **B** **C** **D** **E** **F**

CORSHAM

Cemy

Ladbrook Lane

LACOCK RD

Corsham Road

8

HASTINGS
WILLIAMS GR
OLD SCHOOL YARD
SOUTH RD
KINNEIR CL
STOKES ROAD
STATION ROAD
WAVERLEY CT
NURSERY GDNS

Sewage
Works

Thingley Top

Courtlands

CLEEVEDALE RD
THE CLEEVE
LUDMEAD ROAD
BROADMEAD
WOODBROUGH RD
BROOK DRIVE

Ladbrook
Farm

Byde Mill
Farm

New
Farm

7

LYPIATT
RD

LYPIATT MD
DICKETTS ROAD

Meadowcroft
Farm

Sewage
Works

Thingley
Bridge
Farm

LYPIATT ROAD
FELCROFT

BROADSTONE

Linleys
Farm

Pandown
Farm

Catherine
Court Farm

Coppershell
Farm

69

BROADSTONE

LADBROOK LANE

SILVER STREET

The
Linlays

Coppershell

Willgarrup
Farm

6

Little
Lypiatt
Farm

MONK'S LANE

Gastard
PH

Lanes End
Farm

Moonrakers
Farm

Sandpitts
Farm

Monk's
Park

THE CLOSE
VELLEY HILL

LANES
END
GASTARD LA

Court
Farm

SANDPITTS LA

5

Ridge
Farm

MONK'S PK GD

The
Ridge

B3353

Chapel
Knapp

CHAPEL HILL

Chapel Knapp
Farm

Attwood
Farm

Ridgeside
Farm

VELLEY HILL

68

Mast

GREEN ROAD

Boyds
Farm

WICK LANE

4

Pond
Close
Farm

GREEN ROAD

WATERY LA

Catridge
Farm

PK LA

GOODES HILL

3

67

Daniel's
Wood

Mast

GOODES HL

2

Brittle
Wood

Westlands
Farm

WESTLANDS LANE

Beardwell
Farm

LITTLE NORTH LANE

Whitley
PH

Top Lane

WHITES CR

West
Hill

Purlpit
Bridge

PEARTREE CL

WEST HILL

ORANGE CL
GRANGE CR
BROOK CL
EDEN GR
ARNOLD RD

CORSHAM ROAD

1

Applecroft
Farm

PLANE TREE CL

Slade's
Farm

Whitley
Farm

FIRST LANE

SPRINGFIELD GD
MIDDLE LANE
ASHLEY CL

KENNET AV

B3353

66

Purlpit

PURLPIT

MOUNT
PLEASANT

**A** **B** **C** **D** **E** **F**

87 88 89

85 78

| | A | B | C | D | E | F |
|---|---|---|---|---|---|---|

NOTTON PK

Notton House Sch

Great Notton Farm

Home Farm

Lackham Wood

**8**

Larksnest Farm

Notton

Rake Pond Wood

Weir

Rey Mill

Naish Hill

**7**

CORSHAM ROAD

A350

403

ROSEMARY LA

Cuckoo Bush Farm

White Hall Farm

**Reybridge**

MONS LANE

MONS LANE

New End Farm

BEWLEY LANE

**69**

NETHERCOTE HILL

Mill Farm

Lacock Pottery

CHURCH ST

EAST ST

**Lacock**

Lacock Abbey

Bewley Court

**6**

SANDRITTS LA

WICK LANE

FOLLY LANE

Lacock CE Prim Sch

PO PH

Fox Talbot Museum

HIGH ST

Bewley Common

NT

**5**

Folly Farm

FOLLY LA

HITHER WAY

P

THE WHARF

COWDEN HILL

PH

MELKSHAM ROAD

Packhorse Bridge

Strode Farm

BEWLEY LANE

**68**

Wick Farm

River Avon

Sewage Works

**4**

Earthwork

BOWDEN HILL LANE

403

**3**

Riverside Farm

**67**

Halfway Farm

Queenfield

**2**

WESTLANDS LANE

THE LAURELS

CHAPEL LA

A350

**1**

BEANACRE ROAD

Upper Beanacre Farm

PH

**66**

| 90 | A | B | 91 | C | D | 92 | E | F |
|---|---|---|---|---|---|---|---|---|

85 94

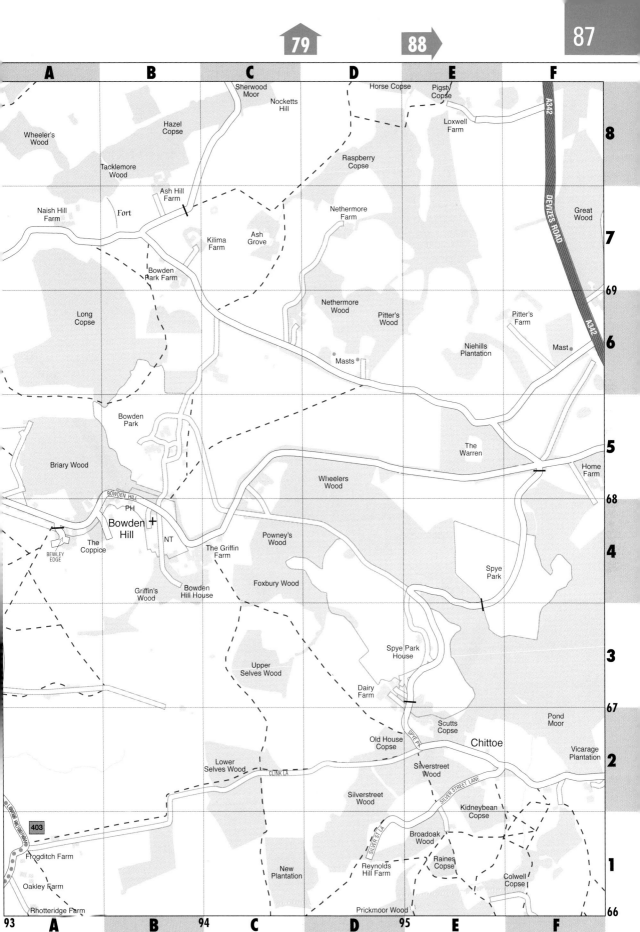

A B C D E F

8
7
69
6
5
68
4
3
67
2
1
66

Wheeler's Wood

Hazel Copse

Sherwood Moor

Nocketts Hill

Horse Copse

Pigsty Copse

Loxwell Farm

A342

DEVIZES ROAD

Great Wood

Tacklemore Wood

Ash Hill Farm

Raspberry Copse

Naish Hill Farm

Fort

Kilima Farm

Ash Grove

Nethermore Farm

Bowden Park Farm

Long Copse

Nethermore Wood

Pitter's Wood

Niehills Plantation

Pitter's Farm

Mast

A342

Bowden Park

Masts

Briary Wood

The Warren

Home Farm

BOWDEN HILL

PH

Bowden Hill

NT

The Coppice

BEWLEY EDGE

Wheelers Wood

Spye Park

The Griffin Farm

Powney's Wood

Griffin's Wood

Bowden Hill House

Foxbury Wood

Spye Park House

Upper Selves Wood

Dairy Farm

SPYE PK

Scutts Copse

Chittoe

Pond Moor

Old House Copse

Vicarage Plantation

Lower Selves Wood

CLINK LA

Silverstreet Wood

SILVER STREET LANE

Silverstreet Wood

Kidneybean Copse

SILVER ST LA

Broadoak Wood

Raines Copse

403

Frogditch Farm

New Plantation

Reynolds Hill Farm

Colwell Copse

Oakley Farm

Rhotteridge Farm

Prickmoor Wood

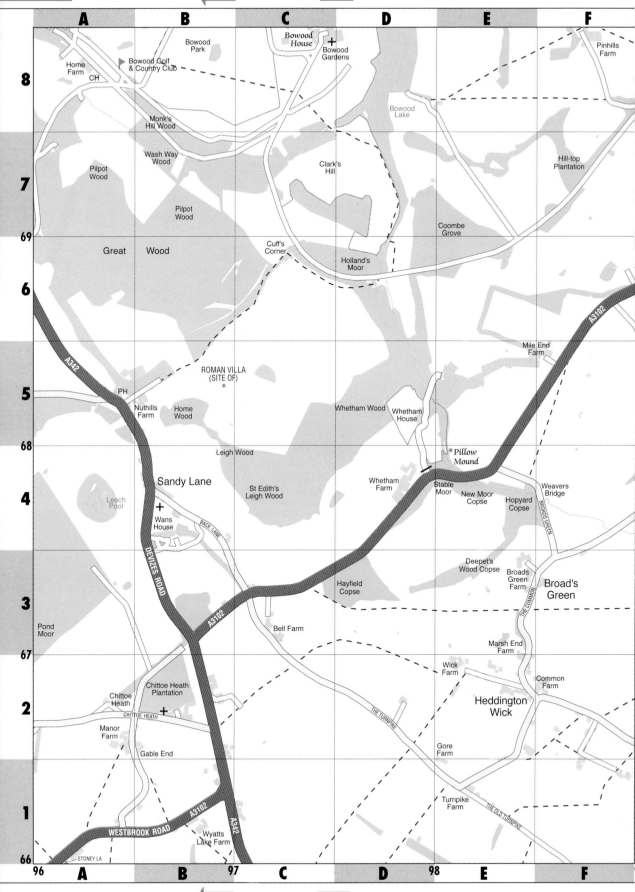

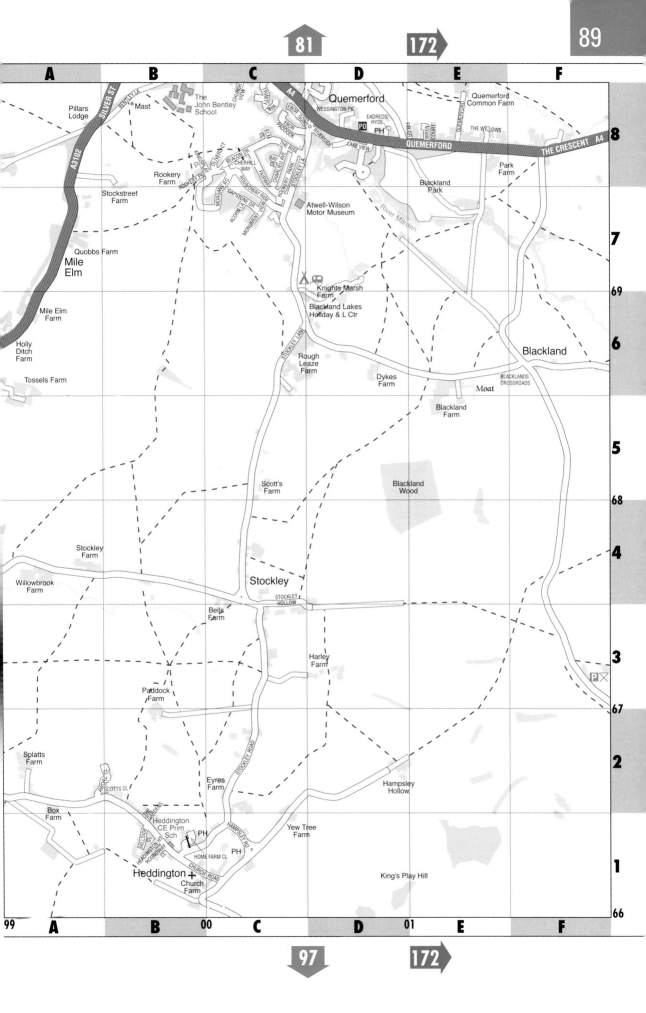

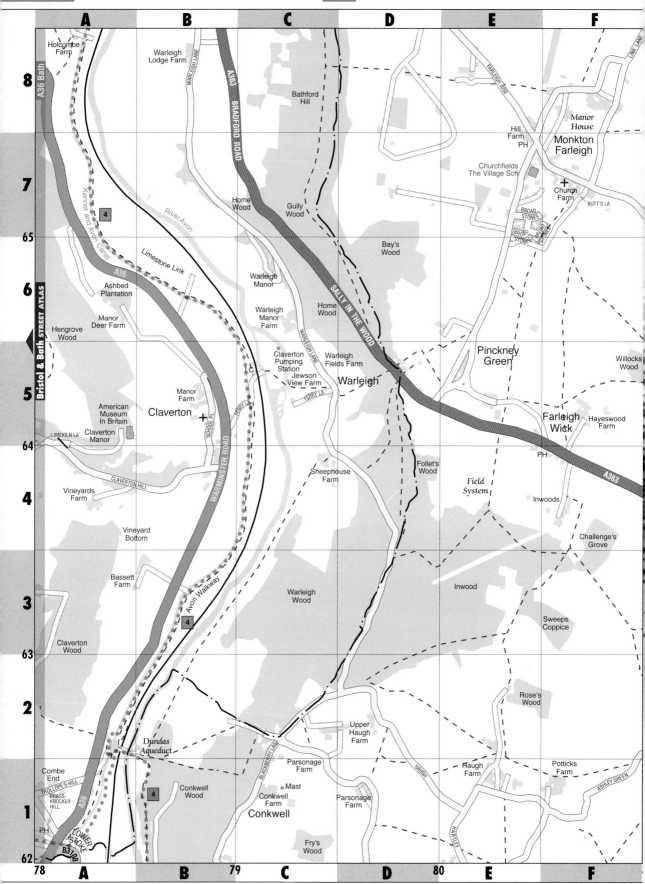

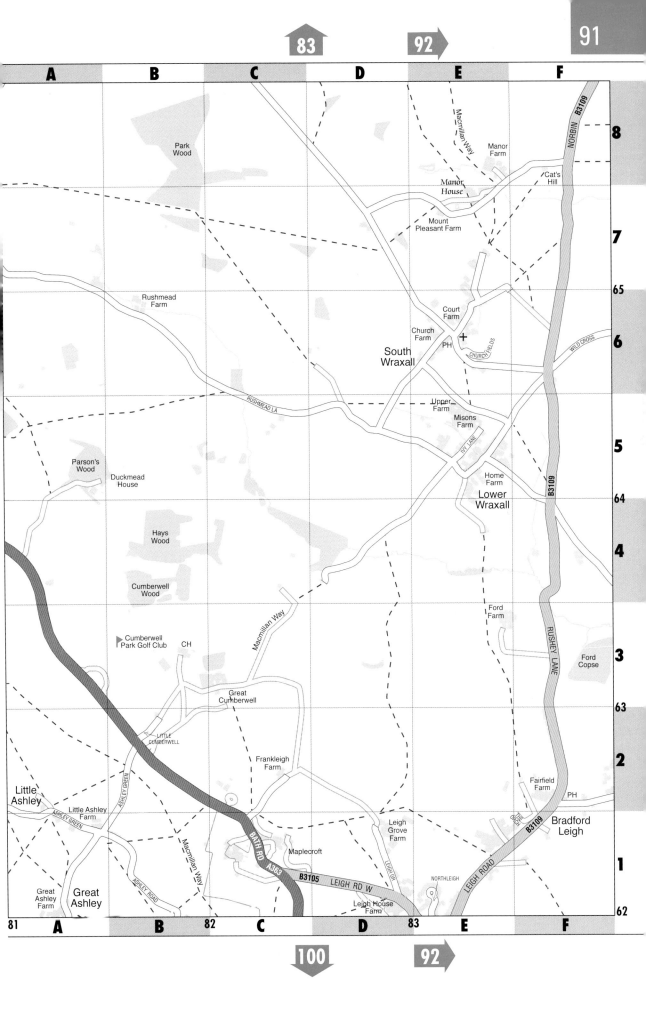

91
84

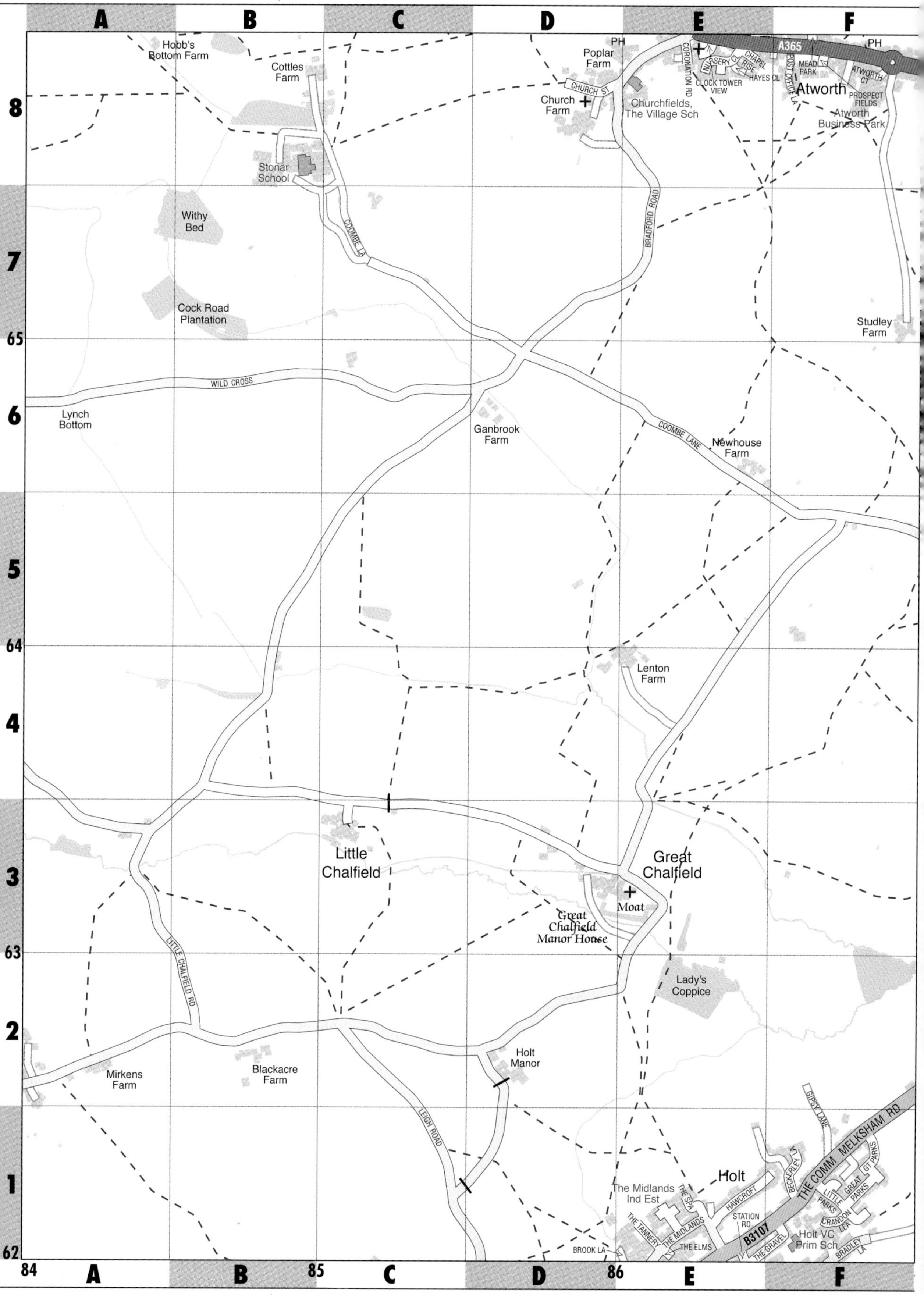

A
B
C
D
E
F
8
7
65
6
5
64
4
3
63
2
1
62
84
85
86
Hobb's Bottom Farm
Cottles Farm
Stonar School
Withy Bed
Cock Road Plantation
COOMBE LA
PH
Poplar Farm
CHURCH ST
Church Farm
Churchfields, The Village Sch
CORONATION RD
NURSERY CL
CHAPEL RISE
CLOCK TOWER VIEW
HAYES CL
A365
POST OFFICE LA
MEAD PARK
ATWORTH CT
Atworth
PROSPECT FIELDS
Atworth Business Park
BRADFORD ROAD
Studley Farm
WILD CROSS
Lynch Bottom
Ganbrook Farm
COOMBE LANE
Newhouse Farm
Lenton Farm
Little Chalfield
Great Chalfield
Moat
Great Chalfield Manor House
Lady's Coppice
LITTLE CHALFIELD RD
Mirkens Farm
Blackacre Farm
Holt Manor
LEIGH ROAD
GIPSY LANE
THE COMM
MELKSHAM RD
BECKERLEY LA
Holt
The Midlands Ind Est
THE SPA
HAWCROFT
THE TANNERY
THE MIDLANDS
STATION RD
THE ELMS
BROOK LA
B3107
THE GRAVEL
LITTLE PARKS
GREAT PARKS
GT PARKS
CRANDON LEA
Holt VC Prim Sch
BRADLEY LA

91
101

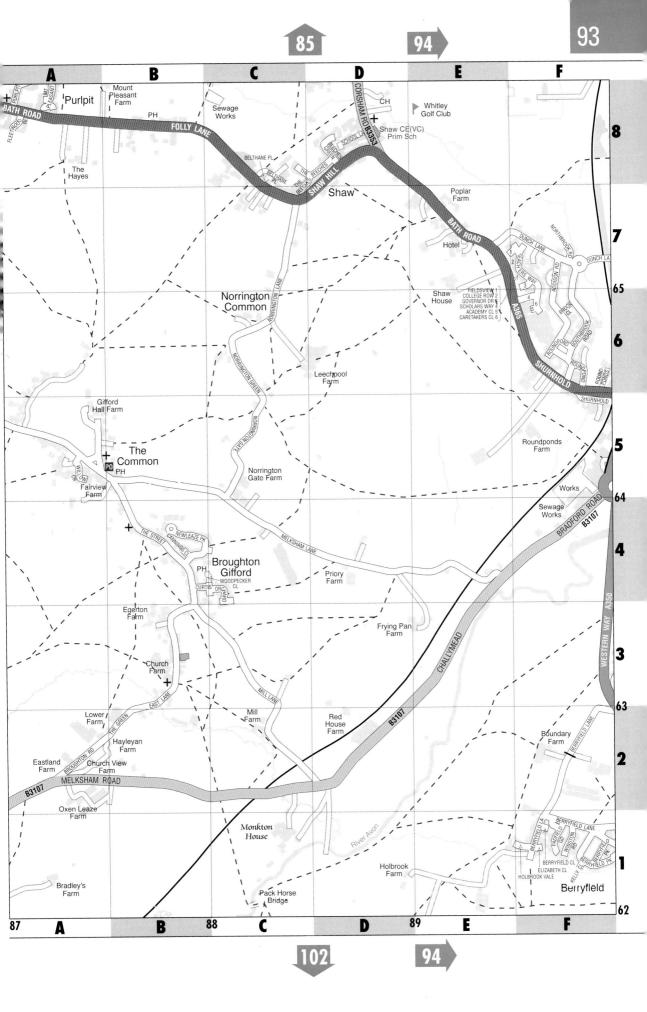

A   B   C   D   E   F

8

7

65

6

5

64

4

3

63

2

1

62

87   A   88   B   C   88   D   89   E   F

BATH ROAD
FLEETWOOD RD
PURLPIT
MT PLEASANT
Purlpit
Mount Pleasant Farm
PH
FOLLY LANE
Sewage Works
CORSHAM RD B3353
CH
Whitley Golf Club
Shaw CE (VC) Prim Sch
SCHOOL LA
BEECHES GREEN
The Hayes
BELTHANE PL
THE BEECHES
BELTHANE PL
SHAW HILL
Shaw
Poplar Farm
BATH ROAD
Hotel
NORRINGTON LANE
Norrington Common
Shaw House
FIELDSVIEW 1
COLLEGE ROW 2
GOVERNOR DR
SCHOLARS WAY 3
ACADEMY CL 5
CARETAKERS CL 6
DUNCH LANE
NORTHBROOK RD
ADDISON RD
BROOK CL
SOUTHBROOK ROAD
TEACHERS WAY
DUNCH LA
A365
SHURNHOLD
ROUND POND
ROUNDPOND
ROUND PONDS
SHURNHOLD
Leechpool Farm
NORRINGTON GREEN
NORRINGTON GATE
Gifford Hall Farm
Roundponds Farm
The Common
PO
PH
WILLOW CR
Fairview Farm
Norrington Gate Farm
Works
Sewage Works
BRADFORD ROAD
B3107
THE STREET
NEWLEAZE PK
CANNINGS CL
MELKSHAM LANE
PH
Broughton Gifford
WOODPECKER CL
CURTIS
ORCHARD
Priory Farm
Egerton Farm
Frying Pan Farm
CHALLYMEAD
WESTERN WAY A350
Church Farm
EAST LANE
MILL LANE
B3107
Lower Farm
THE GREEN
BROUGHTON RD
Hayleyan Farm
Eastland Farm
Church View Farm
MELKSHAM ROAD
B3107
Oxen Leaze Farm
Mill Farm
Red House Farm
Boundary Farm
BERRYFIELD LANE
Monkton House
River Avon
Holbrook Farm
BERRYFIELD LA
PADFIELD CL
WINSTON RD
BERRYFIELD LANE
BERRYFIELD PK
BERRYFIELD CL
ELIZABETH CL
HOLBROOK VALE
KELLY CL
Berryfield
Bradley's Farm
Pack Horse Bridge

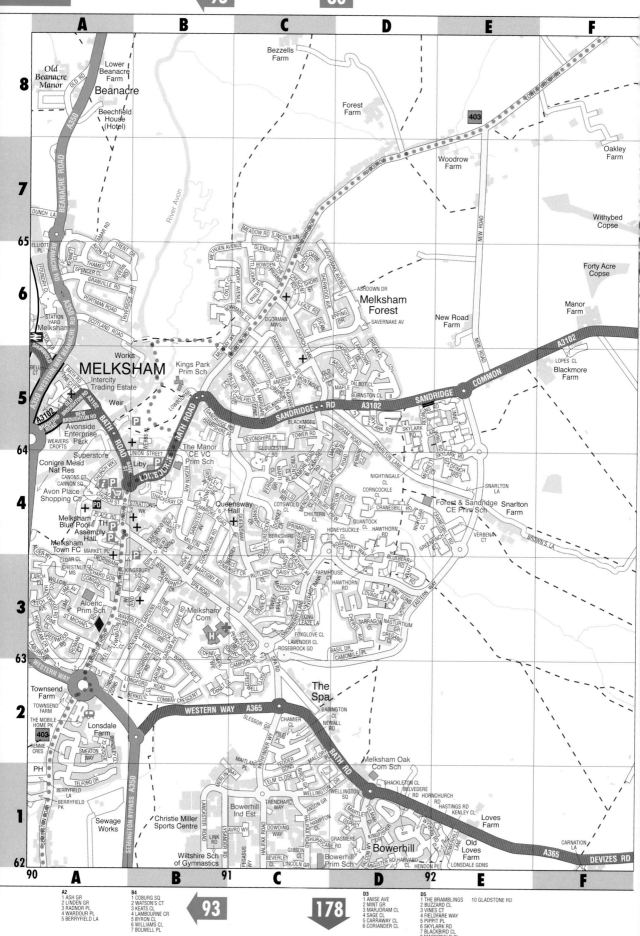

**A2**
1 ASH GR
2 LINDEN GR
3 RADNOR PL
4 WARDOUR PL
5 BERRYFIELD LA

**B4**
1 COBURG SQ
2 WATSON'S CT
3 KEATS CL
4 LAMBOURNE CR
5 BYRON CL
6 WILLIAMS CL
7 BOLWELL PL

**D3**
1 ANISE AVE
2 MINT GR
3 MARJORAM CL
4 SAGE CL
5 CARRAWAY CL
6 CORIANDER CL

**D5**
1 THE BRAMBLINGS
2 BUZZARD CL
3 VINES CT
4 FIELDFARE WAY
5 PIPPIT PL
6 SKYLARK RD
7 BLACKBIRD CL
8 BLACKBIRD CL
9 ASQUITH AVE

10 GLADSTONE RD

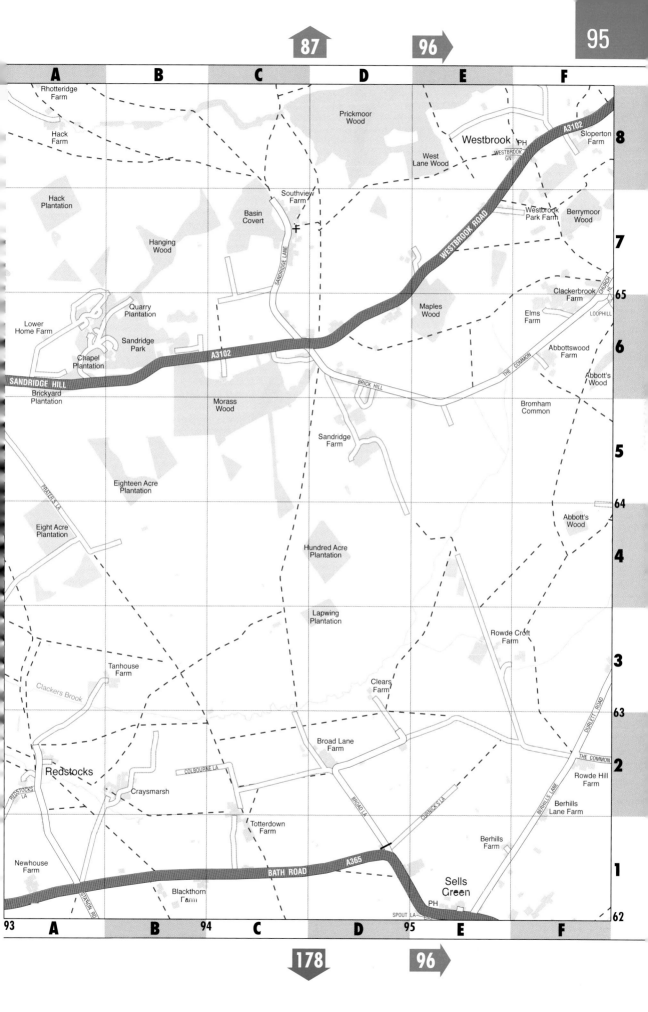

| A | B | C | D | E | F |

A3102

WESTBROOK

**8**

The Coppice

Wyatt's Wood

Bromham House Farm

DEVIZES ROAD

Netherstreet Farm

STONEY LA

GREYSTONES

HORSEPOOL

HIGHFIELD

THE CRESCENT

HIGHFIELD

A342

**7**

Bromham

PH

MINT'S TOP

THE POUND

OLD SCHOOL CL

HIGHFIELD

YARD LANE

CHURCH HL RD

JOCKEY LANE

SCHOOL LA

HIGH ST

BRE... LA

ORCHARD GR

CHURCH HL

HUNT'S MD

St Nicholas CE VC Prim Sch

HAWKSTREET

NETHERSTREET

**65**

CHURCH HL

BARTON CL

PO

SPIRE VIEW

LONGHILL

**6**

Abbott's Wood

NEW ROAD

Hobbs Farm

Moorhouse Farm

**5**

The Fruit Farm

Stills Farm

HAWKSTREET

Homeleigh Farm

St Edith's

PH

NEW ROAD

Lower Hawk Street Farm

Caumans Coppice

ST EDITH'S MARSH

**64**

Burbrook's Wood

Long Pond Wood

Nine Acre Wood

**4**

Durlett Farm

DURLETT ROAD

Clinghill Wood

Horse Lane Copse

HORSE LA

Horse Lane Farm

Marsh Farm

Big Wood

Rowdeford Sch

Withybed Wood

Ashen Wood

The Moors

**3**

Durlett Wood

**63**

Wick Farm

West End Farm

CLOSE LA

Tanis

CONSCINCE LANE

**2**

THE COMMON

COCK ROAD

BUNNIES LA

MAUNDRELL CL

PH

HIGH STREET

Manor Farm

PARADISE LA

A342

DEVIZES ROAD

Sewage Works

COCK ROAD

TOWER VW

ST MATTHEWS CL

SANDS LANE

SPRINGFIELD RD

SCHOLARS PK

Rowde CE Prim Acad

FERRIS CL

Rowde

RONDE CT RD

CHESTNUT

WALNUT CL

ELM CL

MARSH LANE

REED PL

WHEELER PL

B3101

FURLONG CL

Vale Mead

**1**

Smithwick Farm

**62**

96 | A | B | 97 | C | D | 98 | E | F

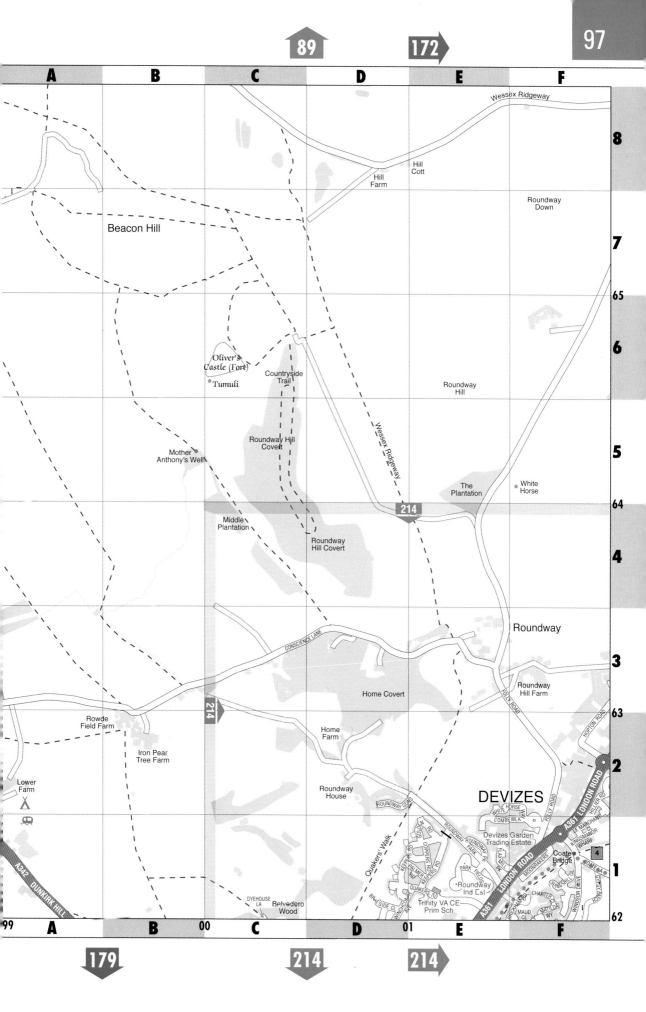

| | A | B | C | D | E | F |

**8**
**7**
65
**6**
**5**
64
**4**
**3**
63
**2**
**1**
62

Wessex Ridgeway

Hill Cott

Hill Farm

Roundway Down

Beacon Hill

Oliver's Castle (Fort)
•Tumuli

Countryside Trail

Roundway Hill

Mother Anthony's Well•

Roundway Hill Covert

Wessex Ridgeway

The Plantation

•White Horse

Middle Plantation

214

Roundway Hill Covert

Roundway

CONSCIENCE LANE

Home Covert

Roundway Hill Farm

FOLLY ROAD

214

Rowde Field Farm

Home Farm

Iron Pear Tree Farm

Lower Farm

Roundway House

DEVIZES

Roundway Gdns

WHITE HORSE
COMBE WLK

Devizes Garden Trading Estate

A361 LONDON ROAD

LE MARCHANT
KINGSMANOR

Coate Bridge

Quaker's Walk

KEEPERS RD
COPPERS RD
PALMERS RD
KEEPERS RD

PARK FIELDS
FLAX MILL

Roundway Ind Est

MOORAKERS

HOPTON ROAD

A361 LONDON ROAD

WINDSOR DRIVE

HILLIER RD

CHARTERS

DYEHOUSE LA
Belvedere Wood

BRAESIDE CL
WINDSOR
MAUD
CL

QUAKERS RD

Trinity VA CE Prim Sch

MATILDA WY

A342 DUNKIRK HILL

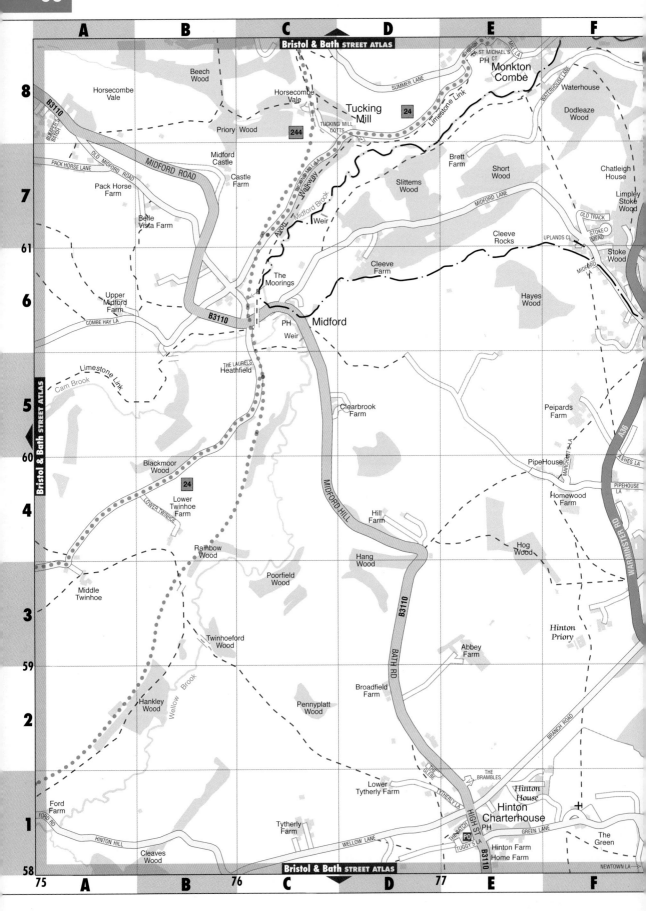

**A** **B** **C** **D** **E** **F**

Horsecombe Vale

Beech Wood

Horsecombe Vale

Monkton Combe

St Michael's PH CT

Waterhouse

8

B3110

BUMPER'S BATCH

Priory Wood

Tucking Mill

24

Dodleaze Wood

Chatleigh House

PACK HORSE LANE

OLD MIDFORD ROAD

MIDFORD ROAD

Midford Castle

TUCKING MILL COTTS

244

Brett Farm

Short Wood

Limpley Stoke Wood

7

Pack Horse Farm

Castle Farm

Walkway

Midford Brook

Weir

Midford Lane

OLD TRACK

STOKE O MEAD

UPLANDS CL

Belle Vista Farm

Avon

Cleeve Rocks

Cleeve Farm

Midford

Stoke Wood

61

Upper Midford Farm

The Moorings

Hayes Wood

6

COMBE HAY LA

B3110

PH

Midford

Weir

Limestone Link

Cam Brook

THE LAURELS

Heathfield

Clearbrook Farm

Peipards Farm

A36

ASHES LA

5

Blackmoor Wood

PipeHouse

MARCHANT'S LA

PIPEHOUSE LA

60

24

Lower Twinhoe Farm

LOWER TWINHOE

Rainbow Wood

Hill Farm

Hog Wood

Homewood Farm

WARMINSTER RD

4

Middle Twinhoe

Poorfield Wood

Hang Wood

MIDFORD HILL

Hinton Priory

3

Twinhoeford Wood

BATH RD

B3110

Abbey Farm

59

Wellow Brook

Pennyplatt Wood

Broadfield Farm

BRANCH ROAD

2

Hankley Wood

THE BRAMBLES

Hinton House

THE GLEBE

FORD RD

Ford Farm

Lower Tytherly Farm

TYTHERLY LA

HIGH ST

Hinton Charterhouse

PH

Green Lane

1

HINTON HILL

Tytherly Farm

WELLOW LANE

PO

TUGGY'S LA

THATCH

B3110

Hinton Farm

Home Farm

The Green

Cleaves Wood

NEWTOWN LA

58

75 **A** **B** 76 **C** **D** 77 **E** **F**

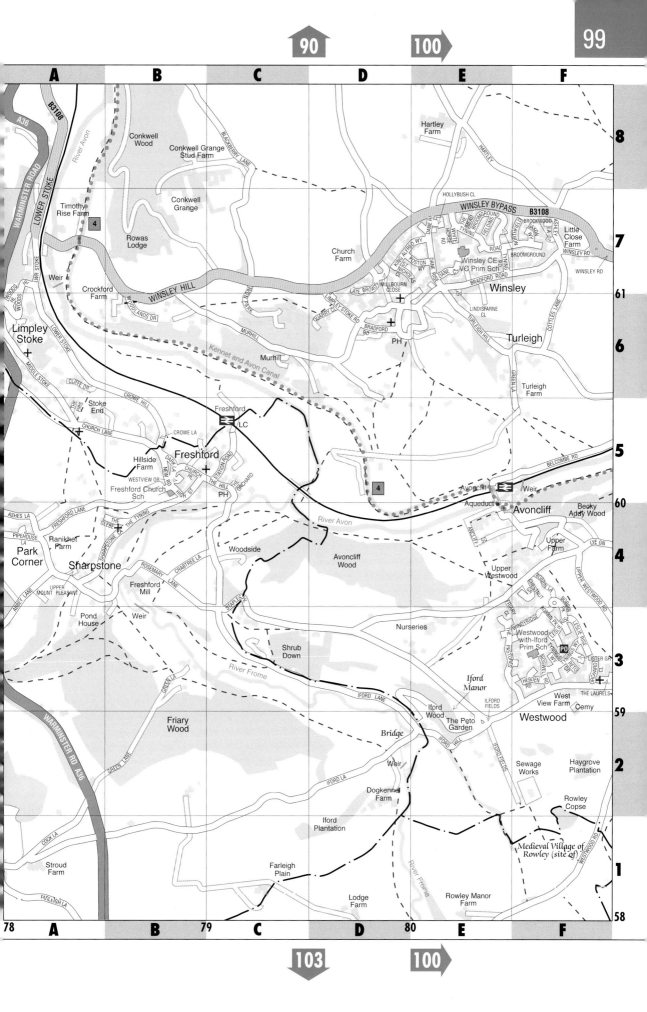

**A** **B** **C** **D** **E** **F**

8

B3108
A36
WARMINSTER ROAD
LOWER STOKE
River Avon

Conkwell Wood
Conkwell Grange Stud Farm
BLACKBERRY LANE
Hartley Farm
HOLLYBUSH CL
HARTLEY
ASHLEY

Timothy Rise Farm
4
Conkwell Grange
Church Farm
Winsley Bypass B3108
BROCKWOOD
BROCK WY
Little Close Farm

7

Rowas Lodge
WHITE HORSE RD
THE BROOK
BROOMGROUND
FIELDS
THE TYNING
NORTHFIELD
Winsley CE VC Prim Sch
BROOMGROUND
Winsley Rd
Winsley Rd

Crockford Farm
Winsley Hill
WOODLANDS DR
KING ALFRED WY
DANE RISE
PISTON WY
DANE
NICHOLAS CL
ST
BRADFORD ROAD
Winsley

61

LWR STOKE
WOODS
WOODS
HILL
MURHILL
KNOR PARK
QUARRY CL
LIMPLEY STOKE RD
LATE BROOKS
BRADFORD RD
MILLBOURN CLOSE
LINDISFARNE CL
TURLEIGH HILL
COTTLES LANE
Turleigh

Limpley Stoke
MIDDLE STOKE
CLIFF DR
CROWE HILL
Murhill
PH
PH
Turleigh Farm
GREEN LA

6

Kennet and Avon Canal

The Firs
Stoke End
CROWE LA
Freshford
LC
Belcombe Rd

5

Church Lane
Hillside Farm
Freshford
DARK LA
CHURCH PL
THE STATION ROAD
THE HILL
THE ORCHARD
Avoncliff
Weir

Freshford Church Sch
NEW RD
HIGH ST
PH
4
Aqueduct
Avoncliff
Becky Addy Wood

60

ASHES LA
FRESHFORD LANE
WESTVIEW OR
THE GLEBE
SHARPSTONE LA
THE TYNING
Woodside
Avoncliff Wood
AVONCLIFF SQ
Upper Farm
LYE GN

Ranikhet Farm
CRABTREE LA
Upper Westwood
UPPER WESTWOOD RD

PIPEHOUSE LA
Park Corner
UPPER MOUNT PLEASANT
Sharpstone
ROSEMARY LANE
Freshford Mill
River Avon
Nurseries
BOBBIN PARK RISE
BOBBIN LA
CHESTNUT
LESLIE RISE
Westwood with-Iford Prim Sch
PO
LISTER GN

4

ABBEY LA
Pond House
Weir
STAPLES LN
Shrub Down
WYNDYRIDGE
FERRY
THE PASTURES
BOSWELL
BOBBIN LA
HEBDEN RD
TYNINGS
ORCHARD
West View Farm
THE LAURELS
Cemy

3

GREEN LA
River Frome
IFORD LANE
Iford Manor
Iford Wood
ILFORD FIELDS
Westwood

59

Friary Wood
Bridge
Weir
IFORD LA
Dogkennel Farm
The Peto Garden
IFORD HILL
IFORD FIELDS
Sewage Works
Haygrove Plantation

2

GREEN LANE
WARMINSTER RD A36
COCK LA
Iford Plantation
River Frome
Rowley Copse

Stroud Farm
FARLEIGH LA
Farleigh Plain
Lodge Farm
Rowley Manor Farm
Medieval Village of Rowley (site of)
WESTWOOD RD

1

58

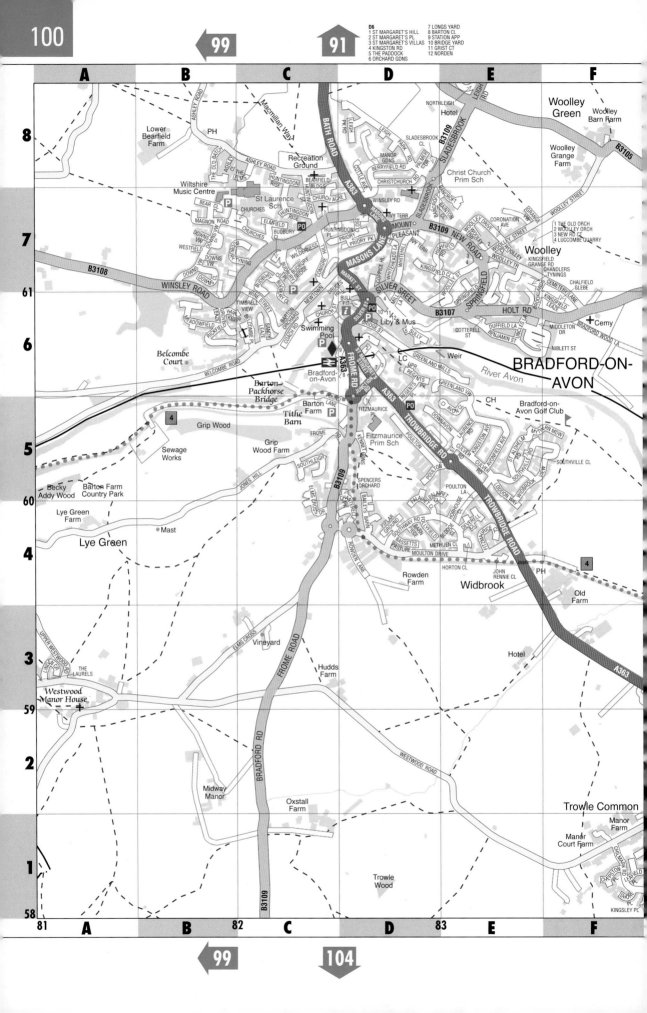

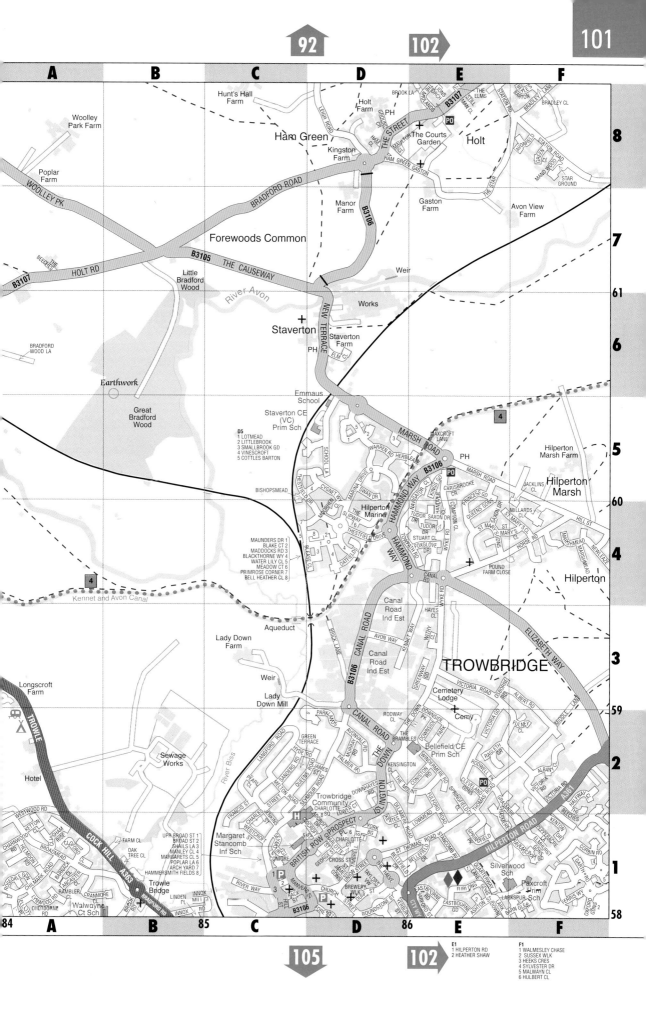

A B C D E F

8
7
61
6
5
60
4
59
3
2
1
58

**Woolley Park Farm**

**Poplar Farm**

WOOLLEY PK

Hunt's Hall Farm

BRADFORD ROAD

Holt Farm

THE STREET

BROOK LA

LIONS

B3107

The Elms

PO

The Courts Garden

**Holt**

STATION ROAD

GREEN CL

BRADLEY CL

MAND MOOR

STAR GROUND

**Ham Green**

Kingston Farm

LEIGH ROAD

HAM GREEN GASTON

Gaston Farm

Avon View Farm

Manor Farm

B3106

THE BEECHES

HOLT RD

B3107

B3105

THE CAUSEWAY

**Forewoods Common**

Little Bradford Wood

River Avon

Weir

Works

NEW TERRACE

BRADFORD WOOD LA

*Earthwork*

Great Bradford Wood

**Staverton**

PH

Staverton Farm

ELM CL

Emmaus School

Staverton CE (VC) Prim Sch

4

Hilperton Marsh Farm

MARSH ROAD

PH

B3106

PO

MARSH ROAD

Hilperton Marsh

D5
1 LOTMEAD
2 LITTLEBROOK
3 SMALLBROOK GD
4 VINESCROFT
5 COTTLES BARTON

WARREN RD HERBLEAN

SCHOOL LA

MARIMA DRIVE

CYGNET WY

SWAN CL

JACKLINS CL

CARISBROOKE CR

KINGS CL

MILLARDS CL

HILL ST

BISHOPSMEAD

THESTFIELD DR

MORDEN CL

THESTFIELD DRIVE

THE SLIPWAY

Hilperton Marina

HAMMOND WAY

TUDOR DR

SAXON CR

COMPTON CL

TUDOR

St MARY'S CL

St MARY'S GDNS

QUEENS GDNS

St MARY'S ST

HORSE RD

MARSHMEAD

MARSHMEAD

NEW LEAZE

MAUNDERS DR 1
BLAKE CT 2
MADDOCKS RD 3
BLACKTHORNE WY 4
WATER LILY CL 5
MEADOW CT 6
PRIMROSE CORNER 7
BELL HEATHER CL 8

BLAKE CL

OATFIELDS

STUART CL

FOXGLOVE DR

HAMMOND WAY

WYKE RD

TOPHILL CL

**Hilperton**

CANAL RD

POUND FARM CLOSE

4

Kennet and Avon Canal

Aqueduct

Lady Down Farm

Canal Road Ind Est

BRICK LANE

CANAL ROAD

AVON WAY

KENNET WAY

WITHY CL

HAYES CL

GREENWAY

ELIZABETH WAY

MIDDLE LANE

**TROWBRIDGE**

Weir

Lady Down Mill

B3106

Canal Road Ind Est

RODWAY CL

Cemetery Lodge

Cemy

Victoria Road

ALBERT RD

FULNEY CL

**Longscroft Farm**

TROWLE

Hotel

River Biss

Sewage Works

PARK ARDS

GREEN TERRACE

LANGFORD ROAD

HYDE RD

MURRAY RD

PALMER RD

AVONVALE RD

THE BRAMBLES

Bellefield CE Prim Sch

KENSINGTON

THE DOWN

ISLINGTON

THE MOUNT

CONISTON

WINDERMERE RD

DOWNSIDE PK

DOWNSIDE PARK

VICTORIA GD

OSBORNE RD

RODWELL PL

RAGLETH GR

SPRINGFIELDS

GRASMERE

CLEVELAND GDNS

ALBAN RD

VICTORIA RD

A361

HILPERTON ROAD

THE BEECHES

KENTON RD

HALFWAY

WESTWOOD RD

KETTON

CHARNWOOD GD

NELSON CL

BROADMEAD

BARRICK CL

LANCASTER CL

RAMBLER CL

CRANMORE CL

COCK HILL

A363

FARM CL

OAK TREE CL

Trowle Bridge

BRADFORD RD

BRICK HILL

LINDEN

INNOX

INNOX MILL CL

PEARL CL

MELTON RD

QUEENS RD

SANDERS RD

SEYMOUR ROAD

FRANCIS STREET

CHARLES STREET

BIRCH ST

Trowbridge Community

CHARLOTTE ST

LOWER RD

CONIGRE

WESTCROFT

MANLEY CL

MARGARETS CL

UPR BROAD ST 1
BROAD ST 2
SHAILS LA 3
MANLEY CL 4
MARGARETS CL 5
POPLAR LA 6
ARCH YARD 7
HAMMERSMITH FIELDS 8

Margaret Stancomb Inf Sch

H

RIVER WAY

MANN'S BACK

P

P

B3106

FORE ST

BRITISH ROW

PROSPECT

YORK BLDGS

CHARLOTTE ST

CROSS ST

GEORGE ST

GEORGE STREET

UNION STREET

St THOMAS ST

CHURCH STREET

BREWERY WLK

ROUNDSTONE ST

CASTLE ST

FIELDING ST

EASTBOURNE GDNS

EASTBOURNE

HILPERTON ROAD

FIRLONG

BYTHESEA RD

Silverwood Sch

Paxcroft Prim Sch

LARKSPUR CL

BARN CL

Walwayne Ct Sch

ROSEDALE GD

CHILMARK RD

CHERBORNE CL

OXFORD GDNS

FERRIS WY

84 A B 85 C D 86 E F 58

E1
1 HILPERTON RD
2 HEATHER SHAW

F1
1 WALMESLEY CHASE
2 SUSSEX WLK
3 HEEKS CRES
4 SYLVESTER DR
5 MALWAYN CL
6 HULBERT CL

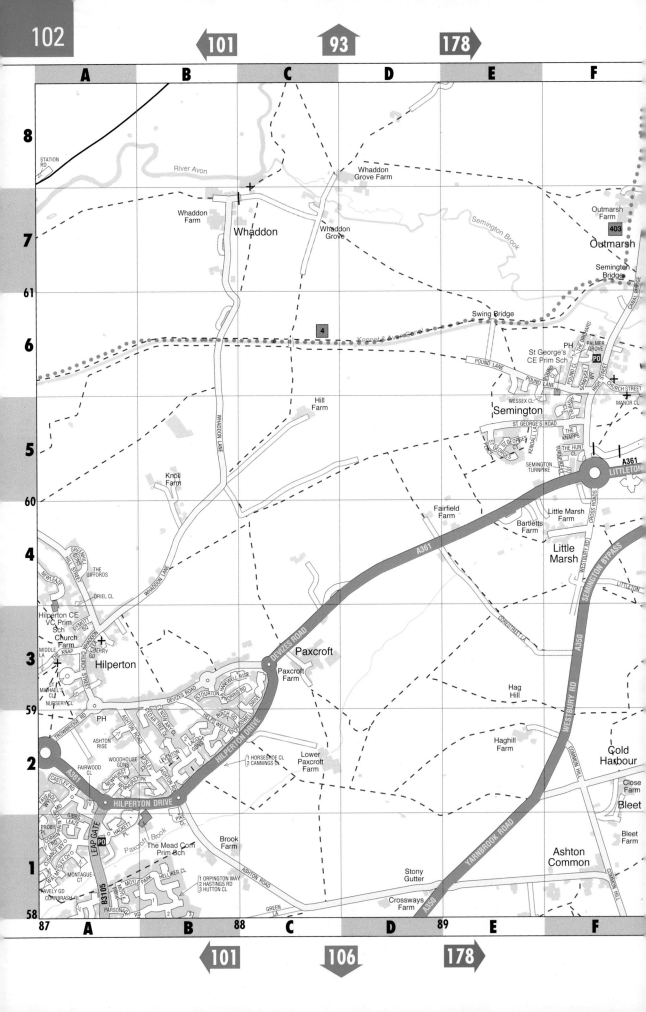

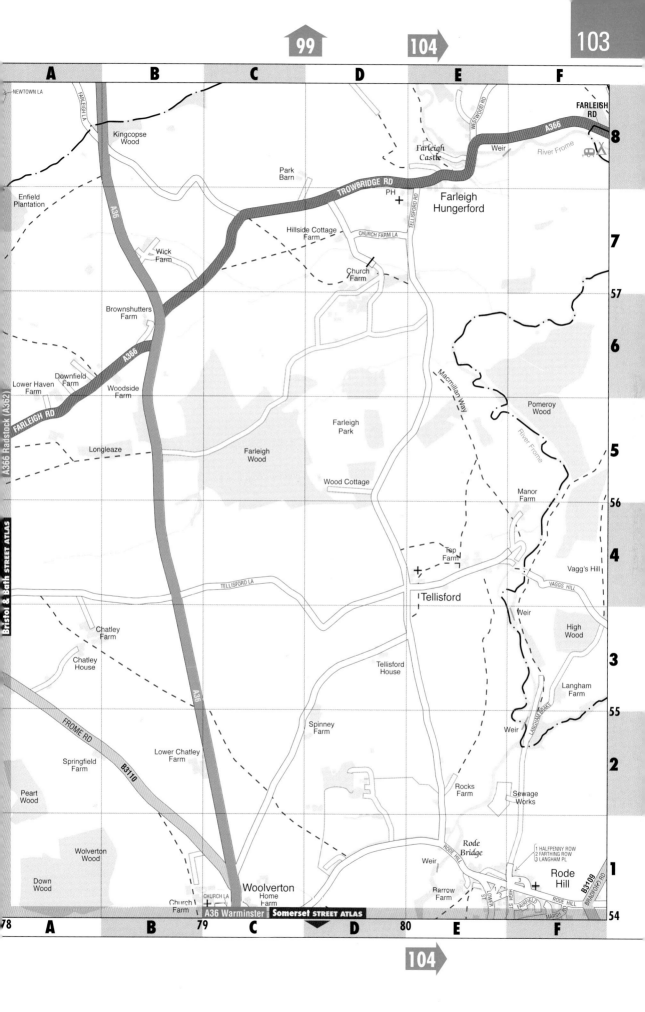

103
100

A B C D E F

8

Stowford Manor Farm

FARLEIGH RD

Snarlton Farm

Weir

7

Stowford Farm

MAGDALEN LA

BRADFORD RD

B3109

Wingfield House

CHAPEL LA

Trowle Farm

TROWBRIDGE RD    A366

Arnold's Hill

London Bridge Farm

London Bridge

Arnolds Hill Farm

Studley Green

SANDFORD PK

KENSINGTON FIELDS

WATERFORD BECK

KINGSWOOD CHASE

FIELDS WY

CAVENDISH DR

REGENTS PL

GREENBANK VIEW

57

Belle Coeur Farm

POMEROY LANE

SHOP LANE

Church Farm

6

Pomeroy Farm

PH

Wingfield

FROME ROAD

MOORES YD

CHURCH LANE

CHAPEL LA

The Mead Com Prim Sch

OAK PARK

Birch Wood

5

Swansbrook Farm

Park Farm

Southwick Country Park

Sleight Wood

56

HOGGINGTON LA

Hoggington Farm

4

Romsey Oak Farm

Vagg's Hill Wood

Hoggington

HOGGINGTON LANE

FLEUR DE LYS DR

FROME ROAD

Southwick

Vaggs Hill Farm

Dillybrook Farm

BRADFORD ROAD

POPLAR TREE LANE

Newpool Farm

FAIRFIELD MS 1
CHANTRY CT 2
SWAN CT 3
THE MOWLEMS 4
CHAPEL CL 5

CORINTHIAN CL

CHANTRY PL GV

3

Vaggs Hill Farm

Arnold Noad Corner

Pound Farm

PH

Southwick CE Prim Sch

WYNSOME ST

CHURCH

FROME ROAD

P

55

Frith Farm

GREEN LANE

Marshfield

Flaxfield Farm

Dunkirk Business Park

Dunkirk Farm

Lamberts Marsh

ORCHARD DR

WESLEY LANE

SOUTHFIELD

HOLLIS WY

BLIND LANE

2

Flexham Farm

MONKLEY LANE

Sparrows Rest Farm

Blue Barn Farm

Poleshole Farm

Whittakers Farm

Hoopers Pool

Marsh Mead

Pole's Hole

B3109

A361

RODE COMMON

1

Rode Common

Rode Common Farm

Hoopers Pool Farm

Mutton Marsh Farm

RODE HILL

54

81          82          83

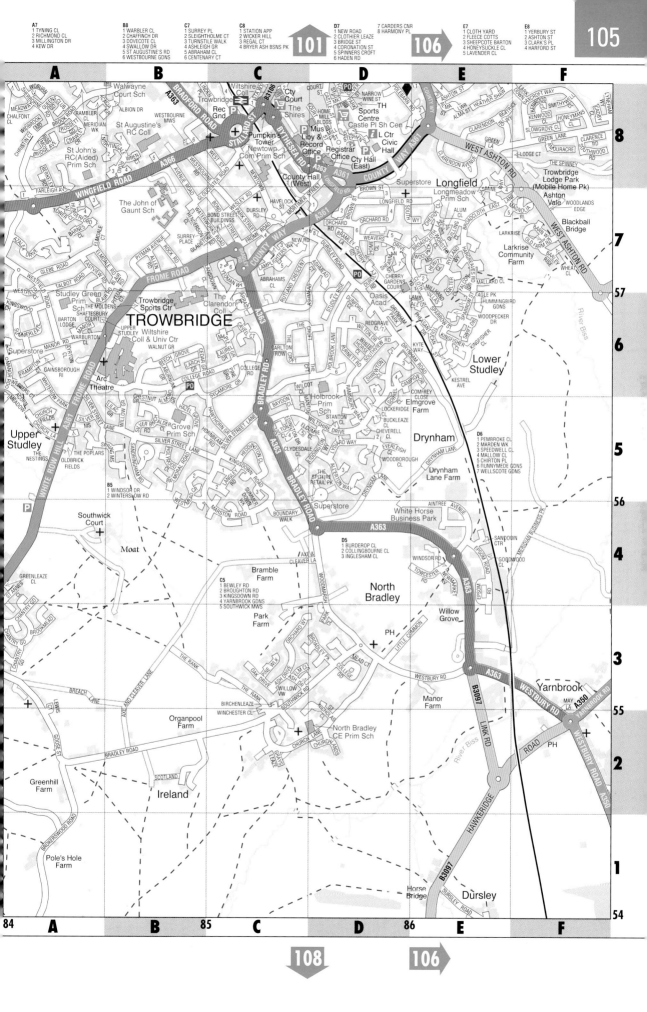

105 102 178

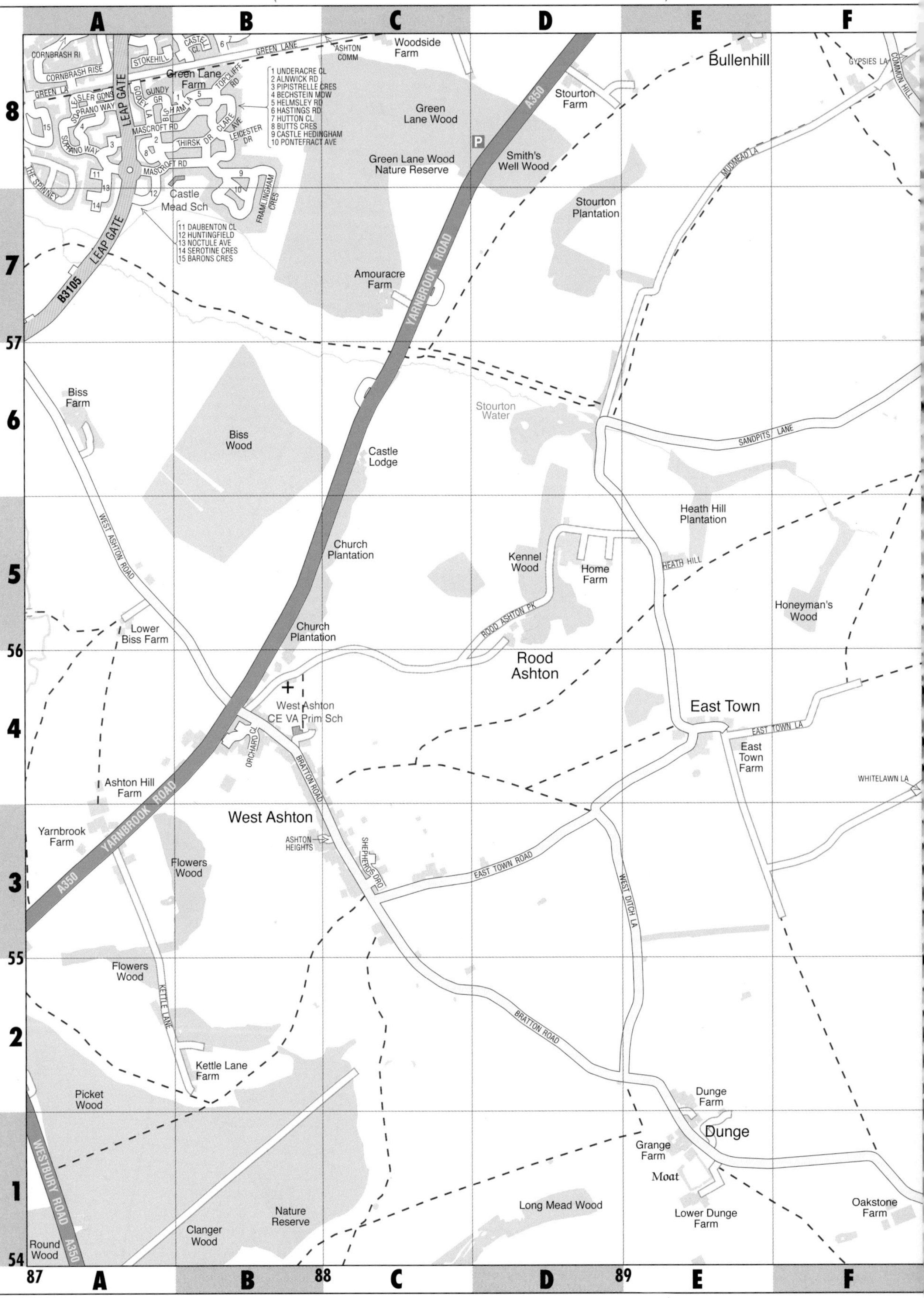
A
B
C
D
E
F
8
7
57
6
5
56
4
3
55
2
1
54
87
88
89
CORNBRASH RI
CORNBRASH RISE
GREEN LA
STOKEHILL
CASTELL CL
GREEN LANE
ASHTON COMM
Woodside Farm
Bullenhill
GYPSIES LA
COMMON HILL
Green Lane Farm
LEAP GATE
GUNDY GR
TOPCLIFFE RD
SOPRANO WAY
MASCROFT RD
THIRSK DR
CLARE AVE
LEICESTER DR
1 UNDERACRE CL
2 ALNWICK RD
3 PIPISTRELLE CRES
4 BECHSTEIN MDW
5 HELMSLEY RD
6 HASTINGS RD
7 HUTTON CL
8 BUTTS CRES
9 CASTLE HEDINGHAM
10 PONTEFRACT AVE
Green Lane Wood
A350
Stourton Farm
P
Smith's Well Wood
Green Lane Wood Nature Reserve
MUDMEAD LA
THE SPINNEY
Castle Mead Sch
FRAMLINGHAM CRES
11 DAUBENTON CL
12 HUNTINGFIELD
13 NOCTULE AVE
14 SEROTINE CRES
15 BARONS CRES
Stourton Plantation
B3105
Amouracre Farm
YARNBROOK ROAD
Biss Farm
Stourton Water
Biss Wood
Castle Lodge
SANDPITS LANE
WEST ASHTON ROAD
Church Plantation
Heath Hill Plantation
Kennel Wood
Home Farm
HEATH HILL
ROOD ASHTON PK
Honeyman's Wood
Lower Biss Farm
Church Plantation
Rood Ashton
West Ashton CE VA Prim Sch
East Town
EAST TOWN LA
ORCHARD CL
BRATTON ROAD
East Town Farm
WHITELAWN LA
Ashton Hill Farm
West Ashton
Yarnbrook Farm
ASHTON HEIGHTS
SHEPHERDS DRO
EAST TOWN ROAD
WEST DITCH LA
Flowers Wood
Flowers Wood
KETTLE LANE
BRATTON ROAD
Kettle Lane Farm
Picket Wood
Dunge Farm
Dunge
Grange Farm
Moat
WESTBURY ROAD
Nature Reserve
Long Mead Wood
Lower Dunge Farm
Oakstone Farm
Clanger Wood
Round Wood

105 109 178

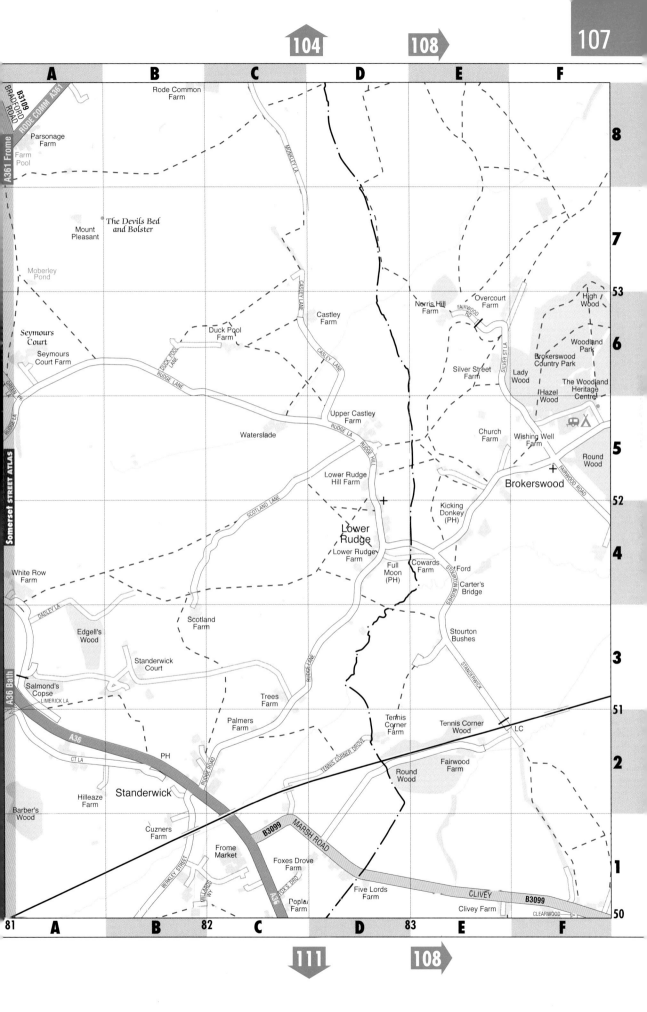

E1
1 SANDALWOOD RD
2 DARTMOOR RD
3 OLDENBURGH RD
4 BRABANT WAY
5 SUFFOLK RD
6 EXMOOR RD
7 PALOMINO PL
8 SALISBURY CL

E2
1 MUSTANG CL
2 CONNEMARA CL

F1
1 PARK VW DR
2 LEIGHTON PK W
3 LAVERTON GN
4 LEIGHTON PK N
5 LEIGHTON PK RD
6 SAND HOLE LA

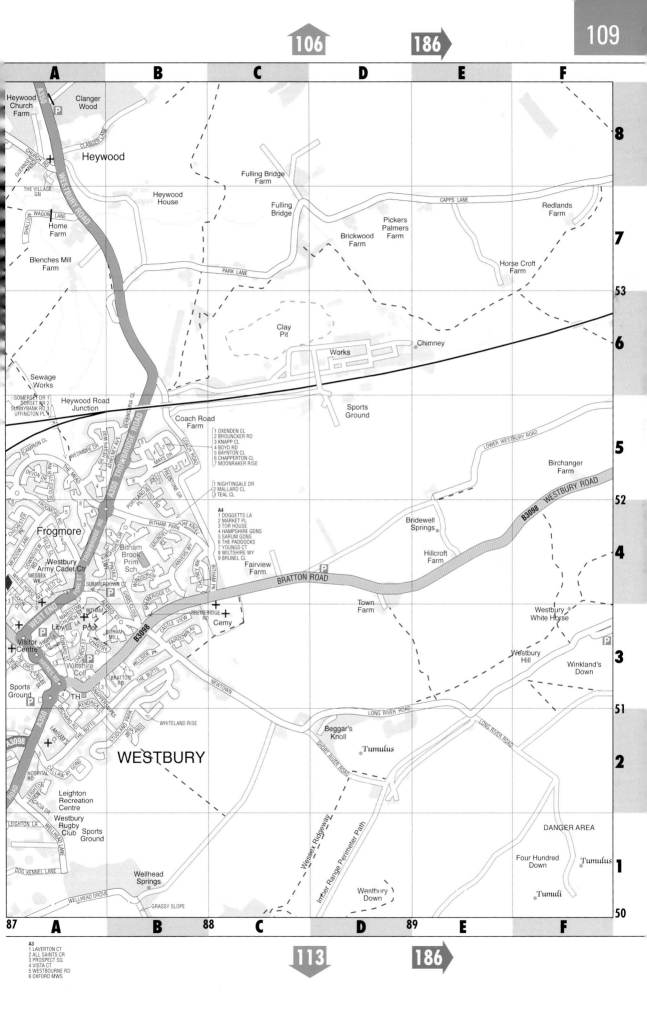

Heywood Church Farm
Clanger Wood
Heywood
Heywood House
THE VILLAGE GN
WAGON LANE
SHALLOW
CHURCH RD
GUERNSEY WAY
WESTBURY ROAD
CLANGER LANE
Home Farm
Blenches Mill Farm
Fulling Bridge Farm
Fulling Bridge
PARK LANE
CAPPS LANE
Brickwood Farm
Pickers Palmers Farm
Redlands Farm
Horse Croft Farm

Clay Pit
Works
Chimney

Sewage Works
SOMERSET DR 1
DORSET DR 2
SUNNYBANK RD 3
UFFINGTON PL 4
Heywood Road Junction
Coach Road Farm
Sports Ground

CAMPION CL
WEDMORE DR
THE MEAD
BERENGRIA CL
TROWBRIDGE ROAD
COACH ROAD
MAYS DR
WILLESPY WAY
ATHELNEY AVE
A350

1 OXENDEN CL
2 BROUNCKER RD
3 KNAPP CL
4 BOYD RD
5 BAYNTON CL
6 CHAPPERTON CL
7 MOONRAKER RISE

1 NIGHTINGALE DR
2 MALLARD CL
3 TEAL CL

A4
1 DOGGETTS LA
2 MARKET PL
3 TOR HOUSE
4 HAMPSHIRE GDNS
5 SARUM GDNS
6 THE PADDOCKS
7 YOUNGS CT
8 WILTSHIRE WY
9 BRUNEL CL

LOWER WESTBURY ROAD
Birchanger Farm
B3098 WESTBURY ROAD

Frogmore
DEVON CL
CHICHESTER
GLOUCESTER WK
MEADOW LANE
DOWNSVIEW
FROGMORE RD
FIELD CL
KINGS MANOR DR
PORTLAND PL
CHEVIOT RD
FREESTONE GR
CIDD
BITHAM PARK
THE KNOLL
ARUNDEL
WINDSOR
CANVERS WY

Bridewell Springs
Hillcroft Farm
Fairview Farm
Westbury Army Cadet Ctr
Westbury Brook Prim Sch
Bitham Brook

West End
WHITE HORSE WK
WESSEX WK
SUMMERDOWN DR
ALFRED ST
BREMERIDGE CL
CHASE
BITHAM PK
BRATTON ROAD
Town Farm
Westbury White Horse

Liby
Pool
MARISTOW
CHURCH LA
BITHAM LA
CASTLE VIEW
FAIRDOWN AV
BITHAM MILL
Cemy
BREMERIDGE RD
SUMMERLEAZE

Visitor Centre
Wiltshire Coll
EDWARD ST
CHURCH ST
CHANTRY
MILLSIDE PK
Westbury Hill
Winkland's Down

Sports Ground
TH
BRATTON RD
THE BUTTS
KENDRICK CL
NEWTOWN
A3098
ORCHARD RD
LANHAM ST
CALLAWAY GDNS
STUDLAND PARK
WHITELAND RISE
LONG RIVER ROAD
LONG RIVER ROAD

WESTBURY
Beggar's Knoll
Tumulus
SHORT RIVER ROAD

Leighton Recreation Centre
Westbury Rugby Club
Sports Ground
LEIGHTON LA
ACACIA DR
HOSPITAL RD
LEIGHTON RD
WELLHEAD LANE
A350
A3098 ROAD
DOG KENNEL LANE

DANGER AREA
Four Hundred Down
Tumulus

Wellhead Springs
WELLHEAD DROVE
GRASSY SLOPE
Wessex Ridgeway
Imber Range Perimeter Path
Westbury Down
Tumuli

A3
1 LAVERTON CT
2 ALL SAINTS CR
3 PROSPECT SQ
4 VISTA CT
5 WESTBOURNE RD
6 OXFORD MWS

218

Somerset STREET ATLAS  A361 Trowbridge

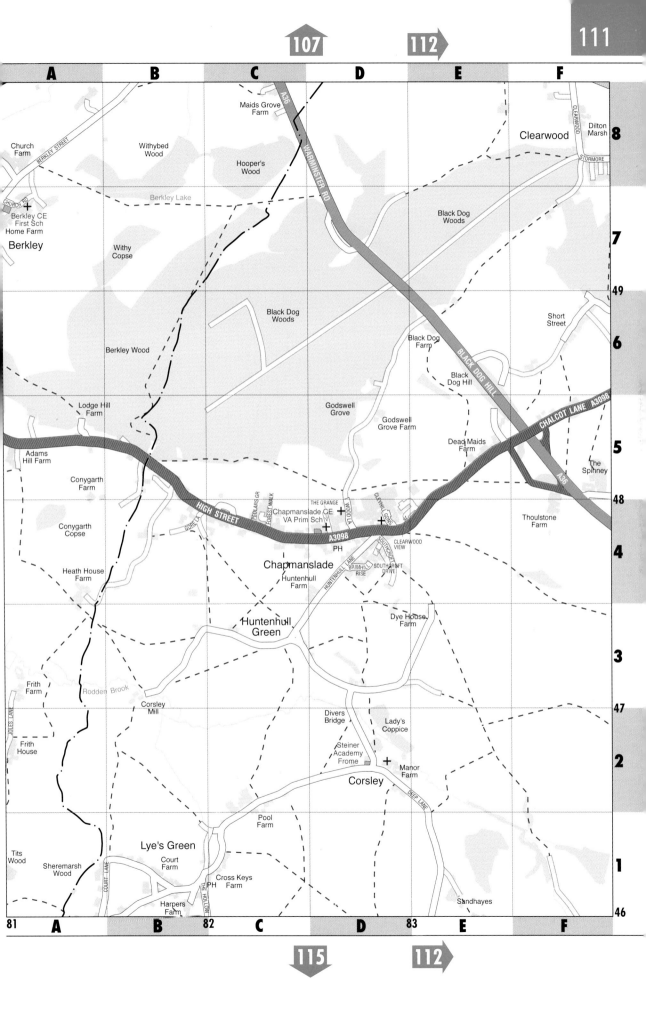

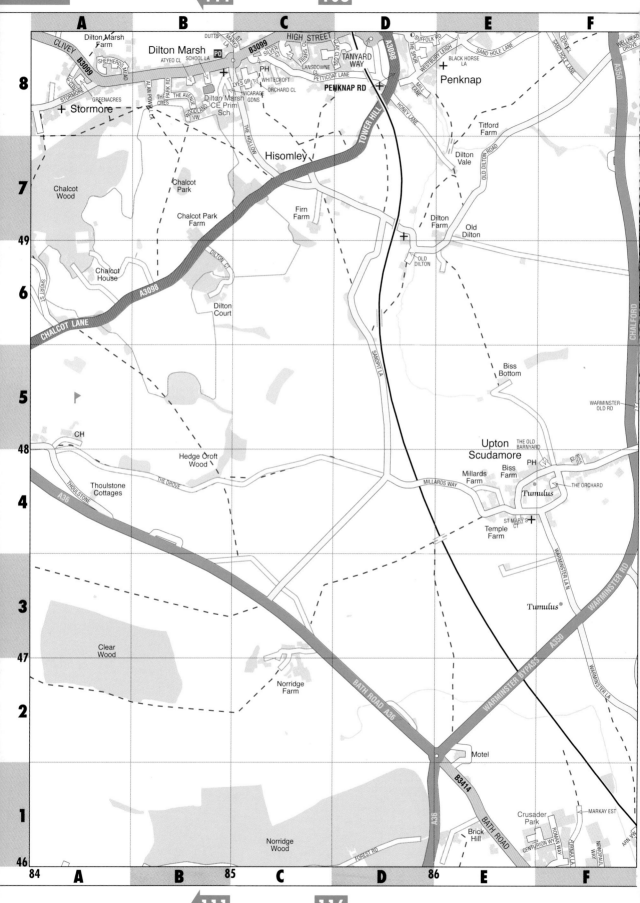

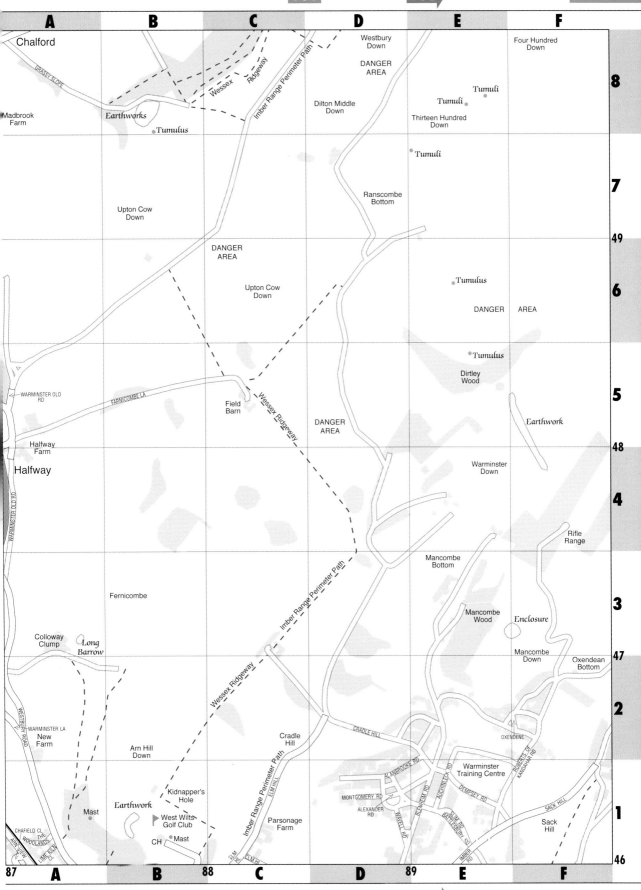

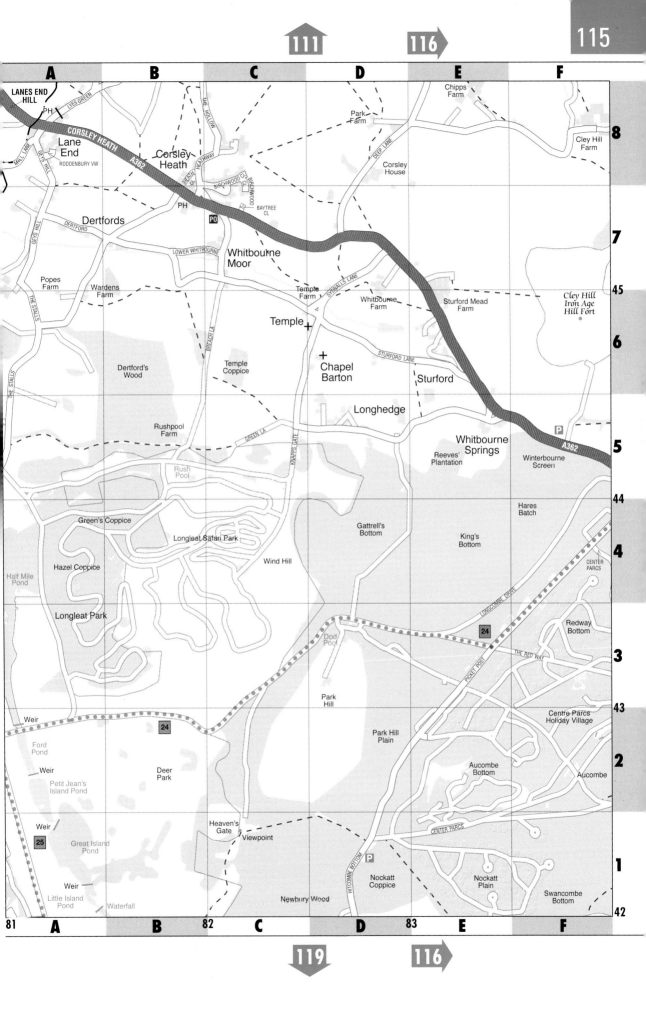

A    B    C    D    E    F

LANES END HILL

PH

LYES GREEN

THE HOLLOW

Park Farm

Chipps Farm

Cley Hill Farm

8

CORSLEY HEATH

Lane End

RODDENBURY VW

MALL LANE

GRYS HILL

A362

Corsley Heath

HEATH CL

HEATH HEATHWAY

BIRCHWOOD CL

BIRCHWOOD

DEEP LANE

Corsley House

PH

PO

BAYTREE CL

7

Dertfords

DERTFORD

GRYS HILL

LOWER WHITBOURNE

Whitbourne Moor

STYNALLS LANE

Whitbourne Farm

Sturford Mead Farm

45

Cley Hill Iron Age Hill Fort

THE STALLS

Popes Farm

Wardens Farm

Temple Farm

Temple ✛

Chapel Barton ✛

STURFORD LANE

Sturford

6

BREACH LA

Dertford's Wood

Temple Coppice

Longhedge

Whitbourne Springs

P

A362

5

Rushpool Farm

GREEN LA

KNAPPS GATE

Reeves' Plantation

Winterbourne Screen

THE STALLS

Rush Pool

44

Green's Coppice

Gattrell's Bottom

King's Bottom

Hares Batch

CENTER PARCS

4

Hazel Coppice

Longleat Safari Park

Wind Hill

LONGCOMBE DRIVE

Redway Bottom

Half Mile Pond

Longleat Park

Dod Pool

24

PICKET POST

THE RED WAY

3

Park Hill

Centre Parcs Holiday Village

43

Weir

24

Ford Pond

Deer Park

Park Hill Plain

Park Hill Plain

Aucombe Bottom

Aucombe

2

Weir

Petit Jean's Island Pond

Heaven's Gate

Viewpoint

CENTER PARCS

25

Weir

Great Island Pond

HITCHCOMBE BOTTOM

P

Nockatt Coppice

Nockatt Plain

Swancombe Bottom

1

Weir

Little Island Pond

Waterfall

Newbury Wood

42

E5
1 THE HOMELANDS
2 SWALLOW CL
3 WREN CL
4 MADDOCK'S HL
5 KINGS CT
6 SOUTH ALLEY

E6
1 PAMPAS CT
2 WOODLAND RD
3 PRINCECROFT LA
4 MELROSE CL
5 MIDDLETON CL
6 CLEY VIEW

E7
1 PRIMROSE WK
2 FREESIA CL
3 WERE CL
4 NORRIDGE VW
5 UPTON CL

F6
1 Warminster
Sambourne CE
Prim Sch

F7
1 CONFERENCE CL
2 GRENADIER CL
3 THE PIPPINS
4 BRAMLEY CL
5 WOODMAN MEAD
6 OBELISK TERR

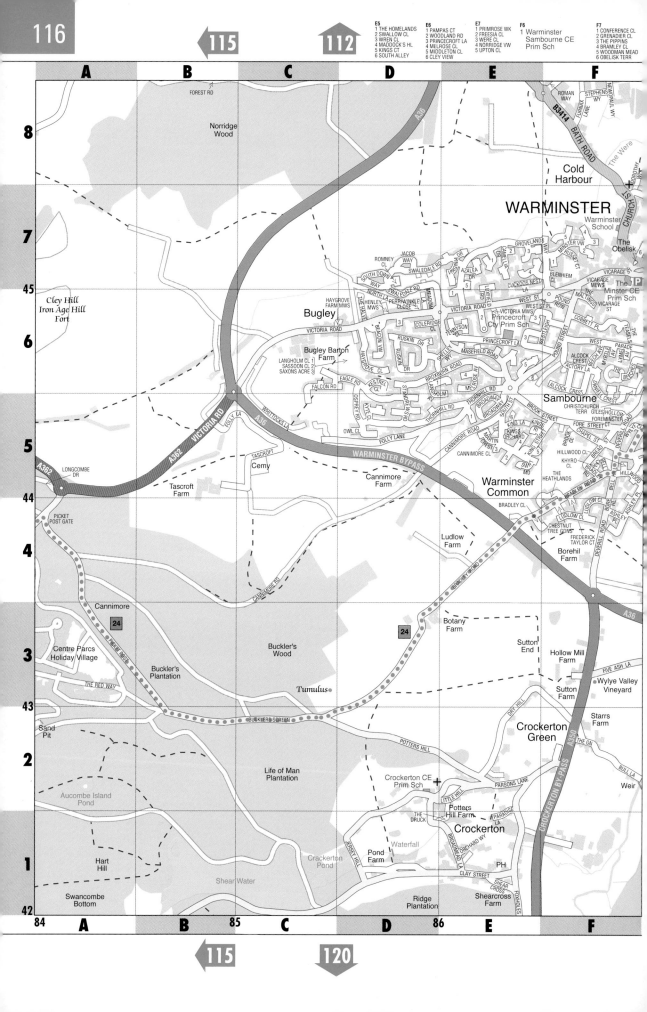

Norridge Wood

FOREST RD

Cold Harbour

ROMAN WAY

B3414 BATH ROAD

WARMINSTER

Warminster School

The Obelisk

Cley Hill Iron Age Hill Fort

Bugley

Bugley Barton Farm

LANGHOLM CL 1
SASSOON CL 2
SAXONS ACRE 3

Sambourne

Warminster Common

LONGCOMBE DR

A362

PICKET POST GATE

Tascroft

Cemy

Tascroft Farm

Cannimore Farm

Warminster Bypass

Ludlow Farm

Borehil Farm

Cannimore

Buckler's Wood

Buckler's Plantation

Botany Farm

Sutton End

Hollow Mill Farm

Wylye Valley Vineyard

THE RED WAY

Tumulus

BUCKLERS SCREEN

POTTERS HILL

Crockerton Green

Starrs Farm

Sand Pit

Life of Man Plantation

Crockerton CE Prim Sch

Potters Hill Farm

Crockerton

Weir

Aucombe Island Pond

Hart Hill

Crockerton Pond

Pond Farm

Waterfall

PH

Shearcross Farm

Swancombe Bottom

Shear Water

Ridge Plantation

Centre Parcs Holiday Village

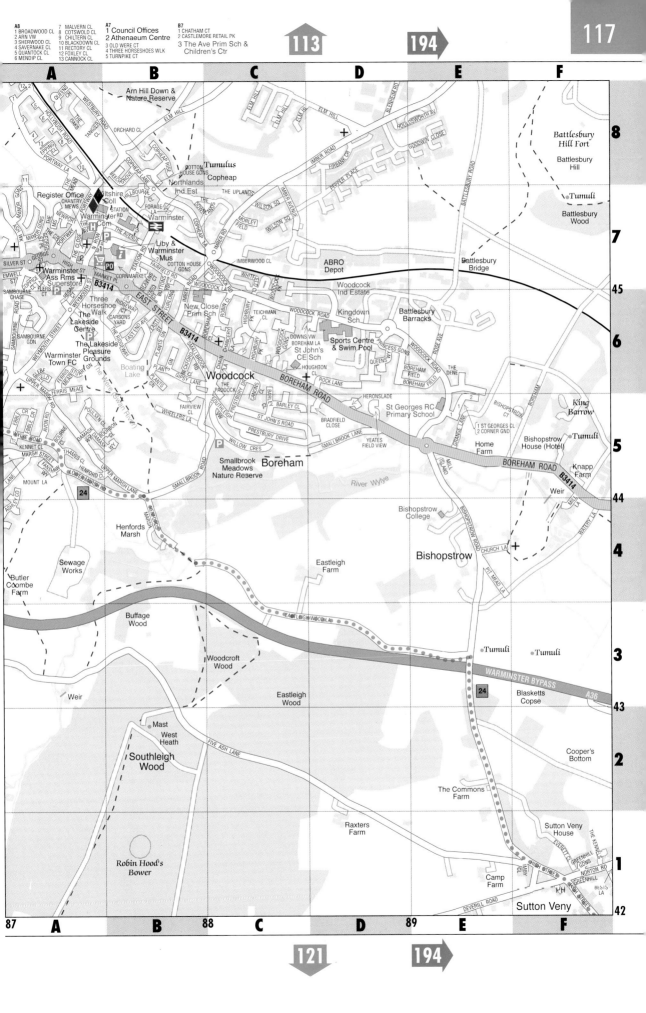

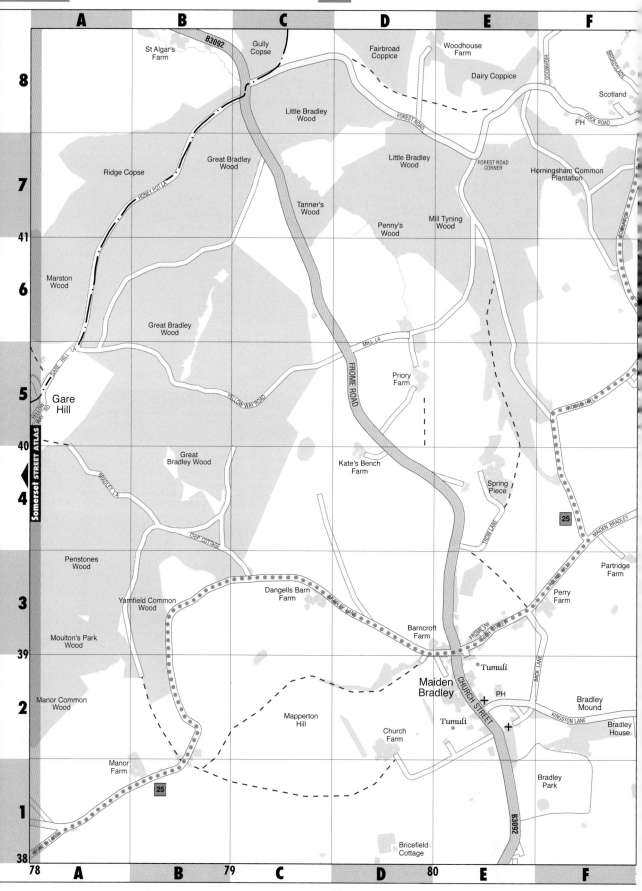

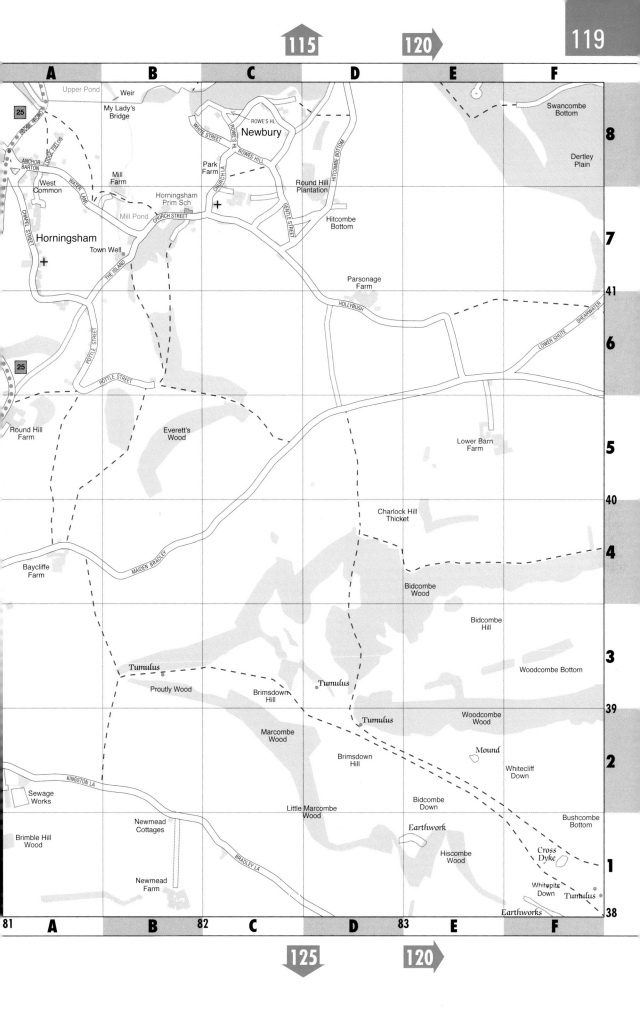

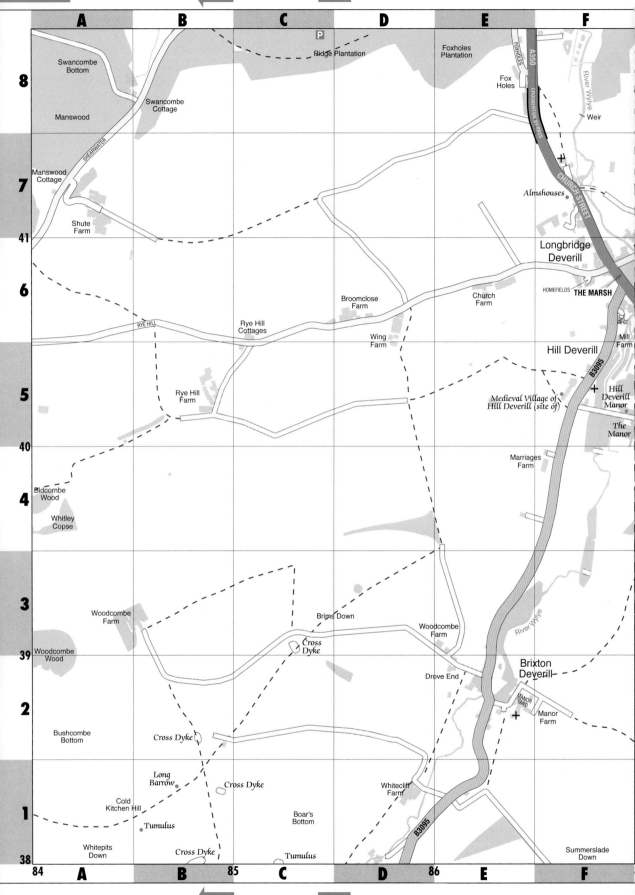

8

Swancombe
Bottom

Ridge Plantation

Foxholes
Plantation

Fox
Holes

Weir

Manswood

Swancombe
Cottage

A350

CROOKWOOD BYPASS

CHURCH STREET

River Wylye

Manswood
Cottage

7

SHEARWATER

Almshouses

Shute
Farm

41

Longbridge
Deverill

6

RYE HILL

Broomclose
Farm

Church
Farm

HOMEFIELDS

THE MARSH

Rye Hill
Cottages

Wing
Farm

Hill Deverill

Mill
Farm

B3095

5

Rye Hill
Farm

Medieval Village of
Hill Deverill (site of)

Hill
Deverill
Manor

40

The
Manor

4

Bidcombe
Wood

Marriages
Farm

Whitley
Copse

3

Woodcombe
Farm

Brins Down

Woodcombe
Farm

River Wylye

39

Woodcombe
Wood

Cross
Dyke

Drove End

Brixton
Deverill

2

Bushcombe
Bottom

Cross Dyke

MANOR WARD

Manor
Farm

Long
Barrow

Cross Dyke

Whitecliff
Farm

Cold
Kitchen Hill

1

Boar's
Bottom

B3095

Summerslade
Down

Whitepits
Down

Tumulus

Cross Dyke

Tumulus

38

Somerset STREET ATLAS

A B C D E F

8

Hick's Park
Wood

Hents Hill
Farm

CANNWOOD LANE

Canwood
Farm

Walters
Farm

Forest Gate
Farm

Lark
Farm

HAMMER STREET

DRULEY HILL

7

Lipgate
Farm

HASSOCKS LA

Horseshoe
Farm

Brewham
House

Border
Farm

Longfield
Farm

Green
Acres

JAMES'S HILL

Jerrards
Farm

37

BORDER LA

STRAP LA

Treetops
Farm

PH

North
Brewham

BRUTON
RD

Cooks
Farm

6

TILE HILL

Brewham Lodge
Farm

Earthwork

Bridge
Farm

Mill
Farm

5

PH

CHARCROFT HILL

Street
Farm

King's
Wood

STREET LANE

36

South
Brewham

Brook
Farm

Haven
Farm

Jack's Castle
Plantation

Tumulus

STREET LANE

Charcroft
Farm

Holland
Farm

Macmillan Way

TOWER ROAD

P

4

CHARCROFT
HILL

Shave
Farm

SHAVE LANE

Alfred's
Tower

Convent
Bottom

3

Hookgate
Farm

Hilcombe
Farm

35

Crawley House
Farm

KINGSETTLE HILL

Hilcombe
Hanging

Cards
Farm

Brewham
Brake Farm

Leland Trail

Berridge

BACK TERR

2

Tower Road
Farm

Hardway
House

Pillinge
Farm

Park
Farm

Brewham
Wood

Beaumont's
Wood

1

Hardway

PH

BARROW WATER LA

Picketts
Farm

Picket's
Copse

Aaron's
Hill

Moss
Cottage

PEN HILL

34

72 A B 73 C D 74 E F

River Brue

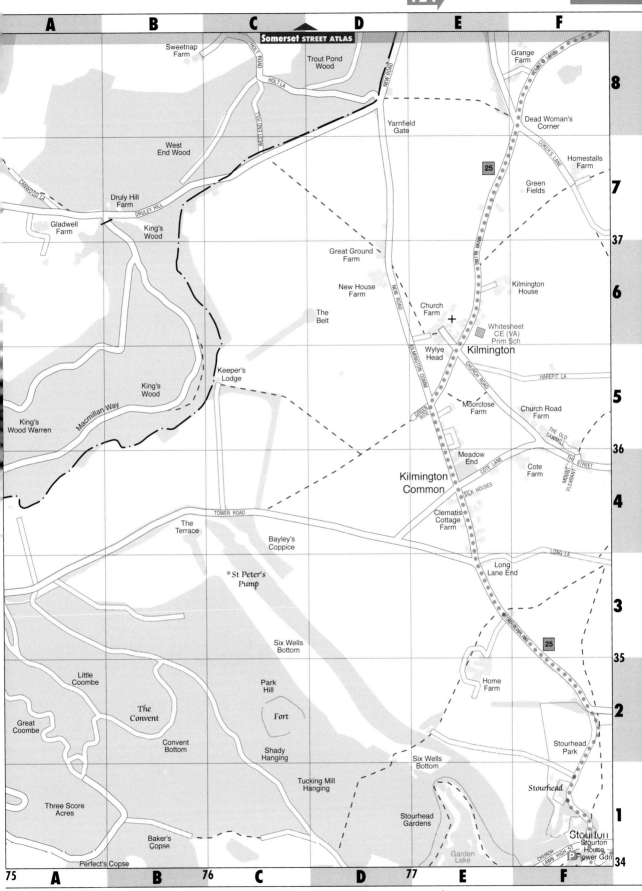

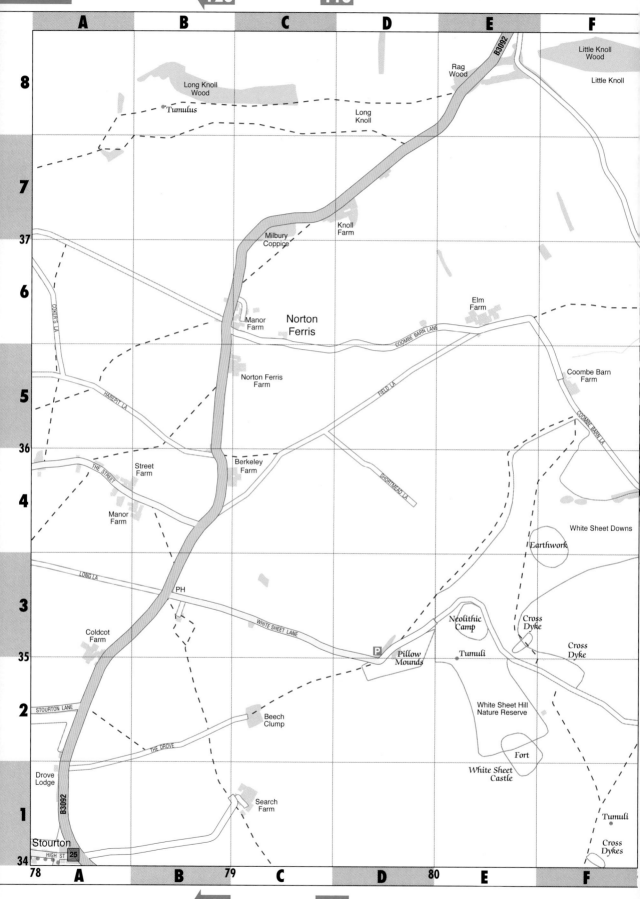

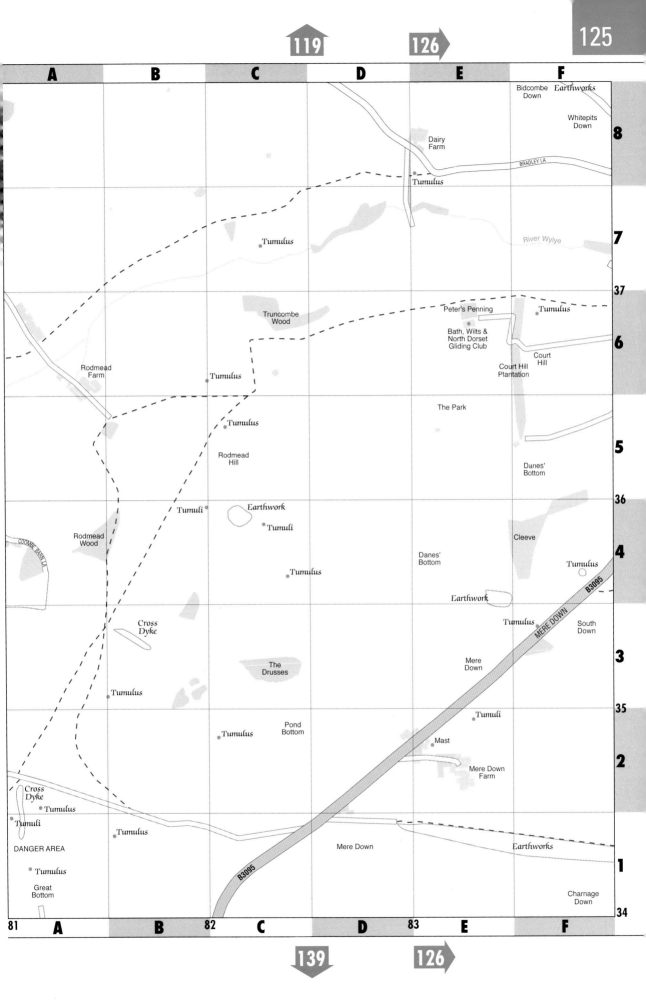

119
126

A  B  C  D  E  F

Bidcombe Down    Earthworks

Whitepits Down

**8**

Dairy Farm

BRADLEY LA

*Tumulus*

River Wylye

**7**

**37**

*Tumulus*

Truncombe Wood

Peter's Penning

*Tumulus*

Bath, Wilts & North Dorset Gliding Club

**6**

Court Hill Plantation

Court Hill

Rodmead Farm

*Tumulus*

The Park

*Tumulus*

Danes' Bottom

**5**

Rodmead Hill

**36**

*Tumuli*    *Earthwork*

Cleeve

*Tumuli*

Danes' Bottom

Rodmead Wood

*Tumulus*

**4**

*Tumulus*

B3095

*Earthwork*

COOMBE BARN LA

*Tumulus*

MERE DOWN

South Down

Cross Dyke

Mere Down

**3**

The Drusses

*Tumulus*

*Tumuli*

**35**

*Tumulus*

Pond Bottom

Mast

**2**

*Tumulus*

Mere Down Farm

Cross Dyke

*Tumulus*

*Tumuli*

*Tumulus*

DANGER AREA

Mere Down

Earthworks

**1**

*Tumulus*

B3095

Great Bottom

Charnage Down

**34**

81  A  B  82  C  D  83  E  F

139
126

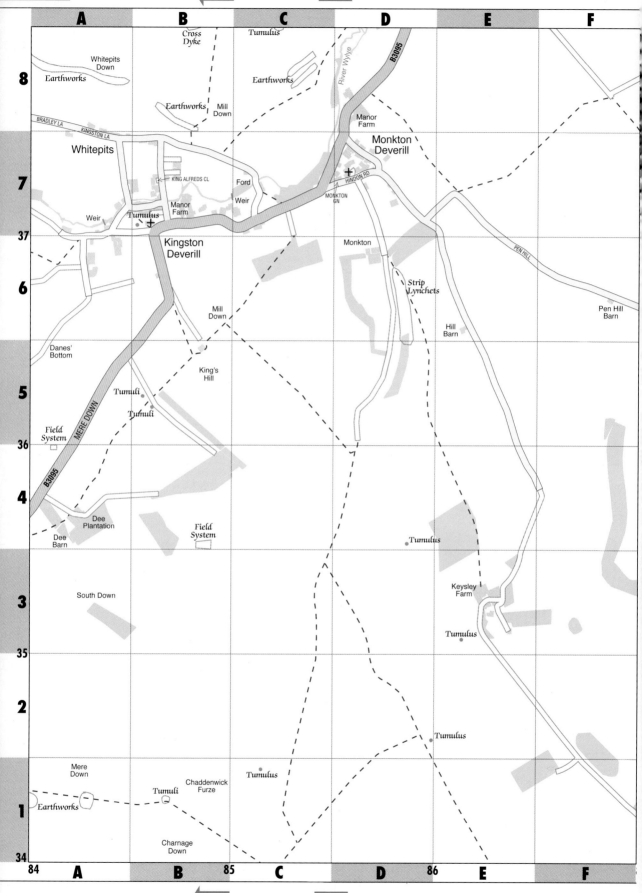

125 140

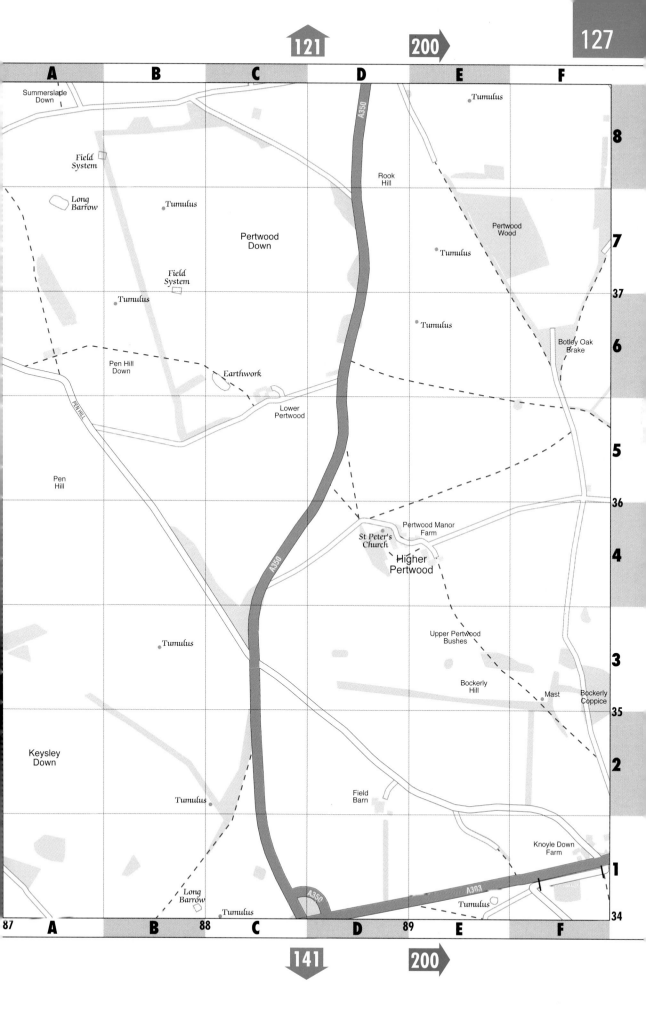

8

Summerslade
Down

Field
System

Long
Barrow

*Tumulus*

Pertwood
Down

Field
System

*Tumulus*

Rook
Hill

*Tumulus*

Pertwood
Wood

7

37

Pen Hill
Down

*Tumulus*

Earthwork

Lower
Pertwood

Botley Oak
Brake

6

Pen
Hill

*Tumulus*

5

St Peter's
Church

Pertwood Manor
Farm

Higher
Pertwood

36

4

*Tumulus*

Upper Pertwood
Bushes

Bockerly
Hill

Mast

Bockerly
Coppice

3

35

Keysley
Down

*Tumulus*

Field
Barn

2

*Tumulus*

Knoyle Down
Farm

A350

1

A350

Long
Barrow

*Tumulus*

A303

*Tumulus*

34

201
196

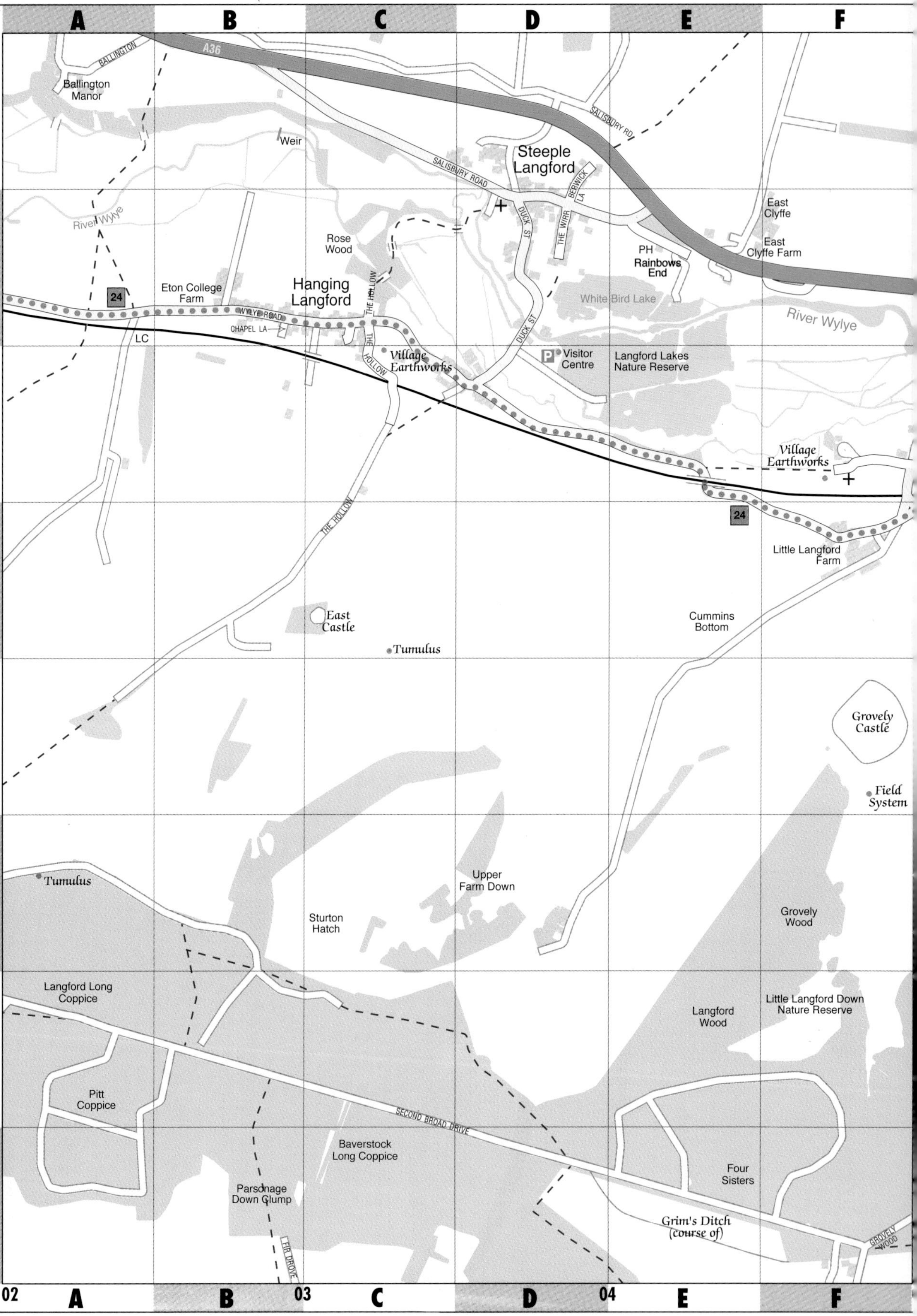

A B C D E F

8

Ballington Manor

Weir

River Wylye

Rose Wood

7

Eton College Farm

Hanging Langford

WYLYE ROAD

CHAPEL LA

LC

THE HOLLOW

A36

SALISBURY ROAD

Steeple Langford

DUCK ST

BERWICK LA

THE WIRR

East Clyffe

East Clyffe Farm

SALISBURY RD

PH Rainbows End

White Bird Lake

River Wylye

37

Village Earthworks

THE HOLLOW

Visitor Centre

P

Langford Lakes Nature Reserve

6

Village Earthworks

24

Little Langford Farm

5

East Castle

Tumulus

Cummins Bottom

Grovely Castle

36

Field System

4

3

Tumulus

Sturton Hatch

Upper Farm Down

Grovely Wood

35

Langford Long Coppice

Langford Wood

Little Langford Down Nature Reserve

2

Pitt Coppice

Baverstock Long Coppice

SECOND BROAD DRIVE

Four Sisters

1

Parsonage Down Clump

THE DRIVE

Grim's Ditch (course of)

GROVELY WOOD

34

02 A 03 B C 04 D E F

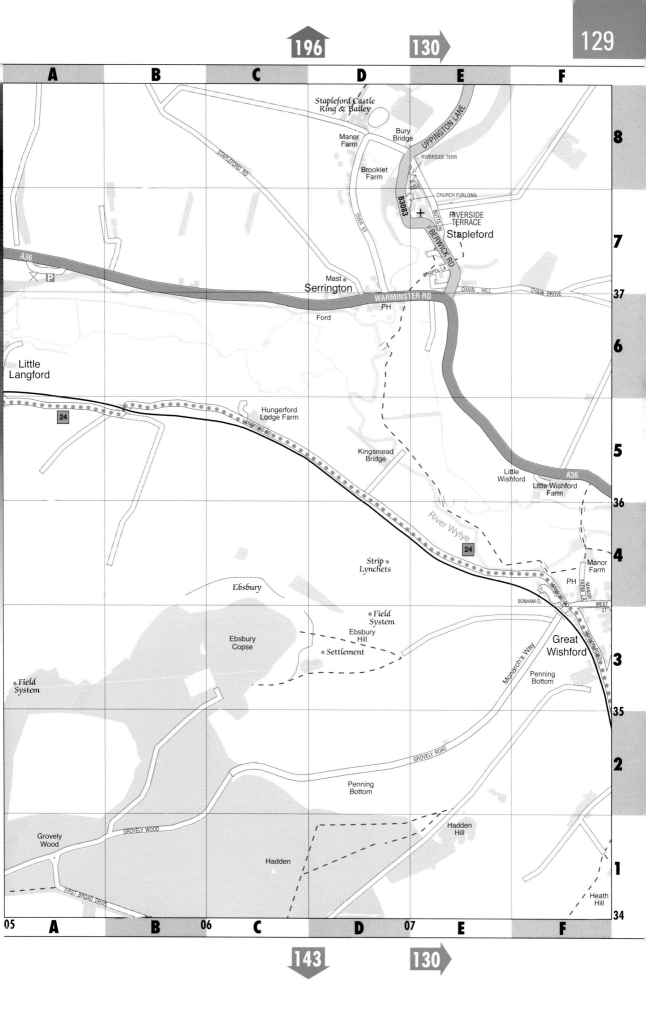

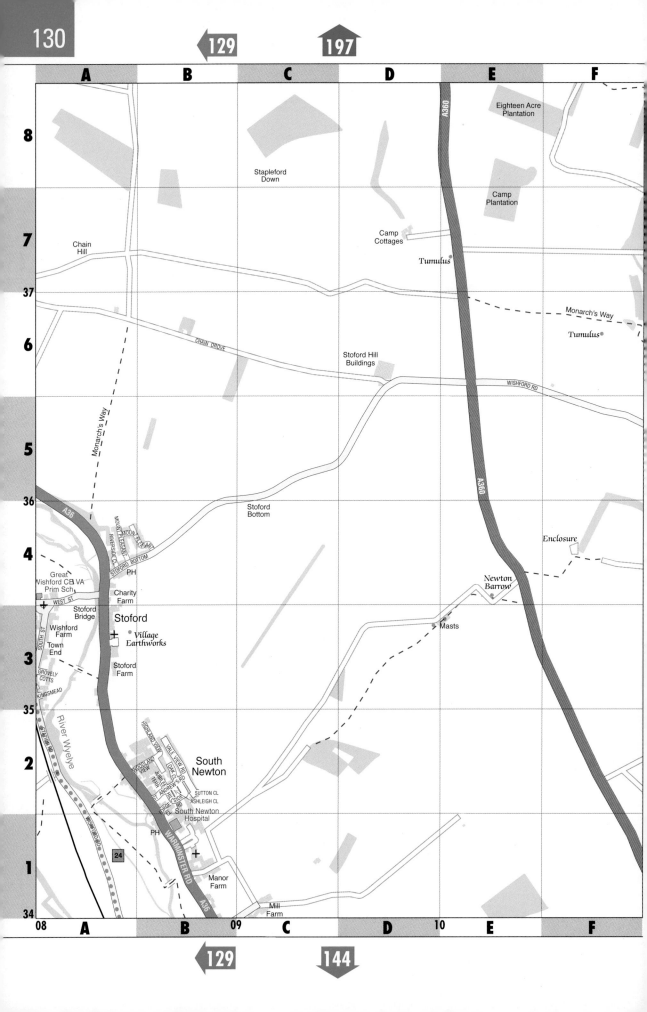

A   B   C   D   E   F

8

Stapleford
Down

Eighteen Acre
Plantation

Camp
Plantation

7

Chain
Hill

Camp
Cottages

*Tumulus*

37

Monarch's Way

*Tumulus*

6

CHAIN DROVE

Stoford Hill
Buildings

WISHFORD RD

Monarch's Way

5

Monarch's Way

A36

36

Stoford
Bottom

Enclosure

4

MOUNT PLEASANT
RIVERSIDE CL
STOFORD BOTTOM
PH

Great
Wishford CB VA
Prim Sch

Charity
Farm

Newton
Barrow

A360

WEST ST

Stoford
Bridge

Stoford

Masts

SOUTH ST

Wishford
Farm

✚ *Village
Earthworks*

3

Town
End

GROVELY
COTTS

Stoford
Farm

KINGSMEAD

35

River Wylye

A36

2

HIGHLAND VIEW
VALE VIEW RD
WOODLAND
VIEW
OAK CL
JUBILEE TERR
ST ANDREW'S RD
BRIDGE CL (SCH)

South
Newton

SUTTON CL
ASHLEIGH CL

South Newton
Hospital

PH

WARMINSTER RD

A36

24

1

Manor
Farm

34

WINSFORD RD

Mill
Farm

08   A   B   09   C   D   10   E   F

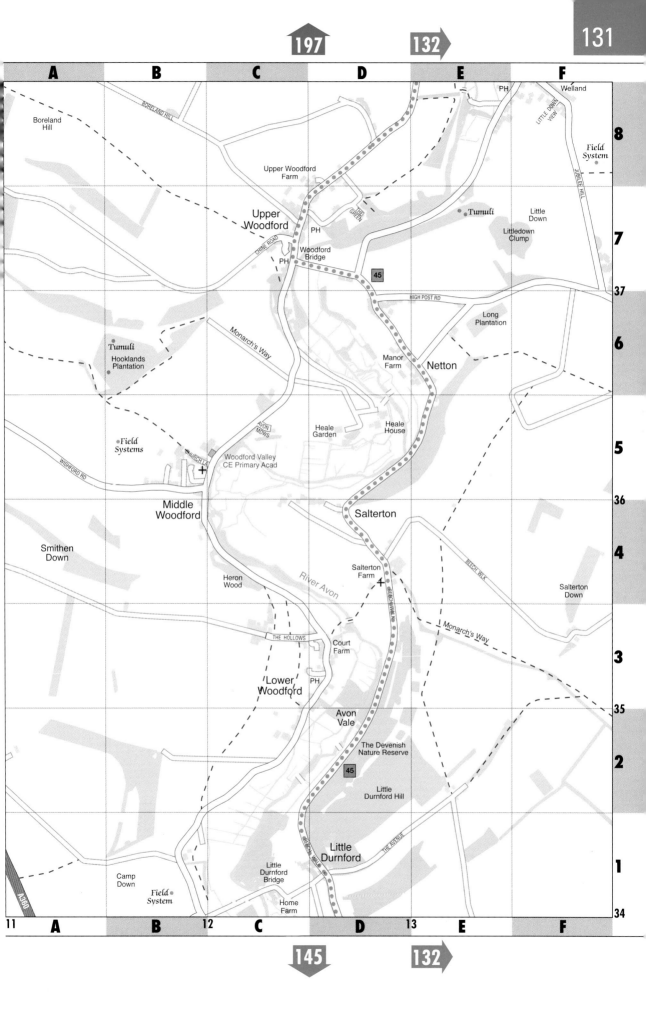

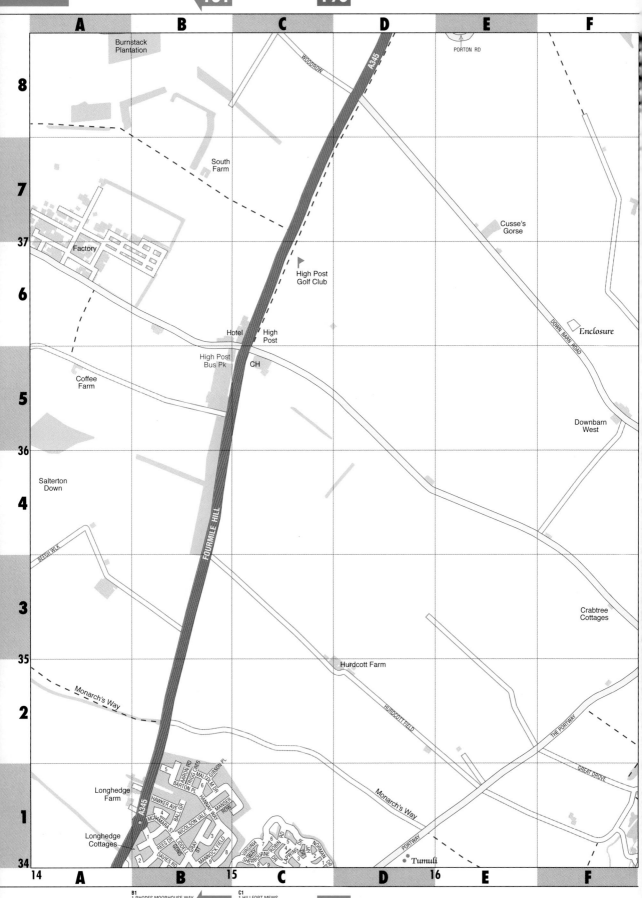

**B1**
1 RHODES MOORHOUSE WAY
2 ROBINSON GR
3 GARLAND MWS
4 WARNEFORD CRES
5 HORNELL CL
6 MIDDLETON TERR
7 CAMPBELL VALE
8 BEAUCHAMP-PROCTOR RISE
9 BARKER CL

**C1**
1 HILLFORT MEWS
2 WALTER WY
3 CURLEW RD
4 KESTREL DR
5 LARK LA
6 BUZZARD RD
7 NORMAN DR
8 ROGER WY
9 BISSINGTON CL

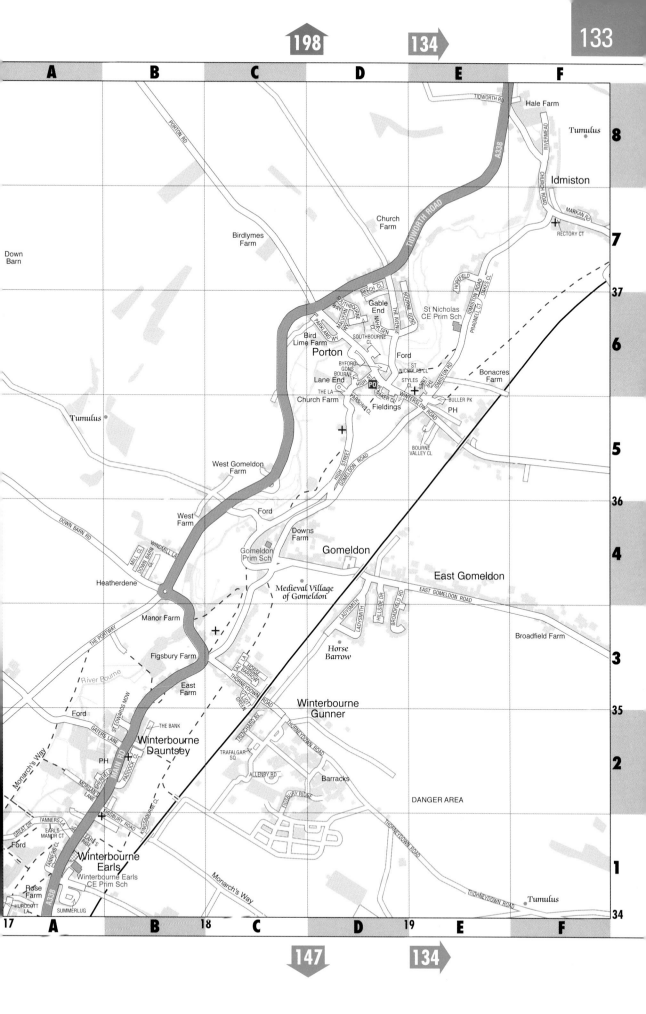

A B C D E F

8
7
37
6
5
36
4
3
35
2
1
34

TIDWORTH RD
Hale Farm
Tumulus
RIVERMEAD
Idmiston
CHURCH ROAD
A338
MARKAN RD
RECTORY CT
Down Barn
Church Farm
Birdlymes Farm
TIDWORTH ROAD
BEECH CL
HOPSFIELD
IDMISTON ROAD
OAKES CL
PRAGNELL CT
St Nicholas CE Prim Sch
SOUTHBOURNE WAY
MALVERN WAY
Gable End
THE AVENUE
BOURNE GDNS
NATHEN CL
SOUTHBOURNE CL
PARKLAND WY
Bird Lime Farm
Porton
Ford
ST NICHOLAS CL
Bonacres Farm
BYFORD GDNS
BOURNE CL
HIGH ST
IDMISTON RD
PO
STYLES CL
SSMS CL
Lane End
THE LA
Church Farm
PARSONS CL
BAKER CL
WINTERSLOW ROAD
BULLER PK
PH
Tumulus
Fieldings
HIGH STREET
GOMELDON ROAD
BOURNE VALLEY CL
West Gomeldon Farm
Ford
Downs Farm
Gomeldon
East Gomeldon
West Farm
DOWN BARN RD
MILL CL
DOWN BARN
WINDMILL LA
Gomeldon Prim Sch
Medieval Village of Gomeldon
EAST GOMELDON ROAD
LADYSMITH
HILLSIDE DR
BROADFIELD RD
Broadfield Farm
Heatherdene
THE PORTWAY
Manor Farm
Figsbury Farm
LADYSMITH
Horse Barrow
River Bourne
East Farm
HORSE BARROW
THORNEYDOWN ROAD
ELIOT GREEN
Winterbourne Gunner
THORNEYDOWN ROAD
Ford
THE BANK
GATERS LANE
ST EDWARDS MDW
MAIN RD
SHERFIELD CL
PADDOCK CL
Winterbourne Dauntsey
TRENCHARD AV
TRAFALGAR SQ
ALLENBY RD
Barracks
Monarch's Way
PH
MORGAN'S LANE
KINGSBOURNE CL
FIGSBURY ROAD
FIGSBURY RIDGE
DANGER AREA
GREAT DR
TANNERS CL
EARLS MANOR CT
EARL'S RISE
TANNERS CL
Winterbourne Earls
Monarch's Way
THORNEYDOWN ROAD
Tumulus
Ford
A338
Rose Farm
Winterbourne Earls CE Prim Sch
HURDCOTT LA
SUMMERLUG

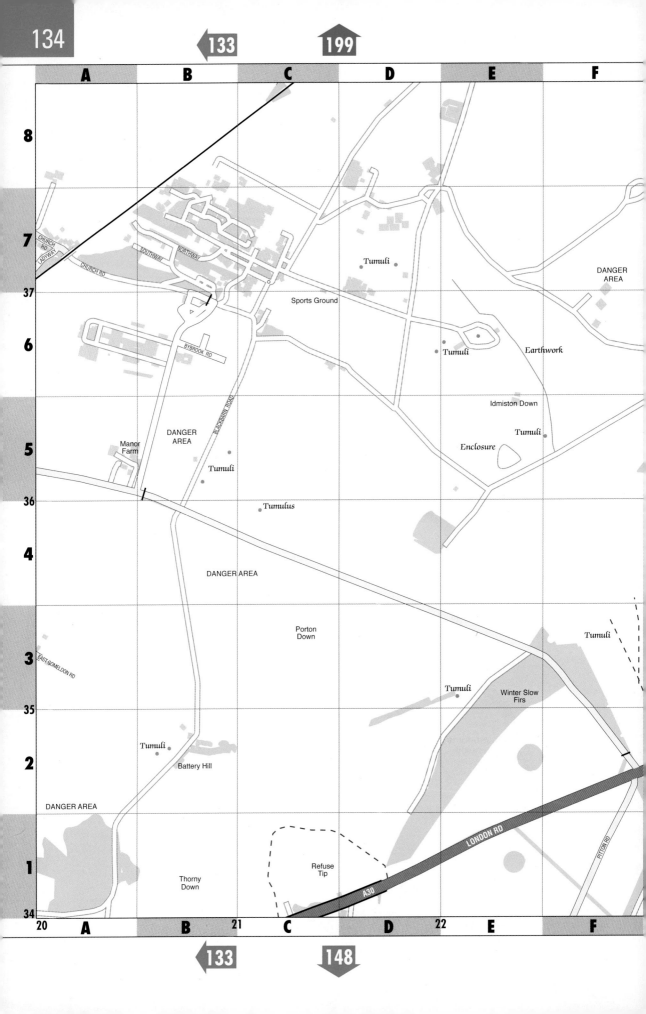
A    B    C    D    E    F

8

7

CHURCH RD
LADYWAY
CHURCH RD
SOUTHWAY
NORTHWAY

Tumuli

DANGER
AREA

37

Sports Ground

BYBROOK RD

6

Tumuli

Earthwork

Idmiston Down

Tumuli

DANGER
AREA

BLACKBARN ROAD

Manor
Farm

Enclosure

5

Tumuli

36

Tumulus

4

DANGER AREA

Porton
Down

Tumuli

EAST GOMELDON RD

3

Tumuli

Winter Slow
Firs

35

Tumuli

Battery Hill

2

DANGER AREA

LONDON RD

PITTON RD

1

Refuse
Tip

A30

Thorny
Down

34

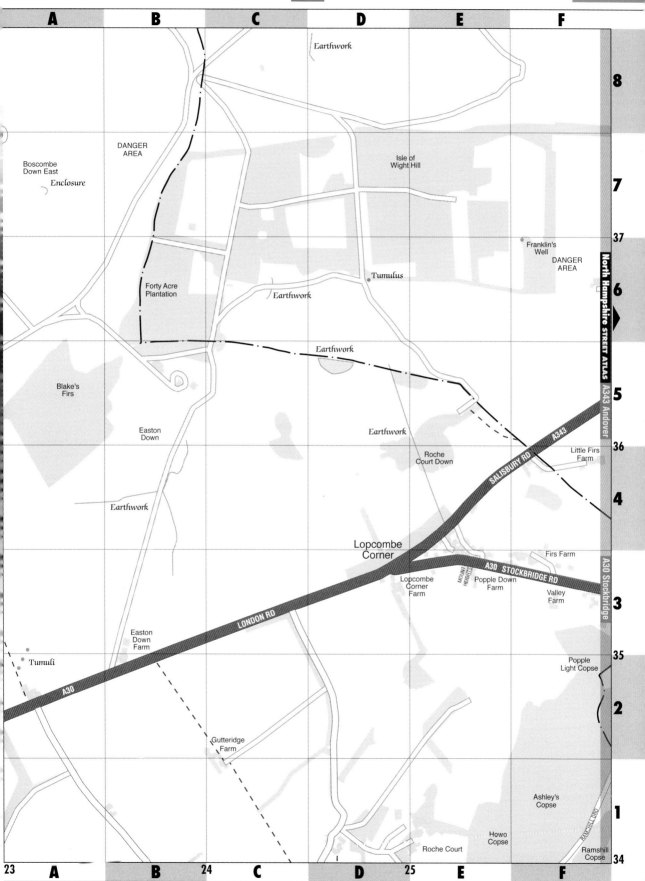

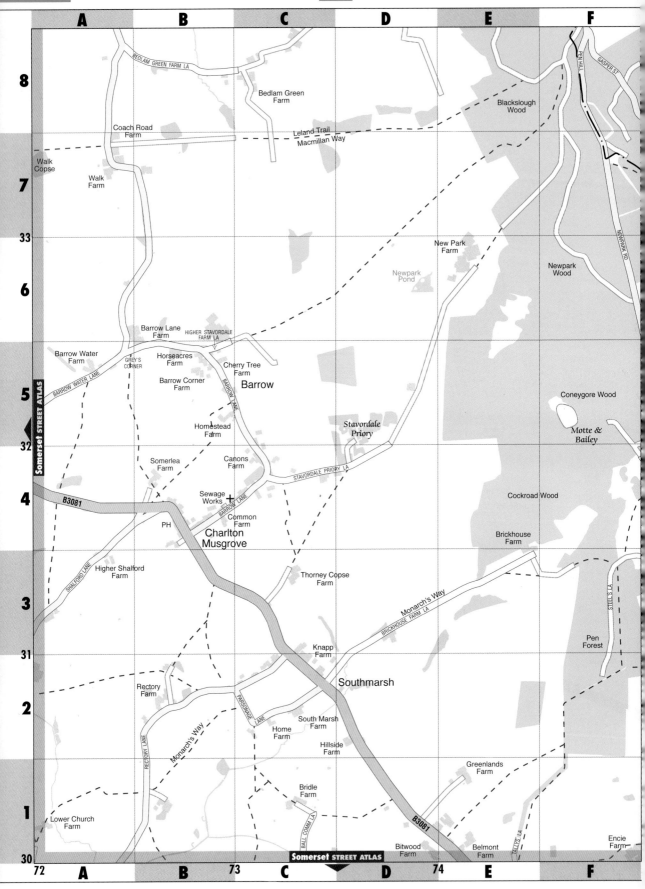

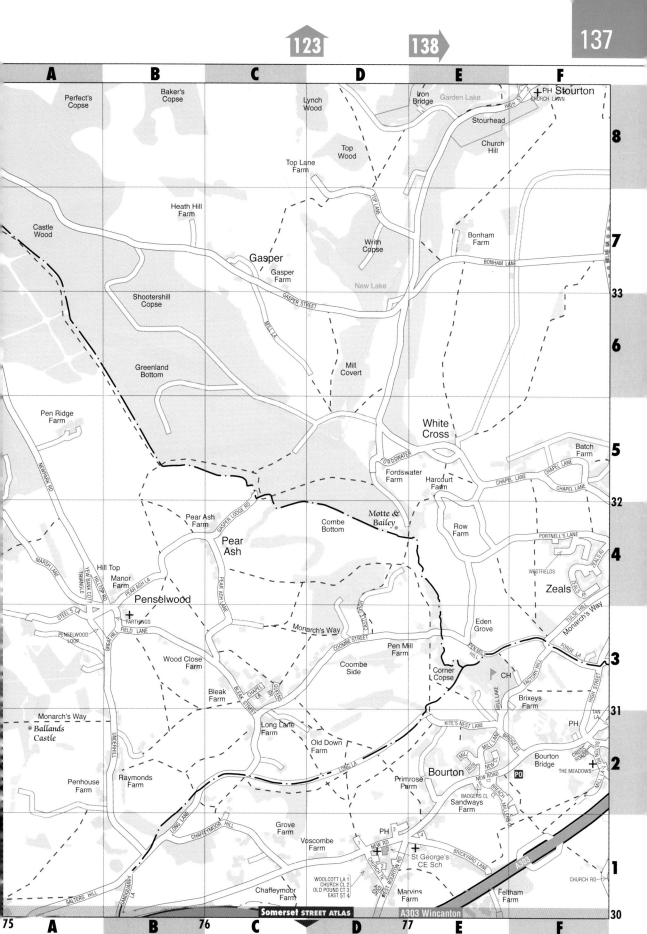

A | B | C | D | E | F

8

Perfect's Copse
Baker's Copse
Lynch Wood
Iron Bridge
Garden Lake
PH Stourton
CHURCH LAWN
HIGH ST
Stourhead
Church Hill

Top Wood
Top Lane Farm
TOP LANE

Heath Hill Farm

Castle Wood

Gasper
Writh Copse
Bonham Farm
BONHAM LANE

7

BELLS DR

33

Gasper Farm
New Lake
GASPER STREET
Shootershill Copse

6

MILL LA

Greenland Bottom
Mill Covert

White Cross

5

Pen Ridge Farm
NEWPARK RD

Fordswater
Batch Farm
CHAPEL LANE
CHAPEL LANE
CHAPEL LANE

Fordswater Farm
Harcourt Farm

32

Pear Ash Farm
GASPER LODGE RD
Combe Bottom
Motte & Bailey
Row Farm
PORTNELL'S LANE

4

Pear Ash
WESTFIELDS
Zeals
ZEALS RI

MARSH LANE
Hill Top
PEAR ASH LANE
TULSE HILL
Monarch's Way

Manor Farm
Penselwood
FARTHINGS
FIELD LANE
Monarch's Way
COOMBE STREET
Pen Mill Farm
Eden Grove
FORGE LA

3

STEEL'S LA
PENSELWOOD LOOP
GREAT HILL
Wood Close Farm
CASTLE LORCH
Coombe Side
PEN MILL HILL
Corner Copse
CHI
FACTORY HILL
Brixeys Farm
HIGH STREET

UNDERHILL
Bleak Farm
CHAPEL LA
BLEAK STREET
QUEENS GR
Long Lane Farm
Old Down Farm
LONG LA
KITE'S NEST LANE
MILL LANE
BRIDGE ST
PH
TAN LA

31

Monarch's Way
Ballands Castle
Penhouse Farm
Raymonds Farm
Bourton
MILL STORE
NEW RD
Bourton Bridge
CROSS ROADS
MILL STORE
THE MEADOWS

2

LONG LANE
CHAFFEYMOOR HILL
Grove Farm
Voscombe Farm
Primrose Farm
Sandways Farm
BADGERS CL
BREACH ST
MILLERS ST
PO
P
+

SALTERS HILL
SANDQUARRY LA
Chaffeymoor Farm
WOOLCOTT LA 1
CHURCH CL 2
OLD POUND CT 3
EAST ST 4
CHURCH TK
WEST BOURTON RD
ASH GN
PH
NEW RD
St George's CE Sch
Marvins Farm
BRICKYARD LANE
A303
Feltham Farm
CHURCH RD

1

Somerset STREET ATLAS
A303 Wincanton

30

75 | A | B | 76 | C | D | 77 | E | F

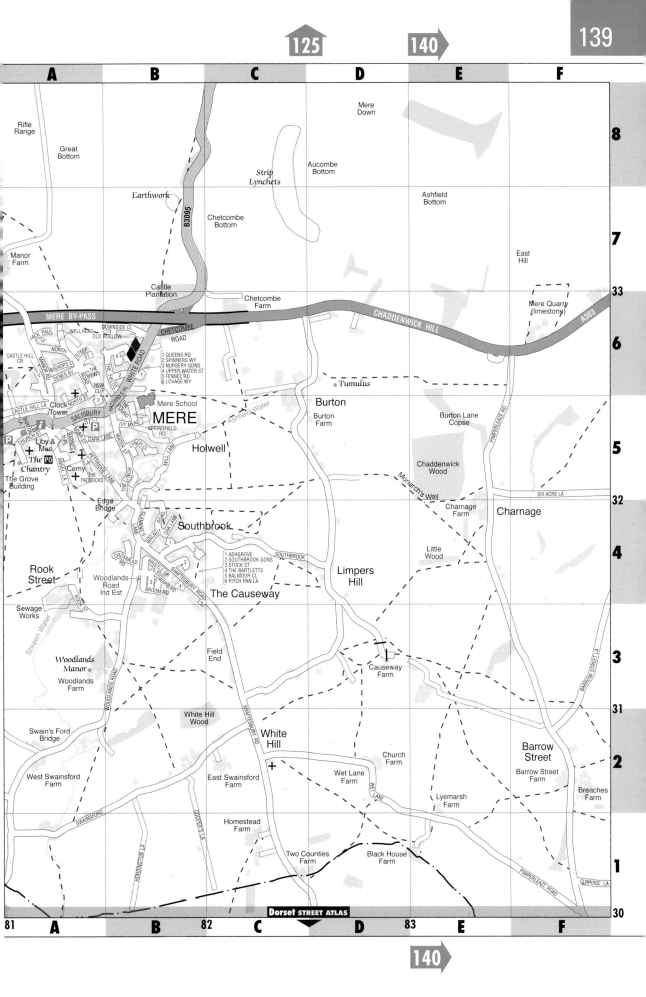

A B C D E F

8
7
33
6
5
32
4
3
31
2
1
30

Rifle Range
Great Bottom
Mere Down
Strip Lynchets
Aucombe Bottom
Ashfield Bottom
Earthwork
Chetcombe Bottom
B3095
Manor Farm
East Hill
Mere Quarry (limestone)
A303
Castle Plantation
Chetcombe Farm
CHADDENWICK HILL
MERE BY-PASS
CHETCOMBE ROAD
DOWNSIDE CL
OLD HOLLOW
WELLHEAD
JACK PAUL CL
NORTH ST
STEEP ST
BISHOPS CL
THE VIEWS
THE FIELDS
HAZZARD'S HILL
WHITE ROAD
1 QUEENS RD
2 SPINNERS WY
3 NURSERY GDNS
4 UPPER WATER ST
5 FENNEL RD
6 LOVAGE WY
Tumulus
CASTLE HILL CR
MANOR RD
DENES AV
NEW CUT
Burton
Burton Farm
Burton Lane Copse
PIMPERLEAZE RD
CASTLE HILL LA
Clock Tower
NORTH ST
SALISBURY
BURTON ST
BOARS HILL
Mere School
IVY MEAD
SPRINGFIELD RD
WATER ST
LYNCH CL
Ashfield Water
Chaddenwick Wood
P
Liby & Mus
CHURCH ST
ANGEL LA
BARNES CL
DARK LANE
MILL LANE
THE LYNCH
Holwell
SIX ACRE LA
The Chantry
PO
RETHRIDGE LANE
Cemy
THE PADDOCKS
Charnage Farm
Charnage
The Grove Building
Edge Bridge
CLEMENT'S LANE
WALNUT ROAD
OAK LANE
Southbrook
1 ASHGROVE
2 SOUTHBROOK GDNS
3 STOCK ST
4 THE BARTLETTS
5 BALMOOR CL
6 PITCH PAN LA
SOUTHBROOK
Little Wood
Monarch's Way
Rook Street
LORDSMEAD RD
BRISTLE GR
COWARD RD
SHAFTESBURY ROAD
Woodlands Road Ind Est
BROOM RD
The Causeway
Limpers Hill
Sewage Works
Shreen Water
ROOK ST
Woodlands Manor
Woodlands Farm
Field End
Causeway Farm
BARROW STREET LA
WOODLANDS ROAD
SHAFTESBURY RD
White Hill Wood
White Hill
Barrow Street
Swain's Ford Bridge
Church Farm
Barrow Street Farm
West Swainsford Farm
East Swainsford Farm
Wet Lane Farm
WET LANE
Lyemarsh Farm
Breaches Farm
HORSINGTON LA
COOPER'S LA
Homestead Farm
SWAINSFORD
Two Counties Farm
Black House Farm
PIMPERLEAZE ROAD
CLINMAGE LA

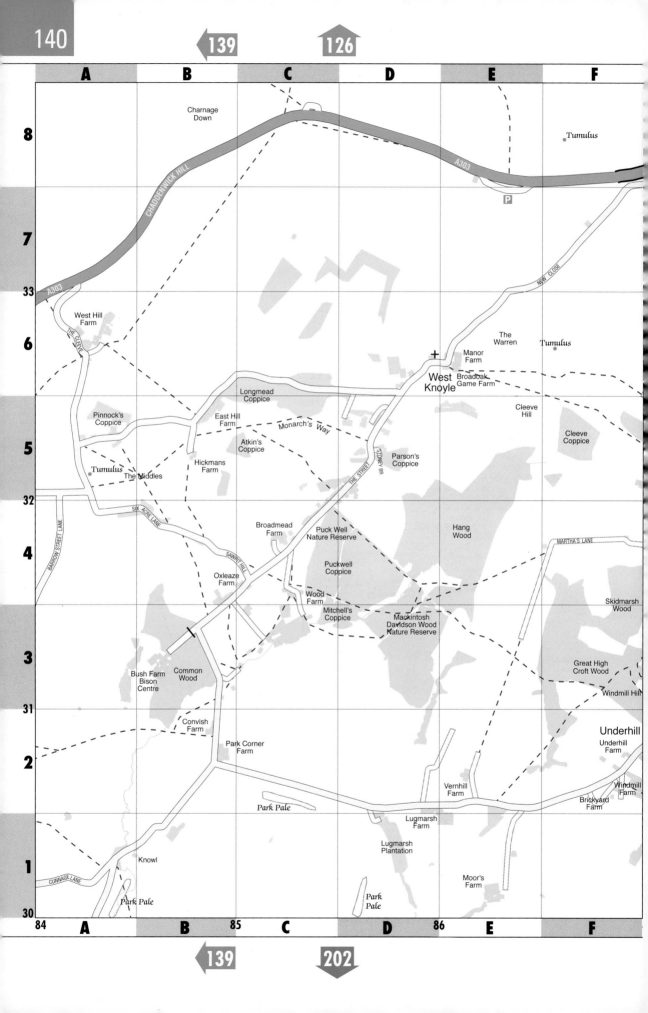

139
126

A B C D E F

8

7

33

6

5

32

4

31

3

2

1

30

Charnage
Down

Tumulus

A303

CHADDENWICK HILL

West Hill
Farm

THE CLEEVE

NEW CLOSE

The
Warren

Tumulus

Manor
Farm

West
Knoyle

Broadoak
Game Farm

Cleeve
Hill

Cleeve
Coppice

Pinnock's
Coppice

Longmead
Coppice

East Hill
Farm

Monarch's Way

Atkin's
Coppice

THE STREET

STONEY BR

Parson's
Coppice

Tumulus

The Middles

Hickmans
Farm

SIX ACRE LANE

BARROW STREET LANE

Broadmead
Farm

Puck Well
Nature Reserve

Hang
Wood

MARTHA'S LANE

SAWPIT HILL

Puckwell
Coppice

Oxleaze
Farm

Wood
Farm

Mitchell's
Coppice

Mackintosh
Davidson Wood
Nature Reserve

Skidmarsh
Wood

Great High
Croft Wood

Windmill Hill

Bush Farm
Bison
Centre

Common
Wood

Convish
Farm

Park Corner
Farm

Underhill

Underhill
Farm

Park Pale

Vernhill
Farm

Windmill
Farm

Brickyard
Farm

Lugmarsh
Farm

CUNNAGE LANE

Knowl

Lugmarsh
Plantation

Moor's
Farm

Park Pale

Park
Pale

84 A 85 C D 86 E F
B

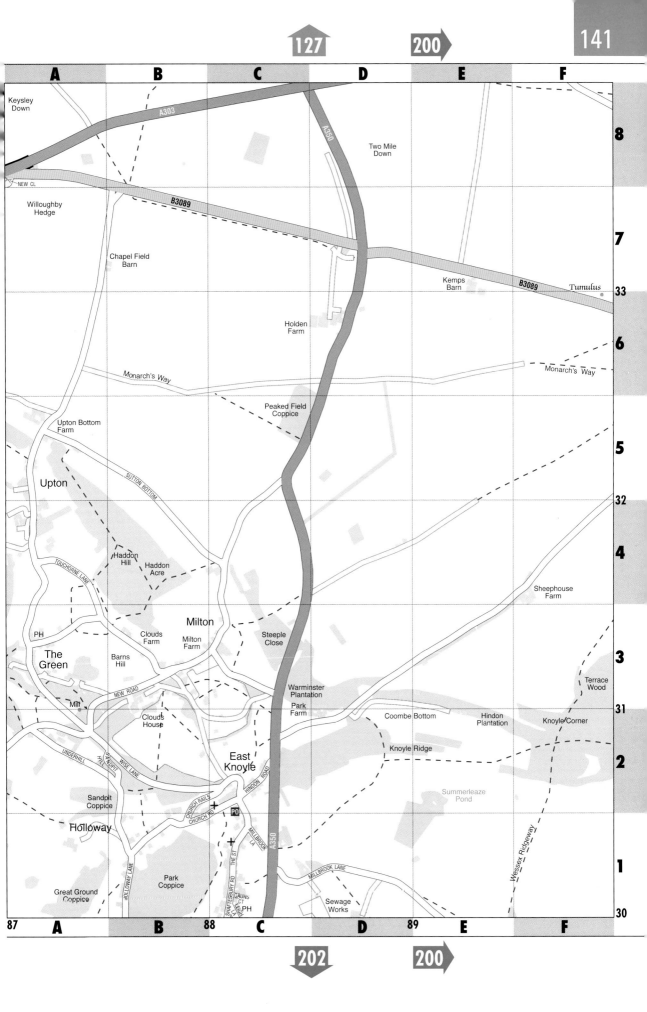

201
128

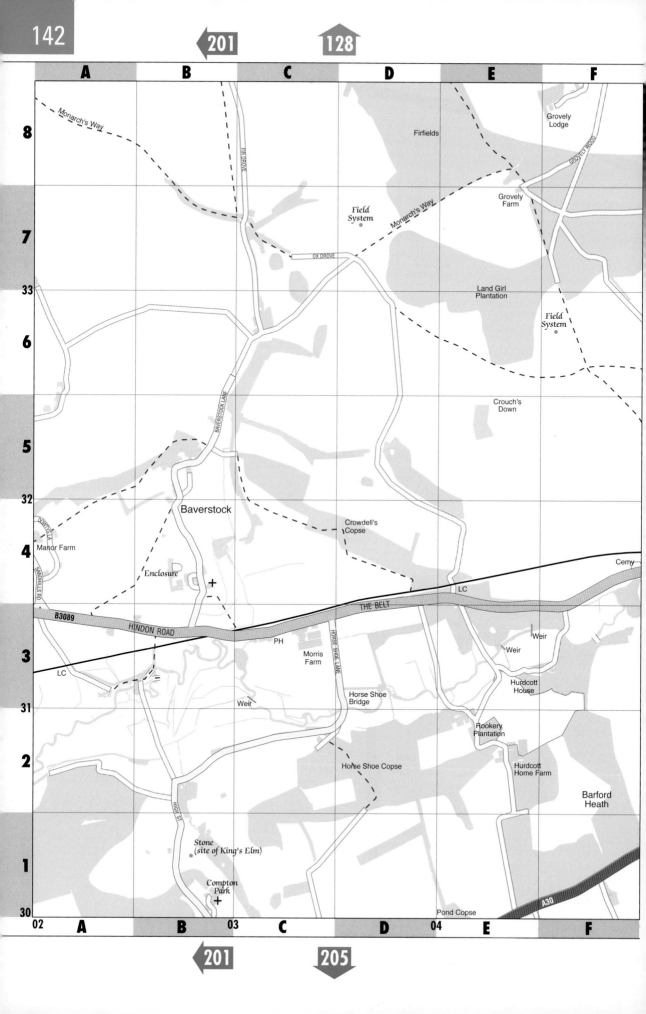

201
205

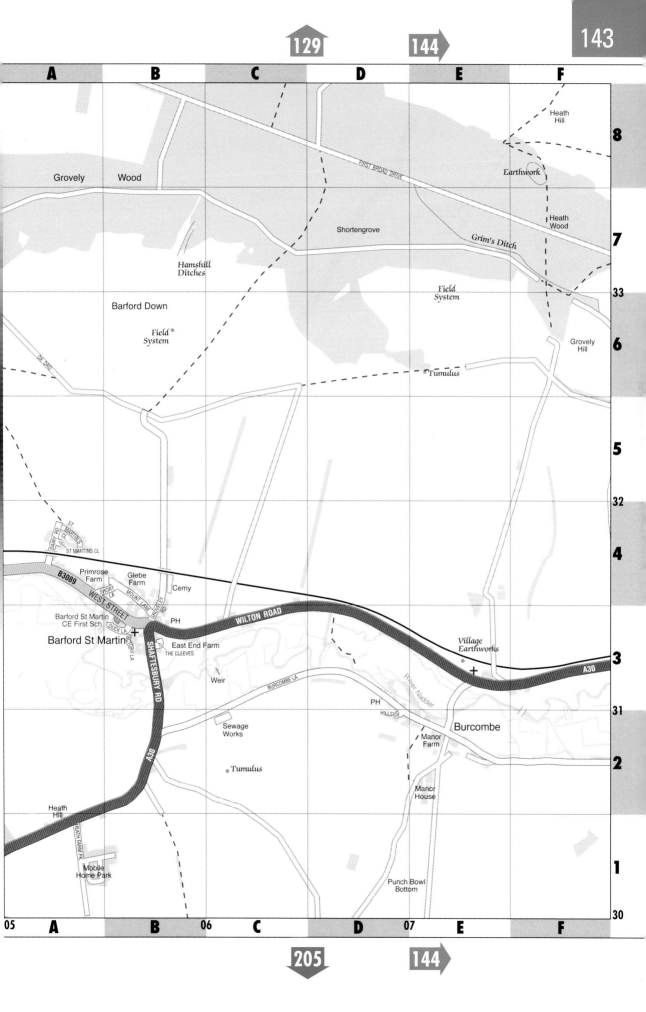

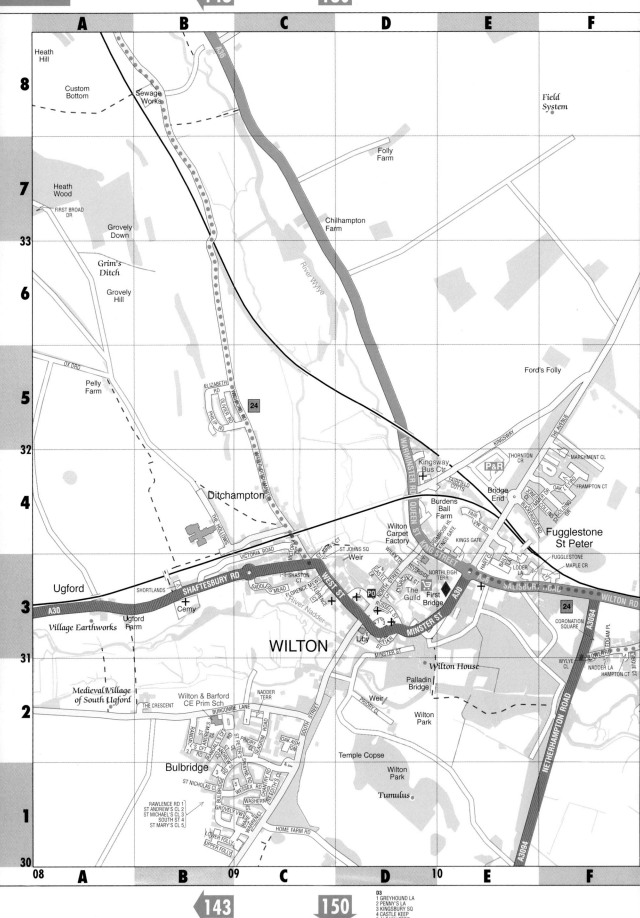

**D3**
1 GREYHOUND LA
2 PENNY'S LA
3 KINGSBURY SQ
4 CASTLE KEEP
5 ALBANY TERR
6 BELL LA
7 CROW LA

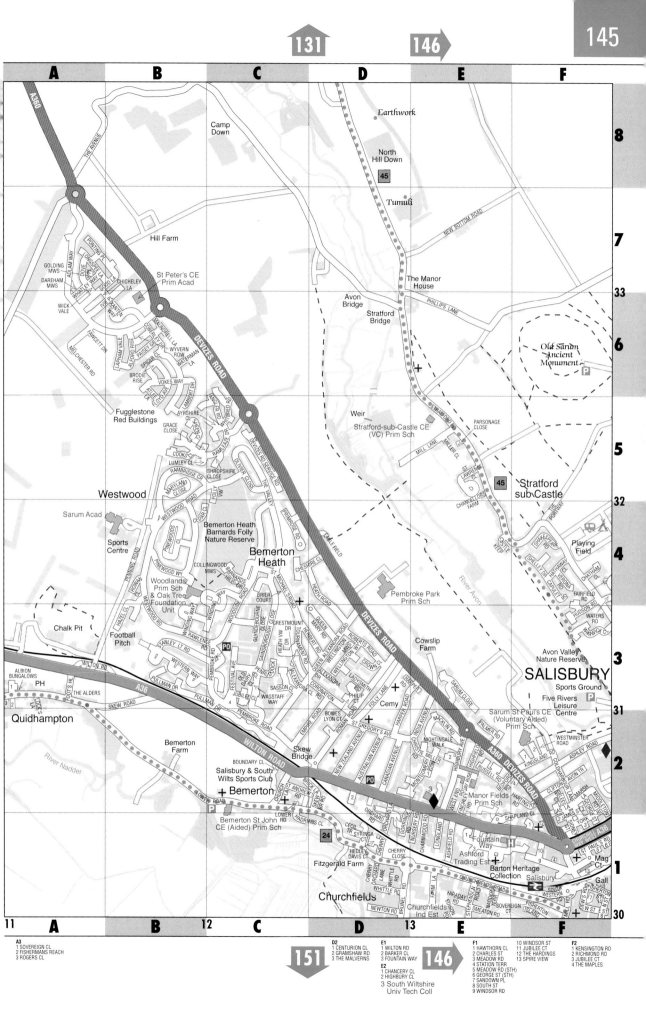

**B8**
1 ROBINSON GR
2 BAZALGETTE LA
3 THOMPSON CL
4 MCLEOD PL

**C8**
1 DEVONALD WAY
2 HENRY LA
3 BUNTING LA
4 WALTER WAY

◄ 145

132

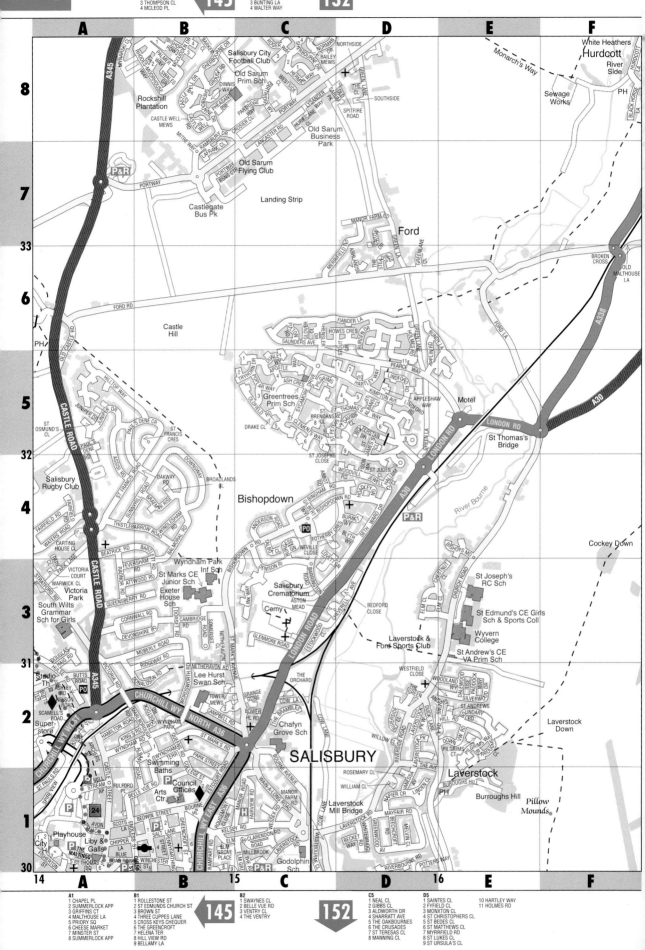

**A1**
1 CHAPEL PL
2 SUMMERLOCK APP
3 GRIFFINS CT
4 MALTHOUSE LA
5 PRIORY SQ
6 CHEESE MARKET
7 MINSTER ST
8 SUMMERLOCK APP

**B1**
1 ROLLESTONE ST
2 ST EDMUNDS CHURCH ST
3 BROWN ST
4 THREE CUPPES LANE
5 CROSS KEYS CHEQUER
6 THE GREENCROFT
7 HELENA TER
8 HILL VIEW RD
9 BELLAMY LA

**B2**
1 SWAYNES CL
2 BELLE VUE RD
3 VENTRY CL
4 THE VENTRY

◄ 145

152

**C5**
1 NEAL CL
2 GIBBS CL
3 ALDWORTH DR
4 SHARRATT AVE
5 THE OAKBOURNES
6 THE CRUSADES
7 ST TERESAS CL
8 MANNING CL

**D5**
1 SAINTES CL
2 FYFIELD CL
3 MONXTON CL
4 ST CHRISTOPHERS CL
5 ST BEDES CL
6 ST MATTHEWS CL
7 MYRRFIELD RD
8 ST LUKES CL
9 ST URSULA'S CL
10 HARTLEY WAY
11 HOLMES RD

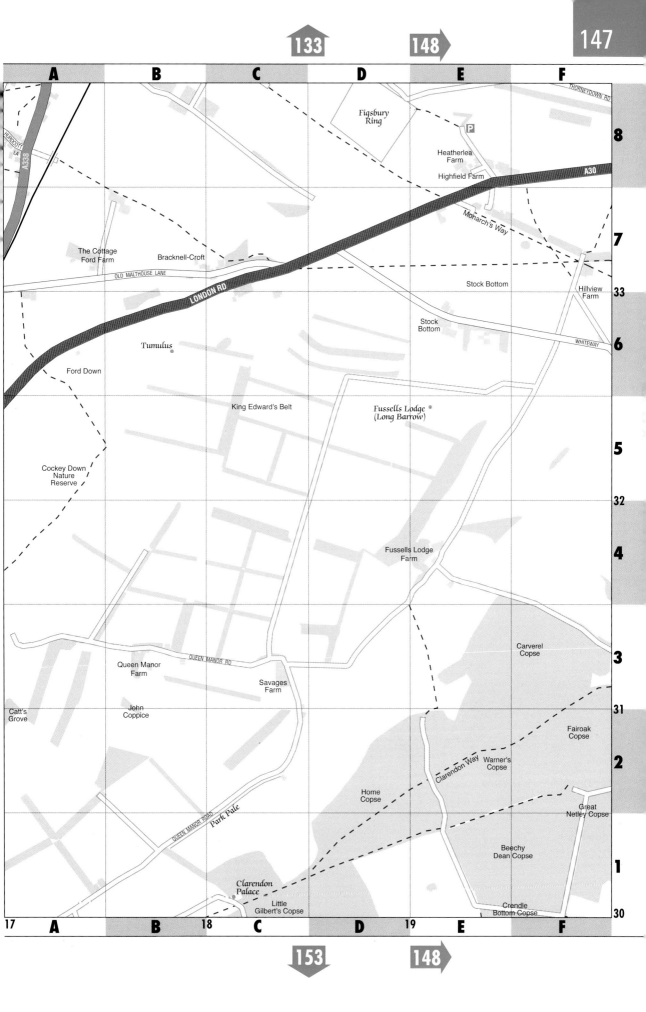

A  B  C  D  E  F

8

THORNEYDOWN RD

Figsbury
Ring

Heatherlea
Farm

Highfield Farm

A30

Monarch's Way

7

The Cottage
Ford Farm

Bracknell-Croft

Stock Bottom

OLD MALTHOUSE LANE

Hillview
Farm

33

LONDON RD

Stock
Bottom

WHITEWAY

Tumulus

6

Ford Down

King Edward's Belt

Fussells Lodge
(Long Barrow)

5

Cockey Down
Nature
Reserve

32

Fussells Lodge
Farm

4

Carverel
Copse

QUEEN MANOR RD

Queen Manor
Farm

3

Savages
Farm

Catt's
Grove

John
Coppice

31

Fairoak
Copse

Clarendon Way

Warner's
Copse

2

Home
Copse

Great
Netley Copse

QUEEN MANOR ROAD

Park Pale

Beechy
Dean Copse

1

Clarendon
Palace

Little
Gilbert's Copse

Crendle
Bottom Copse

30

147
134

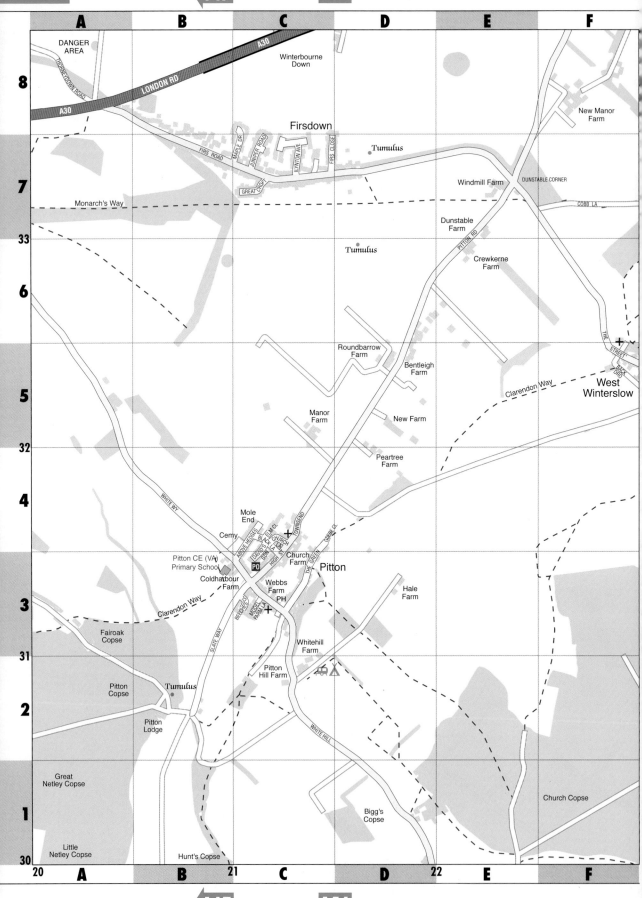

147
154

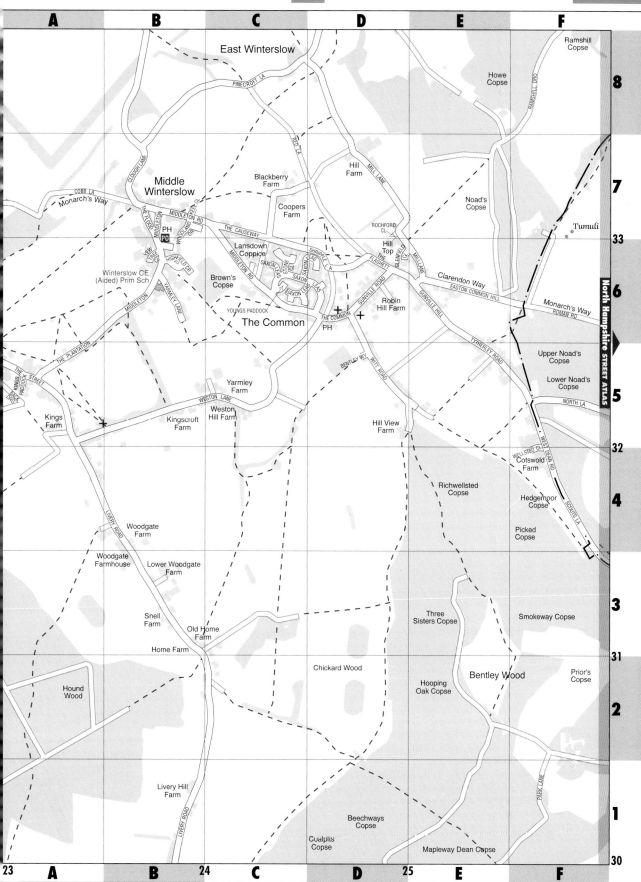

← 205
144
151 →

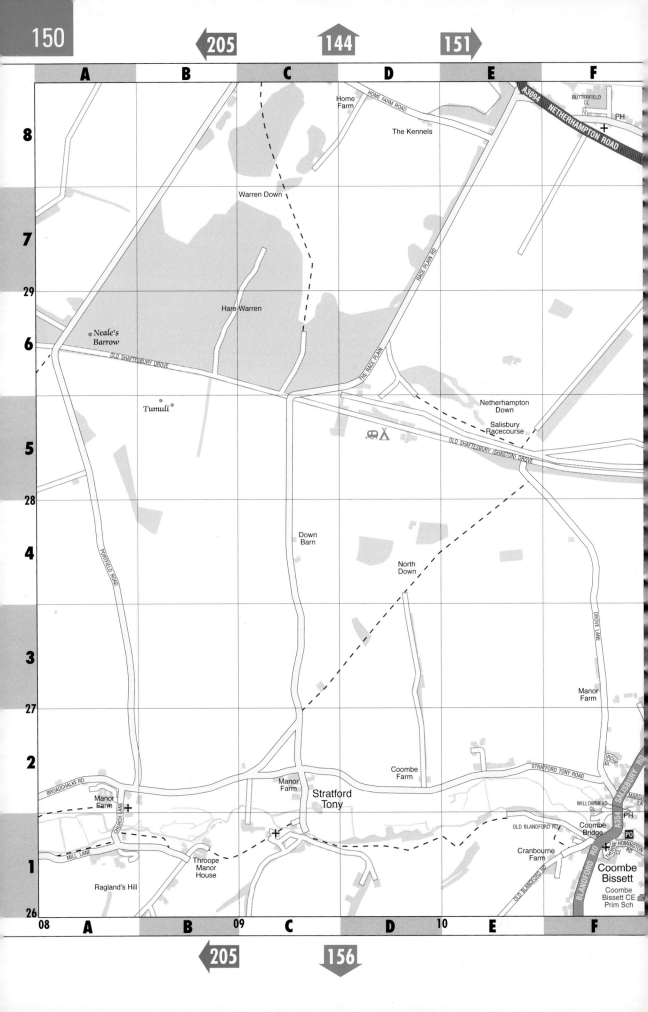

A3094

BUTTERFIELD CL

PH

NETHERHAMPTON ROAD

Home
Farm

HOME FARM ROAD

The Kennels

8

Warren Down

7

RACE PLAIN RD

29

Hare Warren

Neale's
Barrow

6

OLD SHAFTESBURY DROVE

THE RACE PLAIN

Netherhampton
Down

Salisbury
Racecourse

Tumuli

OLD SHAFTESBURY (SHASTON) DROVE

5

28

Down
Barn

PORTFIELD ROAD

4

North
Down

DROVE LANE

Manor
Farm

3

27

DROVE CL

Manor
Farm

2

STRATFORD TONY ROAD

Coombe
Farm

SALISBURY RD

MARSH LA

WILLOWMEAD CL

BROADCHALKE RD

Manor
Farm

CHURCH LANE

Manor
Farm

Stratford
Tony

PH

Coombe
Bridge

OLD BLANDFORD RD

PO

MILL LANE

Throope
Manor
House

Cranbourne
Farm

THORNE HOMINGTON RD

1

Ragland's Hill

BLANDFORD RD

OLD BLANDFORD RD

Coombe
Bissett

Coombe
Bissett CE
Prim Sch

26

08        A        09        B        10        C        D        E        F

← 205
156

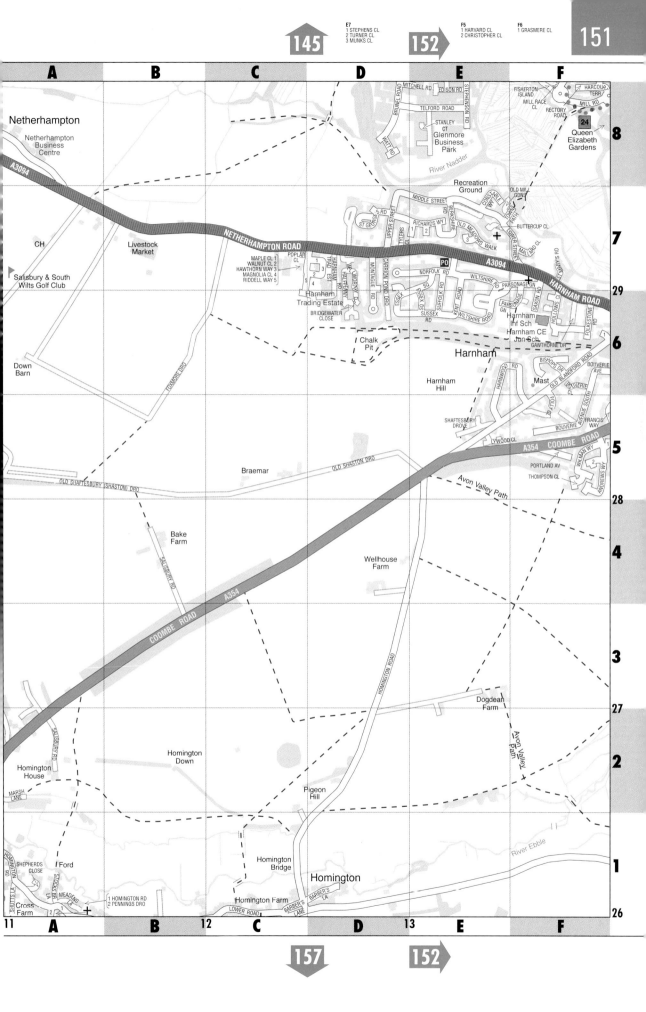

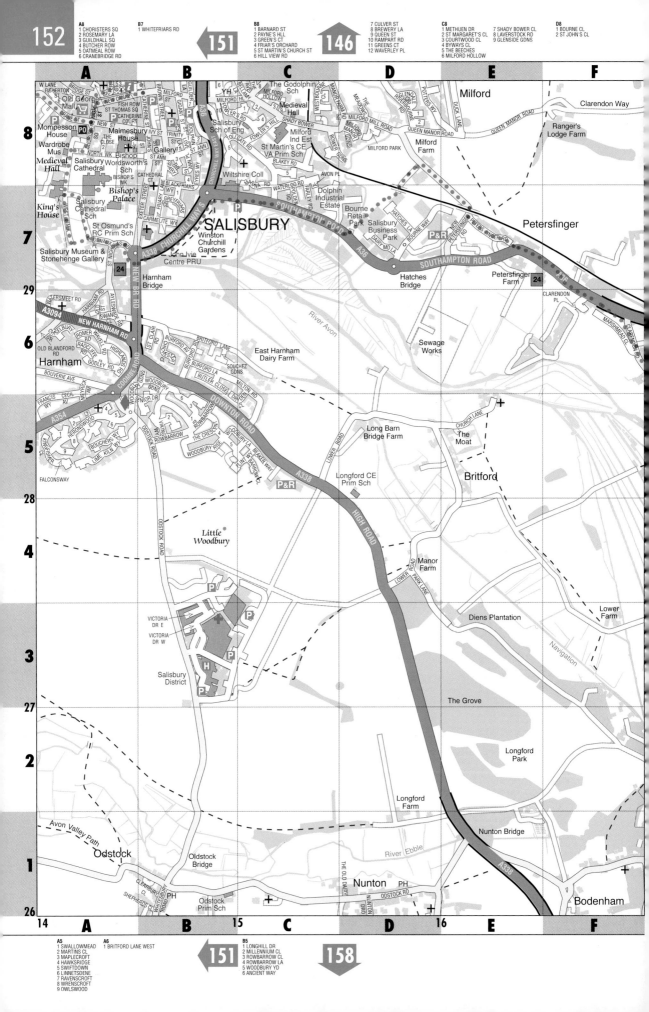

147
154

A B C D E F

8
7
29
6
5
28
4
27
3
2
1
26

Queen Manor Road
Clarendon Way
King Manor Hill
Little Gilbert's Copse
Great Gilbert's Copse
Crendle Bottom Copse
Grimsditch Copse
Grim's Ditch

Ashley Hill
Grimsditch Plantation

Hendon Copse
Long Copse
Rectory Rd

Canon Copse

Morley Plantation
Brickkiln Copse
Clarendon Park

Kennel Farm
A36
Clarendon House

24
South Hampton Rd
Clarendon Road
24

Cupid's Grove

Shute End
Hole Farm
Ivychurch Copse

End Copse
Lower Bigmans Copse
Ivy Church Farm
Old Road
PH
Whitmore's Mdw

River Avon
Shute End Road
Shute End
Silver Wood St
The Green
Clarendon Rd
Common Plantation

Alderbury
Folly La
High St
Southampton Rd
Old Chapel
Oakwood Gr
Bracken Cl

Greenways
Junction Road
Alderbury & West Grimstead CE VA Prim Sch

Silver Street
School Light's La
Tunnel Hill
Foster La
Woodlea Grange
Firs Road
Windmill Cl
Priory Cl
Lee Wy

Longford Pk
Shute End Road
Bowden's Copse
Oak Dr
The Copse
Waleran Cl
Firvale
Firs Rd
Windwk
Twineham Gdn

Longford Castle
Alderbury House
Hightrees Wood
Rectory La
Birch Gr
South Way
Southampton Rd
Canal La
Canalside
Spiders Island
Avon Drive
Eyres Dr
Matrons Cts
Grimstead Rd

Witherington Road
Old Vicarage La
Spelts Copse
Pepperbox Ri
Whaddon
The Sandringhams
Castle Lane
PO
Southampton Cr
A36

Machine Pond Copse
Rectory Farm
WHADDON BSNS PK 1
COLLINGWOOD CL 2
TOZER WAY 3
SPARKES DR 4

Alderbury Farm
1
4
3
2
PH

159
154

17 A 18 B C 19 D E F

153 148

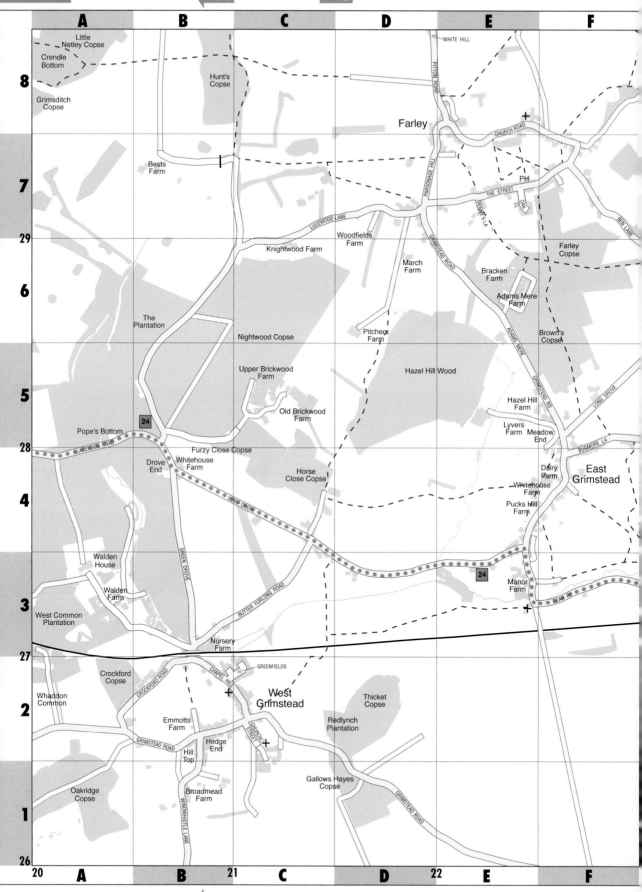

153 160

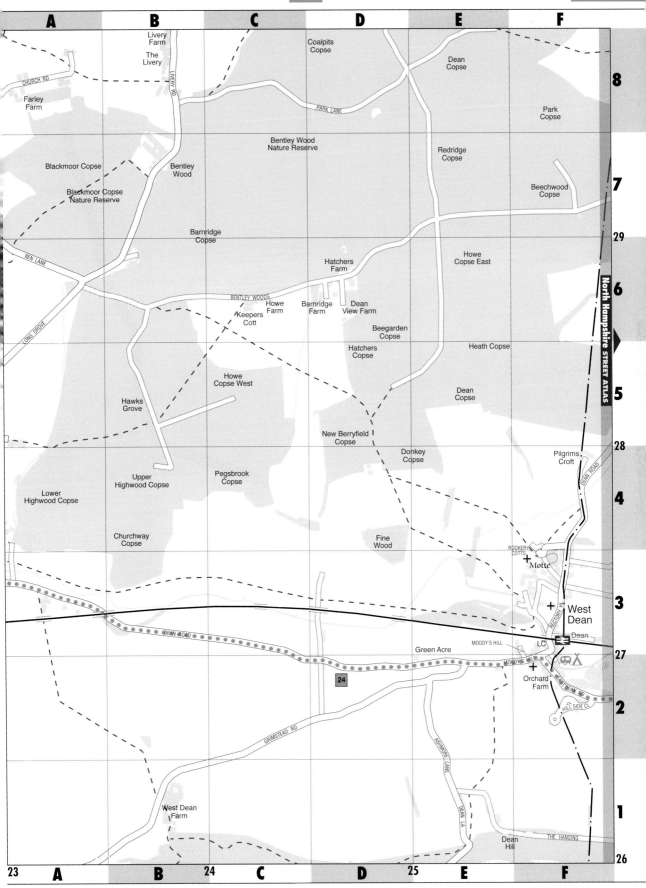

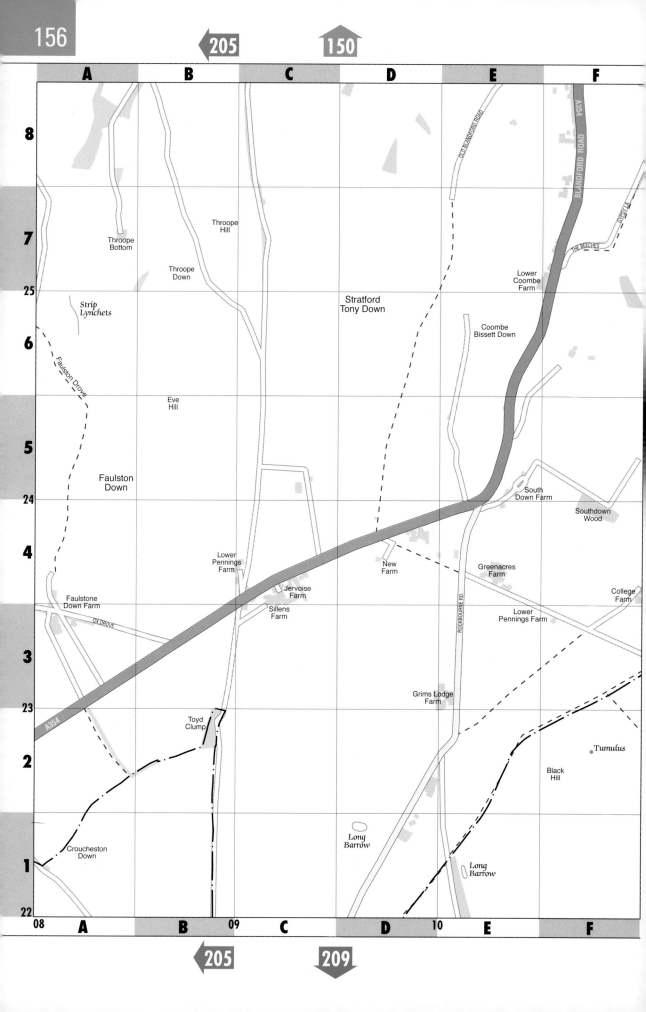

205 150

A B C D E F

8

7

Throope
Hill

Throope
Bottom

Throope
Down

25

Strip
Lynchets

Stratford
Tony Down

6

Faulston Drove

Coombe
Bissett Down

Lower
Coombe
Farm

THE BEECHES

BLANDFORD ROAD

A354

GYPSY LN

Eve
Hill

5

Faulston
Down

24

South
Down Farm

Southdown
Wood

4

Lower
Pennings
Farm

New
Farm

Greenacres
Farm

College
Farm

Faulstone
Down Farm

OX DROVE

Jervoise
Farm

Sillens
Farm

Lower
Pennings Farm

ROOKBOURNE RD

3

A354

23

Toyd
Clump

Grims Lodge
Farm

Tumulus

2

Black
Hill

Long
Barrow

1

Croucheston
Down

Long
Barrow

22

205 209

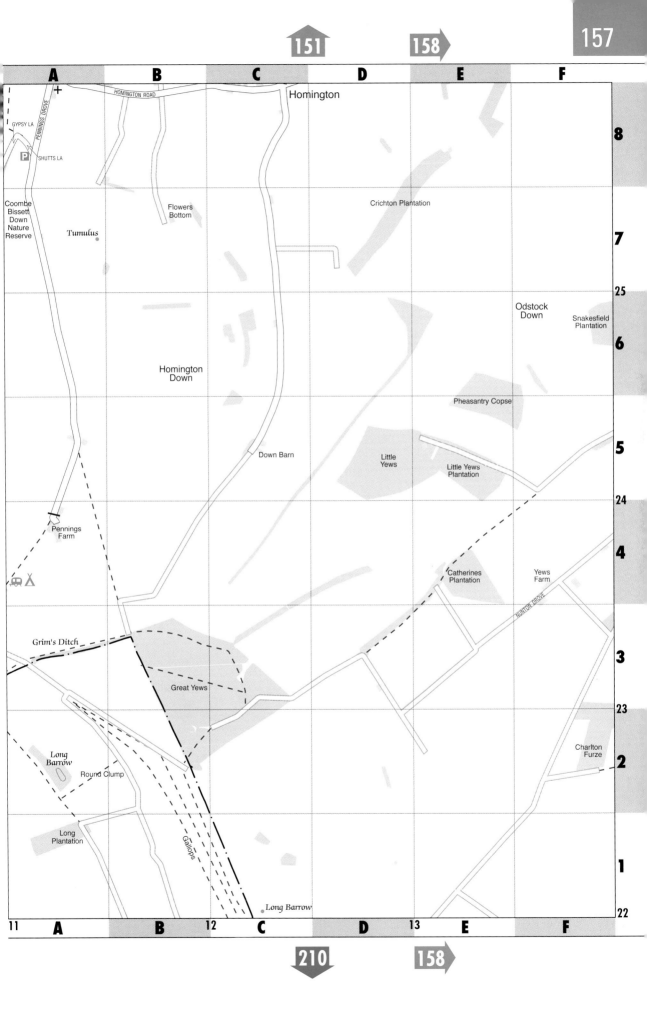

A B C D E F

HOMINGTON ROAD

Homington

GYPSY LA

PENNINGS DROVE

SHUTTS LA

Coombe
Bissett
Down
Nature
Reserve

Flowers
Bottom

Crichton Plantation

*Tumulus*

8

7

25

Odstock
Down

Snakesfield
Plantation

6

Homington
Down

Pheasantry Copse

Down Barn

Little
Yews

Little Yews
Plantation

5

24

Pennings
Farm

Catherines
Plantation

Yews
Farm

NUNTON DROVE

4

*Grim's Ditch*

Great Yews

3

23

Charlton
Furze

*Long
Barrow*

Round Clump

2

Long
Plantation

Gallops

1

Long Barrow

22

11 A B 12 C D 13 E F

| | A | B | C | D | E | F |
|---|---|---|---|---|---|---|

SHEPHERDS CL

Avon Valley Path

Nunton

H New Hall

**8**

NUNTON DROVE

A338

THE HIGHWAY

Bodenham Hill Plantation

**7**

WHITSBURY RD

Fir Plantation

*Earthworks*

THE AVE

Matrimony Farm

**25**

Odstock Copse

Nunton Copse

Charlton Plantation

**6**

NUNTON DROVE

Clearbury Plantation

*Clearbury Ring*

**5**

Charlton Manor Farm

PH

**24**

Clearbury Down

NUNTON DROVE

**4**

North Field Copse

**3**

Warren Plantation

*The Giant's Grave (Long Barrow)*

Giant's Grave Plantation

**23**

*The Giant's Chair (Tumulus)*

**2**

New Court Down Barn

**1**

New Court Down

**22**

A   B   C   D   E   F

8

7

25

6

5

24

4

23

3

2

1

22

Alderbury
Meadows

Hoyels
Copse

Rudghams
Copse

Bunckley's
Copse

Treasurer's
Dean Wood

Nythefield
Copse

Little
Ridghams Copse

Witherington Ring
(Field System)

Witherington Down

Ford

WITHERINGTON ROAD

Witherington
Farm

Warren Field Plantation

Old
Standlynch
Farm

Avon Valley Path

CHAPEL LANE

River Avon

Trafalgar
Park
Farm

CHURCH LANE

LOWER ROAD

Charlton-
All-Saints

Trafalgar
House

Standlynch
Farm

WARRENS LANE

LANGFORD
LA

Barford Down
Farm

A338

SALISBURY RD

Barford
Park

Barford Down

Barford
Park Farm

Trafalgar
Fish Farm

Avon Valley Path

MUDYFORD RD

BARFORD LANE

GRAVEL CL

PARKERS CL

New Court
Farm
Downton
Business
Centre

A36

159
154

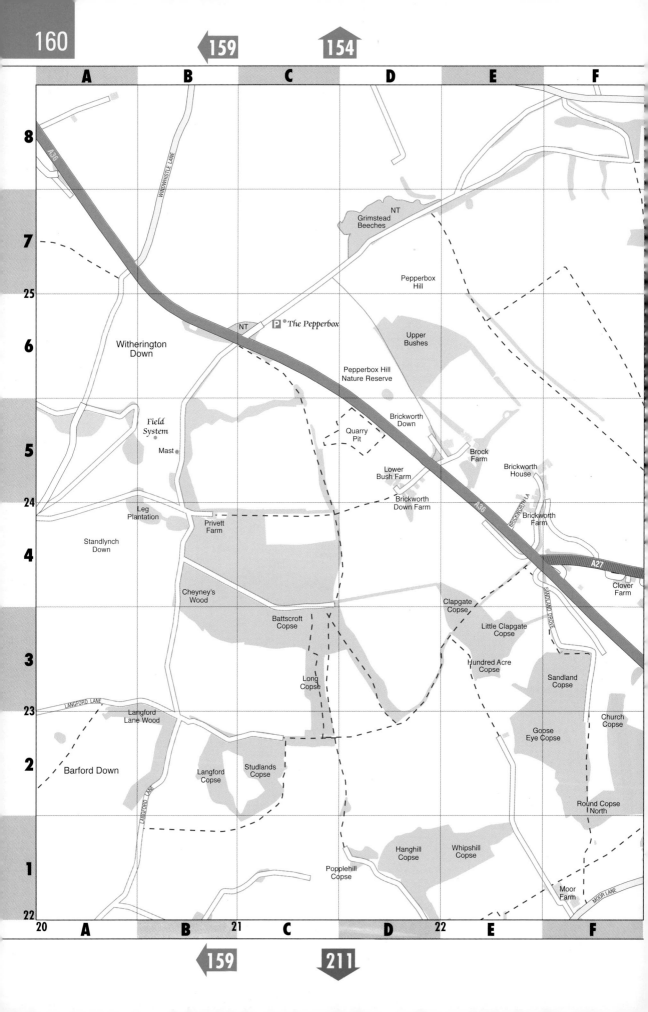

NT
Grimstead
Beeches

Pepperbox
Hill

NT      The Pepperbox

Witherington
Down

Upper
Bushes

Pepperbox Hill
Nature Reserve

Field
System

Brickworth
Down

Quarry
Pit

Mast

Lower
Bush Farm

Brock
Farm

Brickworth
House

Leg
Plantation

Brickworth
Down Farm

Brickworth
Farm

Standlynch
Down

Privett
Farm

Clover
Farm

Cheyney's
Wood

Clapgate
Copse

Battscroft
Copse

Little Clapgate
Copse

Hundred Acre
Copse

Sandland
Copse

Long
Copse

Langford Lane

Langford
Lane Wood

Church
Copse

Goose
Eye Copse

Barford Down

Langford
Copse

Studlands
Copse

Round Copse
North

Hanghill
Copse

Whipshill
Copse

Popplehill
Copse

Moor
Farm

Moor Lane

155
162

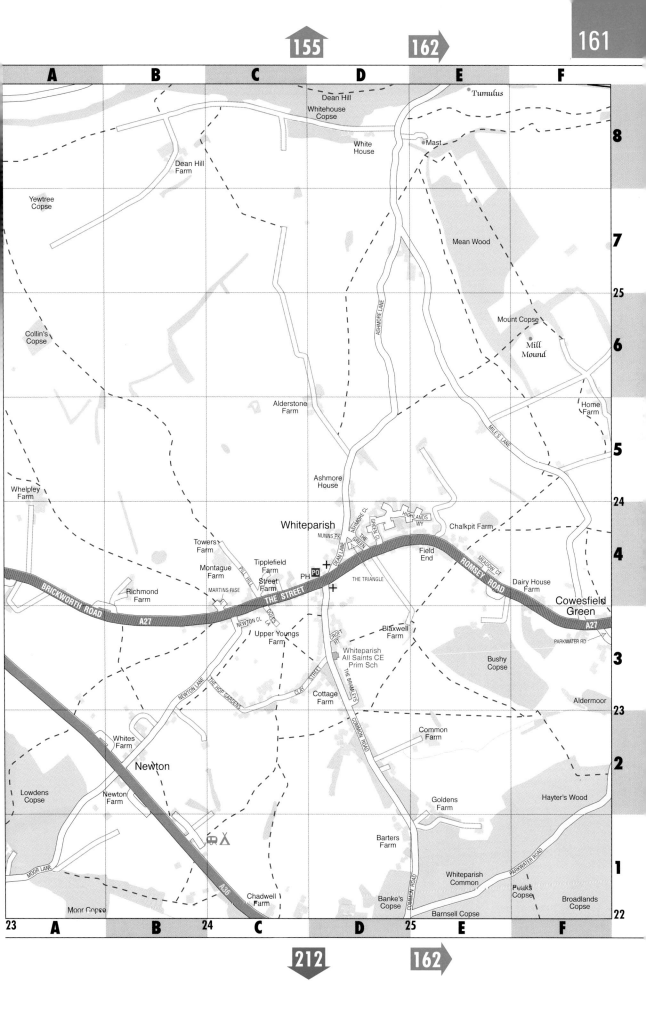

212
162

161

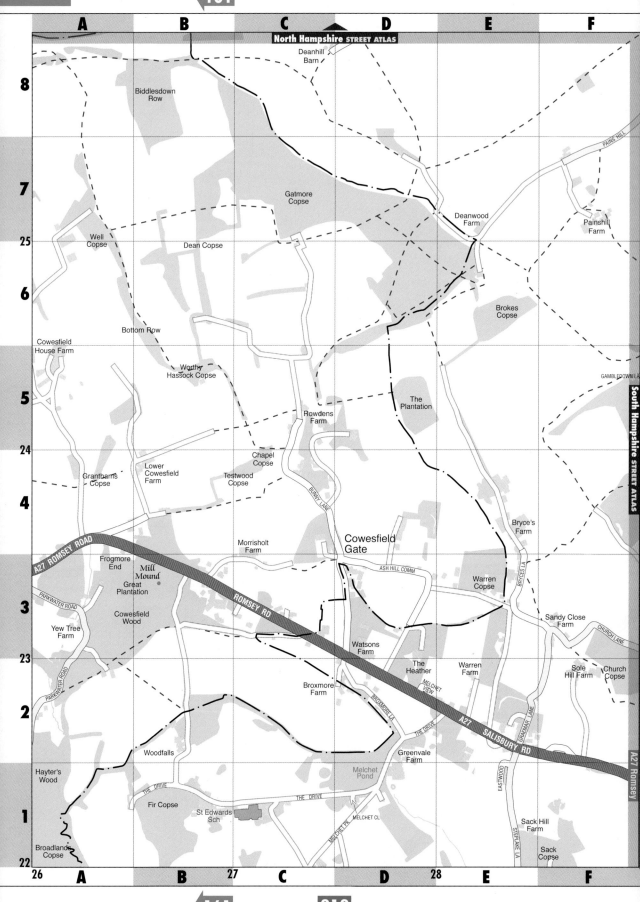

North Hampshire STREET ATLAS

South Hampshire STREET ATLAS

A27 Romsey

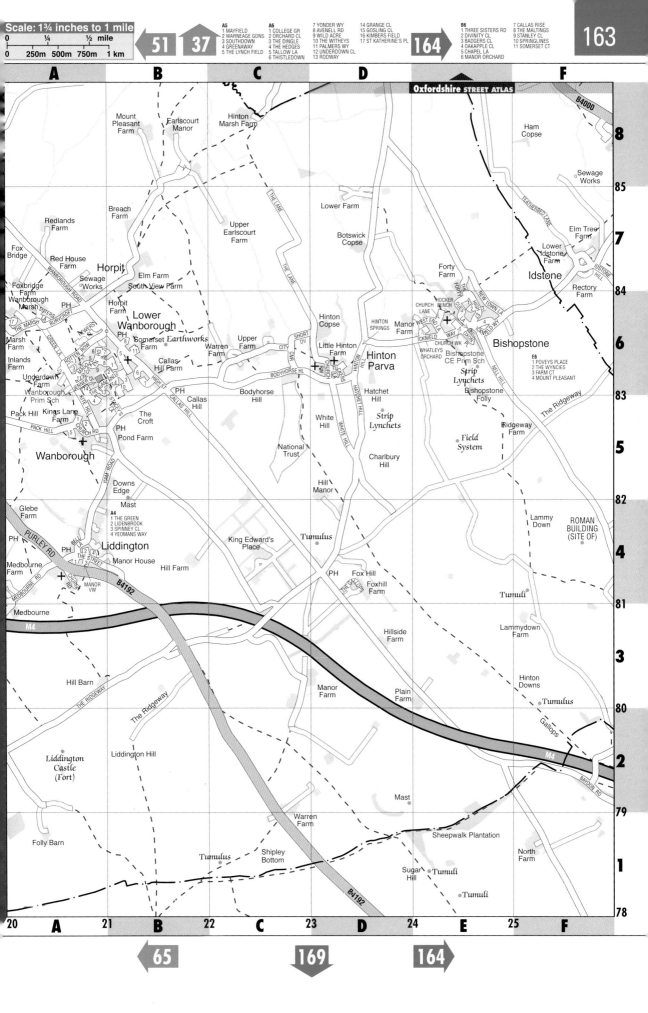

164

A8
1 HIGH ST
2 CHAPEL LA
3 KINGS CL
4 THE LANE
5 COLLEGE FARM LA

163

**Scale: 1¾ inches to 1 mile**

0   ¼   ½ mile
0   250m  500m  750m  1 km

**Oxfordshire STREET ATLAS**

Kingstone
Winslow

Kingstone
Farm

Winslow
Bank

Odstone
Hill

Wayland's Smithy
(Long Barrow)

Ridgeway

B4000

STATION RD

ROUND
PREE

B4507

WIXES PIECE

Ashbury with
Compton Beauchamp
CE (Aided) Prim Sch

Odstone
Coombes

Knighton
Barn

Uffington
Down

Long
Plantation

The Mnr
Hse

BERRYCROFT

WALNUT TREES HILL

WALNUT TREES CL

PO

Kingstone
Coombes

Odstone
Barn

Pingoose
Covert

Cross
Dyke

Idlebush
Barrow

Kingstone
Warren

Lambourn Valley Way

CHURCH LA

Ashbury

ASHBURY HILL

Ashbury Folly

Kingston Warren Down

Ashbury Hill

P

Down
Folly

Settlement

Compton
Bottom

Woolstone
Down

Gallops

Gallops

Idstone
Plantation

Idstone
Hill

HONEYBUNCH
CORNER

Tower
Hill

Field System

Ridgeway

Knighton Down

Tumulus

Whit
Coombe

Wellbottom
Down

Gallops

Hailey
Wood

Odstone
Down

Settlement

Knighton Bushes
Plantation

Gallops

B4000

Crowberry
Tump

Kingstone
Down

Lambourn Valley Way

Middle Wood

Weathercock
Hill

Park Down
Farm

Baldback
Covert

Alfred's
Castle

P

Ashdown
Park

Weathercock

Maddle
Farm

Postdown
Border

Starveall
Farm

Swinley
Down

Ashdown
House

Parkfarm Down

Old Warren

Lye
Leaze

Swinley
Copse

Tumuli

Ashdown
Farm

Halfmoon
Covert

Tumulus

Park
Farm

MADDLE ROAD

Hangman's
Stone

Harley
Bushes

Park Pale

Upper
Wood

Tumulus

Russley Downs

Three
Barrows

Whiteshere

Lambourn
Corner

Kings Farm

HIGH ST

Upper
Lambourn

Earthworks

Bishopstone
Downs

Idstone Down

Dean Bottom

Botley
Bottom

Park Pale

Tumulus

Fognam
Down

Nugent Farm

Cemy

MADDLE RD

Russley Park

Settlement

Botley
Copse

Fognam
Farm

B4000

PH

Gallop

Peaks Downs

Hazelbury
Farm

Gore Lane
Farm

Bailey
Hill

Row
Down

Gallops

MALT SHOVEL LA

White House
Farm

GOOR LANE

Bailey Hill
Copse

Near Down

Gallops

FOLLY ROAD

FOLLY ROAD

Peaks
Wood

Bailey Hill
Farm

Down Farm

M4

Baydon

BAYDON ROAD

FIVEWAYS
CL

Baydon St Nicholas
CE Prim Sch

Baydon Hole
Farm

Farncombe
Farm

East Leaze
Farm

DOWNSMEAD

PO

Hedden's
Copse

M4

Thornslait
Plantation

Farncombe Down

Gallops

BAYDON ROAD

C1
1 ERMIN ST
2 FINCHES LA
3 RUSSLEY GREEN

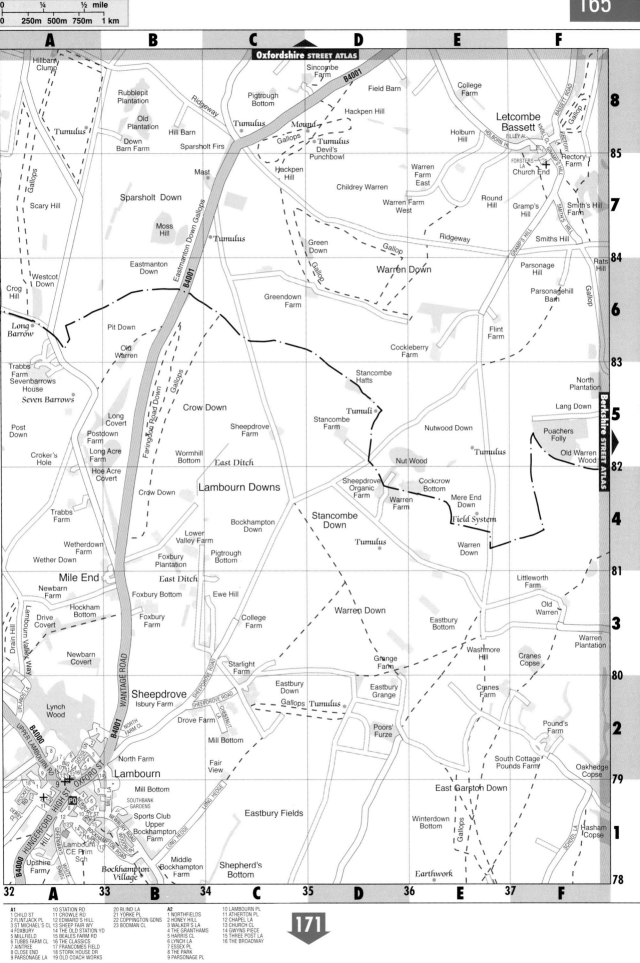

Berkshire STREET ATLAS

171

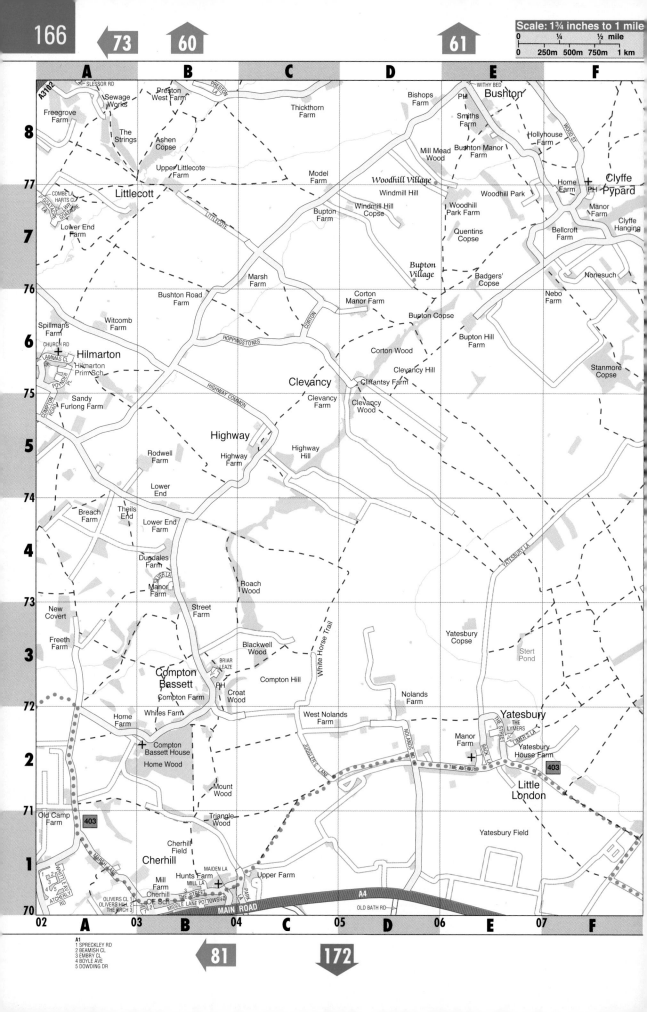

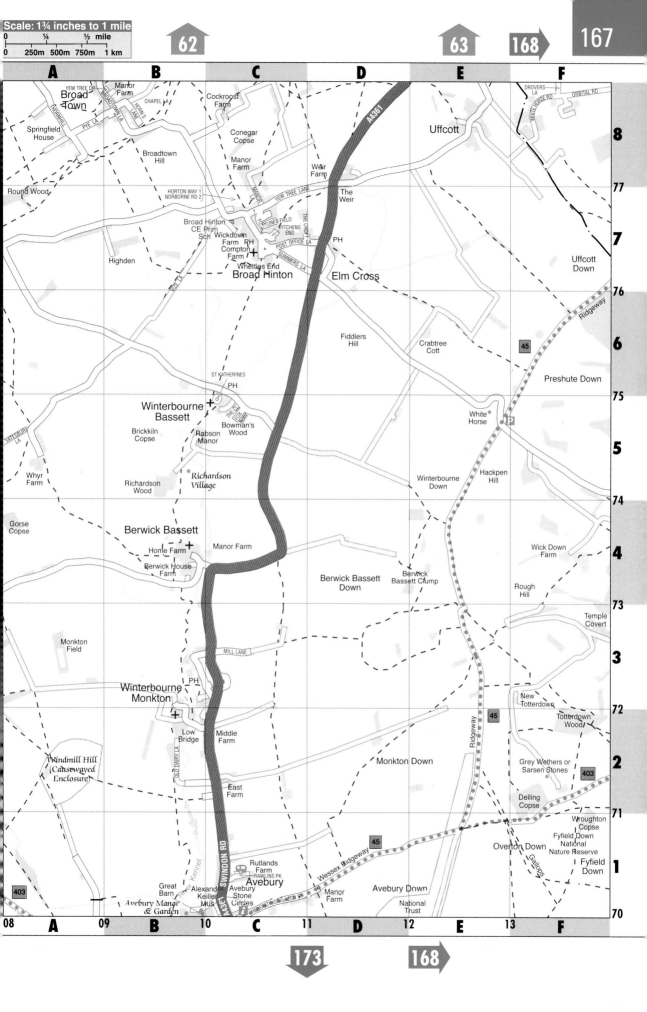

A | B | C | D | E | F

8

Broad Town
Manor Farm
YEW TREE DR
BROADTOWN LA
THORNHILL
PYE LA
HORN'S LANE
CHAPEL LA

Springfield House

Cockroost Farm

Conegar Copse

Uffcott

DROVERS LA
WHITE HORSE RD
ORBITAL RD

Broadtown Hill

Manor Farm

77

Round Wood

HORTON WAY 1
NORBORNE RD 2

Weir Farm

The Weir

Uffcott Down

7

Broad Hinton CE Prim Sch
Wickdown Farm
RH
Compton Farm
YEW TREE LANE
MANOR LA
FORTUNES FIELD
KITCHENS END
POST OFFICE LA
SUMMERS LA
THE CROFT
PH
Elm Cross

Highden
Whettles End
Broad Hinton

Fiddlers Hill

Crabtree Cott

76
Ridgeway

6

St Katherines
PH
Fiddlers Hill

45

Preshute Down

75

Winterbourne Bassett
THE OLD TRACK
Bowman's Wood
Brickkiln Copse
Rabson Manor

White Horse

P

5

YATESBURY LA

Whyr Farm

Richardson Wood
Richardson Village

Winterbourne Down

Hackpen Hill

74

Gorse Copse

Berwick Bassett

Wick Down Farm

4

Home Farm
Berwick House Farm
Manor Farm

Berwick Bassett Down

Berwick Bassett Clump

Rough Hill

73

Temple Covert

Monkton Field

MILL LANE

3

PH
Winterbourne Monkton

New Totterdown

72

Totterdown Wood

Windmill Hill (Causewayed Enclosure)

Low Bridge
Middle Farm
OLD DAIRY LA

Monkton Down

45
Ridgeway

Grey Wethers or Sarsen Stones

403

2

East Farm

Delling Copse

71

403

Rutlands Farm
RAWLINS PK
Avebury

45
Wessex Ridgeway

Manor Farm

Wroughton Copse
Fyfield Down National Nature Reserve

Overton Down

GALLOPS

1

Great Barn
Alexander Keiller Mus
Avebury Stone Circles
River Kennet
A4361 SWINDON RD

Avebury Manor & Garden

Avebury Down

National Trust

Fyfield Down

70

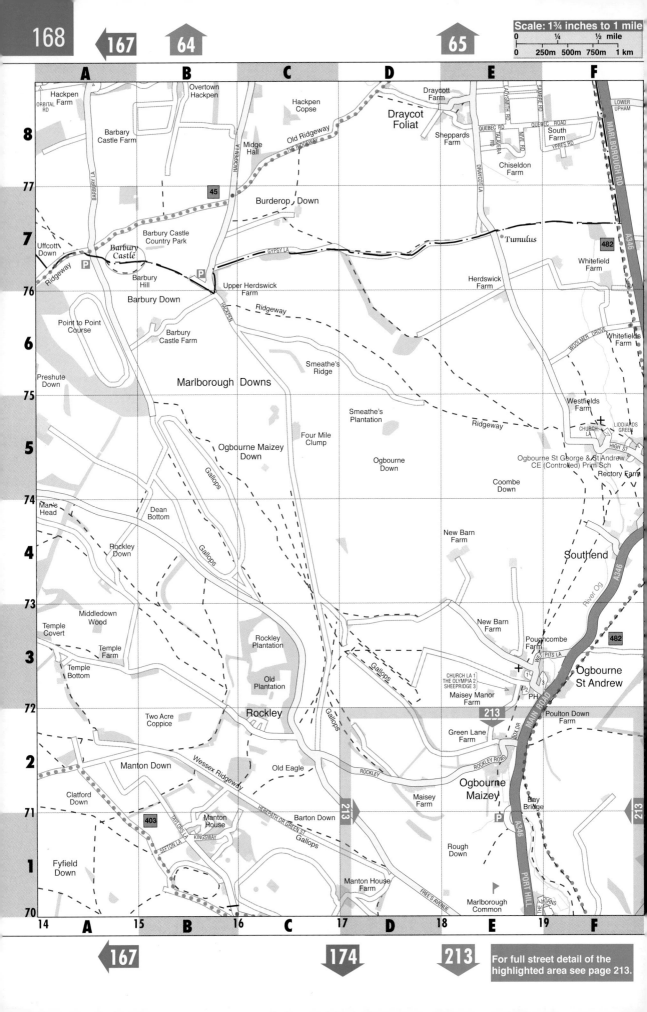

Scale: 1¾ inches to 1 mile

0    ¼    ½    mile

0    250m   500m   750m   1 km

**Row 8:** Hackpen Farm · ORBITAL RD · Overtown Hackpen · Hackpen Copse · Draycott Farm · Draycot Foliat · Sheppards Farm · LADYSMITH RD · SABRE RD · Quebec RD · Quebec ROAD · LOWER UPHAM · Barbary Castle Farm · Midge Hall · Old Ridgeway · THE RIDGEWAY · TALAVERA · TYVE RD · South Farm · YPRES RD

**Row 77:** 45 · Burderop Down · Chiseldon Farm · DRAYCOTT LA

**Row 7:** Uffcott Down · Barbary Castle Country Park · GYPSY LA · Tumulus · 482 · A346 · MARLBOROUGH RD · Ridgeway · P · Barbury Castle · P · Whitefield Farm

**Row 76:** Barbury Hill · Upper Herdswick Farm · HACKPEN · Herdswick Farm · Barbury Down · Ridgeway · WOOLMER DROVE · Whitefields Farm

**Row 6:** Point to Point Course · Barbury Castle Farm · Smeathe's Ridge

**Row 75:** Marlborough Downs · Smeathe's Plantation · Ridgeway · Westfields Farm · CHURCH LA · LIDDIARDS GREEN · HIGH ST

**Row 5:** Preshute Down · Ogbourne Maizey Down · Four Mile Clump · Ogbourne Down · Ogbourne St George & St Andrew CE (Controlled) Prim Sch · Rectory Farm · Gallops

**Row 74:** Man's Head · Dean Bottom · Coombe Down

**Row 4:** Rockley Down · Gallops · New Barn Farm · Southend · River Og · A346

**Row 73:** Middledown Wood · Temple Covert · New Barn Farm

**Row 3:** Temple Farm · Rockley Plantation · Gallops · Poughcombe Farm · PITS LA · Ogbourne St Andrew · CHURCH LA 1 · THE OLYMPIA 2 · SHEEPRIDGE 3 · Maisey Manor Farm · PH

**Row 72:** Temple Bottom · Old Plantation · Rockley · Gallops · 213 · Poulton Down Farm · Green Lane Farm · BOX DR

**Row 2:** Two Acre Coppice · Manton Down · Wessex Ridgeway · Old Eagle · ROCKLEY · Rockley ROAD · Maisey Farm · Ogbourne Maizey · Bay Bridge

**Row 71:** Clatford Down · 403 · TAYLORS LA · KINGSWAY · Manton House · HERPATH OR GREEN ST · Barton Down · 213 · P · A346 · 213

**Row 1:** Fyfield Down · SEFTON LA · Gallops · Manton House Farm · FREE'S AVENUE · Rough Down · Marlborough Common · PORT HILL · THE HORNS

**Row 70:**

14   A   15   B   16   C   17   D   18   E   19   F

167

174

213

For full street detail of the highlighted area see page 213.

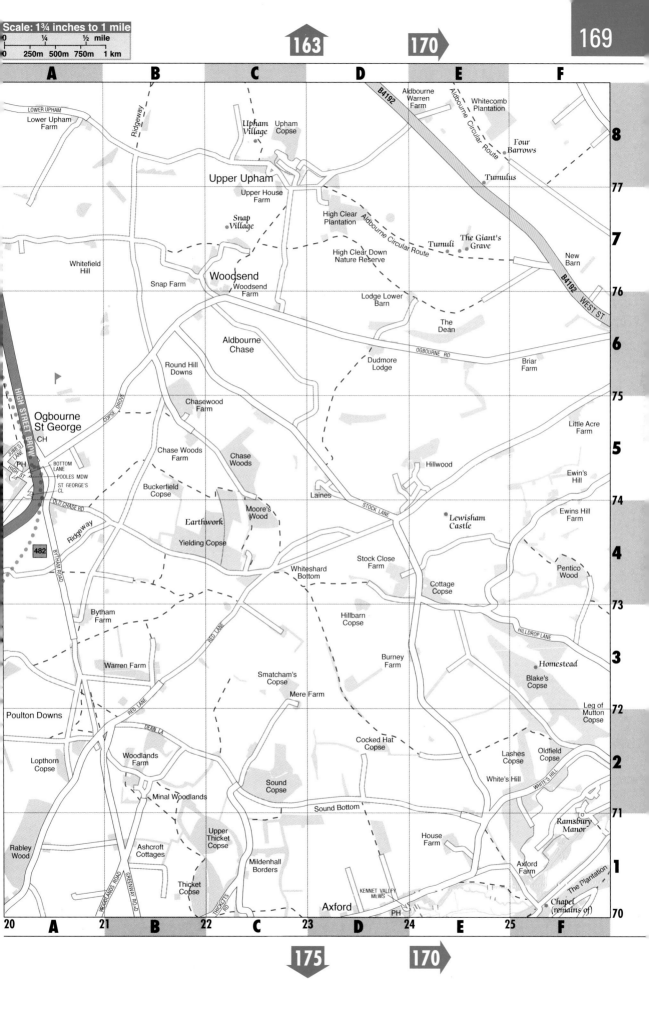

Scale: 1¾ inches to 1 mile

0   ¼       ½   mile
0  250m 500m 750m  1 km

A   B   C   D   E   F

8

77

7

76

6

75

5

74

4

73

3

72

2

71

1

70

LOWER UPHAM
Lower Upham
Farm

Ridgeway

Upham
Village

Upham
Copse

B4192

Aldbourne
Warren
Farm

Whitecomb
Plantation

Aldbourne Circular Route

Four
Barrows

Upper Upham

Upper House
Farm

High Clear
Plantation

Aldbourne Circular Route

Tumulus

Snap
Village

Tumuli

The Giant's
Grave

New
Barn

Whitefield
Hill

High Clear Down
Nature Reserve

B4192  WEST ST

Snap Farm

Woodsend

Woodsend
Farm

Lodge Lower
Barn

The
Dean

OGBOURNE RD

Briar
Farm

Aldbourne
Chase

Dudmore
Lodge

Round Hill
Downs

COPSE DROVE

Chasewood
Farm

Little Acre
Farm

Ogbourne
St George

CH

Chase Woods
Farm

Chase
Woods

Hillwood

Ewin's
Hill

BOTTOM
LANE

POOLES MDW
ST GEORGE'S
CL

Buckerfield
Copse

Laines

STOCK LANE

Lewisham
Castle

Ewins Hill
Farm

JUBB'S
LANE

PH

HIGH ST

OLD CHASE RD

Ridgeway

Moore's
Wood

Earthwork

Yielding Copse

Whiteshard
Bottom

Stock Close
Farm

Cottage
Copse

Pentico
Wood

482

BYTHAM ROAD

RED LANE

Hillbarn
Copse

HILLDROP LANE

Bytham
Farm

Burney
Farm

Homestead

Blake's
Copse

Warren Farm

Smatcham's
Copse

Leg of
Mutton
Copse

Poulton Downs

RED LANE

Mere Farm

Cocked Hat
Copse

Lashes
Copse

Oldfield
Copse

DEAN LA

Woodlands
Farm

White's Hill

WHITE'S HILL

Lopthorn
Copse

Minal Woodlands

Sound
Copse

Sound Bottom

House
Farm

Ramsbury
Manor

NORLANDS ROAD

GREENWAY ROAD

Ashcroft
Cottages

Upper
Thicket
Copse

Axford
Farm

The Plantation

Rabley
Wood

Thicket
Copse

Mildenhall
Borders

THICKET'S RD

KENNET VALLEY
MEWS

Axford

PH

Chapel
(remains of)

20   A   21   B   22   C   23   D   24   E   25   F

# 170

A6
1 RECTORY WOOD
2 SOUTHFIELD
3 CLARIDGE CL
4 TURNPIKE
5 MARLBOROUGH RD
6 THE GARLINGS

7 GLEBE CL
8 ST MICHAEL'S CL
9 BACK LA
10 THE PADDOCKS
11 GODDARDS LA
12 THE KNOLL
13 WESTFIELD CHASE

14 WHITELEY RD
15 HILLWOOD RD
16 HAWKINS RD
17 BARNES YD
18 VALLEY VIEW

← 169

164

Scale: 1¾ inches to 1 mile
0    ¼    ½ mile
0  250m 500m 750m 1 km

| | A | B | C | D | E | F |
|---|---|---|---|---|---|---|

**8** North Field Barn · DOWNSMEAD · NEWTONS WK · BARLEY FIELDS · WALRONDS CL · Baydon · Sewage Works · Farncombe Down · Lodge Farm · Lodge Copse · Lodge Down · Windmill Farm · Farn Combe · Coppington Down

**77** Greenhills · Midge Copse · ERMIN CL · FINCHES LA · ERMIN ST · M4 · BAYDON ROAD · ERMIN STREET · PLATT LANE · Great West Wood · Kingwpod House · Little West Wood · B4000

**7** Lottage Farm · Green Hill · Baydon Hill Farm · Gore's Copse · Woodley's Copse · Coneygre Copse · Common Barn Copse · Hadley Farm · Holly Farm · LAMBOURN BSNS PK · Battens Farm

**76** St Michael's CE Aided Prim Sch · Aldbourne · WEST ST · B4192 · Liby PO · CASTLE ST · STOCK LANE · HAWKINS RD · Pigs Hill Wood · Baydon Wood · St Johns Wood · Membury Service Area · Aerial Business Park · Aerial Farm · Hurst Farm · Dixon's Farm · Lyedown Copse · PH · ERMIN STREET · HUNGERFORD HILL · RAMSBURY RD

**6** THE DOWNS · Housedd's Hill · Long Copse · Hillier's Copse · Paxlet Plantation · Membury Castle (site of) · Membury Farm · Cuckoo Copse · Ford Farm · SOUTH ST · SOUTHWARD LANE · FARM LA · Woodcock Grove

**75** Hoddes Bridge · Baydon Manor · Marridge Hill · Anchor Copse · Balak Farm · Membury Farm · Lyckweed Farm · Moon's Copse · Leigh Farm

**5** Southward Down · Preston · Marridge Hill Wood · Witcha Copse · Tumulus

**74** Crowood Farm · Shell's Wood · Ballard's Copse · Long Barrow · Hunt's Copse · Witcha Farm · Ragnal

**4** Southern Copse · Love's Copse · Hails Grove · Eastridge House · Raffin Stud · Wiltshire Bottom

**73** Pond Wood · Crowood House · Woodlands Farm · Bower Wood · Crooked Soley

**3** Love's Farm · Hilldrop Farm · Boltsridge Copse · Bolstridge Farm · HILLDROP LANE · LOVE'S LANE · Little Wood · Whittonside Farm · Whittonditch · Balaam's Wood · Foxbury Wood · Queen's Copse · Princess Copse

**72** Westfield Copse · LANGFIELDS · Ramsbury Prim Sch · BACK LA · ASHLEY PC · CROWOOD LA · WHITTONDITCH ROAD · Oaken Coppice · Fewley Coppice · King's Copse

**2** Manor Farm · Ramsbury · Liby · PO · PH · OXFORD ST · HIGH ST · New Town · NEWTOWN ROAD · Knighton · Daffy Copse · King's Copse · WHITE'S HILL · MILL LA · Ambrose Farm · LAMPLANDS

**71** Spring Hill · Atherton Coppice · Whitehill Coppice · Weir · River Kennet · B4192 · Manor Farm · Chilton Foliat

**1** The Plantation · Bungalow Bridge Farm · Bridge Farm · Park Coppice · ROMAN VILLA · Littlecote · Hotel · Weir

**70** Darrell's Farm · Great Coppice

| 26 | A | 27 | B | 28 | C | 29 | D | 30 | E | 31 | F |
|---|---|---|---|---|---|---|---|---|---|---|---|

B2
1 HILLDROP CL
2 KNOWLEDGE CRES
3 LAWRENCE MD
4 BURDETT ST
5 ORCHARD CL
6 ISLES RD
7 SWAN'S BOTTOM
8 CHAPEL LA
9 SWAN'S CL

10 TOWNFIELD
11 WHITEHILL CL
12 ATHERTON CL
13 GREEN ACRES
14 THE PADDOCKS
15 TANKARD LANE
16 SCHOLARD'S LA
17 BURDETT ST

← 169

176

165

E7
1 DOWNLANDS
2 BURFORD'S
3 HUMPHREY'S LA
4 COLLEGE WAY
5 THE WALDRONS

171

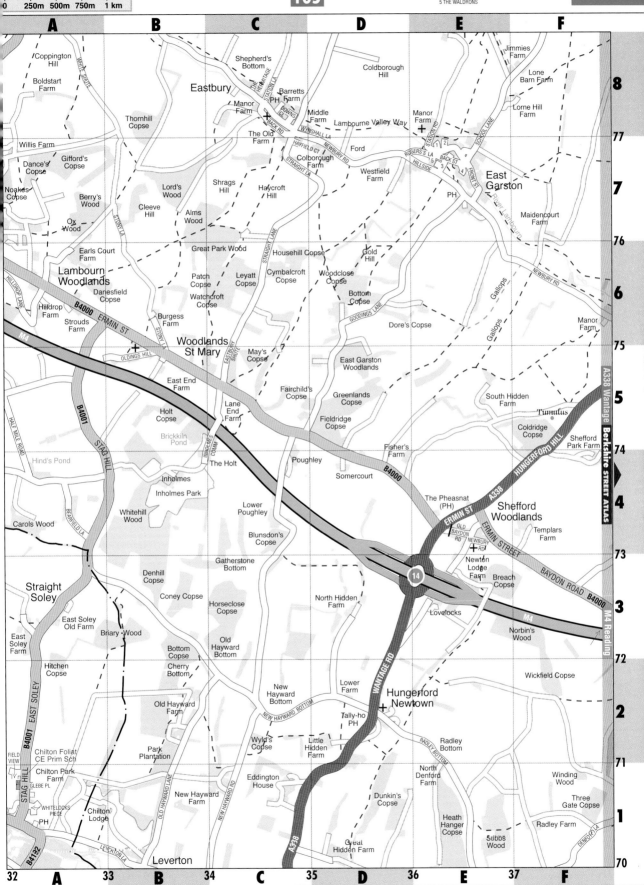

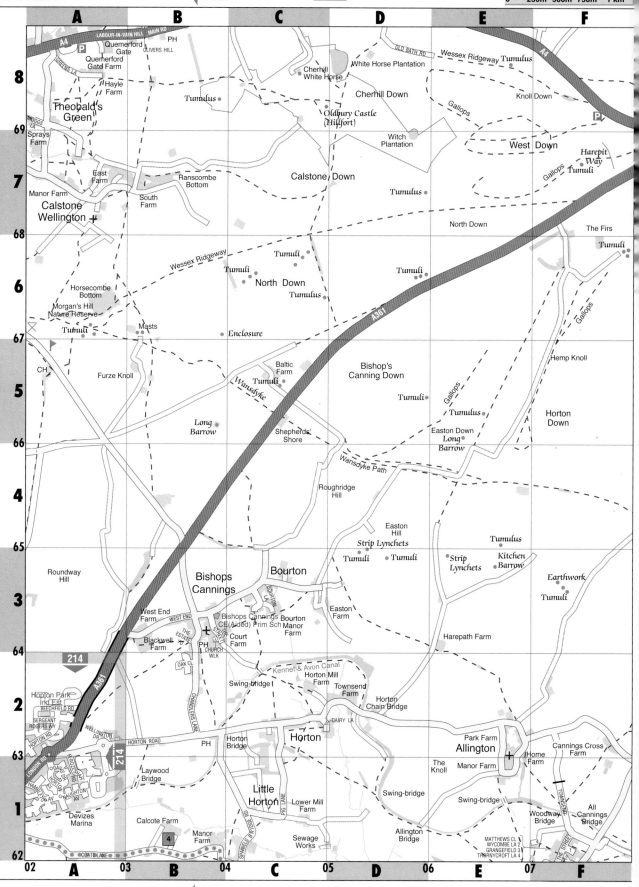

89
166

Scale: 1¾ inches to 1 mile

| 0 | ¼ | ½ mile |
| 0 | 250m | 500m | 750m | 1 km |

**A** **B** **C** **D** **E** **F**

LABOUR-IN-VAIN HILL | MAIN RD
A4
Quemerford Gate
OLIVERS HILL
PH
Quemerford Gate Farm
GREENS LA
P
Hayle Farm

**8**

White Horse Plantation
OLD BATH RD
Wessex Ridgeway Tumulus
A4
Cherhill White Horse
Knoll Down
Cherhill Down
P

Theobald's Green
THOGGS LA
Sprays Farm
Oldbury Castle (Hillfort)
West Down

**69**

Witch Plantation
Harepit Way
Tumuli

**7**

East Farm
Manor Farm
Ranscombe Bottom
Calstone Down
Gallops
Tumulus

Calstone Wellington
South Farm
Tumulus
North Down

**68**

The Firs

Horsecombe Bottom
Wessex Ridgeway
Tumuli
Tumuli
A361
Tumulus
Tumuli

**6**

Morgan's Hill Nature Reserve
North Down
Tumulus
Gallops

**67**

Tumuli
Masts
Enclosure
Baltic Farm
Bishop's Canning Down
Hemp Knoll

CH
Furze Knoll
Wansdyke
Tumuli
Tumuli
Gallops
Horton Down

**5**

Long Barrow
Shepherds Shore
Tumulus
Tumulus
Easton Down Long Barrow

**66**

Wansdyke Path

Roughridge Hill

**4**

Easton Hill
Strip Lynchets
Tumulus

**65**

Roundway Hill
Bishops Cannings
Bourton
Tumuli
Tumuli
Strip Lynchets
Kitchen Barrow
Earthwork
Tumuli

**3**

West End Farm
WEST END
BOURTON LA
Bishops Cannings CE (Aided) Prim Sch
Bourton Manor Farm
Easton Farm
Harepath Farm

West End
THE ESTATE RD
Blackwell Farm
PH
Court Farm
CHURCH WLK

**64**

214
A361
OAK CL
Kennet & Avon Canal
Horton Mill Farm
Swing-bridge
Townsend Farm
Horton Chain Bridge

Hopton Park Ind Est
BEECHFIELD RD
CHANDLERS LANE
DAIRY LA
Park Farm
Cannings Cross Farm

**2**

SERGEANT ROGERS WY
WELLINGTON DR
214
HORTON ROAD
PH
Horton Bridge
Horton
Allington
Home Farm

LONDON RD
HORTON RD
Laywood Bridge
The Knoll
Manor Farm

**63**

OAK DR
NAUGHTON AV
Devizes Marina
Little Horton
PIG LANE
Swing-bridge
Swing-bridge
Woodway Bridge
All Cannings Bridge

**1**

Calcote Farm
Manor Farm
Lower Mill Farm
Allington Bridge
MATTHEWS CL
WYCOMBE LA 2
GRANGEFIELD 3
THORNYCROFT LA 4

4
SPANNELS A FUTURE RD
Sewage Works
THE STREET

**62**

COATE LANE

**02** **A** **03** **B** **04** **C** **05** **D** **06** **E** **07** **F**

97
180

For full street detail of the highlighted area see page 214.

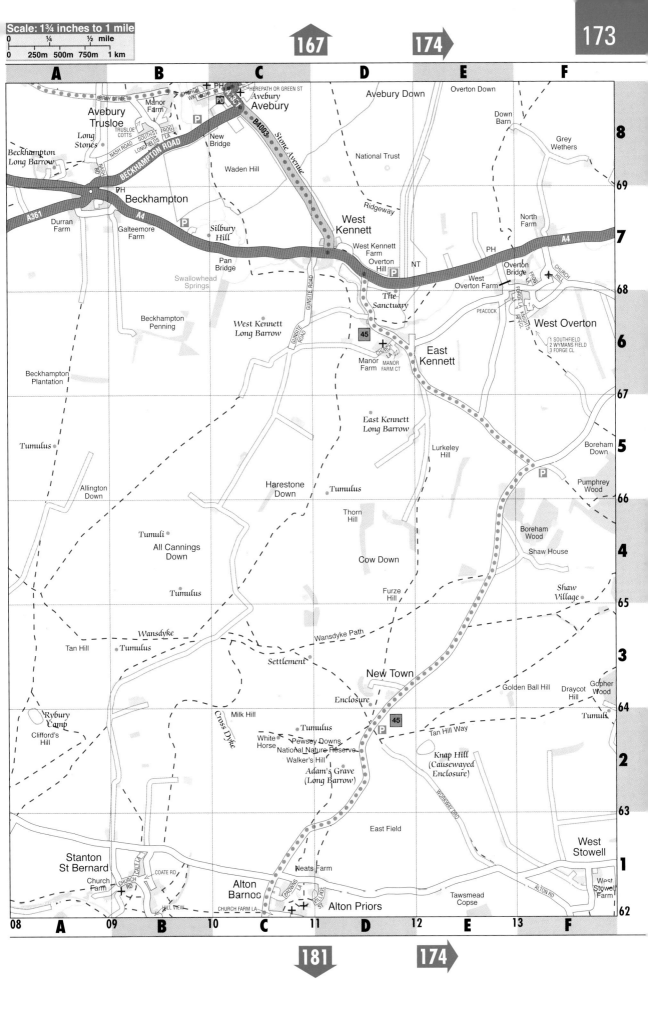

174
173
168
For full street detail of the highlighted area see page 213.
213

Scale: 1¾ inches to 1 mile
0   ¼   ½ mile
0  250m 500m 750m 1 km

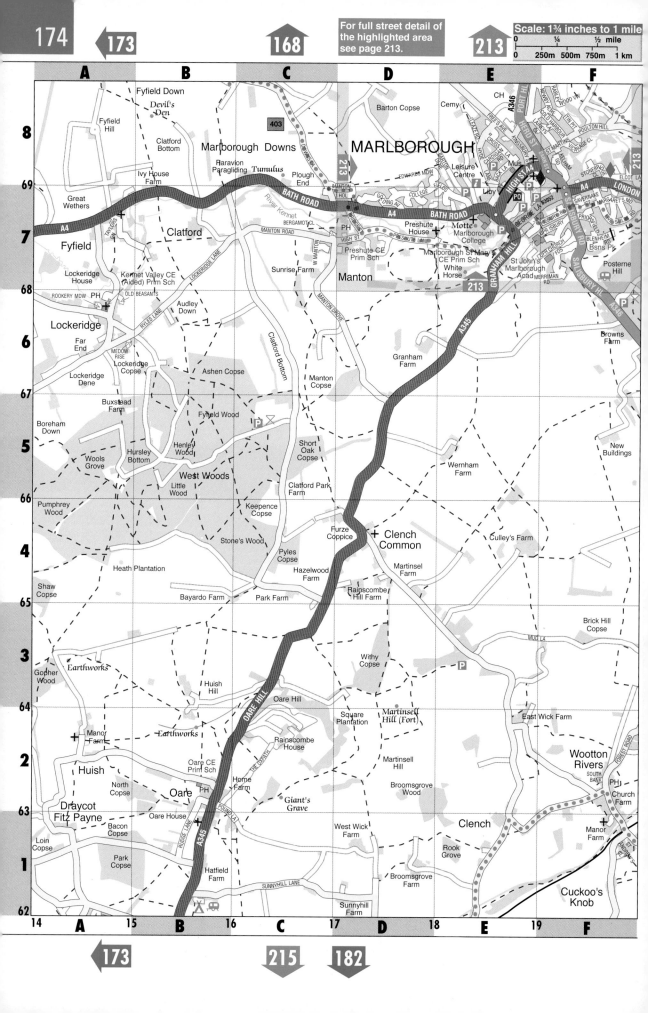

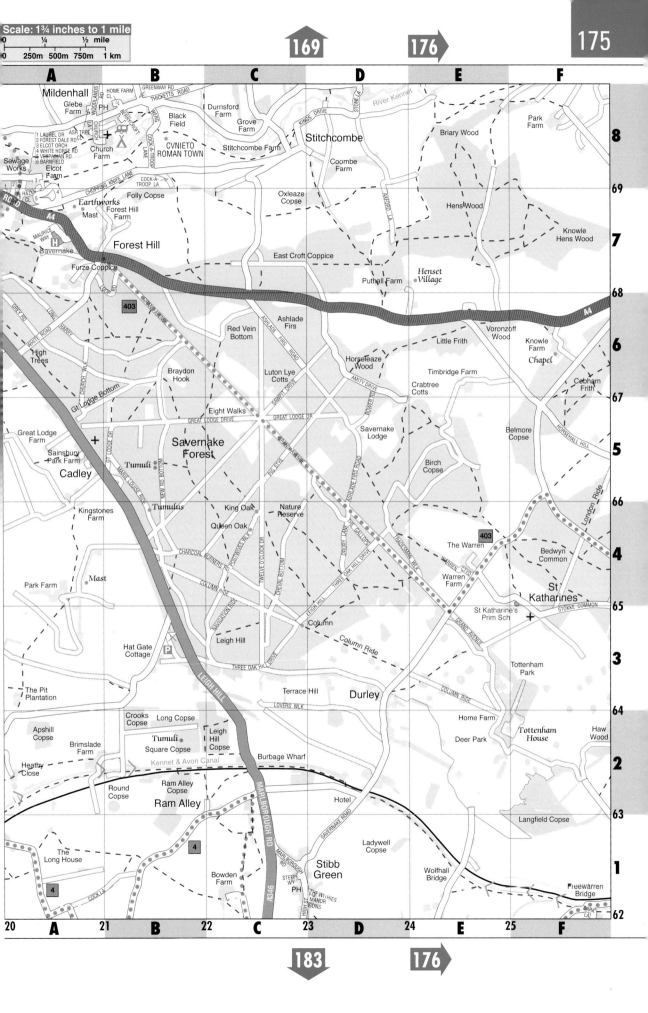

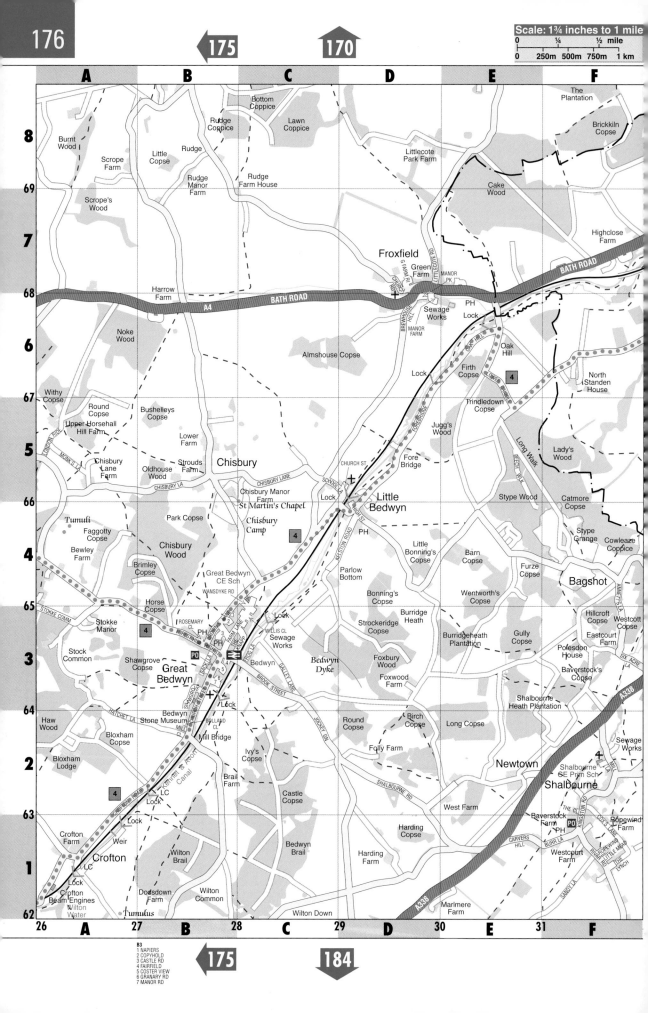

**B6**
1 PRIORY PL
2 SARUM WAY
3 ORCHARD PK CL
4 HILLSIDE RD
5 PRIORY CL
6 LANCASTER CL

7 YORK RD
8 DE MONTFORT GR
9 LIGUIEL CL
10 COMBE VW
11 CHESTNUT WK
12 BEECH SQ
13 WAR MEMORIAL AVE

14 LEWINGTON MS
15 LOURDES CRES
16 JETHRO TULL LA
17 PIDDEN MEAD
18 SANHAM VIEW

**B7**
1 SOMERSET CL
2 WESSEX CL
3 WILTSHIRE CL
4 FREEMANS CL
5 POND PIECE
6 THE CROFT

7 CHERRY GR
8 ST LAWRENCE SQ
9 OAKES COURT
10 HONEYFIELDS
11 ATHERTON RD
12 MOORES PL
13 CHANTRY MD

14 WESTBROOK CL
15 REGENT CL
16 ATHERTON CR
17 CHAPEL CT
18 EVERLAND RD
19 STATION RD
20 NORTHVIEW

21 MACKLIN CL
22 FAIRFIELDS
23 MORLEY PL
24 TARRANT'S HL
25 CLARK'S GDNS
26 BRIDGE ST
27 ALDBOURNE CL

28 UPLANDS
29 WESSEX PL
30 CROWN MEWS
31 ST LAWRENCE SQUARE
32 CHURCH LANE

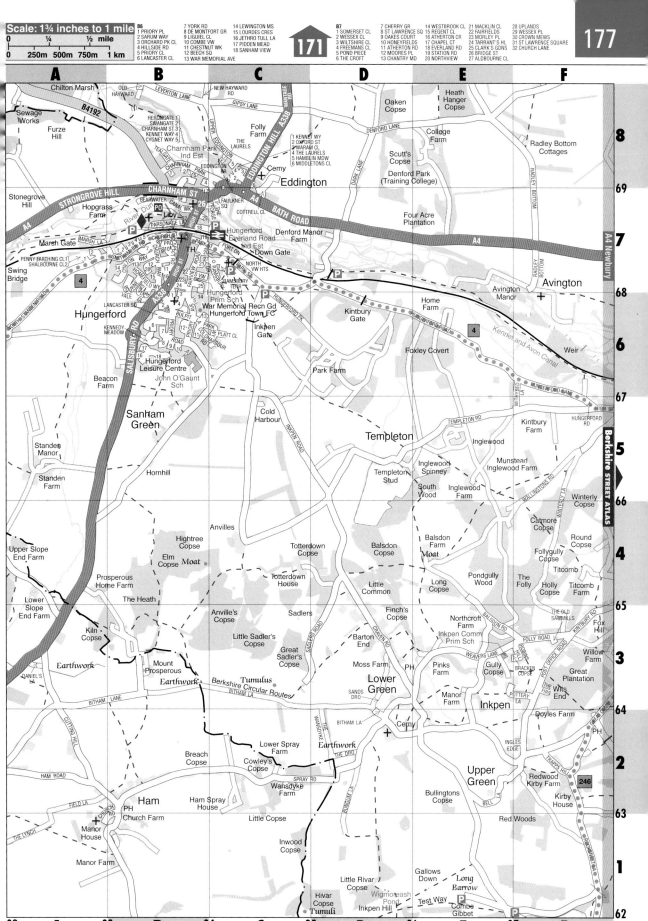

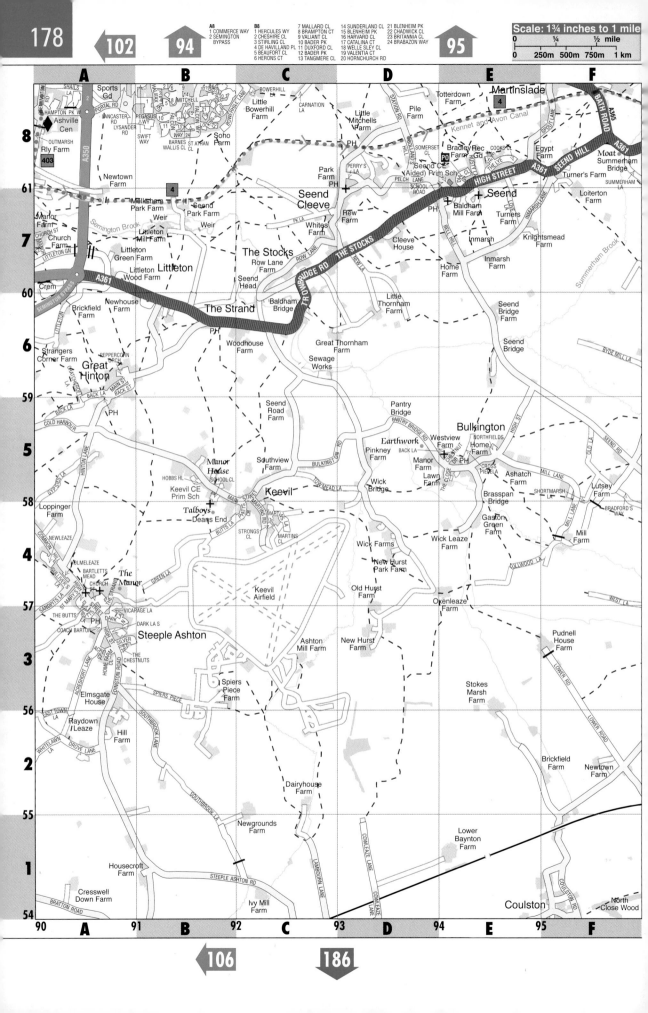

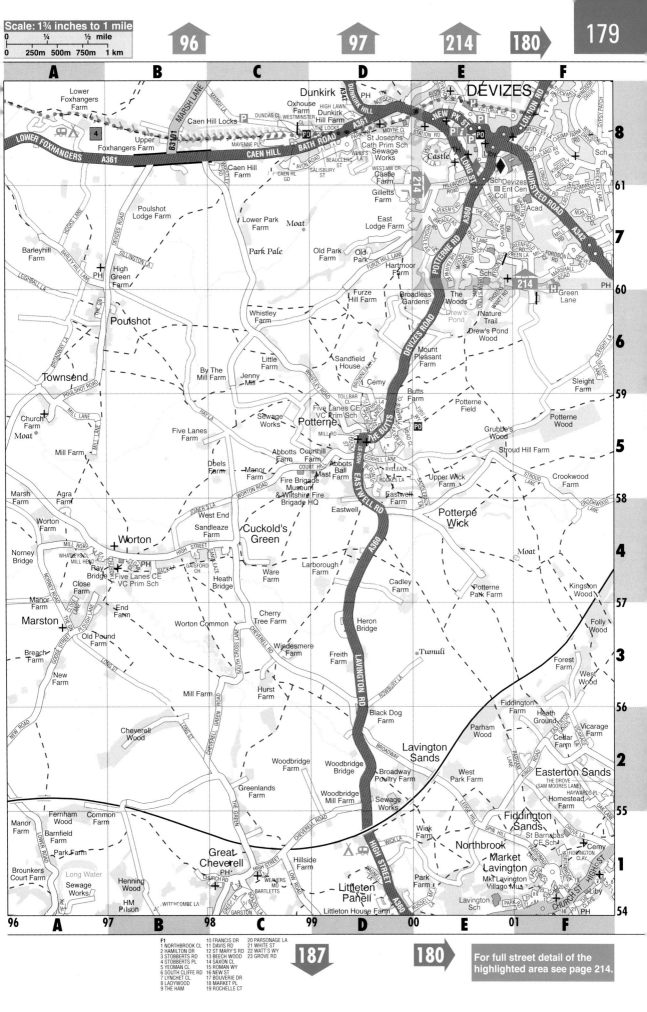

180

For full street detail of the highlighted area see page 214.

214 172

Scale: 1¾ inches to 1 mile

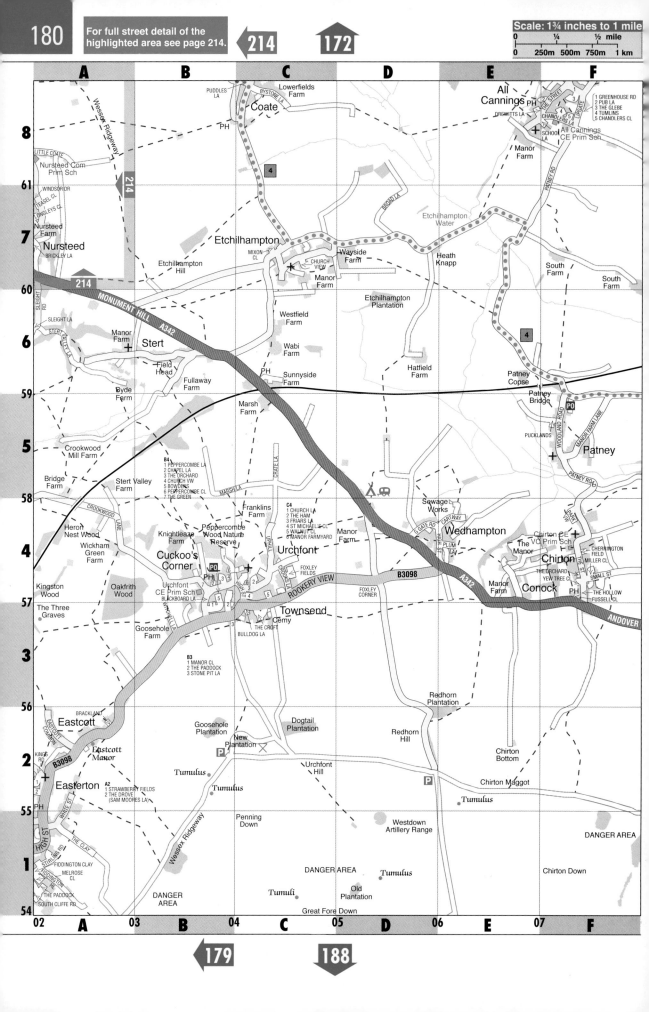

A    B    C    D    E    F

8

Honeystreet
RECTORY CL
Stanton Bridge
PH
Honey Street Farm
45
Hurst's Farm
Sands Farm
THE SANDS
HURST'S LA
Mill Farm
Hanging Stone
Stanton Dairy
PH
SMITHY LA
West End
CHAPEL LA
Church Farm
CHURCH FARM LA
Woodborough
Woodborough Hill
Tawsmead Copse
Picked Hill
Oak Farm
Manor Farm
Wide Water
Kennet & Avon Canal
Lambpit Copse
Cocklebury Farm
Swanborough Tump
Frith Copse
Field Farm
PRIMROSE LA
Rose Farm
DRAGON LANE
4
Bungalow Farm
Woodborough CE Aided Prim Sch
Brow Farm
Nursery Farm
The Plantation
New Barn Farm
Cemy
Bottle Farm
MARTIN'S CL
Stoke Farm
WOODBOROUGH ROAD
Broad Street
PH
Bottlesford
Beechingstoke
Limber Stone Bridge
Mullins Farm
THE IVES
PUCKSHIPTON
GORES LA
Cemy
Vale of Pewsey
STITCHING'S LA
Hilcott
Wilds Farm
Hilcott Farm
Manningford Bohune Common
Locl Wood
Manningford Bruce
CHURCH LA
WICK LANE
YARD'S LANE
WILSFORD ROAD
Butts Farm
North Newton Wood
Manningford Bohune
Hatfield Copse
Marden Henge
Hatfield Farm
The Moors
HATFIELD
Puckshipton House
North Newnton
Manor House
Marden
PH
Sewage Works
Cruck End
CHURCH LA
Wilsford House
Wilsford
Cuttenham Farm
A345
Sports Ground
THE STREET
Woodbridge
Woodbridge
Wood Bridge
PH
PARK RD
River Avon
ROAD
A342
Hinderway Plantation
Coombe Cott
FRIDAY LA
Charlton
Cloud End
Rushall Bridge
France Farm
RUSHALL ROAD
PEWSEY ROAD
Scales Bridge
Castle Plantation
Marden Cowbag
Broadbury Banks
Strip Lynchets
Cleeve Hill
PH
THE GARDENS
Rushall
Rushall CE VA Prim Sch
CHURCH LANE
DEVIZES ROAD
GREEN WAY
Upavon
PEWSEY RD
VICARAGE LA
THE GDNS
Marden Copse
CHARLTON DROVE
HAWKER CE
CHAPEL LA
JARVIS ST
HIGH ST
PH
Pottery
VULCAN DR
GLOSTER CL
PO
FARRIERS FIELD
FAIRFIELD
DEVIZES RD
Marden Covert
Tumulus
Goddard's Cleeve
RUSHALL DROVE
Old Cleeve
ALEXANDER FIELDS
AVON SQ
ANDOVER ROAD
CASTERLEY CL
Sewage Works
Marden Down
Fox Covert
Wilsford Down
Earthwork Charlton Clump
Rushall Hill
Settlement
A345
A342

61
7
60
6
59
5
58
4
57
3
56
2
55
1
54

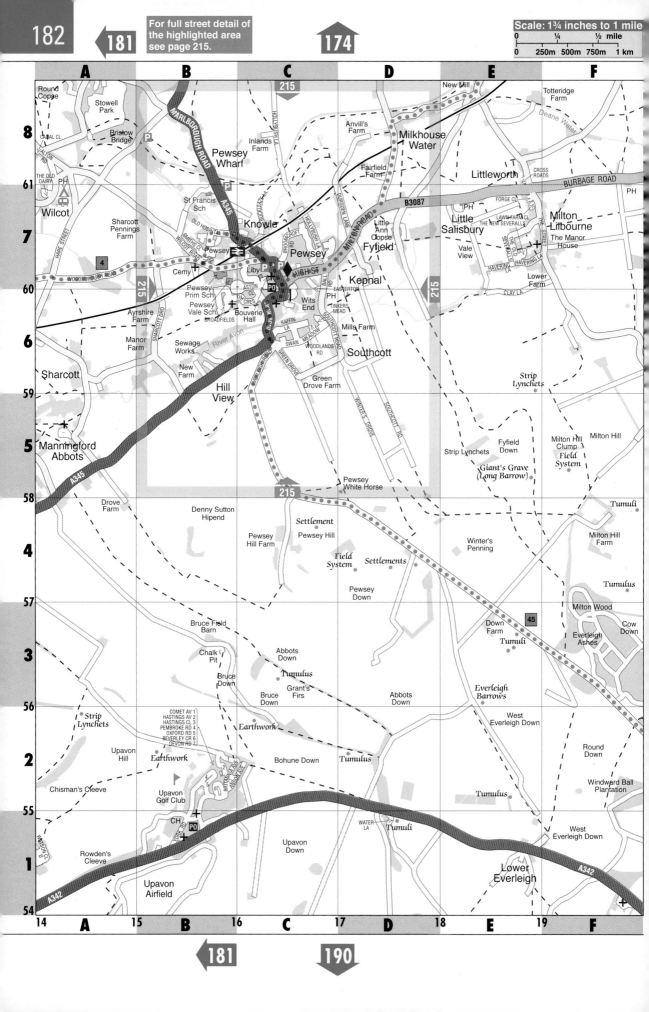

182
181
For full street detail of the highlighted area see page 215.
174
Scale: 1¾ inches to 1 mile
0    ¼    ½   mile
0  250m  500m  750m  1 km

**A** **B** **C** **D** **E** **F**

Round Copse
Stowell Park
MARLBOROUGH ROAD
215
New Mill
Totteridge Farm
Deane Water

**8**

Bristow Bridge
P
Pewsey Wharf
Inlands Farm
HOLLYBUSH LA
Anvill's Farm
Milkhouse Water
CANAL CL
WALTON RD
Littleworth
CROSS ROADS

**61**

THE OLD DAIRY
PH
Wilcot
P
St Francis Sch
Fairfield Farm
B3087
BURBAGE ROAD
PH
A345
OLD HOSPITAL RD
Knowle
DURSDEN LANE
PH
Little Salisbury
FORGE CL
THE NEW SEVERALLS
Milton Lilbourne

**7**

HARE STREET
Sharcott Pennings Farm
4
SMITHS CL
Pewsey
BROOKCROFT RD
HOLLYBUSH LA
Pewsey
MILTON ROAD
Little Ann Copse
Fyfield
THE STREET
The Manor House
WOODBOROUGH ROAD
WILCOT ROAD
Cemy
P P
Liby
HIGH ST
Vale View
HAVERING LA
THE OLD SEVERALLS
Lower Farm

**60**

215
Pewsey Prim Sch
ASTON CL
CRES
PO
Wits End
EASTERTON
Kepnal
BALL RD
CLAY LA
Ayrshire Farm
Pewsey Vale Sch
Bouverie Hall
BROADFIELDS
CLUB LA
RAFFIN LA
SOUTHCOTT ROAD
TINKERS MEAD
Mills Farm

**6**

Manor Farm
SHARCOTT DRO
Sewage Works
SWAN MEADOW
WOODLANDS RD
River Avon
New Farm
GREEN DROVE
Southcott
Sharcott
Hill View
Green Drove Farm
Strip Lynchets

**59**

Manningford Abbots
A345
Pewsey White Horse
WINTER'S DROVE
Strip Lynchets
Fyfield Down
Milton Hill Clump
Field System
Milton Hill

**5**

Drove Farm
215
Denny Sutton Hipend
Settlement
Pewsey Hill
Winter's Penning
Milton Hill Farm
Tumuli

**58**

Pewsey Hill Farm
Field System
Settlements
Pewsey Down
Down Farm
45
Milton Wood
Cow Down
Tumulus

**4**

Everleigh Ashes

**57**

Bruce Field Barn
Chalk Pit
Bruce Down
Abbots Down
Tumulus
Grant's Firs
Abbots Down
Everleigh Barrows
Tumuli

**3**

Bruce Down
Everleigh Ashes

**56**

Strip Lynchets
COMET AV 1
HASTINGS AV 2
HASTINGS CL 3
PEMBROKE RD 4
OXFORD RD 5
BEVERLEY CR 6
DEVON RD 7
Earthwork
West Everleigh Down
Round Down

**2**

Upavon Hill
Earthwork
BRITANNIA LANE
KINGSLEA AVE
Bohune Down
Tumulus
Tumulus
Windward Ball Plantation

Chisman's Cleeve
Upavon Golf Club
WATER LA
Tumuli

**55**

CH
PO
WOODS CL D
WATER LA
WATER LA
West Everleigh Down

**1**

WILSON CL D
Rowden's Cleeve
Upavon Down
Lower Everleigh
A342
A342
Upavon Airfield

**54**

14  **A**  15  **B**  16  **C**  17  **D**  18  **E**  19  **F**

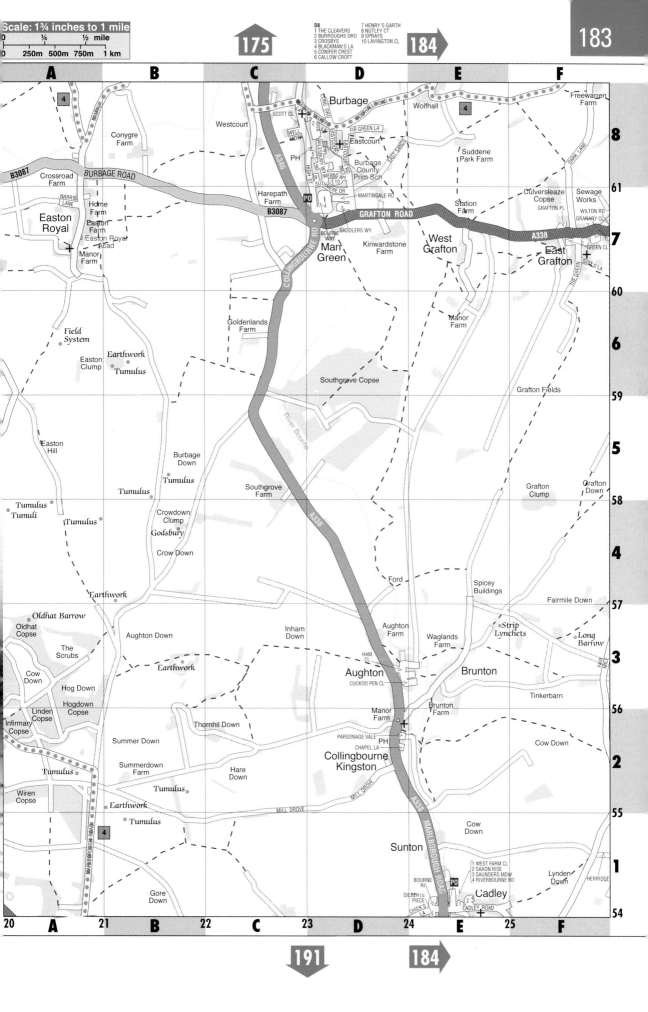

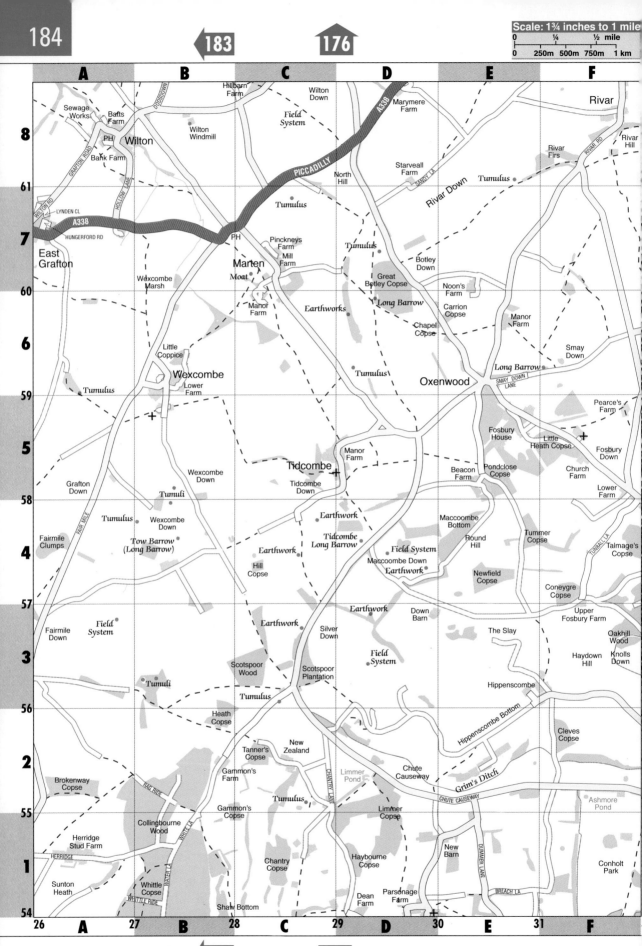

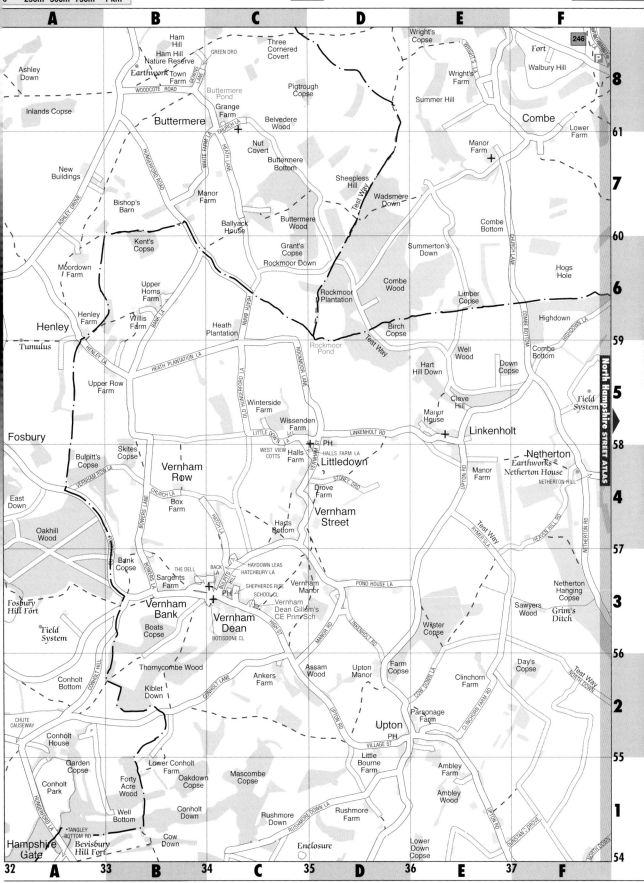

| A | B | C | D | E | F |

**8** Ashley Down, Inlands Copse, Ham Hill, Ham Hill Nature Reserve, Earthwork, Town Farm, Green Dro, Three Cornered Covert, Pigtrough Copse, Wright's Copse, Wright's Farm, Summer Hill, Fort, Walbury Hill, 246, P

**61** Woodcote Road, Buttermere, Buttermere Pond, Grange Farm, Belvedere Wood, Combe, Lower Farm

**7** New Buildings, Bishop's Barn, Manor Farm, Nut Covert, Buttermere Bottom, Sheepless Hill, Wadsmere Down, Test Way, Manor Farm

**60** Moordown Farm, Kent's Copse, Ballyack House, Buttermere Wood, Grant's Copse, Combe Bottom, Combe Wood, Summerton's Down, Hogs Hole

**6** Upper Horns Farm, Henley Farm, Willis Farm, Heath Plantation, Rockmoor Down, Rockmoor Plantation, Combe Wood, Limber Copse, Highdown, Combe Bottom, Highdown La

**59** Henley, Tumulus, Heath Plantation La, Rockmoor Pond, Test Way, Birch Copse, Well Wood, Down Copse, Combe Bottom, Highdown Rd

**5** Upper Row Farm, Old Hungerford La, Winterside Farm, Wissenden Farm, Little Down La, Linkenholt Rd, Hart Hill Down, Manor House, Cleve Hill, Linkenholt, Field System

**58** Fosbury, Bulpitt's Copse, Skites Copse, West View Cotts, Halls Farm, PH, Littledown, Netherton Earthworks, Netherton House, Netherton Hill

**4** East Down, Oakhill Wood, Vernham Row, Church La, Box Farm, Hatch La, Harts Bottom, Drove Farm, Vernham Street, Stoney Dro, Upton Rd, Manor Farm, Heaven Hill Rd, Netherton Rd

**57** Test Way, Rymer's La, Netherton Hanging Copse

**3** Fosbury Hill Fort, Bank Copse, Bowers La, The Dell, Sargents Farm, Back La, Bulpitt's Hill, PH, Haydown Leas, Hatchbury La, Shepherds Rise, School Cl, Vernham Manor, Vernham Dean Gillum's CE Prim Sch, High St, Pond House La, Linkenholt Rd, Wilster Copse, Sawyers Wood, Grim's Ditch

**56** Vernham Bank, Boats Copse, Vernham Dean, Botisdone Cl, Manor Rd

**2** Conholt Bottom, Conholt Hill, Thornycombe Wood, Kiblet Down, Conholt Lane, Ankers Farm, Assam Wood, Upton Manor, Farm Copse, Cow Down La, Clinchorn Farm, Clinchorn Farm Rd, Day's Copse, Test Way, North Down

**55** Chute Causeway, Conholt House, Parsonage Farm, Upton, PH, Village St, Ambley Farm

**1** Garden Copse, Conholt Park, Forty Acre Wood, Lower Conholt Farm, Oakdown Copse, Mascombe Copse, Conholt Down, Rushmore Down, Rushmore Down La, Rushmore Farm, Little Bourne Farm, Ambley Wood, Dunstal Drove, Upton Rd

**54** Hampshire Gate, Hungerford La, Tangley Bottom Rd, Bevisbury Hill Fort, Well Bottom, Cow Down, Enclosure, Lower Down Copse, North Down, Field System

| 32 | A | 33 | B | 34 | C | 35 | D | 36 | E | 37 | F |

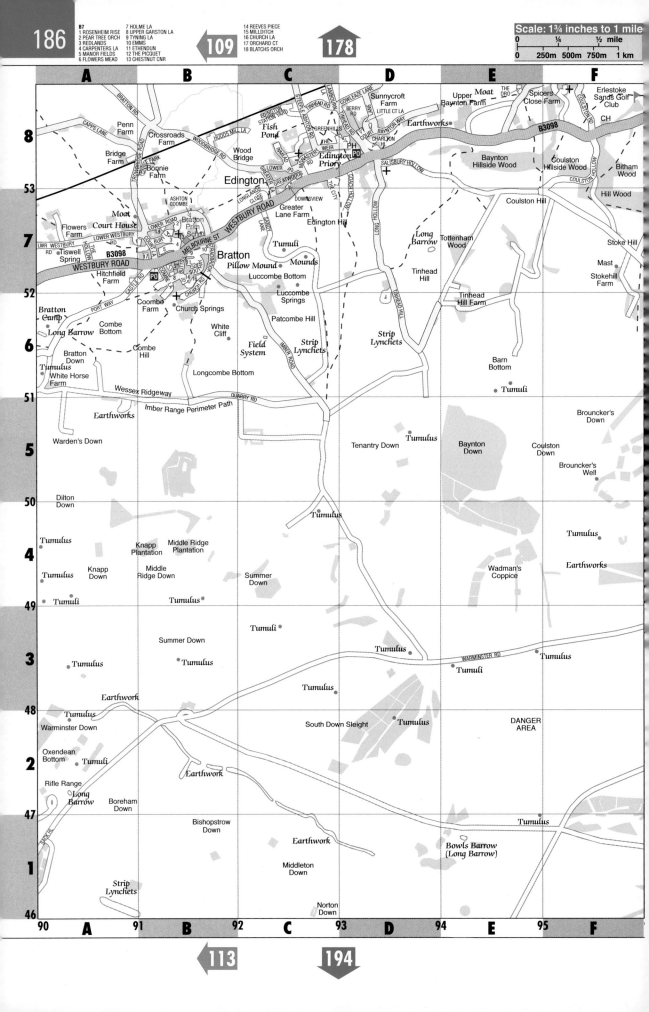

Scale: 1¾ inches to 1 mile
0   ¼   ½ mile
0  250m 500m 750m  1 km

B8
1 WITCHCOMBE CL.

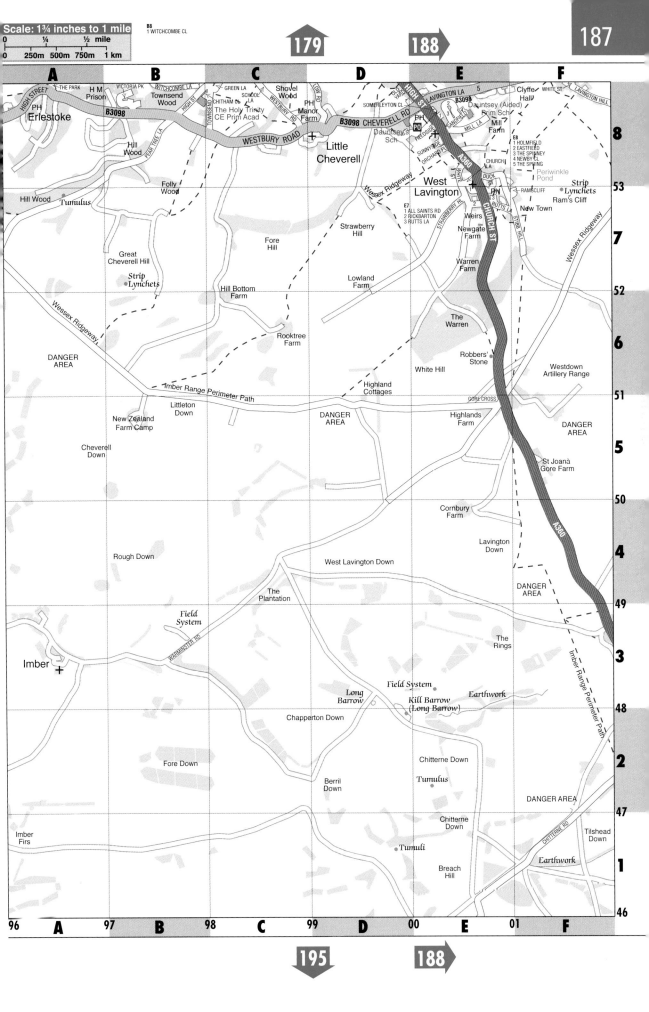

A B C D E F

Wessex Ridgeway

THE CLAY

LAVINGTON HILL

Gibbet Knoll

Great Fore Down

Long Ditch

Earthwork

8

Westdown Artillery Range

Little Hill

53

Wilsford Down

Church Hill

7

Urchfont Down

52

Field System

DANGER AREA

Warren Down

Tumulus

Westdown Artillery Range

Black Heath

6

Earthwork

Ell Barrow (Long Barrow)

51

New Copse Down

Ball Down

Grove Down

Tumulus

Summer Down

Enclosure

Westdown Artillery Range

5

New Copse

Candown Copse

Can Down

50

Enclosure

Rushall Down

DANGER AREA

Barrow Plantation

Long Barrow

East Down

4

West Down Plantation

East Down Plantation

Honeydown Bottom

49

Westdown Artillery Range

Earthwork

Field System

Westdown Artillery Range

3

DANGER AREA

Earthwork

St Thomas A Becket CE Aided Prim Sch

NORTH CROFT

VIMBER PLACE

Tilshead

Earthwork

West Down

48

Horse Down

BACK LA

CANDOWN

PH

A RD

MARVINS CL

Westdown Camp

Nut Park

Orcheston Down

Long Barrow

Imber Range Perimeter Path

CHITTERNE RD

LODGE VIEW

CHAPTER RISE

HIGH STREET

West End

Pembroke Farm

Sewage Works

Long Plantation

Earthwork

2

Earthwork

Silver Barrow

Halfmoon Copse

Tilshead Down

47

White Barrow (Long Barrow)

NT

Orcheston Down

Tumulus

Long Barrow

1

Copehill Down

Imber Range Perimeter Path

Copehill Plantation

A360

DANGER AREA

DANGER AREA

Gallops

46

02 A 03 B 04 C 05 D 06 E 07 F

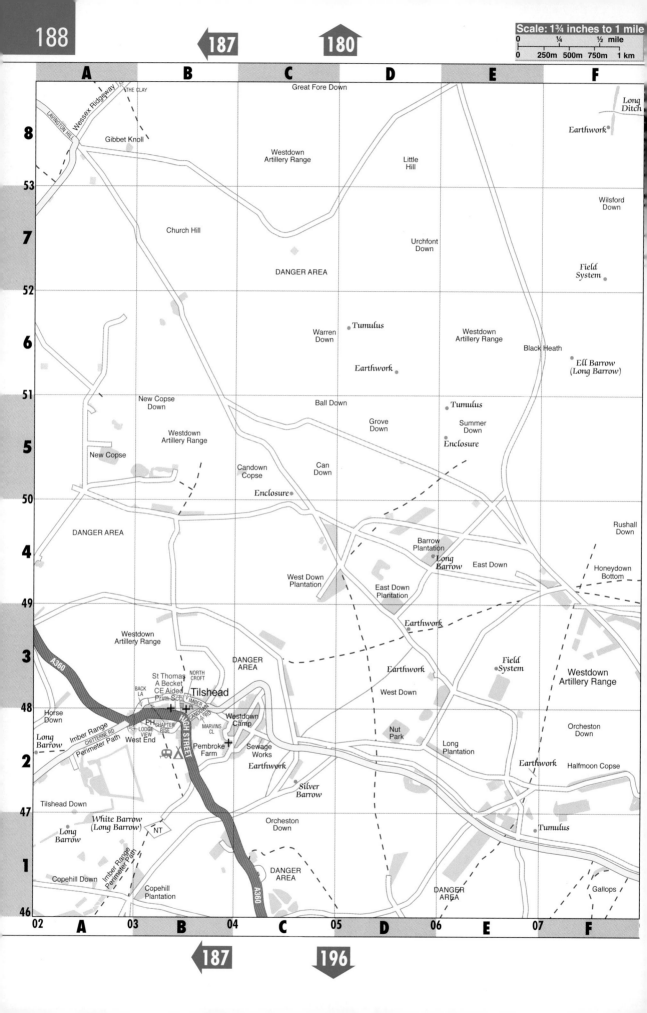

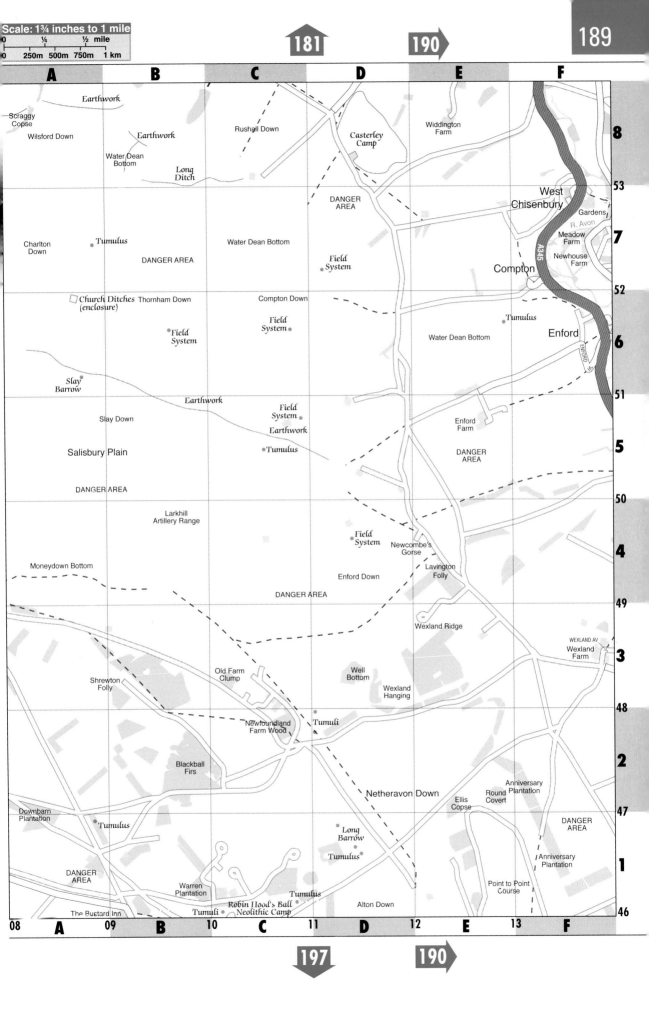

Scale: 1¾ inches to 1 mile

0   ¼   ½ mile
0  250m 500m 750m  1 km

181
190

**A**   **B**   **C**   **D**   **E**   **F**

Earthwork

Scraggy
Copse

Wilsford Down

Earthwork

Rushall Down

Casterley
Camp

Widdington
Farm

**8**

Water Dean
Bottom

Long
Ditch

DANGER
AREA

West
Chisenbury

**53**

Gardens

R. Avon

Charlton
Down

Tumulus

DANGER AREA

Water Dean Bottom

Field
System

Meadow
Farm

Newhouse
Farm

**7**

Compton

**52**

Church Ditches
(enclosure)

Thornham Down

Compton Down

Field
System

Water Dean Bottom

Tumulus

Enford

**6**

Field
System

Field
System

Slay
Barrow

Earthwork

Field
System

Enford
Farm

**51**

Slay Down

Earthwork

DANGER
AREA

**5**

Salisbury Plain

Tumulus

DANGER AREA

**50**

Larkhill
Artillery Range

Field
System

Newcombe's
Gorse

**4**

Moneydown Bottom

Enford Down

Lavington
Folly

DANGER AREA

Wexland Ridge

WEXLAND AV

Wexland
Farm

**3**

Shrewton
Folly

Old Farm
Clump

Well
Bottom

Wexland
Hanging

**48**

Newfoundland
Farm Wood

Tumuli

Blackball
Firs

Netheravon Down

Anniversary
Plantation

Round
Covert

**2**

Ellis
Copse

Downbarn
Plantation

Tumulus

Long
Barrow

Tumulus

DANGER
AREA

**47**

Anniversary
Plantation

**1**

DANGER
AREA

Warren
Plantation

Tumulus

Robin Hood's Ball
Neolithic Camp

Tumulus

Point to Point
Course

The Bustard Inn

Tumulus

Alton Down

**46**

08   **A**   09   **B**   10   **C**   11   **D**   12   **E**   13   **F**

197
190

Scale: 1¾ inches to 1 mile

0   ¼   ½ mile

0   250m   500m   750m   1 km

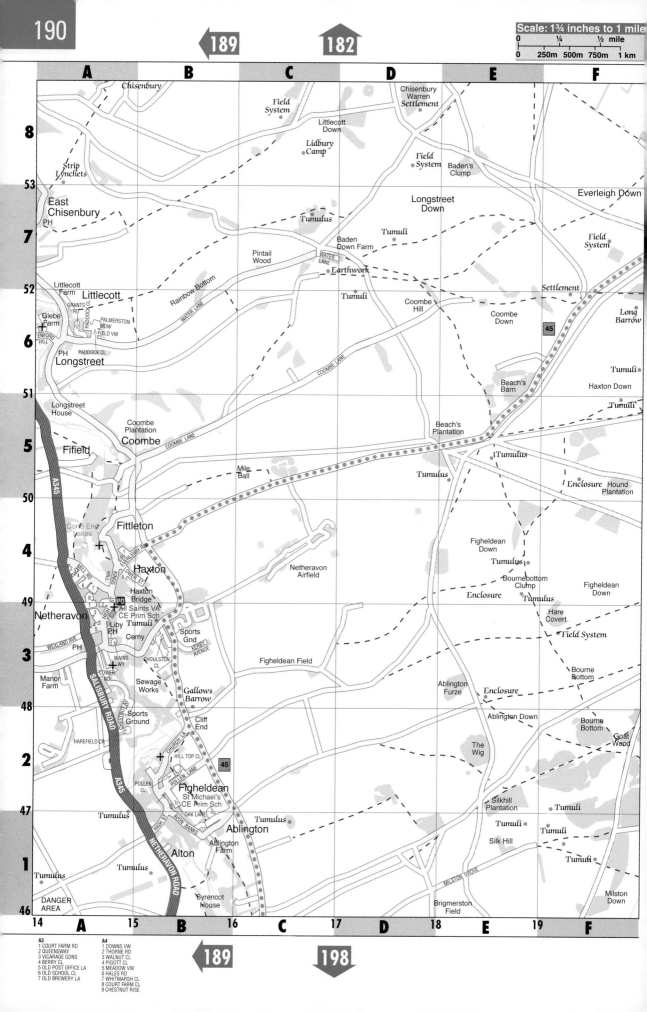

A   B   C   D   E   F

Chisenbury

8

Field System

Chisenbury Warren Settlement

Littlecott Down

Lidbury Camp

Field System

Baden's Clump

53

Strip Lynchets

East Chisenbury

PH

7

Everleigh Down

Longstreet Down

Tumulus

Tumuli

Field System

Baden Down Farm

Pintail Wood

WATER LANE

Earthwork

Settlement

52

Littlecott Farm

Littlecott

Rainbow Bottom

WATER LANE

Tumuli

Coombe Hill

Coombe Down

45

Long Barrow

GRANTS RD

PADDOCK CL

Glebe Farm

ENFORD HILL

PALMERSTON MDW

FIELD VW

6

PH

PADDOCK CL

Longstreet

COOMBE LANE

Tumuli

Haxton Down

Beach's Barn

51

Longstreet House

Beach's Plantation

5

Coombe Plantation

COOMBE LANE

Coombe

Fifield

Tumulus

Tumuli

Mile Ball

Tumulus

Enclosure   Hound Plantation

50

Corse End Lakes

Fittleton

EVERLEIGH RD

4

Figheldean Down

Tumulus

Bournebottom Clump

Figheldean Down

MILL RD

KINGS HILL

LOWER ST

Haxton

Netheravon Airfield

Enclosure

Tumulus

49

Haxton Bridge

All Saints VA CE Prim Sch

Tumuli

Hare Covert

Netheravon

PO

Liby PH

Cemy

KERBY AVENUE

Sports Gnd

Field System

3

WEXLAND AVE

PH

WAINS WY

LOWER RD

CHOULSTON CL

SALISBURY ROAD

Sewage Works

Figheldean Field

Ablington Furze

Enclosure

Bourne Bottom

Manor Farm

CHESTNUT LA

Gallows Barrow

Ablington Down

Bourne Bottom

Goat Wood

48

HAREFIELD CR

Sports Ground

Cliff End

The Wig

2

HILL TOP CL

45

A345

POLLEN CL

POLLEN LANE

CHURCH LA

Figheldean

St Michael's CE Prim Sch

Silkhill Plantation

Tumuli

47

HIGH ST

AVON BANKS

OAK LANE

Tumulus

Ablington

Tumulus

Tumuli

Tumuli

Silk Hill

Tumulus

Alton

Ablington Farm

NETHERAVON ROAD

1

Tumulus

Tumulus

MILSTON DROVE

Tumuli

46

DANGER AREA

Syrencot House

Brigmerston Field

Milston Down

14   A   15   B   16   C   17   D   18   E   19   F

A3
1 COURT FARM RD
2 QUEENSWAY
3 VICARAGE GDNS
4 BERRY CL
5 OLD POST OFFICE LA
6 OLD SCHOOL CL
7 OLD BREWERY LA

A4
1 DOWNS VW
2 THORNE RD
3 WALNUT CL
4 PIGOTT CL
5 MEADOW VW
6 HALES RD
7 WHITMARSH CL
8 COURT FARM CL
9 CHESTNUT RISE

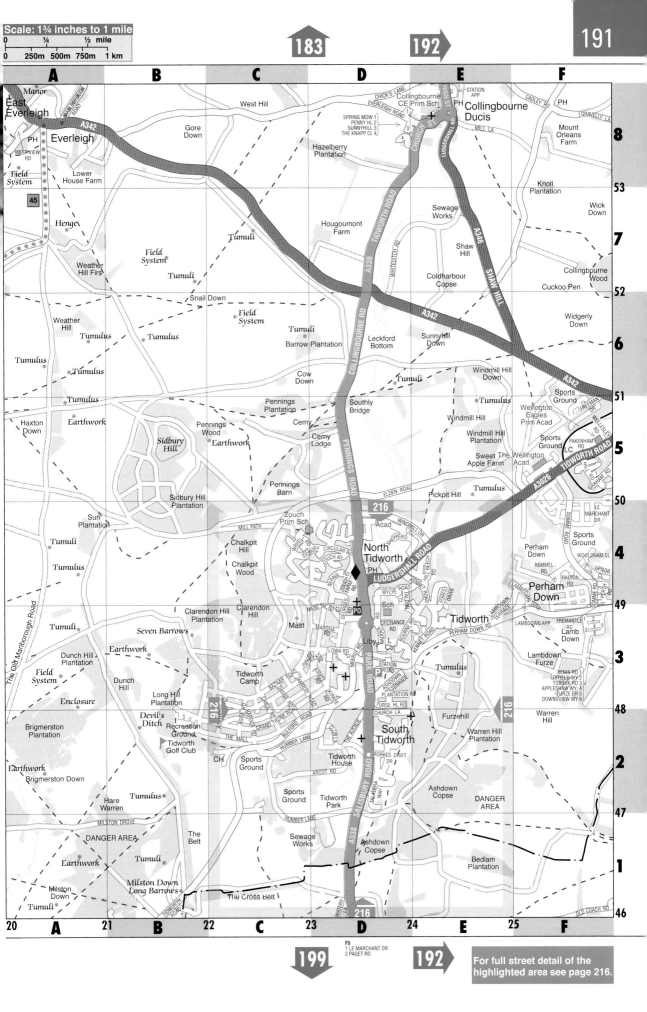

183
192
199
192

Scale: 1¾ inches to 1 mile

0   ¼   ½ mile
0  250m  500m  750m  1 km

**A B C D E F**

**East Everleigh**
Manor

**Everleigh**
PH
WEST VIEW RD
Field System
45
Henge

West Hill

Gore Down

Hazelberry Plantation

**Collingbourne Ducis**
Collingbourne CE Prim Sch
STATION APP
PH
CADLEY RD
PH
GRAVELLY LA
Mount Orleans Farm

SPRING MDW 1
PENNY HL 2
SUNNYHILL 3
THE KNAPP CL 4

CHICK'S LANE
EVERLEIGH ROAD

Knoll Plantation

Wick Down

Lower House Farm

Weather Hill Firs

Field System

Tumuli

Hougoumont Farm

Sewage Works

Shaw Hill

Collingbourne Wood

Coldharbour Copse

Cuckoo Pen

Weather Hill

Tumulus

Tumulus

Snail Down

Field System

Tumuli

Barrow Plantation

Leckford Bottom

Sunnyhill Down

Widgerly Down

Tumulus

Tumulus

Tumulus

Cow Down

Tumuli

Windmill Hill Down

Sports Ground

Haxton Down

Earthwork

Pennings Plantation

Cemy

Southly Bridge

Windmill Hill

Windmill Hill Plantation

Wellington Eagles Prim Acad

Sports Ground

FREEMAN RD
WELLESLEY RD

Sidbury Hill

Pennings Wood

Earthwork

Cemy Lodge

PAKENHAM RD
LC

**TIDWORTH ROAD**

Pennings Barn

Sweet Apple Farm

The Wellington Acad

GRAHAM RD

Sun Plantation

Sidbury Hill Plantation

MILL PATH

Zouch Prim Sch

Acad

Pickpit Hill

Tumulus

ELDEN ROAD

A3026

LE MARCHANT DR

Tumuli

Tumuli

Chalkpit Hill

Chalkpit Wood

SIDBURY RD
WAVENY RD
CIRCULAR RD
ZOUCH AV
NETAVL RD

WINDMILL DR
SHEPPERD

216

**North Tidworth**
PH

**LUDGERSHALL ROAD**

KENNET ROAD

Perham Down

Sports Ground

KEMMEL RD

HALTON RD

**Perham Down**

UPNOR CL

Clarendon Hill Plantation

Clarendon Hill

Mast

MARGHA RD
GEORGES RD
ZOUCH FARM RD

WYLYE RD

Sch

KENNET ROAD

BOURNE RD
FOREST DRIVE

**Tidworth**

LAMBDOWN TERRACE

LAMBDOWN APP

Lamb Down

FREMANTLE RD

BENIN RD 1
LYFIELD WY 2
TOBRUK RD 3
APPLESHAW WY 4
FURZE DR 5
DOWNSVIEW WY 6

Tumuli

Tumulus

Seven Barrows

Earthwork

Clarendon Hill

BAZAAR ROAD
NADDER RD

Liby
L Ctr

ORDNANCE RD

PERHAM DOWN RD

Lambdown Furze

Dunch Hill Plantation

Dunch Hill

Long Hill Plantation

Devil's Ditch

Recreation Ground

Tidworth Camp

216

AGRA RD
ASSAM RD
JELLALABAD
LAMROD RD
BULFORD RD

PATRICIA RD
NIGER RD

STATION ROAD

ASHDOWN TERRACE

PLANTATION RD

FURSE HL RD

Tumulus

Warren Hill

Brigmerston Plantation

Field System

Enclosure

Tidworth Golf Club
CH

THE MALL
HUMBER LANE

Sports Ground

Tidworth House

RORKES DRIFT DR

CHURCH LA

**South Tidworth**

Furzehill

Warren Hill Plantation

216

Earthwork

Brigmerston Down

Hare Warren

Tumulus

MILSTON DROVE

The Belt

Sports Ground

Tidworth Park

ARCOT RD

SALISBURY ROAD
THE AVENUE

TALAVERA WAY

Ashdown Copse

DANGER AREA

**DANGER AREA**

Earthwork

Tumuli

Milston Down Long Barrows

Sewage Works

HUMBER LANE

WATERY LA

Ashdown Copse

Bedlam Plantation

Tumuli

TIDWORTH ROAD

The Cross Belt

216

OLD COACH RD

**20 A 21 B 22 C 23 D 24 E 25 F**

F5
1 LE MARCHANT DR
2 PAGET RD

For full street detail of the highlighted area see page 216.

Scale: 1¾ inches to 1 mile

0   ¼   ½ mile
0   250m   500m   750m   1 km

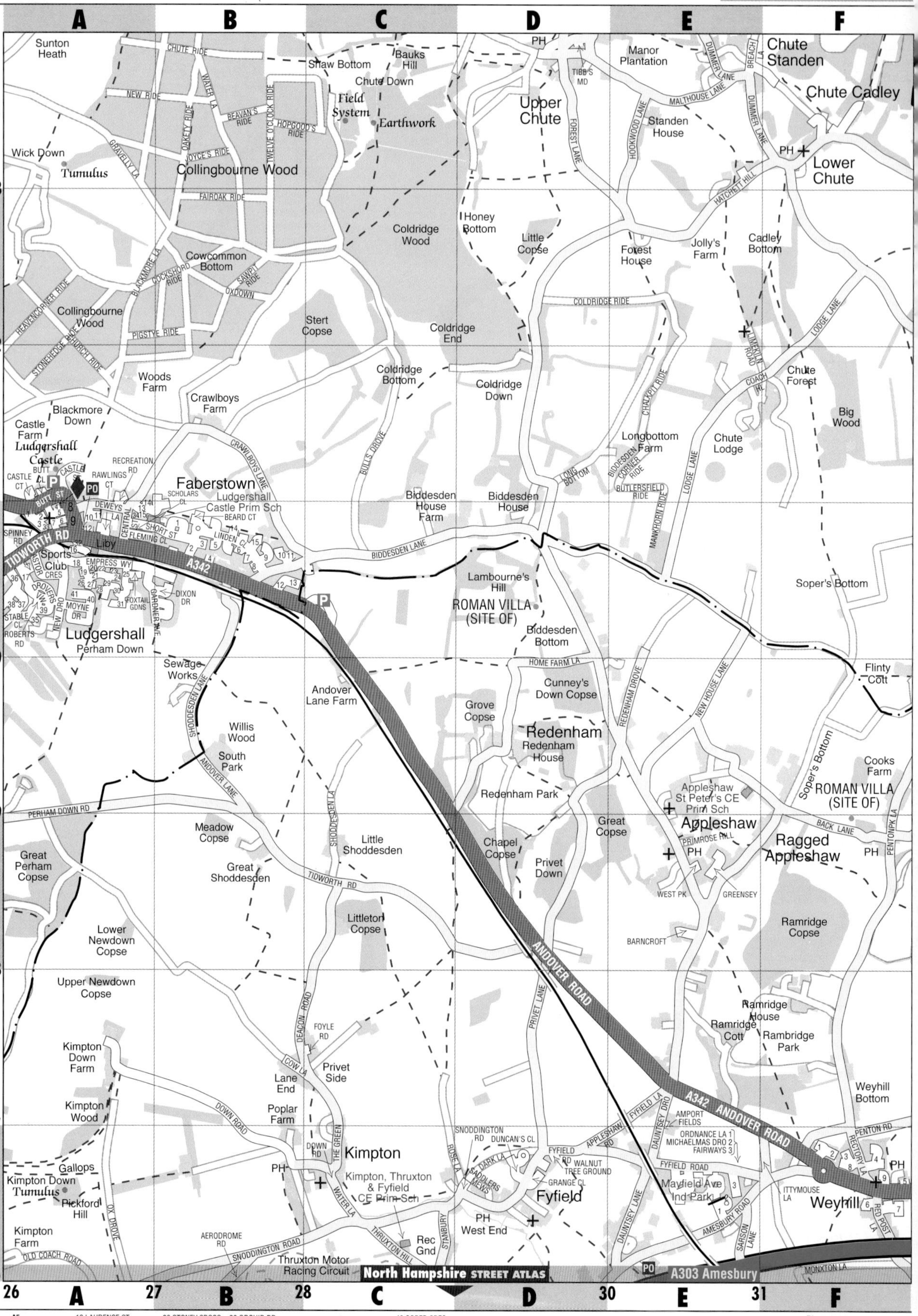

North Hampshire STREET ATLAS

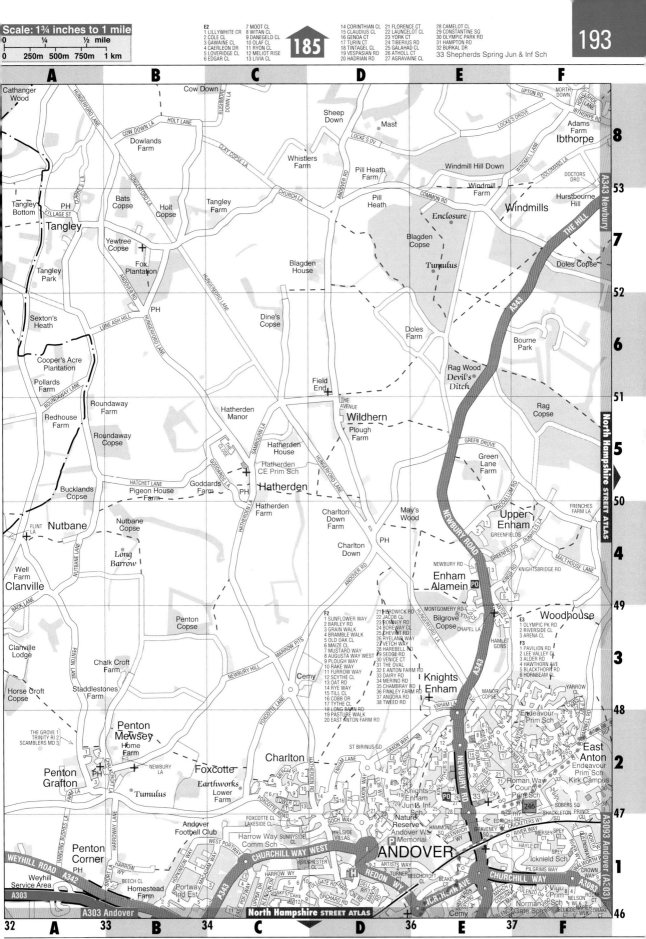

E2
1 LILLYWHITE CR
2 COLE CL
3 GAWAINE DR
4 CAERLEON DR
5 LOVERIDGE CL
6 EDGAR CL

7 MOOT CL
8 WITAN CL
9 DANEGELD CL
10 OLAF CL
11 RYON CL
12 MELIOT RISE
13 LIVIA CL

14 CORINTHIAN CL
15 CLAUDIUS CL
16 GENOA CT
17 TURIN CT
18 TINTAGEL CL
19 VESPASIAN CT
20 HADRIAN CL

21 FLORENCE CT
22 LAUNCELOT CL
23 YORK CT
24 TIBERIUS RD
25 GALAHAD CL
26 ATHOLL CT
27 AGRAVAINE CT

28 CAMELOT CL
29 CONSTANTINE SQ
30 OLYMPIC PARK RD
31 HAMPTON RD
32 BURKAL DR

33 Shepherds Spring Jun & Inf Sch

**F2**
1 SUNFLOWER WAY
2 BARLEY RD
3 GRAIN WALK
4 BRAMBLE WALK
5 OLD OAK CL
6 MAIZE CL
7 MUSTARD WAY
8 AUGUSTA WAY WEST
9 PLOUGH WAY
10 RAKE WAY
11 FURROW WAY
12 SCYTHE CL
13 OAT RD
14 RYE WAY
15 TILL CL
16 COBB DR
17 TYTHE CL
18 LONG BARN RD
19 PASTURE WALK
20 EAST ANTON FARM RD

21 HARDWICK RD
22 JACOB CL
23 ROMNEY RD
24 BOREWAY CL
25 CHEVIOT RD
26 RYELAND WAY
27 VETCH WAY
28 HAREBELL RD
29 SEDGE RD
30 VENICE CT
31 THE OVAL
32 E ANTON FARM RD
33 DAIRY RD
34 MERINO RD
35 CHAMBRAY CL
36 FINLEY CHASE WY
37 ANGORA RD
38 TWEED RD

E3
1 OLYMPIC PK RD
2 RIVERSIDE CL
3 ARENA CL

F3
1 PAVILION RD
2 LEE VALLEY CL
3 ALDER RD
4 HAWTHORN AVE
5 BLACKTHORN RD
6 HORNBEAM CL

218

B1
1 SMEATON RD
2 REITH WY
3 JOULE RD
4 WHITTLE RD
5 ROYCE CL
6 TELFORD GATE

C1
1 STERLING PK
2 CAXTON CL
3 MITCHELL CL
4 WATT CL
5 CHAUCER AV
6 MILTON AV
7 SOPWITH PK
8 LAWNS CL
9 MAY TREE RD

10 APPLE TREE GR
11 STEPHENSON CL
12 THE DROVE

C2
1 BRANCASTER AV
2 BRADWELL CL
3 RICHBOROUGH DR
4 ETHELBERT DR
5 HENGEST CL
6 RECULVER WY
7 BEDE DR
8 PORCHESTER CL
9 AUGUSTINE WY

10 HOME FARM GDNS
11 LITCHFIELD CL
12 BARTON CL
13 DACRE CL

D1
1 GAINSBOROUGH CT
2 STUBBS CT
3 REYNOLDS CT
4 SUTHERLAND CT
5 ALFRED GDNS
6 ST ALPHEGE GDNS
7 ST SWITHIN WY
8 ST BIRSTAN GDNS

D2
1 MARSUM CL
2 OLD ENGLISH DR
3 JUTLAND CR
4 RUNE DR
5 MONEYER RD
6 ANDEFERAS RD
7 ALDRIN CL
8 BORKUM CL
9 CUXHAVEN WAY

D4
1 HAMBURG CL
11 HOLLAND DR
12 MINDEN CL
13 ST THOMAS CL
14 COLLINS CL
15 ARMSTRONG RISE
16 ALTONA GDNS
18 EMDEN RD
19 VERDEN WAY

20 FLENSBURG CL
21 BREMEN GDNS
22 LUBECK DR
23 HATTEM PLACE
24 WETHERBY GDNS
25 PEAKE WAY

E4
1 WESTON CT
2 ATHLONE CT
3 LANDALE CT
4 ALAMEIN RD
5 TOBRUK CL

F1
1 JERVIS CT
2 SOMERVILLE CT
3 TOVEY CT
4 LONDON RD
5 MADRID RD
6 TOLEDO GROVE
7 BEAULIEU CT
8 GRANADA PL
9 WEST WAY

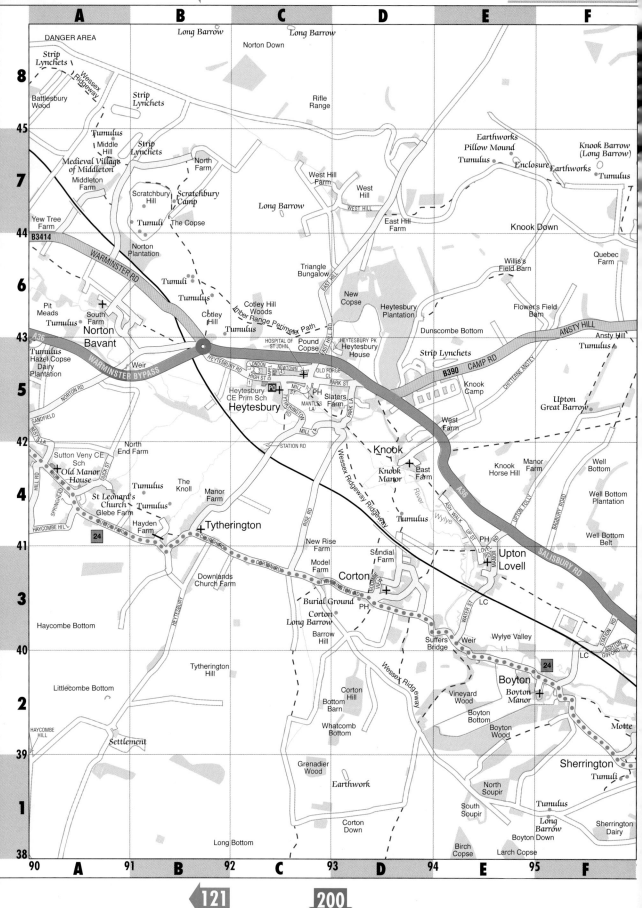

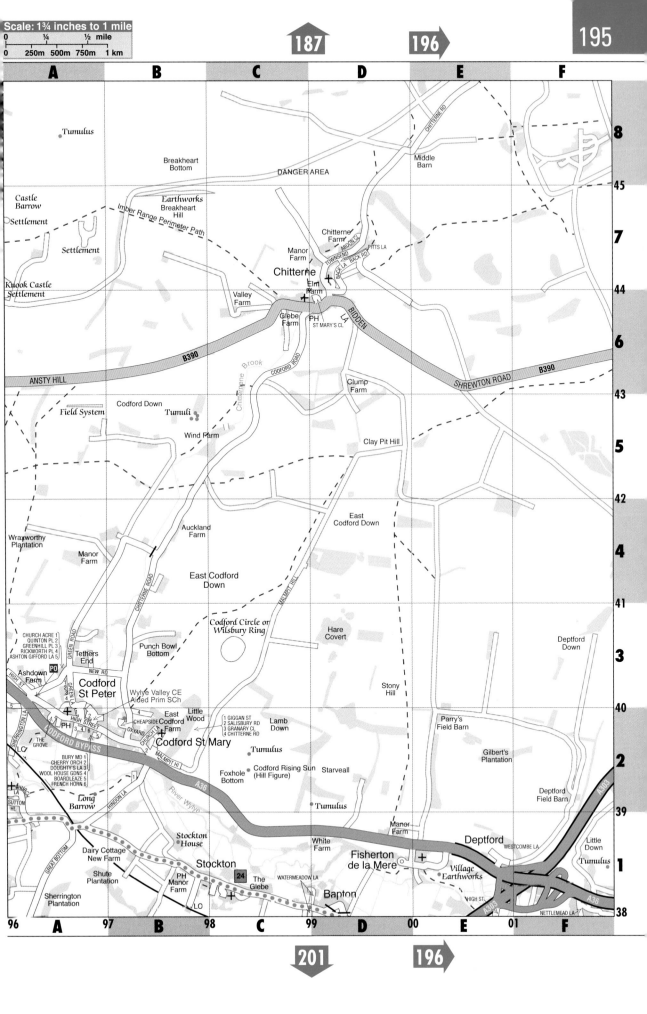

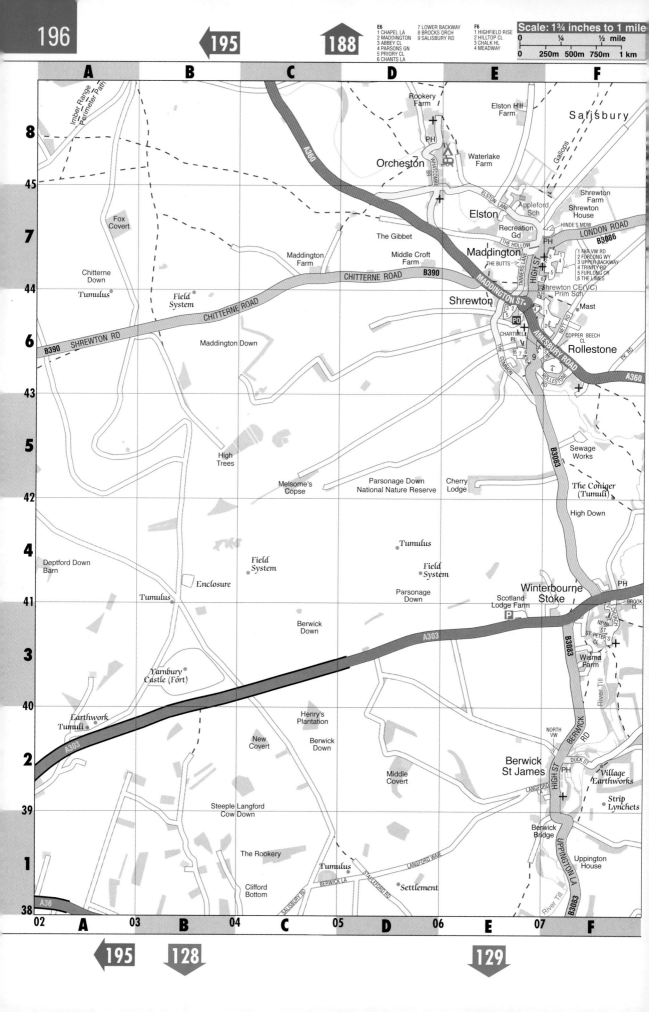

195
188

E6
1 CHAPEL LA
2 MADDINGTON
3 ABBEY CL
4 PARSONS GN
5 PRIORY CL
6 CHANTS LA

7 LOWER BACKWAY
8 BROCKS ORCH
9 SALISBURY RD

F6
1 HIGHFIELD RISE
2 HILLTOP CL
3 CHALK HL
4 MEADWAY

**Scale: 1¾ inches to 1 mile**

0      ¼      ½      mile
0   250m   500m   750m   1 km

## Map labels

Imber Range Perimeter Path

Rookery Farm

Elston Hill Farm

Salisbury

Orcheston

PH

Waterlake Farm

Shrewton Farm

Fox Covert

ELSTON LANE

Appleford Sch

Shrewton House

Elston

Recreation Gd

Shrewton

The Gibbet

Maddington Farm

Maddington

PH

LONDON ROAD

B3086

Chitterne Down

Middle Croft Farm

THE HOLLOW

THE BUTTS

HINDE'S MDW

1 FAR VW RD
2 FURLONG WY
3 UPPER BACKWAY
4 TRINITY RD
5 FURLONG CR
6 THE LIMES

Tumulus

CHITTERNE ROAD

B390

Field System

Shrewton CE (VC) Prim Sch

Shrewton

TANNERS LA

HIGH ST

Mast

B390  SHREWTON RD

Maddington Down

MADDINGTON ST

CHARTWELL PL

PO

Copper Beech Cl

Rollestone

High Trees

THE COMMON

AMESBURY ROAD

A360

ROLLESTONE RD

PK RD

B3083

Sewage Works

Melsome's Copse

Parsonage Down National Nature Reserve

Cherry Lodge

The Coniger (Tumuli)

High Down

Deptford Down Barn

Field System

Tumulus

Field System

Winterbourne Stoke

PH

Enclosure

Parsonage Down

Scotland Lodge Farm

P

NEW ST

CHURCH

BROOK CL

ST PETER'S CL

B3083

Tumulus

Berwick Down

A303

Wisma Farm

River Till

Yarnbury Castle (Fort)

Henry's Plantation

NORTH VW

BERWICK RD

Earthwork

Tumuli

New Covert

Berwick Down

Berwick St James

HIGH ST

PH

DUCK ST

Village Earthworks

Middle Covert

LANGFORD RD

Strip Lynchets

Steeple Langford Cow Down

Berwick Bridge

UPPINGTON LA

Uppington House

The Rookery

Tumulus

LANGFORD WA

Settlement

Clifford Bottom

SALISBURY RD

BERWICK LA

STAPLEFORD RD

River Till

B3083

A36

A360

195
128
129

Grid references: A B C D E F (columns), 38 39 40 41 42 43 44 45 (rows), 02 03 04 05 06 07

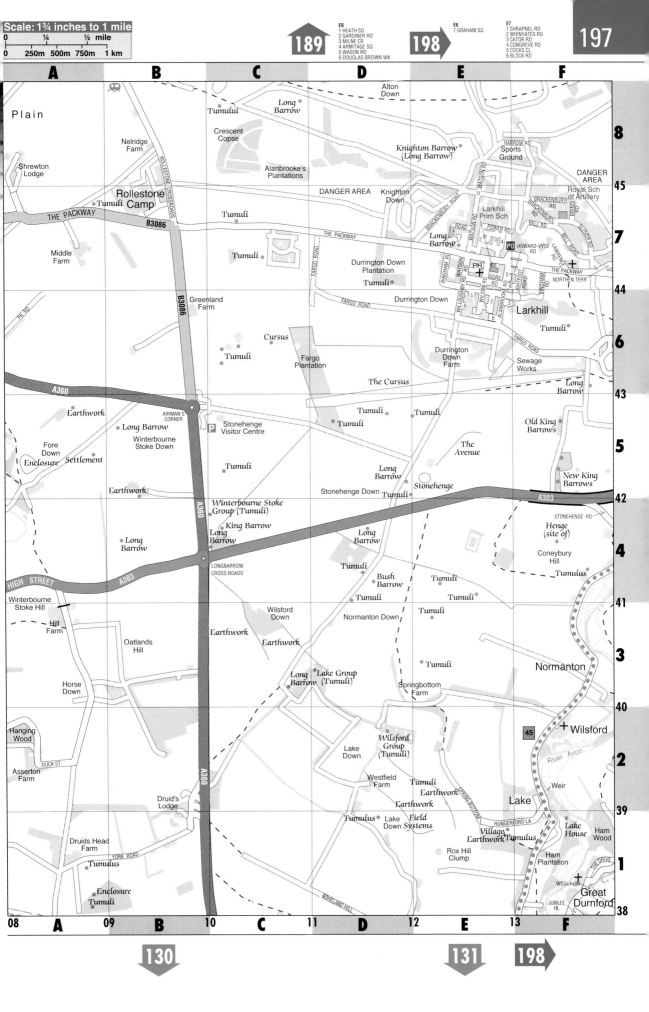

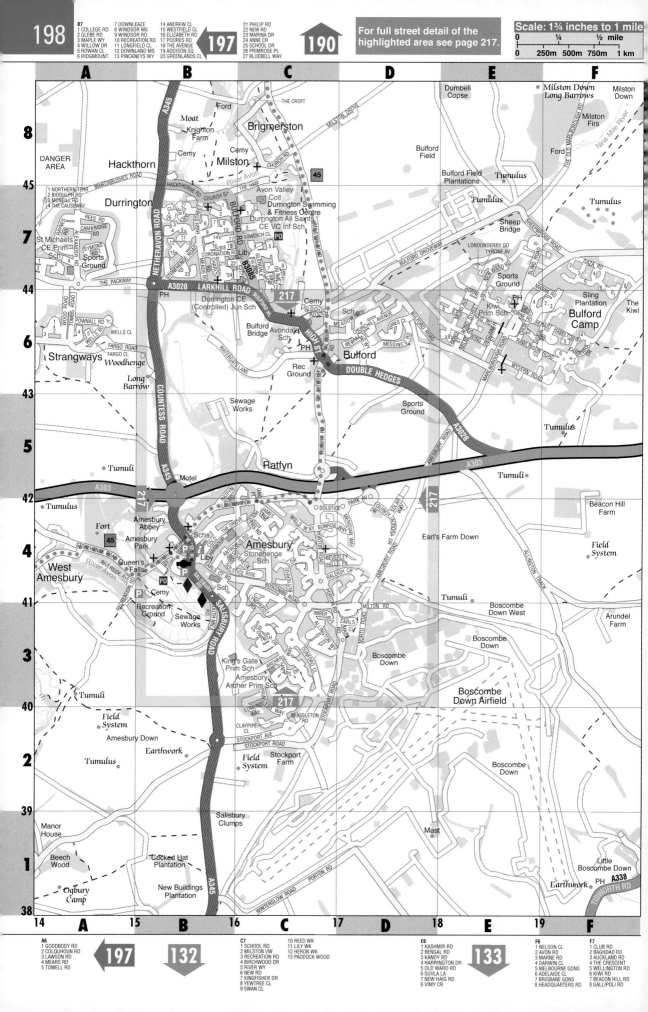

198

B7
1 COLLEGE RD
2 GLEBE RD
3 MAPLE WY
4 WILLOW DR
5 ROWAN CL
6 RIDGMOUNT

7 DOWNLEAZE
8 WINDSOR MS
9 WINDSOR RD
10 RECREATION RD
11 LONGFIELD CL
12 DOWNLAND MS
13 PINCKNEYS WY

14 ANDREW CL
15 WESTFIELD CL
16 ELIZABETH CL
17 POORES RD
18 THE AVENUE
19 ADDISON SQ
20 GREENLANDS CL

21 PHILIP RD
22 NEW RD
23 MARINA CR
24 MARNE CR
25 SCHOOL DR
26 PRIMROSE PL
27 BLUEBELL WAY

197

190

For full street detail of the
highlighted area see page 217.

Scale: 1¾ inches to 1 mile

0      ¼      ½ mile
0   250m 500m 750m 1 km

A6
1 GOODBODY RD
2 COLQUHOUN RD
3 LAWSON RD
4 MEARS RD
5 TOWELL RD

197

132

C7
1 SCHOOL RD
2 MILSTON VW
3 RECREATION RD
4 BIRCHWOOD DR
5 RIVER WY
6 NEW RD
7 KINGFISHER DR
8 YEWTREE CL
9 SWAN CL

10 REED WK
11 LILY WK
12 HERON WK
13 PADDOCK WOOD

E6
1 KASHMIR RD
2 BENGAL RD
3 KANDY RD
4 HARRINGTON DR
5 OLD WARD RD
6 SUVLA LA
7 NEW HAIG RD
8 VIMY CR

133

F6
1 NELSON CL
2 AVON RD
3 MARNE RD
4 DARWIN CL
5 MELBOURNE GDNS
6 ADELAIDE CL
7 BRISBANE GDNS
8 HEADQUARTERS RD

F7
1 CLUB RD
2 BAGHDAD RD
3 AUCKLAND RD
4 THE CRESCENT
5 WELLINGTON RD
6 KIWI RD
7 BEACON HILL RD
8 GALLIPOLI RD

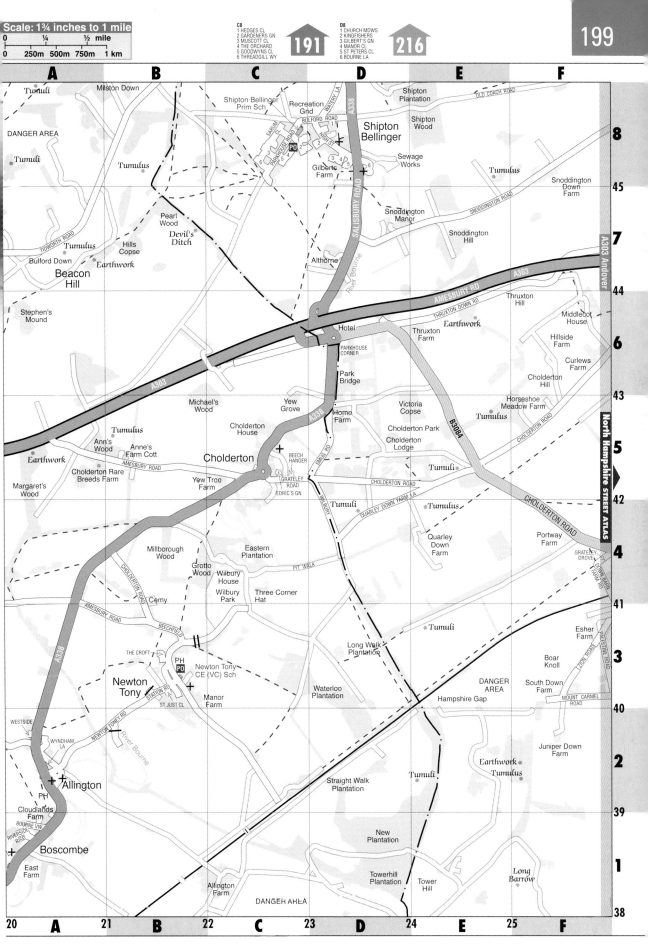

Scale: 1¾ inches to 1 mile

0    ¼    ½ mile

0   250m 500m 750m  1 km

191

216

199

C8
1 HEDGES CL
2 GARDENERS GN
3 MUSCOTT CL
4 THE ORCHARD
5 GOODWYNS CL
6 THREADGILL WY

D8
1 CHURCH MDWS
2 KINGFISHERS
3 GILBERT'S GN
4 MANOR CL
5 ST PETERS CL
6 BOURNE LA

North Hampshire STREET ATLAS

127
194

**Scale: 1¾ inches to 1 mile**

0 ¼ ½ mile
0 250m 500m 750m 1 km

A | B | C | D | E | F

**8**

Long Bottom
Redding Hanging
Tumulus
Well Bottom
Well Bottom
Larch Copse
Nightingale Wood
Park Bottom
Great Bottom
Tumulus

**37**

Starveall
Picket Grove
Wessex Ridgeway
Rowdean Hill
Sherrington Down
Alsesetting Copse
Stockton Down

**7**

Musseldean Copse
Stonehill Copse
Corton Wood
Great Ridge
Longdean Bottom
Stony Hill
Great Bottom
Enclosure
Scrubbed Oak

**36**

West Wood
Pound Copse
Enclosure
Enclosure
Enclosure
Snail-creep Hanging
High Grove

**6**

Cratt Hill
Wessex Ridgeway
Bernwick Bushes
Penning Wood
Point Pond Wood
Chilifinch Hanging
Limekiln Wood
Grim's Ditch
Sherrington Wood
High Park Wood
Gattrell's Copse
Fonthill Bushes

Chilfinch Hill
Tumulus
Tumulus
Hart Coppice

**35**

Chicklade
Chicklade Dairy
Bake Barn
Field System
Tumuli
A303
Woodbine Barn

**5**

Seymour Farm
Down Place
Fonthill Down
Monarch's Way
A303
Wessex Ridgeway
Chicklade Bottom
Chicklade Bottom Farm

**34**

Ox Drove
Cold Berwick Hill
Berwick Down

**4**

Hawking Down
Berwick Down Dairy
Berwick St Leonard
Field Barn Buildings

Two Mile Down
Berwick Glebe Farm
Berwick Farm
Monarch's Way
Kingstead Farm
B3089
Ridge Farm

**33**

High St
PH
P.O
Angel Lane
Doods Hill
Hindon CE VA Prim Sch
P.O
PH
Fonthill Bishop
Ridge Hill

**3**

Crows Top
High St
The Dene
Stops Hill
Hindon
Whitehill
Pinchpenny Clump
Ridge Hill

Wessex Ridgeway
Red House Farm
The Down
The Terraces
Greenwich
Little Ridge Wood
Knap La
Knap Farm
Knap La
Fricker's
Ridge

**32**

Tumuli
Down Dairy
Terrace Farm
Fonthill Gifford
Stop St
Jerrards Farm
Fonthill Stables
Fonthill Lake
Fonthill House
Plowman's Copse

Copper Close
Fonthill Park
Grottos
Caves
Quarry Wood
Grottos
The Bushes
Field System
Ashley Wood
Farnell Copse
Wollard Copse
Paddock La
Mill Lane

**2**

New Close Hanging
Fonthill
Hinkley Hill
Wood La
Fonthill Abbey Wood
PH
Ashley Wood Farm
Weir
Vicarage Barn
Lady Down

**31**

Oddways Hanging
Paddock Wood
Tumulus

Ruddlemoor Farm
Great Western Avenue
Bitham Lake
Fonthill Abbey
Beckford Cl
Hindon Lane
Hillground
Hillstreet Farm

**1**

Bottom Copse
Fonthill Abbey Wood

Clay Hill Wood
Mockeny Wood
Beacon Hill
Lower Lawn House
Grosvenor Dr
Wyndhams Pl
Chilmark Road

**30**

90 | A | 91 | B | 92 | C | 93 | D | 94 | E | 95 | F

141
203

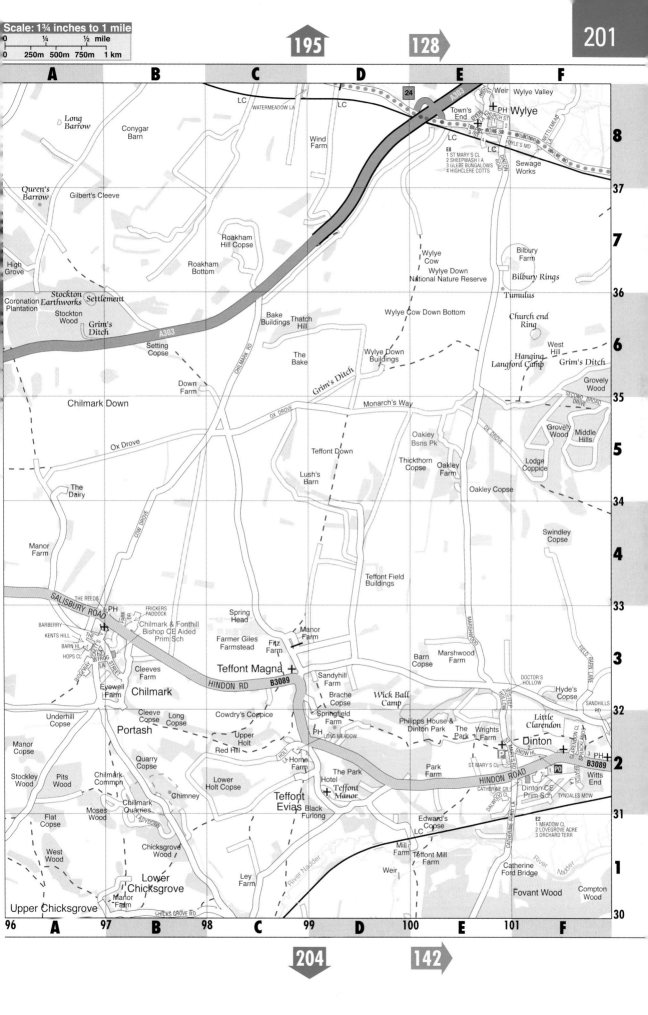

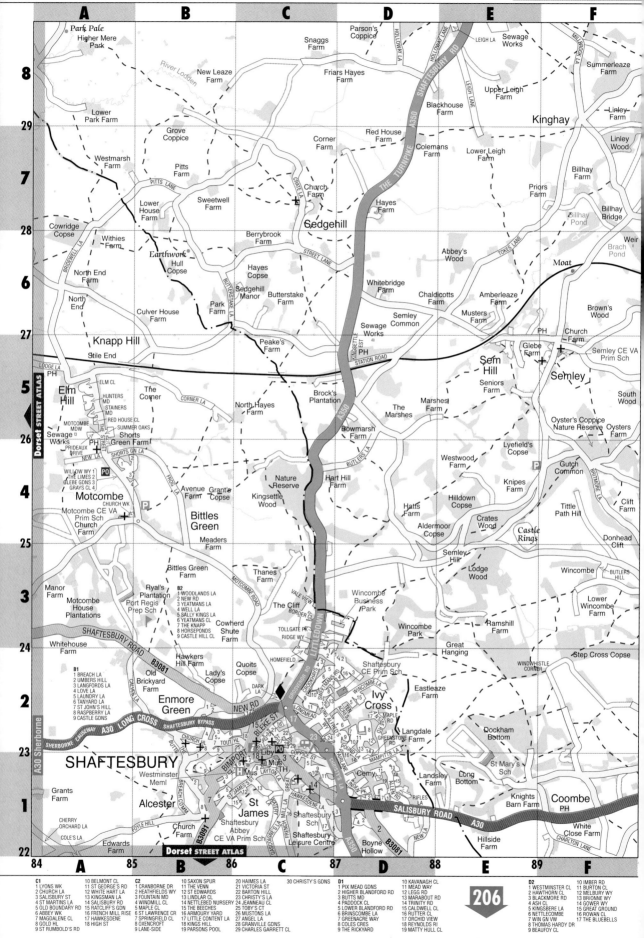

**C1**
1 LYONS WK
2 CHURCH LA
3 SALISBURY ST
4 ST MARTINS LA
5 OLD BOUNDARY RD
6 ABBEY WK
7 MAGDALENE CL
8 GOLD HL
9 ST RUMBOLD'S RD

10 BELMONT CL
11 ST GEORGE'S RD
12 WHITE HART LA
13 KINGSMAN LA
14 SALISBURY RD
15 RATCLIFF'S GDN
16 FRENCH MILL RISE
17 HAWKESDENE
18 HIGH ST

**C2**
1 CRANBORNE DR
2 HEATHFIELDS WY
3 FOUNTAIN MD
4 WINDMILL CL
5 MAPLE CL
6 ST LAWRENCE CR
7 SPRINGFIELD CL
8 OXENCROFT
9 LANE-SIDE

10 SAXON SPUR
11 THE VENN
12 LINDLAR CL
13 NETTLEBED NURSERY
14 THE BEECHES
15 ARMOURY YARD
16 LITTLE CONTENT LA
17 KINGS HILL
18 PARSONS POOL

20 HAIMES LA
21 VICTORIA ST
22 BARTON HILL
23 CHRISTY'S LA
24 JEANNEAU CL
25 TOBY'S CT
26 MUSTONS LA
27 ANGEL LA
28 GRANVILLE GDNS
29 CHARLES GARRETT CL

30 CHRISTY'S GDNS

**D1**
1 PIX MEAD GDNS
2 HIGHER BLANDFORD RD
3 BUTTS MD
4 PADDOCK CL
5 LOWER BLANDFORD RD
6 BRINSCOMBE LA
7 GREENACRE WAY
8 COLES CRES
9 THE RICKYARD

10 KAVANAGH CL
11 MEAD WAY
12 LEGG RD
13 MARABOUT RD
14 TRINITY RD
15 CALDWELL CL
16 RUTTER CL
17 ORCHID VIEW
18 REYNOLDS RI
19 MATTY HULL CL

**D2**
1 WESTMINSTER CL
2 HAWTHORN CL
3 BLACKMORE RD
4 ASH CL
5 KINGSBERE CL
6 NETTLECOMBE
7 WIN GN WE
8 THOMAS HARDY DR
9 BEAUFOY CL

10 IMBER RD
11 BURTON CL
12 MELBURY WY
13 BRIONNE WY
14 GOWER WY
15 GREAT GROUND
16 ROWAN CL
17 THE BLUEBELLS

**B1**
1 BREACH LA
2 UMBERS HILL
3 LANGFORDS LA
4 LOVE LA
5 LAUNDRY LA
6 TANYARD LA
7 ST JOHN'S HILL
8 RASPBERRY LA
9 CASTLE GDNS

**B2**
1 WOODLANDS LA
2 NEW RD
3 YEATMANS LA
4 WELL LA
5 SALLY KINGS LA
6 YEATMANS CL
7 THE KNAPP
8 HORSEPONDS
9 CASTLE HILL CL

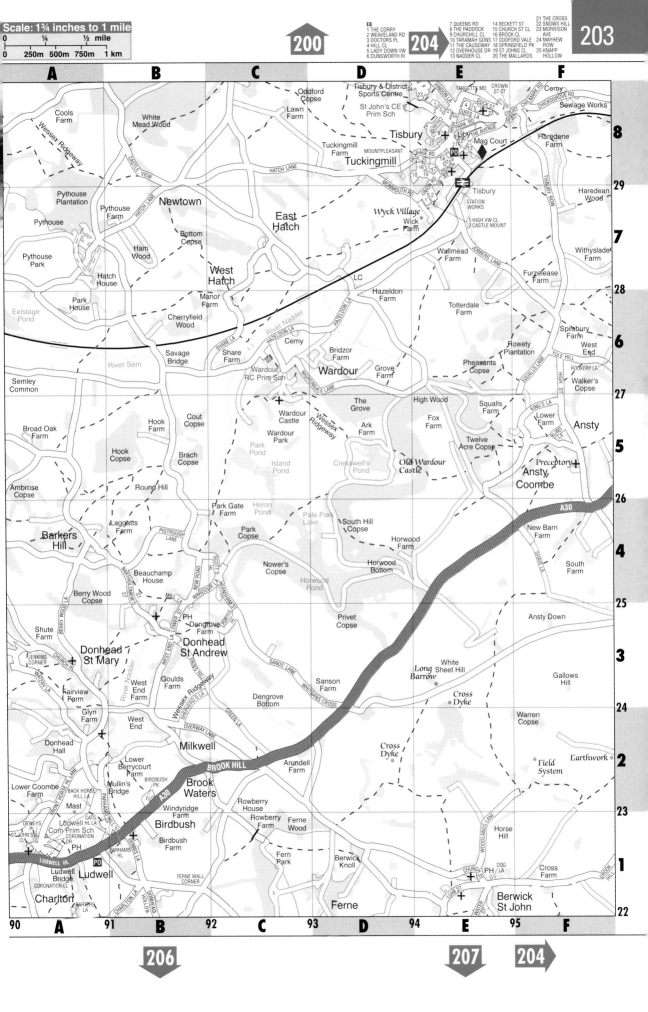

A  B  C  D  E  F

8
29
7
28
6
27
5
26
4
25
3
24
2
23
1
22

Chicksgrove Road
Quarry Farm
LC
Colemans Farm
Ham Cross Farm
CHICKSGROVE RD
Daslett Farm
Fovant Wood
Compton Wood
Apshill Copse
Panters
THE POPLARS
CHURCH LA
Fir Hill Plantation
Fir Hill
Fovant Wood
Woodcock Corner Copse
Chicksgrove
PH
Mill Farm
Longs Farm
MOOR HILL
THE ELMS
CATHERINE FORD LA
Little Wurs Copse
Thorny Bottom
Sutton Mandeville
Great Ground Hill
HOME CL
TISBURY RD
Fovant
MARY BARTERS LA
Greystones
A30 SHAFTESBURY RD
Haredene Wood
Sutton Row
Common Hill Wood
Townsend Wood
Larkhams Farm
PH
Gerrards Farm
SUTTON RD
Dean End
MILL LA
DINTON RD
Pembroke Farm
PH
East Farm
Whitmarsh Wood
Swell Hill Wood
Mast
LAGPOND LA
Church Farm
RECTORY RD
GLASS'S LANE
Dean Copse
TISBURY RD HIGH ST
Ings Farm
PO
Hotel
Fovant Regimental Badges
Castle Ditches (Fort)
Townsend Copse
Chestnut Tree Farm
Manor Farm
Dean Lane Farm
DEAN LANE
West Farm
Chiselbury
Swallowcliffe Wood
Greenlands Farm
Fovant Down
PH
Buxbury Farm
Fovant Down Poultry Farm
Chalk Pit
Gurston Holes
Rookery La
Parsonage Farm
Swallowcliffe
BEAN'S LA
PH
Tumulus
Sheep Well
Fovant Hut
Gurston Knowle
Poles Farm
LOOPER'S LANE
BUXBURY HOLLOW
LARKER'S LA
Red House Farm
Long Barrow
Swallowcliffe Down
Sutton Down
Fifield Down
A30
Swallowcliffe Down
Prescombe Down National Nature Reserve
North Barn
Tumulus
Cross Dyke
Field System
Middle Down
Cross Dyke
North Hill Farm
Church Bottom
Enclosure
Fifield Bavant
HIGH LANE
Ebbesborne Down
Long Bottom
Stowford Bridge
Messcombe Wood
Field System
Prescombe Farm
West End Farm
TOP RD
Norrington Manor
Brooklands Farm
WEST END
DUCK ST
West End
HILLVIEW
POUND ST
THE CROSS
HANDLEY ST
PH
Chalkway Head
Hill Farm
Rookhay Farm
HOLM CL
Alvediston
THE STREET
Church Farm
MAY LA
Ebbesbourne Wake
PH
EBBESBORNE HOLLOW
Barrow Hill
OUIDHAM ST
CHURCH ST
Samways Farm
Manor Farm
PH
ELCOMBE LA
Cleeves Farm
SHEPHERDS CROFT
Hedge End
Windmill Hill
CROOK HILL
Trow Farm
Elcombe Farm
Woodminton Farm
Misselfore
Pincombe Down
Trow Down
Field System
Elcombe Hollow
East Combe Wood
Tumuli
Woodminton Field System
Targetts Farm
Lower Bridmore Farm
Goscombe Copse

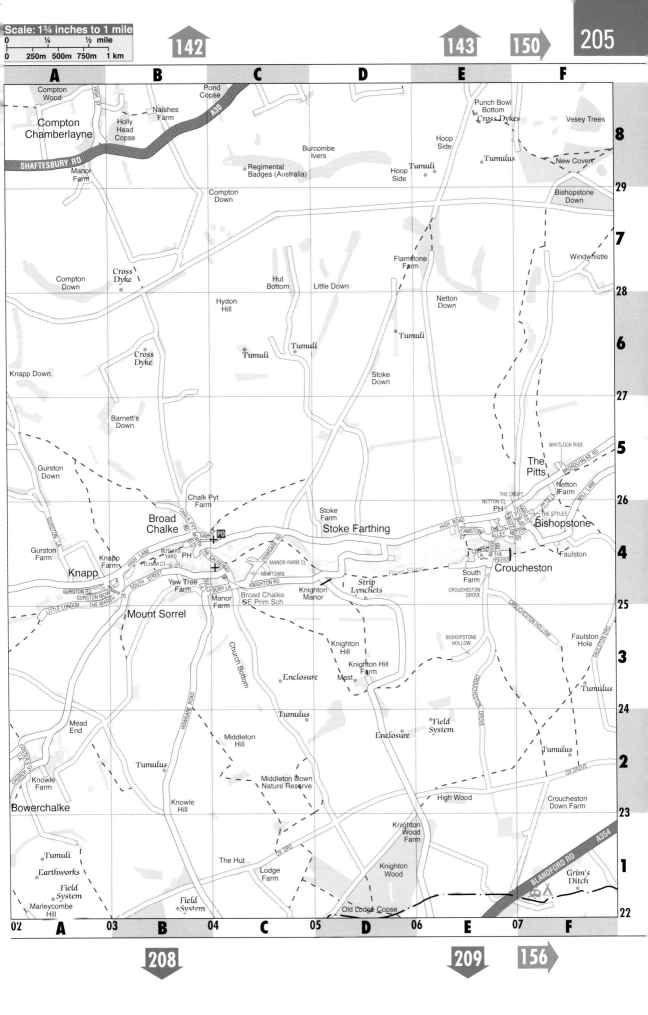

Compton
Wood

Compton
Chamberlayne

Naishes
Farm

Holly
Head
Copse

Pond
Copse

A30

Burcombe
Ivers

Punch Bowl
Bottom
Cross Dykes

Vesey Trees

SHAFTESBURY RD

HIGH ST

Manor
Farm

Compton
Down

Regimental
Badges (Australia)

Hoop
Side

Tumuli

Tumulus

New Covert

Bishopstone
Down

Hoop
Side

Windwhistle

Compton
Down

Cross
Dyke

Hut
Bottom

Little Down

Flamstone
Farm

Netton
Down

Hydon
Hill

Cross
Dyke

Tumuli

Tumuli

Tumuli

Stoke
Down

Knapp Down

Barnett's
Down

WHITLOCK RISE

The
Pitts

BROADCHALKE RD

Gurston
Down

Chalk Pyt
Farm

THE CROFT

NETTON CL

PH

Netton
Farm

MILL LANE

GURSTON LA

CHALK PYT RD NORTH

Broad
Chalke

Stoke
Farm

Stoke Farthing

High Road

THE STYLES

Bishopstone

PITTS LA

HARVEST

NETTON ST

Gurston
Farm

Knapp
Farm

HIGH LANE

BUTLERS
YARD

PELHAM CT

PH

THE CAUSEWAY

HOWGARE RD

MANOR FARM CL

CAMSTON
ST

CHAPEL
LA

THE
CROSS

THE ALLEY

Faulston

Croucheston

Knapp

PO

NEWTOWN

South
Farm

Yew Tree
Farm

GURSTON RD
GURSTON MDW

KNAPP HL

SOUTH STREET

BULLS
BURY LA

KNIGHTON RD

River Elbba

CROUCHESTON
DROVE

LITTLE LONDON

THE MARCH

Manor
Farm

Broad Chalke
SE Prim Sch

Knighton
Manor

Strip
Lynchets

BISHOPSTONE
HOLLOW

Faulston
Hole

Mount Sorrel

Church Bottom

Knighton
Hill

CROUCHESTON HOLLOW

FAULSTON DRO

Mead
End

Knighton Hill
Farm

Enclosure

Mast

Field
System

Tumulus

COSTER'S LA
CHURCH ST

Knowle
Farm

HOWGARE ROAD

Tumulus

Middleton
Hill

Tumulus

Enclosure

CROUCHESTON DROVE

Tumulus

OX DROVE

Bowerchalke

Knowle
Hill

Middleton Down
Nature Reserve

High Wood

Croucheston
Down Farm

Tumuli

Earthworks

The Hut

OX DRO

Lodge
Farm

Knighton
Wood
Farm

BLANDFORD RD

A354

Field
System

Knighton
Wood

Grim's
Ditch

Marleycombe
Hill

Field
System

Old Lodge Copse

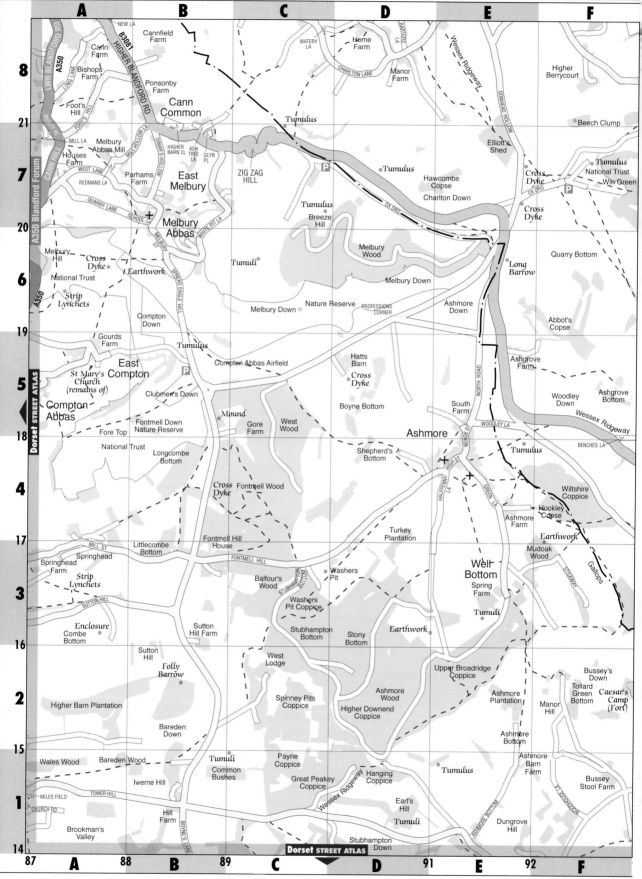

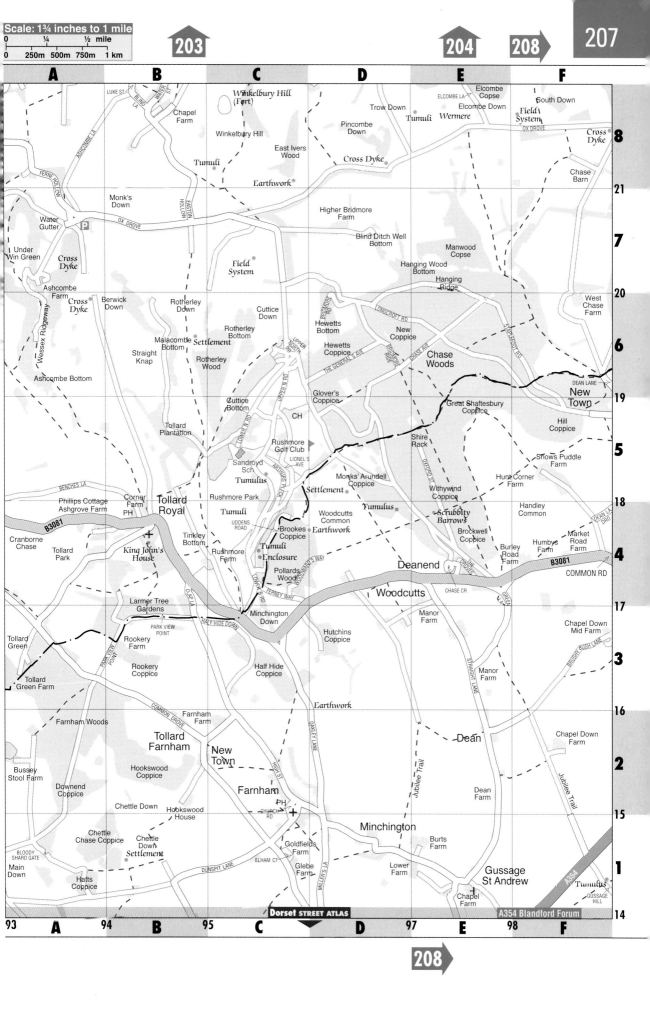

A    B    C    D    E    F

**8**

Winkelbury Hill (Fort)

ELCOMBE LA
Elcombe Copse

Trow Down    Tumuli    Elcombe Down

Wernere    South Down

Field System

Chapel Farm

Winkelbury Hill

OX DROVE    Cross Dyke

East Ivers Wood

Pincombe Down

**21**

Earthwork    Cross Dyke

Chase Barn

FERNE HOLLOW

Monk's Down

OX DROVE    Higher Bridmore Farm

Blind Ditch Well Bottom

Manwood Copse

**7**

Water Gutter

P

Field System

Hanging Wood Bottom

Hanging Ridge

West Chase Farm

**20**

Under Win Green

Cross Dyke

Ashcombe Farm

Cross Dyke

Berwick Down

Rotherley Down

Cuttice Down

Hewetts Bottom

New Coppice

Chase Woods

DEAN LANE

New Town

**6**

Straight Knap

Malacombe Bottom

Settlement

Rotherley Bottom

THE GENERAL'S AVE

Hewetts Coppice

CHASE AVE

Hill Coppice

**19**

Ashcombe Bottom

Rotherley Wood

Glover's Coppice

Great Shaftesbury Coppice

**5**

Tollard Plantation

Cuttice Bottom

CH

Shire Rack

Snows Puddle Farm

Sandroyd Sch

Rushmore Golf Club

LIONEL'S AVE

Monks' Arundell Coppice

Withywind Coppice

Hunt Corner Farm

BENCHES LA

Tumulus

ARTHUR'S PLECK

Settlement

Tumulus

Scrubbity Barrows

Handley Common

**18**

Phillips Cottage
Ashgrove Farm

Corner Farm
PH

Tollard Royal

Rushmore Park

Woodcutts Common
Earthwork

Brockwell Coppice

Burley Road Farm

Humbys Farm

Market Road Farm

DEAN LA DRO

Cranborne Chase

Tollard Park

King John's House

Tinkley Bottom

UDDENS ROAD

Brookes Coppice

Deanend

THE GROVES

B3081

COMMON RD

**4**

Rushmore Farm

Tumuli Enclosure

Woodcutts

CHASE CR

Larmer Tree Gardens

Minchington Down

Hutchins Coppice

Manor Farm

**17**

Tollard Green

Rookery Farm

PARK VIEW POINT

Half Hide Coppice

Manor Farm

Chapel Down Mid Farm

**3**

Tollard Green Farm

Rookery Coppice

Earthwork

Dean

BRUSBY BUSH LANE

**16**

Farnham Woods

COMMON DROVE

Farnham Farm

Tollard Farnham

New Town

Chapel Down Farm

**2**

Bussey Stool Farm

Hookswood Coppice

Farnham

Dean Farm

Downend Coppice

Chettle Down

Hookswood House

PH

**15**

Chettle Chase Coppice

Chettle Down Settlement

CHURCH RD

Minchington

Burts Farm

BLOODY SHARD GATE

Goldfields Farm

Gussage St Andrew

Tumulus

**1**

Main Down

Hatts Coppice

DUNSPIT LANE

ELHAM CT

Glebe Farm

Lower Farm

Chapel Farm

Gussage Hill

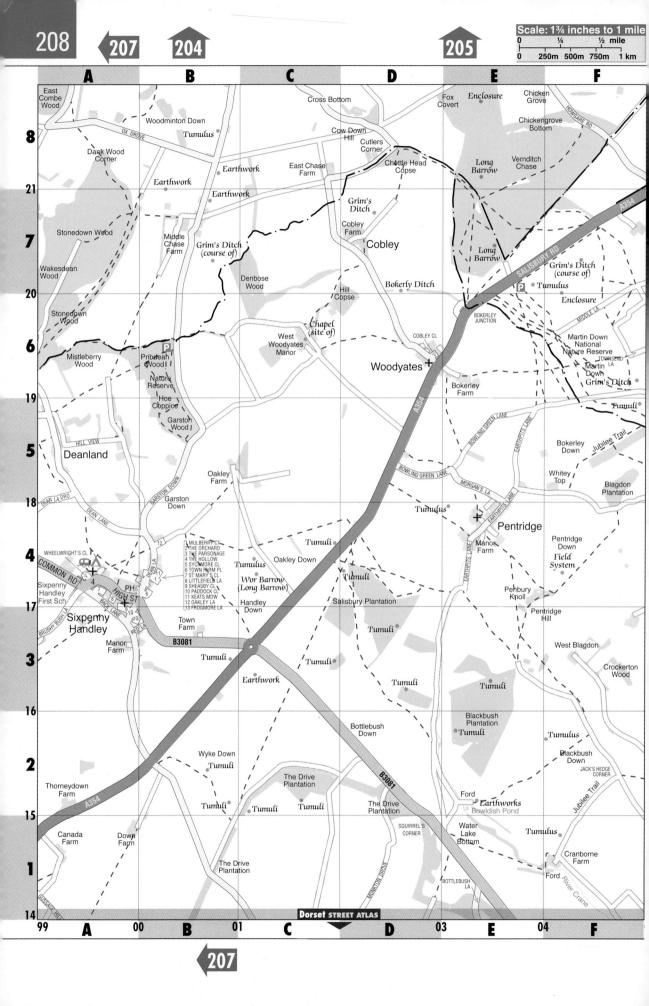

A · B · C · D · E · F

East Combe Wood
Woodminton Down
Cross Bottom
Fox Covert
Enclosure
Chicken Grove
Chickengrove Bottom

OX DROVE
Tumulus
Cow Down Hill
Cutlers Corner
Chettle Head Copse
Long Barrow
Verndich Chase

Dark Wood Corner
Earthwork
Earthwork
East Chase Farm
Grim's Ditch
HOWGARE RD
A354

Stonedown Wood
Middle Chase Farm
Earthwork
Grim's Ditch (course of)
Cobley Farm
Cobley
Long Barrow
SALISBURY RD

Wakesdean Wood
Denbose Wood
Bokerly Ditch
Grim's Ditch (course of)
Tumulus
Enclosure

Stonedown Wood
Pribdeah Wood
West Woodyates Manor
Hill Copse
Chapel (site of)
Bokerley Junction
P
Martin Down National Nature Reserve
MIDDLE LA
TOWNSEND

Mistleberry Wood
Nature Reserve
Hoe Coppice
COBLEY CL
Woodyates
Martin Down
Grim's Ditch

Hill View
Garston Wood
Bokerley Farm
A354
Tumuli

Deanland
Oakley Farm
GARSTON DOWN
Garston Down
BOWLING GREEN LANE
EARTHPITS LANE
Bokerley Down
Jubilee Trail
Blagdon Plantation

DEAN LA DRO
DEAN LANE
Bowling Green Lane
MORGAN'S LA
Whitey Top

1 MULBERRY CT
2 THE ORCHARD
3 THE PARSONAGE
4 THE HOLLOW
5 SYCAMORE CL
6 TOWN FARM PL
7 ST MARY'S CL
8 LITTLEFIELD LA
9 SHEASBY CL
10 PADDOCK CL
11 KEATS MDW
12 OAKLEY LA
13 FROGMORE LA

Wheelwright's CL
COMMON RD
Tumulus
Oakley Down
Tumuli
Pentridge
Pentridge Down Field System

Sixpenny Handley First Sch
HIGH ST
PH
Wor Barrow (Long Barrow)
Salisbury Plantation
Manor Farm
EARTHPITS LANE
Pehbury Knoll

Sixpenny Handley
Town Farm
Handley Down
Tumuli
Pentridge Hill

BRUSHY BUSH LA
BACK LANE
RED LA
Manor Farm
B3081
Tumuli
Tumuli
West Blagdon

Earthwork
Tumuli
Tumuli
Blackbush Plantation
Crockerton Wood

Thorneydown Farm
Wyke Down
Tumuli
Bottlebush Down
Tumulus
Blackbush Plantation
Tumulus

Tumuli
The Drive Plantation
B3081
Tumuli
Blackbush Down
JACK'S HEDGE CORNER

A354
Tumuli
Tumuli
Tumuli
The Drive Plantation
Ford
Earthworks
Bowldish Pond
Jubilee Trail

Canada Farm
Down Farm
SQUIRREL'S CORNER
Water Lake Bottom
Tumulus
Cranborne Farm

BUSSAGE HILL
The Drive Plantation
MONKTON DROVE
BOTTLEBUSH LA
Ford
River Crane

Scale: 1¾ inches to 1 mile

0       ¼              ½    mile
0   250m   500m   750m   1 km

205

156

210

209

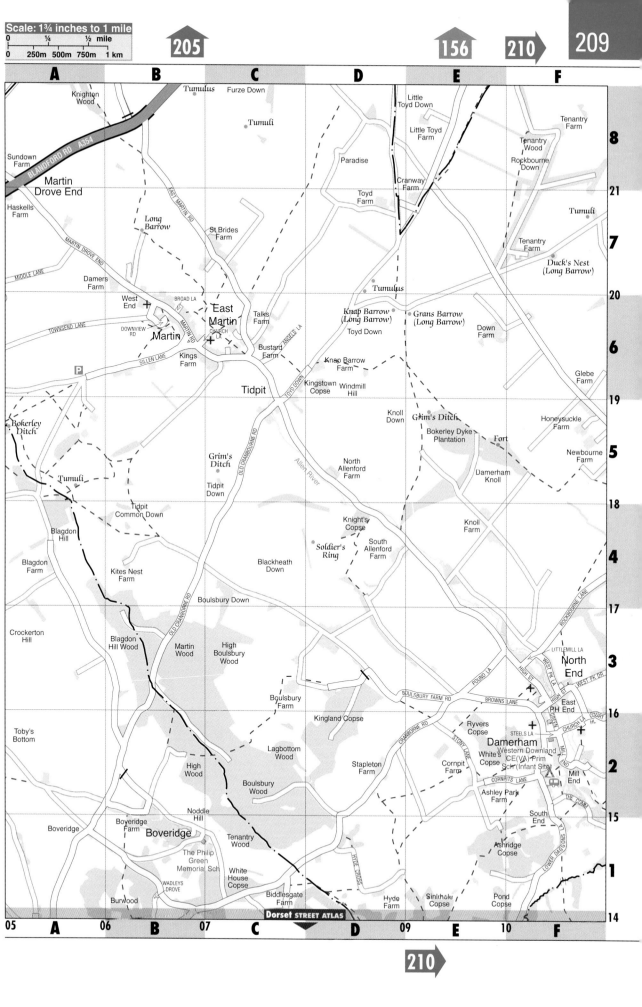

A   B   C   D   E   F

8
21
7
20
6
19
5
18
4
17
3
16
2
15
1
14

Knighton Wood
Tumulus
Furze Down
Tumuli
Little Toyd Down
Little Toyd Farm
Tenantry Farm
Tenantry Wood
Sundown Farm
Paradise
Rockbourne Down
Martin Drove End
BLANDFORD RD A354
Cranway Farm
Toyd Farm
Tenantry Farm
Haskells Farm
Tumuli
St Brides Farm
Duck's Nest (Long Barrow)
Long Barrow
EAST MARTIN RD
MARTIN DROVE END
Damers Farm
Tumulus
MIDDLE LANE
West End
BROAD LA
East Martin
Talks Farm
Knap Barrow (Long Barrow)
Grans Barrow (Long Barrow)
Down Farm
TOWNSEND LANE
DOWNVIEW RD
Martin
CHURCH LA
ANGELS LA
Bustard Farm
Toyd Down
Knap Barrow Farm
SILLEN LANE
Kings Farm
TOYD DOWN
Tidpit
Kingstown Copse
Windmill Hill
Glebe Farm
P
Knoll Down
Grim's Ditch
Honeysuckle Farm
Bokerley Ditch
OLD CRANBOURNE RD
Allen River
Bokerley Dyke Plantation
Fort
Grim's Ditch
North Allenford Farm
Damerham Knoll
Newbourne Farm
Tumuli
Tidpit Down
Tidpit Common Down
Knight's Copse
Knoll Farm
Blagdon Hill
Soldier's Ring
South Allenford Farm
Blagdon Farm
Kites Nest Farm
Blackheath Down
Crockerton Hill
Boulsbury Down
ROCKBOURNE LANE
Blagdon Hill Wood
Martin Wood
High Boulsbury Wood
LITTLEMILL LA
North End
WEST PK LA
HIGH ST
WEST PK DR
Boulsbury Farm
Kingland Copse
BOULSBURY FARM RD
BROWNS LANE
POUND LA
East End
PH
COURT HL
CHURCH LA
Toby's Bottom
Ryvers Copse
STEELS LA
GREEN
MILL END
CRAMBORNE RD
STONY LANE
Damerham
Western Downland CE(VA) Prim Sch (Infant Site)
Lagbottom Wood
Stapleton Farm
Cornpit Farm
White's Copse
Mill End
THE COMM
High Wood
Boulsbury Wood
CORNPITS LANE
Ashley Park Farm
South End
Noddle Hill
LOWER DAGGONS LA
Boveridge Farm
Tenantry Wood
HYDE CROSS
Ashridge Copse
Boveridge
The Philip Green Memorial Sch
WADLEYS DROVE
White House Copse
Biddlesgate Farm
Hyde Farm
Sinkhole Copse
Pond Copse
Burwood

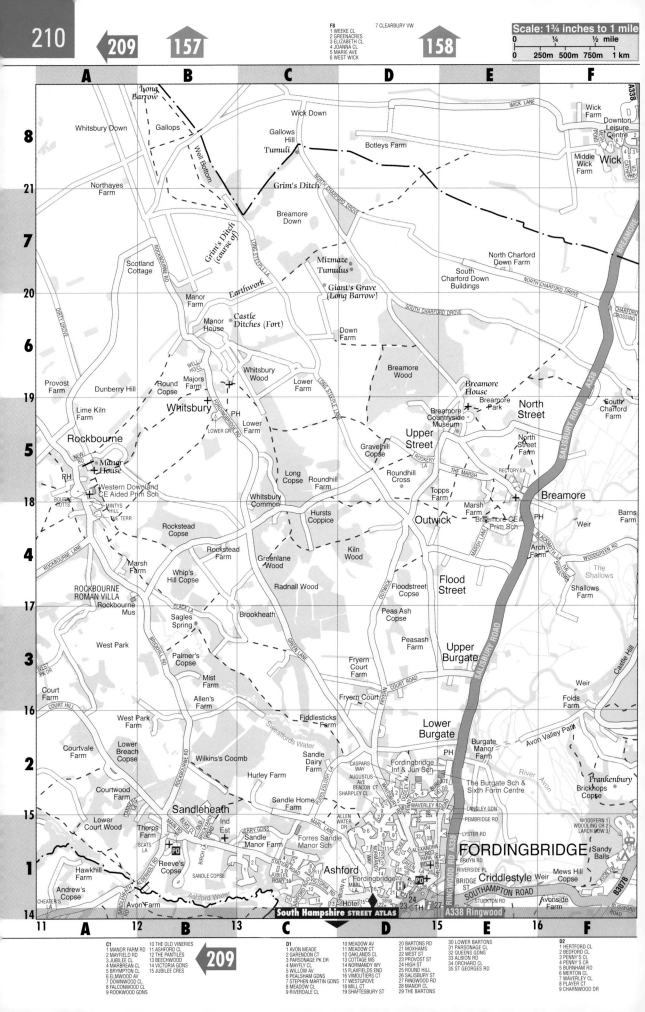

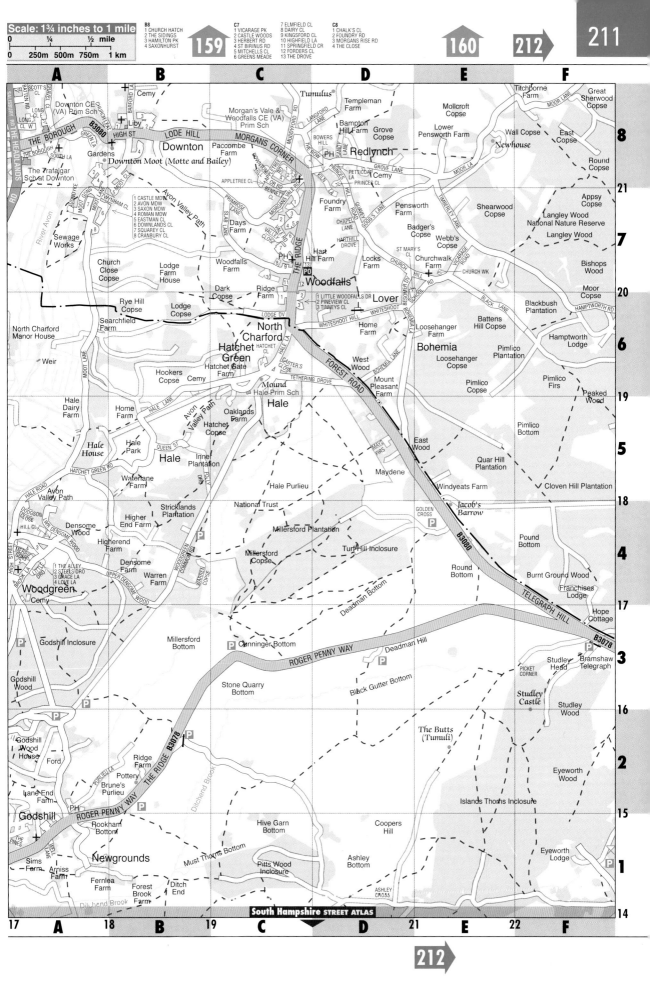

A B C D E F

**8**

Moor Copse
Ivory Copse
Sunt Copse
Glazier's Copse
Earldoms Lodge
Earldoms Farm
Earldoms Earthwork
Barnsell Copse
Peaks Copse
Bush Farm
Landfordwood
Landsbrook Farm
Melchet Park
Melchet Park Farm
Melchetcourt Farm
Boulder Wood
Plaitford Wood
Pilgrims
Hazel Wood
Hazelwood Farm
Short's Farm

**21**

Out Wood
Homan's Copse
Bagfield Copse
Northlands
North Common Farm
Landfordwood Farm
Stock La
White House Farm
Landford
Bracken Farm
Brooklyn Wood Farm
Plaitford Copse
Plaitford Wood Farm
Plaitford Green
Yewtree Farm
Bowles Farm
Gardiner's Farm
Spouts La

**7**

Whitterns Hill Farm
Landford Lodge
Wickets Green Farm
Stock Lane Farm
Southampton Rd
Sandown Farm
Manor Farm
Landford Manor
Manor Farm
Moat
Ford
Compton's Dr
Church La
Gauntletts Farm
Bourne Farm
Bowers Farm
Pound Rd

**20**

Hamptworth Farm
CH
Elmtree Farm
Cuckoo Farm
PH
King's Copse
Whitehouse Farm
Highfield Farm
Landford Glebe
Glebe
Broomside
Elm Farm
Home Farm
Nelson Farm
Giles Lane Ind Est
Furze Farm
Bridgefoot Farm
River Blackwater
Powell's Farm
Lukes Farm
Pembroke Farm
A36 Southampton

**6**

Bath Hole Plantation
Home Farm
Manor Farm Ford
Hamptworth
Hamptworth Rd
Latchmoor Dro
Heath Copse
Landford Captain's Copse
Cherry Tree Farm
PH
NT
Salisbury Road
Partridge Hill Farm
Plaitford
Heatherlands

**19**

Pond Wood
Lyburn Birches
Woodcock Copse
Lane End Farm
Beech Grange
Pine Cl
PO
Landford Bog Nature Reserve
Landford Common Farm
Tumuli
Newlands Farm
Greenhill Farm
Tumulus
West Wellow Common
Sunny Side
Heathlands

**5**

Horse Common
Cloven Hill Plantation
Lyburn Farm
Tumuli
Hamptworth Common
Broomhill
Lyndhurst Rd
Landford Common
New Road
Whitemoor La
Oak La Dr
Pear Tree Dr
Woodside Plantation
Plaitford Common National Trust
Sturtmoor Common
Heathlands

**18**

Tinney's Plantation
Risbury Hill Plantation
Shorthill Farm
The New Forest CE Prim Sch
York Dr
Oak Plantation
Deazle Wood
Dazelwood Farm
Dazel Cnr
Closed Copse
Canada
Plantation Rd
Kingston Pk
Canada Common Rd
Canada Common
Sedgemore Farm

**4**

Browse Green Wood
Franchises Wood
Burnt Tree Copse
Broom Hill Wood
Mire Wood
Lyburn Park Farm
Lyburn House
North La
South Lane
Forest Rd
Woodside
Bottom Rd
Nomansland
Lyndhurst Rd
Barford Farms
Lower Barford Farm
Penn Hungerford Farm
Harley La
NT
Penn Comm Rd
Penn Farm
Lampards Farm
Moorbridge Farm
Furzley
South View Farm
Blackhill La

**17**

Firs Hill Copse
Chapel La
Forest Rd
Wych Gn
Linhay Farm
Bloodoaks Farm
Fry's Copse
Penn Vale
Oak Copse
Furzley Common
Furzley La

**3**

B3078
Crow's Nest Copse
Appsey Copse
Pipers Wait
Forest Road
Two Beeches Bottom
Bramshaw Wood
Parsonage Farm
Bramshaw
Penn Copse
Tumuli
Stagbury Hill
National Trust
Furzley Comm Rd

**16**

Dark Hat Wood
Crow's Nest Bottom
Tumuli
Black Bush Plain
Bramble Hill Hotel
Margaret's Bottom
Stock's Cross
Upper Rowhill Farm
Porters Copse
Vice La
Mount Pleasant Copse
Blenman's Farm
Bramble Hill
Morgans Vale
Rowhill
Pit Copse
Cadnam Common

**2**

Howen Bottom
Longcross Plain
Longcross Pond
Great Wood
Bramshaw Hill Rd
Merry Orch
Long Cross
Burnside Farm
Reservoir Copse
Warren's House
Black Close Copse
Tumuli

**15**

Fritham Lodge
Longcross Plain Rd
Jonesmoor Plain Rd
Roger Penny Way
Coppice of Linwood
Shepherds Copse
Court Farm
B3079
Warren's Park
Poplars Marsh
Kewlake Wood
Rings Copse
Kewlake La

**1**

Fritham
PH
Whitesides Farm
Heatherdean
Fritham House
Coppice of Linwood
Salisbury Trench
Gibbet Wood
Round Hill
Broom Hill Wood
Brook Wood
Brook Hill
Brook Hill Farm
Brook Golf Club
Bramshaw Hill Farm
CH
Bell Inn
Brook
Brook Gn
Warren's Farm
Furze Copse
Manor Farm
Wittsford Dro
Cadnam La

**14**

South Hampshire STREET ATLAS

F6
1 BOTTOM LA
2 ITCHEN CL
3 BOURNE CL
4 THE BEECHES
5 STOUR CL
6 ARUN WY
7 PEARTREE CL
8 NIGHTINGALE CL
9 SPUR OFF MAURY'S LA

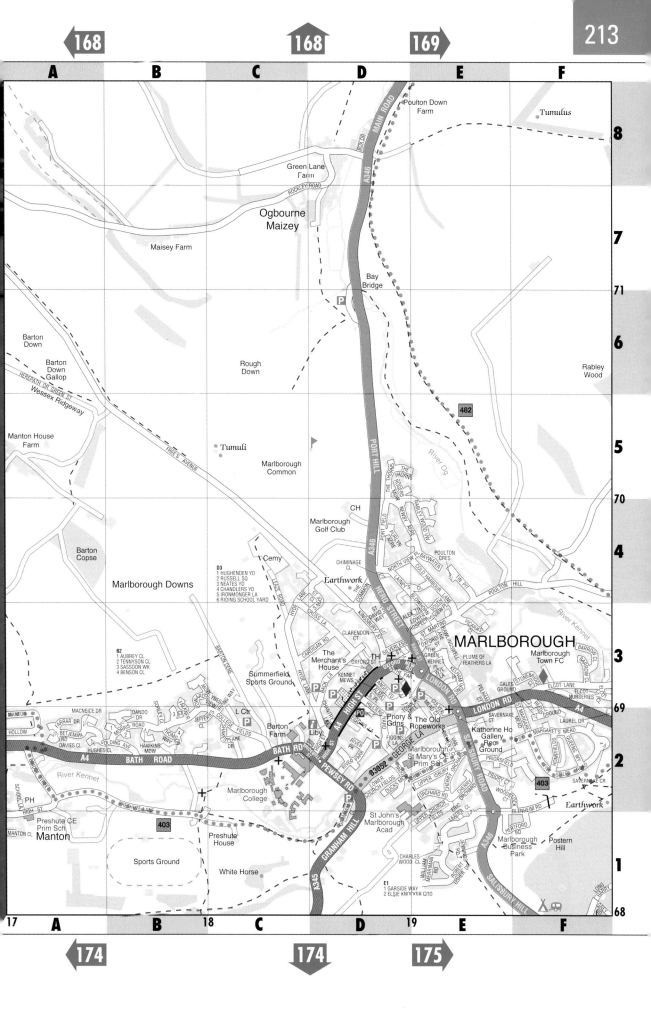

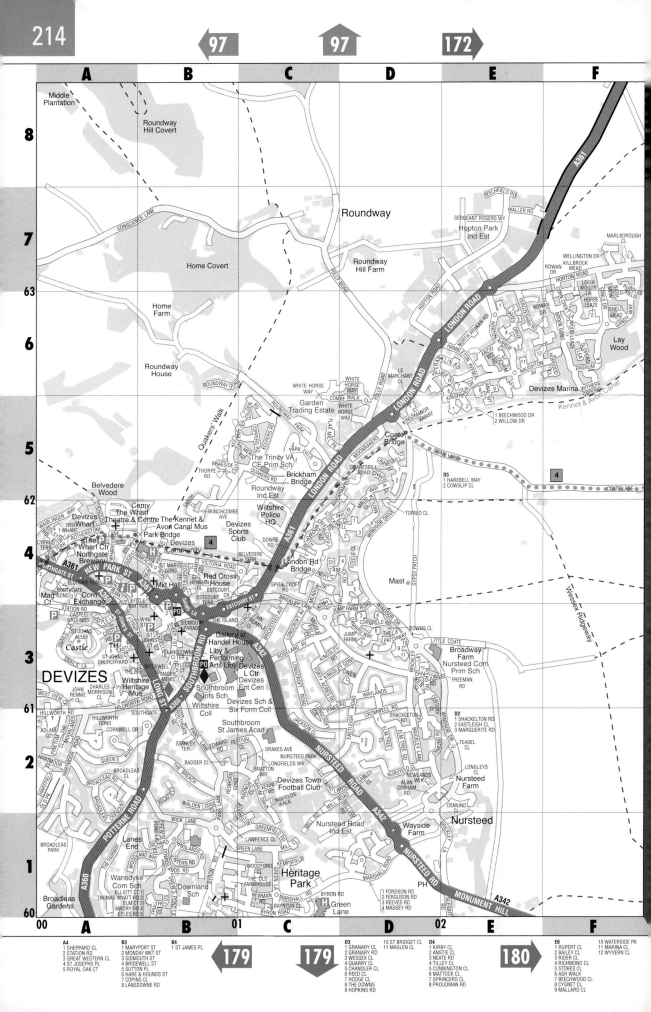

97 97 172

179 179 180

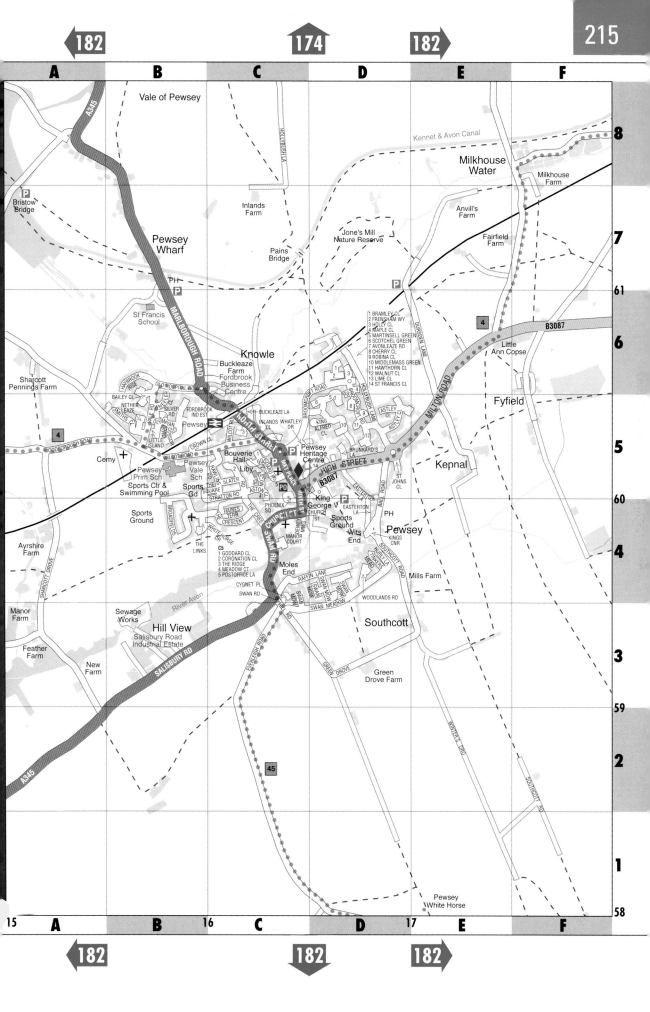

Vale of Pewsey

Bristow Bridge

Pewsey Wharf

Inlands Farm

Pains Bridge

Jone's Mill Nature Reserve

Kennet & Avon Canal

Milkhouse Water

Milkhouse Farm

Anvill's Farm

Fairfield Farm

St Francis School

Knowle

Buckleaze Farm
Fordbrook Business Centre

Sharcott Pennings Farm

B3087

Little Ann Copse

Fyfield

1 BRAMLEY CL
2 FRENSHAM WY
3 HOLLY CL
4 MAPLE CL
5 MARTINSELL GREEN
6 SCOTCHEL GREEN
7 AVONLEAZE RD
8 CHERRY CL
9 ROBINA CL
10 MIDDLEMASS GREEN
11 HAWTHORN CL
12 WALNUT CL
13 LIME CL
14 ST FRANCIS CL

MARLBOROUGH ROAD

HAYBROOK RISE
BAILEY CL
NETHER LEAZE

FORDBROOK LA
IND EST
Pewsey

BUCKLEAZE LA
INLANDS CL
WHATLEY DR

KING ALFRED CL

BROOMCROFT ROAD

HOLLYBUSH LANE

ASTLEY CL

MILTON ROAD

Kepnal

LITTLE ISLAND

WOODBOROUGH ROAD

Cemy

Pewsey Prim Sch

Sports Ctr & Swimming Pool

Sports Gd

Bouverie Hall
Liby

Pewsey Vale Sch

THE SQUARE

SLATER

STRATTON RD

ASTON

MKT PLACE
PO
Pewsey Heritage Centre

Brunkard's
14

HIGH STREET

ST JOHNS CL

Pewsey

BALL ROAD

PH

KINGS CNR

Ayrshire Farm

SHARCOTT DROVE

BROADFIELDS

THE CRESCENT
HAINES CL
PHOENIX SQ

WHITE HORSE DR
THE LINKS

King George V
CHURCH ST
Sports Ground
Wits End

EASTERTON LA

Kepnal

Moles End

RAFFIN LANE
SWAN MDW
SWAN MOW
SWAN MDW
Mills Farm

HURLI LA
UNTERS MEAD

WOODLANDS RD

Manor Farm

Feather Farm

New Farm

Sewage Works

Hill View
Salisbury Road Industrial Estate

River Avon

SALISBURY RD

A345

SWAN RD
SWAN RD
MANOR COURT
CYGNET PL

C5
1 GODDARD CL
2 CORONATION CL
3 THE RIDGE
4 MEADOW CT
5 POSTOFFICE LA

EVERLEIGH ROAD

GREEN DROVE

Green Drove Farm

Southcott

WINTER'S DRO

SOUTHCOTT RD

45

Pewsey White Horse

A345

St Francis School

PH

CROWN CL

WILCOT RD

NORTH STREET

WILCOT ROAD

GODARD RD
RAWLINS RD
SILVER RD
WHEELER CL
OLIVE AN CL

SMITHS

4

B3087

PEWSEY

EASTERTON LA

DURSDEN LANE

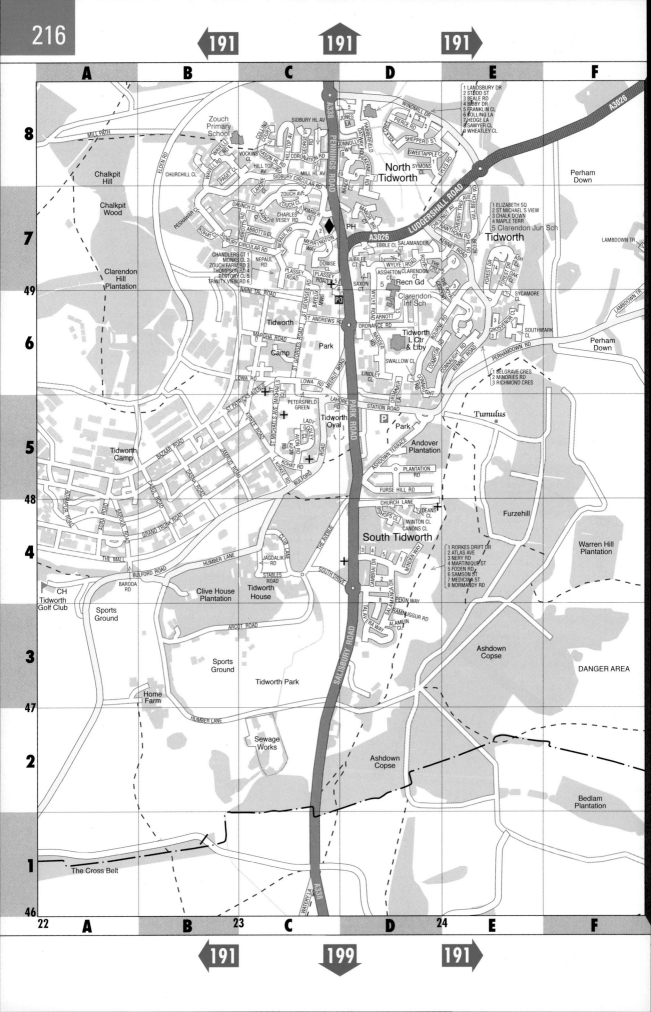

A    B    C    D    E    F

8

Chalkpit Hill

Chalkpit Wood

Zouch Primary School

MILL PATH

Zouch Ave

Clarendon Hill Plantation

CHURCHILL CL

7

ELDEN RD
GASON RD
WAVELL RD
PAGET CL
COLLINS COURT
VOCKINS CL
HILL TOP AV
SIDBURY HL AV
CORONATION RD
HILL TOP AV
MILL HL AV
SIDBURY CIRCULAR RD
PESHAWAR CL
LAHORE RD
KOHAT CT
KARACHI RD
DAUNCH CL
ABBOTTS CL
NEPAUL RD
ZOUCH AVE
ZOUCH CL
CHARLES VESEY RD
KIMBER CL
NAINI TAL ROAD
SIDBURY CIRCULAR RD
NEPAUL RD
PLASSEY ROAD
MERRINGTON WAY
DOWSE CL
PLASSEY ROAD

CHANDLERS CT 1
MONKS CL 2
ZOUCH FARM RD 3
THOMPSON RD 4
RESTORY CL 5
TRINITY VIEW RD 6

North Tidworth

WINDMILL DR
JONES LA
PIERCE RD
SHEPPERD ST
SWEETAPPLE C

HABBERFIELD
CONNAUGHT WY
PICKERNELL RD
CONWAY RD
CONNOLLY RD

SYMONS CL

1 LANDSBURY DR
2 STODD ST
3 BEALE RD
4 BIBBY DR
5 FRANKLIN CL
6 HOLLING LA
7 HEDGE LA
8 SAWYER CL
9 WHEATLEY CL

A3026

Perham Down

1 ELIZABETH SQ
2 ST MICHAEL'S VIEW
3 CHALK DOWN
4 MAPLE TERR
5 Clarendon Jun Sch

Tidworth

LAMBDOWN TR

49

Tidworth

ST ANDREWS ROAD
ST GEORGES ROAD
BATEUX MWS

PO

MANOR BRI
PH

EBBLE CL
JUBILEE CT
ASSHETON
CLARENDON CT
WYLYE ROAD
SAXON CT
ORDNANCE RD
NADDER RD
SWALLOW CL

SALAMANDER CL

Recn Gd

Clarendon Inf Sch

CHESTNUT AV
CHERRY TREE RD
HAWTHORN RD
HILL BEECH RD
KENNET ROAD
THE CREST
THE ROYAL CRESCENT
ROYAL OAK
FOREST DR
FOREST DR
ASH CL
OAK CL
SYCAMORE CL
GROSVENOR CL
SOUTHWARK CL

6

Park

Tidworth L Ctr & Liby

MARGHA ROAD
LOWA RD
MEERUT ROAD
LOWA RD

Camp

ST PATRICKS AVENUE
ST MICHAELS AVE
JAMPUT ROAD
KIRKEE ROAD
BAZAAR ROAD
CABUL ROAD
DASNA ROAD
AGRA ROAD
BAROGH ROAD

Perham Down

COMPTON RD
BOURNE RD
CONNAUGHT RD
KENNET ROAD
PERHAMDOWN RD

1 BELGRAVE CRES
2 MINORIES RD
3 RICHMOND CRES

5

Tidworth Camp

PETERSFIELD GREEN
LADY GOXEY CL
AVON RD
KOHAT RD
BULFORD

LAHORE RD
Tidworth Oval

STATION ROAD
P
Park

Andover Plantation

DRUMMOND RD

Tumulus

48

THE MALL
ADMIRAL ROAD
GRAND TRUNK ROAD
HUMBER LANE
BULFORD ROAD
CLUB LANE
JAGDALIK RD
STABLES ROAD
THE AVENUE
SOUTH DRIVE

ASHDOWN TERRACE
PLANTATION RD
FURSE HILL RD
CHURCH LANE
BISHOPS CLI
WINTON CL
CANONS CL
DEANS CL

South Tidworth

3 4 5 7
CAMBRAI DR
MINDEN WAY

1 RORKES DRIFT DR
2 ATLAS AVE
3 NERY RD
4 MARTINIQUE ST
5 FODEN RD
6 SAMSON ST
7 MEDICINA ST
8 NORMANDY RD

Furzehill

Warren Hill Plantation

4

CH
Tidworth Golf Club

Sports Ground

BARODA RD
ARCOT ROAD

Clive House Plantation

Tidworth House

PEKIN WAY
RANGUGGUR RD
ALAMEIN CL
SALAMANCA DR
TALAVERA WAY

Ashdown Copse

DANGER AREA

3

Home Farm

Sports Ground

Tidworth Park

HUMBER LANE

Sewage Works

Ashdown Copse

2

Bedlam Plantation

1

The Cross Belt

WATER LA
A338

46

22    A    B    23    C    D    24    E    F

SALISBURY ROAD
PARK ROAD
PENNINGS ROAD
A338
LUDGERSHALL ROAD

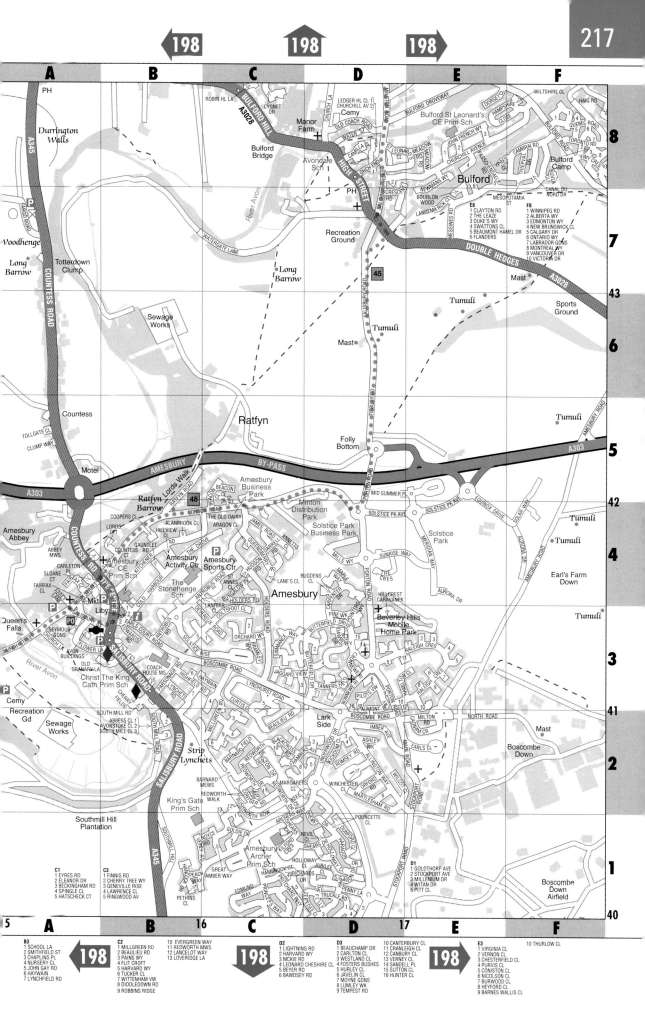

# Frome

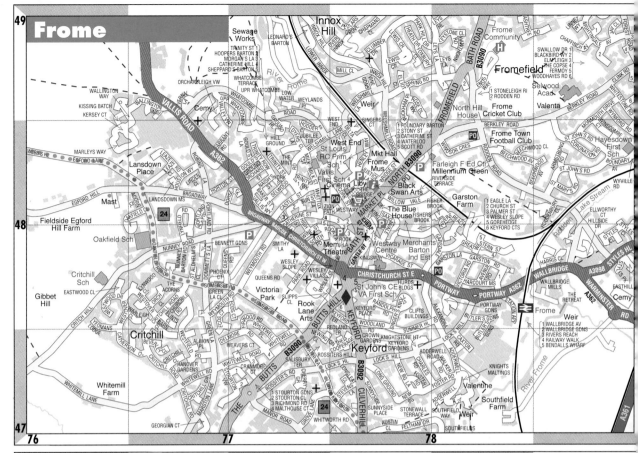

# Andover

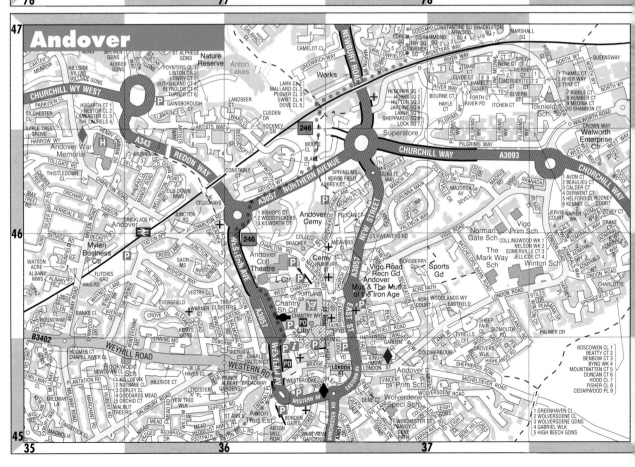

# Index

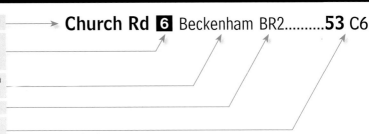

**Place name** May be abbreviated on the map → **Church Rd** **6** Beckenham BR2..........**53** C6

**Location number** Present when a number indicates the place's position in a crowded area of mapping

**Locality, town or village** Shown when more than one place has the same name

**Postcode district** District for the indexed place

**Page and grid square** Page number and grid reference for the standard mapping

**Cities, towns and villages** are listed in CAPITAL LETTERS

**Public and commercial buildings** are highlighted in magenta   **Places of interest** are highlighted in blue with a star *

## Abbreviations used in the index

| | | | | | | | | | |
|---|---|---|---|---|---|---|---|---|---|
| Acad | **Academy** | Comm | **Common** | Gd | **Ground** | L | **Leisure** | Prom | **Promenade** |
| App | **Approach** | Cott | **Cottage** | Gdn | **Garden** | La | **Lane** | Rd | **Road** |
| Arc | **Arcade** | Cres | **Crescent** | Gn | **Green** | Liby | **Library** | Recn | **Recreation** |
| Ave | **Avenue** | Cswy | **Causeway** | Gr | **Grove** | Mdw | **Meadow** | Ret | **Retail** |
| Bglw | **Bungalow** | Ct | **Court** | H | **Hall** | Meml | **Memorial** | Sh | **Shopping** |
| Bldg | **Building** | Ctr | **Centre** | Ho | **House** | Mkt | **Market** | Sq | **Square** |
| Bsns, Bus | **Business** | Ctry | **Country** | Hospl | **Hospital** | Mus | **Museum** | St | **Street** |
| Bvd | **Boulevard** | Cty | **County** | HQ | **Headquarters** | Orch | **Orchard** | Sta | **Station** |
| Cath | **Cathedral** | Dr | **Drive** | Hts | **Heights** | Pal | **Palace** | Terr | **Terrace** |
| Cir | **Circus** | Dro | **Drove** | Ind | **Industrial** | Par | **Parade** | TH | **Town Hall** |
| Cl | **Close** | Ed | **Education** | Inst | **Institute** | Pas | **Passage** | Univ | **University** |
| Cnr | **Corner** | Emb | **Embankment** | Int | **International** | Pk | **Park** | Wk, Wlk | **Walk** |
| Coll | **College** | Est | **Estate** | Intc | **Interchange** | Pl | **Place** | Wr | **Water** |
| Com | **Community** | Ex | **Exhibition** | Junc | **Junction** | Prec | **Precinct** | Yd | **Yard** |

## Index of towns, villages, streets, hospitals, industrial estates, railway stations, schools, shopping centres, universities and places of interest

### A

Aaron Rd SP4 ....... 132 B1
Abberd La SN11 ...... 81 D3
Abberd Way SN11 ....81 C3
Abbess Cl SP4....... 217 B2
Abbey CE VA Prim Sch
The SP3............ 202 B1
Abbey Cl
Chippenham SN15 ..... 79 B5
**3** Shrewton SP3..... 196 E6
Abbey Farm Prim Sch
SN26................20 F1
Abbeyfield Sch SN15...79 B6
Abbey House Gdns *
SN16................28 A3
Abbey La
Amesbury SP4 ....... 217 A4
Hinton Charterhouse
BA2 .............. 99 A3
Swindon SN1 ....... 50 C5
Abbey Meads Com Prim
Sch SN25...........35 A7
Abbey Row SN16 .... 28 A3
Abbey Stadium SN25 ..35 A8
Abbey View Rd SN25...34 E3
Abbey Wlk **6** SP7 .. 202 C1
Abbot Rd SP1........ 146 C4
Abbotsbury Way SN25 .35 A8
Abbots Way GL7....... 4 F7
Abbots Wlk GL7 ...... 2 D4
Abbotts Cl SP9 ..... 216 C7
Abbotts Gdn SN16 .... 28 A3
Abbotts Rd SP9...... 216 C7
Abdon Cl BA12 ..... 195 D7
Abingdon Ct La SN6 ...19 E8
Abington Way SN2... 35 D5
ABLINGTON........ 190 B1
Abney Moor SN3......51 E2
Abotts Cl BA13....... 108 F3
Above Hedges SP5.. 148 C3
Abraham Cl **5** BA14 .105 C7
Abrahams Cl BA14... 105 C7
Acacia Cl SN14 ....... 70 A1
Acacia Cres BA14.... 105 A8
Acacia Dr
Frome BA11.......... 110 C7
Westbury BA13 ...... 109 A2
Acacia Gr SN2 .......35 C2
Academy Cl SN12.....93 F6
Academy Dr SN13 ....76 E2
Acorn Cl SN3.........51 C5

Acorn La SN11........89 C7
Acorn Meadow BA14. 105 A5
Acre Cl BA14 ....... 178 A3
Acre Rise SN14 .......78 A4
Acreshort La BA14... 178 A3
Acres Rd SN10....... 214 C3
Activity Zone Leisure Ctr
SN16................27 F3
ACTON TURVILLE.....52 F6
Acton Turville Rd GL9..52 A4
Adampur Rd SP9 .... 216 A4
Adam's Grave (Long
Barrow) * SN8 ... 173 D2
Adams Mere SP5 .... 154 E6
Adcroft Dr BA14 .... 101 D1
Adcroft St BA14 .... 101 C1
Adderwell BA11 .... 110 A3
Adderwell Cl BA11... 110 A3
Adderwell Rd BA11 .. 110 A3
Addington Cl SN10... 214 C2
Addinsell Rd SN25 ...34 E8
Addison Cres SN14 ...35 F3
Addison Rd SN12 .....93 F6
Addison Sq **19** SP4... 198 B7
Adelaide Cl **6** SP4... 198 F6
Adlam Cl SN10....... 214 A2
Adwalton Cl SN5...... 49 B4
Aerial Bsns Pk RG17. 170 E6
Affleck Cl SN5....... 49 C5
Agra Rd SP9....... 216 A4
Agravaine Cl **27** SP10 193 E2
Aiken Rd SN25.......34 C5
Ailesbury Cl SN15....79 A4
Ailesbury Way SN8 . 183 D8
Ainsworth Rd SN3 ...51 A4
Aintree **7** RG17 ..... 165 A1
Aintree Ave BA14 ... 105 E4
Aintree Dr SN14 ......77 F6
Airman's Cnr SP3.... 197 B5
Aisne Rd SN4........ 65 D1
Akenfield Cl SN25 ....34 F5
Akers Ct SN26........21 C2
Akers Way SN2 ......34 E2
Aki Ct SN26.........21 C2
Alamein Cl SP9 ..... 216 D3
Alamein Rd **4** SP11.. 193 E4
Alan Cobham Rd
SN10................ 214 D2

Alan Powell La BA13 . 112 B8
Alba Cl **11** SN5........48 F8
Albany Cl BA14 ..... 101 F2
Albany Rd SP1....... 146 B1
Albany Terr **5** SP2 .. 144 D3
Alberta Way **2** SP4.. 217 F8
Albert Rd BA14 ..... 101 F3
Albert St SN1........ 50 D4
Albion Bglws SP2.... 145 A3
Albion Cres SN13 .....76 C1
Albion Dr BA14 ..... 105 B8
Albion Rd **33** SP6 .... 210 D1
Albion St SN1 ........50 A5
ALCESTER......... 202 B1
Alcock Crest BA12 ... 116 F6
ALCOMBE..........82 F8
Aldborough Cl **2**
SN5..................49 C6
ALDBOURNE........ 170 A6
Aldbourne Cl
Blunsdon St Andrew
SN2 .............. 35 C6
**27** Hungerford RG17.. 177 B7
Aldbourne Four
Barrows * SN8 ... 169 E8
Aldbourne Rd SN8 .. 170 B7
Aldeburgh Pl BA14... 104 F6
ALDERBURY ....... 153 C3
Alderbury & West
Grimstead CE VA Prim
Sch SP5........... 153 E3
Alder Cl
Swindon SN2 ....... 34 D4
Trowbridge BA14..... 105 B5
Alderholt Rd SP6 .... 210 B1
Alderley Rd **7** SP2 ...34 E7
Alderney Cl **6** SN4 ...48 A2
Alder Rd SN14....... 75 A4
Alders The SP2 ..... 145 A3
ALDERTON..........39 F2
Alderton Rd
Alderton SN14........39 F1
Alderton SN14 ....... 40 C1
Grittleton SN14 ..... 54 D5
Luckington SN14 .... **53** D6
Alderton Way BA14 .. 105 D5
Alder Way SN12 ......94 A4
Alder Wlk **5** BA11 ... 110 B7
Aldhelm Rise SN13 ...84 E7
Aldrin Cl **7** SP10 .... 193 D2
Aldworth Dr **3** SP1.. 146 C5
Alexander Fields
SN9................ 181 F1

Alexander Keiller Mus *
SN8................ 167 B1
Alexander Rd
Malmesbury SN16 .....27 F4
Warminster BA12 .... 113 D1
Alexander Terr SN13 ..77 A1
Alexandra Cl SP2 ... 145 C3
Alexandra Rd
Fordingbridge SP6... 210 D1
Frome BA11........ 110 A4
**1** Swindon SN1 .... 50 C7
Alexandra Terr SN8.. 213 D3
Alfred Gdns **6** SP10 . 193 D1
Alfred St
Swindon SN1 ....... 50 C7
Westbury BA13 ..... 109 A4
Alfred's Twr * BA10.. 122 F3
Alicia Cl **1** SN25......34 C6
Allard Ave **4** SN13...76 C1
ALL CANNINGS..... 180 E8
All Cannings CE Prim Sch
SN10.............. 180 F8
Allenby Rd SP4 ..... 133 C2
Allen Cl SN3......... 50 E2
Allengrove La SN14... 39 C3
Allen Rd
Corsham SN13....... 84 C8
Shaftesbury SP7 .... 202 D1
Trowbridge BA14..... 105 B7
Allen Water Dr SP6 . 210 D2
Alley The
Bishopstone SP5 .... 205 E4
Woodgreen SP6...... 211 A4
ALLINGTON
All Cannings........ 172 E2
Amesbury.......... 199 A2
Chippenham Without .. 69 E3
ALLINGTON BAR..... 69 F2
Allington Rd SN2 .....35 B5
Allington Tk SP4.... 198 E4
Allington Way
Amesbury SP4 ...... 217 D2
**2** Chippenham SN14 .. 70 A1
All Saints Cres **2**
BA13.............. 109 A3
All Saints Rd **1**
SN10.............. 187 E7
All Saints VA CE Prim Sch
SP4............... 190 A3
Alma Pl SN8......... 213 D3
Alma Rd SN8........ 170 A7

Alma St BA14........ 105 E8
Alma Terr SN11.......81 B3
Almond Cl SN13 .....84 C5
Almond Gr BA14.... 105 B5
Alnwick SN5.........49 B4
Alnwick Rd **2** BA14.. 106 A8
Aloeric Prim Sch
SN12................94 A3
Alpine Cl **6** SN5......49 A7
ALTON............ 190 B1
Altona Gdns **17** SP10.193 D2
ALTON BARNES .... 173 C1
Alton Barnes White
Horse * SN8 ..... 173 C2
Alton Cl SN2........35 C5
ALTON PRIORS..... 173 D1
Alton Rd
Avebury SN8....... 173 B8
Wilcot SN8........ 181 F8
Alum Ct BA14....... 105 E7
ALVEDISTON...... 204 B2
Alvescot Rd SN3..... 50 D5
Alveston Cl SN5 ..... 49 D6
Alwyn Ct **4** SN25.... 34 D7
Amazon Way BA13... 108 E4
Amber Ct SN1 ....... 50 D7
Amberley Cl
Calne SN11 ......... 81 A4
Swindon SN25 ...... 35 C4
Amberley Ct SN16 ....27 E2
Ambrose House Business
Ctr SN1.............50 B6
Ambrose Rd SN1 ....50 C2
American Museum in
Britain * BA2........90 A5
Amersham Rd SN3....51 B3
AMESBURY ....... 217 C4
Amesbury Archer Prim
Sch SP4........... 217 C1
Amesbury Bsns Pk
SP4............... 217 B5
Amesbury Bypass
SP4............... 217 B5
Amesbury CC VC Prim
Sch SP4........... 217 B4
Amesbury Cl **4** SN2...35 C6
Amesbury Rd
Amesbury SP4 ...... 217 F4
Amport SP11........ 192 E1
Newton Tony SP4.... 199 A3
Shrewton SP3 ...... 196 E6
Amesbury Sports Ctr
SP4............... 217 C4

### Aar–Ans

Amethyst Rd SN25 ....34 F8
Amity Dr SN8....... 175 D6
Amouracre BA14 .... 105 F8
Ancaster Cl BA14 ... 101 A1
Anchor Barton BA12 . 119 A8
Anchor Rd SN11......81 C2
Ancliff Sq BA15......99 E4
Ancona Cl **12** SN5.....49 A7
Andeferas Rd **6**
SP10............... 193 D2
Anderson Cl SN3 ....51 D3
Anderson Rd SP1.... 146 C4
Andover La SP11 ... 192 B4
Andover Rd
Amport SP11........ 192 E2
Chirton SN10....... 180 F3
Fyfield SP11........ 192 D3
Upavon SN9......... 181 F1
Andover St **3** SN1....50 A5
Andrew Cl **14** SP4... 198 B7
Andrews Cl SN14 .....78 B7
Andrews Way
Calne SN11 ......... 81 B1
Salisbury SP2....... 151 F5
Angelica Cl **6** SN2 .. 34 D4
Angel La
Hindon SP3 ........ 200 A3
Mere BA12......... 139 A5
**27** Shaftesbury SP7.. 202 C2
Angels' La SP6 ..... 209 C6
Angel Yd SN8....... 213 D3
Angler Rd
Salisbury SP2....... 145 C5
Swindon SN5 ....... 49 B7
Anglesey Cl **5** SN5....49 C6
Anglesey Mead SN15 . 43 D4
Angrove Cotts SN16 .. 43 D4
Angrove La SN16 .....43 C4
Angus Cl **5** SN5......49 B7
Anise Cl **4** SN2.......34 C4
Annal Cl BA13....... 108 E3
Anne Cres BA14 .... 105 B7
Annetts Cl SP4 ..... 217 C4
Annett's La RG17 ... 176 F4
Anson Ave
Calne SN11 ......... 81 D4
Upavon Down SN9... 182 B2
Anson Gr SN12 ......94 C1
Anson Pl SN14.......56 C7

Anstey Pl SN15 ... 79 A4
ANSTY ... 203 F5
ANSTY COOMBE ... 203 F5
Ansty Hill BA12 ... 195 A6
Ansty Wlk SN2 ... 35 B6
Anthony Cl SN16 ... 25 C1
Anthony Rd SN4 ... 64 A7
Anton La SP11 ... 193 E4
Antony Rd 5 SN25 ... 34 F7
Antrobus Rd SP4 ... 217 B3
Anvil St SN26 ... 21 C1
Anzio Rd SN10 ... 214 E6
Apollo Cl 1 SN25 ... 34 B7
Apollo Rd SN15 ... 59 E3
Apostle Way SP1 ... 146 C5
Appleford Sch SP3 ... 196 E7
APPLESHAW ... 192 E3
Appleshaw Way
Perham Down SP11 ... 191 F3
Salisbury SP1 ... 146 D5
Appletree Cl SP5 ... 211 C8
Apple Tree Gr 10
SP10 ... 193 C1
Appletree Rd SP5 ... 211 C8
Applewood Cl SN14 ... 78 B8
Applewood Ct SN5 ... 49 D5
Applin Rd SP1 ... 146 D5
Apsley Cl BA14 ... 102 B2
Arabian Ave SN5 ... 34 C2
Arable Rd SN14 ... 78 A4
Aragon Cl SP4 ... 217 C4
Aragon Ct SN3 ... 51 A4
Arcade The 8 SN1 ... 50 B6
Archer Ave 8 SN13 ... 76 C1
Archer Cl SN2 ... 35 F5
Archers Ct SP2 ... 146 A2
Archers The SN6 ... 22 F5
Archers Way SP4 ... 217 C1
Arches La SN16 ... 27 F2
Arch Yard BA14 ... 101 C1
Arcot Rd SP9 ... 216 B3
Arc Theatre BA14 ... 105 A6
Arden Cl SN12 ... 94 C5
Argosy Rd SN15 ... 60 B1
Argus Gn SN25 ... 35 D3
Argyle Dr SN14 ... 70 C3
Argyle St SN2 ... 35 D1
Ariadne Rd 15 SN25 ... 34 B7
Ark The SN10 ... 214 A3
Arkwright Rd SN25 ... 35 D6
Arley Cl SN25 ... 35 A5
Arlingdon Fields
Somerford Keynes GL7 ... 5 F3
Somerford Keynes GL7 ... 6 A3
Arlington Cl SN3 ... 51 B7
Arliss Cl SN25 ... 35 B6
Armfield Rd SN25 ... 20 C1
Armitage Sq 4 SP4 ... 197 E6
Armoury Yd 16 SP7 ... 202 C2
Arms Gdns SN15 ... 57 C1
Armstrong Rd BA11 ... 110 B5
Armstrong Rise 16
SP10 ... 193 D2
Armstrong St 2 SN1 ... 50 C7
Arney Cl SN13 ... 84 E8
Arnfield Moor SN3 ... 51 E2
Arnhem Cross SN15 ... 60 B2
Arn Hill Down & Nature Reserve* BA12 ... 117 B8
Arnhill Rd 5 SN1 ... 50 A2
Arnold Noad Corner
BA14 ... 104 E3
Arnolds Mead SN13 ... 76 F2
Arnold St SN25 ... 34 E7
Arnold Way SN13 ... 84 F6
Arnott Cl SP9 ... 216 D6
Arn View
Cold Harbour BA12 ... 112 F1
2 Warminster BA12 ... 117 A8
Arran Cl 5 SN4 ... 48 A2
Arran Way SN6 ... 22 F7
Arras Cl BA14 ... 105 C6
Arthur Bennett Ct
SN1 ... 50 A5
Arthurs Pleck SP5 ... 207 C5
Artisans La
Swindon SN25 ... 20 C1
6 Swindon SN25 ... 34 C8
Artis Ave SN4 ... 64 B7
Artus Cl 1 SN25 ... 34 E6
Arundel Cl
Chippenham SN14 ... 78 A7
Swindon SN3 ... 50 F3
Arundell Cl BA13 ... 109 B4
Arun Rd SN25 ... 34 F3
Arun Way 6 SO51 ... 212 F6
Ascham Rd SN5 ... 49 A5
Ascot Cl SN14 ... 78 A5
Ascott Cl SN25 ... 34 F7
Ashanti Way SN26 ... 21 D2
Ashbee Cres 6 SN25 ... 34 D8
Ashburnham Cl 7
SN5 ... 49 A4
Ashburn Pl SP6 ... 210 D1
ASHBURY ... 164 A7
Ashbury Ave SN3 ... 51 B7
Ashbury Hill SN6 ... 164 A7
Ashbury with Compton Beauchamp CE Prim Sch SN6 ... 164 A8
Ash Cl
Lyneham SN15 ... 60 B2
4 Shaftesbury SP7 ... 202 D2
Swindon SN5 ... 34 A2
Tidworth SP9 ... 216 E7
Ashcombe La SP5 ... 207 A8
Ash Cres SP1 ... 146 C5
Ashcroft Cotts SN8 ... 169 B1
Ashdown Dr SN12 ... 94 D6
Ashdown Pk* RG17 ... 164 C5
Ashdown Terr SP9 ... 216 D5
Ashdown Way SN2 ... 34 C4
Ash Dr BA14 ... 105 C3
Ashe Cl SN15 ... 70 D1
Ashe Cres SN15 ... 70 D1
Ashen Copse Rd SN4 ... 63 F7
Ashes La
Freshford BA2 ... 99 A4
Kington Langley SN15 ... 70 E7
Sharpstone BA2 ... 99 A4
Ashfield SN6 ... 7 A1
Ashfield Rd
Chippenham SN15 ... 70 D1
Salisbury SP2 ... 145 E1
ASHFORD ... 210 C1
Ashford Cl 11 SP6 ... 210 C1
Ashford Rd
Fordingbridge SP6 ... 210 C1
Swindon SN1 ... 50 B4
Ashford Trad Est
SP2 ... 145 E1
Ash Gdns SN3 ... 36 E4
Ash Gn SP8 ... 137 D1
Ash Gr
1 Melksham SN12 ... 94 A2
Swindon SN2 ... 35 C2
Ashgrove BA12 ... 139 B4
Ash Hill Comm SP5 ... 162 D3
Ashie Cl SN5 ... 34 B2
Ashington Way 4
SN5 ... 49 C5
Ashkirk Cl SN3 ... 50 E6
Ash La SN13 ... 84 C5
Ashlade Firs Rd SN8 ... 175 C6
Ashlands SP4 ... 146 D6
Ashleigh Cl SP2 ... 130 B2
Ashleigh Gr 4 BA14 ... 105 C7
Ashleworth Rd 6
SN25 ... 34 F7
ASHLEY
Ashley ... 3 A2
Box ... 83 A6
Ashley Cl
Atworth/Whitley SN12 ... 85 D1
Bradford-on-Avon BA15 ... 100 B8
Swindon SN3 ... 50 F6
Ashley Coombe
BA12 ... 117 A4
Ashleycross SP6 ... 211 D1
Ashley Dro SN8 ... 185 A7
Ashley Gn SN13 ... 83 A5
Ashley Green
Little Ashley BA15 ... 91 A1
Little Ashley BA15 ... 91 B2
Winsley BA15 ... 90 F1
Ashley La BA15 ... 99 F7
Ashley Piece SN8 ... 170 C2
Ashley Pl BA12 ... 116 F4
Ashley Rd
Bath BA1 ... 82 C2
Bradford-on-Avon BA15 ... 91 B1
Salisbury SP2 ... 145 F2
Ashley Wlk SP4 ... 217 D2
Ashmead BA14 ... 105 D6
Ashmead Ct BA14 ... 105 D7
ASHMORE ... 206 D5
Ashmore Bottom
DT11 ... 206 E1
Ashmore Cl
Swindon SN3 ... 51 C6
Whiteparish SP5 ... 161 D4
Ashmore La
West Dean SP5 ... 155 E2
Whiteparish SP5 ... 161 D6
Ash Rd SN14 ... 75 A5
Ashton Cl SN25 ... 34 C7
Ashton Comm BA14 ... 106 C8
ASHTON COMMON ... 102 F1
Ashton Coombe
BA13 ... 186 B7
Ashton Gifford La
BA12 ... 195 A3
Ashton Heights BA14 ... 106 B3
ASHTON KEYNES ... 6 F1
Ashton Keynes CE Prim Sch
Ashton Keynes SN6 ... 6 E1
Ashton Keynes SN6 ... 17 E8
Ashton Rd
Ashton Keynes SN16 ... 17 E7
Siddington GL7 ... 6 D8
Trowbridge BA14 ... 102 A2
Ashton Rise BA14 ... 102 A2
Ashton Road SN16 ... 17 E6
Ashton St 2 BA14 ... 105 E8
Ash Tree Cl SN8 ... 175 A8
Ash Tree La SP7 ... 206 B7
Ashtree Rd BA11 ... 110 A7
Ashville Ctr SN12 ... 178 A8
Ashwell Cl SN3 ... 50 F5
Ashwicke Rd
Marshfield SN14 ... 74 A4
Marshfield SN14 ... 74 B3
Ash Wlk
Upton Lovell BA12 ... 194 E4
Warminster BA12 ... 117 A7
Ashwood Rd SN13 ... 76 A1
Ashworth Rd SN5 ... 49 E6
Askerton Cl 5 SN5 ... 48 F8
Askew Cl 3 SN5 ... 48 F5
Aspen Cl
Colerne SN14 ... 74 F6
Aspen Cl *continued*
Frome BA11 ... 110 B7
Royal Wootton Bassett SN4 ... 47 E3
Swindon SN25 ... 35 E2
Assart Way SN14 ... 78 A3
Assheton Ct SP9 ... 216 D7
Assisi Rd SP1 ... 146 A4
Astley Cl SN9 ... 215 D5
Aston Cl SN9 ... 215 C5
Aston Mead SP1 ... 146 C3
Astor Cres SP11 ... 192 A5
Astute Pl 12 SN13 ... 76 C1
Atbara Cl SN25 ... 35 A3
Atcherly Rd SN11 ... 166 A1
Athelney Ave BA13 ... 109 B5
Athelstan Mus* SN16 ... 28 A3
Athelstan Rd SN16 ... 27 F4
Athena Ave SN2 ... 35 E1
Athenaeum Ctr 2
BA12 ... 117 A7
Atherton Cl 12 SN8 ... 170 B2
Atherton Cres 16
RG17 ... 177 B7
Atherton Pl 11 RG17 ... 165 A2
Atherton Rd 11 RG17 ... 177 B7
Athlone Cl 2 SP11 ... 193 E4
Atholl Ct 26 SP10 ... 193 E2
Atlas Ave SP9 ... 216 D4
Attlee Cres SN2 ... 35 E3
Attwood Rd SP1 ... 146 A3
Atwell-Wilson Motor Mus* SN11 ... 89 D7
ATWORTH ... 92 F8
Atworth Bsns Pk SN12 ... 92 F8
Atworth Cl SN2 ... 35 B6
Atworth Cl SN12 ... 92 F8
Atworth La
Corsham SN13 ... 84 E4
Neston SN13 ... 84 E4
Atyeo Cl BA13 ... 112 B8
Aubrey Gdns SN2 ... 34 F1
Aubrey Rise 6 SN16 ... 28 A5
Auchinleck Rd BA12 ... 113 E1
Auckland Rd 3 SP4 ... 198 F7
Auden Cl SN25 ... 34 F5
Audley Cl 2 SN5 ... 48 F4
Audley Gate BA13 ... 108 E2
Audley Rd SN14 ... 78 C8
AUGHTON ... 183 D3
Augusta Cl SN25 ... 34 C7
Augusta Way W 8
SP11 ... 193 F2
Augustine Way 9
SP10 ... 193 C2
Augustus Cl SN25 ... 34 B8
Ausden Terr 1 SN1 ... 49 F7
Austen Cres SN3 ... 51 D4
Austin Rd SN5 ... 49 C7
Australian Ave SP2 ... 145 D2
AVEBURY ... 173 C8
Avebury Cl
Calne SN11 ... 81 A3
Westbury BA13 ... 108 F4
Avebury Manor & Gdns*
SN8 ... 167 B1
Avebury Mus* SN8 ... 167 B1
Avebury Rd
Chippenham SN14 ... 78 A6
Swindon SN2 ... 35 B5
Avebury Stone Circles*
SN8 ... 167 C1
AVEBURY TRUSLOE ... 173 B8
Avenell Rd 8 SN4 ... 163 A6
Avening St SN2 ... 35 D1
Avens Cl SN2 ... 34 D4
Avenue De Gien
Malmesbury SN16 ... 27 F6
Malmesbury SN16 ... 28 A6
Avenue La Fleche
SN15 ... 78 D6
Avenue Prim Sch & Children's Ctr The
BA12 ... 117 B7
Avenue Rd
Frome BA11 ... 110 A4
Swindon SN1 ... 50 C4
Trowbridge BA14 ... 105 B8
Avenue The* SP4 ... 197 E5
Avenue The
Cherhill SN11 ... 166 E2
Claverton BA2 ... 90 A4
Durnford SP4 ... 131 D1
18 Durrington/Bulford SP4 ... 198 B7
Porton SP4 ... 133 D6
Salisbury SP1 ... 146 C1
South Tedworth SP9 ... 216 C4
Stanton Fitzwarren SN6 ... 22 B1
Tangley SP11 ... 193 D5
Tisbury SP3 ... 203 E8
Warminster BA12 ... 117 A7
Westbury BA13 ... 109 A3
Wilton SP2 ... 144 F5
Woodford SP2 ... 145 A8
Aviemore Rd 6 SN1 ... 50 A2
Avil's La SN14 ... 56 F6
AVINGTON ... 177 F7
Avocet Cl SN3 ... 51 E6
AVON ... 71 F6
Avon App SP2 ... 146 A1
Avon Bldgs SP4 ... 217 A3
Avon Cl
Bradford-on-Avon BA15 ... 100 E5
Calne SN11 ... 81 A5
AVONCLIFF ... 99 F4
Avoncliff Sta BA15 ... 99 E5
Avon Ct BA1 ... 82 A4
Avondale Prep Sch
SP4 ... 217 D8
Avondown Rd SP4 ... 198 C7
Avon Dr SP5 ... 153 E2
Avondyke SP5 ... 211 A7
Avonfield BA14 ... 101 F8
Avonfield Ave BA15 ... 100 E5
Avonleaze Rd SN9 ... 215 D5
Avonmead SN25 ... 34 F4
Avon Mead SN15 ... 78 F8
Avon Meade 1 SP6 ... 210 D1
Avon Meadow SP5 ... 211 A8
Avon Meadows SP4 ... 131 C5
Avon Mills SN16 ... 28 B2
Avon Park BA2 ... 99 C7
Avon Pl SP1 ... 152 C8
Avon Pl Sh Ctr SN12 ... 94 A4
Avon Rd
Devizes SN10 ... 179 C8
2 Durrington/Bulford SP4 ... 198 F6
Malmesbury SN16 ... 27 F4
Melksham SN12 ... 94 A6
Tidworth SP9 ... 216 C5
Warminster BA12 ... 117 A5
Avon Reach SN15 ... 78 D7
Avon Rise SN14 ... 39 E4
Avonside Enterprise Pk
SN12 ... 94 A5
Avon Sq SN9 ... 181 F1
Avonstoke Cl SP4 ... 217 B2
Avon Terr
Devizes SN10 ... 214 A4
Salisbury SP2 ... 145 F2
Avonvale Rd BA14 ... 101 D2
Avon Valley College
SP4 ... 198 C7
Avon Valley Nature Reserve* SP1 ... 145 F3
Avon View SP6 ... 210 F1
Avon Way
Chippenham SN15 ... 70 F1
Trowbridge BA14 ... 101 D3
Avonweir La SN15 ... 57 F3
Avro Way SN12 ... 94 C1
Awdry Ave SN12 ... 94 C6
Awdry Cl
Chippenham SN14 ... 77 F7
Heddington SN11 ... 89 A2
Awdry Rd SN10 ... 214 B1
Axbridge Cl SN3 ... 51 A5
Axe & Cleaver La
BA14 ... 105 C4
AXFORD ... 169 D1
Axis Bsns Ctr SN5 ... 49 D7
Aylesbury Cl GL7 ... 7 A6
Aylesbury St SN1 ... 50 C7
Ayleswade Rd SP2 ... 152 A6
Aymer Pl SN3 ... 51 C5
Ayr Cl SN14 ... 77 F5
Ayrshire Cl
Salisbury SP2 ... 145 B5
Swindon SN5 ... 49 B7
Ayrton Cl BA14 ... 105 A6
Azalea Cl SN11 ... 81 C1
Azalea Dr
Trowbridge BA14 ... 105 A7
Warminster BA12 ... 116 E7
Azelin Ct SN3 ... 36 B3


## B


Babington Pk 9 SN5 ... 48 F5
Back Dro
West Winterslow SP5 ... 148 F5
West Winterslow SP5 ... 149 A5
Back Hill SN16 ... 28 A3
Back Horse Hill La
SP7 ... 203 A2
Back La
9 Aldbourne SN8 ... 170 A6
Alderton SN14 ... 39 F2
Alderton SN14 ... 40 A2
Blunsdon St Andrew SN26 ... 21 B3
Calne Without SN15 ... 88 B4
Cerney Wick GL7 ... 7 F4
Cherhill SN11 ... 166 E2
Chitterne BA12 ... 195 D7
Great Bedwyn SN8 ... 176 B3
Great Hinton BA14 ... 178 A5
Maiden Bradley with Yarnfield BA12 ... 118 F2
Marlborough SN8 ... 213 D3
Marshfield SN14 ... 74 A8
Penton Grafton SP11 ... 193 A3
Ramsbury SN8 ... 170 B2
Sixpenny Handley SP5 ... 208 A4
Tilshead SP3 ... 188 B3
Vernhams Dean SP11 ... 185 C3
Back Rd
Calne SN11 ... 81 B2
Chitterne BA12 ... 195 D7
Down Ampney GL7 ... 8 E7
Back St
Ashton Keynes SN6 ... 6 F1
East Garston RG17 ... 171 E7
Great Hinton BA14 ... 178 A6
Trowbridge BA14 ... 101 C1
Back Terr BA10 ... 122 F2
Bacon Cl SN1 ... 50 A4
BADBURY ... 65 F5
BADBURY WICK ... 65 D8
Bader Pk 10 SN12 ... 178 B8
Badger Cl
Devizes SN10 ... 214 B2
Badger Cl *continued*
2 Royal Wootton Bassett SN4 ... 47 F2
Badgers Brook SN4 ... 64 A5
Badgers Cl
Bourton SP8 ... 137 E2
3 Wanborough SN4 ... 163 B6
BADMINTON ... 38 F2
Badminton House*
GL9 ... 38 F2
Badminton Pk* GL9 ... 38 F3
Badminton Rd
Acton Turville GL9 ... 52 F7
Little Badminton GL9 ... 38 E6
Bagbury La SN5 ... 33 B1
Bagbury Rd BA12 ... 194 F4
Baghdad Rd 2 SP4 ... 198 F7
BAGSHOT ... 176 F4
Bailey Cl SN9 ... 215 B5
Bailey La SP2 ... 144 E3
Bailey Mews SP4 ... 146 C8
Baileys Barn BA15 ... 100 D5
Baileys Farm Gdns
SN3 ... 51 A6
Baileys La SN6 ... 11 B4
Bailey's Mead SN4 ... 48 A2
Baileys Way SN4 ... 64 B7
Bailiffe Piece SN6 ... 8 D1
Baillie Cl 5 SN25 ... 34 C8
Bainbridge Cl 2 SN5 ... 49 A5
Bainton Cl BA15 ... 100 D7
Baird Cl SN5 ... 49 B8
Bakehouse Cl SN15 ... 78 E6
Baker Cl SP9 ... 216 D8
Bakers Cnr SN13 ... 84 E4
Bakers Ct SN3 ... 36 B2
Bakers Field SN15 ... 60 A3
Bakers Rd SN4 ... 64 B5
Balden Cl SN4 ... 63 F6
Baldwin Cl SN4 ... 65 D4
Bale Cl 6 SN5 ... 48 F5
Ballands Castle*
BA9 ... 137 A2
BALLARD'S ASH ... 47 D5
Ball Comm La BA9 ... 136 C1
Ball Gr SP4 ... 132 B1
Ballie Cl SN25 ... 20 C1
Ballington BA12 ... 128 A8
Ball Rd SN9 ... 215 D4
Balmoor Cl BA12 ... 139 B3
Balmoral Cl
Chippenham SN14 ... 77 F7
Swindon SN3 ... 51 A3
Balmoral Rd
Salisbury SP1 ... 146 B4
Trowbridge BA14 ... 105 B5
Bamford Cl SN5 ... 33 C5
Bampton Gr SN3 ... 50 E6
Banbury Cl SN3 ... 50 F3
Bancroft BA15 ... 100 D7
Bancroft Cl SN5 ... 48 F6
Bankfoot Cl 3 SN5 ... 49 B7
Bank La SP11 ... 185 B6
Bankside SN1 ... 49 F4
Bank St SN12 ... 94 A4
Banks The SN15 ... 59 E4
Bank The SN14 ... 75 C3
Bankwaters Rd SN13 ... 84 B8
Bannerdown Cl BA1 ... 82 B4
Bannerdown Dr BA1 ... 82 A4
Bannerdown Rd BA1 ... 82 C5
Banwell Ave SN3 ... 51 A5
BAPTON ... 195 D1
Barbel Cl SN11 ... 81 B5
Barberry SP3 ... 201 A3
Barbers La SP3 ... 204 A5
Barber's La SP5 ... 151 C1
Barbrook Rd SN1 ... 50 A2
Barbury Castle*
SN4 ... 168 A7
Barbury Castle Ctry Pk*
SN4 ... 168 B7
Barbury Cl
Swindon SN2 ... 34 F3
Swindon SN25 ... 34 F3
Barbury La SN4 ... 168 A7
Barcelona Cres SN4 ... 64 A7
Barcete Cl SN25 ... 34 D7
Bardsey Cl 5 SN4 ... 47 F2
Barford La SP5 ... 159 C1
BARFORD ST MARTIN ... 143 A3
Barford St Martin CE Fst Sch SP3 ... 143 A3
Bargates SN13 ... 83 D6
Barken Rd
4 Chippenham SN14 ... 70 A1
Chippenham SN14 ... 78 A8
Barker Cl 9 SP4 ... 132 B1
BARKERS HILL ... 203 A4
Barkstead Cl 3 SN5 ... 49 B4
Barley Cl
Malmesbury SN16 ... 28 A2
Warminster BA12 ... 117 C5
Barley Fields SN8 ... 170 B8
Barley Hill La SN10 ... 179 A7
Barley Rd 2 SP11 ... 193 F2
Barley Rise BA14 ... 105 F7
Barlow Cl SN25 ... 35 A8
Barnack Cl BA14 ... 101 A1
Barnard Cl SN3 ... 51 B7
Barnard Field SP4 ... 217 C2
Barnard Mews SP4 ... 217 C2
Barnards Hill Dr SP2 ... 145 C4
Barnard St 1 SP1 ... 152 B8
Barn Cl
Chippenham SN14 ... 78 A8
Corsham SN13 ... 76 E1
Barncroft SP11 ... 192 E3
Barn End SN14 ... 74 A8
Barnes Cl
Corston SN16 ... 42 E4
Trowbridge BA14 ... 105 A7
Barnes Gn SN15 ... 45 F6
Barnes Pl BA12 ... 139 A5
Barnes Rd
Chippenham SN14 ... 70 B2
Swindon SN3 ... 36 B6
Barnes Wallis Cl
9 Amesbury SP4 ... 217 E3
Melksham Without BA14 ... 178 B8
Barnes Yd 17 SN8 ... 170 A6
Barnetts Hill SN13 ... 83 F7
Barnfield Cl SN2 ... 49 F7
Barnfield Rd SN2 ... 49 E7
Barnfield Way BA1 ... 82 B4
Barn Glebe BA14 ... 101 E1
Barn Hill SP3 ... 201 A3
Barn Moor Cl SN3 ... 51 E3
Barn Owl Rd SN14 ... 70 B2
Barn Piece
Box SN13 ... 83 D6
Bradford-on-Avon BA15 ... 100 D4
Barnsley Cl SN25 ... 20 B1
Barn St SN8 ... 213 D3
Barnstaple Cl SN3 ... 51 B5
Barnum Ct
2 Swindon SN1 ... 49 F7
Swindon SN2 ... 50 A7
Barn Way BA14 ... 105 F7
Baroda Rd SP9 ... 216 A4
Baron Cl
Lyneham SN15 ... 59 C4
4 Swindon SN3 ... 36 B3
Barons Cres BA14 ... 106 A8
Barons Mead SN14 ... 78 A8
Barracks SN14 ... 74 F4
Barra Cl SN6 ... 22 E6
Barrett La SN15 ... 57 D2
Barrett Way SN4 ... 64 B6
Barrington Cl SN3 ... 51 D3
Barrington Ct SN15 ... 57 C2
Barrington Rd SP1 ... 146 C3
BARROW ... 136 C5
Barrowby Gate SN3 ... 36 A4
Barrow Cl
Marlborough SN8 ... 213 F3
Royal Wootton Bassett SN4 ... 47 E1
Salisbury SP5 ... 152 C5
Barrow Gn SN15 ... 70 E2
Barrow La BA9 ... 136 B5
Barrow St La
Mere BA12 ... 139 F3
West Knoyle BA12 ... 140 A4
Barrows La SP5 ... 212 B7
BARROW STREET ... 139 F2
Barrow Water La
Charlton Musgrove BA9 ... 136 A5
Hardway BA10 ... 122 A1
Barry Glen Cl SN2 ... 35 E1
Barry Pl SN11 ... 79 F2
Barters La SP7 ... 206 D8
Bartholomew Way 4
SN13 ... 84 B8
Bartlett Cl 11 BA11 ... 110 C6
Bartlett Rd SP1 ... 146 B4
Bartletts SN10 ... 179 C1
Bartletts Mead BA14 ... 178 A4
Bartletts The BA12 ... 139 B4
Barton Cl
12 Andover SP10 ... 193 C2
8 Bradford-on-Avon BA15 ... 100 D6
Barton Farm Ctry Pk*
BA15 ... 100 A5
Barton Hill 22 SP7 ... 202 C2
Barton La BA12 ... 139 A5
Barton Lodge BA14 ... 105 A6
Barton Orch BA15 ... 100 C6
Barton Pl SP4 ... 132 B1
Barton Rd SN25 ... 34 E3
Barton Rd 20 SP6 ... 210 D1
Bartons The 29 SP6 ... 210 D1
Barton Way SN16 ... 42 E4
Barwell Ave SN1 ... 49 E2
Basepoint Bsns Ctr
SN5 ... 49 C8
Basevi Cl SN16 ... 27 F4
Bashkir Cl SN5 ... 34 C2
Bashkir Rd BA13 ... 108 E1
Basil Cl SN2 ... 34 D4
Basil Hill Rd SN13 ... 84 C7
Basingstoke Cl 5
SN5 ... 49 A4
Baskerville Rd SN3 ... 51 E7
Bassett Rd OX12 ... 165 F8
Bassetts Pasture
BA15 ... 100 D4
Bassetts The SN13 ... 83 D6
Batch The BA2 ... 98 E1
Bates Way SN25 ... 34 E3
Bathampton St SN1 ... 50 A6
BATHEASTON ... 82 B4
BATHFORD ... 82 B2
Bathford CE VC Prim Sch
BA1 ... 82 C2
Bathford Hill BA1 ... 82 B2
Bath Rd
Atworth SN12 ... 84 D2
Atworth SN12 ... 84 E1
Atworth/Whitley SN12 ... 93 A8
Box SN13 ... 83 A6

**Bath Rd** continued
Bradford-on-Avon BA15. **91** C1
Chippenham Without
SN14 . . . . . . . . . . . . . **77** F5
Colerne SN14 . . . . . . . **74** F3
Corsham SN13 . . . . . . . **77** B4
Cricklade SN6 . . . . . . . . **19** D8
Devizes SN10 . . . . . . . **179** C8
Frome BA11 . . . . . . . . **110** A6
Hinton Charterhouse
BA2 . . . . . . . . . . . . . . **98** D3
Hungerford RG17 . . . . . **176** F7
Marlborough SN8 . . . . . **213** B2
Melksham SN12 . . . . . . **94** A5
Melksham Without SN12 **93** E7
Preshute SN8 . . . . . . . . **174** C7
Royal Wootton Bassett
SN4 . . . . . . . . . . . . . . **47** C1
Seend SN12 . . . . . . . . **95** C1
Swindon SN1 . . . . . . . . **50** C4
Upton Scudamore
BA12 . . . . . . . . . . . . **112** D2
Warminster BA12 . . . . **112** E1
Westonbirt with Lasborough
GL8 . . . . . . . . . . . . . . **25** D8
**Bath Rd Ind Est** SN14. .**78** B6
**Bath Road**
Chippenham SN14 . . . . . **77** E5
Knockdown GL8 . . . . . . . **24** F5
**Bath Road Retail Pk**
SN14 . . . . . . . . . . . . . . . **77** F4
**Bath Spa University
(Corsham Court)**
SN13 . . . . . . . . . . . . . . . **77** A2
**Bath Stone Cres 1**
SN13 . . . . . . . . . . . . . . **76** D1
**Bathurst Rd** SN1 . . . . . . **50** D6
**Batsford Cres** 3 SN25 .**35** A8
**Batten Rd** SP5 . . . . . . . **211** A8
**Battens The 3** SN14 . . . .**70** A1
**Battlesbury Barracks**
BA12 . . . . . . . . . . . . . . **117** E6
*Battlesbury Hill Fort*★
BA12 . . . . . . . . . . . . . . **117** F8
**Battlesbury Rd**
Warminster BA12 . . . . **113** E1
Warminster BA12 . . . . **117** E7
**Battlewell** SN5 . . . . . . . .**33** A3
**Batt's La** SN8 . . . . . . . . **183** F7
**BAVERSTOCK** . . . . . . . **142** B4
**Baverstock La** SP3 . . . **142** B5
**Bawdsey Rd** 6 SP4 . . **217** D2
**Baxter Cl** SN25 . . . . . . . .**35** A7
**Bay Cl** SN11 . . . . . . . . . .**89** C8
**BAYDON** . . . . . . . . . . . . **170** C8
**Baydon Cl**
Swindon SN25 . . . . . . . .**34** F3
Trowbridge BA14 . . . . . **105** C5
**Baydon Gr** SN11 . . . . . . .**81** B4
**Baydon Rd**
Aldbourne SN8 . . . . . . . **164** B1
Great Shefford RG17 . . . **171** F3
**Baydon St Nicholas CE
Prim Sch** SN8 . . . . . **164** C1
**Baydons La** SN15 . . . . . .**78** E6
**Bayes Cl** SN25 . . . . . . . . .**20** C1
**Bayeux Mws** SP9 . . . . . **216** C6
**Bayfield Cl** SN5 . . . . . . . .**34** B2
**Bayleaf Ave** SN2 . . . . . . .**34** D4
**Bayliffes Cl** SN15 . . . . . . .**79** A7
**Baynton Cl** BA13 . . . . . . .**89** C8
**Baynton Way** BA13. . . . **186** D8
**Bayntun Cl**
Bromham SN15 . . . . . . . .**96** A7
Devizes SN10 . . . . . . . . **214** C1
**Baytree Cl** BA12 . . . . . . **115** C7
**Bay Tree Ct** SN2 . . . . . . .**35** C2
**Baywater** SN8 . . . . . . . . **213** E4
**Bazaar Rd** SP9 . . . . . . . **216** B5
**Beacon Cl**
Amesbury SP4 . . . . . . . **217** C4
8 Swindon SN1 . . . . . . . .**49** F4
**Beacon Ct** SP6 . . . . . . . **210** D2
**Beacon Dr** SN11 . . . . . . .**89** C8
**BEACON HILL**
Bromham . . . . . . . . . . . . .**97** B7
Bulford . . . . . . . . . . . . . **199** A7
Hilmarton . . . . . . . . . . . . .**73** E5
**Beacon Hill Rd 7**
SP4 . . . . . . . . . . . . . . . **198** F7
**Beaconsfield Way**
BA11 . . . . . . . . . . . . . . **110** B7
**Beacon View** BA12 . . . . **116** D6
**Beale Cl** SN14 . . . . . . . . . .**78** B7
**Beale Cl** SN14 . . . . . . . . . .**78** A7
**Beale Rd** SP9 . . . . . . . . **216** D8
**Beale's Barton** BA14 . . **101** F8
**Beales Cl** SN1 . . . . . . . . . .**50** B7
**Beales Farm Rd 15**
RG17. . . . . . . . . . . . . . **165** A1
**Beamish Cl 2** SN11 . . **166** A1
**BEANACRE** . . . . . . . . . . .**94** A8
*Beanacre Old Manor*★
SN12. . . . . . . . . . . . . . . .**94** A8
**Beanacre Rd**
Melksham SN12 . . . . . . . .**94** A7
Melksham Without SN12 **86** A1
**Beaney Vw 1** SN2 . . . . . .**34** E2
**Beanlands The** SN4. . . **163** A6
**Bear Cl** BA15 . . . . . . . . **100** B7
**Beard Ct** SP11 . . . . . . . **192** B5
**Beardsley La** SN26 . . . . . .**20** D1
**Bearfield Bldgs** BA15 **100** C8
**Bearfield La** RG17. . . . . **171** A4
**Bearwater** RG17 . . . . . **177** B7
**Beatrice Rd** SP1 . . . . . . **146** A4
**Beatrice St** SN2. . . . . . . .**50** C8
**Beatrice Way** BA14 . . . **105** E8

**Beatty Ct** SN3 . . . . . . . . .**50** D4
**Beauchamp Dr 1**
SP4. . . . . . . . . . . . . . . **217** D3
**Beauchamp-Proctor Rise**
8 SP4 . . . . . . . . . . . . **132** B1
**Beauclerc St** SN10 . . . **179** D8
**Beaufort Ave** SN4. . . . . . .**61** E8
**Beaufort Cl 5** SN12 . . **178** B8
**Beaufort Gn** SN3. . . . . . . .**51** B5
**Beaufort Rd** SN4. . . . . . . .**64** A7
**Beaufort Vw** SN14 . . . . . .**39** E4
**Beaufoy** 3 SP7 . . . . . . . **202** D2
**Beaulieu Cl** SN5 . . . . . . . .**49** C4
**Beaulieu Rd 2** SP4. . . . **217** C2
**Beaumaris Rd** SN5 . . . . . .**49** B5
**Beaumont Rd** SN3 . . . . . .**50** E6
**Beaumont Way** SP4 . . . **217** D2
**Beaven Cl** SN15 . . . . . . . .**78** F4
**Beavens Ct** BA12 . . . . . . **117** B7
**Bechstein Mdw** BA14 **106** A8
**Beck Cl** SN25 . . . . . . . . . . .**35** A3
**Beckerley La** BA14 . . . . . .**92** F1
**Beckett Pl** BA13 . . . . . . **108** F1
**Beckett's La** SP3. . . . . . . .**84** E4
**Beckett St 14** SP3 . . . . **203** E8
**Beckett Strand** SN1 . . . . .**49** E2
**Becket Way** SP1 . . . . . . **146** D1
**Beckford Cl**
Tisbury SP3 . . . . . . . . . **200** D1
Warminster BA12 . . . . **117** B6
**BECKHAMPTON** . . . . . . **173** B7
**Beckhampton (Long
Barrow)**★ SN8 . . . . **173** A8
**Beckhampton Rd**
SN8 . . . . . . . . . . . . . . . **173** B8
**Beckhampton St** SN1 . . .**50** C6
**Beddington Ct** SN2 . . . . . .**36** A5
**Beddoe Cl** BA15 . . . . . . **100** E4
**Bede Dr 7** SP10 . . . . . . **193** C2
**Bedford Cl 2** SP6 . . . . **210** D2
**Bedford Rd**
Salisbury SP2 . . . . . . . **145** E2
6 Swindon SN3 . . . . . . . .**50** F6
**Bedlam Green Farm La**
BA10 . . . . . . . . . . . . . . **136** B8
**Bedlam La** SN6 . . . . . . . . .**22** D8
**Bedwin St** SP1 . . . . . . . . **146** B1
**Bedwyn Cl** SN2 . . . . . . . . .**35** C3
**Bedwyn Dyke**★ SN8 . . **176** C3
**Bedwyn Sta** SN8 . . . . . **176** B3
**Bedwyn Stone Mus**★
SN8. . . . . . . . . . . . . . . **176** B2
**Beech Ave**
Melksham SN12 . . . . . . . .**94** A3
Swindon SN2 . . . . . . . . . .**35** A2
Warminster BA12 . . . . **116** F6
**Beech Cl**
Andover SP11 . . . . . . . **193** B1
Porton SP4 . . . . . . . . . . **133** D4
**Beechcroft Cl** SP10 . . . **193** D1
**Beechcroft Inf Sch**
SN25 . . . . . . . . . . . . . . . .**35** E4
**Beechcroft Rd**
Salisbury SP1 . . . . . . . **146** D1
Swindon SN2 . . . . . . . . . .**35** E4
**Beech Ct** BA11 . . . . . . . . **110** B7
**Beech Dr** SN5 . . . . . . . . . .**34** A2
**Beeches Cl** SP5. . . . . . . **148** C3
**Beeches Gn** SN12 . . . . . .**93** D8
**Beeches La** SN15 . . . . . . .**59** A5
**Beeches The**
Bradford-on-Avon
BA15 . . . . . . . . . . . . **101** A4
Coombe Bissett SP5 . . . **156** F7
Lydiard Millicent SN5. . . .**33** B1
Melksham Without SN12 **93** C7
5 Salisbury SP1 . . . . . **152** C8
15 Shaftesbury SP7. . . **202** C2
Trowbridge BA14 . . . . . **101** F2
Warminster BA12 . . . . **116** F6
4 West Wellow SO51. . **212** F6
**Beechfield** SP4 . . . . . . . **199** B3
**Beechfield Dr** SN10 . . . **214** E5
**Beechfield Rd**
Corsham SN13 . . . . . . . . .**76** E1
Roundway SN10. . . . . . . **214** E7
**Beech Gr**
Highworth SN6. . . . . . . . .**22** F5
Trowbridge BA14 . . . . . **105** B6
**Beech Grange** SP5 . . . **212** C5
**Beech Hanger** SP4 . . . **199** C5
**Beech Hill Rd** SP9 . . . . **216** E7
**BEECHINGSTOKE** . . . . **181** A6
**Beech Lea**
Broad Blunsdon SN26 . . .**21** C1
Meysey Hampton GL7 . . . .**1** A4
**Beech Rd**
Box Hill SN13 . . . . . . . . . .**84** A8
Colerne SN14 . . . . . . . . . .**75** A5
Corsham SN13 . . . . . . . . .**83** E7
**Beech Sq 12** RG17 . . . . **177** B6
**Beech Wlk**
Durnford SP4 . . . . . . . . . **131** C1
Salterton SP4 . . . . . . . . **131** E4
Salterton SP4 . . . . . . . . **132** A4
**Beechwood 13** SP6 . . . **210** C1
**Beech Wood 13** SN10 **179** F1
**Beechwood Ave**
BA11. . . . . . . . . . . . . . **110** A5
**Beechwood Cl**
Frome BA11 . . . . . . . . . **110** A5
Roundway SN10. . . . . . . **214** E6
**Beechwood Rd** SN14. . . . .**78** B8
**Beehive Cl 1** SN5 . . . . . . .**49** A8
**Begle Cl 9** SN25 . . . . . . . .**34** B7
*Belcombe Ct*★ BA15 . . **100** B6
**Belcombe Pl** BA15 . . . . **100** C6

**Belcombe Rd**
Avoncliff BA15 . . . . . . . . .**99** F5
Bradford-on-Avon
BA15 . . . . . . . . . . . . **100** B6
**Belfast Mead** SN15 . . . . .**60** C2
**Belfry Dr** SN14 . . . . . . . . .**41** E1
**Belgrave Cres** SP9 . . . **216** E6
**Belgrave St** SN1 . . . . . . . .**50** C5
**Bellamy La** SP1 . . . . . . . **152** B8
**Bell Cl** BA12 . . . . . . . . . . **116** F1
**Bellefield CE Prim Sch**
BA14 . . . . . . . . . . . . . . **101** E2
**Bellefield Cres** BA14 . . **101** D1
**Belle Vue Rd**
Salisbury SP1 . . . . . . . . **146** A1
Swindon SN1 . . . . . . . . . .**50** D4
**Bell Field The** SN14 . . . .**39** E4
**Bell Gdns** SN3 . . . . . . . . .**36** E4
**Bell Hill**
Seend SN12 . . . . . . . . . **178** E7
Warminster BA12 . . . . . **116** F5
**Bellinger Cl** SN15 . . . . . . .**70** C3
**Bellingham La** SN6 . . . . . .**23** A2
**Bell La**
Inkpen RG17 . . . . . . . . . **177** E2
Lechlade GL7 . . . . . . . . . . .**2** C3
Liddington SN4 . . . . . . . **163** A4
Sutton Benger SN15 . . . . .**57** D2
6 Wilton SP2 . . . . . . . . **144** D3
**Bellot Dr**
3 Corsham SN13 . . . . . . .**76** E1
Corsham SN13 . . . . . . . . .**84** E8
**Bellott Dr** SN13 . . . . . . . . .**84** E8
**Bell Piece** SN15 . . . . . . . .**57** D2
**Bell Rd** SP4 . . . . . . . . . . . **197** F7
**Bells La** BA12 . . . . . . . . . **137** F7
**Bell Sq** SN14 . . . . . . . . . . .**74** A8
**Bell St**
4 Ludgershall SP11 . . . **192** B5
Shaftesbury SP7 . . . . . . **202** C2
**Bellver** SN5 . . . . . . . . . . . .**49** B5
**Belmont Cl**
10 Shaftesbury SP7. . . **202** C1
Swindon SN3 . . . . . . . . . .**36** A4
**Belmont Cres** SN1 . . . . . .**50** A3
**Belsay** SN5 . . . . . . . . . . . .**49** C4
**Belthane Pl** SN12 . . . . . . .**93** C8
**Belvedere Rd**
Bowerhill SN12 . . . . . . . .**94** D1
Swindon SN3 . . . . . . . . . .**51** A3
**Belvedere Terr** SN10. . **214** C4
**Bembridge Cl** SN3 . . . . . .**51** B4
**BEMERTON** . . . . . . . . . . **145** C2
**BEMERTON HEATH** . . . **145** C4
**Bemerton St John CE
Aided Prim Sch**
SP2 . . . . . . . . . . . . . . . **145** C2
**Bences La** SN13 . . . . . . . .**77** A2
**Benches La**
Ashmore SP5 . . . . . . . . **206** F4
Tollard Royal SP5. . . . . . **207** B4
**Bencroft Hill**
Bremhill SN15 . . . . . . . . .**80** B6
Stanley SN15 . . . . . . . . . .**79** F6
**Ben Cross** SN13. . . . . . . .**83** B7
**Bendall's La** SN13 . . . . . .**82** F7
**Bendalls Wharf 8**
BA11. . . . . . . . . . . . . . **110** A4
**Bendy Bow** SN16 . . . . . . .**15** F7
**Benin Rd** SP11. . . . . . . . **191** F3
**Benjamin St** BA15 . . . . **100** E6
**Ben La** SP5 . . . . . . . . . . . **154** F7
**Ben Lane** SP5 . . . . . . . . **155** A6
**Bennett Cl** SP5 . . . . . . . **211** C7
**Bennett Hill Cl 3** SN4 .**47** F2
**Bentham Cl** SN5 . . . . . . . .**49** D6
**Bentham La** SN5. . . . . . . .**33** A8
**Bentley Cl** SN3 . . . . . . . . .**51** A6
**Bentley Gr** SN11 . . . . . . . .**81** C2
**Bentley La**
Calne SN11 . . . . . . . . . . .**81** B1
Quemerford SN11 . . . . . . .**89** B8
**Bentley Way** SP5 . . . . . **149** D5
**Bentley Woods** SP5. . . **155** C6
**Benwell Cl** SN5 . . . . . . . . .**49** C6
**Beranburh Field** SN4 . . .**64** C2
**Berengaria Cl** BA13 . . . **109** B5
**Berenger Cl** SN1. . . . . . . .**50** D3
**Beresford Cl 1** SN3 . . . .**51** C4
**Bergamot Cl** SN8 . . . . . **174** C7
**Bergman Cl** SN25 . . . . . . .**35** B6
**Berhills La** SN10 . . . . . . . .**95** F2
**Bericot La** SN4 . . . . . . . . .**65** E6
**Berkeley Cl**
Melksham SN12 . . . . . . . .**94** A2
South Cerney GL7 . . . . . . . .**6** F8
**Berkeley Lawns** SN3 . . .**50** F3
**Berkeley Rd**
Trowbridge BA14 . . . . . **105** A8
Wroughton SN4 . . . . . . . .**64** B7
**Berkely Cl 2** SN14. . . . . . .**78** A7
**BERKLEY** . . . . . . . . . . . . **111** A7
**Berkley CE Fst Sch**
BA11. . . . . . . . . . . . . . **111** A7
**Berkley Cross** BA11 . . . **110** F6
**BERKLEY DOWN**. . . . . . **110** C5
**Berkley La** BA11 . . . . . . **110** D8
**Berkley Rd** BA11 . . . . . . **110** A5
**Berkley St** BA11 . . . . . . . **107** B1
**Berkshire Dr** SN5 . . . . . . .**49** A7
**Berkshire Rd** SP2 . . . . . **151** E7
*Bermerton Heath &
Barnards Folly Nature
Reserve*★ SP2. . . . . . **145** C4
**Berrington Rd** SN3. . . . . .**51** A3
**Berry Cl 4** SP4 . . . . . . . **190** A3
**Berrycroft**
Ashbury SN6 . . . . . . . . . **164** A7

**Berrycroft** continued
Mildenhall SN8. . . . . . . **175** B8
**BERRYFIELD** . . . . . . . . . .**93** F1
**Berryfield Cl** SN12 . . . . . .**93** F1
**Berryfield La** BA14 . . . . . .**93** F1
**Berryfield Pk** SN12. . . . . .**93** F1
**Berry Rd** BA15 . . . . . . . **100** D8
**Berry Rd** BA13 . . . . . . . **186** D8
**Berry Wood La** SP7 . . . **203** A3
**Bertha's Field** GL9 . . . . . .**24** B4
**Berton St** SN26 . . . . . . . . .**21** C2
**BERWICK BASSETT**. . . **167** B4
**Berwick La**
Steeple Langford SP3 . . **128** D7
Steeple Langford SP3 . . **196** C1
**Berwick Rd**
Berwick St James
SP3. . . . . . . . . . . . . . **196** F3
Stapleford SP3 . . . . . . . **129** E7
**BERWICK ST JAMES**. . **196** F3
**BERWICK ST JOHN** . . . **203** B4
**BERWICK ST
LEONARD**. . . . . . . . . . **200** C4
**Besomer Dro** SP5. . . . . **211** D6
**Bessemer Cl** SN2 . . . . . . .**35** A5
**Bessemer Rd E** SN2 . . . .**35** A4
**Bessemer Rd W** SN2 . . . .**34** F1
**Bess Rd** SN5. . . . . . . . . . .**48** F4
**Bests La** BA12 . . . . . . . . **117** F1
**Best's La** BA12 . . . . . . . **194** A5
**Bethel Rd** SN13 . . . . . . . . .**76** E1
**Betjeman Ave** SN4 . . . . . .**47** E3
**Betjeman Rd** SN8 . . . . . **213** A2
**Betony Cl** SN25 . . . . . . . . .**34** E5
**Bettertons Cl** GL7. . . . . . . .**1** F7
**Bevan Cl** SN2 . . . . . . . . . . .**35** F3
**Beverley** SN5 . . . . . . . . . . .**49** C4
**Beverley Cl** SN12 . . . . . . .**94** C1
**Beverley Cres** SN9 . . . . **182** B2
**Beverley Hills Mobile
Home Pk** SP4 . . . . . . **217** D3
**Beverley Way** SN14 . . . . .**77** F5
**Beversbrook La** SN11. . . .**81** B5
**Beversbrook Rd** SN11. . . .**81** A5
**Beverstone Cl** GL7. . . . . . . .**6** F6
**Beverstone Gr** SN3 . . . . . .**50** F4
**Bevil** SN5. . . . . . . . . . . . . . .**49** A3
*Bevisbury Hill Fort*★
SP11. . . . . . . . . . . . . . **185** A1
**Bevisland** SN3 . . . . . . . . . .**51** C3
**Bewick Cl** GL7 . . . . . . . . . . .**7** A6
**BEWLEY COMMON** . . . . .**86** E5
*Bewley Ct*★ SN15. . . . . . . .**86** F6
**Bewley Edge** SN15. . . . . .**87** A4
**Bewley La** SN15 . . . . . . . .**86** F5
**Bewley Rd 1** BA14 . . . . **105** C5
**Beyer Rd 5** SP4 . . . . . . **217** D2
**Bibby Dr** SP9 . . . . . . . . . **216** D8
**Bibury Rd** SN3 . . . . . . . . . .**50** E5
**Bicton Rd** SN25 . . . . . . . . .**34** F6
**Biddel Springs** SN6 . . . . .**23** B6
**Biddesden La** BA12. . . . **195** D6
**Biddesden La** SP11 . . . **192** C5
**BIDDESTONE** . . . . . . . . . .**76** F8
**Biddestone La** SN14 . . . . .**68** E3
*Biddestone Manor*★
SN14 . . . . . . . . . . . . . . . .**76** F7
**Biddulph Rd** SP4 . . . . . . **198** A7
**Bideford Cl** SN3 . . . . . . . . .**51** A5
**Big La** RG17 . . . . . . . . . . **165** A2
**Bigpool La** SN13 . . . . . . . .**83** A4
**Bilborough Dr 2** SN3 . . .**50** F5
**Bill Turpin Ct** SN3 . . . . . . .**51** B4
**Bimport** SP7 . . . . . . . . . . **202** B1
**Bincknoll** SN5 . . . . . . . . . .**48** B1
**Bincknoll La** SN4 . . . . . . . .**47** F1
**Bindon Cl** SN5 . . . . . . . . . .**49** A5
**Bingham Rd**
Durrington SP4 . . . . . . . **197** E7
Salisbury SP1 . . . . . . . . **146** C4
**Binknoll La** SN4 . . . . . . . . .**47** F1
**Birch Ash** SN2 . . . . . . . . . .**35** F2
**Birch Cl** SN13. . . . . . . . . . .**84** C5
**Birchenleaze** BA14. . . . **105** C3
**Birches The** SN3. . . . . . . .**51** B2
**Birch Gdns** BA14 . . . . . **102** B2
**Birch Glade** SN6 . . . . . . . .**17** F8
**Birch Gr**
Bower Hill SN12. . . . . . . . .**94** C1
Chippenham SN15 . . . . . .**70** E1
Whaddon SP5. . . . . . . . . **153** E2
**Birchill La** BA11 . . . . . . . **110** A1
**Birch St** SN1. . . . . . . . . . . .**49** F5
**Birch Wlk 4** BA11 . . . . **110** B7
**Birchwood Cl** BA12 . . . . **115** C7
**Birchwood Dr 4**
SP4. . . . . . . . . . . . . . . **198** C7
**Birchwood Rd** SN3. . . . . .**36** B2
**Birdbrook Rd** SN2 . . . . . . .**35** E5
**BIRDBUSH**. . . . . . . . . . . **203** B1
**Birdcombe Rd 1** SN5. .**49** C5
**Birds Marsh View**
SN15. . . . . . . . . . . . . . . .**70** E2
**Birkdale Cl 5** SN25 . . . . .**34** D7
**Bisham La** BA14 . . . . . . . **106** A8
*Bishopdale Cl 2* SN5 . . .**34** A1
**BISHOPDOWN**. . . . . . . **146** C4
**Bishopdown Rd** SP1 . . . **146** B3
**Bishop Rd** SN13 . . . . . . . . .**76** D1
**BISHOPS
CANNINGS**. . . . . . . . **172** B3
**Bishops Cannings CE
(Aided) Prim Sch**
SN10. . . . . . . . . . . . . . **172** B3

**Bishops Cannings CE Pri
Sch** SN10. . . . . . . . . **172** B3
**Bishops Cl**
Chippenham SN15 . . . . . .**78** F4
Mere BA12. . . . . . . . . . **139** A6
Tidworth SP9 . . . . . . . . **216** D4
**Bishops Dr** SP2 . . . . . . . **151** F6
**Bishopsfield 6** SN6 . . . . .**19** D8
**Bishopsmead** BA14 . . . . **101** C5
**Bishops Mead** SP1. . . . **146** E4
**BISHOPSTONE**
Shaftesbury . . . . . . . . . **205** F4
Swindon . . . . . . . . . . . . **163** E6
**Bishopstone CE Prim Sch**
SN6. . . . . . . . . . . . . . . . **163** E6
**Bishopstone Hollow**
SN6. . . . . . . . . . . . . . . **205** E3
**BISHOPSTROW**. . . . . . . **117** E4
**Bishopstrow Coll**
BA12. . . . . . . . . . . . . . **117** E4
**Bishopstrow Ct** BA12 **117** E5
**Bishopstrow Rd**
BA12. . . . . . . . . . . . . . **117** E4
**Bishop's Wlk** SP1 . . . . . **152** A8
**Bishop Wordsworth's
Gram Sch** SP1 . . . . . **152** A8
**Bisley** SN16. . . . . . . . . . . . .**29** A6
**Bisley Cl** SN3 . . . . . . . . . . .**51** A5
**Biss Cl** BA12 . . . . . . . . . . **117** F1
**Bissington Cl 9** SN2 . . **132** C3
**Biss Meadow** BA14 . . . . **105** D3
**Bitham Brook Prim Sch**
BA13. . . . . . . . . . . . . . **109** B4
**Bitham La**
Ham RG17 . . . . . . . . . . **177** A3
Westbury BA13 . . . . . . . **109** A3
**Bitham Mill** BA13 . . . . . . **109** B3
**Bitham Pk** BA13 . . . . . . . **109** B4
**Bittern Cl** GL7 . . . . . . . . . . .**7** A6
**Bittern Rd** SN3 . . . . . . . . . .**51** E6
**BITTLES GREEN** . . . . . **202** B4
**Black Acre 4** SN13 . . . . .**84** E8
**Blackbarn Rd** SN4 . . . . **134** B5
**Blackberry Cl** SN14 . . . . . .**70** A2
**Blackberry La**
Brinkworth SN16 . . . . . . . .**30** F3
Brinkworth SN16 . . . . . . . .**31** A2
Potterne SN10 . . . . . . . . **179** D5
Winsley BA15. . . . . . . . . .**90** C1
**Blackbird Cl**
7 Melksham SN12 . . . . . .**94** D5
Swindon SN3 . . . . . . . . . .**51** D7
**Blackbird Way** BA11 . . **110** B6
**Blackboard La** SN10 . . **180** A4
**Black Bridge Rd** SN15. . .**78** F8
**Blackcross** SN15 . . . . . . . .**78** F6
**Blackcross Rd** SP4 . . . . **217** C2
**Black Dog Hill**
Calne Without SN11. . . . . .**80** D2
Chapmanslade BA13. . . **111** E6
**Blackdown Cl 10**
BA12. . . . . . . . . . . . . . **117** A8
**Blackford Dr** SN11. . . . . . .**81** B1
**Blackford La** SN6 . . . . . . .**10** C4
**Blackfriars Way** SP1 . . **152** B8
**Blackhill Rd** SO51. . . . . **212** F3
**Black Horse La**
Westbury BA13 . . . . . . . **108** D1
Westbury BA13 . . . . . . . **112** E8
Winterbourne SP4 . . . . **146** D5
**Blackhorse Way**
Swindon SN1 . . . . . . . . . .**49** F1
Swindon SN1 . . . . . . . . . .**50** A1
**Black La**
Pitton & Farley SP5. . . . **148** C4
Redlynch SP5 . . . . . . . . **211** E6
**BLACKLAND**. . . . . . . . . . .**89** F6
**Blacklands Crossroads**
SN11. . . . . . . . . . . . . . . .**89** G6
**Blackman Gdns** SN1 . . . .**50** D3
**Blackman's La 4**
SN8. . . . . . . . . . . . . . . **183** D8
*Blackmoor Copse Nature
Reserve*★ SP5. . . . . . **155** A7
**Blackmore Cl 1** SN3 . .**51** E7
**Blackmore La** SN8 . . . . **192** A7
**Blackmore Rd**
Melksham SN12 . . . . . . . .**94** C4
3 Shaftesbury SP7. . . . **202** D2
**Blacksmith Cl** SN14 . . . . .**68** F5
**Blackstone Ave** SN3 . . . .**51** C4
**Blackthorn Cl** SN14 . . . . . .**70** A2
**Blackthorn La** SN25 . . . . .**35** B3
**Blackthorn Mews**
SN15. . . . . . . . . . . . . . . .**78** F5
**Blackthorn Way**
BA14. . . . . . . . . . . . . . **101** D4
**Blackwell Cl** SN25 . . . . . . .**20** B1
**Blackworth** SN6 . . . . . . . . .**22** F8
**Bladen Cl** SN4 . . . . . . . . . .**63** F7
**Blagdon Wlk** BA11. . . . . **110** A2
**Blagrove Ind Est** SN1. . . .**49** A2
**Blain Pl**
Royal Wootton Bassett
SN4 . . . . . . . . . . . . . . . .**47** F1
Royal Wootton Bassett
SN1 . . . . . . . . . . . . . . **47/** F2
**Blair Rd** BA14 . . . . . . . . . **105** B7
**Blake Cres** SN3 . . . . . . . . .**36** C7
**Blake Ct** BA14 . . . . . . . . . **101** D4
**Blakehill Farm Nature
Reserve**★ SN6 . . . . . . .**19** A3
**Blakeney Ave** SN3 . . . . . .**51** B5
**Blakesley Cl 3** SN3. . . . . .**50** F4
**Blakey Rd** SP1 . . . . . . . . **152** C8
**Blanchard Rd** SN26 . . . . .**20** B1

**Blandford Alley** SN6 . . . .**23** A5
**Blandford Ct** SN3 . . . . . . .**51** B6
**Blandford Rd**
Bishopstone SP5 . . . . . **205** F1
Coombe Bissett SP5 . . . **150** C1
Martin Drove End SP6 . . **209** A8
**Blatchs Orch 18**
BA13. . . . . . . . . . . . . . **186** B7
**Blaygrove Ind Est** SN1 **49** A2
**Bleak St** BA9 . . . . . . . . . **137** C3
**Blease Cl** BA14 . . . . . . . **101** D4
**BLEET** . . . . . . . . . . . . . . . **102** F2
**Bleke St** SP7 . . . . . . . . . **202** C2
**Blendon Dr** SN14 . . . . . . . .**56** C6
**Blenheim Gdns** SN14 . . . .**56** C6
**Blenheim Pk 21**
SN12. . . . . . . . . . . . . . **178** B8
**Blenheim Rd**
Marlborough SN8. . . . . . **213** F2
Warminster BA12 . . . . . **113** E1
Warminster BA12 . . . . . **117** D8
Wroughton SN4 . . . . . . . .**64** A7
**Blenheim Cl** BA12 . . . . **116** F7
**Bletchley Cl 5** SN3. . . . . .**51** C4
**Blicks Cl** SN14 . . . . . . . . . .**41** F1
**Blicks Hill** SN16 . . . . . . . . .**28** B3
**Blick's Hill** SN16 . . . . . . . .**28** B4
**Blind La**
Ansty SP3 . . . . . . . . . . **203** F5
Berwick St John SP7 . . **204** B8
Southwick BA14. . . . . . . **104** F2
**Blissford Rd** SP6. . . . . . **210** F1
**Blissmore La 8** SP11 **192** F1
**Block Rd 6** SP4 . . . . . . **197** E7
**Bloody Shard Gate**
DT11. . . . . . . . . . . . . . . **207** A1
**Bloomsbury Cl 9** SN13 .**76** D1
**Blossom Dr 9** SN3 . . . . . .**76** D1
**Blounts Cl** SN10 . . . . . . . **179** D5
**Blowhorn St** SN8 . . . . . . **213** D4
**Bluebell Dr** SN14 . . . . . . . .**70** B3
**Bluebell Gr** SN11 . . . . . . . .**81** B5
**Bluebell Mead 7**
SN13. . . . . . . . . . . . . . . .**84** E8
**Bluebell Way 27** SP4. . **198** B7
**Blueberry Rd** SN12. . . . . .**94** D3
**Blue Boar Row** SP1 . . . **146** A1
**BLUE VEIN** . . . . . . . . . . . .**83** D3
**Blunsdon Abbey** SN25 . . .**34** F4
**Blunsdon Hill** SN26 . . . . . .**20** F3
**Blunsdon Rd** SN25 . . . . . .**34** F4
**BLUNSDON ST
ANDREW**. . . . . . . . . . . .**34** E8
**Blunsdon Sta** SN5 . . . . . . .**33** F8
**Blunt Rise** SN26 . . . . . . . .**21** D2
**Blythe Cl**
10 Cricklade SN6. . . . . . .**19** D8
Enham Alamein SP11. . . **193** E3
**Blyth Way** SP1 . . . . . . . . **146** D4
**BMI The Ridgeway Hospl**
SN4. . . . . . . . . . . . . . . . .**64** C6
**Boardleaze** BA12 . . . . . **195** A2
**Boar St** BA12 . . . . . . . . . **139** A5
**Boatman Cl** SN25 . . . . . . .**34** A7
**Bobbin La** BA15. . . . . . . . .**99** F4
**Bobbin Pk** BA15 . . . . . . . .**99** F3
**Bockhampton Rd**
RG17. . . . . . . . . . . . . . **165** A1
*Bockhampton Village*★
RG17. . . . . . . . . . . . . . **165** B1
**BODENHAM** . . . . . . . . . **152** F1
**Bodiam Dr** SN5. . . . . . . . . .**49** D4
**Bodiam Dr N 4** SN5 . . . . .**49** D5
**Bodiam Dr S 3** SN5 . . . . .**49** D4
**Bodkin Hazel La** GL9. . . . .**38** A6
**Bodman Cl** SN15. . . . . . . .**78** F4
**Bodmin Cl** SN3 . . . . . . . . . .**51** A4
**Bodyhorse Hill** SN4. . . . **163** C6
**BOHEMIA** . . . . . . . . . . . . **211** E6
**Bohemia La** SP5 . . . . . . **211** D6
*Bokerley Ditch*★
SP6. . . . . . . . . . . . . . . **209** A5
**Bokerley Junc** SP5. . . . **208** E6
**Boldrewood** SN3 . . . . . . . .**51** D3
*Bolehyde Manor*★
SN14. . . . . . . . . . . . . . . .**69** E4
**Boleyn Cl** SN5 . . . . . . . . . .**49** A6
**Bolingbroke Cl** SN5 . . . . .**47** F6
**Bolingbroke Rd** SN2 . . . . .**34** F2
**Bolland Cl** SN8 . . . . . . . . **176** B2
**Bolland's Hill** SN12 . . . . **178** B8
**Bonaker Cl** SP4 . . . . . . . **133** D6
**Bond St Bldgs** BA14. . . **105** C7
**Bond St**
Durrington/Bulford
SP4. . . . . . . . . . . . . . **198** E6
Trowbridge BA14 . . . . . **105** C7
**Boness Rd** SN4 . . . . . . . . .**64** A7
**Bonham Cl** SP2. . . . . . . . **129** F4
**Bonham La** BA12 . . . . . . **137** E7
**Bonner Cl 10** SN5 . . . . . .**48** F5
**Bonners Cl** SN16 . . . . . . . .**28** A5
**Bonnewe Rise** SP4 . . . . **217** C3
**Bonnie Pk** BA13 . . . . . . . **186** B8
**Boothmead** SN14 . . . . . . .**70** B8
**Borage Cl** SN2 . . . . . . . . . .**34** D5
**Border Cl** SN25 . . . . . . . . .**34** A5
**Border La** BA10. . . . . . . . **122** C7
**BOREHAM** . . . . . . . . . . . **117** C5
**Boreham Cl** BA12 . . . . . . **117** C6
**Boreham Field** BA12. . . **117** D6
**Boreham Rd**
Warminster BA12 . . . . . **117** C6
Warminster BA12 . . . . . **117** E5
Warminster BA12 . . . . . **117** F5

Bore Hill BA12...... 116 F4
Boreland Hill
Great Durnford SP4.....197 D1
Upper Woodford SP4...131 B8
Boreway Cl 24 SP11.. 193 C2
Borkum Cl 8 SP10... 193 D2
Borough Fields SN4.. 47 D2
Borough Parade Sh Ctr
SN15.................. 78 D7
Borough The SP5..... 211 A8
Borrowes Cl 2 SN13..84 F8
BOSCOMBE............ 199 A1
Boscombe Down Airfield
SP4.................. 198 E3
Boscombe Rd
Amesbury SP4........ 217 C3
Swindon SN25........ 34 E4
Bosham Cl 6 SN5.....49 B4
Boswell Rd BA15......99 F3
Bosworth Rd SN5......49 A5
Botany SN6............22 C5
Bothwell Rd SN3......50 F7
Botisdone Cl SP11....185 C3
Botley Copse 1 SN5..34 A4
Bottlebush La BH21.. 208 E1
BOTTLESFORD..........181 D6
Bottom La
Ogbourne St George
SN8................... 169 A5
1 West Wellow SO51.. 212 F6
Bouchers Way SP2.... 152 A5
Boulevard The 3
SN25................34 C5
Boulsbury Farm Rd
SP6................. 209 E3
Boulton Cl BA13......108 E1
Boundary Ave BA11... 110 B5
Boundary Cl
Lyneham SN15........ 59 C3
Swindon SN2.......... 35 F6
Boundary Rd
Chippenham SN15......78 F8
Salisbury SP1........ 146 E2
Boundary Wlk BA14...105 C4
Bourbon Cl BA12..... 117 B5
Bourne Ave SP1...... 146 C2
Bourne Cl
Porton SP4.......... 133 D6
1 Salisbury SP1.......152 D8
Warminster BA12......117 A5
3 West Wellow SO51.. 212 F6
Bourne Gdns SP4.....133 D6
Bourne Hill SP1...... 146 B1
Bourne La 6 SP9..... 199 D8
Bourne Lake Pk SN6..18 E6
Bourne Pk★ SP11... 193 F6
Bourne Rd
Swindon SN2.......... 34 F2
Tidworth SP9........ 216 D6
Bourne Ret Pk SP1... 152 D7
Bourne Rise SN8..... 183 E7
Bourne Vale RG17... 177 B7
Bourne Valley Cl
SP4................. 133 E5
Bourne View SP4..... 199 A1
Bourne Way SP1......152 D7
BOURTON
Bishops Cannings... 172 C3
Bourton............. 137 E2
Bourton Ave SN3......36 B2
Bourton La SN10..... 172 C3
Bouverie Ave
Harnham SP2........ 151 F6
Salisbury SP2........ 152 A6
Swindon SN3.......... 50 D3
Bouverie Ave S SP2.. 151 F5
Bouverie Cl SP2...... 151 F6
Bouverie Dr 17 SN10.179 F1
Bouverie Pk SN14.....56 B5
BOVERIDGE.......... 209 B1
Bow Ct SN1............50 C4
Bowden Cres SN12....94 C6
BOWDEN HILL..........87 B4
Bowden Hill
Bewley Common SN15..86 F5
Bowden Hill SN15..... 87 B5
Bowden Pk★ SN15....87 B5
Bowdich Cl SP4...... 198 C7
Bowd's La SN15........60 A6
BOWERCHALKE........ 205 A2
Bower Gdns SP1..... 152 C8
BOWERHILL............94 D1
Bowerhill Ind Est
SN12.................94 C1
Bowerhill La SN12.....94 E1
Bowerhill Prim Sch
SN12.................94 C1
Bower Hill Rd SP1.... 146 C2
Bower Rd SN8........ 175 D5
Bowers Hill SP5..... 211 D8
Bowers La SP11...... 185 B4
Bowes Lyon Ct SP2.. 145 D3
BOWLDOWN.............70 E8
Bowldown Rd GL8.....25 F8
Bowles Rd SN25.......35 A5
Bowleymead SN3......51 D5
Bowling Gn La
Pentridge SP5....... 208 D5
Swindon SN1.......... 50 C3
Bowls Barrow (Long
Barrow)★ BA12.... 186 E1
Bowman Cl 5 SN4....36 B3
Bowman Ct SN4.......47 C1
Bowmans Ct SN12....94 C6
Bowood Cl SN11......79 F3

Bowood House & Gdns★
SN11..................88 C8
Bowood Rd SN1.......50 B4
Bow Wow GL7..........7 A7
BOX...................83 D6
Boxbush Cl GL7........7 A7
Boxbush Rd GL7........7 A7
Box CE Prim Sch
SN13..................83 C6
Box Dr SN8.......... 213 D8
Boxfields Rd SN13.....83 F7
BOX HILL..............83 F7
Box Hill
Box SN13..............76 A1
Corsham SN13.........83 E7
Box Rd BA1............82 C3
Box View SN14........75 B2
Boydell Cl SN5........49 B8
Boyd Rd BA13........109 B5
Boyle Ave 4 SN11...166 A1
Boyne's La DT11..... 206 B1
BOYTON............. 194 E2
Boyton Manor★
BA12............... 194 E2
Bozley Hill SP7..... 206 A8
Brabant Way 4
BA13................108 E1
Brackenbury 8
SP10................193 C1
Brackenbury Rd SP4..197 E7
Bracken Cl SP5...... 153 D3
Brackland SN10..... 180 A2
Bradbury Cl SN15.....79 A5
Bradene Cl 3 SN4....47 E2
Bradenham Rd SN5....49 A5
BRADENSTOKE.........59 C3
Bradenstoke Abbey★
SN15..................59 B3
Bradfield Cl BA12....117 D5
BRADFORD LEIGH.....91 F1
BRADFORD-ON-
AVON............... 100 E6
Bradford-on-Avon Mus★
BA15................100 D6
Bradford-on-Avon Sta
BA15................100 C6
Bradford-on-Avon
Swimming Pool
BA15................100 C6
Bradford Rd
Atworth SN12.........92 E7
Bathford BA1..........82 B2
Box SN13..............83 E7
Broughton Gifford SN12.93 F4
Corsham SN13.........76 C1
Melksham SN12........94 A5
Rode BA11........... 103 F1
Swindon SN1.......... 50 C4
Wingfield BA14......104 C8
Wingfield BA15......100 C2
Winsley BA15.........99 D6
Bradford Wood La
Bradford-on-Avon
BA15................100 F6
Bradford-on-Avon
BA15................101 A6
Bradley Cl
Holt BA14........... 101 F8
Warminster BA12..... 116 E4
Bradley La
Holt BA14.............92 F1
Kingston Deverill BA12 125 A8
Kingston Deverill BA12 125 F8
Maiden Bradley BA11.118 A4
Maiden Bradley BA12.119 C1
Maiden Bradley with
Yarnfield BA12......118 C3
Bradley Mound★
BA12................118 F2
Bradley Pk★ BA12..118 F1
Bradley Rd
Southwick BA14..... 105 B2
Swindon SN2.......... 35 D4
Trowbridge BA14.... 105 C5
Warminster BA12..... 116 E4
Bradon Forest Sch
SN5...................33 B3
Bradshaw Ct 6 SN25.34 D6
Bradwell Cl 2 SP10.193 C2
Bradwell Moor SN3... 51 D2
Braemar Cl SN3........50 F3
Braemar Rise SP1... 146 B4
Braemore CE Prim Sch
SP6................. 210 E4
Braemor Rd SN11.....81 A4
Braeside Cl SN10.....97 D1
Braithwaite Way 3
BA11................110 C6
Brake Mead SN15.....78 F7
Brakspear Dr SN13...76 E1
Bramble Cl SN2........35 E1
Bramble Ct 7 SN6....19 D8
Bramble Dr
Chippenham SN15.....79 A4
Westbury BA13...... 108 F5
Bramble Hill SO43...212 D2
Bramble Rd SN2.......35 E1
Brambles The
Hinton Charterhouse
BA2.................98 E1
Salisbury SP1....... 146 C2
Trowbridge BA14.... 101 D2
Bramble Wlk 4
SP11................193 F2
Brambling Mews GL7..7 A6
Bramblings The 1
SN12..................94 D5
Bramdean Cl SN25...34 F6

Bramley Cl
Pewsey SN9......... 215 D6
4 Warminster BA12..116 F7
Bramley Dr BA11..... 110 C6
Bramley Hill BA12... 138 F5
Bramley La BA14.... 105 D7
Bramleys The SP5... 161 D3
Bramley Way SP4... 217 C3
Brampton Ct 8
SN12................178 B8
Bramptons The SN5..49 B7
BRAMSHAW.......... 212 E3
Bramshaw Hill Rd
SO43................212 C2
Bramshaw Telegraph★
SP6................. 211 F3
Bramwell Cl SN2......35 E6
Brancaster Ave 1
SP10................193 C2
Branch Rd BA2........98 F2
Branders 4 SN6......19 D8
Brandon Cl SN5.......49 A5
Branksome Rd SN25..34 E3
Branscombe Dr SN4..47 E1
Bransdown Hill
Easton Grey SN16....26 A3
Sherston SN16........25 C7
Brantwood Cl
Swindon SN25.........20 D1
Swindon SN25.........34 C8
Brassknocker Hill BA2.90 A1
Bratch La SP3....... 201 F2
BRATTON............ 186 B7
Bratton Ave SN10... 214 C2
Bratton Camp★
BA13................186 A6
Bratton Cl SN2........35 B5
Bratton Prim Sch
BA13................186 B7
Bratton Rd
Edington BA13...... 186 A8
West Ashton BA14... 106 B4
Westbury BA13...... 109 B3
Westbury BA13...... 109 C4
Braxton Cl 5 SN4...34 C6
Braybrooke Cl 2 SN5..48 F8
Braydon Cl SN2.......35 C5
Braydon La SN6......18 F4
Braydonside
Leigh SN5.............17 F3
Leigh SN6.............18 A2
Purton SN5............32 A6
Bray St SN8......... 173 A8
Breach Cl
Bourton SP8........ 137 E2
Bromham SN15........96 A7
Breach La
Chute SP11......... 184 E1
Chute SP11......... 192 E8
Longhedge BA12.... 115 C6
Royal Wootton Bassett
SN4...................61 B5
1 Shaftesbury SP7.. 202 B1
Southwick BA14..... 105 A3
Breach The SN10... 214 B2
Bread St BA12...... 116 F5
Bream Cl
Calne SN11............81 A5
Melksham SN12........94 D6
BREAMORE........... 210 F5
Breamore Countryside
Mus★ SP6......... 210 D5
Breamore House★
SP6................. 210 E6
Breamore Rd SP5... 210 F7
Brean Rd 3 SN25....34 F7
Brecon Cl
Melksham SN12........94 D4
Swindon SN3.......... 50 E2
Bremen Gdns 21
SP10................193 D2
Bremeridge Cl BA13.109 B3
Bremeridge Rd BA13.109 B3
BREMHILL.............80 E7
Bremhill Cl SN2.......35 C4
Bremhill View SN11...81 A4
Bremilham Rd SN16...27 F4
Bremilham Rise SN16..27 E3
Brendon Wlk SN3.....51 B6
Brentfore St 1 SN1..50 B1
Breton Cl SN5.........34 C2
Breton Rd BA13..... 108 F2
Brettingham Gate
SN3...................64 B8
Brewer Mead SN5....78 F4
Brewer Mws SN13....84 E7
Brewers La SN11......81 C1
Brewery Rd 8 SP1.152 B8
Brewery St SN6........23 A5
Brewery Wlk BA14... 101 D2
Brewhouse Hill SN8.176 D6
Briar Cl
Frome BA11......... 110 B7
Westbury BA13...... 108 F4
Briar Fields SN1.......50 E7
Briar Leaze SN11... 166 B3
Briars Cl SN4..........47 E3
Briarswood Ct SN3...51 D3
Briary Rd GL7.........2 C6
Brickham Rd
Devizes SN10.........97 F1
Swindon SN10....... 214 D5
Brick Hill SN15........95 D6
Brickhouse Farm La
BA9.................136 D3

Brick La
Salisbury SP2....... 145 C2
Trowbridge BA14.... 101 D3
Brickley La SN10.... 214 D2
Bricksteed Ave SN10.214 C3
Brickworth La SP5.. 160 E4
Brickyard La SP8.... 137 E1
Bridewell La SN14...78 B4
Bridewell Sq SN10.. 214 B3
Bridewell St SN10... 213 C2
Bridge Ave BA14.... 105 A8
Bridge Cl GL7..........2 E3
Bridge Ct BA13..... 108 E4
Bridge End Rd
Swindon SN3.........35 F1
Swindon SN3.........36 A1
Bridgeman Cl SN3....36 B2
Bridgemead Cl SN5...49 D7
Bridgemead Ret Pk
SN5...................49 E5
Bridge Rd SP5...... 205 E4
Bridge St
Bourton SP8........ 137 E2
Bradford-on-Avon
BA15................100 D6
Fordingbridge SP6.. 210 D1
26 Hungerford RG17.177 B7
Marlborough SN8... 213 A2
Salisbury SP2....... 152 A8
Swindon SN1.......... 50 B6
3 Trowbridge BA14.105 D7
Bridge The SN15.....78 D7
Bridge Yard 10 BA13.100 D6
Bridleway Prim Sch
SN25..................34 F7
Bridmore Rd SP5... 207 D6
Bridmore Ride SP5.. 207 D6
Bridport Rd SN3......51 B4
Brier Ct SP2........ 145 C4
Briery Cl SN3.........36 A4
Bright Cl 3 SN15....78 F5
Brighton Way SN14...77 F6
Bright St SN2.........50 D8
BRIGMERSTON...... 198 C8
Brimble Hill SN4......64 D5
Brimble Hill Sch
SN25..................34 D8
Brimhill Rise BA13.. 111 D4
Brind Cl SN3..........51 E6
Brindley Cl SN2.......34 E1
Brind Rd SP4........ 197 F7
Brington Rd SN3......51 B8
BRINKWORTH..........45 E5
Brinkworth Cl SN14..77 D7
Brinkworth Earl Danby's
CE Primary Sch SN15.45 E5
Brinkworth Earl Danby's
CE Prim Sch SN15....45 C3
Brinkworth House Bsns &
Events Ctr SN15......45 C6
Brinscombe La 6
SP7................. 202 D1
Brionne Way 13 SP7.202 D1
Brisbane Gdns 7
SP4................. 198 F6
Bristle Gr BA12..... 139 B4
Bristol Rd
Chippenham SN14....78 C8
Chippenham Without
SN14..................69 E2
Easton Grey SN16....26 E4
Luckington SN14......39 D3
Malmesbury SN16.....27 A4
Bristol St
3 Malmesbury SN16..28 A3
Swindon SN1..........50 A6
Britains Cl SN15......57 C2
Britannia Ave SN9.. 182 B2
Britannia Cres SN15..60 B2
Britannia Dr SN11....81 D4
Britannia Pl 6 SN1..50 D4
Britannia Trade Pk
SN3...................35 F3
BRITFORD.......... 152 E1
Britford La SP2...... 152 A6
Britford La W 1 SP2.152 A6
British Row BA14.... 101 C1
Britmore La SP7.... 202 F4
Brittain Cl SN14......77 F7
Britten Rd SN25......34 E7
Brittox The SN10... 214 B3
Brixham Ave SN3.....50 E5
BRIXTON DEVERILL.. 120 E2
Broadacres SN4.......62 B2
BROAD BLUNSDON....21 C2
Broadbury Banks★
SN9................. 181 B2
BROADBUSH...........21 D1
Broad Bush SN26.....21 D1
BROAD CHALKE..... 205 B4
Broad Chalke CE Prim
Sch SP5............ 205 C4
Broadchalke Rd
Bishopstone SP5... 150 A2
Bishopstone SP5... 205 F5
Broadcloth E La
BA14................105 E7
Broadcloth La BA14.. 105 E7
Broad Dr GL8.........25 A8
Broadfield Rd SP4.. 133 D3
Broadfields SN9..... 215 B4
BROAD HINTON..... 167 C7
Broad Hinton CE Prim
Sch SN4............167 D7

Broad Hinton (Hackpen)
White Horse★ SN4. 167 E5
Broad Hinton Rd SN4. 63 D3
Broad La SP6........ 209 B6
Broadlands Cl SP1... 146 B4
Broadleas Cl SN10.. 214 A2
Broadleas Cres SN10. 214 A2
Broadleas Gdns★
SN10................214 A1
Broadleas Pk SN10.. 214 A1
Broadleas Rd SN10.. 214 A2
Broadleaze
Down Ampney GL7.....8 E8
Seagry SN15.........57 D6
Broadly Pk BA14.... 105 D3
Broadmead
Corsham SN13........85 B7
Trowbridge BA14.... 101 A1
Broadmead La BA12. 116 E1
Broadmead Wlk SN3..51 B7
Broadmoor Rd SN3...36 D7
Broads Green SN11...88 F4
Broad Stones BA15...90 E7
BROAD STREET..... 181 C6
BROAD TOWN...... 167 A8
Broad Town CE Prim Sch
SN4...................62 B1
Broadtown La SN4...61 F5
Broadtown Rd SN4...62 B3
Broad Town Rd SN4...62 B3
Broad Town White
Horse★ SN4...... 62 D1
Broadway
Market Lavington
SN10................179 D2
Warminster BA12... 116 E5
Broadway Cl GL7.....10 D7
Broadway Ct GL7......6 F6
Broadway E BA13... 108 D6
Broadway La GL7......7 A5
Broadway Lane GL7...6 F6
Broadway N BA13... 108 C7
Broadway The SN25..35 A3
Broadwood Ave SN13.84 B8
Broadwood Cl 1
BA12................117 A8
Brockley Rise SN2....36 A5
Brocks Orch 8 SP3.. 196 E6
Brockwood SN5.......99 F7
Brokenborough SN14..27 D7
Broken Cross
Calne SN11............81 B3
Laverstock SP4..... 146 F6
BROKERSWOOD..... 107 F5
Brokerswood Ctry Pk★
BA13................107 F5
Brokerswood Rd
BA14................105 A1
BROMHAM............96 A7
Bromley Cl 2 SN3...50 E6
Bronte Cl 2 SN3....51 D4
BROOK............. 212 E1
Brook Cl
Melksham SN12........93 F6
Brookdene SN25......34 E4
Brook Dr SN13........85 B7
Brooke Cl SN16.......28 C2
Brooke Cres SN2......34 C5
Brook End SN14.......39 F5
Brookfield SN6........22 F7
Brook Field Prim Sch
SN5...................49 A8
Brookfield Rise SN12.85 D1
Brookfields SO51.... 212 D6
Brook Gdns SN10... 214 F6
Brook Gn SO43..... 212 D1
BROOK HILL........ 212 D1
Brook Hill
Donhead St Andrew
SP7................. 203 B2
Sherston SN16........40 C8
Brook La
Bradenstoke SN15....59 D3
Holt BA14.............92 D1
Holt BA14........... 101 E8
Westbury BA13...... 108 D4
Woodgreen SP6..... 211 A4
Brooklands
Bradford-on-Avon
BA15................100 F6
Brinkworth SN15......45 E5
Chippenham SN14....78 C5
Royal Wootton Bassett
SN4...................61 E7
Brooklands Ave SN2..34 F1
Brookleaze SN13.....84 E5
Brookline Cl 1 SN2..34 D4
Brook Mdw 1 SN4...64 A5
Brookmead BA14.... 105 A3
Brook Rd BA14...... 101 B1
Brooksby Way
Swindon SN3.........36 B1
Swindon SN3.........51 B8
Brooks Cl SN2........35 C5
Brookside
Crudwell SN16........14 E6
Hullavington SN14.....41 F2

Brookside continued
Landford SP5....... 212 C6
Brookside Cl BA1.....82 A5
Brook St
Chippenham SN14....78 B8
Fovant SP3......... 204 E7
Great Bedwyn SN8.. 176 C3
Warminster BA12... 116 E5
BROOK WATERS.... 203 B2
Brook Way SN11......81 C3
Brookwell Cl SN14...70 C7
Broomcroft Rd SN9. 215 C5
Broome Manor La
SN3...................50 F2
BROOMFIELD..........55 A1
Broomfield
Chippenham SN15....70 D2
Yatton Keynell SN14..68 E8
Broom Gdns SN14.....55 F8
Broomgrounds SN15..99 E7
Broomhill SP5....... 212 C5
Broom Rd BA12..... 139 B4
Brotherton Cl SN15..78 F5
BROUGHTON
GIFFORD............93 C4
Broughton Gifford
SN3...................50 F4
Broughton Grange 6
SN3...................50 F4
Broughton Rd
Broughton Gifford
SN12..................93 A2
2 Trowbridge BA14. 105 C5
Brouncker Rd BA13. 109 B5
Brouncker's Well★
BA12................186 F5
Browning Cl 1 SN3..36 B3
Brownings The SN13..83 D5
Brownleaze La SN10.179 D6
Browns Dr
7 Corsham SN13....76 C1
1 Corsham SN13....84 C1
Brown's Folly★ BA1..82 C1
Browns La
Alton SN8.......... 173 C1
Damerham SP6..... 209 E3
Brown's La SN8..... 176 B3
Brown St
3 Salisbury SP1... 146 B1
Salisbury SP1....... 152 B8
Trowbridge BA14.... 105 D7
Brow The SN25........34 E4
Broxburn Rd BA12.. 116 D6
Broxmore La SO51.. 162 D2
Bruce St SN2..........49 F7
Bruddel Gr SN3.......50 E2
Bruges Cl SN15.......78 F7
Brunel Cl
Corsham SN13........76 F1
Westbury BA13..... 109 A4
Brunel Cres SN2......50 B8
Brunel Ct SN15.......78 B6
Brunel Ctr The SN1..50 B6
Brunel Rd SP2...... 145 D1
Brunel Way
Box SN13..............83 D6
Calne SN11............81 C6
Frome BA11......... 110 C7
Brunkard's La SN9.. 215 D5
Brunswick St SN1.....50 C4
BRUNTON........... 183 E3
Brushy Bush La SP5. 207 F3
Bruton Rd BA10..... 122 A6
Bruton Wlk SN3......51 A4
Bruyn Rd SP6....... 210 E1
Bryans Cl Rd SN11...81 B3
Bryanston Way SN3..51 C6
Bryant Rd SN25......34 C5
Bryces La SP5...... 162 E3
Brydes Rd 21 SP11.. 192 A5
Bryer Ash Bsns Pk 4
BA14................105 C8
Brympton Cl 5 SP6. 210 D1
Brynards Hill SN4.....47 C1
Bryony Way SN2......34 D4
Bryworth La GL7......2 A6
Buckeridge Rd SP2.. 144 F4
Buckhorn Dr SN2.....34 D4
Buckhorn Row SN13..84 E8
Budbury Circ BA15.. 100 C7
Budbury Cl BA15.... 100 C7
Budbury Pl BA15.... 100 C7
Budbury Ridge BA15.100 C7
Budbury Tyning
BA15................100 C7
Bude Rd SN5..........49 F6
Budge La BA11...... 114 A8
Buettell Way SN16....27 F5
Bugdens Cl SP4.... 217 D4
BUGLEY.............. 116 C6
Bugmore La SP5.... 154 F4
Buie Cl SN5...........34 B2
BULBRIDGE.......... 144 B1
Bulbridge Rd SP2... 144 B1
BULFORD........... 217 E8
BULFORD CAMP.... 198 F6

**Bulford Droveway**
SP4 . . . . . . . . . . . . 198 D7
**Bulford Hill** SP4 . . . 217 C8
**Bulford Rd**
  Bulford SP4 . . . . . . 217 F8
  Durrington/Bulford
  SP4 . . . . . . . . . . . . 198 B7
  Shipton Bellinger SP9 . 199 C8
  South Tedworth SP9 . . 216 A4
**Bulford St Leonard's CE**
  **Prim Sch** SP4 . . . . 217 E8
**BULKINGTON** . . . . . . 178 E5
**Bulldog La** SN10 . . . . 180 C3
**BULLENHILL** . . . . . . 106 E8
**Buller Pk** SP4 . . . . . 133 E5
**Buller St** SN2 . . . . . . 35 D1
**Bullfinch Cl** SN3 . . . . 51 D6
**Bull La** BA12 . . . . . . 116 F2
**BULLOCK'S HORN** . . . . 15 E1
**Bullock's Horn La**
  Charlton SN16 . . . . . 29 D7
  Hankerton SN16 . . . . 15 D1
**Bull Pit** BA15 . . . . . 100 D6
**Bulls La**
  Box SN13 . . . . . . . . . 83 D6
  Broad Chalke SP5 . . . 205 B4
**Bulpit La** RG17 . . . . . 177 B6
**Bulpits Hill** SP11 . . . 185 C3
**Bumper's Batch** BA2 . . 98 A8
**Bumpers Fram Ind Est**
  SN14 . . . . . . . . . . . 70 A1
**Bumpers Way** SN14 . . . 70 A1
**Bunce Rd** SN3 . . . . . . 36 A2
**Bungalow Pk** SN15 . . . 59 B3
**Bungalows The** SN2 . . 35 C2
**Bunnies La** SN10 . . . . 96 D2
**Bunns La** BA11 . . . . . 114 A2
**Bunny La** SP5 . . . . . . 162 C4
**Buntings The** SN3 . . . 51 D7
**Bupton Village** ★ . . . . 166 D7
**BURBAGE** . . . . . . . . . 183 D8
**Burbage Prim Sch**
  SN8 . . . . . . . . . . . . 183 D8
**Burbage Rd**
  Easton SN9 . . . . . . . 183 A8
  Milton Lilbourne SN9 . 182 F7
  Swindon SN2 . . . . . . 35 C6
**Burbage Wharf** ★
  SN8 . . . . . . . . . . . . 175 C2
**BURCOMBE** . . . . . . . . 143 E2
**Burcombe La**
  Barford St Martin
  SP3 . . . . . . . . . . . . 143 C3
  Wilton SP2 . . . . . . . 144 B2
**Burcot Cl** SN25 . . . . . 34 C7
**Burden Cl** SN3 . . . . . . 36 C1
**Burden Rd** SN26 . . . . 20 D1
**Burderop Barns** SN4 . . 64 E4
**Burderop Cl**
  **1** Trowbridge BA14 . . 105 D5
  Wroughton SN4 . . . . 64 B8
**Burdett St 4** SN8 . . . 170 B2
**Burford Ave**
  Salisbury SP2 . . . . . 152 B6
  Swindon SN3 . . . . . . 50 E6
**Burford La** SP2 . . . . 152 B6
**Burford Rd**
  Little Faringdon GL7 . . 2 E7
  Salisbury SP2 . . . . . 152 B6
**Burford's 2** RG17 . . . 171 E7
**Burford St** GL7 . . . . . 2 C4
**Burford Stone La**
  Hannington SN6 . . . . 11 B1
  Hannington SN6 . . . . 11 D1
  Hannington SN6 . . . . 22 C8
**Burgate Fields** SP6 . . 210 D2
**Burgate Sch & Sixth**
  **Form The** SP6 . . . . 210 E2
**Burgess Cl** SN3 . . . . . 36 A1
**Burgess Gn** SP1 . . . . 146 C4
**Burghley Cl** SN3 . . . . 51 A4
**Burkal Dr 32** SP10 . . 193 E2
**Burlands Rd** SN15 . . . 78 E6
**Burleaze** SN15 . . . . . . 78 C5
**Burlington Pl** SN13 . . 84 D8
**Burne Jones Ave**
  Swindon SN25 . . . . . 34 D8
  Swindon SN26 . . . . . 20 D1
**Burnet Cl**
  Melksham SN12 . . . . . 94 B2
  Swindon SN2 . . . . . . 34 D5
**Burnett Rd** BA14 . . . . 105 D6
**Burnet Way** SP1 . . . . 146 D4
**Burnham Rd**
  **5** Fordingbridge
  SP6 . . . . . . . . . . . . 210 D2
  **4** Malmesbury SN16 . 28 A4
  Swindon SN3 . . . . . . 51 B6
**Burnhams Cl 1**
  SP10 . . . . . . . . . . . 193 E2
**Burnivale** SN16 . . . . . 28 A3
**Burn Rd** SN13 . . . . . . 76 E1
**Burnston Cl** SN12 . . . 94 D5
**Burns Way** SN2 . . . . . 35 E4
**Burr La** SN8 . . . . . . . 176 F1
**Burroughs Cl** SN1 . . . 146 E2
**Burroughs Dro 2**
  SN8 . . . . . . . . . . . . 183 D8
**BURTON**
  Mere. , . . . . . . . . . . 139 D3
  Nettleton . . . . . . . . 53 B4
**Burton Cl 11** SP7 . . . 202 D2
**Burton Farm Cl** SN14 . 53 B3
**Burton Hill**
  Corston SN16 . . . . . . 43 A7
  Malmesbury SN16 . . . 28 B2

**Burton Rd**
  Acton Turville GL9 . . . 52 F6
  Acton Turville GL9 . . . 53 A5
**Burtons La** SN13 . . . . 83 C5
**Burwood Cl 7** SP4 . . 217 E3
**Bury Camp (Hill Fort)** ★
  SN14 . . . . . . . . . . . 67 B1
**Burycroft** SN4 . . . . . 163 A6
**Bury Fields** SN5 . . . . 33 D1
**Bury Hill (Settlement)** ★
  SN6 . . . . . . . . . . . . 18 B1
**Bury La**
  Bratton BA13 . . . . . . 186 B7
  Broad Chalke SP5 . . . 205 C4
**Bury Mead** BA12 . . . . 195 A4
**Burytown La** SN26 . . . 21 C2
**Buscot Cl** SN25 . . . . . 34 E7
**Buscot Old Parsonage** ★
  SN7 . . . . . . . . . . . . 12 D8
**BUSCOT WICK** . . . . . . 12 D8
**Bush Barrow** ★ SP4 . . 197 D4
**Bush Farm Bison Ctr** ★
  BA12 . . . . . . . . . . . 140 B3
**BUSHTON** . . . . . . . . . 166 E8
**Bustlers Hill** SN16 . . . 40 D8
**Bute Cl** SN6 . . . . . . . 22 F7
**Butleigh Rd** SN25 . . . 34 C7
**Butler Cl** SP2 . . . . . . 152 B6
**Butlers Cl** SN16 . . . . . 25 C1
**Butlers Ct La** GL7 . . . 2 B4
**Butler's Field** GL7 . . . 2 C5
**Butler's Gdns** BA11 . . 110 A4
**Butlers Yard** SP5 . . . 205 B4
**Butt Cl** SP11 . . . . . . 192 A6
**Buttercup Cl**
  Chippenham SN14 . . . 70 B3
  Harnham SP2 . . . . . . 151 F7
**Butterfield Cl** SP2 . . 150 F8
**Butterfield Dr** SP4 . . 217 D3
**Butterfly World** ★ SN1 . 48 F1
**Butter Furlong Rd**
  SP5 . . . . . . . . . . . . 154 C3
**BUTTERMERE** . . . . . . 185 B8
**Buttermere** SN3 . . . . 51 E3
**Butterstake La** SP7 . . 202 B6
**Butterworth St** SN1 . . 50 A5
**Butt La** SP5 . . . . . . . 205 E4
**Buttons Yd** BA12 . . . . 117 B7
**Butts Cl** SN14 . . . . . . 76 E7
**Butts Cres** BA14 . . . . 106 A8
**Butts Hill** SP3 . . . . . . 129 E7
**Butts La**
  Kilmington BA12 . . . . 123 E6
  Steeple Ashton BA14 . 178 A3
**Butt's La** BA15 . . . . . 90 F7
**Butts Mead 3** SP7 . . 202 D1
**Butts Rd**
  Chiseldown SN4 . . . . 65 D5
  Salisbury SP1 . . . . . 146 A2
**Butt St** SP11 . . . . . . 192 A5
**Butts Terr** SP2 . . . . . 146 A2
**Butts The**
  Aldbourne SN8 . . . . . 170 A6
  Biddestone SN14 . . . . 76 D7
  Bratton BA13 . . . . . . 186 B7
  Chippenham SN15 . . . 78 B8
  Crudwell SN16 . . . . . 14 E6
  Lydiard Millicent SN5 . 48 C8
  Potterne SN10 . . . . . 179 D5
  Shaftesbury SP7 . . . . 202 B2
  Shrewton SP3 . . . . . 196 E7
  Steeple Ashton BA14 . 178 A3
**Butts (Tumuli) The** ★
  SP6 . . . . . . . . . . . . 211 E2
**Buxbury Hollow** SP3 . . 204 B6
**Byams Ride** GL8 . . . . 25 B7
**By Brook Valley CE Prim**
  **Sch** SN14 . . . . . . . 68 F5
**Bybrook View** SN13 . . 76 A2
**Bydemill Gdns** SN6 . . . 22 E1
**Byers Cl** SN25 . . . . . . 35 A8
**Byfield Way** SN3 . . . . 51 B8
**Byford Gdns** SP4 . . . . 133 D6
**Byrd Cl 13** SN5 . . . . 48 F5
**Byre Cl** SN6 . . . . . . . 19 D7
**Byron Ave** SN4 . . . . . 47 F2
**Byron Cl**
  **11** Ludgershall SP11 . 192 A5
  **5** Melksham SN12 . . 94 B4
**Byron Ct** SN3 . . . . . . 36 E5
**Byron Rd** SN10 . . . . . 214 B1
**Byron St 3** SN1 . . . . 50 C5
**Bytham Rd** SN8 . . . . 169 A4
**Bythebrook** SN14 . . . 70 B3
**Bythesea Rd** BA14 . . 105 C8
**Byways Cl 4** SP1 . . . 152 C8

## C

**Cabot Dr** SN5 . . . . . . 48 F6
**Cabul Rd** SP9 . . . . . . 216 B5
**Cadby Cl** SN14 . . . . . 105 F8
**Caddy La** BA12 . . . . . 138 F5
**CADLEY** . . . . . . . . . . 175 A5
**Cadley Cl** SN2 . . . . . . 35 D2
**Cadley Clay Shooting Gd**
  SN8 . . . . . . . . . . . . 175 A5
**Cadley Rd** SN8 . . . . . 183 E1
**Cadnam Cres** SP4 . . . 217 E2
**Cadnam La** SO51 . . . . 212 F1
**Caen Hill** SN10 . . . . . 179 C8
**Caen Hill Gdns** SN10 . . 179 C8

**Caen Hill Locks** ★
  SN10 . . . . . . . . . . . 179 C8
**Caen View** SN1 . . . . . 49 E4
**Caerleon Dr 4** SP10 . . 192 E2
**Caesar Rd** SP10 . . . . 193 E2
**Caesar's Camp (Fort)** ★
  DT11 . . . . . . . . . . . 206 F2
**Cagney Dr** SN25 . . . . 35 A5
**Caird Lawns** SN10 . . . 214 C2
**Cairndow Way** SN2 . . 35 E5
**CALCUTT** . . . . . . . . . 20 A7
**Calcutt St** SN6 . . . . . 19 E8
**Calder Cl** SN25 . . . . . 34 F5
**Calder House Sch**
  SN14 . . . . . . . . . . . 75 D6
**Caldwell Cl 15** SP7 . . 202 D1
**Calf La** SN8 . . . . . . . 173 B1
**Calgary Dr 5** SP4 . . . 217 F8
**Callaghan Cl 2** SN3 . . 36 B2
**Callas Hill** SN4 . . . . . 163 B5
**Callas Rise 7** SN4 . . . 163 B6
**Callaway Gdns** BA13 . . 109 A2
**Callenders** SN5 . . . . . 49 E5
**Callington Rd** SN5 . . . 34 B6
**Calliope Cres** SN25 . . 35 D3
**Callow Croft** SN8 . . . 183 D8
**CALLOW HILL** . . . . . . 46 D6
**Callows Cross** SN15 . . 46 C6
**CALNE** . . . . . . . . . . . 81 B2
**Calne Heritage Ctr** ★
  SN11 . . . . . . . . . . . 81 B2
**CALNE MARSH** . . . . . 81 C4
**Calne Rd** SN15 . . . . . 60 A1
**Calstock Rd** SN25 . . . 34 B6
**CALSTONE**
  **WELLINGTON** . . . . . 172 A7
**Calvert Rd** SN3 . . . . . 50 E6
**Calves La** SP7 . . . . . . 202 A2
**Camargue Rd** BA13 . . 108 E1
**Cambrai Rd** SN4 . . . . 65 D1
**Cambria Bridge Rd**
  SN1 . . . . . . . . . . . . 50 A5
**Cambria Pl** SN1 . . . . . 50 A5
**Cambridge Cl** SN3 . . . 50 F4
**Cambridge Rd** SP1 . . . 146 B3
**Camden Cl** SN5 . . . . . 49 A5
**Camellia Dr** BA14 . . . 116 E7
**Camelot Cl 28** SP10 . . 193 E2
**Cameron Cl** SN3 . . . . 36 A1
**Camilla Cl** SP4 . . . . . 217 D8
**Camomile Dr 25**
  SP11 . . . . . . . . . . . 192 A5
**Campbell Rd** SP1 . . . . 146 B2
**Campbell Vale 7**
  SP4 . . . . . . . . . . . . 132 B1
**Campden Rd** SN3 . . . 50 E5
**Campion Cl**
  Calne SN11 . . . . . . . 81 B5
  Westbury BA13 . . . . . 109 A5
**Campion Dr**
  Melksham SN12 . . . . . 94 C2
  Trowbridge BA14 . . . 105 D6
**Campion Gate** SN5 . . 48 F5
**Camp Rd** BA12 . . . . . 194 E5
**Camton Rd** SN5 . . . . 48 F7
**CANADA** . . . . . . . . . 212 F4
**Canada Comm Rd**
  SO51 . . . . . . . . . . . 212 F4
**Canada Rd** SO51 . . . . 212 F5
**Canada Rise** SN10 . . . 179 F1
**Canadian Ave** SN2 . . . 145 D2
**Canal Bridge** BA14 . . 102 F6
**Canal Cl**
  Calne SN11 . . . . . . . 81 A2
  Wilcot SN8 . . . . . . . 182 A8
**Canal La** SP5 . . . . . . 153 E2
**Canal Rd**
  Chippenham SN15 . . . 78 F5
  Trowbridge BA14 . . . 101 D3
**Canal Rd Ind Est**
  BA14 . . . . . . . . . . . 101 D3
**Canalside** SP5 . . . . . 153 E2
**Canal Way** SN10 . . . . 214 E6
**Canal Wlk**
  Hungerford RG17 . . . 177 B7
  Swindon SN1 . . . . . . 50 B6
**Canberra Dr** SP4 . . . . 198 F6
**Canberra Rd** SN4 . . . . 64 E3
**Candown Rd** SP3 . . . . 188 B2
**Canford Cl** SN3 . . . . . 51 C6
**CANN COMMON** . . . . 206 B8
**Canney Cl** SN4 . . . . . 65 D4
**Canney The** SN4 . . . . 65 D4
**Cann Hill** SP7 . . . . . . 206 A2
**Cannimore Cl** BA12 . . 116 E5
**Cannimore Rd**
  Warminster BA12 . . . 116 C4
  Warminster BA12 . . . 116 D5
**Cannings Cl**
  Broughton Gifford
  SN12 . . . . . . . . . . . 93 C4
  **2** Hilperton BA14 . . 102 B2
**Cannock Cl 13** BA12 . . 117 A8
**Cannon Sq** SN12 . . . . 94 A4
**Cannon St** SN1 . . . . . 50 C5
**Cannwood La** BA10 . . 122 D8
**Canon Dr** GL7 . . . . . . 2 E3
**Canons Cl**
  Tidworth SP9 . . . . . . 216 D4
  Warminster BA12 . . . 117 C5
**Canons Ct** SN12 . . . . 94 A4
**Canons Yard Ind Est**
  SN4 . . . . . . . . . . . . 61 E8
**Cantax Hill** SN15 . . . . 86 C6
**Cantelo Cl** SN25 . . . . 34 F7
**Canterbury Cl**
  **10** Amesbury SP4 . . 217 D3
  Swindon SN3 . . . . . . 50 F3

**Canterbury St** SN14 . . 78 C8
**Cantors Way** SN16 . . 17 C2
**Canwood La** BA10 . . . 123 A7
**Capella Cres 17** SN25 . 34 B7
**Capesthorne Dr** SN25 . 34 E6
**Capitol Cl** SN3 . . . . . 36 C1
**Capps La** BA13 . . . . . 109 F7
**Caprice Cl 1** SN5 . . . 49 A7
**Capulet Rd** SP1 . . . . . 145 E4
**Caradon Wlk** SN5 . . . 34 C7
**Caraway Dr** SN2 . . . . 34 A4
**Carders Cnr 7** BA14 . . 105 D7
**Cardigan Cl** SN3 . . . . 50 E4
**Cardigan Rd** SN8 . . . . 213 C3
**Cardwell Cl 1** SN3 . . 51 B7
**Caretakers Cl** SN12 . . 93 F6
**Carey Cl** SN5 . . . . . . 49 A5
**Carfax Cl 1** SN1 . . . . 50 C6
**Carfax St** SN1 . . . . . . 50 C6
**Cargill Pl** SN16 . . . . . 15 F8
**Carisbrooke Cres**
  BA14 . . . . . . . . . . . 101 E5
**Carisbrook Rd** SN12 . . 94 B3
**Carisbrook Terr** SN4 . . 65 C3
**Carleton Pl** SP4 . . . . 217 A4
**Carlisle Ave** SN3 . . . . 50 D3
**Carlton Cl 2** SP4 . . . 217 D3
**Carlton Gate** SN3 . . . 50 F1
**Carlton Row** BA14 . . . 105 C6
**Carman Cl** SN3 . . . . . 36 B3
**Carmelite Way** SP1 . . 152 B7
**Carmel Wlk** SN3 . . . . 50 F1
**Carnarvon Cl** SN14 . . 78 A7
**Carnation La** SN12 . . . 178 C8
**Carnegie Rd** SN11 . . . 81 C4
**Carnival Cl** SN16 . . . . 28 A6
**Carpenter Cl 5** SN15 . 78 C7
**Carpenter Dr** SP4 . . . 217 D4
**Carpenters** SN6 . . . . . 19 D7
**Carpenters Cl** SN15 . . 25 D1
**Carpenter's Cl** SN11 . . 80 F4
**Carpenters La**
  **4** Bratton BA13 . . . 186 B7
  Swindon SN2 . . . . . . 50 D8
**Carp Rd** SN11 . . . . . . 81 A5
**Carrick Cl** SN15 . . . . . 79 A8
**Carriers Cl** SN16 . . . . 25 C1
**Carrion Pond Dro**
  SP2 . . . . . . . . . . . . 151 D7
**Carroll Cl** SN3 . . . . . . 50 F4
**Carronbridge Rd** SN5 . 49 B6
**Carr St** SN1 . . . . . . . 50 B6
**Carshalton Rd** SN3 . . 51 B3
**Carsons Yd** BA12 . . . . 117 B6
**Carstairs Ave** SN3 . . . 51 A3
**Carter Cl** SN25 . . . . . 35 C6
**Carter's Cl** SP6 . . . . . 211 C6
**Cartway** SN10 . . . . . 180 E4
**Cartwright Dr** SN5 . . . 49 B8
**Carver Cl** SN3 . . . . . . 36 C2
**Carvers Hill** SN8 . . . . 176 E1
**Cary Glen** SN5 . . . . . 79 A4
**Casley La** BA11 . . . . . 107 C7
**Caspian Cl** SN3 . . . . . 34 C3
**Caspian Gdns** BA13 . . 108 F1
**Cassini Dr**
  Swindon SN25 . . . . . 34 B6
  **8** Swindon SN25 . . 34 B7
**Casson Rd** SN3 . . . . . 36 A2
**Castell Cl** BA14 . . . . . 106 B8
**Casterbridge La 3**
  SP11 . . . . . . . . . . . 192 F1
**Casterbridge Rd**
  Swindon SN3 . . . . . . 34 D5
  **6** Swindon SN25 . . 34 C5
**Castian Mews** SN5 . . 49 A7
**Castle Barrow** ★
  BA12 . . . . . . . . . . . 195 A7
**CASTLE COMBE** . . . . 68 A7
**Castle Combe Motor**
  **Racing Circuit** ★
  SN14 . . . . . . . . . . . 68 C6
**Castle Combe Motte &**
  **Baileys** ★ SN14 . . . 67 F8
**Castle Ct** SP11 . . . . . 192 A6
**Castle Ditches Hill Fort** ★
  SP3 . . . . . . . . . . . . 204 A7
**Castle Dore** SN5 . . . . 49 A5
**CASTLE EATON** . . . . 10 B4
**Castlefield Cl 3** SN5 . 49 C6
**Castlefields** SN11 . . . . 81 A4
**Castlegate Bsns Pk**
  SP4 . . . . . . . . . . . . 146 B7
**Castle Grounds**
  SN10 . . . . . . . . . . . 214 A4
**Castle Hedingham**
  BA14 . . . . . . . . . . . 106 B8
**Castle Hill Cl 9** SP7 . . 202 B2
**Castle Hill Cres** BA12 . 139 A6
**Castle Hill (Fort)** ★
  SN26 . . . . . . . . . . . 21 D3
**Castle Hill La** BA12 . . 139 A5
**Castle Keep**
  Salisbury SP1 . . . . . 145 E4
  **4** Salisbury SP2 . . . 144 D3
**Castle La**
  Aldbury SP5 . . . . . . 153 E1
  Devizes SN10 . . . . . 214 A3
  Wilton SP2 . . . . . . . 144 D3
**Castle Meadow** SP5 . . 211 A8
**Castle Mead School**
  BA14 . . . . . . . . . . . 106 B8
**Castle Orch** BA9 . . . . 137 D3

**Castle Prim Sch**
  SP11 . . . . . . . . . . . 192 B5
**Castle Rd**
  Rratton BA13 . . . . . . 186 A6
  Devizes SN10 . . . . . 214 A3
  **3** Great Bedwyn SN8 . 176 B3
  Salisbury SP1 . . . . . 146 A3
**Castle St**
  Aldbourne SN8 . . . . . 170 A6
  Calne SN11 . . . . . . . 81 B2
  **8** Ludgershall SP11 . 192 A5
  Mere BA12 . . . . . . . 138 F5
  Salisbury SP2 . . . . . 146 A2
  Trowbridge BA14 . . . 105 D8
**Castleton Rd** SN5 . . . 49 A7
**Castle View**
  Westbury BA13 . . . . . 109 B3
  West Tisbury SP3 . . . 203 B8
**Castle View Rd**
  Chiseldown SN4 . . . . 65 E4
  Swindon SN3 . . . . . . 36 C1
**Castle Well Dr** SP4 . . 146 B8
**Castle Wlk** SN11 . . . . 81 A2
**Castle Woods 2** SP5 . 211 C7
**Castley Rd** BA14 . . . . 102 A2
**Catalina Ct 17** SN12 . . 178 B8
**CATCOMB** . . . . . . . . 73 D6
**Catcomb St** SN11 . . . 73 D6
**Cathedral Ct** SP1 . . . 152 B8
**Catherine Cres**
  Dinton SP3 . . . . . . . 201 E2
  Downton SP5 . . . . . . 210 F8
**Catherine Ct** SP1 . . . 152 A8
**Catherine Ford La**
  Dinton SP3 . . . . . . . 201 E1
  Fovant SP3 . . . . . . . 204 E8
**Catherine St**
  Salisbury SP1 . . . . . 152 B8
  **5** Swindon SN1 . . . 50 B6
**Catherine Way** BA1 . . 82 A5
**Catherine Wayte Cl**
  SN25 . . . . . . . . . . . 34 F4
**Catherine Wayte Prim**
  **Sch** SN25 . . . . . . . 34 F5
**Catmint Cl** SN2 . . . . . 34 D4
**Cator Rd 3** SP4 . . . . 197 E7
**Cats Hill La** SP7 . . . . 203 A1
**Catterick Cl 7** SN14 . . 77 F6
**Caulfield Rd** SN2 . . . . 50 D8
**Causeway Cl** SN15 . . . 78 E7
**CAUSEWAY THE** . . . . 139 C4
**Causeway The**
  Brinkworth SN15 . . . . 45 D6
  Broad Chalke SP5 . . . 205 B4
  Chippenham SN15 . . . 78 E7
  **11** Tisbury SP3 . . . . 203 E8
**Cavell Ct** BA14 . . . . . 105 C6
**Cavendish Cl** SN11 . . . 81 D3
**Cavendish Dr** BA14 . . 104 F6
**Cavendish Sq** SN3 . . . 51 A4
**Caversham Cl** SN3 . . . 50 F5
**Cavie Cl** SN5 . . . . . . 49 A8
**Cawte Mews** SN3 . . . 36 A4
**Caxton Cl**
  **2** Andover SP10 . . . 193 C1
  **3** Swindon SN5 . . . 50 F4
**Caxton Rd** BA11 . . . . 110 A3
**Cayenne Pk** SN2 . . . . 34 C4
**Cecil Ave** SN2 . . . . . 152 A5
**Cecil Rd** SN3 . . . . . . 51 A6
**Cecil Terr** SP2 . . . . . . 145 D1
**Cedar Cl**
  Melksham SN12 . . . . . 94 A3
  Salisbury SP2 . . . . . 145 B4
  Worton SN10 . . . . . 179 B4
**Cedar Glen** SN5 . . . . 33 B4
**Cedar Gr**
  Chippenham SN15 . . . 70 E1
  Trowbridge BA14 . . . 105 B6
**Cedars Cl** SN2 . . . . . 35 A2
**Cedars The** SN16 . . . 28 F2
**Cedar Tree Cl** BA14 . . 102 B2
**Celandine Way** SN14 . 70 B2
**Celsus Gr** SN1 . . . . . 50 A3
**Cemetery La** BA15 . . 100 F7
**Centenary Cl** BA14 . . 102 B2
**Centenary Ct 6**
  BA14 . . . . . . . . . . . 105 C7
**Center Parcs**
  Longhedge BA12 . . . 115 C1
  Longhedge BA12 . . . 115 F4
**Central St** SP11 . . . . 192 A5
**Central Trad Est** SN3 . 50 D3
**Centre The** SP4 . . . . 217 A4
**Centre Wlk Ave** GL9 . 38 F2
**Centurion Cl**
  Chippenham SN15 . . . 79 A5
  **1** Salisbury SP2 . . . 145 D2
**Centurion Way**
  Swindon SN3 . . . . . . 51 C8
  Warminster BA12 . . . 112 C1
**Century Rd** SN5 . . . . 34 B1
**Ceres Pl** SN11 . . . . . 81 D4
**Ceres Rd** SN26 . . . . . 21 A1
**CERNEY WICK** . . . . . 7 F5
**Cerney Wick La** GL7 . . 7 D5
**Chaddenwick Hill**
  SN1 . . . . . . . . . . . . 49 C2
**Chadwick Cl 22** SN12 . 178 B8
**Chaffeymoor Hill**
  SP8 . . . . . . . . . . . . 137 B1
**Chaffinch Ave** BA11 . . 110 B6

**Chaffinch Dr 2**
  BA14 . . . . . . . . . . . 105 B8
**Chafield Cl** BA12 . . . . 113 A1
**Chafyn Gr Sch** SP1 . . 146 C2
**Chain Dro**
  South Newton SP3 . . 130 B6
  Stapleford SP3 . . . . . 129 F7
**Chain Hill** SP3 . . . . . . 129 E7
**Chain La** BA12 . . . . . 117 C6
**Chalcot La**
  Chapmanslade BA13 . 111 F5
  Upton Scudamore
  BA13 . . . . . . . . . . . 112 A6
**Chalfield Cres** SN12 . . 94 C5
**Chalfield Glebe** BA15 . 100 F6
**Chalfont Cl** BA14 . . . . 105 A8
**CHALFORD** . . . . . . . 113 A8
**Chalford**
  Westbury BA12 . . . . . 112 F6
  Westbury BA13 . . . . . 108 F1
**Charlford Ave** SN15 . . 51 B7
**Chalkcroft La** SP11 . . 193 A2
**Chalk Down** SP9 . . . . 216 E7
**Chalk Hill 3** SP3 . . . 196 F6
**Chalk Pyt Rd** SP5 . . . 205 B4
**Chalk's Cl 1** SP5 . . . 211 C8
**Challis Ct 5** SP11 . . . 192 B5
**Challows La** SN14 . . . 76 D8
**Challymead** SN12 . . . 93 E3
**Chalvedon Gn** SN3 . . 51 A5
**Chamberlain Rd**
  Chippenham Without
  SN14 . . . . . . . . . . . 77 F7
  Swindon SN3 . . . . . . 36 B4
**Chambers Ave** SP4 . . 217 C2
**Chambon Cl** SN16 . . . 17 A2
**Champneys Rd 6**
  BA11 . . . . . . . . . . . 110 A7
**Chancellor Cl** SN15 . . 48 F6
**Chancel Way** GL7 . . . 2 C4
**Chancery Cl 1** SP2 . . 146 C2
**Chancery La** SN14 . . . 117 C6
**Chandler Cl** SN3 . . . . 50 D5
**Chandlers Cl** SN10 . . . 180 F8
**Chandlers Ct**
  North Tidworth SP9 . . 216 C4
  Tidworth SP9 . . . . . . 216 C7
**Chandlers La**
  All Cannings SN10 . . . 180 F8
  Bishops Cannings
  SN10 . . . . . . . . . . . 172 B2
**Chandler's La 1** SN8 . 170 A7
**Chandlers Tynings**
  BA15 . . . . . . . . . . . 100 E7
**Chandler Way 3** SN15 . 78 F4
**Chandos Cl** SN5 . . . . 49 A6
**Chanterelle Pk** BA15 . 100 D5
**Chantry Ct**
  Southwick BA14 . . . . 104 F3
  Westbury BA13 . . . . . 109 A3
**Chantry Gdns** BA14 . . 104 F3
**Chantry La**
  Chute SP11 . . . . . . . 184 C2
  Marlborough SN8 . . . 213 D2
**Chantry Mead 13**
  RG17 . . . . . . . . . . . 177 B7
**Chantry Mews** BA12 . . 117 A7
**Chantry Rd**
  Swindon SN2 . . . . . . 34 F2
  Wilton SP2 . . . . . . . 144 C1
**Chantry The** ★ BA12 . 139 A5
**Chants Cl** SN3 . . . . . 196 E6
**CHAPEL BARTON** . . . 115 D6
**Chapel Cl**
  Kempsford GL7 . . . . 10 D6
  Southwick BA14 . . . . 104 F3
**Chapel Cnr** SN14 . . . 41 F1
**Chapel Ct 17** RG17 . . 177 B7
**Chapel Hill**
  Broad Blunsdon SN26 . 21 B2
  Gastard SN13 . . . . . 85 E5
  Grimstead SP5 . . . . . 154 B2
  Lacock SN15 . . . . . . 86 C6
**CHAPEL KNAPP** . . . . 85 D5
**Chapel La**
  Acton Turville GL9 . . . 53 A6
  Andover SP11 . . . . . 193 E3
  Bishopstone SP5 . . . 205 E4
  Box SN13 . . . . . . . . . 83 D5
  Broad Town SN4 . . . 167 B8
  Chippenham SN15 . . . 78 E7
  Collingbourne Kingston
  SN8 . . . . . . . . . . . . 183 D2
  Corsham SN13 . . . . . 84 E4
  Downton SP5 . . . . . . 159 B5
  Hanging Langford SP3 . 128 B3
  Hankerton SN16 . . . . 15 C2
  **12** Lambourn RG17 . 165 A2
  **5** Ludgershall SP11 . 192 A5
  Melksham Without SN12 . 86 A1
  Minety SN16 . . . . . . 17 A2
  Nomansland SP5 . . . 212 C4
  Pen Selwood BA9 . . . 137 C3
  **8** Rambury SN8 . . . 170 B2
  Redlynch SP5 . . . . . 211 D7
  **1** Shrewton SP3 . . . 196 E6
  South Marston SN3 . . 36 E5
  Stapleford SP3 . . . . . 129 E7
  Upavon SN9 . . . . . . 181 D5
  **2** Wanborough SN4 . 163 B6
  Wingfield BA14 . . . . 104 C6
  Woodborough SN9 . . 181 D7
  Zennor BA12 . . . . . . 137 E5
**Chapel Mews** SN15 . . 78 E7

Chapel Orch **6** SN4 . . 163 B6
Chapel Path SN14 . . . . . 75 B3
Chapel Pl **1** SP2 . . . . . 146 A1
CHAPEL PLAISTER . . . . .84 A5
Chapel Plaister SN13 . .83 F4
Chapel Rd
 **2** Ashbury SN6 . . . . . 164 A8
 Heytesbury BA12 . . . . 194 C5
 Kempsford GL7 . . . . . 10 D7
Chapel Rise SN12 . . . . .92 E8
Chapel Row
 Bathford BA1 . . . . . . . 82 C2
 Luckington SN14 . . . . . 39 E4
Chapel St
 Horningsham BA12 . . . 119 A4
 Studley SN11 . . . . . . 80 A2
 Swindon SN2 . . . . . . . 50 D8
 Warminster BA12 . . . . 116 F5
Chapel Way SN16 . . . . 14 D6
Chapel Wlk GL9 . . . . . .24 B3
Chaplins Pl **3** SP4 . . 217 B3
CHAPMANSLADE . . . . . 111 C4
Chapmanslade CE Prim
 Sch BA13 . . . . . . . . . 111 C4
Chapperton Cl BA13 . 109 B5
Chapter Rise SP3 . . . . 188 B2
Charcoal Burners Rd
 SN8 . . . . . . . . . . . . . 175 B4
Charcroft Hill BA10 . 122 A5
Charfield Cl SN3 . . . . . 51 A4
Charlbury Cl SN25 . . . .34 C3
CHARLCUTT . . . . . . . . .72 F4
Charles Garrett Cl **39**
 SP7 . . . . . . . . . . . . . 202 C2
Charles McPherson Gdns
 SN3 . . . . . . . . . . . . . .51 C5
Charles Morrison Cl
 SN10 . . . . . . . . . . . . 214 A3
Charles Rd SP4 . . . . . 198 B7
Charles St
 Corsham SN13 . . . . . . .76 F2
 **2** Salisbury SP2 . . . 145 F1
 Trowbridge BA14 . . . . 101 C1
Charles Vesey Rd
 SN9 . . . . . . . . . . . . . 216 C7
Charlham La GL7 . . . . . .8 D7
Charlieu Ave SN11 . . . . 89 C8
Charlock Path SN25 . . .34 E5
Charlotte Ct BA14 . . . 101 D1
Charlotte Mews SN3 . . 50 D4
Charlotte Sq BA14 . . . 101 D1
Charlotte St BA14 . . . 101 D1
CHARLTON
 Andover . . . . . . . . . . 193 C2
 Donhead St Mary . . . . 203 A1
 Malmesbury . . . . . . . . 29 A6
 Pewsey . . . . . . . . . . . 181 D3
CHARLTON-ALL-
 SAINTS . . . . . . . . . . 159 A4
Charlton Cl SN2 . . . . . 35 D5
Charlton Dro SN9 . . . . 181 D2
CHARLTON HEATH . . . 29 D6
Charlton Hill BA13 . . . 186 D8
Charlton La SP7 . . . . . 202 F1
CHARLTON
 MUSGROVE . . . . . . . 136 B4
Charlton Pk SN16 . . . . 14 D1
Charlton Pk★ SN16 . . .28 E7
Charlton Rd SN16 . . . . .28 E5
Charlwood Rd SN13 . . .84 F8
Charminster Cl SN3 . . .51 C6
CHARNAGE . . . . . . . . . 137 B7
Charnham La RG17 . . . 177 B8
Charnham Pk RG17 . . . 177 B8
Charnham Pk Ind Est
 RG17 . . . . . . . . . . . . 177 B8
Charnwood Dr **9**
 SP6 . . . . . . . . . . . . . 210 D2
Charnwood Rd
 Salisbury SP2 . . . . . . 145 E1
 Trowbridge BA14 . . . . 101 A1
Charolais Dr SN1 . . . .49 A7
Charter Cl **3** SN10 . . 214 D5
Charterhouse Dr **4**
 BA11 . . . . . . . . . . . . 110 C7
Charterhouse Rd
 Wroughton SN4 . . . . . .63 F6
 **5** Wroughton SN4 . . 64 A6
Charter Prim Sch
 SN15 . . . . . . . . . . . . .78 F6
Charter Rd SN1 . . . . . 78 D7
Chartley Gn **1** SN5 . . 49 A5
Chartwell Pl SP3 . . . . 196 E6
Chartwell Rd SN25 . . . .34 F7
Chase Ave SP5 . . . . . . 207 E6
Chase Cres SP5 . . . . . . 207 E4
Chase Wood SN5 . . . . .34 A2
Chastleton Rd SN25 . . .34 E7
Chatfield SN25 . . . . . . 20 D1
Chatham Cl SP1 . . . . . 146 A5
Chatham Ct **1** BA12 . 117 B7
Chatsworth Rd SN25 . . .34 F5
Chaucer Ave **5** SP10 193 C1
Chaucer Cl SN4 . . . . . .47 E3
Chaveywell Ct SN11 . . .81 B2
Cheapside BA12 . . . . . 195 A2
Cheater's La SP6 . . . . 210 A1
Cheddar Cl BA11 . . . . . 110 C7
Cheddar Rd SN25 . . . . .34 E3
CHEDGLOW . . . . . . . . . .7 E2
Chedworth Gate SN3 . .50 F1
Cheese Mkt **5** SP1 . 146 A1
Cheese Wharf★ SN7 . . .2 F1
Chelmsford Rd SN5 . . .49 C7
Cheltenham Dr SN14 . .78 A5

Cheltenham St SN1 . . .50 B7
Chelwood Cl SN14 . . . .78 B6
CHELWORTH . . . . . . . . .4 C1
Chelworth Ind Est
 SN6 . . . . . . . . . . . . . .19 A5
CHELWORTH LOWER
 GREEN . . . . . . . . . . . .19 A5
Chelworth Rd SN6 . . . .19 B6
Chelworth Road
 Chelworth Upper Green
 SN6 . . . . . . . . . . . . .18 F6
 Chelworth Upper Green
 SN6 . . . . . . . . . . . . 19 A6
CHELWORTH UPPER
 GREEN . . . . . . . . . . . .19 A6
Chemical Rd BA13 . . . 108 C6
CHENEY MANOR . . . . . .34 F1
Cheney Manor Ind Est
 SN2 . . . . . . . . . . . . . .34 E1
Cheney Manor Rd SN2 34 F2
Cheney Pl SN2 . . . . . . .34 E1
Chepston Pl BA14 . . . . 100 F1
Chepstow Cl
 **4** Chippenham SN14 . .78 A5
 Swindon SN5 . . . . . . . 49 C3
Cheraton Cl SN3 . . . . . .51 B7
Cherbury Wlk SN3 . . . . .51 A6
CHERHILL . . . . . . . . . . 166 B1
Cherhill CE Sch SN11 166 B1
Cherhill Ct SN25 . . . . . .34 E3
Cherhill Way SN11 . . . .89 C8
Cherhill White Horse★
 SN11 . . . . . . . . . . . . 172 C8
Cherrington Field
 SN10 . . . . . . . . . . . . 180 F4
Cherry Cl
 Pewsey SN9 . . . . . . . 215 D5
 Salisbury SP2 . . . . . . 145 D1
Cherry Gdns BA14 . . . 102 A3
Cherry Gdns Ct BA14 . 105 D7
Cherry Gr **7** RG17 . . 177 B7
Cherry Orch
 Codford St Peter
 BA12 . . . . . . . . . . . . 195 A2
 Highworth SN6 . . . . . . 23 A5
 Marlborough SN8 . . . . 213 E2
Cherry Orch E SN2 . . . .35 E2
Cherry Orch La
 Cann SP7 . . . . . . . . . 202 A1
 Luckington SN14 . . . . 39 C5
 Salisbury SP2 . . . . . . 145 D1
Cherry Orch N SN2 . . . .35 E2
Cherry Orch W SN2 . . .35 D2
Cherry Rd SN14 . . . . . .75 A5
Cherry Tree Ave SP9 . 216 E7
Cherry Tree Ct SN11 . .81 B4
Cherry Tree Gr SN2 . . .35 C2
Cherry Tree La SN6 . . 19 D8
Cherry Tree Way **2**
 SP4 . . . . . . . . . . . . . 217 C3
Chervil Cl **3** SN2 . . . .34 C4
Cherwell SN26 . . . . . . 20 D1
Chesford Cl SN3 . . . . . .51 A3
Cheshire Cl
 **2** Bower Hill SN12 . . 178 B8
 Swindon SN5 . . . . . . . 145 C4
Chesterfield Cl
 **3** Amesbury SP4 . . 217 E3
 **4** Swindon SN5 . . . 49 C6
Chester St SN1 . . . . . . 50 B6
Chesters The SN5 . . . . .49 C6
Chester Way SN14 . . . .78 A5
Chestnut Ave
 Netheravon SP4 . . . . . 190 A2
 Swindon SN2 . . . . . . . 35 C3
 Tidworth SP9 . . . . . . . 216 D7
Chestnut Cl
 Acton Turville GL9 . . . 53 A6
 Down Ampney GL7 . . . 8 D7
 Frome BA11 . . . . . . . . 110 B7
 Rowde SN10 . . . . . . . . 96 D2
 Salisbury SP1 . . . . . . 146 D3
Chestnut Cnr **13**
 BA13 . . . . . . . . . . . . 186 B7
Chestnut Dr SN10 . . . 178 E5
Chestnut Gr
 Sutton Benger SN15 . . 57 C2
 Trowbridge BA14 . . . . 105 B5
 Westbury BA13 . . . . . 108 F3
 Westwood BA15 . . . . . .99 F4
Chestnut Grange
 SN13 . . . . . . . . . . . . 76 D1
Chestnut La RG17 . . . 165 C2
Chestnut Mews SN12 . .94 A3
Chestnut Rd
 Chippenham SN14 . . 78 B8
 Sutton Benger SN15 . . . 57 D2
Chestnut Springs SN5 33 D1
Chestnut Tree Gdns
 BA12 . . . . . . . . . . . . 116 F4
Chestnut Wlk **11**
 RG17 . . . . . . . . . . . . 177 B7
Chetcombe Rd BA12 . 139 B6
Chevalier Cl **13** SN5 . .48 F8
Cheverell Ave SP1 . . . 146 C3
Cheverell Cl BA14 . . . 105 D5
Cheverell Gn Rd
 SN10 . . . . . . . . . . . . 179 C2
Cheverell Rd
 Cheverell Parva SN10 . 179 C1
 West Lavington SN10 . 187 D8
Cheviot Cl
 Swindon SN5 . . . . . . . 49 A6
 Trowbridge BA14 . . . . 105 B8
Cheviot Rd **25** SP11 . 193 F2
Chevral Cl SN14 . . . . . .70 B2
Cheyney Wlk BA13 . . . 109 B4

Chichester Cl SP2 . . . 152 B6
Chichester Pk BA13 . . 109 A4
Chickerell Rd SN3 . . . . .51 A4
CHICKLADE . . . . . . . . . 200 A5
CHICKSGROVE . . . . . . 204 B8
Chicksgrove Rd
 Sutton Mandeville
 SP3 . . . . . . . . . . . . . 204 C8
 Tisbury SP3 . . . . . . . 203 F8
Chicks Grove Rd SP3 . 201 B1
Chick's La SN8 . . . . . . 183 E1
Chicory Cl SN2 . . . . . . .34 C3
Chiffchaff Cl GL7 . . . . .7 A6
Child St **1** RG17 . . . . 165 A1
CHILMARK . . . . . . . . . . 201 B3
Chilmark & Fonthill
 Bishop CE Aided Prim
 Sch SP3 . . . . . . . . . . 201 B3
Chilmark Rd
 Stockton SP3 . . . . . . . 201 C6
 Tisbury SP3 . . . . . . . 200 F1
 Trowbridge BA14 . . . . 100 F1
 Trowbridge BA14 . . . . 101 A1
Chiltern Cl
 Melksham SN12 . . . . . 94 C4
 **9** Warminster BA12 . . 117 A8
CHILTON FOLIAT . . . . . 170 F1
Chilton Foliat CE Prim
 Sch RG17 . . . . . . . . 171 A2
Chilton Gdns SN25 . . . .34 F3
Chilton Way RG17 . . . 177 C8
Chilvester Hill SN11 . .80 E2
Chilworth Cl **5** SN25 . .34 E6
Chine Rd SP4 . . . . . . . 131 C7
Chip Cottage BA11 . . . 118 B4
CHIPPENHAM . . . . . . . .78 E7
Chippenham Cl **4**
 SN25 . . . . . . . . . . . . .35 B6
Chippenham Com Hospl
 SN15 . . . . . . . . . . . . .78 C6
Chippenham La SN14 . .77 B7
Chippenham Lane
 SN14 . . . . . . . . . . . . .77 C7
Chippenham Mus &
 Heritage Ctr★ SN15 . .78 E2
Chippenham Rd
 Biddestone SN14 . . . . . .76 F7
 Chippenham SN14 . . . . 77 B7
 Corsham SN13 . . . . . . .76 F2
 Corsham SN13 . . . . . . .77 B4
 Corston SN16 . . . . . . . 42 E4
 Lyneham & Bradenstoke
 SN15 . . . . . . . . . . . . 59 E3
 Marshfield SN14 . . . . 74 A8
 Marshfield SN14 . . . . 74 C8
Chippenham Sta SN15 .78 E8
Chipper La SP1 . . . . . . 146 A1
CHIRTON . . . . . . . . . . . 180 F4
Chirton Pl **5** BA14 . . 105 D6
Chirton CE Prim Sch
 SN10 . . . . . . . . . . . . 180 F4
CHISBURY . . . . . . . . . . 176 B5
Chisbury Camp★
 SN8 . . . . . . . . . . . . . 176 C4
Chisbury La SN8 . . . . . 176 C5
Chiselbury Gr SP2 . . . 152 A6
CHISELDON . . . . . . . . . 65 D3
Chiseldon Ct SN4 . . . . 65 D4
Chiseldon Prim Sch
 SN4 . . . . . . . . . . . . . .65 E4
Chissell Brook SN11 . .81 B4
Chitham Cl SN10 . . . . 187 C8
CHITTERNE . . . . . . . . . 195 C7
Chitterne Anstey
 BA12 . . . . . . . . . . . . 194 E5
Chitterne Rd
 Chitterne BA12 . . . . . 195 E8
 Codford St Mary BA12 . 195 B2
 Shrewton SP3 . . . . . . 196 B6
 Tilshead SP3 . . . . . . . 187 F1
 Tilshead SP3 . . . . . . . 188 A2
CHITTOE . . . . . . . . . . . .87 E2
Chittoe Heath SN15 . . .88 A2
Chivers Rd
 Chippenham SN15 . . . . 78 E5
 Devizes SN10 . . . . . . . 214 D3
Chives Way SN2 . . . . . .34 D4
Chobham Cl SN2 . . . . . 36 A5
CHOLDERTON . . . . . . . 199 C5
Cholderton Rare Breeds
 Farm★ SP4 . . . . . . . 199 A5
Cholderton Rd
 Amport SP4 . . . . . . . . 199 D5
 Quarley SP4 . . . . . . . . 199 F5
Chopping Knife La
 SN8 . . . . . . . . . . . . . 175 A7
Choristers Sq **1** SP1 . 152 A8
Choulston Cl SP4 . . . . 190 B3
Christ Church Prim Sch
 BA15 . . . . . . . . . . . . 100 E8
Christchurch Rd
 BA15 . . . . . . . . . . . . 100 D8
Christchurch Terr
 BA12 . . . . . . . . . . . . 116 F5
CHRISTIAN
 MALFORD . . . . . . . . .58 B2
Christian Malford CE
 Prim Sch SN15 . . . . .58 A2
Christie Cl SN3 . . . . . . 51 D4
Christie Miller Rd
 SP2 . . . . . . . . . . . . . 145 E2
Christie Miller Sports Ctr
 SN12 . . . . . . . . . . . . .94 B1
Christin Ct BA14 . . . . 105 A8
Christopher Cl **2**
 SP2 . . . . . . . . . . . . . 151 F5
Christopher Dr SN15 . .79 A4

Christ the King RC Prim
 Sch SP4 . . . . . . . . . 217 B3
Christy's Gdns **30**
 SP7 . . . . . . . . . . . . . 202 C2
Christy's La **23** SP7 . 202 C2
Chubb Cl SN16 . . . . . . .28 A5
Chudleigh SN5 . . . . . . .49 B4
Church Acre
 Bradford-on-Avon
 BA15 . . . . . . . . . . . . 100 C7
 Codford BA12 . . . . . . 195 A3
 Seagry SN15 . . . . . . . 57 F6
Church Cl
 Bath BA1 . . . . . . . . . . 82 B2
 Bourton SP8 . . . . . . . 137 D1
 **13** Lambourn RG17 . . 165 A2
Church End SN5 . . . . . 33 D3
Church End Cl SN15 . . .60 A2
Churches BA15 . . . . . 100 C7
Church Farm
 **9** Swindon SN3 . . . 36 B3
 Yatton Keynell SN14 . . .68 F5
Church Farm La
 Alton Barnes SN8 . . . 173 C1
 Farleigh Hungerford
 BA2 . . . . . . . . . . . . . 103 D7
 South Marston SN3 . . 36 E4
 Woodborough SN9 . . . 181 D7
Church Farm Mews
 SN15 . . . . . . . . . . . . .60 A2
Church Farm Rd SN6 . .8 D4
Churchfield SN25 . . . . .34 F4
CHURCHFIELDS . . . . . 145 D1
Churchfields BA15 . . . .91 E6
Church Fields BA14 . . 105 A5
Churchfields Academy
 SN3 . . . . . . . . . . . . . .50 F5
Churchfields Ind Est
 SP2 . . . . . . . . . . . . . 145 E1
Churchfields Rd SP2 . 145 E1
Churchfields the Village
 Sch BA15 . . . . . . . . .90 E2
Churchfields, the Village
 School SN12 . . . . . . .92 E8
Church Furlong **3** SP4 129 C2
Church Ground SN3 . . .36 F4
Church Hatch **1** SP5 211 B8
Church Hill
 Bromham SN15 . . . . . .95 F7
 Donhead St Mary SP7 . 203 A3
 Limpley Stoke BA2 . . . 99 B5
 Nettleton SN14 . . . . . . 53 B3
 Redlynch SP5 . . . . . . . 211 D7
 Shaftesbury SP7 . . . . . 202 B2
 West Overton SN8 . . . 173 F7
 Wroughton SN4 . . . . . .63 F5
Church Hill Rise SN15 .96 A7
Churchill Ave
 Broad Blunsdon SN26 . 21 C2
 Durrington/Bulford
 SP4 . . . . . . . . . . . . . 217 D8
 Melksham SN12 . . . . . 94 D5
Churchill Cl
 Calne SN11 . . . . . . . . 81 C1
 North Tidworth SP9 . . 216 B8
 **3** Royal Wootton Bassett
 SN4 . . . . . . . . . . . . . .47 F3
 **9** Tisbury SP3 . . . . 203 E8
Churchill Ct SP2 . . . . 144 D3
Churchill Est SP3 . . . . 203 E8
Churchill Way SN13 . . .76 F3
Churchill Way E SP1 . 146 B1
Churchill Way N SP1 . 146 A2
Churchill Way S SP1 . 152 B7
Churchill Way W
 Salisbury SP2 . . . . . . 146 A1
Church La
 Amesbury SP4 . . . . . . 217 A3
 Ashbury SN6 . . . . . . . 164 A7
 Ashton Keynes SN6 . . . .6 E1
 Bishopstone SN6 . . . . 163 E6
 Bishopstone SN6 . . . . 150 A1
 Bishopstrow BA12 . . . 117 E4
 Box SN13 . . . . . . . . . 83 C5
 **16** Bratton BA13 . . . 186 B7
 Britford SP5 . . . . . . . 152 E5
 Brokenborough SN16 . . 27 D7
 Buttermere SN8 . . . . . 185 C7
 Codford St Peter BA12 . 195 B2
 **5** Cricklade SN6 . . . 19 D8
 Damerham SP6 . . . . . 209 F2
 Dauntsey SN15 . . . . . . 44 E1
 Dauntsey SN15 . . . . . . 45 A1
 Down Ampney GL7 . . . 8 D6
 Downton SP5 . . . . . . . 159 A5
 Durrington/Bulford
 SP4 . . . . . . . . . . . . . 217 D8
 East Kennet SN8 . . . . 173 D6
 Fovant SP3 . . . . . . . . 204 D8
 Great Somerton SN15 . . 44 E1
 Hankerton SN16 . . . . . 15 C2
 Hawkesbury GL9 . . . . 38 E5
 **32** Hungerford RG17 . 177 B7
 Inglesham GL7 . . . . . . .2 B1
 Kington Langley SN15 . 70 E6
 Limpley Stoke BA2 . . . 99 A5
 **6** Ludgershall SP11 . 192 A5
 Lyneham SN15 . . . . . . 60 A2
 Marshfield SN14 . . . . 74 A8
 Martin SP6 . . . . . . . . 209 B6
 Melchet Park & Plaitford
 SO51 . . . . . . . . . . . . 212 E7
 Melksham SN12 . . . . . 94 C6
 Middle Woodford SP4 . 131 B5
 Mildenhall SN8 . . . . . 175 A8
 Monkton Combe BA2 . . 98 E8
 Newbury BA12 . . . . . 119 C8

Church La continued
 Norton SN16 . . . . . . . 41 D5
 Ogbourne St Andrew
 SN8 . . . . . . . . . . . . . 168 E3
 Ogbourne St George
 SN8 . . . . . . . . . . . . . 168 F5
 Pitton & Farley SP5 . . 148 C4
 Rushall SN9 . . . . . . . . 181 E2
 Salisbury SP2 . . . . . . 145 C2
 **2** Shaftesbury SP7 . . 202 C1
 Sherfield English SO51 162 F3
 Sherrington BA12 . . . . 194 F2
 Shipton Moyne GL8 . . 26 E8
 Sopworth SN14 . . . . . 24 D1
 South Cerney SN5 . . . . .6 F7
 Stanton Fitzwarren SN6 . 22 B1
 Stanton St Quintin SN14 56 B5
 Stanton St Quintin SN14 56 C6
 Tidworth SP9 . . . . . . . 216 D4
 Trowbridge BA14 . . . . 105 A5
 Vernhams Dean SP11 . 185 B4
 Westbury BA13 . . . . . 108 E1
 West Lavington SN10 . 187 E8
 Wingfield BA14 . . . . . 104 C6
 Woolverton BA2 . . . . . 103 C1
Churchlands BA14 . . . 105 D2
Church Lawn
 Stourton BA12 . . . . . . 123 F1
 Stourton BA12 . . . . . . 137 F8
Church Farm Mews
 SN15 . . . . . . . . . . . . .60 A2
Church Leat SP5 . . . . 211 A8
Church Mdws **1**
 SP9 . . . . . . . . . . . . . 199 D8
Church Piece SN15 . . . 57 D2
Church Pk SN15 . . . . . 59 C3
Church Pl
 Lydiard Millicent SN5 . .33 C1
 Lydiard Millicent SN5 . .48 C8
 Swindon SN1 . . . . . . . 50 A6
Church Rails SP3 . . . . 141 B1
Church Rd
 Biddestone SN14 . . . . 76 B7
 Bourton SP8 . . . . . . . 137 F1
 Bratton BA13 . . . . . . . 186 B6
 Calne Without SN11 . . 80 A2
 Cheverell Magna SN10 179 B1
 Christian Malford SN15 . 58 A2
 Derry Hill/Studley SN11 .79 F2
 East Knoyle SP3 . . . . . 141 B1
 Farley SP5 . . . . . . . . 155 A8
 Farnham DT11 . . . . . . 207 C2
 Froxfield SN8 . . . . . . . 176 B7
 Ham SN8 . . . . . . . . . 177 A1
 Heddington SN13 . . . . .89 B1
 Hilmarton SN11 . . . . . .73 F3
 Idmiston SP4 . . . . . . . 133 F8
 Iwerne Minster DT11 . 206 A1
 Kemble GL7 . . . . . . . . .4 F7
 Kempsford GL7 . . . . . 10 E6
 Kington Langley SN15 . 70 E6
 Lechlade-on-Thames GL7 2 D4
 Liddington SN4 . . . . . 163 A4
 Luckington SN14 . . . . 39 C4
 Milston SP4 . . . . . . . . 198 C8
 Norleaze BA13 . . . . . . 108 F8
 Pitton & Farley SP5 . . 154 E7
 St Paul Malmesbury Without
 SN16 . . . . . . . . . . . . 43 A3
 Salisbury SP1 . . . . . . 146 E3
 Sherston GL8 . . . . . . . 25 B5
 Silton SP8 . . . . . . . . . 138 A1
 Stanton St Bernard
 SN8 . . . . . . . . . . . . . 173 B1
 Stanton St Quintin SN14 56 B5
 **2** Swindon SN1 . . . . 50 D4
 Tytherington BA12 . . . 194 B4
 Wanborough SN4 . . . . 163 A4
 Woodborough SN9 . . . 181 D7
Church Ri SN14 . . . . . .53 B3
Church Ride SP11 . . . . 192 A6
Church Rise SN13 . . . . .84 C5
Church Row SN14 . . . . 163 D6
Church St Cl **15** SP3 . 203 E8
Church St
 Amesbury SP4 . . . . . . 217 A3
 Atworth SN12 . . . . . . . 92 D8
 Bath BA1 . . . . . . . . . . 82 B2
 Berwick St John SP7 . . 203 E1
 Bowerchalke SP5 . . . . 204 F1
 Bower Chalke SP5 . . . 205 A2
 Bradford-on-Avon
 BA15 . . . . . . . . . . . . 100 C6
 Calne SN11 . . . . . . . . 81 B2
 Chiseldown SN4 . . . . . 65 D4
 Collingbourne Ducis
 SN8 . . . . . . . . . . . . . 191 E8
 Corsham SN13 . . . . . . 77 A2
 Great Bedwyn SN8 . . . 176 B2
 Grimstead SP5 . . . . . . 154 C2
 Horningsham BA12 . . . 119 B7
 Hungerford RG17 . . . . 177 B7
 Keevil BA14 . . . . . . . . 178 A4
 Lacock SN15 . . . . . . . 86 D6
 Little Bedwyn SN8 . . . 176 D5
 Longbridge Deverill
 BA12 . . . . . . . . . . . . 120 F7
 Maiden Bradley with
 Yarnfield BA12 . . . . . 118 E2
 Market Lavington SN10 179 F1
 Melksham SN12 . . . . . 94 A4
 Mere BA12 . . . . . . . . 139 A5
 Pewsey SN9 . . . . . . . 215 D4
 Purton SN5 . . . . . . . . 33 C4
 Royal Wootton Bassett
 SN4 . . . . . . . . . . . . . .47 C2
 Semington BA14 . . . . 102 F6

Church St continued
 Sherston SN16 . . . . . . 25 C1
 Southwick BA14 . . . . . 104 F3
 Swindon SN3 . . . . . . . 36 B3
 Tisbury SP3 . . . . . . . 203 E8
 Trowbridge BA14 . . . . 101 D1
 Warminster BA12 . . . . 116 F7
 Westbury BA13 . . . . . 108 C4
 West Lavington SN10 . 187 F7
 Winterbourne Stoke
 SP3 . . . . . . . . . . . . . 196 F3
 Wylye BA12 . . . . . . . . 201 E8
Church Tk SP8 . . . . . . 137 D1
Church View
 Calne SN11 . . . . . . . . 81 C1
 Castle Eaton SN6 . . . . 10 B4
 Chippenham SN14 . . . 70 C2
 Quemerford SN11 . . . .89 C8
 Sutton Benger SN15 . . 57 D2
Churchward Ave SN2 . .35 A1
Churchward Dr BA11 . 110 C7
Churchward Sch SN26 .20 E2
Churchway SN26 . . . . .21 C2
Church Way
 Hungerford RG17 . . . . 177 B7
 **7** Swindon SN3 . . . 36 B3
Church Wlk
 Ashton Keynes SN6 . . . .6 E1
 Avebury SN8 . . . . . . . 173 B8
 Bishops Cannings
 SN10 . . . . . . . . . . . . 172 B3
 Bishopstone SN6 . . . . 163 E6
 Devizes SN10 . . . . . . 214 C3
 Melksham SN12 . . . . . 94 A4
 Motcombe SP7 . . . . . . 202 A4
 Redlynch SP5 . . . . . . . 211 E7
 Swindon SN2 . . . . . . . 35 E3
Church Wlk N SN25 . . .34 F3
Church Wlk S SN2 . . . .34 F3
Churn Cl SP4 . . . . . . . . .6 F7
Chur St SP4 . . . . . . . . 198 E6
CHUTE CADLEY . . . . . 192 F8
Chute Causeway
 SP11 . . . . . . . . . . . . 185 A2
Chute Cswy SP11 . . . . 184 E2
CHUTE STANDEN . . . . 192 F8
Cinders End SN14 . . . . 78 D8
Circle The SN2 . . . . . . .35 C2
Cirencester Rd
 Fairford GL7 . . . . . . . . . .1 F7
 Latton GL7 . . . . . . . . . .7 E8
 South Cerney SN5 . . . . .6 F8
Cirencester Way
 Swindon SN2 . . . . . . . 50 D8
 Swindon SN25 . . . . . . 35 D2
Citrine Cl SN25 . . . . . . 20 F1
City Cnr SN4 . . . . . . . . 163 C6
City The SN12 . . . . . . . .94 A5
Clack La SP6 . . . . . . . . 210 B3
Clanfield Rd SN3 . . . . .51 B5
Clanger La BA13 . . . . 109 A4
CLANVILLE
 Penton Grafton . . . . . 193 A4
 Stanton St Quintin . . . 56 E4
Clanville Way SN15 . . .56 E3
Clapham Cl **6** SN25 . .34 E3
Clap La SP5 . . . . . . . . 207 B4
Clardon La SN5 . . . . . .33 C6
Clare Ave BA14 . . . . . 106 B8
Clarence Cl **18** SP11 . 192 A5
Clarence Rd
 Chippenham SN14 . . . . .77 F7
 Trowbridge BA14 . . . . 105 F8
Clarence St SN1 . . . . . .50 C6
Clarendon Ave BA14 . . 105 E8
Clarendon Cl SP3 . . . . 201 F2
Clarendon Coll The
 BA14 . . . . . . . . . . . . 105 C6
Clarendon Ct
 Marlborough SN8 . . . . 213 D3
 Tidworth SP9 . . . . . . . 216 D7
Clarendon Dr SN4 . . . .47 E1
Clarendon Infs Sch
 SP9 . . . . . . . . . . . . . 216 D6
Clarendon Jun Sch
 SP9 . . . . . . . . . . . . . 216 D6
Clarendon Pal★ SP5 . 147 C1
Clarendon Rd
 Alderbury SP5 . . . . . . 153 D3
 Clarendon Park SP5 . . 152 F6
 Grimstead SP5 . . . . . . 154 A4
 Salisbury SP1 . . . . . . 146 C1
 Trowbridge BA14 . . . . 105 E8
Clare Wlk SN5 . . . . . . . 49 B4
Claridge Cl **3** SN8 . . 170 A4
Clark Ave SN11 . . . . . . .81 C5
Clarke Dr SN5 . . . . . . . 49 B8
Clarkes Field SN16 . . . .17 B1
Clarke's La SP11 . . . . . 193 A7
Clarkes Leaze SN14 . . .68 F6
Clark's Gdns **25** RG17 177 B7
Clarks Hay GL7 . . . . . . .4 F8
Clark's Pl **3** BA14 . . 105 E8
Clary Rd SN2 . . . . . . . .34 D5
Classics The **16** RG17 165 A1
CLATFORD . . . . . . . . . 174 B7
Clattinger Farm Nature
 Reserve★ SN16 . . . . .16 F2
Claudius Cl **15** SP10 . 193 E2
CLAVERTON . . . . . . . . .90 B5
Claverton Hill BA2 . . . .90 A4
Claverton Pumping Sta★
 BA1 . . . . . . . . . . . . . .90 C5
Clay Cl BA13 . . . . . . . . 112 C8
Claydon Rd **6** SN25 . .34 E7
Clay Fields GL8 . . . . . . .26 C6
Clayfurlong Gr GL7 . . . .4 F8
Clayhill Copse SN5 . . .34 A2

Clays Cl SN2 . . . . . . . . . 35 E3
Clay St
  Little Somerford SN15 . . 44 C6
  Longbridge Deverill
    BA12 . . . . . . . . . . . . . 116 E1
  Whiteparish SP5 . . . . . 161 C3
Clays The SN10 . . . . . . 179 F1
Clay The SN10 . . . . . . . 180 A1
Clayton Rd SP4 . . . . . . 217 E8
Clearbury Ring★
  SP5 . . . . . . . . . . . . . . 158 C5
Clearbury Vw **7** SP5 . 210 F8
CLEARWOOD . . . . . . . 111 F8
Clearwood
  Dilton Marsh BA13 . . . 107 F1
  Westbury BA13 . . . . . . 111 F8
Clearwood View
  BA13 . . . . . . . . . . . . . 111 D4
Cleasby Cl SN5 . . . . . . . 49 D6
Cleavers The **1** SN8 . 183 D8
Cleaves Ave SN14 . . . . . 75 A3
Cleevedale Rd SN13 . . . 85 A8
Cleeve Lawns SN3 . . . . . 50 F3
Cleeves Cl SN5 . . . . . . . 49 A6
Cleeves The SP3 . . . . . 143 B3
Cleeve The
  Corsham SN13 . . . . . . . 85 A8
  West Knoyle BA12 . . . . 140 A6
Clementine Rd **4**
  SN25 . . . . . . . . . . . . . . 34 B7
Clement's La BA12 . . . 139 B4
CLENCH . . . . . . . . . . . 174 E1
CLENCH COMMON . . . 174 D4
CLEVANCY . . . . . . . . . 166 C6
Clevedon Cl SN3 . . . . . . 51 A6
Cleveland Gdns BA14 101 C2
Cleveland Rd SN2 . . . . . 34 C3
Cleveland Way BA13 . 108 E2
Cleverley Way SN11 . . . 81 B1
CLEVERTON . . . . . . . . . 44 D8
Cleverton Ct SN2 . . . . . 35 C5
Cleves Cl SN5 . . . . . . . . 49 A6
Cleyhill Gdns BA13 . . . 111 D5
Cley Hill (Hill Fort)★
  BA12 . . . . . . . . . . . . . 116 A6
Cley View **6** BA12 . . 116 E6
Cliffe Dr BA2 . . . . . . . . . 99 A6
Cliffords SN6 . . . . . . . . . 19 C8
Cliff Rd SN16 . . . . . . . . . 40 C8
Clift Ave SN15 . . . . . . . . 70 E1
Clift Cl SN13 . . . . . . . . . 84 A8
Clifton Cl SN14 . . . . . . . 78 B8
Clifton Rd SP2 . . . . . . . 145 F2
Clifton St SN1 . . . . . . . . 50 B5
Clifts Bldgs BA11 . . . . . 110 A4
Clinchorn Farm Rd
  SP11 . . . . . . . . . . . . . 185 E2
Clink Farm Ct **6**
  BA11 . . . . . . . . . . . . . 110 C6
Clink La SN12 . . . . . . . . 87 C2
Clink Rd BA11 . . . . . . . 110 E6
Clinton Cl SN5 . . . . . . . . 48 F4
Clipsham Rise BA14 . . 101 A1
Clive Parade SN2 . . . . . 35 D3
Clivey BA13 . . . . . . . . . 107 E1
CLOATLEY . . . . . . . . . . . 15 E2
Cloatley Cres SN4 . . . . . 61 E8
CLOATLEY END . . . . . . . 16 B1
Cloatley Manor★
  SN16 . . . . . . . . . . . . . . 15 D2
Cloatley Mdws Nature
  Reserve★ SN16 . . . . . 15 E2
Cloatley Rd SN16 . . . . . . 15 C2
Cloche Way SN2 . . . . . . 35 C3
Clock Tower Vw SN12 . . 92 E8
Cloford Cl BA14 . . . . . . 101 A1
Cloister Gdn★ SN16 . . . 28 A3
Close End **8** RG17 . . 165 A1
Close La
  Marston SN10 . . . . . . . 179 A3
  Rowde SN10 . . . . . . . . . 96 D2
Close The
  Bulkington SN10 . . . . . 178 E5
  Chippenham SN14 . . . . . 77 E8
  Corsham SN13 . . . . . . . 85 C6
  Kington St Michael SN14 70 A8
  Laverstock SP4 . . . . . . 146 D8
  Lechlade GL7 . . . . . . . . . 2 C5
  Lydiard Millicent SN5 . . 48 D8
  Melksham SN12 . . . . . . 94 B3
  **4** Redlynch SP5 . . . . 211 C8
  Salisbury SP1 . . . . . . . 152 A8
  Tangley SP11 . . . . . . . 193 C5
  Warminster BA12 . . . . 117 A7
Clothier Leaze **2**
  BA14 . . . . . . . . . . . . . 105 D7
Cloth Yd **1** BA14 . . . 105 E7
Cloudberry Rd SN25 . . . 34 C5
Clough La SP5 . . . . . . . 149 B7
Clouts Wood **5** SN5 . . 34 A2
Clouts Wood Nature
  Reserve★ SN4 . . . . . . 63 F4
Clover Cl SN12 . . . . . . . 94 C3
Clover Dean SN14 . . . . . 78 A6
Clover Gdns **23** SP11 . 192 A5
Clover Gr SN11 . . . . . . . 81 D5
Clover La
  **8** Cricklade SN6 . . . . 19 D8
  Durrington/Bulford
    SP4 . . . . . . . . . . . . . 198 B2
Cloverlands SN25 . . . . . 34 D4
Clover Pk SN2 . . . . . . . . 34 D4
Clubhouse Pl **2** SN13 . 76 C1
Club La SP9 . . . . . . . . . 216 C6
Club Rd **1** SP4 . . . . . 198 F7
Clump Way SP4 . . . . . . 217 A5
Clydesdale Cl
  **5** Swindon SN5 . . . . . 49 A7

Clydesdale Cl continued
  Trowbridge BA14 . . . . . 105 C5
Clydesdale Rd SN13 . . . 83 D5
CLYFFE PYPARD . . . . . 166 F8
Coach Barton BA14 . . . 178 A3
Coach Hill SP11 . . . . . . 192 E6
Coach Hollow BA13 . . . 186 D8
Coach Ho Mews SP4 . . 217 B3
Coach Rd
  Bradford-on-Avon
    BA15 . . . . . . . . . . . . 100 C6
  Westbury BA13 . . . . . . 109 B5
Coalpit Rd BA1 . . . . . . . 82 A4
Coalway La BA11 . . . . . 110 C7
COATE
  Bishops Cannings . . . . 180 C8
  Chiseldon . . . . . . . . . . . 51 C2
Coate La
  Devizes SN10 . . . . . . . . 97 F1
  Devizes SN10 . . . . . . . 214 E5
Coate Rd SN8 . . . . . . . . 173 B1
Coate Water Ctry Pk★
  SN3 . . . . . . . . . . . . . . . 51 A1
Coate Water Nature
  Reserve★ SN3 . . . . . . 51 B1
Coatside Way SN3 . . . . . 51 D1
Cobb Dr **18** SP11 . . . . 193 F2
Cobbett Cl SN25 . . . . . . 35 A7
Cobbett Pl BA12 . . . . . 116 F6
Cobb La
  Middle Winterslow
    SP5 . . . . . . . . . . . . . 149 A7
  Winterslow SP5 . . . . . . 148 F7
Cobden Rd SN2 . . . . . . . 50 A8
Cob Hill SN25 . . . . . . . . 34 B3
COBLEY . . . . . . . . . . . . 208 D7
Cobley Cl SP5 . . . . . . . 208 D6
Cob Pl BA13 . . . . . . . . . 108 F1
Coburg Sq **1** SN12 . . . 94 B4
Cochran Ave SN14 . . . . . 78 C5
Cock-a-Troop La
  SN8 . . . . . . . . . . . . . . 175 B8
Cock Hill BA14 . . . . . . . 101 A1
Cock La BA2 . . . . . . . . . . 99 A1
Cocklebury La SN15 . . . . 70 F1
Cocklebury Rd SN15 . . . 78 E8
Cock Rd
  Horningsham BA12 . . . 118 F8
  Rowde SN10 . . . . . . . . . 95 F2
Cocks Cl **5** SP4 . . . . . 197 E7
Codford Bypass
  BA12 . . . . . . . . . . . . . 195 C3
Codford Circ or Wilsbury
  Ring★ BA12 . . . . . . . . 195 C3
Codford Rd BA14 . . . . . 195 C6
Codford Rising Sun (Hill
  Figure)★ BA12 . . . . . 195 C2
CODFORD ST MARY . 195 B2
CODFORD ST
  PETER . . . . . . . . . . . . 195 A3
Cody Cl BA13 . . . . . . . . 109 B5
Coffin Cl SN6 . . . . . . . . . 23 A6
Coker's La
  Kilmington BA12 . . . . . 123 F7
  Kilmington BA12 . . . . . 124 A6
Colbert Pk SN25 . . . . . . 34 E4
Colborne Cl SN15 . . . . . 79 B5
Colbourne St SN1 . . . . . 50 D7
Colchester Cl SN5 . . . . . 49 D4
COLD HARBOUR
  Great Hinton . . . . . . . . 102 F2
  Warminster . . . . . . . . . 116 F8
Cold Harbour SP4 . . . . 217 B3
Coldharbour La SP2 . . 145 F2
Cold Harbour La SN8 . 213 E4
Coldharbour Rd
  RG17 . . . . . . . . . . . . . 177 B6
Colebrook Inf Acad
  SN3 . . . . . . . . . . . . . . . 51 C8
Colebrook Rd SN3 . . . . . 36 B1
Cole Cl
  **2** Andover SP10 . . . . 193 C2
  Malmesbury SN16 . . . . 28 C1
  Swindon SN3 . . . . . . . . 51 D6
Cole Hill BA12 . . . . . . . 108 F1
Colemans Cl SN11 . . . . . 81 C3
Coleridge Cl
  Royal Wootton Bassett
    SN4 . . . . . . . . . . . . . . 47 E3
  Warminster BA12 . . . . 116 D6
Coleridge Rd SN25 . . . . 34 F6
COLERNE . . . . . . . . . . . 75 B3
Colerne Airfield SN14 . 74 E3
Colerne CE Prim Sch
  SN14 . . . . . . . . . . . . . . 75 B3
Colerne Industrial Pk
  SN14 . . . . . . . . . . . . . . 75 A3
Colerne Pk★ SN14 . . . . 75 F6
Coles Cres **8** SP7 . . . 202 D1
Cole's La SP7 . . . . . . . . 202 A1
Coles's La SP5 . . . . . . . 212 A7
Collard Cl SN1 . . . . . . . . 50 B2
College Cl SN15 . . . . . . . 78 F8
College Farm La **5**
  SN6 . . . . . . . . . . . . . . 164 A8
College Fields SN8 . . . 213 C2
College Gdns BA14 . . . 105 D3
College Gr **1** SN4 . . . 163 A6
College Rd
  **1** Durrington/Bulford
    SP4 . . . . . . . . . . . . . 198 B7
  Purton SN5 . . . . . . . . . . 33 C4
  Trowbridge BA14 . . . . . 105 C5
  Trowbridge BA14 . . . . . 105 C6
College Row SN12 . . . . . 93 F7
College St
  Salisbury SP1 . . . . . . . 146 B1
  Swindon SN1 . . . . . . . . 50 C6

College Way **4** RG17 . 171 E7
Collen Cl **1** SN14 . . . . 78 A7
Collett Ave SN2 . . . . . . . 35 A1
Collett Pl SN6 . . . . . . . . . 8 C3
Collett Way BA11 . . . . . 110 C7
Collingbourne CE Prim
  Sch SN8 . . . . . . . . . . . 191 E8
Collingbourne Cl **2**
  BA14 . . . . . . . . . . . . . 105 D5
COLLINGBOURNE
  DUCIS . . . . . . . . . . . . 191 E8
COLLINGBOURNE
  KINGSTON . . . . . . . . 183 D2
Colling La SP9 . . . . . . . 216 D8
Collingsmead SN3 . . . . . 51 C5
Collingwood Cl SP5 . . . 153 F1
Collingwood Cres
  SN25 . . . . . . . . . . . . . . 35 D3
Collingwood Wlk **4**
  SP10 . . . . . . . . . . . . . 193 F1
Collins Cl **15** SP10 . . . 193 D2
Collins Ct SP9 . . . . . . . 216 C8
Collins La SN5 . . . . . . . . 33 E5
Colman Pk SN25 . . . . . . 35 A6
Coln Cres SN25 . . . . . . . 35 A4
Coln House Sch GL7 . . . . 1 F6
Colquhoun Rd **2**
  SP4 . . . . . . . . . . . . . . 198 A6
Colston Cl SN3 . . . . . . . . 51 A4
Colston Rd SN10 . . . . . 214 A4
Coltsfoot Cl SP4 . . . . . . 217 C3
Column Ride SN8 . . . . . 175 E3
COMBE . . . . . . . . . . . . 185 F8
Combe Bottom SP11 . . 185 F5
Combe Hay La BA2 . . . . 98 A6
Combe La
  Bratton BA13 . . . . . . . 186 B7
  Hilmarton SN11 . . . . . . 73 F6
Combe View
  **10** Hungerford RG17 . 177 B6
  Yatton Keynell SN14 . . . 68 F5
Combe Wlk
  Devizes SN10 . . . . . . . . 97 E1
  Devizes SN10 . . . . . . . 214 E5
Comet Ave SN9 . . . . . . 182 B2
Comet Cl SN15 . . . . . . . 60 B2
Comet Cres SN11 . . . . . 81 D4
Comfrey Cl
  Swindon SN2 . . . . . . . . 34 D4
  Trowbridge BA14 . . . . . 105 E6
Commerce Bsns Ctr
  BA13 . . . . . . . . . . . . . 108 E7
Commerce Cl BA13 . . . 108 E7
Commerce Park
  BA11 . . . . . . . . . . . . . 110 D8
Commercial Rd
  Devizes SN10 . . . . . . . 214 A4
  Swindon SN1 . . . . . . . . 50 B5
Common Dro DT11 . . . 207 B3
Common Hill
  Cricklade SN6 . . . . . . . . 19 B7
  Great Hinton BA14 . . . 102 F2
  Steeple Ashton BA14 . . 106 F8
COMMON PLATT . . . . . 33 F2
Common Platt
  Peatmoor SN5 . . . . . . . 34 A2
  Purton SN5 . . . . . . . . . . 33 F2
Common Rd
  St Paul Malmesbury Without
    SN16 . . . . . . . . . . . . . 27 D1
  Sixpenny Handley SP5 . 207 F4
  Whiteparish SP5 . . . . . 161 C1
Common Slip SN15 . . . . 78 E7
COMMON THE
  Brinkworth . . . . . . . . . . 46 B7
  Broughton Gifford . . . . 93 B5
  Winterslow . . . . . . . . . 149 C6
Common The
  Bromham SN15 . . . . . . 95 E6
  Holt BA14 . . . . . . . . . . . 92 F1
  Kington Langley SN15 . . 70 E6
  Marlborough SN8 . . . . 213 D4
  Minety SN16 . . . . . . . . . 17 C1
  Shrewton SP3 . . . . . . . 196 E6
  The Common SP5 . . . . 149 D6
Commonweal Rd SN1 . 50 B3
Commonweal Sch The
  SN1 . . . . . . . . . . . . . . . 50 B3
Commonwood La
  SN16 . . . . . . . . . . . . . . 40 D5
Comm Rd BA12 . . . . . . 118 F7
COMPTON . . . . . . . . . . 189 F7
COMPTON ABBAS . . . 206 A5
Compton Abbas Airfield
  SP5 . . . . . . . . . . . . . . 206 C5
COMPTON BASSETT . 166 B3
COMPTON
  CHAMBERLAYNE . . . 205 A8
Compton Cl
  **4** Swindon SN3 . . . . . 51 C4
  Trowbridge BA14 . . . . . 101 E4
Compton Gdns BA11 . . 110 C7
Compton Pk★ SN13 . . 142 C1
Compton Rd SP9 . . . . . 216 D6
Compton's Dr SO51 . . 212 E7
Conan Doyle Wlk SN3 . 51 C4
Concorde Cres GL7 . . . . 1 F6
Concord Wlk SN3 . . . . . 51 A5
Conference Cl **1**
  BA12 . . . . . . . . . . . . . 116 F7
Congreve Rd **4** SP4 . 197 E7
Conholt Hill SP11 . . . . . 185 A2
Conholt La SP11 . . . . . . 185 B2
Conholt Pk★ SP11 . . . . 184 F1
Conifer Crest **5** SN8 . 183 D8
Conifers The SN16 . . . . . 17 A2
Coniger the (Tumuli)★
  SP3 . . . . . . . . . . . . . . 196 F5

Conigre BA14 . . . . . . . . 101 C1
Conigre Cl SN12 . . . . . . 94 A3
Conigre Hill BA15 . . . . 100 C7
Conigre Mead Nature
  Reserve★ SN12 . . . . . 94 A4
Conisborough SN5 . . . . . 49 C5
Coniston Cl **5** SP4 . . 217 E3
Coniston Rd
  Chippenham SN14 . . . . 77 F6
  **7** Chippenham SN14 . . 78 A6
  Trowbridge BA14 . . . . . 101 E2
CONKWELL
  90 C1
Conkwell BA15 . . . . . . . . 90 C2
Connaught Rd SP9 . . . . 216 D6
Connelly Cl **4** SN25 . . 34 C5
Connemara Cl **2**
  BA13 . . . . . . . . . . . . . 108 C2
Connolly Way SP9 . . . . 216 D8
CONOCK . . . . . . . . . . . 180 E4
Conrad Cl SN3 . . . . . . . . 51 D4
Conscience La SN10 . . 214 A7
Constable Rd SN2 . . . . . 35 C2
Constable Way SP2 . . . 151 E7
Constantine Sq **29**
  SP10 . . . . . . . . . . . . . 193 E2
Convent The★ BA10 . . 123 B2
Conway Cres SN12 . . . . 94 B2
Conway Rd
  Chippenham SN14 . . . . 78 A7
  Swindon SN3 . . . . . . . . 51 C3
Conyers Cl **5** SN5 . . . . 48 F4
Conyger Rd SP4 . . . . . . 217 C2
Cookham Rd SN25 . . . . . 34 C7
Cook Rd **5** SN8 . . . . . 170 A7
Cooks Cl
  Hullavington SN14 . . . . 56 D6
  Salisbury SP2 . . . . . . . 145 B5
  Seend SN12 . . . . . . . . 178 E4
COOMBE
  Donhead St Mary . . . . 202 F1
  Enford . . . . . . . . . . . . . 190 B5
Coombe Barn La
  Kilmington BA12 . . . . . 124 D5
  Kilmington BA12 . . . . . 125 A4
COOMBE BISSETT . . . 150 F1
Coombe Bissett CE Prim
  Sch SP5 . . . . . . . . . . . 150 F1
Coombe Cl SN4 . . . . . . . 64 C5
Coombe La
  Atworth SN12 . . . . . . . . 92 C7
  Enford SN9 . . . . . . . . . 190 C6
Coombe Rd
  Salisbury SP2 . . . . . . . 151 F5
  Swindon SN25 . . . . . . . 34 F3
Coombe Road SP5 . . . . 151 B3
Coombe St BA9 . . . . . . 137 D3
Coombe View BA12 . . . 194 D3
Cooper Cl SN26 . . . . . . . 20 B1
Cooper Fields SN25 . . . 35 A5
Coopers Cl
  Amesbury SP4 . . . . . . 217 B4
  **2** Malmesbury SN16 . 28 A5
Cooper's La BA12 . . . . 139 B1
Coopers Mdw SN14 . . . 68 F6
Cooper Way SN11 . . . . . 81 B1
Cop Croft SN11 . . . . . . . 81 B3
COPED HALL . . . . . . . . . 47 F4
Copenacre SN16 . . . . . . 16 D2
Copenacre Way SN13 . 76 C1
Copheap La BA12 . . . . 117 B7
Copheap Rise BA12 . . . 117 B8
Copper Beech Cl SP3 196 F6
Copper Beeches SN6 . . 22 F5
Coppershell SN13 . . . . . 85 D6
Coppers Rd SN10 . . . . 214 C5
Coppice Cl
  Chippenham SN14 . . . . 78 B5
  Swindon SN2 . . . . . . . . 34 D3
  Warminster BA12 . . . . 117 A7
Coppice Hill BA15 . . . . 100 D7
Coppice La SN16 . . . . . . 15 E8
Coppice St SP7 . . . . . . . 202 C1
Copse Ave SN1 . . . . . . . 50 E8
Copse Dro SN8 . . . . . . . 169 B5
Copse The
  Alderbury SP5 . . . . . . . 153 D2
  Frome BA11 . . . . . . . . 110 B6
Copse View **2** SN16 . . 28 B2
Copyhold **2** SN8 . . . . 176 B3
Coral Cl **5** SN25 . . . . . 34 F8
Corbin Rd BA14 . . . . . . 101 F1
Corby Ave SN3 . . . . . . . 50 E3
Corestreet La BA14 . . . 102 E3
Corfe Cl SN25 . . . . . . . . 35 A4
Corfe Cres SN11 . . . . . . 81 A4
Corfe Rd
  Melksham SN12 . . . . . . 94 B3
  Swindon SN25 . . . . . . . 49 B4
Coriander Way SN2 . . . . 34 D5
Corinium Way SN3 . . . . . 36 C1
Corinthian Cl
  **14** Andover SP10 . . . . 193 E2
  Southwick BA14 . . . . . 104 E3
Cornbrash BA11 . . . . . . 110 D7
Cornbrash Rise BA14 . 102 A1
Corn Cft La SN10 . . . . . 214 F6
Corncockle Cl SN12 . . . 94 D4
Corner Gd BA12 . . . . . . 117 C5
Corner La SP7 . . . . . . . 202 B5
Cornfield Rd SN10 . . . . 214 D3
Cornflower Cl SN11 . . . . 81 C5
Cornflower Rd **3**
  SN25 . . . . . . . . . . . . . . 34 D5
Cornflower Way
  **31** Ludgershall SP11 . 192 A5
  Melksham SN12 . . . . . . 94 B3
Corn Gastons SN16 . . . . 27 E3

Cornmarket BA12 . . . . 117 B7
Cornmarsh Way SN3 . . . 51 E7
Cornpits La SP6 . . . . . . 209 E2
Cornwall Ave SN2 . . . . . 35 A1
Cornwall Cres SN12 . . . 94 C4
Cornwall Rd SP1 . . . . . 146 A3
Cornwell Cres SN10 . . 214 A2
Cornwood Rd **6** SN1 . 50 B4
Coronation Ave BA15 . 100 E7
Coronation Cl
  Christian Malford
    SN15 . . . . . . . . . . . . . 58 A1
  Donhead St Mary SP7 . 203 A1
  **2** Pewsey SN9 . . . . . 215 C5
  Sutton Benger SN15 . . . 57 F1
Coronation Dr SP7 . . . 203 A1
Coronation Rd
  Atworth/Whitley SN12 . 92 C8
  Durrington/Bulford
    SP4 . . . . . . . . . . . . . 198 B2
  Frome BA11 . . . . . . . . 110 B5
  **3** Ludgershall SP11 . . 192 B5
  Melksham SN12 . . . . . . 94 B3
  Salisbury SP2 . . . . . . . 145 D3
  Tidworth SP9 . . . . . . . 216 C8
  Wroughton SN4 . . . . . . 64 A6
Coronation Sq SP2 . . . 144 F3
Coronation St
  Fairford GL7 . . . . . . . . . . 1 F7
  **4** Trowbridge BA14 . . 105 D7
Coronel Cl SN2 . . . . . . . 36 A4
Corporation St SN2 . . . . 50 C7
Corral Cl SN5 . . . . . . . . . 34 A1
Corry The **1** SP3 . . . . 203 E8
CORSHAM . . . . . . . . . . . 85 A8
Corsham St★ SN13 . . . 77 A2
Corsham Media Pk
  SN13 . . . . . . . . . . . . . . 84 C6
Corsham Pk★ SN13 . . . 77 B8
Corsham Prim Sch
  Corsham SN13 . . . . . . . 77 B1
  Corsham SN13 . . . . . . . 85 B8
  **6** Rudloe SN13 . . . . . 84 B8
Corsham Rd
  Atworth/Whitley SN12 . 85 D1
  Lacock SN13 . . . . . . . . 85 D5
  Swindon SN2 . . . . . . . . 35 C5
Corsham Regis Prim Sch
  SN13 . . . . . . . . . . . . . . 76 F2
Corsham Sch The
  SN13 . . . . . . . . . . . . . . 76 F1
Corsham Sports Club
  SN13 . . . . . . . . . . . . . . 77 A1
CORSLEY . . . . . . . . . . . 111 D2
CORSLEY HEATH . . . . 115 B8
Corsley Heath BA12 . . 115 A8
Corston SN9 . . . . . . . . . . 42 F5
CORSTON . . . . . . . . . . 194 D3
Corton Cl SN4 . . . . . . . . 64 D3
Corton Rd BA12 . . . . . . 194 C3
Cory Way BA13 . . . . . . 108 E2
Cosford Cl SN4 . . . . . . . 64 D3
Cossington Sq BA13 . . 108 E5
Cossor Rd SN9 . . . . . . . 215 B5
Coster's La SP5 . . . . . . 205 A2
Coster View **5** SN8 . . 176 B3
Cosway Ct SN1 . . . . . . . 36 C1
Cote La BA12 . . . . . . . . 123 E4
Cotley Pl **4** BA12 . . . 194 C5
COTMARSH . . . . . . . . . . 62 B4
Cotswold Cl
  Calne SN11 . . . . . . . . . 81 D2
  Melksham SN12 . . . . . . 94 C4
  **8** Warminster BA12 . . 117 A8
COTSWOLD
  COMMUNITY . . . . . . . . 6 D4
Cotswold Community The
  / Old Farmhouse SN6 . 6 C4
Cotswold Water Pk★
  SN6 . . . . . . . . . . . . . . . 6 F4
Cotswold Water Pk
  Gateway Ctr★ GL7 . . . 7 E6
Cottage Mews **13**
  SP6 . . . . . . . . . . . . . . 210 D1
Cottars Cl **3** SN3 . . . . 36 B3
Cotterell St BA15 . . . . . 100 E6
Cottington Cl SN5 . . . . . 49 A4
Cottle Ave BA15 . . . . . . 100 D8
Cottle Mead SN13 . . . . . 84 E8
Cottles Barton **5**
  BA14 . . . . . . . . . . . . . 101 D5
Cottles La BA15 . . . . . . . 99 F5
Cotton House Gdns
  Warminster BA12 . . . . 117 B7
  Warminster BA12 . . . . 117 B8
Cottrell Cl RG17 . . . . . . 177 C7
Couch La SN10 . . . . . . . 214 A4
Coulston SN14 . . . . . . . 178 C1
Coulston Hollow
  BA13 . . . . . . . . . . . . . 186 F8
Coulston Rd
  Corsham SN13 . . . . . . . 77 A3
  Coulston BA13 . . . . . . 186 F8
Council Houses The
  SN15 . . . . . . . . . . . . . . 44 A4
Country Park Way
  SN4 . . . . . . . . . . . . . . . 61 C8
County Bsns Pk SN1 . . . 50 F8
County Rd SN1 . . . . . . . 50 D7
County Way SN14 . . . . 101 C1
Course Mdw SN25 . . . . 34 A2
Courtenay Rd SN3 . . . . . 51 A6
Court Farm Cl **8**
  SP4 . . . . . . . . . . . . . . 190 A4

Court Farm Rd **1**
  SP4 . . . . . . . . . . . . . . 190 A3
Courtfields SN6 . . . . . . . . 8 C4
Court Gdns
  Bath BA1 . . . . . . . . . . . 82 A3
  Stanton St Quintin SN14 56 B4
Court Hill
  Damerham SP6 . . . . . . 209 F2
  Potterne SN10 . . . . . . 179 C5
Court La
  Bathford BA1 . . . . . . . . 82 B1
  Bratton BA13 . . . . . . . 186 B7
  Corsley BA12 . . . . . . . 111 B1
  Edington BA13 . . . . . . 186 D8
Court St Cl SP3 . . . . . . . 203 E8
Courts Gdns The★
  BA14 . . . . . . . . . . . . . 101 E8
Courtsknap Ct **6** SN1 . 50 A5
Court St
  Sherston SN16 . . . . . . . 25 C1
  Tisbury SP3 . . . . . . . . 203 E8
  Trowbridge BA14 . . . . . 105 D8
Courtwood Cl **3**
  SP1 . . . . . . . . . . . . . . 152 C8
Cove House Gdns SN6 . . 6 F1
Coventry Cl SN4 . . . . . . . 64 B7
COVINGHAM . . . . . . . . . 51 D7
Covingham Dr SN3 . . . . 51 C8
Covingham Pk Prim Sch
  SN3 . . . . . . . . . . . . . . . 51 C7
Covingham Sq SN3 . . . . 51 C7
Coward Rd BA12 . . . . . 139 B4
Cowbridge Cres SN16 . 28 C1
Cow Down La SP11 . . . 185 E2
Cowdrey Cl SN5 . . . . . . . 49 B4
Cow Dro SP3 . . . . . . . . 201 B4
COWESFIELD
  GREEN . . . . . . . . . . . 161 F4
Cow La
  Kimpton SP11 . . . . . . . 192 B2
  Laverstock SP1 . . . . . . 146 C1
Cowleaze
  Chippenham SN14 . . . . 78 F8
  Swindon SN25 . . . . . . . 34 A3
Cowleaze Cres SN4 . . . . 63 F6
Cowleaze La BA13 . . . . 186 D8
Cowleaze Wlk SN2 . . . . 35 F4
Cowley Way SN15 . . . . . 57 D1
Cowleaze Wlk SN2 . . . . 35 F4
Cowslip Bank **8** SN13 . 84 E8
Cowslip Gr SN11 . . . . . . 81 B5
Cowslip Way
  Chippenham SN14 . . . . 70 B3
  East Anton SP11 . . . . . 193 F2
Cow St SN5 . . . . . . . . . . 19 B1
Coxhill La SN10 . . . . . . 179 D5
Cox's Hill
  Ashton Keynes SN6 . . . . 6 E2
  Calne SN11 . . . . . . . . . 81 B2
Cox's La SN8 . . . . . . . . 176 F1
Coxstalls SN4 . . . . . . . . . 47 D2
Crab La BA12 . . . . . . . . 138 A7
Crab Mill La SN16 . . . . . 28 E1
Crab Tree Cl SN16 . . . . . 27 F3
Crabtree Copse SN5 . . . 34 A2
Crabtree La BA2 . . . . . . 99 B4
Cradle Hill BA12 . . . . . 113 D2
Crampton Rd SN3 . . . . . 51 A7
Cranborne Chase SN2 . 34 C4
Cranborne Dr **1** SP7 202 C2
Cranborne Rd SP6 . . . . 209 E2
Cranbury Cl SP5 . . . . . . 211 A3
Crandon Lea BA14 . . . . . 92 F1
Cranebridge Rd SP2 . . 152 A8
Crane Furlong SN6 . . . . 23 A7
Cranesbill Cl SN10 . . . 214 D5
Cranesbill Rd
  Devizes SN10 . . . . . . . 214 D5
  Melksham SN12 . . . . . . 94 D4
Crane St SP1 . . . . . . . . 152 A8
Cranmore Ave SN3 . . . . 51 A3
Cranmore Cl BA14 . . . . . 92 F1
Cranwell Cl **6** SN14 . . 78 A6
Cratchcroft La BA14 . 178 A6
Crate La SP7 . . . . . . . . 202 C7
Craven Rd RG17 . . . . . 177 D3
Crawford Cl SN5 . . . . . . 49 A4
Crawlboys La SP11 . . . 192 B6
Crawley Ave SN3 . . . . . . 36 B1
Crawley Cres BA14 . . . 105 A8
Craybourne Rd SN12 . . 94 C6
Crays The SN12 . . . . . . . 94 C5
Crench Comm Airfield
  SN8 . . . . . . . . . . . . . . 174 E4
Crescent Rd
  Durrington/Bulford
    SP4 . . . . . . . . . . . . . 217 D7
  Melksham SN12 . . . . . . 94 C6
Crescent The
  Bromham SN15 . . . . . . 96 C7
  Calne SN11 . . . . . . . . . 89 F8
  Chiseldown SN4 . . . . . . 65 C3
  **4** Durrington/Bulford
    SP4 . . . . . . . . . . . . . 198 F7
  Pewsey SN9 . . . . . . . . 215 B4
  Swindon SN5 . . . . . . . . 33 F2
  Westbury BA13 . . . . . . 109 A3
  Wilton SP2 . . . . . . . . . 144 B2
Cresswell Dr BA14 . . . . 102 B2
Cresswell La SN15 . . . . . 44 B8
Cres The SP2 . . . . . . . . 152 B5
Crestmount Dr SP2 . . . . 151 A5
Creswells SN13 . . . . . . . 84 F8
Creswick SN25 . . . . . . . 20 D1
Cricketts La SN15 . . . . . 78 F5

CRICKLADE . . . . . . . . . . . 19 E7
Cricklade Leisure Ctr
  SN6 . . . . . . . . . . . . . . . . . 19 C8
Cricklade Manor Prep
  SN6 . . . . . . . . . . . . . . . . . 19 E7
Cricklade Mus★ SN6 . . 19 E8
Cricklade Rd
  Highworth SN6 . . . . . . . . . 22 F5
  Purton SN5 . . . . . . . . . . . . 19 C2
  Swindon SN25 . . . . . . . . . 35 D1
Cricklade St SN1 . . . . . . . 50 D5
CRIDDLESTYLE . . . . . . . 210 E1
Crieff Cl SN3 . . . . . . . . . . 51 B6
Crispin Cl 5 SN3 . . . . . . 36 B3
CROCKERTON . . . . . . . . 116 E1
Crockerton By-Pass
  Crockerton Green
    BA12 . . . . . . . . . . . . . . 116 F2
  Longbridge Deverill
    BA12 . . . . . . . . . . . . . . 120 F7
Crockerton CE Prim Sch
  BA12 . . . . . . . . . . . . . . . 116 D2
CROCKERTON
  GREEN . . . . . . . . . . . . 116 F2
Crockford Rd SP5 . . . . 154 B2
Croft Cl SN6 . . . . . . . . . . . 8 C4
Croft Hts SP5 . . . . . . . . 161 D3
Croft La SN6 . . . . . . . . . . . 8 C4
CROFTON . . . . . . . . . . . . 176 A1
Crofton Beam Engines★
  SN8 . . . . . . . . . . . . . . . . 176 A1
Crofton Rd SN8 . . . . . . 176 A1
Croft Prim Sch The
  SN1 . . . . . . . . . . . . . . . . . 50 D3
Croft Rd
  6 Hungerford RG17 . . . 177 B7
  Swindon SN1 . . . . . . . . . . 50 C1
Croft Sports Hall SN1 . 50 D3
Croft The
  Bishopstone SP5 . . . . . 205 E5
  Broad Hinton SN4 . . . . 167 D7
  Milston SP4 . . . . . . . . . 198 C8
  Newton Tony SP4 . . . . . 199 B3
  Trowbridge BA14 . . . . . 105 C6
  Urchfont SN10 . . . . . . . 180 C3
Crombey St SN1 . . . . . . 50 B5
Cromer Cl SN3 . . . . . . . . 51 D3
Cromhall La SN14 . . . . . 69 A7
Cromhall Lane SN14 . . 68 F7
Crompton Rd SN25 . . . . 35 D6
Cromwell SN5 . . . . . . . . 49 B3
Cromwell Rd SN10 . . . 214 D2
Crooked Cnr SN8 . . . . 170 A6
CROOKED SOLEY . . . . 170 F3
Crookhays SP7 . . . . . . . 202 C2
Crook Hill SP5 . . . . . . . 204 A1
Crooks La SN10 . . . . . . 180 C4
Crookwood La SN10 . . 179 F4
Croome Cl SN25 . . . . . . 34 B8
Crosbys 3 SN8 . . . . . . 183 D8
Crosby Wlk SN3 . . . . . . 51 A3
Croscombe Gdns
  BA11 . . . . . . . . . . . . . . . 110 D6
Cross Hayes La SN16 . . 28 A3
Crossing La SN15 . . . . . 71 B3
CROSS KEYS . . . . . . . . . 77 A3
Cross Keys
  Biddestone SN14 . . . . . . 76 F6
  Corsham SN14 . . . . . . . . 77 A4
Cross Keys Chequer 5
  SP1 . . . . . . . . . . . . . . . . 146 B1
Cross Keys Rd SN13 . . . 77 A3
Cross La SN8 . . . . . . . . . 213 D3
Crosslanes SN5 . . . . . . . 33 F8
Crossling La SN16 . . . . . 16 E3
Cross Roads
  Bourton SN6 . . . . . . . . . 137 F2
  Latton GL7 . . . . . . . . . . . . 8 B6
  Semington BA14 . . . . . . 102 F4
Cross St
  Swindon SN1 . . . . . . . . . . 50 C5
  Trowbridge BA14 . . . . . 101 D1
Cross The
  Bishopstone SP5 . . . . . 205 E4
  Ebbesborne Wake SP5 204 D3
  21 Tisbury SP3 . . . . . . 203 E8
Cross Tree Cres GL7 . . 10 C7
Crossways SN4 . . . . . . . 46 D6
Crossways Ave SN25 . . 35 C3
Crosswood Rd SN3 . . . . 51 A3
CROUCHESTON . . . . . . 205 F4
Croucheston Dro
  SP5 . . . . . . . . . . . . . . . . 205 E3
Croucheston Hollow
  SP5 . . . . . . . . . . . . . . . . 205 E4
Crowdy's Hill Sch SN2 35 D2
Crowe Hill BA2 . . . . . . . . 99 B6
Crowe La BA2 . . . . . . . . . 99 B5
Crow La 7 SP2 . . . . . . 144 D3
Crowle Rd 11 RG17 . . 165 A1
Crown Cl
  Chippenham SN15 . . . . . 79 A5
  Pewsey SN9 . . . . . . . . . 215 B5
  Salisbury SP2 . . . . . . . . 145 D3
Crown La 4 SP11 . . . . 192 A5
Crown Mews 30
  RG17 . . . . . . . . . . . . . . . 177 B7
Crown Way SP10 . . . . . 193 F1
Crowood La SN8 . . . . . 170 B2
CRUDWELL . . . . . . . . . . . 14 E6
Crudwell CE Prim Sch
  SN16 . . . . . . . . . . . . . . . . 14 E6
Crudwell La
  Crudwell SN16 . . . . . . . . 14 B6
  Long Newnton GL8 . . . . 13 D6

Crudwell Rd
  Malmesbury SN16 . . . . . 28 B5
  Murcott SN16 . . . . . . . . . 14 D3
Crudwell Way SN25 . . . 35 C6
Crusader Pk BA12 . . . . 112 F1
Crusades The 6 SP1 146 C5
Cruse Cl SN14 . . . . . . . . 77 F8
Ct La BA11 . . . . . . . . . . . 107 A2
CUCKOLD'S GREEN . . 179 C4
Cuckoo Cl SN14 . . . . . . . 68 B7
Cuckoo Pen Cl SN8 . . 183 D3
Cuckoo's Corner 180 B4
CUCKOO'S CORNER . . 180 B4
CUCKOO'S KNOB . . . . 174 F1
Cuckoo's Mead SN3 . . . 51 E6
Cuckoos Nest La
  BA12 . . . . . . . . . . . . . . . 116 E7
Cues La SN6 . . . . . . . . . . 163 E7
Cuffs La SP3 . . . . . . . . . 203 E8
Culborne Rd SN1 . . . . . . 50 B2
CULKERTON . . . . . . . . . . . 3 A5
Cullerne Rd SN3 . . . . . . 36 C1
Cullerns The SN3 . . . . . 23 A6
Culpepper Cl 6 SN3 . . 51 A4
Culver Gdns 9 SN16 . . 28 A3
Culverhouse Rd SN1 . . 50 E7
Culvermead Cl SN8 . . 213 E3
Culver Rd BA15 . . . . . . 100 E5
CULVERSLADE . . . . . . . 66 A2
Culver St 7 SP1 . . . . . 152 B8
Culverwell Rd SN14 . . . 78 A7
Cumberland Rd SN3 . . . 50 E6
Cunetio Rd SN3 . . . . . . . 51 C8
Cunnage La BA12 . . . . 139 F1
Cunningham Rd SN2 . . 35 A2
Curie Ave SN1 . . . . . . . . . 50 A4
Curlcroft Rd SN13 . . . . . 84 D7
Curlew Dr SN14 . . . . . . . 70 A2
Curlew Rd 3 SP4 . . . . 132 C1
Curnicks The SN4 . . . . . 65 C4
Cursus The★ SP4 . . . . 197 D6
Cursus The GL7 . . . . . . . . 2 C5
Curtis Orch SN12 . . . . . . 93 B4
Curtis St SN1 . . . . . . . . . . 50 B5
Curzon Cl SN11 . . . . . . . 81 A3
Curzon St SN11 . . . . . . . 81 A3
Cusance Way BA14 . . . 102 A1
Cuthwine Pl GL7 . . . . . . . 2 C5
Cutting Hill RG17 . . . . . 177 A2
Cuttle La SN14 . . . . . . . . 76 E8
Cutts Cl SN15 . . . . . . . . . 46 A7
Cvnieto Roman Town★
  SN8 . . . . . . . . . . . . . . . . 175 B8
Cygnet Dr SP4 . . . . . . . 217 C8
Cygnet Pl SN9 . . . . . . . 215 C4
Cygnet Way BA14 . . . . 101 D5
Cygney Way RG17 . . . 177 B8
Cyppa Ct SN15 . . . . . . . . 78 E6
Cypress Gr SN2 . . . . . . . 35 A3
Cypress Way 7
  BA11 . . . . . . . . . . . . . . . 110 C7
Cypress Wlk SN14 . . . . . 74 F6
Cyprus Terr SN10 . . . . 214 A4

## D

Dace Rd SN11 . . . . . . . . . 81 B4
Dacre Cl 13 SP10 . . . . 193 C2
Dacre Rd SN3 . . . . . . . . . 51 A6
Dadley La BA11 . . . . . . 107 A3
Dairy Cl
  Chippenham SN14 . . . . . 78 A3
  8 Redlynch SP5 . . . . . 211 C7
Dairy La SN10 . . . . . . . . 172 D2
Dairy Mdw La SP1 . . . 152 D7
Dairy Mws SN13 . . . . . . 76 F2
Dairy Rd
  Barford St Martin
    SP3 . . . . . . . . . . . . . . 143 A4
  Chiseldon SN4 . . . . . . . . 64 F4
Daisy Cl
  Melksham SN12 . . . . . . . 94 C3
  Swindon SN2 . . . . . . . . . 34 C3
Dakota Dr SN11 . . . . . . . 81 D4
Dalby Strand SN1 . . . . . 49 E2
Dalefoot Cl SN5 . . . . . . . 34 A1
Dales Cl SN25 . . . . . . . . . 35 A7
Dales Rd BA13 . . . . . . . 108 E2
Dalewood Rise SP1 . . 146 E2
Dallas Ave SN14 . . . . . . 51 B7
Dallas Rd SN14 . . . . . . . 78 C8
Dalton Cl SN3 . . . . . . . . . 50 F7
Dalwood Cl
  Dinton SP3 . . . . . . . . . 201 E2
  Swindon SN3 . . . . . . . . . 51 B3
Damask Way BA12 . . . 117 A5
DAMERHAM . . . . . . . . . 209 F2
Dammas Bsns Ctr
  SN1 . . . . . . . . . . . . . . . . . 50 D4
Dammas La SN3 . . . . . . 50 D4
Damson Cres 11 SN25 34 C5
Damson Orch BA1 . . . . . 82 A4
Damy Gn SN13 . . . . . . . . 84 E5
Dance Ct 6 SN6 . . . . . . 19 D7
Dando Dr SN8 . . . . . . . 213 B2
Dane Cl BA15 . . . . . . . . 100 E3
Danegeld Cl 9 SP10 . 193 E2
Dane Rise BA15 . . . . . . . 99 E7
Danes Cl SN15 . . . . . . . . 78 F5
Danestone Cl SN5 . . . . 48 F7
Daneway SN25 . . . . . . . . 20 B1
Daniel Cl 9 SN1 . . . . . . 49 F4
Daniell Crest BA13 . . . 116 F6
Daniel's Well★ SN16 . . 28 A3
Danvers Mead SN15 . . 79 A4
Danvers Rd SN13 . . . . . 76 E1
Danvers Way BA13 . . . 109 B4
Darby Cl SN2 . . . . . . . . . 34 C1

Darcey Cl SN5 . . . . . . . . 48 F6
Darcy Cl SN15 . . . . . . . . 78 F8
Darius Way SN25 . . . . . 35 A6
Dark La
  Berkley BA11 . . . . . . . . 110 E8
  Castle Combe SN14 . . . . 68 B7
  Grafton SN8 . . . . . . . . . 175 F1
  Kintbury RG17 . . . . . . . 177 D8
  Limpley Stoke BA2 . . . . . 99 B5
  Mere BA12 . . . . . . . . . . 139 A5
Dark La N BA14 . . . . . . 178 A3
Dark La S BA14 . . . . . . 178 A3
Darling Cl SN3 . . . . . . . . 36 A1
Darnley Cl SN3 . . . . . . . . 50 F6
Dart Ave SN25 . . . . . . . 217 C4
Dartmoor 7 SN1 . . . . . 49 F4
Dartmoor Rd 2
  BA13 . . . . . . . . . . . . . . . 108 E1
Darwin Cl
  4 Durrington/Bulford
    SP4 . . . . . . . . . . . . . . 198 F6
  Swindon SN3 . . . . . . . . . 51 B7
Dasna Rd SP9 . . . . . . . 216 B5
Daubenton Cl BA14 . . 106 A8
Daunch Cl SP9 . . . . . . . 216 B7
DAUNTSEY . . . . . . . . . . . 45 B1
Dauntsey Acad Prim Sch
  SN10 . . . . . . . . . . . . . . . 187 E8
Dauntsey Dro SP11 . . 192 E1
Dauntsey La SP11 . . . . 192 E1
DAUNTSEY LOCK . . . . . 59 B5
Dauntsey Pk★ SN15 . . 44 E2
Dauntsey Rd
  Great Somerford SN15 . 44 C2
  Little Somerford SN15 . . 44 D4
Dauntsey's (Aided) Prim
  Sch BA13 . . . . . . . . . . . 187 E8
Dauntsey's Sch
  West Lavington BA13 . . 187 D8
  West Lavington SN10 . . 187 D8
Davenham Cl SN3 . . . . . 51 A3
Davenwood SN2 . . . . . . . 35 F4
Dave Watkins Ct SN2 . . 35 F3
David's Gdn SP5 . . . . . 148 C3
David Stoddart Gdns
  SN2 . . . . . . . . . . . . . . . . . 35 B1
Davies Cl SN8 . . . . . . . . 213 A2
Davies Dr SN10 . . . . . . 214 E6
Davies Rd SP4 . . . . . . . 132 B1
Davis Pl SN1 . . . . . . . . . . 50 B6
Davis Rd 11 SN10 . . . . 179 F1
Davy Dr SN11 . . . . . . . . . 81 D3
Dawbeney Dr SP4 . . . . 217 D3
Dawes Cl GL7 . . . . . . . . . . 1 A5
Dawlish Rd SN3 . . . . . . . 51 B5
Dawneys The SN16 . . . . 14 E6
Day Ho La SN3 . . . . . . . . 51 C2
Day's Cl SN3 . . . . . . . . . . 36 A1
Days Ct SN10 . . . . . . . . 214 E6
Day's La SN5 . . . . . . . . . . 56 D2
Days Rise SN25 . . . . . . . 35 A3
Dazel Cnr SO51 . . . . . . 212 D4
Deacon Cl SN3 . . . . . . . 213 A2
Deacon Rd SP11 . . . . . 192 B2
Deacon St SN1 . . . . . . . . 50 B5
DEAN . . . . . . . . . . . . . . . 207 E2
Dean Cl
  Frome BA11 . . . . . . . . . 110 C6
  Melksham SN12 . . . . . . . 94 C6
DEANEND . . . . . . . . . . . 207 E4
Deanery Dr SN1 . . . . . . . 49 E2
Dean La
  Fovant SP3 . . . . . . . . . . 204 D7
  Mildenhall SN8 . . . . . . 169 B2
  Sixpenny Handley SP5 . 207 F6
  West Dean SP5 . . . . . . . 155 E2
  Whiteparish SP5 . . . . . . 161 D4
Dean La Dro SP5 . . . . . 207 F4
DEANLAND . . . . . . . . . . 208 A5
Dean Rd
  East Grimstead SP5 . . . 154 F3
  West Dean SP5 . . . . . . . 155 B3
Deans Cl SP9 . . . . . . . . 216 D4
Deansfield SN6 . . . . . . . . 19 D7
Dean St SN1 . . . . . . . . . . 49 F5
Dean Sta SP5 . . . . . . . . 155 F3
Deansway SN15 . . . . . . . 70 D2
Dearle Rd SN26 . . . . . . . 20 D1
Deben Cres SN25 . . . . . 34 F5
Deburgh St SN2 . . . . . . . 49 F6
Deep La BA12 . . . . . . . . 111 D2
Deere Ave SN14 . . . . . . . 78 A3
Deerhurst Way 1
  SN5 . . . . . . . . . . . . . . . . . 49 D4
Deer Pk★ SP4 . . . . . . . 198 B6
Defroscia Cl SN11 . . . . . 81 D4
De Havilland Pl 4
  SN12 . . . . . . . . . . . . . . 178 B8
Delamere Dr SN3 . . . . . 36 A4
Delamere Rd BA14 . . . 101 D2
Delft Cres 1 SN25 . . . . 34 F8
Delius Cl SN25 . . . . . . . . 34 E8
Dell The SP11 . . . . . . . . 185 B3
Delta Bsns Pk SN5 . . . . 49 D6
Delta Office Pk SN5 . . . 49 D5
De Montfort Gr 8
  RG17 . . . . . . . . . . . . . . . 177 B6
Demorgancres SN26 . . 20 D1
Dempsey Rd BA12 . . . . 113 E1
Denbeck Wood SN5 . . . 49 B6
Denbigh Cl SN3 . . . . . . . 50 E3
Denby Rd 4 SN25 . . . . 34 E7
Deneb Dr SN25 . . . . . . . 34 B7
Denes Ave BA12 . . . . . 139 A6
Dene The
  Hindon SP3 . . . . . . . . . . 200 B3

Dene The continued
  Warminster BA12 . . . . . 117 E6
Denford La RG17 . . . . . 177 D8
Denholme Rd SN3 . . . . . 51 A3
Denison Rise SP1 . . . . 146 C3
Dennis La SP7 . . . . . . . 203 B1
Dennis St SN5 . . . . . . . . 49 C7
Denton Dr SP4 . . . . . . . 217 C2
DEPTFORD . . . . . . . . . . 195 E1
Derby Cl
  Chippenham SN15 . . . . . 78 F5
  Lamborn RG17 . . . . . . . 165 A1
Derby Ct SN3 . . . . . . . . . 50 E6
Derriads Gn SN14 . . . . . 78 A7
Derriads La 3 SN14 . . . 77 F6
Derryfields SN16 . . . . . . 17 E8
DERRY FIELDS . . . . . . . . 17 F8
DERRY HILL . . . . . . . . . . 79 F2
Derry Hill CE (VA) Prim
  Sch SN11 . . . . . . . . . . . . 80 A2
Derry Pk SN16 . . . . . . . . 17 C2
Derry The SN6 . . . . . . . 17 F8
Dertford BA12 . . . . . . . 115 A7
DERTFORDS . . . . . . . . . 115 B7
Derwent Dr SN2 . . . . . . . 35 F4
Desborough SN5 . . . . . . 49 A3
Deva Cl SN3 . . . . . . . . . . 51 D8
De Vaux Pl SP1 . . . . . . 152 A7
Devenish Nature
  Reserve★ SP4 . . . . . . 131 D2
Deverell Cl SN15 . . . . . 100 E4
Devereux Cl 8 SN5 . . . . 48 F5
Devereux Mws 9
  SN16 . . . . . . . . . . . . . . . . 28 A5
Devereux Rd SP4 . . . . 217 B3
Deverill Rd
  Sutton Veny BA12 . . . . . 117 E1
  Warminster BA12 . . . . . 116 F4
Devils Bed & Bolster
  The★ BA11 . . . . . . . . . 107 A8
DEVIZES . . . . . . . . . . . . 214 A3
Devizes Castle★
  SN10 . . . . . . . . . . . . . . . 214 A4
Devizes Com Hospl
  SN10 . . . . . . . . . . . . . . . 214 B4
Devizes Enterprise Cen
  SN10 . . . . . . . . . . . . . . . 214 C3
Devizes Leisure Ctr
  SN10 . . . . . . . . . . . . . . . 214 B3
Devizes Rd
  Box SN13 . . . . . . . . . . . . 83 E4
  Bromham SN15 . . . . . . . 88 B4
  Calne Without SN11 . . . . 87 F7
  Charlton SN9 . . . . . . . . 181 D2
  Derry Hill/Studley SN11 .79 F1
  Hilperton BA14 . . . . . . . 102 C3
  Potterne SN10 . . . . . . . 179 D6
  Poulshot SN10 . . . . . . . 179 B7
  Rowde SN10 . . . . . . . . . . 96 F2
  Salisbury SP2 . . . . . . . . 145 E2
  Swindon SN1 . . . . . . . . . 50 D4
  Trowbridge BA14 . . . . . 102 B3
  Wroughton SN4 . . . . . . . 64 B6
Devizes Sports Club
  SN10 . . . . . . . . . . . . . . . 214 C4
Devizes White Horse★
  SN10 . . . . . . . . . . . . . . . . 97 F5
Devon Cl 5 SN14 . . . . . 77 F6
Devon Dr SN3 . . . . . . . . 109 A5
Devon Rd
  Swindon SN2 . . . . . . . . . 35 B1
  Upavon Down SN9 . . . . 182 B2
Devonshire Pl SN12 . . . 94 C5
Devonshire Rd SP1 . . . 146 A5
Dewberry Cl SN2 . . . . . . 34 F4
Dew Cl SN13 . . . . . . . . . . 85 A8
Dewey Cl SN4 . . . . . . . . . 65 F4
Dewey Mws SN9 . . . . . 215 C4
Deweys La SP11 . . . . . . 192 A5
Dew Pond Cl SN25 . . . . 34 B3
Dew's Rd SP2 . . . . . . . . 145 F1
Dew Way SN11 . . . . . . . 81 D6
Dexter Cl SN5 . . . . . . . . . 49 B7
Dial Cl SN12 . . . . . . . . . 178 E8
Diamond Cres
  Swindon SN25 . . . . . . . . 20 F1
  Swindon SN25 . . . . . . . . 34 F8
Dianmer Cl SN4 . . . . . . . 47 F5
Dickens Ave SN13 . . . . . 76 F2
Dickens Cl SN3 . . . . . . . . 51 D3
Dickenson Rd SN25 . . . 34 C5
Dicketts Rd SN13 . . . . . 85 A7
Dickson Rd SN15 . . . . . . 60 A1
Dickson Way 2 SN15 . . 78 F5
Diddledown Rd 8
  SP4 . . . . . . . . . . . . . . . . 217 C2
DIDMARTON . . . . . . . . . 24 C3
Didmarton Rd GL9 . . . . 24 A3
Dilton Cl BA14 . . . . . . . 105 C5
Dilton Ct BA13 . . . . . . . 112 B6
DILTON MARSH . . . . . . 112 B8
Dilton Marsh CE Prim
  Sch BA13 . . . . . . . . . . . 112 B8
Dilton Marsh Sta
  BA13 . . . . . . . . . . . . . . . 108 C1
Dimmer Dr SP2 . . . . . . 144 F4
Dinah's Hollow SP7 . . 203 A1
Dingle The 3 SN4 . . . . 163 A6
Dinmore Rd SN25 . . . . . 34 F6
Dinnis Way SP4 . . . . . . 146 B8
DINTON . . . . . . . . . . . . . 201 F2
Dinton CE Prim Sch
  SP3 . . . . . . . . . . . . . . . . 201 F2
Dinton Cl 10 SN25 . . . . 34 F7
Dinton Rd
  Fovant SP3 . . . . . . . . . . 204 E8
  Wylye BA12 . . . . . . . . . . 201 E8

Dione Cres SN25 . . . . . . 34 B7
Dior Dr SN4 . . . . . . . . . . . 61 E8
Discover Salisbury
  (Medieval Hall)★
  SP1 . . . . . . . . . . . . . . . . 152 A8
Distillery Mdws Nature
  Reserve★ SN16 . . . . . . 31 B7
DITCHAMPTON . . . . . . 144 C4
DITTERIDGE . . . . . . . . . . 83 B8
Divinity Cl 2 SN4 . . . . 163 B6
Dixon St SN1 . . . . . . . . . . 50 B5
Dixon Way
  Calne SN11 . . . . . . . . . . . 81 B4
  Swindon SN5 . . . . . . . . . 49 C6
Dobbin Cl SN3 . . . . . . . . 51 E7
Dobson Cl 1 SN25 . . . . 35 A8
Dockle Way SN2 . . . . . . . 35 F4
Doctors Hill SN13 . . . . . 83 B5
Doctor's Hollow SP3 . 201 F2
Doctors Pl 3 SP3 . . . . 203 E8
Dodford La SN15 . . . . . . 58 D6
Dodgson Cl SP6 . . . . . . 211 A4
Dodsdown SN8 . . . . . . . 184 B8
Doggetts La BA13 . . . . 109 A4
Dog Kennel La BA13 . . 109 A1
Dog La SP7 . . . . . . . . . . 203 E1
DOGRIDGE . . . . . . . . . . . 32 F3
Dogridge SN5 . . . . . . . . . 33 A3
Dog Trap La SN16 . . . . . 16 E1
Dolina Rd SN25 . . . . . . . 34 D6
Dolphin Ind Est SP1 . . 152 D7
Dolphin St SP1 . . . . . . . 152 B8
Donaldson Rd SP1 . . . 146 A2
Doncaster Cl SN14 . . . . 77 F5
Don Cl SN25 . . . . . . . . . . 35 A4
Doncombe Hill SN14 . . 74 E7
Doncombe La SN14 . . . 75 A6
Donhead Hollow SP7 206 E8
DONHEAD ST
  ANDREW . . . . . . . . . . 203 B3
DONHEAD ST MARY . 203 A3
Donnington Gr SN3 . . . 50 F4
DORCAN . . . . . . . . . . . . . 51 D5
Dorcan Acad The SN3 . 51 D6
Dorcan Bsns Village
  SN3 . . . . . . . . . . . . . . . . . 51 E6
Dorcan Ind Est SN3 . . . 51 E5
Dorcan Way SN3 . . . . . . 51 A8
Dorchester Rd SN3 . . . . 50 F3
Dores Ct SN3 . . . . . . . . . 35 E3
Dores Rd SN2 . . . . . . . . . 35 D3
Doris Archer Ct SN2 . . 35 B2
Dormers The SN6 . . . . . 23 A6
Dorney Cl BA13 . . . . . . 108 F1
Dorney Rd SN25 . . . . . . 34 C8
Dorothy Wlk BA12 . . . 116 F6
Dorset Cl SP4 . . . . . . . . 217 E8
Dorset Cres SN12 . . . . . 94 C3
Dorset Dr BA13 . . . . . . 109 A5
Dorset Gn SN2 . . . . . . . . 34 F2
Dorset Rd SP1 . . . . . . . 146 B3
Doubledays SN6 . . . . . . 19 D8
Double Hedges SP4 . . 217 E2
Doughty's La SP21 . . . 195 A2
Douglas Brown's Wlk 8
  SP4 . . . . . . . . . . . . . . . . 197 E6
Douglas Haig Rd
  SP1 . . . . . . . . . . . . . . . . 146 A3
Douglas Rd 5 SN3 . . . . 50 F6
Doulting Ct BA11 . . . . . 110 D7
Doulton Cl SN25 . . . . . . 34 D7
Dovecote Cl 3 BA14 . . 105 B8
Dovecote Dr SN13 . . . . . 76 F2
Dovedale 7 SN25 . . . . . 34 F7
Dovers La BA1 . . . . . . . . 82 C2
Dovers Pk BA1 . . . . . . . . 82 C2
Dover St
  Chippenham SN14 . . . . . 78 C7
  Swindon SN1 . . . . . . . . . 50 C5
Doves La SN25 . . . . . . . 161 C3
Dovetrees SN3 . . . . . . . . 51 D7
Doveys Terr SN15 . . . . . 70 E7
Dowding Ave SN13 . . . . 84 B8
Dowding Dr 5 SN11 . . 166 A1
Dowding Way SN12 . . . 94 C1
Dowlais Ct 2 SN25 . . . . 34 C6
Dowland Ct SN3 . . . . . . 34 E8
Dowling St SN1 . . . . . . . 50 C5
DOWN AMPNEY . . . . . . . 8 D7
Down Ampney House★
  GL7 . . . . . . . . . . . . . . . . . . 8 D6
Down Ampney Rd GL7 . 8 D6
Downavon BA15 . . . . . 100 D5
Down Barn Cl SP4 . . . 133 B4
Down Barn Rd
  Winterbourne SP4 . . . . 132 F6
  Winterbourne Gunner
    SP4 . . . . . . . . . . . . . . 133 A4
Downham Mead SN15 .78 F8
Downhayes Rd BA14 . 101 D2
Downing St SN14 . . . . . 78 C8
Downland Rd
  Calne SN11 . . . . . . . . . . . 81 A2
  Swindon SN2 . . . . . . . . . 34 D4
Downlands 1 RG17 . . . 171 E7
Downlands Ct SP5 . . . . 211 A7
Downlands The BA12 . 117 B7
Downland Way 12
  SP4 . . . . . . . . . . . . . . . . 198 B7
Downleaze 7 SP4 . . . . 198 B7
Down Rd
  Kimpton SP11 . . . . . . . 192 B2
  Marshfield SN14 . . . . . . 66 C2
Downs Cl
  Bradford-on-Avon
    BA15 . . . . . . . . . . . . . 100 B7
  Devizes SN10 . . . . . . . . 214 D3
  Lambourn RG17 . . . . . . 171 C8

Downside Cl BA12 . . . 139 A6
Downside Pk BA14 . . . 101 E2
Downs La SN4 . . . . . . . . 185 B8
Downslands Rd SN10 214 B1
Downsmead SN8 . . . . . 164 B1
Downs Rd SN4 . . . . . . . . 65 E4
Downs The SN8 . . . . . . 170 A5
Downs View BA13 . . . . 186 C7
Downs View
  Bradford-on-Avon
    BA15 . . . . . . . . . . . . . 100 B7
  Highworth SN6 . . . . . . . . 23 A6
  1 Netheravon SP4 . . . 190 A4
  Royal Wootton Bassett
    SN4 . . . . . . . . . . . . . . . 47 D1
  Warminster BA12 . . . . . 117 C6
Downsview Rd BA13 . . 109 A4
Downs View Rd SN3 . . . 50 F2
Downsview Way
  SP11 . . . . . . . . . . . . . . . 191 F3
Downsway SP1 . . . . . . . 146 B4
Downs Way SN3 . . . . . . . 51 E2
Down The
  Hindon SP3 . . . . . . . . . . 200 B3
  Trowbridge BA14 . . . . . 101 D2
DOWNTON . . . . . . . . . . . 211 B8
Downton Bus Ctr
  SP5 . . . . . . . . . . . . . . . . 159 A1
Downton CE Prim Sch
  SP5 . . . . . . . . . . . . . . . . 211 A8
Downton Hill SP5 . . . . 211 C8
Downton L Ctr SP5 . . . 210 F8
Downton Meml Gdns★
  SP5 . . . . . . . . . . . . . . . . 211 A8
Downton Rd
  Salisbury SP2 . . . . . . . . 152 B5
  Swindon SN2 . . . . . . . . . 35 B5
Down View SN14 . . . . . . 78 A7
Downview Rd SP6 . . . . 209 B6
Down View Rd SP1 . . . 146 E2
Downwood Cl 7
  SP6 . . . . . . . . . . . . . . . . 210 C1
Dowse Cl SP9 . . . . . . . . 216 C7
Dowse Rd SN10 . . . . . . 214 C4
Dowtys La SP3 . . . . . . . 142 A4
Doyle Cl 1 SN25 . . . . . . 34 C5
Dragonfly Rd 3 SN3 . . 51 B8
Dragon La SN9 . . . . . . . 181 F6
Drain Hill RG17 . . . . . . 165 A2
Drake Cl SP1 . . . . . . . . 146 C5
Drake Cres SN14 . . . . . . 77 F6
Drake Rd SP10 . . . . . . 193 F1
Drakes Ave SN10 . . . . 214 C2
Drakes Mdw SN3 . . . . . 50 F7
Drakes Mdw Bsns Pk
  SN3 . . . . . . . . . . . . . . . . . 50 F7
Drake's Way SN3 . . . . . 50 F6
Drakes Way Bsns Ctr
  SN3 . . . . . . . . . . . . . . . . . 51 A7
DRAYCOT CERNE . . . . . 56 F1
DRAYCOT FITZ
  PAYNE . . . . . . . . . . . . 174 A2
Draycot La SN4 . . . . . . 168 E8
Draycot Rd SN4 . . . . . . . 65 C3
Draycott SN3 . . . . . . . . . 51 A5
Draymans Ct SN4 . . . . . 61 D8
Dr Behr Ct SN2 . . . . . . . 35 B2
Dresser Cl SN26 . . . . . . 20 D2
Drewitts La SN10 . . . . . 180 E8
Drew's Pond La SN10 214 B1
Drew St SN2 . . . . . . . . . . 49 E7
Drifton Hill SN14 . . . . . . 88 E7
Drive The
  Durnford SP4 . . . . . . . . 197 F1
  Melchet Park & Plaitford
    SO51 . . . . . . . . . . . . . 162 C3
  Swindon SN3 . . . . . . . . . 51 B7
Drove Cl SP5 . . . . . . . . 150 F2
Drove La
  Coombe Bissett SP5 . . 150 A3
  Market Lavington SN10 179 F1
  Steeple Ashton BA14 . . 178 A2
Drove Prim Sch SN1 . . 50 D6
Drove Rd SN1 . . . . . . . . . 50 D5
Drovers Green SN14 . . . 68 F4
Drovers La
  Wroughton SN4 . . . . . . . 63 E4
  Wroughton SN4 . . . . . . 167 F8
Drovers Vw SP11 . . . . . 192 A5
Droves The SP5 . . . . . . 207 F4
Drove The
  Amesbury SP4 . . . . . . . 217 B4
  Hawkeridge BA13 . . . . 108 D7
  13 Redlynch SP5 . . . . . 211 C5
Dr The SN4 . . . . . . . . . . . 61 A7
Druces Hill BA15 . . . . . 100 C7
Druids Cl SN11 . . . . . . . . 81 A3
Druley Hill
  North Brewham BA10 . . 122 F7
  Witham Friary BA10 . . . 123 B7
Drummer La SP9 . . . . . 216 D5
Drury Cl SN5 . . . . . . . . . . 47 F6
Drury La SN8 . . . . . . . . . 175 D4
Dryden Cl SP2 . . . . . . . 152 B3
Dryden St SN1 . . . . . . . . 50 B5
Dry Hill BA12 . . . . . . . . 116 C2
DRYNHAM . . . . . . . . . . . 105 E5
Drynham La BA14 . . . . 105 D6
Drynham Rd BA14 . . . . 105 D6
Duchess Way SN2 . . . . . 35 C4
Duck La
  Barford St Martin
    SP3 . . . . . . . . . . . . . . 143 B3
  Laverstock SP1 . . . . . . 152 E8
  Salisbury SP1 . . . . . . . . 146 D2
Duck Pool La BA11 . . . 107 B6

Ducks Meadow SN8 . 213 D2
Duck's Nest (Long
  Barrow)★ SP6 ..... 209 F7
Duke St
  Berwick St James
  SP3............196 F2
  Berwick St James SP3. 197 A2
  Ebbesborne Wake SP5. 204 C3
  Potterne SN10......179 D5
  Steeple Langford SP3 128 D7
  Sutton Veny BA12....194 A4
  Tisbury SP3 ........203 E8
  West Lavington SN10. 187 E8
Dudley Ave SP6......210 D2
Dudley Rd SN3 .......50 F6
Dudmore Rd SN3 . 50 D6
Duffield La BA15.....100 E6
Duke Cres [10] SN13...76 C1
Dukes Cl SN2.........35 E5
Dukes Field GL7.......8 D7
Duke's La BA12......118 A1
Duke St BA14........101 D1
Duke's Way SP4 .....217 E8
Dukwick La SN14 ....74 A3
Dulverton Ave SN3...51 A5
Dumbarton Terr [2]
  ..................50 C5
Dumb Post Hill SN11...80 D6
Dummer La SP11 .....184 E1
Dummer Way SN15 ...79 A5
Dunbar Rd SN14......64 A7
Dunbeath Rd SN2....35 E1
Dunbeath Rd SN2....35 E1
Duncan's Cl SP11....192 D1
Duncan St SN11 ......81 B5
Dunch La SN12 .......93 F7
Dundas Aqueduct★
  BA2..............90 B2
Dundas Cl SN10 ....179 C8
DUNFIELD ...........10 A8
Dunfield Loop GL7...10 B8
Dunford Cl
  Amesbury SP4 ......217 D1
  Trowbridge BA14....105 D6
DUNGE ..............106 E1
Dunhills La SP11.....193 F4
DUNKIRK .............179 D8
Dunkirk Bsns Pk
  BA14..............104 D2
Dunkirk Hill
  Devizes SN10......179 D8
  Rowde SN10 ........97 A1
Dunley Cl SN25......34 D7
Dunley Way SP1.....146 C5
Dunnet Cl SN11......81 B4
Dunnington Rd SN4...61 D8
Dunns La SN14 ......68 B8
Dunn's La SP8.......138 A1
Dunraven Cl SN3.....50 F4
Dunsford Cl SN1.....49 F4
Dunsley Vale SN11...50 E4
Dunspit La DT11.....207 B1
Dunstable Cnr SP5...148 E7
Dunstan's Dro SP11..185 E1
Dunster Cl SN3.......50 E3
Dunvant Rd SN25.....34 C7
Dunwich Dr SN5......49 D4
Dunworth Rise [6]
  SP3..............203 E8
Durham St SN1........50 C5
Durlett Rd SN10......95 F2
DURLEY .............175 D3
Durley Pk SN13......84 D6
Durnford Rd SN2.....35 C5
DURRINGTON ........198 B7
Durrington bAll Saints CE
  VC Infs Sch SP4 ...198 C7
Durrington CE
  (Controlled) Jun Sch
  SP4..............198 B6
Durrington Swimming &
  Fitness Ctr SP4....198 C7
Durrington Walls★
  SP4..............217 A8
Durrington Wlk SN2...35 C5
Dursden La SN9......215 E6
DURSLEY ...........105 C1
Dursley Rd
  Heywood BA13......108 F8
  North Bradley BA13..105 C1
Dussek Pl [2] SN25...34 E7
Dutts
  Dilton Marsh BA14...112 B8
  Westbury BA13.....100 E6
Duxford Cl [11] SN12. 178 B8
Dydale Rd SN3.......34 C6
Dyehouse La SN10...214 A4
Dyer La BA12........201 E8
Dyer's Cl SN15.......79 A6
Dyke Mews SN4 .....65 D4
Dymocks La BA12....121 F8
Dymott Sq BA14.....102 A3
Dyrham Ct [1] SN25...34 F7
Dyson Campus SN16...27 F6
Dyson Rd SN25......34 E8

**E**

Eadreds Hyde SN11...89 D8
Eagle Cl SN3 .........51 E7
Eagle Field SN1.....145 D4
Eagle Pk BA14.......105 E6
Eagle Rd BA12.......116 D6
Ealing Way SN2......34 F6
Earl Cl SN5..........48 F7
Earls Cl SP4.........217 E2
Earls Cnr SN16.......15 E8

Earls Ct Rd SP4......217 B3
Earls Manor Ct SP4...133 A1
Earl's Rise SP4 .....133 A1
Earthpits La SP5.....208 E4
Easdale St SN25 .....34 D8
East Allcourt GL7......2 C4
EAST ANTON ........193 F2
East Anton Farm Rd [20]
  SP11.............193 F2
Eastbourne Gdns
  BA14.............101 E1
Eastbourne Rd BA14. 101 E1
EASTBURY ...........171 C8
Eastbury Shute
  RG17.............171 C5
Eastbury Way SN25...34 E7
EAST CHISENBURY ..190 A7
EAST COMPTON ....206 A5
EASTCOTT ..........180 A2
Eastcott Comm SN10 180 A2
Eastcott Hill [5] SN1...50 C5
Eastcott Rd SN1......50 C5
Eastcourt SN14.......40 E1
Eastcourt Rd SN8....183 D8
Eastdean Rd SP5....155 F2
East Dr [6] SN25......34 F8
East Dunley Cotts
  SN14..............40 E1
EAST END............74 A8
East End Ave BA12...117 B6
East End La
  Cleverton SN15 ....44 D7
  Little Somerford SN15. 44 D5
Eastern Ave
  Chippenham SN15...78 F8
  Swindon SN3 .......50 E6
EASTERTON .........180 A2
Easterton La SN9....215 D4
EASTERTON SANDS .179 F2
EAST EVERLEIGH ...191 A8
Eastfield
  Ashton Keynes SN6 ...6 F1
  [2] Littleton Panell
  SN10.............187 E8
EAST GARSTON ....171 E7
EAST GOMELDON ..133 E4
East Gomeldon Rd
  SP4..............133 E4
EAST GRAFTON ....183 F7
EAST GRIMSTEAD ..154 F4
EAST HATCH ........203 C7
Easthill BA11........110 B4
East Hill BA12.......194 C6
East Hill Rd BA12....194 C5
EAST KENNETT.....173 E6
East Kennett (Long
  Barrow)★ SN8 ....173 D5
EAST KNOYLE ......141 C2
East La SN12 ........93 B3
Eastlake SN25 ......20 C1
Eastlands Way SN15...70 E1
EASTLEAZE ..........49 B6
Eastleaze Rd SN5...49 C6
Eastleigh Cl [4] BA11. 110 A7
Eastleigh Rd SN10...214 D2
Eastleigh Wood La
  BA12.............117 D3
Eastman Cl SP5.....211 B7
EAST MARTIN ......209 C6
East Martin Rd SP6...209 B7
EAST MELBURY ....206 B7
Eastmere SN3........51 E3
EASTON ............77 D2
Easton Comm Hill
  SP5..............149 E6
EASTON GREY ......26 C3
Easton Grey Rd GL8...26 A7
Easton Hollow SP5...207 B7
Easton La SN14......77 F3
EASTON ROYAL .....183 A7
Easton Royal Academy
  SN9..............183 A7
Easton Sq SN16......25 D1
EASTON TOWN ......25 D1
Easton Town
  Sherston SN16......25 C1
  Sherston SN16......40 E8
East Portway SP10...193 C1
EASTRIP ............75 C4
Eastrip La SN14......75 C3
Eastrop SN6.........23 B5
Eastrop Inf Sch SN6...23 A5
East Sands SN8......183 D8
East St
  Bourton SP8.......137 E1
  Hindon SP3 ........200 A4
  Lacock SN15 .......86 D6
  Salisbury SP2......145 F1
  [10] Swindon SN1 ....50 B6
  Warminster BA12...117 B6
EAST TOWN ........106 E4
East Town La BA14...106 E4
East Town Rd BA14...106 D3
EAST TYTHERTON ..72 B2
Eastview Rd BA14...105 A7
Eastville Rd SN25....35 C3
Eastwell Rd SN10...179 D5
East Wichel Prim Sch
  SN1..............50 B2
East Wichel Way
  Swindon SN1.......49 F2
  Swindon SN1.......50 A2
  Swindon SN1.......50 B1
EAST WINTERSLOW . 149 C8
Eastwood SO51......162 E4
Eastwood Ave SN4...47 E1
EAST WOODLANDS .114 B5

East Woodlands Rd
  BA11.............114 A7
Eastwoods BA1......82 B3
East Yewstock Cres
  SN15..............70 C1
Eaton Cl [1] SN3......51 A4
Eaton Wood [6] SN5...34 A2
Ebbesborne Hollow
  SP5..............204 D2
EBBESBORNE
  WAKE ...........204 C2
Ebble Cl SP9 ........216 D7
Ebble Cres BA12.....117 A5
Ebor Cl SN25........34 F7
Ebor Gdns SN11......89 C8
Ebor Paddock SN11...89 C8
Eccleston Cl SN3.....51 B3
Echo Lodge Mdws Nature
  Reserve★ SN15 ....46 E7
Ecklington SN3......51 C5
Edale Moor SN3.....51 E3
EDDINGTON .........177 C8
Eddington Hill RG17. 177 C8
Eddleston Rd [2] SN1...50 A4
Edelweiss Cl [29] SP11 192 A5
Edencroft SN6........23 B8
Eden Gr SN12........85 D1
Eden Pk Cl BA1......82 A4
Eden Pk Dr BA1......82 A4
EDEN VALE .........108 E3
Eden Vale Rd BA13...108 F3
Edgam Pl SP2.......144 F3
Edgar Cl [6] SP10 ....193 E2
Edgar Row Cl [1] SN4...64 A6
Edgecorner La SN14...53 A3
Edgehill SN5.........49 B3
Edgeware Rd SN1.....50 C6
Edgeworth Cl [4] SN5...49 B7
Edinburgh Rd SN11...81 F1
Edinburgh St SN2....35 D1
Edinburgh Way SN11. 84 E7
EDINGTON ..........186 C8
Edington Cl SN5.....49 B5
Edington Dr BA14....105 C5
Edington Priory★
  BA13.............186 C8
Edington Rd BA14...178 A3
Edington Station Yard
  BA13.............186 C8
Edison Bsns Pk SN3...51 D5
Edison Rd
  Salisbury SP2......151 E8
  Swindon SN3 .......51 D5
Edith New Cl [4] SN5...34 E3
Edmonton Way [3]
  SP4..............217 E8
Edmund St SN1......50 C5
Edrich Sq SP10 .....193 E1
Edric's Gn SP4......199 C5
Edridge Cl SN15.....78 F8
Edridge Pl [1] SN13...76 E1
Education Cen The
  SN1..............50 F8
Education La
  Great Cheverell SN10 187 C8
  Westbury BA13 ....112 B8
Education Pl BA2.....90 B5
Edward Rd SN10....214 B2
Edward Richardson &
  Phyllis Amey Nature
  Reserve★ GL6......2 C6
Edwards Hill [12]
  RG17.............165 A1
Edwards Meadow
  SN8..............213 B3
Edwards Rd SP4.....217 B3
Edward St BA13......109 A3
Egdon Cl [9] SN25....34 D6
Egerton Cl SN3......51 B7
Eglantyne Ave SN26...20 D1
Eider Ave SN15......60 A1
Elbe Way SP10......193 D2
Elborough Rd SN2...34 D3
ELCOMBE............63 E5
Elcombe SN1........49 D1
Elcombe Ave [3] SN4...64 A6
Elcombe Cl BA14....105 C5
Elcombe Gdns SN10. 214 A4
Elcombe La
  Alvediston SP5.....204 B2
  Alvediston SP5.....207 E8
Elcot Cl SN8........213 F3
Elcot La SN8........213 F3
Elcot Orch SN8......175 A8
ELDENE.............51 C5
Eldene Dr SN3......51 C4
Eldene Prim Sch SN3. 51 C5
Elden Rd
  North Tidworth SP9. 191 D5
  Tidworth SP9......216 B8
Elder Cl SN2.........34 C3
Elder Cl [3] SN13.....84 E8
Eleanor Ct [6] SP11...192 A5
Elgar Cl SN25........34 E7
Elgin Dr SN2.........35 E1
Elgin Ind Est SN2....35 E1
Elham Ct DT11......207 C1
Eliot Cl SN3.........51 D3
Elizabeth Cl
  [5] Downton SP5....210 H4
  Melksham Without SN12 93 F1
Elizabeth Dr SN10...214 C4
Elizabeth Gdns GL7...1 A5
Elizabeth Pl SN15....79 A4
Elizabeth Rd
  [16] Durrington/Bulford
  SP4..............198 B7

Elizabeth Rd continued
  Wilton SP2........144 B5
Elizabeth Sq SP9....216 E7
Elizabeth Way BA1...101 F3
Elley Gn SN13........84 E6
Ellingdon Rd SN4....63 F7
ELLIOTS GREEN ....114 D8
Elliott Cl SN3........214 B1
Elliott Gn SP4.......133 C3
Elliott Pl BA14......101 A1
Ellworthy Ct BA11...110 B4
Elm Cl
  Bower Hill SN12.....94 C1
  Calne SN11.........89 C8
  [8] Ludgershall SP11. 192 B5
  Lyneham SN15......60 B2
  Motcombe SP7......202 A5
  Pitton & Farley SP5..148 C4
  Rowde SN10 .......96 D1
  Royal Wootton Bassett
  SN4..............47 E4
  Salisbury SP1......146 D3
  Staverton BA14....101 D6
  Trowbridge BA14...105 C3
ELM CROSS ........167 D7
Elm Ct SN10 ........214 B1
Elmdale BA14.......105 A4
Elmdale Rd BA14....105 A7
Elmer Cl SN16.......28 A5
Elm Farm Cl SN16...16 D2
Elmfield SN11 ......100 C7
Elmfield Cl [7] SP5...211 C7
Elm Gr
  Calne SN11.........81 B1
  Corsham SN13......76 E1
  Salisbury SP1......146 C1
  Swindon SN5 .......49 A8
  Westbury BA13.....108 E3
Elm Gr Pl SP1......146 B1
Elm Gr Rd SP1......146 B1
Elm Hayes SN13.....85 A7
ELM HILL...........202 A5
Elm Hill BA14.......113 C1
Elmhurst Est BA1....82 A4
Elmhurst Rd BA14...108 F1
Elmina Rd SN1......50 C7
Elm Leigh BA11.....110 C6
Elmore SN3..........51 C5
Elm Pk SN4..........47 D1
Elm Rd
  Colerne SN14.......75 A5
  Swindon SN2 .......35 A2
Elms Cl SP6.........210 B1
Elms Cross BA15....100 C5
Elms Cross Dr BA15..100 C5
Elms The
  Bradford-on-Avon
  BA15.............100 B8
  Highworth SN6......22 F5
  Holt BA14..........92 E1
  Swindon SN5 .......48 F8
Elmswood Cl SN2....35 E5
Elm Tree Cl SN10...214 D2
Elm Tree Gdns SN10. 214 D2
Elm View GL7.........5 F4
Elmwood SN15......78 F7
Elmwood Ave [6] SP6 210 C1
Elsham Way SN25...35 A5
ELSTON............196 E7
Elston La SP3.......196 E7
Elstree Way
  Haydon Wick SN25...34 F6
  Swindon SN25 ......35 A7
Eltham Cl SN5.......48 F4
Elver Cl [9] SN3......51 B8
Ely Cl SN5...........49 C4
Ely Ct SN4..........64 A5
Embankment SN1....50 D3
Embry Cl [3] SN11...166 A1
Emden Rd [18] SP10..193 D2
Emerald Cres SN26...21 A1
Emerson Cl SN25.....35 A6
Emery Gate SN15....78 E7
Emlyn Sq SN1.......50 B6
Emmanuel Cl SN25...35 A4
Emmaus Sch BA14...101 D5
Emmet Hill SN16.....50 A0
Emmett Hill Mdws Nature
  Reserve★ SN16....16 D1
Emms La [10] BA13...186 B7
Empire Rd SP2......145 C2
Empress Way SN1...192 A5
Emwell St BA12......117 A7
Endeavour Prim Sch
  SP11.............193 F2
Endeavour Rd [6] SN3. 51 B8
Endless St SP1......146 A1
ENFORD............189 F6
Enford Ave SN2......35 C6
Enford Hill SN9......189 F6
Engineer Rd BA13...108 C6
ENGLANDS..........78 F5
Englefield SN4.......47 E1
ENHAM ALAMEIN ...193 E4
Enham La SP10......193 D3
ENMORE GREEN ...202 B2
Enos Way BA11......110 A6
Ensor Cl SN25.......35 A8
Enstone Cl [2] SN2...34 E2
Epping Cl BA12......117 A8
Epping Dr SN12......94 C6
Epsom Cl SN14......77 F6
Epsom Rd BA14.....105 E4
Equinox Dr SP4......217 E4
Erin Ct [1] SN1.......50 A2
Eriskay Gdns BA13..108 F2
Eriskay Pl SN5.......34 B3
Erleigh Dr SN15.....78 C7

ERLESTOKE ........187 A8
Erlestoke Way SN25...35 C6
Ermin Cl SN8........170 C8
Ermin St RG17......171 A6
Ermin St
  [1] Baydon SN8....164 C1
  Baydon SN8.......170 C8
  Blunsdon St Andrew
  SN26.............20 F2
  Swindon SN2 .......35 B8
Erneston Cres SN13...76 F1
Ernle Rd SN11........81 C4
Erskine Barracks
  SP2..............144 F4
Escott Cl [4] SN15...78 F4
Eshton Wlk SN3.....51 A3
Esmead SN15........78 F8
Espringham Pl SN2...35 E4
Essex Pl [7] RG17....165 A2
Essex Sq SN15......151 D6
Essex Wlk SN3......51 A3
Estate Yd The SN10..172 B3
Estcourt Cres SN10. 214 B4
Estcourt Rd SP1....146 B1
Estcourt St SN10....214 B5
Estcourt Terr SN10.. 214 B5
Estella Cl SN25......34 D6
Eston Medieval Village
  of★ SN14.........69 D8
ETCHILHAMPTON ..180 C7
Ethelbert Dr [4] SP10. 193 C2
Ethelred Pl SN13.....76 E1
Ethendun [11] BA13..186 B7
Euclid St SN1........50 C6
Euridge SN14.........75 E5
Europa & Brittania Pk
  SN3..............51 A8
Euro Way SN1........48 F3
Evans Cl SN15.......70 E1
Eveleigh Rd SN4.....47 E2
Evelyn Cl BA1........82 B3
Evelyn St SN1.......50 D3
Evening Star
  Royal Wootton Bassett
  SN4..............61 F8
  Royal Wootton Bassett
  SN5..............48 A1
EVEN SWINDON ....49 E6
Even Swindon Prim Sch
  SN2..............49 E6
Eveque Ct SP2......144 F3
Everett Cl BA12.....117 F1
Evergreen Ind Pk GL7...6 F5
Evergreens Cl SN3...36 C1
Evergreen Way [10]
  SN4..............217 C2
Everland Rd [18] RG17. 177 B7
Everland Rd Ind Est
  RG17.............177 C7
EVERLEIGH .........191 A8
Everleigh Barrows★
  SN9..............182 E3
Everleigh Cl BA14...105 D5
Everleigh Rd
  Collingbourne Ducis
  SN8..............191 D8
  Pewsey SN9.......215 C3
  Swindon SN2 .......35 C5
Ewden Cl SN1.......50 B2
EWEN...............5 C8
Ewen Rd
  Ewen GL7..........5 E6
  Siddington GL7......6 C7
Eworth Cl SN5.......48 F5
Exbury Cl [2] SN25...35 A4
Exe Cl SN4..........217 A8
Exeter Cl SN14......77 F6
Exeter House Specl Sch
  SP1..............146 B3
Exeter St
  Salisbury SP1......152 B7
  Swindon SN1.......50 B6
Exmoor Cl [1] SN2...34 C4
Exmoor Rd [6] BA13..108 E1
Exmouth St SN1......50 A5
Eyam Rd SN1........50 A1
Eyles Rd
  Devizes SN10......214 B1
  North Tidworth SP9..216 D8
Eyre Cl [1] SN25......34 D6
Eyres Dr SP5........153 E2
Eyres Way SP1......152 B8
Eysey SN6...........9 A2

**F**

FABERSTOWN ......192 B6
Factory Hill SP8.....137 F3
Factory La
  Barford St Martin
  SP3..............143 B3
  Warminster BA12...116 F6
Fairdown Ave BA13..109 B3
Fairfax Cl
  Amesbury SP4 .....217 A4
  Swindon SN3 .......50 F7
Fairfield
  [1] Cricklade SN6 ...19 D0
  [4] Great Bedwyn SN8. 176 B3
  Minety SN16........17 B1
  Rode BA11.........103 F1
  Royal Wootton Bassett
  SN4..............47 E3
Fairfield Cl
  Frome BA11........110 A7
  Marshfield SN14 ....74 A8
Fairfield Cotts SP2..144 E4

**Duc–Far 227**

Fairfield Farm Coll
  BA13.............108 C1
Fairfield Meadows
  BA14.............104 F3
Fairfield Rd
  Salisbury SP1......146 A4
  Warminster BA12...117 B7
Fairfields [22] RG17...177 B7
Fairfoot Cl SN14.....78 A7
FAIRFORD...........1 E7
Fairford Airfield GL7...1 E1
Fairford Cres SN25...35 C5
Fairford Rd GL7......2 B4
Fairground The [2]
  SP11.............192 F1
Fairhaven BA13.....108 D1
Fairholme Way SN2...35 F4
Fairlane SP7........202 C1
Fairlawn SN3........51 D3
Fairleigh Rise SN15...70 F7
Fair Mile
  Collingbourne Kingston
  SN8..............183 D3
  Grafton SN8.......184 A4
Fairview
  Colerne SN14......75 C6
  Swindon SN1........50 B5
Fairview Cl BA12.....117 B5
Fairview Rd
  [1] Andover SP11....192 F1
  Hungerford RG17...177 B7
  Salisbury SP1......146 C1
Fair View Rd SP2....144 E4
Fairwater Ct SN4....64 A5
Fairway
  Calne SN11.........89 C8
  Melksham SN12.....94 C5
Fairways
  Amport SP11........192 E1
  Dilton Marsh BA13..108 D1
Fairway The SN10...214 A1
FAIRWOOD..........108 B4
Fairwood Cl BA14....102 A2
Fairwood Rd
  Dilton Marsh BA13..108 C3
  North Bradley BA13..107 F5
Falcon Dr BA14......105 E4
Falconer Mews SN25..35 B6
Falcon Rd
  Calne SN11.........81 D3
  Warminster BA12...116 C6
Falconscroft SN3.....51 C8
Falconsway SP2......152 A5
Falcon Way SN12.....94 D1
Falconwood Cl [8]
  SP6..............210 C1
Falkirk Rd SN4......64 A7
Falklands Rd SN4....64 E3
Falkner Cl SN8......213 B3
Fallow Field Cl SN14. 70 B2
Falmouth Gr SN3....50 E4
Fanshaw Way BA12..117 A5
Fanstones Rd SN3...51 C4
Fantley La SP8......138 E1
Faraday Pk SN3.....51 E5
Faraday Rd
  Salisbury SP2......145 E1
  Swindon SN3 .......51 E5
Fareham Cl SN3.....51 B5
Farfield La SN3......19 E4
Fargo Cl SP4.........198 A6
Fargo Rd SP4........217 A7
Faringdon Rd
  Lechlade-on-Thames
  GL7..............2 E3
  [2] Swindon SN1 ....50 B6
Farleigh Ave
  Melksham SN12.....94 B3
  Trowbridge BA14...105 A7
Farleigh Castle★
  BA2..............103 E8
Farleigh Cl
  [1] Chippenham SN14. 77 F6
  Westbury BA13 ....108 F4
Farleigh Cres SN3....50 E3
FARLEIGH
  HUNGERFORD ....103 E7
Farleigh La
  Hinton Charterhouse
  BA2..............99 A1
  Hinton Charterhouse
  BA2..............103 A8
Farleigh Pk★ BA2...103 D5
Farleigh Rise
  Farleigh Hungerford
  BA14.............103 F8
  Norton St Philip BA2. 103 A5
  Wingfield BA14 ....104 A8
Farleigh Rise
  Bath BA1..........82 C2
  Monkton Farleigh BA1. 82 D1
FARLEIGH WICK....90 F5
FARLEY............154 D8
Farley Cl BA11......110 C6
Farley Rd SP1.......152 C7
Farman Cl SN3......51 C4
Farm Cl BA11.......101 A1
Farm Ct [3] SN6.....163 E6
Farmer Cl SN15......70 E1
Farmer Cres SN25...35 C6
Farmer Giles
  Farmstead★
  SP3..............201 C3
Farmhouse Cl SN15...78 F4
Farmhouse Dr SN15. 78 A4

Gawthorne Dr SP2 . . . 151 F6
Gaynor Cl SN25 . . . . . . .35 A6
Gay's Pl SN2 . . . . . . . .35 F4
Gayton Way SN3 . . . . . .51 B8
Gaza Rd SP4 . . . . . . . . 198 F7
Geneville Rise **3**
SP4 . . . . . . . . . . . . . . 217 C3
Genoa Ct **16** SP10 . . . 193 E2
Gentle St BA12 . . . . . . 119 C7
George Cl SN11 . . . . . . .81 C3
George Gay Gdns **7**
SN3 . . . . . . . . . . . . . . . .50 F4
George La SN8 . . . . . . 213 D2
George St Pl BA12 . . . . 117 A7
George St (South) **6**
SP2 . . . . . . . . . . . . . . 145 F1
George St
Salisbury SP2 . . . . . . . 145 F1
Swindon SN1 . . . . . . . .50 A6
Trowbridge BA14 . . . . 101 D1
Warminster BA12 . . . . 117 A7
George VI Rd SP7 . . . 216 C8
Gerard Wlk SN5 . . . . . .49 A6
Germain's La SN14 . . . 76 A6
Geys Hill BA12 . . . . . . 115 A7
Giant's Cave (Long
Barrow)★ SN14 . . . . . .39 C2
Giant's Chair The
(Tumulus)★ SP5 . . 158 E2
Gibb Rd
Castle Combe SN14 . . . 54 A1
Castle Combe SN14 . . . 68 B8
Gibbs Cl
**2** Salisbury SP1 . . . 146 C5
Swindon SN3 . . . . . . . .51 E7
Westbury BA13 . . . . . 109 B4
Gibbs Ct SN13 . . . . . . .76 D1
Gibbs La SN14 . . . . . . .55 F8
Gibbs Leaze BA14 . . . . 102 A1
GIBB THE . . . . . . . . . . .53 F3
Gibson Cl SN12 . . . . . . .94 C1
Gibson Pl SP4 . . . . . . . 132 B1
GIDDEAHALL . . . . . . . . 68 D2
Gifford Rd SN3 . . . . . . .36 B3
Giffords The BA14 . . . 102 A4
Gigant St
Salisbury SP1 . . . . . . . 152 B8
Swallowcliffe SP3 . . . . 204 A6
Giggan St BA12 . . . . . 195 B2
Gilbert's Gn **3** SP9 . . 199 D8
Gilberts La SN6 . . . . . . .23 A5
Gilberts Piece SN8 . . . 183 E1
Gilbert Way SP1 . . . . . 146 C4
Giles Ave **1** SN6 . . . . 19 D7
Giles La SO51 . . . . . . . 212 E7
Giles La Ind Est SP5 . . 212 E7
Giles Rd **3** SN25 . . . . 34 D6
Gilhespy Way BA13 . . 109 A5
Gillingham Rd
Mere BA12 . . . . . . . . . 138 E4
Silton SP8 . . . . . . . . . . 138 A1
Gilling Way SN3 . . . . . . 51 D6
Gilman Cl SN25 . . . . . . .35 A8
Gilmore Ct SN6 . . . . . . .23 A5
Gilmore Rd SN16 . . . . . .28 A6
Gimson Cres SN25 . . . . 20 C1
Giotto Cl **11** SN25 . . . . 34 B7
Gipsy La
Chippenham SN15 . . . . 78 D6
Frome BA11 . . . . . . . . 110 B7
Holt BA14 . . . . . . . . . . .92 F2
Hungerford RG17 . . . . 177 C8
Swindon SN2 . . . . . . . . 50 E8
Warminster BA12 . . . . 117 B5
Gladstone Rd
Chippenham SN15 . . . . 78 D7
Trowbridge BA14 . . . . 105 B7
Gladstone St SN1 . . . . .50 C7
Gladys Plumley Gdns
SN2 . . . . . . . . . . . . . . . 50 C8
Glass's La SP3 . . . . . . 204 D7
Glebe Bglws **3** BA12 201 E8
Glebe Cl
**7** Aldbourne SN8 . . 170 A6
Pitton & Farley SP5 . . . 148 C4
Glebe Field BA12 . . . . 117 A6
Glebe Gdns SP7 . . . . . 202 A4
Glebe La
Kemble GL7 . . . . . . . . . . 4 F7
Landford SP5 . . . . . . . 212 C6
Wroughton SN4 . . . . . . .63 F7
Glebelands **3** BA12 . 194 C5
Glebe Pl
Chilton Foliat RG17 . . . 171 A1
Highworth SN6 . . . . . . .23 A6
Glebe Rd
**2** Durrington/Bulford
SP4 . . . . . . . . . . . . . . 198 B7
Royal Wootton Bassett
SN4 . . . . . . . . . . . . . . . 47 D1
Trowbridge BA14 . . . . 105 A7
Glebe The
All Cannings SN10 . . . . 180 F8
Calne SN11 . . . . . . . . . .81 C3
Freshford BA2 . . . . . . . 99 B4
Hinton Charterhouse
BA2 . . . . . . . . . . . . . . . 98 D2
Glebe Way SN13 . . . . . .76 E1
Gleed Cl SN5 . . . . . . . . .32 F4
Glendale Cres SP1 . . . 152 D8
Glendale Dr SN14 . . . . .78 E6
Glendale Rd SP4 . . . . . 198 C7
Gleneagles Cl SN15 . . .78 F7
Glenfield Cl SP5 . . . . . 149 D6
Glenmore Bsns Pk
SP2 . . . . . . . . . . . . . . 151 E8
Glenmore Rd
Haydon Wick SN25 . . . .34 C5

Glenmore Rd continued
Salisbury SP1 . . . . . . . 146 C3
Glenside SN12 . . . . . . . .94 C6
Glenville Cl SN4 . . . . . .61 E8
Glenwood Cl SN1 . . . . .50 C2
Glevum Cl SN5 . . . . . . . 33 C5
Glevum Rd SN3 . . . . . . .36 C1
Globe St SN1 . . . . . . . . 50 C4
Gloucester Cl **3** SN14 .78 A6
Gloucester Rd
Calne Without SN11 . . . .81 F1
Trowbridge BA14 . . . . 105 B7
Gloucester Sq SN12 . . .94 C4
Gloucester St
**8** Malmesbury SN16 . . 28 A3
Swindon SN1 . . . . . . . . 50 B7
Gloucester Wlk BA13 . 109 A4
Glover Rd SP4 . . . . . . . 197 F7
Glyndebourne Cl
SP2 . . . . . . . . . . . . . . 145 C3
Glyn Pl SP7 . . . . . . . . . 206 B7
GOATACRE . . . . . . . . . .73 F7
Goatacre La SN11 . . . . .73 F7
Goblins Pit Cl **3** SN13 .76 C1
Goddard Ave SN13 . . . . 50 B4
Goddard Cl **1** SN25 . . 215 C5
Goddard Pk Com Prim
Sch SN3 . . . . . . . . . . . 51 B5
Goddard Rd SN9 . . . . . 215 D5
Goddards La **11** SN8 . 170 A6
Godley La BA14 . . . . . . 106 A8
Godley Rd SP2 . . . . . . 152 A6
Godolphin St SN5 . . . . .49 A3
Godolphin Prep Sch
SP1 . . . . . . . . . . . . . . 146 C1
Godolphin Sch The
SP1 . . . . . . . . . . . . . . 152 C8
GODSHILL . . . . . . . . . 211 F2
Godwin Ct **9** SN1 . . . . 50 D4
Godwin Rd SN3 . . . . . . .36 B3
Godwins Cl SN12 . . . . . .84 E1
Gogg's La SP5 . . . . . . . 211 D7
Goldcrest Wlk SN3 . . . .51 E7
Golden Cross SP6 . . . . 211 E4
Golden Rd SN10 . . . . . 214 C5
Goldfinch Rd SN12 . . . .94 E1
Gold Hill **8** SP7 . . . . . 202 C1
Golding Ave SN8 . . . . . 213 A2
Golding Gr SP2 . . . . . . 144 F4
Goldney Ave SN14 . . . . .78 C7
Goldsborough Cl SN5 . 49 B6
Gold View SN1 . . . . . . . .49 F4
GOMELDON . . . . . . . . 133 D4
Gomeldon Medieval
Village of★ SP4 . . . 133 C4
Gomeldon Prim Sch
SP4 . . . . . . . . . . . . . . 133 C4
Gomeldon Rd SP4 . . . . 133 D5
Gooch Cl BA11 . . . . . . 110 C7
Gooch St SN1 . . . . . . . .50 C7
Goodbody Rd **1**
SP4 . . . . . . . . . . . . . . 198 A6
Goodes Hill SN13 . . . . . 85 D3
Goodings La RG17 . . . 171 D6
Goodwin Cl BA12 . . . . 117 E8
Goodwood Cl BA14 . . . 105 E4
Goodwood Way **3**
SN14 . . . . . . . . . . . . . .77 F5
Goodwyns Cl **5** SP9 . 199 C8
Goor La SN8 . . . . . . . . . 164 B2
Goose Gn RG17 . . . . . . 165 A2
Gooselands
Crudwell SN16 . . . . . . .14 D5
Westbury BA13 . . . . . . 108 F2
Goose St
Marston SN10 . . . . . . . 179 A3
Southwick BA14 . . . . . 105 A2
Gordon Gdns **4** SN1 . .50 C6
Gordon Rd **5** SN1 . . . .50 C6
Gore Cl SN25 . . . . . . . . .34 F6
Gore Cross SN10 . . . . . 187 E5
Gore La BA13 . . . . . . . . 111 B4
Gore Rd SP4 . . . . . . . . 197 E7
Gores La SN9 . . . . . . . . 181 C5
Gornall Rd SN13 . . . . . .84 F6
Gorringe Rd SP2 . . . . . 145 D1
GORSE HILL . . . . . . . . . 35 D1
Gorse Hill Sch &
Children's Centre
SN2 . . . . . . . . . . . . . . . 35 D1
Gorse Pl **5** SN13 . . . . .84 E8
Gosditch
Ashton Keynes SN6 . . . . 6 F1
Ashton Keynes SN6 . . . . 17 E8
Latton SN6 . . . . . . . . . . . 8 C4
Gosling Cl **15** SN4 . . . 163 A6
Gosse Ct SN3 . . . . . . . . 50 E2
Goughs Way SN4 . . . . . .47 E2
Gould Cl **1** SP11 . . . . 192 A5
Goulding Cl **3** SN3 . . .36 B2
Governor Dr SN12 . . . . .93 F7
Gower Cl
Swindon SN2 . . . . . . . . .35 F2
**1** Swindon SN5 . . . . . 48 F5
Gower Rd **14** SP7 . . . 202 D2
Grace Cl SP2 . . . . . . . . 145 B5
Grace La SP6 . . . . . . . . 211 A4
Grafton Pl SN8 . . . . . . 183 F7
Grafton Rd
Burbage SN8 . . . . . . . . 183 D7
Swindon SN2 . . . . . . . . 35 C5
Graham Sq **7** SP4 . . . 197 E6
Graham St SN1 . . . . . . .50 D7
Grailey Cl SN3 . . . . . . . .51 C4
Grain Wlk **3** SP11 . . . 193 F2
Gramp's Hill OX12 . . . 165 F7
Gramshaw Rd **2**
SP2 . . . . . . . . . . . . . . 145 D2

Granary Cl
Codford St Mary
BA12 . . . . . . . . . . . . . 195 B2
Corston SN16 . . . . . . . .42 F4
East Grafton SN8 . . . . 183 F7
**4** Swindon SN5 . . . . . 48 F8
Granary Rd **6** SN8 . . 176 B3
Grand Ave SN8 . . . . . . 175 E3
Grandison Cl SN5 . . . . .49 A6
Grand Trunk Rd SP9 . . 216 B4
Grange Cl
Atworth/Whitley SN12 . 85 D1
Fyfield SP11 . . . . . . . . 192 D1
Highworth SN6 . . . . . . .23 A5
**14** Wanborough SN4 . 163 A6
Grange Dr SN3 . . . . . . . .36 B1
Grangefield SN10 . . . . 172 F1
Grange Gdns SP1 . . . . 146 C2
Grange Inf Sch SN3 . . .36 B3
Grange Jun Sch SN3 . . .36 B2
Grange La
St Paul Malmesbury Without
SN16 . . . . . . . . . . . . . 43 B5
Warminster BA12 . . . . 117 E5
GRANGE PARK . . . . . . .48 F5
Grange Pk Way SN5 . . .48 F5
Granger Cl SN15 . . . . . .78 F4
Grange Rd BA11 . . . . . 110 A7
Grange View BA15 . . . 100 F8
Granham Cl SN8 . . . . . 213 D1
Granham Hill SN8 . . . . 213 D1
Granica Cl **5** SN25 . . .34 D6
Grans Barrow (Long
Barrow)★ SP6 . . . . 209 E6
Grantham Cl SN5 . . . . .49 B3
Granthams The **4**
RG17 . . . . . . . . . . . . . 165 A2
Grantley Cl SN3 . . . . . . .51 A3
Grants Rd SN9 . . . . . . 190 A6
Granville Gdns **28**
SP7 . . . . . . . . . . . . . . 202 C2
Granville Rd SN12 . . . . .94 A6
Granville St SN1 . . . . . . 50 C6
Grasmere
Bower Hill SN12 . . . . . .94 D1
Swindon SN3 . . . . . . . . 51 E3
Trowbridge BA14 . . . . 101 E2
Grasmere Cl **1** SP2 . . 151 F6
Graspan Rd **12** SP11 . 192 B5
Grassy Slope
Westbury BA13 . . . . . . 109 B1
Westbury BA13 . . . . . . 113 A8
Grateley Rd SP4 . . . . . 199 C5
Gravel Cl SP5 . . . . . . . . 211 A8
Gravel The BA14 . . . . . .92 E1
Graveney Sq SP10 . . . 193 E1
Grayling Cl **9** SN11 . . .81 B1
Grays Cl SP7 . . . . . . . . 202 A4
Grays Leaze BA14 . . . . 105 C2
Gray St SP4 . . . . . . . . . 132 B1
Graythwaite Cl **3**
SN25 . . . . . . . . . . . . . .34 F6
GREAT ASHLEY . . . . . .91 A1
Great Barn★ SN8 . . . 167 B1
GREAT BEDWYN . . . . 176 B3
Great Bedwyn CE Prim
Sch SN8 . . . . . . . . . . 176 B4
Great Bottom
Sherrington BA12 . . . . 200 F8
Stockton BA12 . . . . . . 195 A1
GREAT CHALFIELD . . .92 E3
Great Chalfield Manor★
BA14 . . . . . . . . . . . . . 92 D3
GREAT CHEVERELL . . 179 C1
Great Croft SP5 . . . . . . 148 C7
Great Dro SP4 . . . . . . . 132 F1
Great Drove SP4 . . . . . 132 F1
GREAT DURNFORD . . 197 F1
Greater La BA13 . . . . . 186 C8
GREATFIELD . . . . . . . . .47 F8
Great Ground **15** SP7 202 D2
Great Hill BA9 . . . . . . . 137 B3
GREAT HINTON . . . . . 178 A6
Great La SP7 . . . . . . . . 202 C1
Great Lodge Dr SN8 . . 175 B5
Great Mead SN14 . . . . .78 F8
Great Parks BA14 . . . . .92 F1
Great Roc Rd BA13 . . . 108 E3
Great Rose La
Broad Blunsdon SN26 . . 21 A6
Swindon SN6 . . . . . . . . 20 F6
GREAT SOMERFORD . .44 B2
Great Western Acad
SN26 . . . . . . . . . . . . . .20 C2
Great Western Ave
SP3 . . . . . . . . . . . . . . 200 B1
Great Western Hospl The
SN3 . . . . . . . . . . . . . . . 51 D1
Great Western St **7**
BA11 . . . . . . . . . . . . . 110 A4
Great Western Way
SN5 . . . . . . . . . . . . . . . 48 F3
Great Wethers★
SN8 . . . . . . . . . . . . . . 174 A7
GREAT WISHFORD . . . 129 F3
Great Wishford CE VA Fst
Sch SP2 . . . . . . . . . . 130 A4
Greatwoods BA13 . . . . 186 C8
Grebe Cl GL7 . . . . . . . . . 7 A6
Greenacres
Dilton Marsh BA13 . . . 112 A8
**6** Downton SP5 . . . . 210 F8
Green Acres **13** SN8 . 170 B2
Greenacres Way SN11 . 80 F4
Greenacre Way **7**
SP7 . . . . . . . . . . . . . . 202 D1
Greenaway **4** SN4 . . 163 A5
Greenbank Vw BA14 . 104 F6

Greenbridge Ind Est
SN3 . . . . . . . . . . . . . . . 51 A7
Greenbridge Rd SN3 . . .51 A7
Greenbridge Retail Pk
SN3 . . . . . . . . . . . . . . . 36 A1
Greenbridge Ret Pk
SN3 . . . . . . . . . . . . . . . 51 A8
Green Cl
Damerham SP6 . . . . . . 209 F2
East Grafton SN8 . . . . 183 F7
Holt BA14 . . . . . . . . . . 101 F8
Whiteparish SP5 . . . . . 161 D4
Greencroft St SP1 . . . 146 B1
Greencroft The **6**
SP1 . . . . . . . . . . . . . . 146 B1
Green Dro
Buttermere SN8 . . . . . 185 C8
Fovant SP3 . . . . . . . . . 204 B3
Grimstead SP5 . . . . . . 154 B4
Pewsey SN9 . . . . . . . . 215 D3
Smannell SP11 . . . . . . 193 E5
Greene St
Swindon SN25 . . . . . . . 20 C1
Swindon SN25 . . . . . . . 34 C8
Green Farm Rise
SN8 . . . . . . . . . . . . . . 176 D7
Greenfield Rd SN10 . . 214 C1
Greenfields
Grimstead SP5 . . . . . . 154 C2
Smannell SP11 . . . . . . 193 F4
South Marston SN3 . . . 36 E5
Greenfield Vw SN6 . . . .18 F6
Greenfinch Cl SN12 . . .94 D4
Green Gate Rd SN10 . . 180 D4
Greenham Wlk SN3 . . .51 B6
Greenhill
Neston SN13 . . . . . . . . 84 D6
Sutton Veny BA12 . . . . 117 F1
Westwells SN13 . . . . . . 84 D7
GREEN HILL . . . . . . . . . 32 D1
Greenhill Gdns
Sutton Veny BA12 . . . . 117 F1
Trowbridge BA14 . . . . 102 A4
Greenhill Pl BA12 . . . . 195 A3
Greenhill Rd SN2 . . . . .34 E2
Greenhills BA13 . . . . . 186 C8
Greenhouse Rd SN10 180 F8
Green La
Ashmore SP5 . . . . . . . 206 E4
Cheverell Magna SN10 179 C1
Codford BA12 . . . . . . . 195 A3
Colerne SN14 . . . . . . . .75 A3
Deanend SP5 . . . . . . . 207 E4
Devizes SN10 . . . . . . . 214 B1
Downton SP5 . . . . . . . 211 A8
Fordingbridge SP6 . . . 210 D1
Hinton Charterhouse
BA2 . . . . . . . . . . . . . . . 98 E1
Laverstock SP4 . . . . . . 146 D8
Longhedge BA12 . . . . 115 C5
Rockbourne SP6 . . . . . 210 C3
Salisbury SP1 . . . . . . . 146 D6
Sherston SN16 . . . . . . .25 C1
Southwick BA14 . . . . . 104 D2
Steeple Ashton BA14 . . 102 C1
Trowbridge BA14 . . . . 105 E8
Westbury BA13 . . . . . . 108 F2
Winsley BA15 . . . . . . . . 99 F6
Green La Hospl SN10 . 214 C1
Green La Ind Est SN12 .92 E8
Greenland Mills
BA15 . . . . . . . . . . . . . 100 D6
Greenlands **1** BA12 . 194 C5
Greenlands Cl **20**
SP4 . . . . . . . . . . . . . . 198 B7
Greenlands Rd SN2 . . .35 E3
Greenland View
BA15 . . . . . . . . . . . . . 100 D6
Greenlane Cl SP4 . . . . 146 D6
Green La Wood Nature
Reserve★ BA14 . . . 106 C8
Greenleaze Cl BA14 . . .69 F8
Green Mdw Ave SN25 . .34 F4
GREENMEADOW . . . . .34 F3
Greenmeadow Prim Sch
SN25 . . . . . . . . . . . . . .35 A4
Green Pk La BA11 . . . . 107 A6
Green Rd
Codford BA12 . . . . . . . 195 A3
Corsham SN13 . . . . . . .85 B4
Swindon SN2 . . . . . . . . 35 E3
Green Ride BA12 . . . . . 123 E5
Greensand Cl **10** SN25 .34 F7
Greens Cl SN14 . . . . . . .41 F1
Green's Ct **3** SP1 . . . 152 B8
Greensey SP11 . . . . . . 192 E3
Greens La SN11 . . . . . . 172 A8
Green's La SN4 . . . . . . .64 B5
Greens Meade **6**
SP5 . . . . . . . . . . . . . . 211 C7
Green St SN8 . . . . . . . . 167 C1
Greenstone Rd SP7 . . 202 D1
Green Terr BA14 . . . . . 101 C2
GREEN THE . . . . . . . . 141 A3
Green The
Alderbury SP5 . . . . . . . 153 C3
Biddestone SN14 . . . . .76 E8
Brokenborough SN16 . .27 D7
Calne SN11 . . . . . . . . . .81 B2
Cheverell Magna SN10 179 C2
Dauntsey SN15 . . . . . . .59 A8
Fairford GL7 . . . . . . . . . .1 E4
Highworth SN6 . . . . . . .22 F5
**1** Liddington SN4 . . . 163 A4
Lyneham & Bradenstoke
SN15 . . . . . . . . . . . . . .60 A4
Marlborough SN8 . . . . 213 E3
Oaksey SN16 . . . . . . . . .15 F7

Green The continued
Pitton & Farley SP5 . . . 148 C3
Salisbury SP1 . . . . . . . 152 B8
Upper Woodford SP4 . . 131 D7
Whiteparish SP5 . . . . . 161 D4
Greentrees Prim Sch
SP1 . . . . . . . . . . . . . . 146 C5
Green Valley Ave
SN25 . . . . . . . . . . . . . .34 F4
Greenway Ave SN15 . . 70 D1
Greenway Cl SN3 . . . . .51 B7
Greenway Ct SN15 . . . 70 D2
Greenway Dr SN15 . . . .73 F8
Greenway Gdns
Chippenham SN15 . . . . 70 D1
Trowbridge BA14 . . . . 101 E3
Greenway La SN15 . . . 70 D2
Greenway Pk SN15 . . . 70 D1
Greenway Rd SN8 . . . 169 B1
Greenways RG17 . . . . 165 A1
GREENWICH . . . . . . . . 200 C3
Greenwich Cl SN25 . . .35 A5
Greenwood Ave SP1 . 146 D1
Greenwood Gr **4**
SN25 . . . . . . . . . . . . . .34 C6
Greenwood Pl **6**
SN25 . . . . . . . . . . . . . .34 D7
Greenwood Rd SN12 . .94 A3
Gregor Dr SN11 . . . . . . 81 D3
Gregory Cl
Box SN13 . . . . . . . . . . . 83 D6
Sutton Benger SN15 . . 57 C1
Grenadier Cl **2** BA12 116 F7
Gresham Cl SN3 . . . . . .50 F6
Greyfriars Cl SP1 . . . . 152 B7
Greyhound La **1**
SP2 . . . . . . . . . . . . . . 144 D3
Grey's Cnr BA9 . . . . . . 136 A5
Greystones SN13 . . . . .96 B8
Greywethers Ave SN3 .50 E3
Grey Wethers or Sarsen
Stones★ SN8 . . . . . 167 F3
Grierson Cl SN11 . . . . . .81 B3
Griffin Alley **6** SN16 . .28 A3
Griffins Ct **3** SP2 . . . 146 A1
Griffiths Cl SN3 . . . . . . .36 B1
Grimstead Beeches★
SP5 . . . . . . . . . . . . . . 160 D7
Grimstead Rd
Alderbury SP5 . . . . . . . 153 F1
East Grimstead SP5 . . 154 E5
West Dean SP5 . . . . . . 155 C2
Grimstead Road SP5 . 134 D6
Grindal Dr SN5 . . . . . . .48 F5
Grist Ct **11** BA15 . . . . 100 D6
GRITTENHAM . . . . . . . .46 C2
GRITTLETON . . . . . . . . 54 D5
Grocyn Cl SN14 . . . . . . .75 B3
Grosmont Dr SN5 . . . . .49 B5
Grosvenor close SP9 . . 216 E1
Grosvenor Dr SP3 . . . . 200 E1
Grosvenor Rd
Shaftesbury SP7 . . . . . 202 C2
Swindon SN1 . . . . . . . . 50 A4
Ground Cnr BA14 . . . . 101 D8
Groundstone Way
Corsham SN13 . . . . . . . 76 C1
**2** Corsham SN13 . . . 84 C8
Groundwell SN25 . . . . .35 C6
Groundwell Ind Est
SN25 . . . . . . . . . . . . . .35 D6
Groundwell Rd SN1 . . .50 D5
Grouse Rd
Calne SN11 . . . . . . . . . .81 B5
Old Sarum SP4 . . . . . . 146 B8
Grove Hill SN6 . . . . . . . .23 A7
Grove La
Kington St Michael
SN14 . . . . . . . . . . . . . .69 F8
Redlynch SP5 . . . . . . . 211 D8
Yatton Keynell SN14 . . .69 A6
Grovelands Ave SN1 . . .50 C3
Grovelands Way
BA12 . . . . . . . . . . . . . 116 E7
Grove Leaze BA14 . . . 100 B6
Grove Rd SP3 . . . . . . . 143 B3
Grove Orch SN6 . . . . . .22 F7
Grove Prim Sch
BA14 . . . . . . . . . . . . . 105 B5
Grove Rd
Corsham SN13 . . . . . . .77 A1
**23** Market Lavington
SN10 . . . . . . . . . . . . . 179 F1
Sherston SN16 . . . . . . 40 C8
Groves St SN2 . . . . . . . .49 F6
Groves The SN25 . . . . . .35 B3
Grove The
Codford St Peter
BA12 . . . . . . . . . . . . . 195 A2
Crudwell SN16 . . . . . . . .4 C1
Penton Mewsey SP11 . 193 A2
Warminster BA12 . . . . 117 A7
Grundys SN3 . . . . . . . . . 51 D3
Gryphon Cl BA13 . . . . 108 E3
Guernsey La SN25 . . . . 34 D6
Guernsey Mead
BA13 . . . . . . . . . . . . . 109 A8
Guilder La SP1 . . . . . . . 152 B8

Guildford Ave SN3 . . . .50 F3
Guildhall Sq **3** SP1 . . 152 A8
Guild The (Wilton)
SP2 . . . . . . . . . . . . . . 144 E3
Gullet The SN13 . . . . . .83 F7
Gulliver's La BA14 . . . 178 A4
Gundry Cl
Chippenham SN15 . . . . 78 F5
Devizes SN10 . . . . . . . 214 C4
Gundy Gr BA14 . . . . . . 106 A8
Gunner St SP4 . . . . . . . 198 E6
Gunsite Rd SN8 . . . . . . 173 C6
Gunville Hill SP5 . . . . . 149 E6
Gunville Rd SP5 . . . . . 149 D6
Guppy St SN2 . . . . . . . . .49 F7
Gurston La SP5 . . . . . . 205 A4
Gurston Meadow
SP5 . . . . . . . . . . . . . . 205 A4
Gurston Rd SP5 . . . . . . 205 A4
Gussage Hill
Gussage St Andrew
BH21 . . . . . . . . . . . . . 208 A1
Gussage St Andrew
SP5 . . . . . . . . . . . . . . 207 F1
GUSSAGE ST
ANDREW . . . . . . . . . 207 E1
Guthrie Cl SN11 . . . . . . .81 C4
Guyers La SN13 . . . . . . .76 D2
Gwyns Piece **14**
RG17 . . . . . . . . . . . . . 165 A2
Gypsies La BA14 . . . . . 106 F8
Gypsy La
Coombe Bissett SP5 . . 156 F7
Coombe Bissett SP5 . . 157 A8
Draycot Foliat SN4 . . . 168 C7
Swindon SN25 . . . . . . . 35 F1
Gypsy Patch SN10 . . . .97 F1

**H**

Habberfield SP9 . . . . . 216 D8
Habrel's Cl SN15 . . . . . .78 F6
Hackett Cl SN3 . . . . . . .35 E4
Hackleton Rise SN3 . . .51 B8
Hackney Way BA13 . . . 108 E3
Hackpen SN8 . . . . . . . . 168 B6
Hackpen Cl SN4 . . . . . .64 B7
Hackpen La SN4 . . . . . 168 B8
HACKTHORN . . . . . . . . 198 A8
Hackthorne Rd SP4 . . 198 A8
Haddon **14** SN5 . . . . .48 F5
Haddons Cl SN16 . . . . .27 D2
Haden Rd **6** BA14 . . . 105 D7
Hadleigh Cl SN5 . . . . . .49 C6
Hadleigh Rise SN2 . . . .36 A5
Hadrian Rd **20** SP10 . 193 E2
Hadrians Cl
Salisbury SP2 . . . . . . . 145 C1
Swindon SN3 . . . . . . . . 36 C1
Swindon SN3 . . . . . . . . 51 C8
Haig Cl SN2 . . . . . . . . . .35 E4
Haig Rd SP4 . . . . . . . . . 217 F8
HAILSTONE HILL . . . . . .8 A1
Haimes La **20** SP7 . . . 202 C2
Haines Terr SN9 . . . . . 215 C4
HALCOMBE . . . . . . . . . .27 E3
HALE . . . . . . . . . . . . . . 211 C5
Hale House★ SP6 . . . 211 A5
Hale La SP6 . . . . . . . . . 211 B5
Hale Prim Sch SP6 . . . 211 C6
Hale Rd SP6 . . . . . . . . . 211 A5
Hales Castle★ BA11 . 114 D5
Hales Cl SN15 . . . . . . . .59 E4
Hales Rd **6** SP4 . . . . . 190 A4
Half Hide Down SP5 . . 207 B3
Half Mile Rd RG17 . . . 171 A5
Halfpenny La SP5 . . . . 206 E4
Halfpenny Rd SP2 . . . 151 D7
Halfpenny Row BA11 . 103 E1
HALFWAY . . . . . . . . . . 113 A4
Halfway Cl BA14 . . . . . 101 F2
Halfway Firs SN13 . . . .76 C1
HALF WAY FIRS . . . . . .76 C1
Halfway La SN8 . . . . . . 170 C2
Halifax Cl SN4 . . . . . . . .64 A7
Halifax Rd SN12 . . . . . .94 C1
Hallam Moor SN3 . . . . .51 E2
Hall Cl SN4 . . . . . . . . . .64 A6
Halls Farm La SP11 . . 185 C4
Hallsfield SN6 . . . . . . . . .8 D1
Hallum Cl SP1 . . . . . . . 146 D4
Halton Cres SN4 . . . . . .64 E3
Halton Rd SP11 . . . . . . 191 F4
Halve The BA14 . . . . . . 101 D1
HAM . . . . . . . . . . . . . . 177 B2
Hambidge La GL7 . . . . . .2 C5
Hamble Ct SP10 . . . . . 193 F1
Hamble Rd SN25 . . . . . .34 F4
Hambleton Ave SN10 214 E6
Hamblin Meadow
RG17 . . . . . . . . . . . . . 177 B8
Hamburg Cl **10** SP10 . 193 D2
Ham Cl
Collingbourne Kingston
SN8 . . . . . . . . . . . . . . 183 D3
Holt BA14 . . . . . . . . . . 101 D8
Trowbridge BA14 . . . . 101 B1
HAM GREEN . . . . . . . . 101 C8
Ham Green Gaston
BA14 . . . . . . . . . . . . . 101 C8
Ham Hill Nature
Reserve★ SN8 . . . . 185 B8
Hamilton Cl
Amesbury SP4 . . . . . . 217 E3

**Hamilton Cl** continued
Swindon SN3 . . . . . . . . . .**50** F7
**Hamilton Dr**
Chippenham SN14 . . . . . .**77** F5
**2** Market Lavington
SN10 . . . . . . . . . . . . . . . .**179** F1
**Hamilton Pk 3** SP5. . **211** B8
**Hamilton Rd** SP1 . . . . **146** A2
**Ham La**
Biddestone SN14 . . . . . .**76** C8
Kempsford GL7 . . . . . . . .**10** E6
South Cerney GL7 . . . . . . .**6** F6
South Cerney GL7 . . . . . . .**7** A6
**Hamlet Cl** SN15 . . . . . . .**70** D1
**Hamlet Gdns** SP11 . . **193** E3
**Hamlet The** SN15 . . . . . .**70** E1
**Hammersmith Fields**
BA14 . . . . . . . . . . . . . . . .**101** C1
**Hammer St** BA10 . . . . **122** C7
**Hammond Cl** SN6 . . . . . .**23** A5
**Hammonds** SN6 . . . . . . .**19** E8
**Hammond Way** BA14.**101** D4
**Hampshire Cl**
Durrington/Bulford
SP4. . . . . . . . . . . . . . . . .**217** E8
**7** Swindon SN5 . . . . . .**49** A7
**HAMPSHIRE GATE**. . . **185** A1
**Hampshire Gdns**
BA13. . . . . . . . . . . . . . . .**109** A4
**Hampshire Pl** SN12 . . . .**94** B5
**Hampsley Rd** SN13. . . . .**89** C1
**Hampstead Way** SN25. .**34** F7
**HAMPTON**. . . . . . . . . . . .**22** D5
**Hampton Cl** SN12 . . . . . .**94** C1
**Hampton Ct**
Quidhampton SP2 . . . . **144** F2
Swindon SN5 . . . . . . . . . .**48** F5
**Hampton Dr** SN5 . . . . . .**48** F5
**HAMPTON HILL**. . . . . . . .**22** E2
**Hampton Rd 31** SP11.**193** E2
**HAMPTWORTH**. . . . . . . **212** B6
**Hamptworth Rd** SP5 .**211** F6
**Ham Rd**
Ham RG17 . . . . . . . . . . .**177** A2
Liddington SN4. . . . . . . **163** A5
**Hamshill Ditches**★
SP3. . . . . . . . . . . . . . . . .**143** B7
**HAM THE**. . . . . . . . . . . **108** E5
**Ham The**
Durrington/Bulford
SP4. . . . . . . . . . . . . . . . .**198** C7
Kington St Michael SN14**70** A8
**9** Market Lavington
SN10 . . . . . . . . . . . . . . . .**179** F1
Westbury BA13 . . . . . . . **108** E5
**Hamworthy Rd** SN3 . . . .**51** C6
**Hanbury Rd** SN3 . . . . . . .**51** A4
**Hancock Cl** SN15 . . . . . . .**79** A5
**Handel St** SN2 . . . . . . . . .**50** C8
**Handley St** SP5 . . . . . . **204** D3
**Hanewell Rise** BA14.**102** B2
**Hanging Bushes La**
SP11. . . . . . . . . . . . . . . .**193** A1
**HANGING
LANGFORD**. . . . . . . . . **128** C2
**Hanging Langford**
Camp**★** BA12. . . . . . . . **201** F6
**Hanging Stone**★
SN9. . . . . . . . . . . . . . . . .**181** B7
**Hanging The** SP5. . . . **155** F1
**Hangman's Stone**★
RG17. . . . . . . . . . . . . . . .**164** F4
**Hanker Cl** SN26. . . . . . . .**20** D1
**HANKERTON**. . . . . . . . . .**15** C2
**Hankerton Priory**
SN16. . . . . . . . . . . . . . . .**15** B4
**Hankerton Rd** SN16. . . .**16** C2
**Hanks Cl** SN16. . . . . . . . .**28** A5
**Hannah Way** SP4 . . . . **132** B1
**HANNINGTON**. . . . . . . . .**22** B7
**Hannington Cl** SN2 . . . .**35** B6
**HANNINGTON WICK**. . . .**11** A4
**Hanover Cl** BA14 . . . . **101** E4
**Hanover Ct** SN3 . . . . . . . .**51** D7
**Hanson Cl 1** SN5. . . . . .**49** B8
**Hanwell Cl 4** SN25 . . . .**34** B8
**Ha'penny Bridge**★ GL7 .**2** C3
**Happy Land** SN6 . . . . . . .**18** A8
**Haragon Dr** SP4 . . . . . **217** D1
**Harbour Cl** SN25. . . . . . .**34** F3
**Harbour Mdw** SN2 . . . . .**34** F3
**Harcourt Mews 5**
BA14. . . . . . . . . . . . . . . .**110** A4
**Harcourt Rd** SN2 . . . . . .**50** A4
**Harcourt Terr** SP2 . . . .**151** F8
**Hardenhuish Ave**
SN15. . . . . . . . . . . . . . . .**70** C1
**Hardenhuish La** SN14.**70** B1
**Hardenhuish Pk**★
SN14. . . . . . . . . . . . . . . .**70** C2
**Hardenhuish Sch**
SN14. . . . . . . . . . . . . . . .**70** C2
**Hardens Cl** SN15. . . . . . .**79** A5
**Hardens Mead** SN15 . . .**79** A5
**Hardhams Rise** SN13..**84** F8
**Hardie Cl** SN3. . . . . . . . . .**36** A1
**Harding St 6** SN1 . . . . .**50** B6
**HARDWAY**. . . . . . . . . . . **122** A1
**Hardwick Cl** SN25 . . . . .**35** A5
**Hardy Cl** SN25. . . . . . . . . .**34** D6
**Hardyfair Cl** SP11. . . . **192** F1
**Harebell Cl** SN25 . . . . . .**34** D5
**Harebell Rd 23** SP11 .**193** F2
**Hare Cl** SN2 . . . . . . . . . . .**35** F5
**Harefield Cres** SP4 . . **190** A2

**Hare Knapp** BA15. . . . **100** B6
**Harepit La**
Kilmington BA12 . . . . . **123** F5
Kilmington BA12 . . . . . **124** A5
**Harepit Way**★ SN11 .**172** F7
**Haresdown Hill**
Rodmarton GL7 . . . . . . . . .**3** F7
Rodmarton GL7 . . . . . . . . .**4** A7
**HARESFIELD**. . . . . . . . . . .**23** B8
**Hares Patch** SN14 . . . . .**70** B2
**Hare St**
Bremhill SN15 . . . . . . . . .**72** C5
Pewsey SN9 . . . . . . . . . .**182** A7
**Hare Warren Cl** SP2 . **144** C1
**Harford Cl** SN15 . . . . . . .**78** F5
**Harford St 1** BA14 . . **105** E8
**Hargreaves Rd**
Swindon SN25 . . . . . . . . .**35** D6
Trowbridge BA14. . . . . **105** E7
**Harlech Cl** SN5. . . . . . . . .**49** B4
**Harlestone Rd** SN3 . . . .**51** B8
**Harley La** SO51 . . . . . . **212** E3
**Harmony Pl 8** BA14 . **105** D7
**HARNHAM**. . . . . . . . . . . **151** E6
**Harnham CE Jun Sch**
SP2. . . . . . . . . . . . . . . . .**151** F6
**Harnham Inf Sch** SP2.**151** F6
**Harnham Rd** SP2 . . . . **151** F7
**Harnham Trad Est**
SP2. . . . . . . . . . . . . . . . .**151** D7
**Harnham Trading Est**
SP2. . . . . . . . . . . . . . . . .**151** D7
**Harnish Way** SN14 . . . . .**70** B2
**Harnwood Rd** SP2 . . . .**151** E6
**Harper Rd** SP2 . . . . . . .**151** E6
**Harpers La 3** SN16 . . . .**28** A3
**Harper's La** SN14 . . . . . .**27** F3
**Harptree Cl** SN5 . . . . . . .**49** A8
**Harrier Cl** SN11 . . . . . . . .**81** A5
**Harriers The** SN3 . . . . . .**51** C7
**Harrington Dr 4**
SP4 . . . . . . . . . . . . . . . . .**198** E6
**Harrington Wlk** SN3 . . .**51** A7
**Harris Cl**
Frome BA11. . . . . . . . . . **110** B4
**5** Lambourn RG17 . . . **165** A2
**Harris La** SN9. . . . . . . . .**183** A7
**Harris Rd**
Ashton Keynes SN6 . . . . . .**7** A1
Calne SN11 . . . . . . . . . . .**81** C5
Swindon SN2 . . . . . . . . . .**35** A2
**Harroway La** SP11 . . . **193** B1
**Harrow Cl**
Swindon SN25 . . . . . . . . .**35** F1
Swindon SN3 . . . . . . . . . .**36** A1
**Harrow Gr** SN15 . . . . . . .**60** B2
**Harrow Rd** SP4 . . . . . . .**197** E8
**Harrow Way** SN11 . . . .**193** B1
**Harrow Way Com Prim
Sch** SP10 . . . . . . . . . . **193** C1
**Hart Cl**
Swindon SN25 . . . . . . . . .**35** F1
Swindon SN3 . . . . . . . . . .**36** A1
**Hartfield** SN4 . . . . . . . . . .**61** E8
Wilton SP2 . . . . . . . . . . .**144** E3
**Hartham La** SN13 . . . . . .**76** E5
**Harthill Dro** SP5 . . . . . .**211** D7
**Hartington Rd**
Salisbury SP2. . . . . . . . **145** E2
Swindon SN25 . . . . . . . . .**34** C7
**Hartland Cl** SN3. . . . . . . .**51** A5
**Hartley**
Winsley BA15. . . . . . . . . .**90** E1
Winsley BA15. . . . . . . . . .**99** E8
**Hartley Way** SP1 . . . . **146** D5
**Hartmoor Cl** SN10 . . . .**214** A2
**Hartmoor Rd** SN10 . . .**214** A2
**Harts Cl** SN11 . . . . . . . . .**166** A7
**Harts La** SN14 . . . . . . . . .**76** E8
**Hartsthorn Cl** SN2 . . . .**34** D3
**Harvard Cl**
**16** Bower Hill SN12 . . **178** B8
**1** Salisbury SP2 . . . . **151** F5
**Harvester Cl 7** SN5. . .**48** F8
**Harvest La** SP5 . . . . . . .**205** F4
**Harvey Cl** SN14 . . . . . . . .**78** A4
**Harvey Gr** SN12 . . . . . . . .**34** F2
**Hassocks La** BA10 . . . .**122** A7
**Hastings Ave** SN9 . . . .**182** B2
**Hastings Ct** SN9 . . . . . .**182** B2
**Hastings Dr**
Calne SN11 . . . . . . . . . . .**81** D4
Lyneham SN15. . . . . . . . .**60** B2
**Hastings Rd**
Corsham SN13. . . . . . . . .**85** A8
Trowbridge BA14. . . . . **102** B1
Trowbridge BA14. . . . . **106** B8
**Hatchbury La** SN15 . . **185** C3
**Hatcher's Cres** SN26. . .**21** B2
**Hatches La** SP1. . . . . . .**152** D7
**Hatchet Cl** SP6 . . . . . . .**211** C6
**Hatchet Hill** SN4 . . . . .**163** D6
**Hatchet La** SP11 . . . . . **193** B5
**Hatch La**
Vernhams Dean SP11 .**185** C4
West Tisbury SP3. . . . . .**203** C8
**Hatch Rd** SN3 . . . . . . . . . .**36** B4
**Hatfield Cl 4** SN25 . . . .**34** E4
**Hatfields** SN10. . . . . . . .**181** A5
**Hathaway Cl** SP1 . . . . **145** F4
**Hathaway Ret Pk**
SN15. . . . . . . . . . . . . . . .**78** C8
**HATHERDEN**. . . . . . . . . **193** C5
**Hatherden CE Prim Sch**
SP11. . . . . . . . . . . . . . . .**193** C5
**Hatherell Rd** SN15 . . . . .**78** F4

**Hatherhall Cl** SN3 . . . . .**36** C2
**Hatherleigh Ct** SN3 . . . .**51** B6
**Hatherley Rd** SN3. . . . . .**51** B7
**Hathersage Moor** SN3 .**51** E2
**Hattem Pl 23** SP10 . . . **193** D2
**Hatton Gr** SN3. . . . . . . . . .**50** F6
**Hatton Way** SN13 . . . . . .**76** E1
**Haugh** BA15. . . . . . . . . . . .**90** D1
**Havard Way 2** SP4 . . .**217** D2
**Havelock Sq** SN1 . . . . . .**50** B6
**Havelock St**
Swindon SN1 . . . . . . . . . .**50** B5
Trowbridge BA14. . . . . **105** C7
**Haven Cl** SN3. . . . . . . . . . .**51** B8
**Havering La** SN9. . . . . .**182** E7
**Havisham Dr** SN25. . . . .**34** D6
**Hawcroft** BA14 . . . . . . . .**92** E1
**Hawfinch Cl** SN3. . . . . . .**51** E5
**Hawker Ave** SP4 . . . . . .**132** B1
**HAWKERIDGE**. . . . . . . . **108** E8
**Hawkeridge Pk** BA13 **108** E5
**Hawkeridge Rd** BA14 **105** C2
**Hawker Rd** SN3. . . . . . . . .**51** C4
**Hawkesdene 17** SP7 . .**202** C1
**Hawkesdene La** SP7 . .**202** C1
**Hawkins Cl** SN15 . . . . . . .**78** F5
**Hawkins Meadow**
SN8. . . . . . . . . . . . . . . . .**213** B2
**Hawkins Rd 16** SN8 . .**170** A6
**Hawkins St**
**3** Swindon SN1 . . . . . .**49** F7
Swindon SN2 . . . . . . . . . .**50** A7
**Hawksdge 4** SP2 . . . .**152** A5
**Hawkstreet** SN15 . . . . . .**96** B6
**Hawkswood** SN3 . . . . . . .**51** D8
**Hawk's Worth Cl 6**
BA11. . . . . . . . . . . . . . . .**110** C7
**Hawksworth Trad Est**
SN2. . . . . . . . . . . . . . . . .**50** A8
**Hawksworth Way** SN2 .**50** A7
**Hawthorn Ave** SN2. . . . .**35** C6
**Hawthorn Cl**
Calne SN11 . . . . . . . . . . .**81** D5
Pewsey SN9 . . . . . . . . . .**215** D5
**Hawthorn Cl** SN4 . . . . . .**61** F8
**1** Salisbury SP2 . . . . . **145** F1
**2** Shaftesbury SP7. . . .**202** C2
**Hawthorn Gr** BA14. . . .**105** C5
**Hawthorn Rd**
Bowerhill SN12 . . . . . . . .**94** D3
Chippenham SN15 . . . . .**70** E1
Frome BA11. . . . . . . . . . **110** A6
Tidworth SP9 . . . . . . . . .**216** D7
**Hawthorn Way** SP2 . .**151** D7
**HAXTON**. . . . . . . . . . . . . .**197** A4
**Haybrook Rise** SN9 . . .**215** B6
**Haycombe Hill**
Sutton Veny BA12 . . . . .**194** A4
Sutton Veny SP3. . . . . . .**121** F4
Tytherington SP3 . . . . .**194** A2
**Haydock Cl 4** SN14.. .**77** F5
**Haydon Cl** SN25 . . . . . . .**34** E5
**Haydon Ct Dr** SN25 . . . .**34** E5
**Haydon End La**
Haydon Wick SN25 . . . . .**34** D6
**3** Swindon SN25 . . . . .**34** E5
**HAYDON WICK**. . . . . . . . .**34** E5
**Haydon Wick Prim Sch**
SN25. . . . . . . . . . . . . . . .**34** E4
**Haydown Leas** SP11 . .**185** C3
**Hayes Cl**
Atworth SN12 . . . . . . . . .**92** E8
Trowbridge BA14. . . . . **101** E3
**Hayesdown Fst Sch**
BA11. . . . . . . . . . . . . . . .**110** B5
**HAYES KNOLL**. . . . . . . . . .**19** E2
**Hayes Knoll** SN5. . . . . . .**33** F8
**Hayes Knoll Sta** SN5 . . .**19** F2
**Haye's La** GL9 . . . . . . . . . .**38** C2
**Hayfield** SN14 . . . . . . . . . .**74** A8
**Hayfield Ct** RG17. . . . . .**171** C7
**Haygrove Cl** BA12. . . . **116** D6
**Haygrove Farm Mws**
BA12. . . . . . . . . . . . . . . .**116** C6
**Hay La** SN5 . . . . . . . . . . . .**48** F6
**Hayle Rd** SN5. . . . . . . . . . .**49** F6
**Hayman Cres** SN3 . . . . . .**50** E2
**Haynes Cl** SN3. . . . . . . . . .**51** C4
**Haynes Rd** BA13 . . . . . .**109** A3
**Hay St** SN14 . . . . . . . . . . .**74** A8
**Haystack Ave** SN14 . . . .**78** A4
**Haywain 6** SN4 . . . . . .**217** B3
**Haywain** SN25 . . . . . . . . .**35** C6
**Hayward Cl**
Chippenham SN15 . . . . .**78** F5
Swindon SN25 . . . . . . . . .**35** A6
**Hayward Pl** BA13 . . . . **108** F5
**Haywards** GL7. . . . . . . . . .**10** E6
**Haywards Pl** SN10 . . . .**179** F2
**Hazeland** SN15 . . . . . . . . .**80** C5
**Hazelbury Cres** SN3. . . .**51** A4
**Hazelbury Hill** SN13. . . .**83** D6
**Hazelbury Manor Gdns**★
SN13. . . . . . . . . . . . . . . .**83** D7
**Hazel Cl**
Marlborough SN8. . . . . .**175** A7
Salisbury SP2. . . . . . . . **145** B3
**Hazel Copse** SN14. . . . . .**77** F6
**Hazeldon La** SP3 . . . . . .**203** D6
**Hazel End** SN4. . . . . . . . . .**47** E1
**Hazel Gr**
Calne SN11 . . . . . . . . . . .**81** B1

**Hazel Gr** continued
Swindon SN2 . . . . . . . . . .**35** C3
Trowbridge BA14. . . . . **105** B5
**Hazel Way**
Colerne SN14. . . . . . . . . .**75** A5
**6** Corsham SN13 . . . . .**76** E1
**Hazelwood Academy**
SN5. . . . . . . . . . . . . . . . .**49** C4
**Hazelwood Rd** SN12 . . .**94** A3
**Hazlemere Cl** SN3 . . . . . .**51** B4
**Hazzard's Hill** BA12..**139** B5
**Headington Hts** SN11 . .**89** B1
**Headlands** SN2 . . . . . . . . .**35** E3
**Headlands Trad Est Rd**
SN25. . . . . . . . . . . . . . . .**35** E2
**Headley Cl** SN4 . . . . . . . .**64** D3
**Headquarters Rd**
**8** Durrington/Bulford
SP4. . . . . . . . . . . . . . . . .**198** F6
Westbury BA13 . . . . . . .**108** C6
**Heale Gdn**★ SP4 . . . . **131** D5
**Heath Ave** SN15 . . . . . . .**57** C2
**Heath Barn** SP11 . . . . .**185** C6
**Heath Cl** BA12. . . . . . . . **115** B8
**Heathcote Cl** SN5. . . . . .**49** B8
**Heathcote Rd** SN12 . . . .**94** C5
**Heather Ave** SN12 . . . . .**94** C4
**Heather Cl** BA13 . . . . . .**108** F4
**Heather Shaw**
**2** Trowbridge BA14. . **101** C1
Trowbridge BA14. . . . . **105** B8
**Heather Way** SN11 . . . . .**81** C1
**Heath Farm Pk** SP3 . .**143** A1
**Heathfield** SN15 . . . . . . .**70** E2
**Heathfields Way 2**
SP7. . . . . . . . . . . . . . . . .**202** C2
**Heath Hill** BA14 . . . . . .**106** E5
**Heath La**
Buttermere SN8 . . . . . . .**185** C7
Great Somerford SN15 . .**43** D2
**Heathlands The** BA12 **116** F5
**Heath Plantation La**
SP11. . . . . . . . . . . . . . . .**185** B5
**Heath Rd** SP2. . . . . . . . .**145** D4
**Heath Sq 1** SN4 . . . . . .**197** E6
**Heath View Dr** SP2 . . .**145** C3
**Heathway** BA12 . . . . . . **115** C8
**Heath Way** SN3 . . . . . . . .**51** B8
**Heaton Cl** SN25. . . . . . . .**35** A6
**Heaven Hill Rd** SP11 . .**185** F4
**Heaven's Gate**★
BA12. . . . . . . . . . . . . . . .**115** C4
**Heavens Rise** SN16 . . . .**17** F7
**Hebden Cl 5** SN25 . . . . .**34** E7
**Hebden Rd** BA15. . . . . . .**99** F3
**Hector Rd 2** SN25. . . . .**34** C7
**HEDDINGTON**. . . . . . . . . .**89** B1
**Heddington CE Prim Sch**
SN11. . . . . . . . . . . . . . . .**89** B1
**Heddington Cl**
Swindon SN2 . . . . . . . . . .**35** B5
Trowbridge BA14. . . . . **105** C5
**HEDDINGTON WICK**. . . .**88** E2
**Hedgeditch La** GL8 . . . . .**26** D7
**Hedge La** SP9 . . . . . . . . .**216** D8
**Hedge Row** SN5 . . . . . . . .**79** A4
**Hedgerow La** SN4 . . . . . .**61** F8
**Hedges Cl**
**1** Shipton Bellinger
SP9. . . . . . . . . . . . . . . . .**199** C8
Swindon SN3 . . . . . . . . . .**36** B3
**Hedgesparrow La**
SN13. . . . . . . . . . . . . . . .**83** B7
**Hedges The 4** SN4 . . .**163** A6
**Heeks Cres 3** BA14. . **101** F1
**Heights The** SN1. . . . . . .**50** A4
**Hei-lin Way 2** SP11 . .**192** A5
**Helena Rd** SN25 . . . . . . .**34** C8
**Helena Terr 7** SP1 . . .**146** B1
**Helliker Cl** BA14 . . . . . .**102** B1
**Helmdon Rd** BA14 . . . .**101** A1
**Helmsdale** SN25. . . . . . . .**34** F4
**Helmsdale Wlk** SN3. . . .**51** A4
**Helmsley Rd** BA14 . . . .**106** B8
**Helps Well Rd** BA14. . .**102** B2
**Helston Rd** SN3. . . . . . . . .**51** A5
**Henchard Cres 7**
SN2. . . . . . . . . . . . . . . . .**34** C5
**Henderson Cl** BA14 . . .**105** B7
**Henford Cl** BA12. . . . . .**117** A5
**Henfords Marsh**
BA12. . . . . . . . . . . . . . . .**117** B4
**Hengest Cl 5** SP10 . . .**193** C2
**HENLEY**
Box . . . . . . . . . . . . . . . . . .**83** C4
Buttermere . . . . . . . . . .**185** A6
**Henley Ave** SN11 . . . . . .**81** D3
**Henley Dr** SN6. . . . . . . . . .**23** A7
**Henley La**
Box SN13 . . . . . . . . . . . . .**83** C4
Henley SN8 . . . . . . . . . .**185** A5
**Henley Mws** BA12. . . . .**116** D6
**Henley Rd 2** SN3. . . . . . .**51** A4
**Henloke Way** SN16 . . . .**28** C2
**Henman Cl**
Devizes SN10 . . . . . . . .**214** B4
Swindon SN25 . . . . . . . . .**35** A5
**Henn La** SN15 . . . . . . . . . .**57** C6
**Henry's Garth 7**
SN8. . . . . . . . . . . . . . . . .**183** D8
**Henry St 9** SN1. . . . . . . .**50** B6
**Henset Village**★ SN8. **175** E7
**Hensler Dr** SP4 . . . . . . .**146** C6
**Hepworth Rd 6** SN25..**34** F6
**Herbert Ludlow Gdns**
SN15. . . . . . . . . . . . . . . .**59** C3
**Herbert Rd**
**3** Redlynch SP5 . . . . .**211** C7

**Herbert Rd** continued
Salisbury SP2. . . . . . . . **145** C3
**Herbleaze** BA14 . . . . . .**101** D5
**Hercules Rd** SN11 . . . . . .**81** D4
**Hercules View** SN15 . . .**59** F4
**Hercules Way 1**
SN2. . . . . . . . . . . . . . . . .**178** B8
**Herdsman Cl** SN14. . . . .**78** A4
**Herd St** SN8 . . . . . . . . . .**213** D4
**Herdwick Rd 21** SP11 **193** F2
**Hereford Cl** SN14 . . . . . .**78** A5
**Hereford Lawns** SN3. . .**50** F3
**Herepath** SN8 . . . . . . . . .**167** C1
**Herepath or Green St**
SN8. . . . . . . . . . . . . . . . .**168** C1
**HERITAGE PARK**. . . . . . **214** C1
**Herman Miller Ind Est**
SN14. . . . . . . . . . . . . . . .**78** B5
**Hermitage La** SN2 . . . . .**35** E3
**Hernsham St** SP7. . . . .**203** C4
**Heronbridge Cl 2**
SN5. . . . . . . . . . . . . . . . .**49** C5
**Heron Cl** SN11 . . . . . . . . .**81** D3
**Herongate** RG17 . . . . . .**177** B8
**Heronscroft** SN3. . . . . . .**51** D7
**Herons Ct 6** SN12 . . . .**178** B8
**Heronslade** BA12 . . . . .**117** D5
**Heronswood** SP2 . . . . .**152** A5
**Heron Way** SN14. . . . . . .**77** F6
**Heron Wlk 12** SP4 . . . .**198** C7
**Herridge** SN8. . . . . . . . . .**184** A1
**Herschell Cl 7** SN25. . .**34** B7
**Hertford Cl**
**1** Fordingbridge
SP6. . . . . . . . . . . . . . . . .**210** D2
**4** Swindon SN3 . . . . . .**50** F2
**Hertford Rd** SN8. . . . . .**213** F1
**Hesketh Cres** SN1 . . . . .**50** D3
**Hewers Cl** SN4 . . . . . . . .**163** A6
**Hewitt Cl**
Swindon SN3 . . . . . . . . . .**51** C4
Trowbridge BA14. . . . . **105** E7
**Hewlett Cl** SN15 . . . . . . .**79** A5
**Hexham Cl**
**4** Chippenham SN14 . . .**77** F6
Swindon SN5 . . . . . . . . . .**49** B5
**Heyford Cl 8** SP4 . . . . **217** E3
**Heygate** SN25 . . . . . . . . . .**20** D1
**HEYTESBURY**. . . . . . . . . **194** C5
**Heytesbury** BA12 . . . . .**194** B3
**Heytesbury CE Prim Sch**
BA12. . . . . . . . . . . . . . . .**194** C5
**Heytesbury Pk** BA12. .**194** C5
**Heytesbury Rd** BA12 . .**194** B5
**Heytsbury Gdns 4**
SN5. . . . . . . . . . . . . . . . .**48** F4
**HEYWOOD**. . . . . . . . . . . .**109** A8
**Heywood Cl** SN2. . . . . . . .**35** B5
**Heywood Prep Sch**
SN13. . . . . . . . . . . . . . . .**77** A2
**Hicks Cl** SN4 . . . . . . . . . . .**64** A6
**Hidcot Ct** SN25 . . . . . . . .**34** C7
**High Bannerdown**
BA1. . . . . . . . . . . . . . . . .**82** B4
**Highbury Ave** SP2 . . . .**145** E2
**Highbury Cl 2** SP2 . . .**145** E2
**Highbury Pk** BA12 . . . .**117** C6
**Highbury Prim Sch**
SP2. . . . . . . . . . . . . . . . .**145** E2
**Highclere Ave** SN3. . . . .**50** F4
**Highclere Cotts 4**
BA12. . . . . . . . . . . . . . . .**201** C8
**Highdown La** SP11. . . .**185** F6
**Highdown Way** SN25. . .**35** A7
**Higher Barn Cl** SP7 . .**206** B7
**Higher Blandford Rd**
Cann Common SP7 . . . .**206** A8
**2** Shaftesbury SP7. . . .**202** D1
**Higher Mere Pk**★
BA12. . . . . . . . . . . . . . . .**202** A8
**HIGHER PERTWOOD**. . .**127** E4
**Higher Stavordale Farm**
La BA9 . . . . . . . . . . . . . .**136** B5
**Highfield** SN15 . . . . . . . . .**96** C7
**Highfield Cl** BA14. . . . . .**102** F5
**Highfield Cres** SP5 . . . .**149** B6
**Highfield La 10** SP5 . . .**211** C7
**Highfield Rd**
Amesbury SP4 . . . . . . . .**217** B3
Bradford-on-Avon
BA15 . . . . . . . . . . . . . . .**100** D7
Salisbury SP2. . . . . . . . **145** E2
**Highfield Rise 1**
SP3. . . . . . . . . . . . . . . . .**196** F6
**Highfold** SN4 . . . . . . . . . . .**47** F1
**Highgate Cottage** SN4 .**46** F5
**High Ground** SN25. . . . . .**20** B1
**Highgrove Cl** SN11. . . . . .**81** D2
**High La** SP5 . . . . . . . . . . .**205** B4
**Highland Cl**
**8** Swindon SN5 . . . . . .**49** A1
Westbury BA13 . . . . . . .**108** C1
**Highlands** SN10 . . . . . . .**179** D5
**Highlands Cl** SN13. . . . . .**84** A8
**Highlands Rd** SP2 . . . . .**152** A6
**Highlands Way** SP5 . . .**161** D4
**Highland View**
South Newton SP2. . . . .**130** A2
South Newton SP2. . . . .**130** B2
**High Lane** SP5 . . . . . . . .**204** F4
**High Lawn** SN10 . . . . . .**179** D8
**High Mead** SN4 . . . . . . . .**47** F2
**Highmoor Copse** SN5 . .**34** A1
**Highnam Cl** SN3 . . . . . . . .**36** A1
**High Post Bsns Pk**
SP4. . . . . . . . . . . . . . . . .**132** B5

**High Post Rd** SP4 . . . .**131** E6
**High Rd**
Ashton Keynes SN6 . . . . . .**6** F1
Bishopstone SP5 . . . . . .**205** E4
Britford SP5. . . . . . . . . .**152** D4
**Highridge Cl** SN5. . . . . . .**33** A3
**High St Brow** SN8. . . . . **169** A6
**High St**
Alderbury SP5 . . . . . . . .**153** C3
Amesbury SP4 . . . . . . . .**217** A3
Ansty SP3. . . . . . . . . . . .**203** F6
**1** Ashbury SN6. . . . . .**164** A8
Ashmore SP5 . . . . . . . . .**206** E4
Avebury SN8. . . . . . . . . .**173** B8
Badminton GL9 . . . . . . . .**38** E2
Bath BA1. . . . . . . . . . . . . .**82** D2
Berwick St James SP3. .**196** F2
Bishopstone SN6 . . . . . .**163** E6
Bourton SP8. . . . . . . . . .**137** F3
Box SN13 . . . . . . . . . . . . .**83** C5
Broad Blunsdon SN26 . . .**21** E1
Bromham SN15 . . . . . . . .**96** A7
Bulford SP4 . . . . . . . . . .**217** D8
Burbage SN8 . . . . . . . . .**175** C1
Calne SN11 . . . . . . . . . . .**81** B3
Chapmanslade BA13 . .**111** B4
Cheverell Magna SN10 .**179** C1
Chippenham SN15 . . . . .**78** D7
Chiseldown SN4. . . . . . . .**65** D4
Codford BA12. . . . . . . . .**195** A2
Codford St Mary BA12. .**195** A3
Colerne SN14. . . . . . . . . .**75** B3
Collingbourne Ducis
SN8 . . . . . . . . . . . . . . . .**191** E8
Compton Chamberlayne
SP3. . . . . . . . . . . . . . . . .**142** B1
Compton Chamberlayne
SP3. . . . . . . . . . . . . . . . .**205** A8
Corsham SN13. . . . . . . . .**77** A1
Cricklade SN6 . . . . . . . . .**19** E8
Damerham SP6 . . . . . . .**209** F3
Deptford BA12. . . . . . . .**195** E1
Downton SP5 . . . . . . . . .**211** B8
Durrington/Bulford
SP4. . . . . . . . . . . . . . . . .**198** B7
Erlestoke SN10 . . . . . . .**187** A8
Farnham DT11 . . . . . . . .**207** C2
Figheldean SP4 . . . . . . .**190** B1
**24** Fordingbridge SP6 **210** D1
Fovant SP3. . . . . . . . . . .**204** E7
Great Bedwyn SN8 . . . .**176** B3
Great Cheverell SN10 . .**187** B8
Heytesbury BA12. . . . . .**194** C5
Highworth SN6. . . . . . . . .**23** A5
Hindon SP3 . . . . . . . . . .**200** A4
Hinton Charterhouse
BA2 . . . . . . . . . . . . . . . .**98** E1
Hungerford RG17. . . . . .**177** B7
Idmiston SP4 . . . . . . . . .**133** D5
Kempsford GL7 . . . . . . . .**10** C7
Lacock SN15 . . . . . . . . . .**86** D5
Lambourn RG17. . . . . . .**164** F3
Lechlade GL7 . . . . . . . . . . .**2** C4
Limpley Stoke BA2. . . . . .**99** B5
Little Bedwyn SN8 . . . . .**176** D4
Littleton Panell SN10 . .**187** D8
**1** Ludgershall SP11 . .**192** A5
Maiden Bradley with
Yarnfield BA12. . . . . . .**118** A3
Malmesbury SN16 . . . . . .**28** A3
Market Lavington SN10.**179** F1
Marlborough SN8. . . . . .**213** A1
Marshfield SN14 . . . . . . .**74** A8
Melksham SN12. . . . . . . .**94** A4
Meysey Hampton GL7 . . .**1** A5
Netheravon SP4 . . . . . . .**190** A3
Ogbourne St George
SN8 . . . . . . . . . . . . . . . .**168** F5
Pewsey SN9 . . . . . . . . . .**215** D5
Pitton & Farley SP5 . . . .**148** C3
Porton SP4. . . . . . . . . . .**133** D6
Purton SN5. . . . . . . . . . . .**33** B4
Ramsbury SN8 . . . . . . . .**170** B2
Rode BA11. . . . . . . . . . . .**103** F1
Rowde SN10 . . . . . . . . . .**96** D2
Royal Wootton Bassett
SN4 . . . . . . . . . . . . . . . .**47** D1
Salisbury SP1. . . . . . . . .**152** A8
Seend SN12 . . . . . . . . . .**178** E8
Semington BA14 . . . . . .**102** F6
**18** Shaftesbury SP7.. .**202** C1
Sherston SN16. . . . . . . . .**40** C8
Shipton Bellinger SP9 . .**199** D8
Shrewton SP3 . . . . . . . .**196** E7
Sixpenny Handley SP5 .**208** B4
South Cerney GL7 . . . . . . .**6** F6
Steeple Ashton BA14. . .**178** A3
Stourton with Gasper
BA12 . . . . . . . . . . . . . .**123** F1
Sutton Benger SN15 . . . .**57** C2
Sutton Veny BA12 . . . . .**117** F1
Swindon SN25 . . . . . . . . .**34** E4
Swindon SN1 . . . . . . . . . .**50** D4
Tilshead SP3 . . . . . . . . .**188** B2
Tisbury SP3 . . . . . . . . . .**203** E8
Upavon SN9 . . . . . . . . . .**181** F2
Urchfont SN10 . . . . . . . .**180** C4
Vernhams Dean SP11 .**185** C3
Wanborough SN4. . . . . .**163** B6
Warminster BA12 . . . . .**117** A7
Westbury BA13 . . . . . . .**109** A3
West Lavington SN10 . .**179** D1
Winterbourne Stoke
SP3. . . . . . . . . . . . . . . . .**197** A4
Woodgreen SP6. . . . . . .**211** A4
Worton SN10 . . . . . . . . .**179** B4
Wroughton SN4. . . . . . . .**64** A5
Wylye BA12 . . . . . . . . . .**201** E8

**High St** continued
Yatton Keynell SN14 ....68 F5
Zeals SN6............138 A3
**High View Cl** SP3 ...203 E7
**HIGHWAY**.............166 B5
**Highway Comm**
 SN11...............166 B6
**Highway The** SP5.....158 F5
**Highwood** BA12......118 F8
**Highwood Cl 4** SN2.. 34 D4
**HIGHWORTH**............23 B5
**Highworth Ind Est**
 SN6..................23 A7
**Highworth Rd**
 Highworth SN6...... 22 D1
 Shrivenham SN4 ......37 F8
 Shrivenham SN6 ......23 E1
 South Marston SN3.. 36 E6
**Highworth Recn Ctr**
 SN6..................22 F5
**Highworth Warneford**
 Sch SN6.............23 A4
**HILCOTT**..............181 D5
**Hillary Cl** SN25.......35 C4
**Hill Beech Rd** SP9 .. 216 E5
**Hillbourne** BA12 .. 117 B7
**Hill Cl 4** SP3........203 E8
**Hill Cnr Rd** SN15.....70 E2
**HILL CORNER**........110 E7
**Hillcote Hospl** SP1.. 146 C1
**Hillcrest**
 Colerne SN14....... 75 C6
 Malmesbury SN16 .... 28 B2
**Hillcroft** SN11........81 C2
**HILL DEVERILL** ......120 F5
**Hill Deverill Manor** *
 BA12...............120 F5
**Hill Deverill Medieval**
 **Village of** * BA12... 120 F5
**Hilldrop Cl 1** SN8 .. 170 B2
**Hilldrop La**
 Lambourn RG17.....171 A6
 Ramsbury SN8.......169 F3
**Hillfort Mews 1** SP4. 132 C1
**Hill Hayes** SN14...... 41 D2
**Hill Hayes La** SN14....41 E1
**Hillier Cres** SN11 .... 81 D3
**Hillier Rd** SN10 .....214 D6
**Hilliers Yd** SN8 ..... 213 D3
**Hillingdon Rd** SN3....51 B4
**Hillmead Dr** SN5......34 B1
**Hillmead Ent Pk** SN5..49 B8
**Hillocks The** SN4 .....60 B5
**Hill Rd**
 Norton Bavant BA12.. 194 A4
 Pewsey SN9.........215 C3
 Salisbury SP1.......146 E2
 Sutton Veny BA12... 121 F6
**Hill Rise** SN15........70 E2
**Hillside**
 Burcombe SP2.......143 D2
 Leigh SN6........... 18 C5
 Nettleton SN14 .... 53 A4
**Hill Side** SP3.........129 E8
**Hillside Ave** SN1......50 A4
**Hillside Cl**
 Heddington SN11..... 89 B1
 Mere BA12..........138 E5
 West Tytherley SP5... 155 F2
**Hillside Ct** SN1.......50 A4
**Hillside Dr**
 Frome BA11.........110 B4
 Winterbourne SP4....133 D3
**Hillside Pk** BA13..... 109 B3
**Hillside Rd**
 4 Hungerford RG17... 177 B6
 South Newton SP2.... 130 B2
**Hillside Villas** SP10 . 193 D1
**Hillside Way** SN26.....21 A1
**Hill St** BA14.........101 C1
**Hill The**
 Limpley Stoke BA2.... 99 C5
 Little Somerford SN15.. 44 B6
**Hill Top Ave** SN4.... 216 C8
**Hill Top Cl 2** SP3... 196 F6
**Hilltop Cl** SP4...... 190 B2
**Hilltop Rd** BA9.......137 A4
**Hilltop Way** SP1.....146 A5
**Hillview** SP5.........204 C3
**HILL VIEW**...........215 B3
**Hill View**
 Deanland SP5.......208 A5
 Stanton St Bernard
 SN8................173 B1
 Stanton St Bernard
 SN8................181 B8
 9 Swindon SN25.....34 A2
**Hillview Cl** SP4......217 B4
**Hill View Rd**
 6 Salisbury SP1.....152 B8
 Swindon SN3........ 36 C1
**Hill Vw La** SN15......59 D3
**Hillwell** SN16.........15 B2
**Hillwood Cl** BA12....116 F5
**Hillwood La** BA12....116 F5
**Hillwood Rd 15** SN8.. 170 A6
**Hillyard Cl 3** SN5....48 F4
**Hilly Fields** SN13......84 E8
**HILMARTON**..........166 A6
**Hilmarton Ave 1** SN2..35 C5
**Hilmarton Prim Sch**
 SN11...............166 A6
**HILPERTON**..........102 A3
**Hilperton CE VC Prim Sch**
 BA14...............102 A3
**Hilperton Dr** BA14 .. 102 A2
**HILPERTON MARSH** . 101 F5

**Hilperton Rd 1**
 BA14...............101 E1
**Hilton Cl** SN1........50 D6
**Hinde's Meadow** SP3. 196 F7
**HINDON**.............200 B3
**Hindon La**
 Codford St Mary
 BA12...............195 B2
 Tisbury SP3.........200 D1
**Hindon Rd**
 Chilmark SP3.......201 A4
 Chilmark SP3.......201 B3
 East Knoyle SP3..... 141 C2
 Kingston Deverill BA12 126 D7
**Hinkson Cl** SN25......34 F8
**Hinton Cl** SN25........34 E1
**HINTON**
 **CHARTERHOUSE** .....98 E1
**Hinton Hill**
 Bishopstone SN6.... 163 D6
 Hinton Charterhouse
 BA2................ 98 A1
**Hinton Ho** * BA2......98 E1
**Hinton La** BA14...... 178 A5
**HINTON PARVA**.......163 D6
**Hinton Priory** * BA2.. 98 F3
**Hinton Springs** SN6.. 163 D6
**Hinton St** SN2........ 50 D8
**HISOMLEY**...........112 C7
**Hitchings 4** SN6..... 19 D7
**Hitchings Cl** SN16.....28 A6
**Hitchings Skilling**
 SN14................75 B3
**Hitch Rd** SN14....... 35 B8
**Hitcombe Bottom**
 Horningsham BA12...115 D1
 Newbury BA12.......119 D8
**Hither Cl** SN14....... 78 A8
**Hither Spring** SN13.. 84 F8
**Hither Way** SN15..... 86 D5
**Hoadley Gn** SP1.....146 D4
**Hobbes Cl** SN16.......27 F4
**Hobbs Hill** BA14..... 178 B5
**Hobbs Wlk** SN11......77 A1
**Hobhouse Cl** BA15... 100 E4
**Hobley Dr** SN3........36 A3
**Hocketts Cl** SN15..... 60 A3
**Hodds Hill** SN5........34 B2
**Hodge La** SN16........27 F4
**Hodges Barn Gdns** *
 GL8.................26 F8
**Hodges Dr 8** SN16 ... 28 A5
**HODSON**............. 65 A5
**Hodson Rd** SN4....... 65 C4
**HOGGINGTON**.......104 D4
**Hoggington La** BA14. 104 D4
**Hoggs La** SN5......... 33 A4
**Holbein Cl 6** SN5 ....49 A5
**Holbein Ct** SN5.......49 A5
**Holbein Field 12** SN5..49 A5
**Holbein Mews 5** SN5..49 A5
**Holbein Pl** SN5........49 A5
**Holbein Sq 10** SN5....49 A5
**Holbein Wlk 11** SN5...49 A4
**Holborn** SN5..........48 E8
**Holborn Hill** OX12 .. 165 E8
**Holbrook La** BA14.... 105 D6
**Holbrook Prim Sch**
 BA14...............105 D6
**Holbrook Vale** SN12 .. 93 F1
**Holbrook Way** SN1.... 50 B6
**Holcombe La** BA2..... 82 A1
**Holdcroft Cl** SN26.....21 C2
**Holden Cres** SN25.....35 A6
**Holders Rd** SP4......217 C4
**Holford Cres** GL7.....10 E6
**Holinshead Pl 4** SN5. 49 A5
**Holinshed Mews 3**
 SN5.................49 A5
**Holland Cl** SN15......79 A4
**Holland Dr 11** SP10 . 193 D2
**Holliday Cl** SN25...... 35 A6
**Hollies La** BA1........82 A6
**Hollins Moor** SN3.....51 D2
**Hollis Gdns** SN14.....39 E4
**Hollis Way** SN14..... 104 F3
**HOLLOWAY**..........141 A1
**Holloway** SN16........28 A3
**Holloway Cl**
 Amesbury SP4.......217 D1
 Swindon SN25....... 35 A8
**Holloway Hill** SN14 .. 66 E8
**Holloway La** SP3..... 141 B1
**Hollow La** SN8....... 184 A7
**Hollows Cl** SP2...... 151 F6
**Hollow St** SN15........43 F2
**Hollows The** SP2.....144 B4
**Hollow The**
 Bratton BA13....... 186 A7
 Chirton SN10.......180 F4
 Corsley BA12.......111 B1
 Dilton Marsh BA13... 112 C8
 Shrewton SP3.......196 E7
 Sixpenny Handley SP5. 208 A4
 Steeple Langford SP3. 128 C5
**Hollow Way** SN15......59 D3
**Hollybush** BA12...... 119 D6
**Hollybush Cl**
 Acton Turville GL9 ... 53 A6
 Chippenham Without
 SN14................70 A2
 Winsley BA15........99 E7
**Hollybush La**
 Pewsey SN8.........215 C8
 Pewsey SN9.........215 D6
**Hollybush Rd** BA12 .. 117 A8
**Holly Cl**
 Bower Chalke SP5.... 204 F2
 Calne SN11..........81 C1

**Holly Cl** continued
 Pewsey SN9.........215 D6
 Swindon SN2.........35 A2
**Holly Cres 6** SN13....84 E8
**Holly Ct** BA11........110 B7
**Holly Dr** SN14.........74 F6
**Holmbury Cl** BA11... 110 C6
**Holme La 7** BA13.... 186 B7
**Holmes Cl** SN15.......78 F4
**Holmes Rd** SP1......146 D5
**Holmfield**
 1 Littleton Panell
 SN10...............187 E8
 Sherston SN16....... 25 C1
**Holmleigh** SN25.......34 E4
**Holmoak Ct 5** SN3 .. 50 D4
**Holne Rd** SN11........50 A1
**Holst Rd** SN25........34 E8
**HOLT**.................92 E1
**Holt La**
 Tangley SP11....... 193 B8
 Teffont SP3......... 201 C2
 Witham Friary BA11.. 123 C8
**Holt Rd**
 Bradford-on-Avon
 BA15...............100 E6
 Bradford-on-Avon
 BA15...............101 A7
 Witham Friary BA11.. 123 C8
**Holt VC Prim Sch**
 BA14................92 F1
**HOLWELL**............139 B5
**Holy Cross Catholic Prim**
 Sch SN3............. 50 D5
**Holy Family Cath Prim**
 Sch SN3............. 51 B6
**Holy Rd Church** * SN3.50 E4
**Holy Rood Cath Inf Sch**
 SN1................. 50 C5
**Holyrood Cl** BA15... 105 B5
**Holy Trinity CE Acad**
 SN11................81 C1
**Holy Trinity CE Prim**
 **Acad** BA13......... 187 B8
**Holy Trinity CE Prim**
 **Acad The** SN10..... 187 B8
**Home Cl**
 Chiseldown SN4..... 65 C4
 Fovant SP3......... 204 D8
 Trowbridge BA14... 105 D7
**Homefarm** SN6........22 F6
**Home Farm Cl**
 Heddington SN11..... 89 B1
 Mildenhall SN8......175 D8
 Steeple Ashton BA14. 178 A3
**Home Farm Gdns 10**
 SP10...............193 C2
**Home Farm La** SN6... 22 B7
**Home Farm Rd** SP2 .. 144 C1
**Homefield**
 Mere BA12..........138 F5
 Motcombe SP7......202 C2
 Royal Wootton Bassett
 SN4................ 47 E2
**Homefields**
 Longbridge Deverill
 BA12...............120 F6
 Marlborough SN8... 213 F2
**Home Fields** SN14..... 68 F5
**Homefield Way** RG17. 177 B7
**Home Gd**
 Cricklade SN6....... 19 C8
 Swindon SN2........ 35 E6
**Homelands The 1**
 BA12...............116 E5
**Home Mead 5** SN13.. 76 E1
**Home Mill Bldgs**
 BA14...............105 D8
**Homes Mead 7** SN13. 76 D1
**Homestead Cl** SN14.. 78 A4
**HOMINGTON**.........151 D1
**Homington Rd**
 Britford SP5........151 D3
 Coombe Bissett SP5. 151 A1
 Coombe Bissett SP5. 157 B8
**Honeybone Cl** GL7......1 F6
**Honeybone Wlk** SN3.. 51 D7
**Honeybrook Cl** SN14.. 78 B8
**Honeybunch Cnr**
 SN8................164 C6
**Honeyfields 10** RG17. 177 B7
**Honey Garston** SN11. 81 C3
**Honey Hill 2** RG17... 165 A2
**Honey Knob Hill** SN14..55 F1
**Honey La**
 Norton SN16........ 41 E6
 Westbury BA13..... 112 D8
**Honeylight View 3**
 SN25................35 A6
**Honeymans Cl** BA14 . 105 F8
**Honeymead** SN11.... 81 C3
**Honey Pot La** BA11 .. 118 B7
**Honeysuckle Cl**
 Calne Without SN11...80 F4
 Chippenham Without
 SN14................70 B3
 Melksham SN12..... 94 D4
 Swindon SN25...... 34 D5
 4 Trowbridge BA14. 105 E7
**Honiton Rd** SN3.......51 B5
**HOOK**................34 A1
**Hook Cl** SN5..........34 A1
**Hooks Hill** SN5........33 C4
**Hooks La** SN10...... 179 A7
**Hook St**
 Hook SN4............47 F6

**Hook St** continued
 Swindon SN5........48 F4
**HOOK STREET**.........48 F4
**Hookwood La** SP11 .. 192 E8
**Hoopers Pl** SN1........50 D4
**Hop Gdns The** SP5... 161 C3
**Hopgood Cl** SN10.... 214 F6
**Hopkinson Way**
 SP10...............193 B1
**Hoppingstones** SN11. 166 B6
**Hops Cl** SP3......... 201 A3
**Hopton Cl** SN5........49 B3
**Hopton Pk Ind Est**
 SN10...............214 E7
**Hopton Rd** SN10..... 214 D6
**Horace St** SN2........49 F7
**Horcott Rd**
 Fairford GL7..........1 F6
 Peatmoor SN5...... 34 B2
 Swindon SN5....... 34 A2
**Horder Mews** SN3..... 50 D4
**Horefield** SP4........133 E7
**Horham Cres** SN3..... 51 A4
**Hornbeam Cl 1**
 BA11...............110 C6
**Hornbeam Cres** SN12. 94 A3
**Hornbeam Ct** SN2..... 35 B2
**Hornbeam Rd** BA14.. 105 C5
**Hornbury Cl** SN16.....17 A2
**Hornbury Hill**
 Minety SN16........ 17 A2
 Upper Minety SN16... 16 E2
**Hornchurch Rd 20**
 SN2................178 B8
**Horne Cl** SN25........ 20 D1
**Hornell Cl 5** SP4.....132 B1
**Horne Rd** SP4....... 198 E6
**HORNINGSHAM**.......115 B7
**Horningsham Prim Sch**
 BA12...............115 B7
**Hornsey Gdns** SN2....36 A5
**Horn's La** SN4.......167 B8
**HORPIT**.............. 163 B7
**Horsdown** SN14....... 53 C4
**Horse Barrow** * SP4. 133 D3
**Horsebrook Pk** SN11.. 81 B2
**Horsebrook The** SN11. 81 C2
**Horsefair La** SN15..... 59 C3
**Horse Fair La** SN6.....19 E8
**Horse La** SN15........96 C4
**Horse Leaze** SN10 .. 214 F6
**Horsell Cl 2** SN4......47 E2
**Horseponds 8** SP7... 202 B2
**Horsepool** SN15...... 96 B8
**Horse Rd** BA14...... 101 F4
**Horseshoe Cl 1**
 BA14...............102 B2
**Horseshoe Cres** SN5.. 34 A1
**Horseshoe La** SP11 .. 193 F8
**Horse Shoe La** SP3 .. 142 C3
**Horseshoe Sq** SN26... 21 C2
**Horsey Down** SN6 .... 19 C8
**Horsington La** SP8.... 139 B1
**Horsley Cl 2** SN25.... 34 B8
**Horta Cl** SN26........ 20 D1
**HORTON**.............172 C2
**Horton Ave** SN10 ... 214 E6
**Horton Cl** BA15...... 100 E4
**Horton Rd**
 Bishops Cannings
 SN10...............172 B2
 Devizes SN10.......214 F7
 Swindon SN2....... 35 E6
**Horton Way** SN4..... 167 C7
**Hospital of St John**
 BA12...............194 C5
**Hospital Rd** BA13 ... 109 A2
**Hossil La** SN6.........22 B1
**Houghton Cl** BA12... 117 C6
**Houldsworth Ave**
 BA12...............117 D8
**House Field** SN25.....34 A3
**Howard Cl** SN3........50 F6
**Howard-Vyse Rd**
 SP4................197 F7
**Howgare Rd**
 Broad Chalke SP5... 205 B2
 Broad Chalke SP5... 208 F8
**Howse Gdn** SN2.......50 A8
**Hreod Parkway Sch**
 SN2.................34 E3
**Hubble View** SN25.....34 A8
**Hubert Hamilton Rd**
 SP4................198 E6
**Huddleston Cl** SN2.... 50 D8
**Hudds Mill La** BA13 . 186 B8
**Hudson Rd**
 Amesbury SP4.......217 C4
 Malmesbury SN16.....27 F4
 Salisbury SP1....... 145 F3
**Hudson Way** SN25.... 35 A5
**HUDSWELL**............84 C8
**Hudswell La** SN13..... 84 C8
**Hughes Cl** SN8...... 213 A2
**Hughes St** SN2........49 F7
**Hugo Dr** SN25........ 35 A6
**HUISH**...............174 A2
**Hulbert Cl**
 Corsham SN13....... 76 E1
 6 Chippenham BA14 . 101 F1
 4 Trowbridge BA14. 105 E7
**HULLAVINGTON**.......41 E1
**Hullavington Airfield**
 SN14................56 A7
**Hullavington CE Prim Sch**
 SN14................41 F1
**Hull Rd 4** SN2........34 E2
**Hulse Rd** SP1........146 A2
**Humber La** SP9...... 216 B4

**Hummingbird Gdns**
 BA14...............105 E6
**Humphrey's La 3**
 RG17...............171 E7
**Hungerdown La** SN14..78 A6
**HUNGERFORD** ...... 177 A6
**Hungerford Ave**
 BA14...............105 A7
**Hungerford Hill**
 Great Shefford RG17. 171 F4
 Lambourn RG17.....165 A1
**Hungerford La**
 Andover SP10....... 193 E3
 Chute SP11.........185 A1
 Kintbury RG17......177 F6
 Lake SP4...........197 E1
 Tangley SP11....... 193 A8
**Hungerford Leisure Ctr**
 RG17...............177 B6
**HUNGERFORD**
 **NEWTOWN** ....... 171 D2
**Hungerford Prim Sch**
 RG17...............177 B7
**Hungerford Rd**
 Buttermere SN8.....185 B7
 Calne SN11.........81 B4
 Chippenham SN15.... 70 D1
 Grafton SN8........184 A7
 Hungerford RG17.... 177 D6
 Kintbury RG17......177 F5
**Hungerford Sta**
 RG17...............177 C7
**Hunsdon Cl** SN3......51 A6
**Hunt Cl The** BA14 .. 102 F5
**HUNTENHULL**
 **GREEN** ........... 111 C3
**Huntenhull La** BA13.. 111 D4
**Hunter Cl** SN11...... 81 D3
**Hunters Chase** BA13. 108 F2
**Huntersfield** SN16.... 25 D1
**Hunters Field** SN14.. 78 A4
**Hunter's Gr** SN2..... 35 B1
**Hunters Mead** SP7... 202 A5
**Hunters Meadow**
 SN14................68 F5
**Huntingdon Pl** BA15. 100 C7
**Huntingdon Rise**
 BA15...............100 C7
**Huntingdon St** BA15 . 100 C8
**Huntingdon Way** SN14 78 A6
**Huntingfield** BA14... 106 A7
**Huntingford Rd** SP8 . 138 F1
**Huntley Cl** SN3.......50 F7
**Hunts Hill** SN26...... 21 B2
**Huntsland** SN4....... 47 F2
**Hunts Mead** SN15.....96 A7
**Hunts Mill Rd** SN4....61 A8
**Hunts Rise** SN3...... 36 C7
**Hunt St** SN1.........50 C5
**HURDCOTT**...........146 F8
**Hurdcott Field** SP4 . 132 D2
**Hurdcott La**
 Winterbourne SP4... 146 F8
 Winterbourne Earls
 SP4................133 A1
**Hurley Cl 5** SP4.....217 D3
**Hurly La** SN9........ 215 D4
**Hurricane Dr** SN11.... 81 D3
**Hurricane Rd** SN12...94 C1
**Hurst Cres** SN2...... 35 C3
**Hurst's La** SN9...... 181 C7
**Hutton Cl**
 Trowbridge BA14.... 102 B1
 Trowbridge BA14.... 106 B8
**Huxley Cl** GL7.........7 A7
**Hyam Cotts** SN16.....27 C4
**HYDE**................ 35 D7
**Hyde Cross** SP6..... 209 D1
**Hyde La**
 Marlborough SN8... 213 C3
 Purton SN5......... 33 C4
**Hyde Rd**
 Royal Wootton Bassett
 SN4................ 47 F1
 Swindon SN2........ 35 D6
 Trowbridge BA14... 101 C2
**Hyde The** SN5....... 33 D4
**Hylder Cl** SN2....... 34 D4
**Hyson Cres 6** SP11 . 192 B5
**Hysopp Cl** SN2...... 34 C4
**Hythe Rd** SN1........50 B5

**I**

**IBTHORPE** .......... 193 F8
**Icknield Sch** SP10 .. 193 F1
**Icknield Way**
 Andover SP10....... 193 E2
 Bishopstone SN6.... 163 E6
**Icomb Cl** SN5........49 C4
**Idlebush Barrow** *
 SN7................164 E7
**IDMISTON**........... 133 F8
**Idmiston Rd** SP4.... 133 E6
**Idovers Dr** SN5...... 49 C4
**IDSTONE**............ 163 F7
**Idstone Hill** SN6.... 163 F7
**Idstone Rd** SN6..... 164 A7
**Ittley Rd** SN2....... 49 F8
**Iford Fields**
 Westwood BA15..... 99 E2
 Westwood BA15..... 99 E3
**Iford Hill** BA15...... 99 E3
**Iford La**
 Freshford BA15..... 99 D3
 Westwood BA2...... 99 D2
 Iford Manor * BA15...99 E3

**Iles Ct** SN11......... 73 F7
**Ilett Cres** SN25...... 20 B1
**Ilkeston Rd** SN25.....34 C7
**Ilynton Ave** SP5..... 148 C7
**Image Rd** SN26...... 20 C1
**IMBER**.............. 187 A3
**Imber Ave**
 Amesbury SP4....... 217 D2
 Warminster BA12.... 117 C7
**Imber Pl** SP3....... 188 B3
**Imber Rd**
 Bratton BA12....... 186 C6
 10 Shaftesbury SP7.. 202 D2
 Warminster BA12.... 117 D8
**Imber Wlk Rear** SN2.. 35 B6
**Imberwood Cl** BA12.. 117 C7
**Imby Cl** BA12....... 117 F1
**Imperial Way** BA11.. 110 D7
**India Ave** SP2....... 145 E2
**Indigo Gdns** BA13... 108 F3
**Indigo La** BA13..... 108 F3
**Ingles Edge** RG17... 177 E2
**INGLESHAM**............2 B1
**Inglesham Cl 3**
 BA14...............105 D5
**Inglesham Rd 5**......35 C4
**Inglesham Village** *
 SN6..................2 B1
**Inglewood Rd** RG17.. 177 E5
**Ingram Pl** BA13..... 108 F4
**Ingram Rd** SN12..... 94 D5
**Ingram St** SN16...... 28 A3
**INKPEN**............. 177 E3
**Inkpen Community Prim**
 Sch RG17........... 177 E3
**Inkpen Rd** RG17.... 177 C5
**Inlands Cl** SN9...... 215 C5
**Inmarsh La** SN12.... 178 E7
**Inmead** BA13....... 186 C8
**Innox Mill Cl** BA14 .. 101 B1
**Innox Rd** BA14...... 101 B1
**Intercity Trad Est**
 SN12................94 A5
**Interface Distribution Pk**
 SN4.................47 F1
**Inverary Rd** SN4......64 A7
**Ipswich St** SN2...... 50 C8
**IRELAND**............105 B2
**Ironstone Cl** SN25....34 E7
**Irston Way 4** SN5....49 B4
**Irvine Cl** SN26....... 20 D2
**Irving Way** SN8..... 213 C3
**Isambard Com Sch**
 SN25................34 D7
**Isambard Way** SN25 . 34 D7
**Isbury Rd** SN8...... 213 E2
**Isis Cl**
 Calne SN11......... 81 A4
 Swindon SN25...... 35 A3
**Islandsmead** SN3.....51 C6
**Island The** SN10.... 214 B3
**Islay Cres** SN6....... 22 F6
**Isles Rd 6** SN8..... 170 B2
**Islington** BA14...... 101 D1
**Islington St** SN1...... 50 C6
**Itchen Cl 2** SO51.... 212 F6
**Ivies The** SN9....... 181 F5
**IVY CROSS**.......... 202 D2
**Ivy Fields** SN13......77 A2
**Ivy La**
 Broad Blunsdon SN26. 21 B2
 Chippenham SN15.... 78 D7
 South Wraxall BA15... 91 E5
**Ivy La Prim Sch** SN15. 78 D7
**Ivy Mead** BA12..... 139 B5
**Ivy Rd** SN15......... 78 D7
**Ivy Rd Ind Est** SN15 . 78 D7
**Ivy St** SP1.......... 152 B8
**Ivy Terr** BA15....... 100 D7
**Ixworth Cl 10** SN5....49 A7

**J**

**Jackaments Barn** GL7....4 B6
**Jacklins Cl** BA14..... 101 F5
**Jack Paul Cl** BA12 .. 139 A6
**Jack's Hedge Cnr**
 BH21...............208 F2
**Jacksom's La** SN15 ... 70 D5
**Jackson Cl**
 3 Corsham SN13.....84 F8
 Devizes SN10.......214 C2
**Jack Thorne Cl 4**
 SN5.................34 A2
**Jacob Cl 22** SP11 ... 193 F2
**Jacob's Barrow** *
 SP5................211 E4
**Jacobs Piece** GL7......1 E6
**Jacobs Wlk** SN3......51 D4
**Jacob Way** BA12.... 116 D7
**Jade Cl** SN25........ 20 F1
**Jagdalik Rd** SP9.... 216 C4
**Jaggards La** SN13 .... 84 D5
**Jaggard Way** SP4 ... 217 C3
**Jagoda Ct 7** SN25... 34 D6
**James Ave** SN11...... 81 D3
**James Cl** SN15........79 A4
**James Rd** SP4....... 217 C4
**James's Hill** BA10 .. 122 A7
**James St**
 Salisbury SP1....... 145 F1
 Trowbridge BA14... 101 D2
**James Watt Cl** SN2 .. 50 A7
**Jamrud Rd** SP9..... 216 B5

**Janesmoor Plain Rd**
SO43. . . . . . . . . . . . . . **212** B1
Janus Rd SN26. . . . . . . **21** A1
Jarvis St SN9. . . . . . . **181** F2
**Jasmine Cl**
Calne SN11. . . . . . . . . **81** B1
Chippenham SN14. . . . . **70** A1
Swindon SN2. . . . . . . . **34** D4
Jasmine Way BA14 . . . **105** E7
Jason Cl SN25. . . . . . . **34** A7
Jasper Cl SN5. . . . . . . **20** F1
Javelin Cl **6** SP4 . . . . **217** D3
Jay Cl BA11. . . . . . . . **110** B6
Jay Dr SP4 . . . . . . . . . **132** C1
Jeanneau Cl **24** SP7. . **202** C2
Jebb Cl SN26. . . . . . . . **20** D1
Jefferies Ave SN2. . . . . **35** D2
Jefferies Cl SN8 . . . . . **213** B2
Jeffreycl SN26. . . . . . . **20** D1
Jekyll Cl SN25. . . . . . . **20** C1
Jellicoe Cl SP10 . . . . . **193** F1
Jenkins Cl SN26 . . . . . . **21** D2
Jenkins St BA14 . . . . . **101** C1
Jenner Cl SN4. . . . . . . **163** A6
Jenner La **4** BA14. . . . **28** A5
Jenners Yard SN6 . . . . . **19** C8
**Jenni Manners Ct 2**
SN5. . . . . . . . . . . . . . . **49** D6
Jennings St SN2. . . . . . **49** F6
Jenson Ave BA11. . . . . **110** D8
**Jerram Gall The ★**
SP1. . . . . . . . . . . . . . **152** B8
Jersey Hill BA12. . . . . **116** D1
Jersey Pk SN5. . . . . . . . **49** B8
Jervis Ct **1** SN10 . . . . **193** F1
Jewel Cl **2** SN5. . . . . . **48** F5
Jewell Cl SN11. . . . . . . **146** D4
Joanna Cl **4** SP5 . . . . **210** F8
Jobbers La SP3 . . . . . . **203** E7
Jockey La SN15. . . . . . . **96** A7
John Alder Cl SN4 . . . . **65** C3
John Aubrey Cl SN14 . . **68** F6
**John Bentley Sch**
SN11. . . . . . . . . . . . . **89** B8
**John Betjeman Cl 1**
SN16. . . . . . . . . . . . . . **28** A5
**John French Way**
SP4. . . . . . . . . . . . . . **217** E8
John Gay Rd **5** SP4. . **217** B3
**John Herring Cres**
SN3. . . . . . . . . . . . . . . **36** A1
**John Ivie Ctr Pru**
SP1. . . . . . . . . . . . . . **152** B8
John of Gaunt Rd GL7. . **10** D6
**John of Gaunt Sch The**
BA14. . . . . . . . . . . . . **105** B4
**John O'Gaunt Sch**
RG17. . . . . . . . . . . . . **177** B6
**John Rennie Cl**
Bradford-on-Avon
BA15 . . . . . . . . . . . . **100** E4
Devizes SN10. . . . . . . **214** A2
**John Rumble Cl**
SN10. . . . . . . . . . . . . **214** C3
**John Ruskin Rd**
Swindon SN25. . . . . . . **34** C8
Swindon SN26. . . . . . . **20** D1
**Johnson Way 35**
SP11. . . . . . . . . . . . . **192** A5
John St SN1. . . . . . . . . **50** B6
Joiner La SN1 . . . . . . . . **50** D4
Jole Cl SN2. . . . . . . . . . **35** E5
Joles La BA11. . . . . . . **110** F1
Jolliffe St **7** SN1. . . . . **50** A5
Jones Cl SP2 . . . . . . . . **144** F4
Jones Hill BA15. . . . . . **100** C5
Jones La SP9 . . . . . . . . **216** D8
**Jone's Mill Nature
Reserve ★** SN9 . . . . **215** D7
Jopp Cl **9** SN5. . . . . . . **34** C5
Jordan Cl SN1. . . . . . . . **78** F5
Joseph St **4** SN1. . . . . **50** A5
Joule Rd **3** SP10 . . . . **193** B1
Joyce Cl SN5. . . . . . . . . **35** A6
Jubb's La SN8 . . . . . . . **169** A5
**Jubilee Cl**
Bermerton Heath
SP2. . . . . . . . . . . . . . **145** C3
**3** Sandleheath SP6 . . **210** C1
Westbury BA13 . . . . . **109** A3
**Jubilee Ct**
North Tidworth SP9 . . . **216** C1
**3** Salisbury SP2. . . . . **145** F2
Jubilee Est SN5. . . . . . . **33** C5
Jubilee Gdns GL7. . . . . . **6** F7
Jubilee Hill SP4 . . . . . **197** F1
**Jubilee Rd**
Chippenham SN15. . . . . **70** E1
Devizes SN10. . . . . . . **214** D3
Sandleheath SP6 . . . . . **210** C1
Swindon SN2. . . . . . . . **34** D3
Jubilee Terr SP2 . . . . . **130** B2
Juggler's La SN11. . . . . **166** C2
Juliana Cl **2** SN5. . . . . **49** A7
Jump Farm SN10 . . . . . **214** D3
Jump Farm Rd SN10. . . **214** C3
**Junction Rd**
Alderbury SP5 . . . . . . . **153** C2
Bradford-on-Avon
BA15 . . . . . . . . . . . . **100** D6
**Juniper Cl**
Calne SN11 . . . . . . . . . **81** D5
Swindon SN3. . . . . . . . **51** B8
Juniper Dr SP1 . . . . . . **146** A5
Juniper Rd SP5 . . . . . . **148** C7

**Juno Gdns** SN6. . . . . . **22** F4
Juno Way SN1. . . . . . . . **49** F4
Jupiter Cl SN26. . . . . . . **21** A1
Jutland Ave SN25 . . . . . **35** D3
**Jutland Cres 3**
SP10 . . . . . . . . . . . . . **193** D2

**K**

Kandahar SN8. . . . . . . **170** A7
Kandy Rd **3** SP4. . . . . **198** E6
Karachi Cl SP9. . . . . . . **216** C7
Karslake Cl SN3. . . . . . . **51** C4
Kashmir Rd **1** SP4. . . **198** E6
**Katherine House Gall ★**
SN8. . . . . . . . . . . . . . **213** E2
Katherine's Wlk GL7. . . . . **2** D4
Katifer La SN16. . . . . . . **28** A3
Kavanagh Cl **10** SP7. . **202** D1
Keates Cl BA14 . . . . . . **101** D1
**Keats Cl**
**3** Melksham SN12. . . . **94** B4
Royal Wootton Bassett
SN4 . . . . . . . . . . . . . . **47** F3
Keats Cres SN2 . . . . . . . **35** F4
Keats Mdw SP5. . . . . . **208** B4
**Keble Cl**
Lechlade GL7. . . . . . . . . **2** D5
Swindon SN3 . . . . . . . . **51** C7
**Keel Cl**
Amesbury SP4 . . . . . . **217** C2
Middle Winterslow SP5 **149** B7
Keels SN6. . . . . . . . . . . **8** C1
Keepers Rd SN10 . . . . **214** C5
KEEVIL . . . . . . . . . . . **178** C5
Keevil Airfield BA14. . **178** C4
**Keevil CE Prim Sch**
BA14. . . . . . . . . . . . . **178** B5
Kelham Cl **8** SN3. . . . . . **50** F4
Kelham Gdns SN8 . . . **213** E3
Kelk Cres SP9 . . . . . . . **216** D8
KELLAWAYS . . . . . . . . . **71** E4
Kellsboro Ave SN4. . . . . **63** F7
Kelly Cl SN12. . . . . . . . . **93** F1
Kelly Gdns SN25 . . . . . . **34** F6
Kelmscot Rd SN25. . . . . **35** C3
Kelmscott Rd GL7 . . . . . . **2** F3
Kelsey Rd SP1. . . . . . . **146** B1
Kelso Ct **3** SN14. . . . . . **78** A5
Kelston Rd SN3. . . . . . **176** C4
Kelvin Rd SN3. . . . . . . . **51** A7
KEMBLE . . . . . . . . . . . . . **4** E7
**Kemble Bsns Pk** GL7. . . **4** A3
**Kemble Dr**
Swindon SN2. . . . . . . . **50** A7
Swindon SN5. . . . . . . . **49** F7
**Kemble Enterprise Pk**
GL7. . . . . . . . . . . . . . . **4** A6
Kemble Rd GL7. . . . . . . . **4** B8
Kembles Cl SN16. . . . . . **28** C2
Kemble Sta GL7 . . . . . . . **4** B8
**KEMBLE WICK** . . . . . . . . **4** E4
Kemerton Wlk SN3 . . . . **51** A3
Kemmel Rd SP11 . . . . **191** F4
Kemp Cl SN10 . . . . . . . **214** C3
Kempe La SN26. . . . . . . **20** D1
**Kempsfield** SN10 . . . . **214** C1
KEMPSFORD. . . . . . . . **10** E6
**Kempsford CE Prim Sch**
GL7. . . . . . . . . . . . . . **10** C7
Kemp's La BA11 . . . . . **110** F7
**Kempton Pk Ct 10**
SN14. . . . . . . . . . . . . . **77** F6
Kencot Ct **5** SN3. . . . . . **35** C6
Kendal SN5. . . . . . . . . . **49** B4
Kendall La BA14 . . . . . **102** E5
Kendrick Cl BA13. . . . . **109** A3
Kendrick Ind Est SN2 . . **49** E8
Kenilworth Gdns SN12 **94** B3
**Kenilworth Lawns**
SN3. . . . . . . . . . . . . . . **50** F3
Kenley Cl SN12. . . . . . . **94** E1
Kennedy Ave SN12. . . . . **85** D1
Kennedy Dr SN3 . . . . . . **51** D4
**Kennedy Meadow**
RG17. . . . . . . . . . . . . **177** B6
Kennel Dr GL9. . . . . . . . **38** E2
Kennet Ave SN25. . . . . . **35** B3
**Kennet & Avon Canal
Mus The ★** SN10 . . . **214** B4
**Kennet Cl**
Melksham SN12 . . . . . . **94** A6
Warminster BA12 . . . . **117** A5
Kennet Gdns BA15. . . . **100** D5
Kennet Mews SN8 . . . . **213** D3
Kennet Pl SN8. . . . . . . **213** E3
**Kennet Rd**
Devizes SN10. . . . . . . **214** C2
South Tedworth SP9. . . **216** E6
Wroughton SN4. . . . . . . **64** A7
**Kennett Valley CE Prim
Sch** SN8. . . . . . . . . . **173** D8
**Kennet Valley CE Prim
Sch** SN8. . . . . . . . . . **174** A6
**Kennet Valley Mews**
SN8. . . . . . . . . . . . . . **169** D1
**Kennet Way**
Hungerford RG17. . . . . **177** B8
Hungerford RG17. . . . . **177** C8
Trowbridge BA14. . . . . **101** D3
Ken Savage Cl SN4 . . . . **51** A6
Kensington Cl BA14. . . **101** D2
**Kensington Fields**
BA14. . . . . . . . . . . . . **104** F7

**Kensington Rd 1**
SP2. . . . . . . . . . . . . . **145** F2
Kensington Way SN14 . **77** F7
Kent Cl SN14. . . . . . . . . **78** A6
Kent End SN6. . . . . . . . . **7** A1
Kent End Cl SN6 . . . . . . . **7** A1
Kent End Field SN6 . . . . . **7** A1
Kenton Cl SN3. . . . . . . . **51** B6
Kenton Dr BA14. . . . . . **101** F1
**Kent Rd**
Salisbury SP2. . . . . . . **151** E6
Swindon SN1. . . . . . . . **50** B4
Kents Hill SP3. . . . . . . **201** A3
Kenwin Cl SN3 . . . . . . . **36** B2
Kenwood Cl BA14. . . . . **105** F8
Keohler Cl SN26. . . . . . . **20** C2
KEPNAL . . . . . . . . . . . **215** E5
Kerby Ave SP4. . . . . . . **190** B3
Kerrs Way SN4 . . . . . . . **64** A6
**Kerry Cl**
Derry Hill/Studley
SN11 . . . . . . . . . . . . . **79** F2
Swindon SN5. . . . . . . . **49** A7
Kershaw Rd SN3. . . . . . **51** B8
Kestrel Ave BA14 . . . . **105** E6
**Kestrel Cl**
Calne SN11 . . . . . . . . . **81** A5
Warminster BA12 . . . . **116** D6
**Kestrel Dr**
Swindon SN3 . . . . . . . . **51** E6
**4** Winterbourne SP4 . **132** C1
Keswick Rd SN3. . . . . . **51** B3
Kettle La SN3. . . . . . . . **106** A2
Ketton Cl BA14. . . . . . . **101** A1
Kew Dr **4** BA14. . . . . . **105** A7
Kewlake La SO51. . . . . **212** F1
**Keyneston Rd**
Swindon SN3. . . . . . . . **50** F5
Swindon SN3. . . . . . . . **51** C6
Keynsham Wlk SN3. . . . **51** B4
Khyro Cl BA12 . . . . . . . **116** F5
Kibblewhite Cl SN5. . . . **33** B3
Kickdom Cl SP4. . . . . . **217** D2
Kidston Way SN13 . . . . . **84** A8
Kiel Dr SP10. . . . . . . . . **193** D2
Kilben Cl SN5. . . . . . . . . **48** F7
Kilby Cres SN5. . . . . . . . **35** A8
Kilda Rd SN6. . . . . . . . . **22** E7
Kilford Cl SP4. . . . . . . . **217** C1
**Kill Barrow (Long
Barrow) ★** BA12 . . . **187** D3
KILMINGTON . . . . . . . **123** E5
**Kilmington Comm**
BA12. . . . . . . . . . . . . **123** E5
**KILMINGTON
COMMON.** . . . . . . . . **123** D4
**Kiln Cl**
Alderbury SP5 . . . . . . **153** F1
Devizes SN10 . . . . . . . **214** D3
**Kiln La**
Redlynch SP5. . . . . . . **211** D8
Swindon SN4. . . . . . . . **34** F1
Kilns The SN11. . . . . . . **81** C4
Kilsby Dr SN3. . . . . . . . **51** B8
Kilsyth Cl SN5 . . . . . . . . **49** B5
Kilve Cl SN3. . . . . . . . . **51** B6
Kilverts Cl SN14 . . . . . . **78** A6
Kimber Cl SP9. . . . . . . **216** C7
Kimberley Rd SN3 . . . . . **51** A4
**Kimbers Field 16**
SN4. . . . . . . . . . . . . . **163** A6
Kimbolton Cl **6** SN5. . . **49** A4
Kimmeridge Cl SN5. . . . **51** C6
KIMPTON. . . . . . . . . . **192** C1
**Kimpton Thruxton &
Fyfield CE Prim Sch**
SP11. . . . . . . . . . . . . **192** C1
King Alfred Cl SN9. . . . **215** D5
King Alfreds Cl BA12. . **126** B7
King Alfred St SN15. . . . **78** C8
**King Alfred's Way**
SP7. . . . . . . . . . . . . . **202** C2
King Alfred Way BA15. . **99** D7
King Arthur's Way
SP10 . . . . . . . . . . . . . **193** E2
**King Barrow ★**
Bishopstone BA12. . . . **117** F5
Winterbourne Stoke
SP4. . . . . . . . . . . . . . **197** C4
King Charles Rd SN11 . . **81** C4
Kingdom Ave BA13 . . . **108** D5
**Kingdom Cres 1**
SN25. . . . . . . . . . . . . . **34** D8
Kingdom Sch BA12 . . . **117** D6
King Edward Cl SN11. . . **81** B4
**Kingfisher CE Acad**
SN1. . . . . . . . . . . . . . . **49** E4
**Kingfisher Cl**
Salisbury SP2. . . . . . . **152** A5
Trowbridge BA14. . . . . **105** E6
Kingfisher Ct **7** SN11. . **81** B5
**Kingfisher Dr**
Bower Hill SN12. . . . . . **94** D1
Devizes SN10. . . . . . . **214** E5
**7** Durrington/Bulford
SP4. . . . . . . . . . . . . . **198** C7
Swindon SN3 . . . . . . . . **51** D7
Westbury BA13. . . . . . **109** A4
Kingfisher Pl GL7. . . . . . **7** B7
Kingfishers **2** SP9. . . **199** D8
Kingham Cl SN14 . . . . . **78** B6
**King Henry Dr**
Chippenham SN15. . . . . **79** A4
Swindon SN5. . . . . . . . **48** F4

**King John St 3** SN1. . **50** D4
King La BA12. . . . . . . . **116** E5
**King Oak ★** SN8. . . . . **175** C4
**Kings Ave**
Chippenham Without
SN14 . . . . . . . . . . . . . **77** F6
Corsham SN13 . . . . . . . **76** F2
Highworth SN6. . . . . . . **23** A5
Kingsbere La **5** SP7. . **202** D2
Kingsbourne Cl SP4 . . **133** B1
Kingsbury Cl SN12. . . . . **94** B3
Kingsbury Sq **3** SP2. . **144** D3
**Kingsbury St**
Calne SN11 . . . . . . . . . **81** B2
Marlborough SN8. . . . . **213** D3
Kings Cl **3** SN6. . . . . . **164** A8
Kings Cnr SN9. . . . . . . **215** D4
Kingscote Cl **1** SN5. . . **48** F8
Kings Ct **5** BA12 . . . . . **116** E5
KINGSDOWN
Box. . . . . . . . . . . . . . . . **82** F3
Stratton St Margaret. . . **35** F5
**Kingsdown Gr** BA1. . . . **82** F2
**Kingsdown Ind Est**
SN2. . . . . . . . . . . . . . . **36** A6
Kingsdown La SN25. . . . **35** D8
**Kingsdown Rd**
Stratton St Margaret
SN2. . . . . . . . . . . . . . . **36** A6
Swindon SN2. . . . . . . . **35** F5
**3** Trowbridge BA14 . . **105** C5
Kingsdown Sch SN2 . . . **35** F5
Kings Dr SN8. . . . . . . . **175** C8
Kingsettle Hill BA10. . **122** C2
Kingsfield SN15 . . . . . . **100** D7
**Kingsfield Grange Rd**
BA15. . . . . . . . . . . . . **100** E7
**Kingsfield Leaze**
BA15. . . . . . . . . . . . . **100** F6
Kingsford Cl **9** SP5. . . **211** C7
Kings Gate SP2. . . . . . **144** E4
Kings Gdns BA14 . . . . . **101** E5
KINGSHILL . . . . . . . . . . **50** B5
Kings Hill **18** SP7 . . . . **202** C2
Kingshill Rd SN1. . . . . . **50** A4
**King's House ★** SP1. . **152** A7
King's La SP3. . . . . . . . **203** F5
**7** Shaftesbury SP7. . . **202** B2
Knap The BA14 . . . . . . **102** A3
KINGTON. . . . . . . . . . **170** D2
**Knighton Barrow (Long
Barrow) ★** SP4 . . . . **197** E8
Knighton Rd SP5 . . . . . **205** C4
**Knightsbridge Rd**
SP11. . . . . . . . . . . . . **193** F4
**Knights Cl**
**1** Chippenham SN15. . **78** F4
West Overton SN8 . . . . **173** F6
KNIGHTS ENHAM. . . . **193** E3
**Knights Enham Prim Sch**
SP10. . . . . . . . . . . . . **193** E2
**Knights Maltings**
BA11. . . . . . . . . . . . . **110** A3
KNOCKDOWN. . . . . . . . **24** F5
**Knockdown Rd**
Sherston GL9. . . . . . . . **25** B2
Sherston SN16. . . . . . . **25** C1
Knole Cl **4** SN25. . . . . . **34** F7
Knoll Cl OX12. . . . . . . **165** F8
**Knoll The**
**12** Aldbourne SN8. . . . **170** A6
Kempsford GL7 . . . . . . **10** D7
Malmesbury SN16 . . . . **28** B2
Westbury BA13. . . . . . **109** B4
Knolton Wlk SN3 . . . . . **51** A4
KNOOK. . . . . . . . . . . . **194** D4
**Knook Barrow (Long
Barrow) ★** BA12. . . . **194** F7
**Knook Castle ★** BA12. **195** A4
**Knook Manor ★**
BA12. . . . . . . . . . . . . **194** D4
Knowlands SN6. . . . . . . **23** A7
KNOWLE. . . . . . . . . . . **215** C6
**Knowledge Hill 2**
SN8. . . . . . . . . . . . . . **170** B2
**Knowle The 1** SN13. . . **84** F8
Knowsley Rd SN3. . . . . . **51** A4
Kohat Cl SP9 . . . . . . . . **216** B7
Komat Rd SP9. . . . . . . **216** C5
Kopernik Rd SN25 . . . . . **34** D6
Kyneton Way SN14. . . . **70** A8
Kyte Cl BA12. . . . . . . . **116** D5
Kyte Way BA14 . . . . . . **105** E6

**L**

**Labour-in-Vain Hill**
SN11. . . . . . . . . . . . . **172** A8
**Labrador Gdns 7**
SP4. . . . . . . . . . . . . . **217** F8
Laburnam Dr SN4. . . . . **47** E3
**Laburnum Cl 8**
BA11. . . . . . . . . . . . . **110** B7
Laburnum Dr SN12 . . . . **94** A3
Laburnum Gr BA14. . . . **105** B6
Laburnum Rd SN2 . . . . . **35** C3
Lacemakers Rd SN16 . . **28** A5
Lackham Cir SN14 . . . . . **78** B6
**Lackham Coll of
Agriculture** SN15. . . . **78** E1
**Lackham Ctry Pk ★**
SN15. . . . . . . . . . . . . . **78** F1
**Lackham Mus** SN15 . . . **78** F1
LACOCK. . . . . . . . . . . . **86** D5
**Lacock Abbey ★** SN15. **86** D5
**Lacock CE Prim Sch**
SN15. . . . . . . . . . . . . . **86** D5
Lacock Gdns BA14 . . . . **102** B2

**Lacock Pottery ★**
SN15. . . . . . . . . . . . . . **86** D6
**Lacock Rd**
Corsham SN13. . . . . . . **85** D8
Swindon SN2. . . . . . . . **35** C4
Ladbrook La SN13 . . . . . **77** C1
Ladds La SN15. . . . . . . . **78** E7
**Lady Coventry Rd**
SN15. . . . . . . . . . . . . . **78** F7
**Lady Diana Ct 13**
SP11. . . . . . . . . . . . . **192** A5
**Ladydown**
Calne SN11 . . . . . . . . . **81** B4
Lower Chicksgrove
SP3. . . . . . . . . . . . . . **201** B1
Lady Down View **5**
SP3. . . . . . . . . . . . . . **203** E8
Ladyfield Rd SN14 . . . . . **78** B7
Lady Godley Cl SP9 . . . **216** C5
**Lady Jane Wlk 22**
SP11. . . . . . . . . . . . . **192** A5
**Lady La**
Broad Blunsdon SN25 . . **21** B1
Swindon SN2. . . . . . . . **34** F7
**Lady Margaret
Hungerford
Almshouse ★**
SN13. . . . . . . . . . . . . . **77** A1
Lady Mead SN6. . . . . . . **19** D8
Ladysmith SP4 . . . . . . **133** D3
**Ladysmith Rd**
Chiseldon SN4. . . . . . . . **65** D1
Salisbury SP2. . . . . . . **145** D3
Ladyway SP4. . . . . . . . **134** A7
Ladywood **8** SN10. . . . **179** F1
Lafranc Cl SP4. . . . . . . **146** B7
Laggar The SN13 . . . . . . **77** A2
Lagos St **3** SN1 . . . . . . **50** C7
Lagpond La SP3. . . . . . **204** B7
Lahore Cl SP9 . . . . . . . **216** C7
Lahore Rd SP9. . . . . . . **216** C5
Laines Head SN14 . . . . . **70** C2
**Lainesmead Prim Sch**
SN3. . . . . . . . . . . . . . . **50** E5
Lainey's Cl SN8. . . . . . **213** D4
LAKE. . . . . . . . . . . . . **197** F2
**Lake Group (Tumuli) ★**
. . . . . . . . . . . . . . . . . **197** D3
**Lake House ★** SP4. . . . **197** F1
**Lakeside**
Fairford GL7. . . . . . . . . . **1** F4
South Cerney GL7. . . . . . **7** B7
Swindon SN3. . . . . . . . **50** E3
Lakeside Cl SP10 . . . . . **193** C1
Lake View SN11 . . . . . . . **89** D8
Lake Vw SN4 . . . . . . . . . **61** A7
Lalique Cl SN25. . . . . . . **20** D1
Lamb Ale Gn BA14 . . . . **105** D6
Lambdown App SP11. . **191** F3
**Lambdown Terr**
North Tidworth SP11 . . **216** E4
Perham Down SP11 . . . **191** F4
Lambe Cl GL7. . . . . . . . . **1** E6
Lambert Cl SN5. . . . . . . **49** B3
Lamberts SN14 . . . . . . . **78** A8
LAMBOURN. . . . . . . . **165** B2
Lambourn Ave SN3 . . . . **50** E3
**Lambourn CE Prim Sch**
RG17. . . . . . . . . . . . . **165** A1
**Lambourne Cr 4**
SN12. . . . . . . . . . . . . . **94** B4
Lambourne Cres SN12 . **94** B4
Lambourn La BA13. . . . **186** C5
**Lambourn Pl 10**
RG17. . . . . . . . . . . . . **165** A2
**LAMBOURN
WOODLANDS** . . . . . **171** A4
Lambrok Cl BA14 . . . . . **104** F6
Lambrok Rd BA14. . . . . **104** F6
Lammas Cl SN11. . . . . **166** A6
Lamora Cl **12** SN5. . . . . **48** F8
Lampeter Rd SN25. . . . . **34** C6
**Lamplighters Wlk**
BA14. . . . . . . . . . . . . **105** A4
Lanac Rd SN3 . . . . . . . . **36** A1
Lancashire Dr SN14. . . . **78** A4
Lancaster Cl **6** RG17. . **177** B6
Lancaster Mews SN3 . . **36** C6
Lancaster Pl SN3 . . . . . . **36** C6
**Lancaster Rd**
Bower Hill SN12. . . . . . **94** B4
Kempsford GL7. . . . . . . **10** E6
Wroughton SN4. . . . . . . **64** A6
**Lancaster Sq**
Hungerford RG17. . . . . **177** B6
Lyneham SN15. . . . . . . **60** A2
Lancefield Pl SN13. . . . . **76** E2
Landale Cl **3** SP11 . . . . **193** E4
LANDFORD. . . . . . . . . **212** C6
LANDFORD WOOD. . . . **212** D8
Landor Rd SN25. . . . . . . **34** F8
Landsbury Dr SP9 . . . . **216** D8
LANE END. . . . . . . . . . **115** A8
Lane's Cl SP4. . . . . . . . **217** C4
Lanes End SN13. . . . . . . **85** D5
**Lanes End Hill**
Corsley BA12. . . . . . . . **115** A8
Lane End BA12. . . . . . . **115** A8
Lane-side **9** SP7. . . . . **202** C2
**Lane The**
**4** Ashbury SN6 . . . . . **164** A8
Bishopstone SN4. . . . . **163** C4
Lanfear Cl SP4. . . . . . . **217** C4
Langdale Dr SN5 . . . . . . **49** B3
Langdean Rd **5** SN1. . . **50** B1
Langet GL7. . . . . . . . . . . **6** E6
Langfields SN8. . . . . . . **170** A2

Langford Gr SN3.......50 E6
Langford La
 Berwick St James
  SP3............196 E2
 Downton SP5.......159 F2
 Downton SP5.......160 A3
Langford Rd
 Great Wishford SP2...129 F4
 Little Langford SP3...129 C5
 Trowbridge BA14......101 C2
Langfords La 3 SP7..202 B1
Langford Waie SP3...196 D1
Langham Brake BA2..103 F2
Langham Pl BA11.....103 F1
Langholm Ave BA12..116 D6
Langholm Cl BA12...116 D6
LANGLEY BURRELL...71 A3
Langley Fitzurse CE Prim
 Sch SN15..........70 E6
Langley Gdn SP6....210 E2
Langley Pk SN15.....70 E1
Langley Pk SN15.....70 F1
Langley Rd
 Chippenham SN15....70 E1
 Swindon SN5........34 B1
 Trowbridge BA14....105 C5
Langley Wood National
 Nature Reserve★
 SP5............211 F7
Lang Mws SN26.......21 C2
Langport Cl 1 SN5...49 B4
Langstone Way SN5...49 C6
Lanham's Cl BA13....109 A2
Lanhill (Long Barrow)★
 SN14..............69 B2
Lanhill View SN14....70 B2
Lanhydrock Cl 9 SN5.49 A4
Lansbury Dr SN2......35 F4
Lansdown Cl
 Melksham SN12......94 D6
 Trowbridge BA14....105 B7
Lansdowne Cl
 Calne SN11.........81 A4
 Dilton Marsh BA13...112 C8
Lansdowne Cres SN11.79 F2
Lansdowne Terr
 SN10............214 A3
Lansdown Gr SN15....70 D1
Lansdown Rd SN1.....50 B4
Lapwing Cl 1 SN3....51 E6
Lapwing Cres SN14...70 B2
Lapwing Dr SP4......132 C1
Lapwing Rd SN12.....94 D5
Larch Cl
 Melksham SN12......94 A3
 Swindon SN25.......35 D2
Larchfield Cl BA11...110 B7
Larch Gr BA14......105 B6
Larchmore Cl SN25...35 A3
Larch Rd SN14.......74 F6
Larch Row SP6......210 F1
Lark Cl SP9........216 D7
Lark Down BA14.....101 E1
Larkham Rise SN15...78 F6
LARKHILL...........197 F6
Larkhill Prim Sch
 SP4............197 E7
Larkhill Rd SP4.....198 B7
Lark La 5 SP4......132 C1
Larkrise BA14......105 F7
Larksfield SN3.......51 C8
Larkspur BA14......101 E1
Larkspur Dr SN11....81 D5
Larmer Tree Gdns★
 SP5............207 B3
Latchmoor Dro SP5..212 C6
Late Broads BA14....99 D7
Latham Rd SP4.....197 F6
Latimer Gdns SN14...41 E1
LATTON............8 C4
Latton Cl SN2.......35 B6
Latton Wharf SN6.....8 E1
Laughton Way SN25...35 A6
Launcelot Cl 22 SP10.193 E2
Laundry La 5 SP7...202 D1
Laura Pl SN13.......83 F7
Laurel Cl BA11.....110 B7
Laurel Dr
 Chippenham SN14....78 C6
 Colerne SN14.......74 F6
 Marlborough SN8...213 F2
Laurel Gr BA14.....105 E7
Laurels The
 Hungerford RG17....177 C8
 Melksham Without SN12 86 A1
 Westwood BA15......99 F3
Laurence Ct 10 SP11.192 A5
Lavender Cl
 Melksham SN12......94 C3
 5 Trowbridge BA14...105 E7
Lavender Ct BA11....110 B7
Lavender Dr SN11....81 B1
LAVERSTOCK........146 E2
Laverstock Pk SP1...146 C1
Laverstock Pk W
 SP1............146 D2
Laverton Ct 1 BA13.109 A3
Laverton Gn 3 BA13.108 F1
Laverton Rd BA13....108 F1
Lavington Cl 10 SN8.183 D8
Lavington Comp Sch
 SN10............179 E1
Lavington Hill SN10...187 F8
LAVINGTON SANDS...179 E2
LAWN..............50 F3
Lawn Farm Cl SN9...182 E7

Lawn La SN6.........22 A5
Lawn Prim Sch SN3...50 F2
Lawns The SN4.......47 D2
Lawrence Cl
 4 Amesbury SP4....217 C3
 Devizes SN10......214 C1
 Swindon SN3........51 C4
Lawrence Dr SN11....81 D3
Lawrence Mead 3
 SN8............170 B2
Lawrence Rd SP4....197 F7
Lawson Rd 3 SP4...198 A6
Lawton Cl SN3.......51 A3
LEA................28 F1
Lea Cl SN25.........35 A7
LEAFIELD..........84 E7
Leafield Ind Est SN13.84 E6
Leafield Pl BA14....100 F1
Leafield Rd SN13....84 E6
Leafield Way SN13...84 E6
Leafy La SN13.......76 A1
Lea & Garsdon CE Prim
 Sch SN16..........28 A2
Lea House SN16.......28 D1
Leamington Gr SN3...50 F2
Leap Gate
 Hilperton BA14.....102 A1
 Trowbridge BA14....106 A7
 Trowbridge BA14....106 A8
Leatler Cl SP3......204 D8
Leaze Rd
 Marlborough SN8...213 C4
 Melksham SN12......94 C6
Leaze St SN1........50 A2
Leaze The
 Ashton Keynes SN6....6 F1
 Durrington/Bulford
  SP4............217 E8
 South Cerney GL7.....6 F6
LECHLADE-ON-
 THAMES............2 D4
Lechlade Rd
 Buscot SN7.........2 E2
 Highworth SN6.......23 A7
 Inglesham SN6......12 A6
 Lechlade-on-Thames GL7..2 C2
 Little Faringdon GL7...2 F7
Ledge Hill SN10....179 E2
Ledger Hill Cl SP4...217 D8
Leech La GL8........25 C4
Lee Cres SN15......105 C4
Leehurst Swan SP1...146 B2
Lees Ct SP2........145 F2
Legate Cl SN15......79 B5
Legg Rd 12 SP7.....202 D1
Leicester Dr BA14...106 B8
Leicester St SN1.....50 D6
LEIGH..............18 C5
LEIGH DELAMERE.....55 C3
Leighfield Cl 8 SN1..50 C5
Leigh Gr BA15.......91 E1
Leigh La
 East Knoyle SP3....141 C1
 East Knoyle SP3....202 E8
 Leigh Pk Rd BA15...100 D8
 Leigh Pk Way BA13..108 E1
Leigh Rd
 Bradford-on-Avon
  BA15............91 E1
 Holt BA14..........92 C1
 Swindon SN2........35 C4
 Westbury BA13.....108 F1
Leigh Rd W
 Bradford-on-Avon
  BA15............91 D1
 Bradford-on-Avon
  BA15............100 E8
Leighton Ave SN3....50 F4
Leighton Gn BA13...109 A2
Leighton La BA13...109 A1
Leighton Pk N 4
 BA13............108 F1
Leighton Pk Rd 5
 BA13............108 F1
Leighton Pk W 2
 BA13............108 F1
Leigh Woods La
 SN10............214 F6
Leisler Gdns BA14...106 A8
Leland Cl 5 SN16....28 A5
Lena Cl 26 SP11....192 A5
Lennards The GL7.....7 A7
Lennox Dr SN3.......50 E6
Lenta Bsns Ctr SN1...50 B6
Lenton Cl 1 SN14....77 F7
Leonard Cheshire Cl 4
 SP4............217 D2
Lesley Anne Skeete Ct
 SN3............51 B4
Leslie Cl SN5.......49 A4
Leslie Rd BA15......99 F3
LETCOMBE
 BASSETT..........165 F8
Lethbridge Prim Sch
 SN1.............50 C3
Lethbridge Rd SN1...50 C3
Letterage Rd SN5....34 A2
Levell Ct 12 SP11...192 A5
Leven SN5..........49 A3
Leventon Pl BA14...102 B2
Leversedge Rd 2
 BA11............110 A7
LEVERTON..........171 B1
Leverton Gate SN3...50 F1

Leverton La RG17...171 B1
Lewington Cl SN12...94 A3
Lewington Mews 14
 RG17............177 B6
Lewis Cl
 Corsham SN13......84 D8
 Swindon SN25.......34 F6
Lewis Ct BA14......105 A3
Lewisham Castle★
 SN8............169 E4
Lewisham Cl SN25...34 F3
Leylands Rd
 Corsham SN13......76 B1
 2 Rudloe SN13......84 B8
Leys Hill BA14......110 A6
Leys La BA11.......110 A6
Leystone Cl BA11...110 A6
Ley The SN13........83 D5
Lichen Cl 3 SN2.....34 D4
Lickhill Rd SN11.....81 A4
Lidbrook SN11.......81 B4
Lidbury Camp★ SN9.190 C8
Liddel Gdns SP4....132 B1
Liddiards Gn SN8...168 F5
LIDDINGTON........163 B4
Liddington Castle (Fort)★
 SN4............163 A2
Liddington St SN2...35 C3
Liddington Way
 BA14............105 D5
Liden Dr SN3........51 D4
Liden Prim Sch SN3..51 D3
Light Cl SN13.......77 A2
Lightfoot Rd SP4...197 F7
Lightning Rd
 1 Amesbury SP4...217 D2
 Calne SN11.........81 D3
Light's La SP5......153 C2
Light The SN16......27 F3
Liguiel Cl 9 RG17...177 B6
Lilac Cl SN2........35 B2
Lilac Gr BA14......105 B5
Lilac Way SN11......81 B1
Lilian Cl 8 SN25....34 C6
Lilian Lock Gdns SN2.35 C5
Lillywhite Cres 1
 SP10............193 E2
Lilypad St 5 SN3....51 B8
Lily Wlk 11 SP4.....198 C7
Lime Ave
 Badminton GL9......38 C1
 Melksham SN12......94 A3
Lime Cl
 Frome BA11.......110 B7
 Lyneham & Bradenstoke
  SN15............60 C2
 Pewsey SN9.......215 D6
Lime Kiln SN4.......47 D3
Lime Kiln Cl BA12...113 A1
Limekiln Hill GL7.....4 B7
Limekiln La BA2......90 A5
Limekiln Rd SP11...192 E6
Lime Kiln Sports Ctr
 SN4............47 D3
Lime Kiln Way SP2..152 A5
Lime Rd SN14.......75 A5
Limerick La BA11...107 A2
Limer's La SN11....166 E2
Limes Ave SN2.......35 B3
Limes Pl SN6.........8 C4
Limes Rd GL7.........4 F7
Limes The
 Badminton GL9......38 E2
 Motcombe SP7.....202 A4
 Porton SP4.......133 E6
 Shrewton SP3......196 E7
 South Ceney GL7.....7 A6
Limestone Dr
 6 Corsham SN13....76 D1
 Corsham SN13......84 D8
Lime Tree Cl SN11...81 A3
Lime Trees SN15.....58 A2
LIMPERS HILL......139 D4
LIMPLEY STOKE.....99 B6
Limpley Stoke Rd
 BA15............99 D6
Lincoln Gn SN12.....94 C7
Lincoln Gr SN12.....94 C1
Lincoln St SN1......50 C6
Linden Ave SN3......35 C3
Linden Cl
 Calne SN11.........81 B2
 Colerne SN14.......74 F6
 Ludgershall SP11...192 B5
 Royal Wootton Bassett
  SN4............47 E3
 Salisbury SP1.....146 D1
Linden Cres BA15...100 A3
Linden Gr 2 SN12....94 A2
Linden Lea GL7.......8 E8
Linden Pk SP7......202 D1
Linden Pl BA14.....101 B1
Linden Way SN5......34 A2
Lindford Rd SP1....146 D5
Lindisfarne 1 SN4....48 A2
Lindisfarne Cl BA15..99 F7
Lindlar Cl 13 SP7...202 C2
Lindley Cl SP9......216 D6
Lineacre Cl SN5.....48 F4
Lingen Cl 12 SP10...193 D2
Lingfield Cl 3 SP11..77 F5
Link Ave SN5........49 B5
LINKENHOLT.......185 E5
Linkenholt Rd
 Little Down SP11...185 D5
 Vernhams Dean SP11.185 D3

Link La BA15........83 A1
Link Leisure Ctr SN5.49 B5
Link Rd BA13......108 E7
Links The
 Corsham SN13......84 B7
 Pewsey SN9.......215 B4
Link Way SP1.......146 C3
Linley Cl SN11......50 C2
Linley Rd SN26......21 C2
LINLEYS THE........85 B6
Linnet La SN12......94 E5
Linnet Rd SN11......81 C5
Linnetsdene
 6 Salisbury SP2...152 A5
 Swindon SN3........51 C8
Linnet Way BA11...110 B6
Linslade SN2........50 A7
Linslade St SN2......49 F6
Linsvale Cl BA11...110 C5
Linsvale Dr BA11...110 C5
Lionel's Ave SP5...207 C5
Lions Orch BA14....101 E8
Lipgate SN10......180 F8
Lipman Way SN3.....28 C2
Liskeard Way SN5...49 B4
Lisle Cl SN5........49 A5
Lismore Rd SN6......22 E6
Lister Gr BA15.......99 F3
Lister Rd SN4........64 B7
Litchfield Cl 11 SP10.193 C2
Litherland Cl SN14...78 B6
LITTLE ASHLEY......91 A1
Little Ave SN2.......35 A1
LITTLE BADMINTON...38 E5
Little Badminton La
 SN16............28 F2
LITTLE BEDWYN....176 D1
Little Brittox SN1...214 A3
Littlebrook 2 BA14.101 D5
LITTLE CHALFIELD...92 C3
Little Chalfield Rd
 BA14............92 B2
Little Challows SN14..76 D7
LITTLE CHEVERELL...187 D8
Little Clarendon★
 SP3............201 F2
Little Comm BA14...105 D3
Little Content La 17
 SP7............202 C2
Littlecote SN11.....166 B7
Littlecote Cl 3 SN5...49 D5
Littlecote Rd
 Chippenham SN14....78 A6
 Froxfield SN8......176 D7
Littlecote Roman Villa★
 RG17............170 D1
LITTLECOTT
 Enford...........190 A6
 Hilmarton........166 A7
Little Ct La BA13...186 D8
Little Cumberwell
 BA15............91 B2
Littledown SP7.....202 C2
LITTLE DOWN.......185 D4
Little Down SN14....78 B7
Little Down La SP11.185 C5
Little Down View
 SP4............131 F8
Little Dro SP6......211 A4
LITTLE DURNFORD...131 D1
Little End SN14......74 A8
Little Englands
 Chippenham SN14....78 E6
 Chippenham SN15....78 E6
LITTLE FARINGDON....2 F8
Littlefield La SP5...208 A4
Little Ground 7 SN25..34 A2
Little Hill BA12.....116 E2
LITTLE HORTON....172 C1
Little Ingleburn SN16.28 A2
Little Island SN9...215 B5
Littlejohn Ave SN12...94 C6
LITTLE LANGFORD...129 A6
LITTLE LONDON....166 E2
Little London
 Heytesbury BA12...194 C5
 Mount Sorrel SP5...205 A3
 1 Swindon SN1.....50 D4
LITTLE MARSH......102 F4
Littlemead SN13.....83 B5
Little Mead SN8....176 F1
Littlemill La SP6...209 F3
Little Parks BA14....92 F1
Little Pk Cl SN15....59 F1
Little Rose La SN26..20 F5
LITTLE SALISBURY...182 E7
Little Sands SN14....68 F5
LITTLE SOMERFORD...44 B5
LITTLETON.........178 B7
Littleton
 Great Hinton BA14..102 F4
 Semington BA14....102 E5
LITTLETON DREW....53 C6
Littleton Drew La GL9.53 A6
LITTLETON PANELL...179 D1
Little Woodbury★
 SP5............152 B4
Little Woodfalls Dr
 SP5............211 C6
LITTLEWORTH.......85 B8
Littleworth La SN12..85 C2
Livery Rd
 West Dean SP5....155 B7
 Winterslow SP5....149 B4
Livia Cl 3 SP10......193 E2
Lockem Rd SN10....214 E6
LOCKERIDGE.......174 A6
Lockeridge Cl BA14.105 D5

Lockeridge La SN8..174 B7
Locke's Dro SP11...193 E8
Locking Cl SN12....178 B8
Locks Cross SN13....84 E5
Locksgreen Cres 1
 SN2.............34 E3
Lock's Hill BA11....110 A3
Lockside SN15......78 F5
Locks La
 Purton SN5.........33 B5
 Widham SN5........33 B6
Lock's La SP2......145 A3
Locks The SN10....179 D8
Lockswell Cl SN15...79 A4
Loddon Way BA15...100 E5
Lode Hill SP5......211 B8
Loder La SP2.......144 E3
Lodersfield GL7......2 C4
Lodge Cl SN11......81 A3
Lodge Ct BA14.....105 F8
Lodge Dr 6 SP11...192 F1
Lodge Dro SP5.....211 C6
Lodge Fields BA12..119 A8
Lodge Hill BA11....110 F5
Lodge La SP11......192 E6
Lodge Rd
 Chippenham SN15....79 A5
 Horningsham BA12..119 A8
Lodge Vw SP3......188 A2
Lodowicks SN11......80 D7
Logan Cl 3 SN2......50 E6
Loiret Cres
 Malmesbury SN16....27 F6
 Malmesbury SN16....28 A6
Lomond Cl SN5......34 B2
Londonderry Gdns
 SP4............198 E7
London La SN5......17 C1
London Rd
 Amesbury SP4.....217 B4
 Bishops Cannings
  SN10............214 E6
 Box SN13..........83 D7
 Calne SN11.........81 B2
 Chippenham SN15....78 F6
 Firsdown SN4.....148 B8
 Laverstock SP4....147 B6
 Marlborough SN8...213 E4
 Meysey Hampton GL7...1 A5
 Salisbury SP1.....146 C3
 Shrewton SP3......196 F7
London Rd E BA1....82 A3
London Ride SN8...176 A5
London St SN1......50 B6
Long Acre SN5......33 B4
Long Barn Rd 18
 SP11............193 F2
Longbarrow Cross Roads
 SP4............197 C4
Long Barrow Rd SN11.81 A3
Long Bottom SP11..192 D6
LONGBRIDGE
 DEVERILL........120 F6
Long Cl
 Chippenham SN15....78 F6
 Downton SP5......211 A8
Long Cl Ave SN11....76 B1
Long Cl W SP5.....211 A8
Longcombe Dr
 Corsley BA12.......115 E3
 Warminster BA12...116 A5
Longcot Cl SN3......36 A1
Longcroft Ave SN10.214 C3
Longcroft Cres SN10.214 C3
Longcroft Rd
 Berwick St John SP5.207 D6
 Devizes SN10......214 C3
LONG CROSS........138 B5
Long Cross
 Bramshaw SO43....212 C2
 Shaftesbury SP7...202 B2
Longcross Plain Rd
 SO43............212 B2
LONG DEAN.........68 C4
Long Dro
 Burbage SN8......183 D8
 Grimstead SP5....154 B4
Long Drove
 East Grimstead SP5.154 F5
 East Grimstead SP5.155 A6
Longfellow Dr 7 SN25.35 A8
Longfellow Cres SN4.47 F3
LONGFIELD........108 E8
Longfield 11 SP4...198 B7
Longfield Rd BA14..105 D7
Longfields SN8.....173 B8
Longfields Wlk SN10.214 C2
Longford Castle★
 SP5............153 A2
Longford CE (VC) Prim
 Sch SP5..........152 D5
Longford Pk★ SP5..152 E2
Longford Rd SP5...153 A2
Longford Rd SN12...94 C2
Long Ground
 4 Corsham SN13....76 D1
 Corsham SN13......84 D8
Long Harry SN8....213 F1
LONGHEDGE........115 D5
Long Hedge RG17...165 B1
Long Hill BA12.....138 F5
Longhill Dr 1 SP2...152 B5
Long Hollow BA13..186 D2
Long La
 Bourton SP8......137 D1

Long La continued
 Bourton SP8......137 D2
 Cann SP7........206 A8
 Kilmington BA12...123 F3
 Stourton with Gasper
  BA12............124 A3
Longland SP2......145 E1
Longlands GL7........1 E7
Longlands Cl BA13..186 C7
Longleat
 Longhedge BA12...115 A5
 Warminster BA12...115 A5
Longleat Gdns SN2...35 C4
Longleat House★
 BA12............114 F3
Longleat Safari Pk★
 BA12............115 B4
Longleaze SN4.......47 E3
Long Leaze SN14....53 C1
Long Leaze La SN12..94 C3
Longleaze Prim Sch
 SN4.............47 E3
Longleys Cl SN10...214 E2
Longmead SP7.....202 C2
Long Meadow SP3..201 D2
Longmeadow Prim Sch
 BA14............105 E7
LONG NEWNTON.....13 C5
Long Ridings SN4....70 C2
Long River Rd BA13.109 D2
Long Row SN6.......10 B4
Longsplatt SN13.....83 D3
Long Steeple La SP6.210 C6
Longstock Ct SN5....49 A4
Longstone Rd 1 SN14.70 A1
Long Stones★ SN8...173 A8
LONGSTREET.......190 A6
Longs Yard 7 BA15.100 D5
Longthorpe Cl SN5...49 D4
Lonsdale Cl SN26....21 C2
Lonsdale Gdns
 Bowerhill SN12......94 E1
 Melksham SN12......94 A2
Loophill SN13........96 A6
Loop Rd SN8.......175 A7
Lopcombe Cnr SP4..135 D3
LOPCOMBE
 CORNER..........135 D3
Lopes Way BA13....108 F4
Lords Cl SN4........64 E3
Lords Croft SP4....217 B4
Lord's Hill SP3.....121 C3
Lord's La SN15......78 E7
Lord's Mead SN14...78 A8
Lordsmead Rd BA12.139 A4
Lorne St SN1........50 A5
Lotmead 1 BA14....101 D5
Lottage Rd SN8....170 A7
Lottage Way 2 SN8.170 A7
Lotts The SN6.......17 F8
Loughborough Cl 1
 SN5.............48 F4
Louise Rayner Pl SN14.78 E7
Lourdes Cres 15
 RG17............177 B6
Louviers Way SN1....50 C2
Lovage La SN11......81 B5
Lovage Way BA12...139 B6
Loveage Cl 3 SN2....34 D4
Love La
 Box SN13..........83 F7
 Salisbury SP1.....152 B8
 4 Shaftesbury SP7..202 B1
 Woodgreen SP6....211 A4
Lovell Cl SN3........51 D7
Lovel Rd BA12......194 E3
LOVER.............211 D6
Loveridge Cl
 5 Andover SP10....193 E2
 Swindon SN2........35 E6
Love's La SN8......170 B3
Lovett Gn SP1.....146 C4
Lowa Rd SP9.......216 B6
Lowbourne SN12.....94 B4
Lowden SN15........78 C7
Lowden Ave SN14....78 C8
Lowden Hill SN15....78 C7
Lower Alma St BA14.105 E8
Lower Backway 7
 SP3............196 E6
Lower Bartons 30
 SP6............210 D1
Lower Blandford Rd
 Cann SP7........206 A8
 5 Shaftesbury SP7..202 D1
LOWER BLUNSDON....21 B3
LOWER BURGATE....210 D2
LOWER
 CHICKSGROVE.....201 B1
Lower Churchfields
 SN8............213 D2
LOWER CHUTE......192 F8
Lower Ct BA14......101 D1
Lower Daggons La
 SP6............209 F1
Lower Densome Wood
 SP6............211 A4
LOWER EVERLEIGH...182 E1
Lower Folly SP2....144 B1
Lower Goatacre
 SN11............166 A7

Lower Gr SP6........210 B5
LOWER GREEN....177 D3
Lower Ho SN16.......15 B8
Lower Kingsdown Rd
　Box SN13.........83 A4
　Kingsdown BA1......82 E2
Lower Marsh Rd
　BA12............117 A5
Lower Mill SN25.......34 B2
Lower Mill Est GL7.....6 A1
Lower Mill La GL7.....6 A1
LOWER MOOR.......17 A4
Lower N Rd SP5......207 C5
Lower Pavenhill SN5...32 E5
Lower Prospect SN8. 213 E3
Lower Rd
　Bratton BA13.......186 B7
　Britford SP5........152 C5
　Coombe Bissett SP5 .151 C1
　Downton SN5.......159 B4
　Edington BA13......186 C8
　Erlestoke BA13......178 F2
　Netheravon SP4......190 A3
　Odstock SP5........152 D4
　Salisbury SP2.......144 F2
LOWER RUDGE......107 D4
LOWER SEAGRY......57 F7
Lower Shockerwick La
　BA1.............82 D4
Lower Shute BA12....119 F6
Lower S Rd SP5......207 C4
Lower St
　Donhead St Andrew
　SP7.............203 B3
　Netheravon SP4......190 A4
　Rode BA11.........103 E1
　Salisbury SP2.......151 E7
LOWER STANTON ST
　QUINTIN..........56 D6
Lower Stoke
　Limpley Stoke BA2....99 A4
　Monkton Combe BA2...90 A1
LOWER STRATTON...36 B2
LOWER STUDLEY....105 E6
Lower Twinhoe BA2...98 B4
Lower Upham
　Draycot Foliat SN8...168 F8
　Upper Upham SN8...169 A8
Lower Wadswick
　SN13.............84 B3
LOWER
　WANBOROUGH....163 B6
Lower Westbury Rd
　BA13.............109 E5
Lower Wharf SN10...214 A4
Lower Whitbourne
　BA12.............115 B7
Lower Widhill Farm La
　SN26.............20 D3
LOWER WOODFORD. 131 C3
Lower Woodrow
　Melksham Without
　SN12.............86 F1
　Melksham Without SN12 87 A1
LOWER WRAXALL....91 E5
LOWER ZEALS......138 D5
Lowes Cl 2 SN5.....34 B2
Low La SN11........81 D2
Lowmead BA14......101 E1
Low Rd SN10.......179 C1
Loxley Cl SN12......94 B6
Loxley Wlk SN3......51 B3
Loyalty St SN14......78 C7
Lubeck Dr 22 SP10.. 193 D2
Luccombe Quarry
　BA15.............100 E4
Lucerne Cl
　Royal Wootton Bassett
　SN4............. 47 D4
　10 Swindon SN5.....48 F8
Lucetta Rise 6 SN25.. 34 D5
Lucewood La SP5... 154 C7
Luckett Way SN11.....81 C4
LUCKINGTON.......39 E4
Luckington Comm Sch
　GL9.............38 E5
Luckington Com Sch
　SN14.............39 E5
Luckington Ct* SN14.. 39 F5
Luckington Rd
　Acton Turville GL9.... 53 B7
　Luckington SN14.....39 D2
　Sherston SN14......40 B7
Lucknam Pk* SN14 .. 75 B6
Lucknam Pk SN14....75 C7
Ludborne Pl BA13....108 D1
Luddesdown Rd SN5...49 C4
LUDGERSHALL......192 A5
Ludgershall Castle*
　SP11.............192 A6
Ludgershall Rd
　Collingbourne Ducis
　SN8.............191 B8
　4 Swindon SN1......49 F4
　Tidworth SP9.......216 D2
Ludgershall Sports Club
　SP11.............192 A5
Ludlow Cl
　Chippenham SN15.....79 A5
　10 Frome BA11......110 C6
　Swindon SN3........50 F4
　Warminster BA12....116 F4
　Westbury BA13......108 F4
Ludmead Rd SN13....85 A8
LUDWELL..........203 A1

Ludwell Com Prim Sch
　SP7.............203 A1
Ludwell (Hill) SP7.....203 A1
　SN14.............53 E2
Lukas Cl SN25.......34 F7
Luke St SP7.........203 E1
Lulworth Rd SN25....34 E3
Lumb Cl SN25.......20 C1
Lumley Cl
　2 Swindon SN5.....49 A4
　Westwood SP2......203 C8
Lumley Wlk 8 SP4...217 D3
Luna Cl 19 SN25.....34 B7
Lupin Cl SN11.......81 D5
Luxfield Rd BA12.....116 E7
Lyall Cl SN25........34 F8
Lyburn Rd SP5.......212 A5
Lycetts Orch SN13....83 D6
Lyddon Way SN25....34 F4
Lydford Cl 4 SN5.....49 A8
Lydiard Fields Bsns Pk
　SN5.............48 E3
Lydiard Gn SN5......33 A1
LYDIARD GREEN.....48 B8
LYDIARD MILLICENT. 33 D1
Lydiard Millicent CE Prim
　Sch SN5.........48 B8
Lydiard Pk* SN5.....48 A4
Lydiard Pk Academy
　SN5.............48 F5
LYDIARD PLAIN.....32 B1
Lydiard Rd SN14.....78 A6
LYDIARD TREGOZE.. 48 E6
Lydiard Way BA14...105 D5
Lydiard Gn SN15.....58 B2
Lye Gn BA15.........99 F4
LYE GREEN........100 A4
Lyes Gr BA13........112 B8
Lyes Green BA12.....115 A8
LYE'S GREEN.......111 B1
Lye The SN12.......178 E8
Lyme Ave BA12......116 F6
Lymers The SN11....166 E2
Lyme Way SN25......35 A5
Lynch Cl BA12.......139 B5
Lynchet Cl 7 SN10...179 F1
Lynchets Rd SP4.....217 B3
Lynchfield Rd 7 SP4 217 B3
Lynch Field The 5
　SN4.............163 A5
Lynch La 6 RG17....165 A2
Lynch The SN8......176 F1
Lynden Cl SN3.......184 A7
Lyndhurst Cres SN3...51 A6
Lyndhurst Rd
　Amesbury SP4......217 C3
　Bramshaw SO51......212 D3
　Brook SO43........212 E1
　Landford SP5.......212 C6
LYNEHAM..........60 B2
Lyneham Cl SN2......35 B6
Lyneham Prim Sch
　SN15.............60 B2
Lyneham Way BA14...105 E8
Lynmouth Rd SN5....49 A4
Lynt Farm Cotts SN6...12 B6
Lynt Farm La SN6.....12 B6
Lynton Rd SN2.......34 E1
Lynt Rd SN6.........12 A5
Lynwood Gr SN2......34 D3
Lynwood Rd BA14....101 A1
Lyons Wlk 1 SP7.....202 C1
Lypiatt SN13.........84 F6
Lypiatt Mead SN13....85 A8
Lypiatt Prim Sch SN13 .84 F6
Lypiatt Rd SN13......85 A7
Lypiatt View SN6......19 C7
Lysander Rd
　Bower Hill SN12......94 B1
　Laverstock SP4......146 C8
　Melksham Without
　SN12.............178 B8
Lysley Cl SN15.......79 A5
Lyster Rd SP6.......210 E1
Lytchett Way SN3.....51 C6
Lytham Cl SN15......78 F7
Lywood Cl SP2.......151 E5

**M**

MacAdam Way SP10. 193 B1
MacCullum Rd SP11 . 193 E4
Macie Dr SN13.......84 E8
Mackay Cres
　Swindon SN25......20 C1
　Swindon SN25......34 B8
MacKenzie Cl 1 SN3 . 51 D4
Mackintosh Davidson
　Wood Nature Reserve*
　BA12.............140 D3
MacKlin Cl 21 RG17.. 177 B7
MacKlin Rd SP2......145 E2
Mackmurdo Ave SN25 20 D1
MacNeice Dr SN3....213 A2
MADDINGTON......196 E7
Maddington 2 SP3... 196 E7
Maddington St SP3... 196 E7
Maddle Rd RG17.....164 E4
Maddock's Hill 4
　BA12.............116 E5
Maddocks Rd BA14...101 D4
Magdalene Cl SN3....36 F4
Magdalene La 7
　SP7.............202 C1
Magdalen La BA14...104 B7
Magdalen Rd SN4....34 A6

Magic Rdbt SN1......50 E6
Magister Rd SN12....94 D1
Magnolia Cl
　1 Frome BA11......110 C7
　Harnham SP2......151 D7
Magnolia Ct SN2......35 B2
Magnolia Gdns SN5...49 B7
Magnolia Rise
　Calne SN11.........81 B1
　Trowbridge BA14....105 E7
Magnon Rd BA15.....100 B7
Magpie La SN3.......51 E6
Magpie Mews SN10.. 214 B3
Maida Vale 3 SN25...34 D6
MAIDEN BRADLEY... 118 D2
Maiden Bradley
　Horningsham BA12...119 B4
　Maiden Bradley BA12.. 118 F4
Maidencroft Cotts
　GL7.............10 E6
Maiden La SN11.....166 B1
Maiden St SN11......50 B4
Main Dr
　Swindon SN25......34 F8
　Westonbirt GL8......25 C8
Main Rd
　Amesbury SP4......217 D2
　Cherhill SN11......166 B1
　Christian Malford SN15. 58 E5
　Ogbourne St Andrew
　SN8.............213 D8
　St Paul Malmesbury Without
　SN16.............42 E4
　Sutton Benger SN15...57 F2
　Winterbourne Dauntsey
　SP4.............133 B2
Main St E BA13......108 C6
Main St
　Great Hinton BA14...178 A6
　Westbury BA13......108 C6
Maisey Mws SN16.....17 F7
Maitland Cl SN15.....79 A4
Maitland Rd SN3......51 A7
Maize Cl 6 SP11.....193 D4
Maizey Rd SN5.......20 D1
Majestic Cl 4 SN5....49 A7
Malcolm Dr SP4.....132 B1
Maldwyn Cl 9 SN5...48 F8
Mallard Ave SN15.....60 B1
Mallard Cl
　7 Bower Hill SN12...178 B8
　Calne SN11.........81 D2
　Salisbury SP2.......151 F7
　Swindon SN3........51 E6
　Trowbridge BA14....105 E7
　Westbury BA13......109 B8
Mallards The
　South Cerney GL7.....7 A5
　20 West Tisbury SP3 . 203 E8
Mallory Pl SN12......94 C2
Mallow Cl
　2 Swindon SN2.....34 D4
　4 Trowbridge BA14.. 105 D6
Mall The
　South Tedworth SP9.. 216 A4
　Swindon SN5........50 B3
MALMESBURY.......28 B3
Malmesbury Abbey*
　SN16.............28 A3
Malmesbury CE Prim Sch
　Malmesbury SN16.....27 F5
　Malmesbury SN16.....28 A4
Malmesbury Gdns
　SN3.............51 A5
Malmesbury House*
　SP1.............152 A8
Malmesbury Ind Est
　SN16.............28 A4
Malmesbury Primary
　Care Ctr SN16......28 B1
Malmesbury Rd
　Chippenham SN15....70 C1
　Kemble GL7.........4 C6
　Leigh SN5..........17 E3
　Lower Stanton St Quintin
　SN14.............56 C8
　Minety SN16........17 A1
　Minety SN16........31 A8
Malmesbury Swimming
　Pool SN16.........27 E4
Malmpit Hill
　Codford BA12......195 B2
　Codford St Mary BA12.195 C4
Malone Ave SN25.....35 B8
Malory Cl
　Swindon SN25......20 D1
　Swindon SN25......34 D8
Malthouse Cl
　Ashbury SN6.......164 A8
　Broad Blunsdon SN26 .21 C2
Malthouse La
　Chute SP11........192 E8
　4 Salisbury SP2....146 A1
Malt House La SP11.. 193 F4
Maltings The
　Malmesbury SN16.....28 A3
　Royal Wootton Bassett
　SN4.............47 D1
　Salisbury SP2.......146 A4
　8 Wanborough SN4.. 163 B6
　Warminster BA12....116 F6
　Yatton Keynell SN14...68 F6
Malt Shovel La RG17. 164 F2
Malvern Cl
　Melksham SN12......94 D4
　7 Warminster BA12.. 117 A8
Malvern Rd SN2......35 C1

Malvern Way SP4... 133 D6
Malwany Cl 5 BA14.. 101 F1
Mampitts La SP7.....202 D1
Manchester Rd SN1...50 C7
Mandarin Cl GL7......6 F6
Mand Wood BA14....101 F8
Mane Way
　Westbury BA13......108 E2
　Westbury Leigh BA13. 108 D1
Manley Cl BA11......101 C1
Manners Way SN4.....63 E1
Manning Cl 8 SP1...146 C5
MANNINGFORD
　ABBOTS.........182 A5
MANNINGFORD
　BOHUNE.........181 F4
MANNINGFORD
　BRUCE..........181 F5
Mannington La SN5...49 D5
Mannington Pk SN2...49 F7
Mannington Ret Pk
　SN1.............49 E4
Mannock Field SP4.. 132 B1
Manor Ave GL7.......2 E3
Manor Bridge Ct
　SP9.............217 D7
Manor CE VC Prim Sch
　The SN12.........94 B4
Manor Cl
　Broad Blunsdon SN26 .21 C2
　28 Fordingbridge SP6 210 D1
　Semington BA14.....102 F5
　4 Shipton Bellinger
　SP9.............199 D8
　Trowbridge BA14....105 A6
　Wroughton SN4......64 B5
Manor Copse SP11... 193 E3
Manor Cotts SN14.....24 D1
Manor Cres SN2......34 F2
Manor Ct SN9.......215 C4
Manor Dr BA1........82 B2
Manor Farm Cl
　Broad Chalke SP5....205 C4
　Upper Seagry SN15...57 D5
Manor Farm Ct
　East Kennet SN8....173 D6
　Purton Stoke SN5....19 C2
Manor Farm Dr SN15 .57 C2
Manor Farm La
　Great Wishford SP2...129 F4
　Patney SN10.......180 F5
　Shorncote GL7.......6 B7
Manor Farm Rd
　Salisbury SP2.......146 C1
　1 Sandleheath SP6 . 210 C1
Manor Fields 5
　BA13.............186 B7
Manor Fields Prim Sch
　SP2.............145 E2
Manor Gdns
　Bradford-on-Avon
　BA15.............100 D8
　Burbage SN8.......175 D1
　Swindon SN2........34 F2
　Warminster BA12....117 A7
Manor Ho SN14.......68 C5
Manor House Cl SN4...47 D3
Manor House The*
　SN9.............182 F7
Manor La
　Baydon SN8........170 C8
　Broad Hinton SN4...167 C7
Manor Mdws SN3.....36 E4
Manor Orch SN6......19 E8
Manor Pk
　Froxfield SN8.......176 D6
　Great Somerford SN15 .44 A2
　South Marston SN3....36 E4
Manor Rd
　Chippenham SN14.....78 A8
　Corsham SN13.......76 F2
　7 Great Bedwyn SN8. 176 B3
　Mere BA12.........138 F7
　Mere BA12.........139 A6
　Salisbury SP1.......146 C1
　Swindon SN1........49 F5
　Trowbridge BA14....105 A6
　Upton Lovell BA12...194 E3
　Vernhams Dean SP11. 185 D3
Manor The*
　Keevil BA14........178 A4
　Longbridge Deverill
　BA12.............120 F5
Manor View SN16.....28 F2
Manor Vw SN4......163 A4
Manor Yard BA12....120 E2
Mansion House Mews
　SN13.............77 A1
Mantell Cl BA13......108 F8
Mantles La BA12.....194 C5
MANTON..........213 A1
Manton Cl
　Marlborough SN8....213 A1
　Trowbridge BA14....105 C6
Manton Dro SN8.....174 C6
Manton Hollow SN8 . 213 A2
Manton Rd SN8.....174 C7
Manton St SN2.......50 D4
Manvers St BA14.....101 C1
Maple Cl
　Calne SN11.........81 B1
　Harnham SP2.......151 D7
　Melksham SN12......94 D5
　Pewsey SN9........215 D6
　Royal Wootton Bassett
　SN4.............61 E7
　Salisbury SP1.......146 A2
　Wroughton SN4......64 B6
Maple Cres
　7 Ludgershall SP11.. 192 B5
　Wilton SP2.........144 F3

Maplecroft 3 SP2... 152 A5
Maple Ct 8 BA11.....110 A7
Maple Dr
　Firsdown SP5.......148 C8
　Royal Wootton Bassett
　SN4.............47 E4
Maple Gr
　Swindon SN2........35 C2
　Trowbridge BA14....105 C6
Maple Terr 4 SP9...216 E7
Maple Way
　Amesbury SP4......217 D4
　Chippenham SN15....70 D2
　3 Durrington/Bulford
　SP4.............198 B7
Mapperton Hill SP8.. 138 E1
Marabout Rd 13 SP7. 202 D1
Maranatha Christian Sch
　SN6.............22 C1
Marbeck Cl SN25.....34 E7
Marbrean Cl 4 SP6.. 210 C1
Marchant's La BA2....98 F4
March Cl SN25.......35 A6
Marchment Cl SP2...144 F4
MARDEN..........181 A4
Marden Ave SN1......49 C2
Marden Henge*
　SN9.............181 B5
Marden Vale CE Acad
　SN11.............81 C4
Marden Way SN11....81 A2
Marden Wlk 2 BA14.105 C6
Margaret Leckie Ct 5
　SN3.............50 F6
Margarets Cl SP4.....217 D2
Margaret Stancomb
　Infants' Sch BA14....101 C1
Margery Holroyd Rise
　SN16.............27 F3
Margha Rd SP9.....216 C6
Marie Ave 5 SP5.... 210 F8
Marigold Cl
　Melksham SN12......94 C3
　Swindon SN2........34 D4
Marina Dr BA14......101 D4
Marina Rd
　23 Durrington/Bulford
　SP4.............198 B7
　Salisbury SP1.......152 C7
Marine Cl SN4........64 B7
Mariner Rd SN25.....34 B7
Maristow St BA13....109 A3
Marjoram Cl 4 SN2...34 D5
Markan Rd SP4......133 F7
Markay Est BA12.....112 F1
Markenfield 2 SN5...49 D4
Market Hill SN11......81 B3
Market La 4 SN16....28 A3
MARKET
　LAVINGTON......179 E1
Market Lavington Mus*
　SN10.............179 F1
Market Mead SN14...78 F8
Market Pl
　Box SN13..........83 D7
　Castle Combe SN14...68 A7
　Chippenham SN15....78 E7
　Colerne SN14.......75 B3
　Lechlade GL7........2 C4
　18 Market Lavington
　SN10.............179 F1
　Marshfield SN14.....74 A8
　Pewsey SN9........215 C5
　Warminster BA12....117 A7
　2 Westbury BA13... 109 A4
Market Pl The SN10.. 214 A4
Market Sq The 4 SN3 50 D4
Market St
　Bradford-on-Avon
　BA15.............100 D7
　Swindon SN1........50 B6
　Trowbridge BA14....105 D8
Markham Cl SN3......50 F7
Markham La SN4......63 E3
Markham Rd SN4.....64 A5
Markova Gr 9 SN25...34 B7
Markton Cl 3 SN25...34 C6
MARLBOROUGH.... 213 F3
Marlborough Bsns Pk
　SN8.............213 E1
Marlborough Cl
　SN10.............214 F7
Marlborough Coll
　SN8.............213 C2
Marlborough Craft Ctr*
　SN8.............213 D2
Marlborough Ct SN14.78 C7
Marlborough La SN1...50 D3
Marlborough Leisure Ctr
　SN8.............213 C3
Marlborough Rd
　5 Aldbourne SN8...170 A6
　Bulford SP4........198 E6
　Burbage SN8.......175 C1
　Chiseldon SN3......51 C2
　Collingbourne Ducis
　SN8.............183 E1
　Draycot Foliat SN4.. 168 F8
　Everleigh SN8......183 A1
　Liddington SN4......51 E1
　Pewsey SN9........215 B6
　Royal Wootton Bassett
　SN4.............61 E7
　Salisbury SP1.......146 A2
　Swindon SN3........50 D3
　Wroughton SN4......64 B6
Marlborough St 5
　SN1.............50 A5

Marlborough White
　Horse* SN8.......213 C1
Marl La SP6.........210 D1
Marlowe Ave SN3.....50 F7
Marlowe Way SN4....47 F3
Marlstones The SN1...50 B4
Marne Rd 3 SP4.....198 F6
Marney Rd SN5.......49 A5
MARR GREEN......183 D7
Marshall Rd
　Roundway SN10.....214 D1
　Swindon SN5........49 B8
Marshall St SN14......78 C7
Marshall Way BA11...110 D8
Marsh Cl SN25.......34 A3
Marsh Farm La SN1...50 C7
MARSHFIELD.......74 A8
Marshfield Path GL9...38 A8
Marshfield Prim Sch
　SN14.............74 B8
Marshfield Rd SN15...78 C8
Marshfield Way SN3...36 A2
Marshgate SN1.......50 F8
Marsh Gr 6 SN13....76 C1
Marsh La
　Breamore SP6......210 E4
　Cherhill SN11......166 A1
　Coombe Bissett SP5 . 150 F2
　Hungerford RG17....177 A7
　Nettleton SN14......53 C4
　Pen Selwood BA9....137 A4
　Rowde SN10.........96 D2
　Salisbury SP2.......145 F2
Marshmead BA14....101 F4
Marshmead Cl SP5... 152 F6
Marsh Rd
　Berkley BA11.......107 C1
　Rode BA11.........103 F1
　Trowbridge BA14....101 E5
　Marsh BA12.........117 A5
Marsh The SN4.......51 F3
Marshwood SP3.....201 E3
Marsland Rd SN2.....35 D2
MARSTON..........179 A3
Marston Ave SN4.....35 D4
MARSTON HILL......1 C4
Marston Hill GL7......1 C5
Marston Hill Farm La
　GL7.............1 D3
MARSTON MEYSEY.. 9 D7
MARSTON.........184 C7
Martha's La SP3......140 F4
Marti Cl SN12........94 C4
Martigny Rd SN12....94 B3
MARTIN..........209 B6
Martins Rd
　SP4.............198 A7
Martin Cl SP9.......216 E6
Martin Crest BA12....116 E5
Martin Dro End SP6.. 209 A7
MARTIN DROVE END. 209 A8
Martinfield SN3......51 D7
Martingale Rd SN8.. 183 D7
Martingate SN13......77 A1
Martinique St SP9... 216 D7
Martin Rd SP6......209 B6
Martins Cl
　Chippenham SN15....79 A4
　2 Salisbury SP2.... 152 A5
　Steeple Ashton BA14. 178 C4
Martin's Cl SN9......181 C6
Martins Croft SN14....75 B3
Martinsell Gn SN9....181 F1
Martinsell Hill (Fort)*
　SN8.............174 D2
Martins La BA14.....178 C4
MARTINSLADE......178 C5
Martins Rd BA14.....178 C5
Martins Rise SP5.....161 C4
Martin's St 4 SP7....202 C1
Martin Way SN11.....81 D3
Martlesham Rd SP4.. 217 D2
Martlet Cl SN12......94 D1
Martor Ind Est SN14...66 A2
Marvins Cl SP3......188 B2
Mary Barters La SP3. 204 E8
Maryland Cl SP2.....145 B5
Mascroft Rd BA14....106 A8
Masefield SN4........47 F3
Masefield Ave SN2....35 E3
Masefield Rd BA12....116 E6
Maskeleyne Way SN4 .63 F6
Maslen La SN13......83 F7
Mason Rd SN25......35 B6
Masons La BA15.....100 C8
Masons The SN5......33 A3
Masons Way SN13....76 D1
Massey Cl SN15......78 E5
Massey Rd 4 SN10 . 214 D1
Massinger Wlk SN3...50 F6
Matford Hill SN15.....79 A8
Mathews Cl SN25.....20 D1
Matilda Piece 5 SN6 19 D7
Matilda Way SN10...214 D4
Matley Moor SN3......51 E6
Matravers Cl BA13...108 F3
Matrons Cotts SP5...153 F1
Matthews Cl SN10...172 C1
Mattocks Path 2 SN1 .50 B1
Matty Hull Cl 19 SP7. 202 C1
Maud Cl SN10.......214 D4
Maud Heath Ct SN15..78 E8
Maud Heath's Cswy
　Chippenham SN15....70 C1
　Langley Burrell Without
　SN15.............71 B3

Maud Heath's Mon★ SN11 . . . . . . . . . . .80 C8
Maud Heath's Stone★ SN11 . . . . . . . . . . .80 C8
Maulton Cl BA14. . . . 101 D8
Maunders Dr BA14. . . .101 D4
Maundrell Cl SN10. . . . 96 D2
Maundrell Rd SN11. . . .81 C5
Maunsell Way SN4. . . . .63 F7
Maur Cl SN15. . . . . . . .78 C7
Maurice Way SN8. . . . 175 A7
Maurys La SO51 . . . . . 212 F6
Maxcroft La BA14. . . .101 E5
Maxey Cl SN5. . . . . . . .49 B8
Maxwell St SN1. . . . . . .50 A6
Maybold Cres 8 SN2 . 34 D5
May Cl SN2. . . . . . . . . .35 C1
Mayenne Pl SN10. . . . 179 C8
Mayfair Pl SP1. . . . . . 146 D1
Mayfield 1 SN4 . . . . 163 A5
Mayfield Ave Ind. Pk SP11. . . . . . . . . . . . 192 E1
Mayfield Cl
  4 Shipton Bellinger SP9. . . . . . . . . . . . 199 C8
  Swindon SN3. . . . . . .51 B7
Mayfield Rd 2 SP6 . . 210 C1
Mayfly Cl 4 SP6. . . . 210 D1
Mayfly Rd SN25. . . . . . .34 A7
May La
  Ebbesbourne Wake SP5. . . . . . . . . . . . 204 D3
  Yarnbrook BA14. . . . 105 F3
Mayo Cl SN13. . . . . . . .76 E2
Mays Dr BA13 . . . . . . 109 B5
Mays Firs SP6 . . . . . . 211 D5
May's La SN4. . . . . . . . .65 D4
Maytree Cl 6 BA11 . . 110 B7
May Tree Rd 9 SP10. . . . . . . . . . . . 193 C1
Mazurek Way SN25. . . . .34 E6
McArthur Glen Designer Outlet Village SN2 . . .50 A6
McKie Rd 3 SP4 . . . . 217 D2
Mcnamara St SN4. . . . 132 B1
McNeill Rd SP4. . . . . 198 A7
Mead Com Prim Sch The BA14. . . . . . . . . 102 B1
Mead Cl BA14 . . . . . . 105 D3
Meadens La SP5. . . . . 151 A1
Meade Rd 2 SP11 . . . 192 B5
Meadland SN13. . . . . . .76 E1
Meadow Ave 10 SP6. . . . . . . . . . . . 210 D1
Meadow Bridge Sch SN5. . . . . . . . . . . . . .19 E8
Meadow Cl
  Chippenham SN14 . . . .78 A7
  1 Dinton SP3 . . . . . 201 E2
  8 Fordingbridge SP6. . . . . . . . . . . . 210 D1
  Upper Minety SN16 . . 16 D2
  Yatton Keynell SN14 . . .68 F6
Meadowcroft SN2 . . . . .35 F3
Meadow Ct
  11 Fordingbridge SP6. . . . . . . . . . . . 210 D1
  Pewsey SN9. . . . . . . 215 C5
  Trowbridge BA14. . . . 101 D4
  Whiteparish SP5 . . . . 161 E4
Meadow Dr SN10 . . . . 214 C3
Meadowfield BA15. . . 100 B6
Meadow La
  Little Somerford SN15. . 44 A5
  Warminster BA12 . . . 116 D6
  Westbury BA13 . . . . 109 A4
Meadow Pk BA1. . . . . .82 B3
Meadow Rd
  Durrington/Bulford SP4. . . . . . . . . . . . 217 E8
  Melksham SN12. . . . . .94 C7
  3 Salisbury SP2. . . . 145 F1
Meadow Rd (South) 5 SP2. . . . . . . . . . . . 145 F1
Meadow Rise SN8 . . . 174 A6
Meadow Springs SN5. .48 E8
Meadows The
  Bourton SP8. . . . . . 137 F2
  Lydiard Tregoze SN5 . . .47 F5
  Salisbury SP1. . . . . 152 D8
Meadowsweet Cl 2 SN25. . . . . . . . . . . . .34 E5
Meadowsweet Dr SN11. . . . . . . . . . . . .80 F3
Meadow View
  5 Fittleton SP4. . . . 190 A4
  Kempsford GL7 . . . . 10 C7
  Lechlade-on-Thames GL7. . . . . . . . . . . . . 2 D5
Meadow Way
  Chiseldon SN4. . . . . .65 E7
  South Cerney GL7 . . . .7 F6
  Westbury BA13. . . . . 109 A3
  Winsley BA15. . . . . . .99 E7
Meadway
  4 Shrewton SP3 . . . 196 F6
  Wingfield BA14 . . . . 105 A8
Mead Way
  11 Shaftesbury SP7. . . 202 D1
  Swindon SN5 . . . . . . 34 B2

Meares Dr SN5 . . . . . . .49 B8
Mears Rd 4 SP4. . . . 198 A6
Medbourne La . . . . . . 163 A3
Medbourne Rd SN4. . . 163 A4
Medgbury Pl SN1. . . . . 50 D6
Medgbury Rd SN1. . . . .50 C6
Medicina St SP9. . . . . 216 D4
Medieval Hall Salisbury★ SP1. . . . . . . . . . . . 152 A8
Medina Way SN2 . . . . .35 F4
Medlar Ct SN2. . . . . . .35 B2
Medway SN25. . . . . . . .34 F4
Medway Rd SN25. . . . . .34 F4
Meerut Rd SP9 . . . . . 216 C6
Melbourne St SN3. . . . .50 F3
Melbourne Gdns 5 SP4. . . . . . . . . . . . 198 B6
Melbourne St BA13 . . 186 B7
MELBURY ABBAS. . . . 206 B7
Melbury Abbas Mill★ SP7. . . . . . . . . . . . 206 A7
Melbury Down★ SP5 206 C6
Melbury St SP7. . . . . 206 B6
Melbury Way 12 SP7 . 202 D2
Melchet Cl SO51. . . . . 162 D1
Melchet Pk
  Melchet Park and Plaitford SO51. . . . . . . . . . . 162 C1
  Plaitford SO51. . . . . 212 D8
Melchet Vw SO51. . . . 162 D2
Melfort Cl SN5. . . . . . .34 B2
Meliot Rise 12 SP10 . . 193 E2
MELKSHAM. . . . . . . . .94 A5
Melksham Blue Pool SN12. . . . . . . . . . . . .94 A4
Melksham Cl SN2. . . . . .35 B6
Melksham Com Hospl SN12. . . . . . . . . . . . .94 B3
MELKSHAM FOREST. . 94 D6
Melksham La SN13. . . . .93 C4
Melksham Oak Com Sch SN12. . . . . . . . . . . . 94 D1
Melksham Rd
  Chippenham SN14 . . . .78 B5
  Chippenham SN15 . . . .78 B5
  Holt BA14. . . . . . . . .92 F1
  Holt SN12. . . . . . . . .93 A2
  Lacock SN15 . . . . . . .86 D5
Melksham Sta SN12. . . .94 A6
Mellow Gd SN25. . . . . .34 E5
Melrose Ave BA12 . . . 116 E6
Melrose Cl
  Easterton SN10 . . . . 180 A1
  1 Swindon SN5 . . . . 49 C6
  4 Warminster BA12. . 116 E6
Melsome Rd SN15 . . . . .59 F1
Melstock Rd SN25 . . . . .34 C6
Melton Rd BA14 . . . . . 101 C2
Melusine Rd 4 SN3 . . .51 B8
Melville Cl 3 SN3 . . . .50 F6
Melvin Cl SP1 . . . . . . 146 D1
Mendip Cl
  3 Frome BA11. . . . . 110 A7
  Melksham SN12. . . . . .94 C4
  Swindon SN25 . . . . . .35 C3
  6 Warminster BA12. . 117 A8
Mendip Dr BA11 . . . . 110 A7
Menham Cl SN2 . . . . . 35 D2
Mercer Cl SN25. . . . . . .20 C1
Merchants House The★ SN8. . . . . . . . . . . . 213 D3
Mercia Ave SP10. . . . 193 C2
MERE. . . . . . . . . . . . 139 B5
Mere Ave SN14 . . . . . .41 F1
Mere By-Pass BA12. . . 139 A6
Mere Castle★ BA12. . 138 F6
Mere Down
  Kingston Deverill BA12. . . . . . . . . . . . 125 F3
  Kingston Deverill BA12 126 A5
Mere Mus★ BA12. . . . 139 A5
Mere Sch BA12 . . . . . 139 B5
Meriden Wlk SN3. . . . .51 B4
Meridian Wlk BA14 . . 105 A8
Meriton Ave SN13 . . . .77 A1
Merlin Cl 23 SP10 . . . 193 E2
Merlin Rd 1 SN11. . . .81 B5
Merlin Theatre BA11 . 110 A7
Merlin Way
  Bower Hill SN12. . . . . 94 B1
  Stratton St Margaret SN3 . . . . . . . . . . . .51 D8
  Swindon SN3 . . . . . . 36 D1
Merrifield Rd SP4 . . . 146 C6
Merrington Way SP9. 216 C7
Merrivale Gr SN3 . . . . .50 C5
Merry Orch SO43 . . . 212 D2
Mersey St SP10. . . . . 193 F1
Merton Ave SN2 . . . . 35 D4
Merton Cl 6 SP6. . . . 210 D2
Merton St 2 SN1. . . . .50 C6
Mervyn Webb Pl SN2 . 50 D8
Mesh Pond SP5. . . . . 210 D8
Methuen Ave SN12 . . . .94 B6
Methuen Cl BA15 . . . 100 E4
Methuen Dr 1 SP1 . . 152 C8
Methuen Pk
  Chippenham SN13 . . . .77 F4
  Chippenham SN14 . . . .77 F4
  5 Chippenham SN14 . .77 F5
Methuen Way SN13. . . .76 F2
Metis Cl SN25. . . . . . .34 B8
Mews The
  Highworth SN6. . . . . 23 A6
  Lydiard Millicent SN5. . .48 B3
  Warminster BA12 . . . 117 A7
Meynell Cl SN25. . . . . .34 F8

Meyrick Ave SP2. . . . 152 A5
Meysey Cl GL7. . . . . . . .1 A5
MEYSEY HAMPTON. . . .1 A5
Michaelmas Dro SP11. . . . . . . . . . . . 192 E1
Michael Pym's Rd SN16. . . . . . . . . . . . .28 A5
Middle Farm Cl SN15 . .45 B8
Middle Farm Ct GL7 . . 10 D7
Middle Field SN10. . . 214 C3
Middle Gd
  Cricklade SN6 . . . . . 19 C8
  Fovant SP3. . . . . . . 204 E7
Royal Wootton Bassett SN4 . . . . . . . . . . . 48 A2
Middle Green La SN15 .45 B1
MIDDLEHILL. . . . . . . .83 A6
Middle La
  Atworth/Whitley SN12 . .85 D1
  Cherhill SN11. . . . . . 166 B1
  Martin SP5. . . . . . . 208 F6
  Martin SP5. . . . . . . 209 A7
  Trowbridge BA14. . . . 101 F2
Middleleaze Dr SN5 . . .48 F8
Middlemass Gn SN9 . . 215 D5
Middlemead La
  Hannington SN6. . . . . 22 B8
  Hannington Wick SN6 . 11 A1
Middle St SP1 . . . . . . 151 E7
Middle Stoke BA2 . . . . .99 A6
Middleton
  Middle Winterslow SP5. . . . . . . . . . . . 149 B6
  The Common SP5. . . 149 B7
Middleton Cl
  Swindon SN3 . . . . . . .50 F6
  5 Warminster BA12. . 116 E6
Middleton Medieval Village of★ BA12. . . 194 A7
Middleton Rd
  Salisbury SP2. . . . . . 145 F2
  The Common SP5. . . 149 B7
Middletons Cl RG17. . 177 C8
Middleton Terr 6 SP4. . . . . . . . . . . . 132 B1
MIDDLEWICK. . . . . . . 76 D3
Middlewick La SN13 . . 76 D3
MIDDLE WINTERSLOW. . . . 149 B7
MIDDLE WOODFORD. . . . . . 131 B4
MIDFORD. . . . . . . . . . .98 C6
Midford Hill BA2. . . . . .98 C4
Midford La
  Limpley Stoke BA2. . . . 98 E7
  Limpley Stoke BA2. . . .98 F6
Midford Rd BA2 . . . . . .98 B7
Midhurst Ave SN3 . . . . .51 B5
Midlands Ind Est The BA14. . . . . . . . . . . . 92 E1
Midlands The BA14 . . . .92 E1
Mid Summer Pl SP4 . 217 E5
Midwinter Cl SN5. . . . .34 B2
Midwinter Gdns SN3. . .36 A2
MILBOURNE. . . . . . . . .28 D4
Milbourne La SN16 . . . .28 C4
Milbourne Pk SN16 . . . .28 C4
Milbourne Way SN14 . .78 C5
MILDENHALL. . . . . . . 175 A8
Mildenhall Way SN3 . . .36 B6
Mildmay Cl 12 SN5. . . .48 F5
Mile Dr SN15. . . . . . . .44 E1
MILE ELM. . . . . . . . . .89 A7
MILE END. . . . . . . . . 165 A3
Miles Field DT11. . . . . 206 A1
Miles Lane SP5. . . . . . 161 E5
Miles's La SP5. . . . . . 161 E5
Milestone Way SN15 . .70 C2
MILFORD. . . . . . . . . . 152 E8
Milford Hill SP1 . . . . . 152 B8
Milford Hollow 6 SP1. . . . . . . . . . . . 152 C8
Milford Ind Est SP1 . . 152 C8
Milford Manor Gdns SP1. . . . . . . . . . . . 152 D8
Milford Mill Rd SP1. . 152 D8
Milford Pk SP1 . . . . . 152 D8
Milford St
  Salisbury SP1. . . . . . 152 B8
  Swindon SN1 . . . . . . 50 C6
Milford Way SN5 . . . . .78 F4
MILKHOUSE WATER . 215 E8
MILKWELL. . . . . . . . . 203 B2
Millais Cl SN25 . . . . . . .20 C1
Milland Cl SN25. . . . . . 35 B6
Millard Cl 2 SN15. . . . .78 F4
Millard Rd 5 SN25 . . . 35 A8
Millards Cl BA14. . . . . 101 F4
Millards Way
  Standerwick BA11. . . 107 B1
  Upton Scudamore BA12. . . . . . . . . . . . 112 E4
Millbourn Cl BA15. . . . .99 D7
Millbrook 2 SP1 . . . . 146 B2
Millbrook La SN13 . . . 141 C1
Millbrook Prim Sch SN5. . . . . . . . . . . . .49 A3
Mill Cl
  Devizes SN10. . . . . . 214 C1
  Great Bedwyn SN8 . . 176 B2
  Longbridge Deverill BA12. . . . . . . . . . . . 120 F6
  South Cerney GL7 . . . .7 A7
  Winterbourne SP4 . . . 133 A4
  Wroughton SN4 . . . . .64 B6

Millditch 15 BA13 . . . 186 B7
Mill Dro SN8 . . . . . . . 183 C1
Mill End SP6. . . . . . . . 209 F2
Millennium Cl 2 SP2. . . . . . . . . . . . 152 B5
Millennium Visitor Ctr★ GL7. . . . . . . . . . . . . .6 B4
Miller Cl
  Chirton SN10. . . . . . 180 F4
  Salisbury SP1. . . . . . 145 E5
  Swindon SN5 . . . . . . .48 F8
Millers Cl SP8 . . . . . . 137 E2
Miller's La DT11 . . . . 207 D1
Millfield 6 RG17 . . . 165 A1
Millgreen Rd 1 SP4 . 217 C2
Millgrove St SN25 . . . . 34 D7
Millhand Villas BA14. . 105 E7
Mill Head SN10 . . . . . 179 A4
Mill Hill Ave SP9. . . . . 216 C8
Mill Hollow La SP7. . . 206 A7
Milling Cl SN6 . . . . . . . .7 A1
Millington Dr 3 BA14. . . . . . . . . . . . 105 A4
Mill Island BA12 . . . . 117 E5
Mill La
  Bishopstone SP5 . . . 150 A1
  Bishopstow BA11. . . . 117 F4
  Bourton SP8. . . . . . 137 E2
  Box SN13 . . . . . . . . .83 C7
  Bradford-on-Avon BA15. . . . . . . . . . . 100 D6
  Broughton Gifford SN12 93 C3
  Bulkington SN10 . . . 178 E5
  Castle Eaton SN6. . . . 10 A4
  Cherhill SN11. . . . . . 166 B1
  Chilmark SP3 . . . . . 200 F2
  Fairford GL7. . . . . . . . 1 F7
  Fovant SP3. . . . . . . 204 D8
  Gasper BA12 . . . . . 137 C6
  Hawkeridge BA13 . . . 108 E7
  Heytesbury BA12. . . . 194 C5
  Lambourn RG17 . . . 165 B1
  Lechlade GL7. . . . . . . 2 F4
  Little Somerford SN15. . .43 F5
  Maiden Bradley BA12 . 118 D5
  Malmesbury SN16 . . . .28 A3
  Melbury Abbas SP7 . . 206 A7
  Mere BA12. . . . . . . 139 B5
  Monkton Combe BA2. . .98 E8
  Poulshot SN10 . . . . . 179 A5
  Ramsbury SN8. . . . . 170 B2
  St Paul Malmesbury Without SN16 . . . . . . . . . . . 42 E1
  Salisbury SP1. . . . . . 145 E5
  Selwood BA11. . . . . 114 F8
  Shalbourne SN8. . . . 176 F2
  Somerford Keynes GL7 . .2 A2
  Stanton Fitzwarren SN6 22 A2
  Swindon SN1 . . . . . . 49 E2
  Swindon SN1 . . . . . . 50 A3
  The Common SP5. . . 149 E6
  Westbury BA13 . . . . 112 D8
  West Lavington SN10 . 187 E8
  Winterbourne Monkton SN4 . . . . . . . . . . . 167 C3
  Winterslow SP5. . . . 149 D7
  Zeale SP8. . . . . . . . 137 F2
Mill Lake SP8. . . . . . 137 E2
Mill Lane BA12 . . . . . 115 A8
Mill Path SP9. . . . . . . 216 D4
Mill Race Cl SP2 . . . . 151 F8
Mill Rd
  Devizes SN10. . . . . . 214 C1
  Netheravon SP4. . . . 190 A4
  Potterne SN10 . . . . . 179 D5
  Salisbury SP2. . . . . . 145 F1
  Worton SN10. . . . . . 179 A4
Mill St
  Calne SN11. . . . . . . . 81 B2
  Fontmell Magna SP7. . 206 A3
  Heytesbury BA12. . . . 194 C5
  Trowbridge BA14. . . . 105 D8
Millstone Cl SN4. . . . . .47 F1
Mill Stream App SP2. 146 A1
Mills Way SP4 . . . . . . 217 D4
Milne Cres 3 SP4 . . . 197 E6
Milne Rd SP4 . . . . . . 198 E6
Milne Way SN3 . . . . . 36 B5
MILSTON . . . . . . . . . 198 B8
Milston Ave SN2. . . . . .35 C5
Milston Down (Long Barrows)★ SP4 . . . 198 E8
Milston Dro SP4. . . . . 190 E1
Milston Rd
  Bulford SP4. . . . . . . 198 C4
  Durrington/Bulford SP4. . . . . . . . . . . . 217 D8
Milston View 2 SP4 . 198 C5
MILTON . . . . . . . . . . 141 B3
Milton Ave
  6 Andover SP10. . . . 193 C1
  Melksham SN12. . . . . .94 B4
MILTON LILBOURNE . 182 F7
Milton Pl GL7. . . . . . . . 1 F6
Milton Rd
  Amesbury SP4 . . . . . 217 E2
  Pewsey SN9. . . . . . . 215 F5
  Salisbury SP2. . . . . . 152 B6
  Swindon SN1 . . . . . . 50 B6
Milton St GL7. . . . . . . . 1 F6
Milton's Way SN4. . . . .47 F2
Milverton Ct SN3 . . . . .51 A5
MINCHINGTON. . . . . 207 D1
Minden Cl 13 SP10 . . 193 D2
Minden Way SP9 . . . . 216 D4
Minerva Hts SN26. . . . .21 A1

MINETY. . . . . . . . . . . .17 B2
Minety CE Prim Sch SN16. . . . . . . . . . . . .17 B2
MINETY COMMON. . . . 31 C8
Minety La SN16 . . . . . . 16 A7
Minety Rd SN2. . . . . . .35 B5
Minnow Cl
  5 Calne SN11. . . . . . 81 B5
  Swindon SN25 . . . . . 34 A7
Minories Rd SP9. . . . . 216 E6
Minot Cl SN16 . . . . . . .28 A5
Minster CE Prim Sch The BA12. . . . . . . . . . . . 116 F7
Minster Cl SN25 . . . . .34 F7
Minster St
  7 Salisbury SP1. . . . 146 A1
  Wilton SP2. . . . . . . 144 D3
Minster View BA12 . . 116 F7
Minster Way SN14 . . . .78 A5
Mint Cl SN2 . . . . . . . . 34 D4
Minton Distribution Pk SP4. . . . . . . . . . . . 217 C4
Minty's Top SN15. . . . .96 A7
Mir Cres 3 SN25 . . . . .34 B7
MISSELFORE. . . . . . . 204 F1
Mitchell Cl
  3 Andover SP10. . . . 193 C1
Royal Wootton Bassett SN4 . . . . . . . . . . . 47 D1
Mitchell Dr
  Bower Hill SN12. . . . . 178 B8
  Westonbirt GL8 . . . . . 25 D8
Mitchell Rd SP9. . . . . 216 D8
Mitchells Cl 5 SP5 . . 211 C7
Mizmaze★ SP6. . . . . 210 D7
Moat Rd BA13 . . . . . 108 D6
Moberly Rd SP1. . . . . 146 B3
Model Farm La SP5. . 148 C3
Moffat Rise SN16. . . . . .28 A5
Moggs La SN11. . . . . 172 A8
Moldens The BA14. . . 105 B6
Mompesson Ho★ SP2. . . . . . . . . . . . 152 A8
Monastery Rd BA13. . 186 C8
Monet Cl SN25. . . . . . .34 B7
Moneyer Rd 5 SP10 . 193 D2
Monkeys Jump SO51. 212 F5
Monkley La
  Rode BA11. . . . . . . 107 C8
  Rode BA11. . . . . . . 104 C1
Monks Cl
  North Tidworth SP9 . . 216 C7
  Tidworth SP9. . . . . . 216 C7
Monks Dr SN3. . . . . . .84 B8
Monk's La SN13 . . . . . .85 B6
Monks Pk SN16. . . . . . .28 B4
Monks Pk Gdns SN13 . .85 B5
Monks Way SN15 . . . . .79 A4
Monks Wlk GL7. . . . . . . 2 E3
Monkton Cl SN3 . . . . . .51 B4
MONKTON COMBE. . . .98 E8
MONKTON DEVERILL. . . . . . 126 D7
MONKTON FARLEIGH . .90 F7
Monkton Gn BA12 . . . 126 D7
Monkton Hill SN15 . . . .78 D7
Monkton House★ SN12. . . . . . . . . . . . .93 C1
Monkton Pk SN15. . . . .78 F7
Monkton Pk Prim Sch SN15. . . . . . . . . . . . .78 E7
Monmouth Cl 4 SN3 . .50 F4
Monmouth Dr BA11. . 110 B5
Monmouth Rd SP3. . . 203 D8
Mons Ave SP4 . . . . . 198 E6
Mons La SN15 . . . . . . 86 D8
Montague Cl SN15. . . . .79 A4
Montague Ct BA14. . . 102 A1
Montague Pl SN12. . . . .94 C5
Montague Rd SP2 . . . 151 D7
Montagu St SN2. . . . . .49 F7
Monteagle Cl SN5 . . . . 49 A4
Montgomery Ave SN12 .94 C5
Montgomery Gdns SP2. . . . . . . . . . . . 145 E2
Montgomery Rd
  Enham Alamein SP11. . 193 E3
  Warminster BA12 . . . 113 D1
Montreal Way 8 SP4. . . . . . . . . . . . 217 F8
Montrose Cl SN2. . . . . .34 E2
Monument Hill SN10. 214 C1
Monument View SN11 .89 C7
Monxton Cl 3 SP1. . . 146 D5
Moody's Hill SP5. . . . 155 E2
Moon Cl SN14 . . . . . . .75 D2
Moonraker Rise BA13. . . . . . . . . . . . 109 B5
Moonrakers SN10 . . . 214 D5
Moor Barton SN13. . . . .84 D6
Moore Cl SN4 . . . . . . .64 C8
Moore's Pl 12 RG17 . 177 B7
Moores Yd BA14 . . . 104 C6
Moorgate GL7. . . . . . . .2 B4
MOOR GREEN. . . . . . . 84 D6
Moorhen Cl
  Swindon SN3. . . . . . 51 E5
  Trowbridge BA14. . . . 101 D4
Moor Hill SP3 . . . . . . 204 D8
Moorings The SN1. . . . .50 A5
Moor La
  Charlton Heath SN16. . .29 D6
  Whiteparish SP5 . . . . 161 A1
Moorlands SN15. . . . . .70 E2
Moorlands The SN10 . 214 A2
Moor Lane SP5 . . . . . 160 F1

Moormead Rd SN4 . . . .64 B6
Moor Pk SN13 . . . . . . .84 C6
Moors Cl SN15. . . . . . .70 C5
Moot Cl
  7 Andover SP10. . . . 193 E2
  Downton SP5 . . . . . 211 B7
Moot Gdns SP5 . . . . . 211 A7
Moot La SP5. . . . . . . 211 A7
Moot (Motte & Bailey) The★ . . . . . . . . . . . 211 B8
Mopes La SN5 . . . . . . .33 C7
Moray Rd SN2 . . . . . . .35 E1
MOREDON. . . . . . . . . .34 E3
Moredon Pk SN2 . . . . 34 D3
Moredon Prim Sch SN2. . . . . . . . . . . . .34 E3
Moredon Rd SN25. . . . .34 F3
Moresby Cl SN5 . . . . . .49 C6
Morgan's La
  Pentridge SP5 . . . . . 208 E5
  Winterbourne SP4. . . 133 A2
Morgans Rise Rd 3 SP5. . . . . . . . . . . . 211 C8
Morgans Vale SO43 . . 212 D2
Morgans Vale Rd SP5. . . . . . . . . . . . 211 C7
Morgan's Vale & Woodfalls CE Prim Sch SP5. . . . . . . . . . . . 211 C8
Morgan Wlk BA13 . . . 108 E2
Morie Cl SN5. . . . . . . .34 B1
Morley Field BA12. . . 117 C7
Morley Pl 28 RG17 . . 177 B7
Morley St SN1. . . . . . .50 C5
Morris Cl BA1. . . . . . . .82 B3
Morris La
  Bath BA1. . . . . . . . . 82 B3
  Devizes SN10. . . . . . 214 B3
Morrison St SN2. . . . . .49 F7
Morris Rd SN8. . . . . . 213 B2
Morris St SN2 . . . . . . .49 E6
Morse Cl
  Chippenham SN15 . . . .78 E4
  Malmesbury SN16 . . . .28 A4
Morse Gdns SN5. . . . . .49 C6
Morse St SN1. . . . . . . .50 C5
Morstone Rd SN4 . . . . 61 D8
Mortimer Cl 5 SN5. . . .49 B7
Mortimer St BA14. . . 105 C7
Mortimores SN14 . . . . .75 B2
Moses Mead SN25 . . . . 34 A3
Moss Mead SN14 . . . . .77 F8
MOTCOMBE. . . . . . . 202 A4
Motcombe CE VA Prim Sch SP7. . . . . . . . . . . . 202 B2
Motcombe Rd SP7. . . 202 B2
Moulton Dr BA15 . . . 100 D4
MOUNTAIN BOWER. . .66 F4
Mountain Wood BA1. . .82 B2
Mount Carmel Rd SP11. . . . . . . . . . . . 199 F3
Mountford Manor Prim Sch SN3. . . . . . . . . . . . .50 F6
Mount Hts SP5 . . . . . 135 E3
Mountings The SN4. . . .64 B8
Mount La
  Barford St Martin SP3. . . . . . . . . . . . 143 B4
  Warminster BA12 . . . 117 A5
Mountpleasant SP3. . 203 D8
Mount Pleasant
  Atworth SN12 . . . . . .85 A1
  Atworth/Whitley SN12 . .93 A8
  4 Bishopstone SN6 . . 163 E6
  Bradford-on-Avon BA15. . . . . . . . . . . 100 D7
  Chippenham SN14 . . . .70 A1
  Kilmington BA12 . . . 123 F4
  Lechlade GL7. . . . . . . 2 C4
  South Newton SP2. . . 130 A4
Mountsfield BA11. . . . 110 A2
MOUNT SORREL. . . . 205 B3
Mount The BA14 . . . . 101 D2
Mowlems The BA14. . 104 F3
Moxhams 21 SP6 . . . 210 D1
Moyle Pk BA14 . . . . . 102 A1
Moyne Cl SN10 . . . . . 179 D8
Moyne Gdns 7 SP4. . 217 D3
Mucha SN25. . . . . . . . 20 D1
Muddyford Rd
  Downton SP5 . . . . . 159 F1
  Redlynch SP5 . . . . . 211 C8
Mud La SN5 . . . . . . . .32 F2
Mudmead La BA14. . . 106 E8
Muirfield SN25 . . . . . . 34 D7
Mulberry Cl SN14. . . . .70 B1
Mulberry Ct
  Frome BA11. . . . . . . 110 B7
  Sixpenny Handley SP5. 208 B4
Mulberry Gr
  Swindon SN2 . . . . . . 35 A2
  Swindon SN25 . . . . . 35 A2
Mulcaster Ave SN5 . . . .48 F5
Mullins Cl SN14. . . . . .75 A3
Mundy Ave SN3. . . . . .51 C4
Munks Cl 3 SP2. . . . . 151 E7
Munnings Ct 2 SP10. . . . . . . . . . . . 193 C1
Munro Cl SN3 . . . . . . .50 E6
MURCOTT. . . . . . . . . .14 F4
Murdock Rd SN3 . . . . .51 C6
Murhill BA2. . . . . . . . . .99 C6
Murrayfield SN15. . . . .70 E1
Murray Rd BA14 . . . . 101 D2

Murray Wlk SN12 . . . . . .94 B5
Muscott Cl 3 SP9 . . . .199 C8
Muscovey Cl SN15 . . . . . .60 A2
Mustang Cl 1 BA13. .108 E2
Mustang Way SN5 . . . .34 C2
Mustard Way 7
SP11. . . . . . . . . . . . . .193 F2
Mustons La 28 SP7. . .202 C2
Mycroft Rd 2 SN25. . .34 D6
Myrrfield Rd 7 SP1. .146 D5
Myrtle Ave BA12 . . . .116 F6
Myrtle Gdns SN2. . . . .35 C2
Mythern Meadow
BA15. . . . . . . . . . . . .100 E5

**N**

Nadder Cl 13 SP3 . . . .203 E8
Nadder La SP2 . . . . . .144 F2
Nadder Rd SP9 . . . . . .216 D6
Nadder Terr SP2. . . . .144 C2
Nahalsen Cl SN4 . . . .133 D6
Naini Tal Rd SP9. . . . .216 C6
Nantwich SN5. . . . . . . .49 A3
Napier Cl SN2 . . . . . . . .50 A7
Napier Cres SP1 . . . .146 D1
Napiers 1 SN8 . . . . . .176 B3
Napier Wlk SP10. . . .193 F1
Narrow Wine St
BA14. . . . . . . . . . . . .105 D8
Nash Cl 3 SN25 . . . . . .35 A8
Nash La SN15. . . . . . . .56 B1
Nash Rd SN8 . . . . . . .173 A8
National Monuments
Records Ctr★ SN2. . .50 A7
Naughton Ave SN10. .214 E6
Naunton Rd SN3. . . . . .51 A6
Navigator Cl BA14 . .101 E4
Neal Cl 1 SP1. . . . . .146 C5
Neale Ct SN13 . . . . . . .76 F1
Neale's Barrow★
SP2. . . . . . . . . . . . . .150 A6
Neeld Cl SN14 . . . . . . .68 F6
Neeld Cres SN14. . . . .78 B8
Neighbridge GL7 . . . . . .5 F1
Neigh Bridge Ctry Pk★
GL7. . . . . . . . . . . . . . . .5 F2
Nell Hill SN6. . . . . . . . .22 A7
Nelson Cl 1 SP4 . . . .198 F6
Nelson Rd SP2. . . . . .146 A2
Nelson St SN1. . . . . . . .49 F5
Nelson Wlk SP10 . . . .193 F1
Nepaul Rd SP9 . . . . . .216 C7
Neptune Cres 2 SN3 .51 B8
Neptune Rd BA13. . . .108 F5
Nery Rd SP9. . . . . . . .216 D4
Ness Cl 1 SN5. . . . . . . .34 B2
Nestings The BA14. . .105 A5
Nestleton Cl SN11. . . .81 B1
NESTON. . . . . . . . . . . .84 E6
Neston Cres SN13 . . . .84 E6
Neston Gdns SN13. . . .84 B7
Neston Pk★ SN13 . . . .84 E3
Neston Prim Sch
SN13. . . . . . . . . . . . . .84 E6
NETHERAVON. . . . . . .190 A3
Netheravon Cl SN11. .146 B3
Netheravon Rd
Durrington SP4 . . . .198 B7
Figheldean SP4 . . . .190 B1
Salisbury SP1. . . . . .146 B2
Nethercote Hill SN15 .86 D6
NETHERHAMPTON. . . .151 A8
Netherhampton Bsns Ctr
SP2. . . . . . . . . . . . . .151 A8
Netherhampton Rd
Netherhampton SP2 .150 F8
Quidhampton SP2 . . .144 F1
Nether Leaze SN9 . . .215 B5
Nethermore SN13 . . . .84 D6
Netherstreet SN15. . . .96 D6
NETHERTON. . . . . . . .185 F4
Netherton Cl SN3. . . . .51 B4
Netherton Hill SP11. .185 F4
Netherton House★
SP11. . . . . . . . . . . . .185 F4
Netherton Rd SP11 . .185 F4
Nettlebed Nursery 14
SP7. . . . . . . . . . . . . .202 C2
Nettlecombe 6 SP7 .202 D2
Nettlemead La
Deptford BA12. . . . .195 F1
Wylye BA12. . . . . . . .201 F8
NETTLETON. . . . . . . . .53 C1
NETTLETON GREEN. . . .53 B1
Nettleton Rd SN14. . . .53 B3
NETTLETON SHRUB. . . .67 C7
NETTON. . . . . . . . . . .131 E6
Netton Cl SP5 . . . . . .205 E4
Netton St SP5 . . . . . .205 E4
Nett Rd SP4. . . . . . . .196 F6
Nevil Cl SP4. . . . . . . .217 D1
Neville Cl SP1 . . . . . .146 C4
Neville Terr SN15. . . . .57 D1
Nevis Cl SN5. . . . . . . .34 B2
Newall Tuck Rd SN15 .78 F7
Newark Cl SN5 . . . . . . .49 B3
New Bottom Rd SP4 .145 E7
Newbourne Gdns
SN14. . . . . . . . . . . . .56 D6
New Bridge Cl SN2 . . .50 C7
New Bridge Rd SP1. .152 A2
New Bridge Sq 5
SN1. . . . . . . . . . . . . .50 C7

New Broughton Rd
SN12. . . . . . . . . . . . .94 A5
New Brunswick Cl 4
SP4. . . . . . . . . . . . . .217 F8
Newburgh Pl SN6. . . . .22 F6
Newburn Cres SN1 . . .49 F5
NEWBURY . . . . . . . . .119 C8
Newbury Ave SN11 . . .80 F4
Newbury Dr
Chippenham SN14 . . . .77 F5
Swindon SN5 . . . . . . .49 B3
Newbury Rd
Andover SP10 . . . . . .193 E2
Lambourn RG17. . . . .165 B1
Newbury St RG17 . . .165 A1
Newby Acre SN8. . . .213 D4
Newby Cl 4 SN10 . . .187 E8
New Canal SP1. . . . . .152 A8
Newcastle St SN1. . . . .50 D6
New Cl
Bourton SP8. . . . . . .137 E2
West Knoyle BA12. . .140 E7
West Knoyle SP3. . . .141 A8
New Close Prim Sch
BA12. . . . . . . . . . . .117 B6
New Coll SN3. . . . . . . .50 F5
New Coll Wlk SN3. . . . .50 F5
Newcombe Dr SN2 . . .50 A7
Newcombe Trad Est
SN2. . . . . . . . . . . . . .50 B7
New Cres SN11 . . . . .192 A5
Newcroft Cl SN11. . . . .81 B4
Newcroft Rd SN11 . . . .81 B4
New Cut BA12 . . . . . .139 A6
New Dro SP11 . . . . . .192 A5
Newfield Cl BA13 . . . .108 F4
New Forest CE Prim Sch
The SP5. . . . . . . . . .212 C4
NEWGROUNDS. . . . . . .211 B1
New Haig Rd 7 SP4 .198 E6
New Hall Hospl SP5. .158 F8
Newhall St SN1. . . . . .50 B5
New Harnham Rd
SP2. . . . . . . . . . . . . .152 A6
New Hayward Bottom
RG17. . . . . . . . . . . . .171 C2
New House La SP11. .192 E4
Newhurst Pk BA14. . .102 A2
Newill Cl SN26. . . . . . .20 D1
New King Barrows★
SP4. . . . . . . . . . . . . .197 F5
New La
Cann SP7 . . . . . . . . .202 D1
Cann Common SP7 . .206 A8
Seend SN12. . . . . . .178 D7
Newland Rd SN25. . . . .35 A3
Newlands Cl SN15 . . . .70 E7
Newlands Rd SN13. . . .77 A1
New Lawns SN12 . . . . .94 B4
Newleaze
Steeple Ashton BA14 .178 A4
Trowbridge BA14. . . .101 F4
Newleaze Pk SN12. . . .93 B4
Newlyn Cl SN26. . . . . .20 D1
Newman Rd SN10. . . .214 C1
Newmans View SN25 .34 A2
Newmans Way SP4. . .217 E7
Newmarket Ave
BA14. . . . . . . . . . . .105 E4
Newmarket Cl 9
BA14. . . . . . . . . . . . .77 F6
Newmeadow Copse
SN5. . . . . . . . . . . . . .34 A1
Newnton Farm La GL8 .13 C4
Newnton Gr SN16. . . . .27 E4
Newnton Rd GL8. . . . .13 A5
Newopaul Way
Warminster BA12 . . .112 F1
Warminster BA12 . . .116 F8
Newpark Rd
Charlton Musgrove
BA9. . . . . . . . . . . . .136 F6
Penselwood BA9. . . .137 A5
New Pk Rd SN10. . . .214 B4
New Pk St SN10 . . . .214 A4
Newport BA12. . . . . .117 A7
Newport St SN1 . . . . .50 D3
New Rd
Bath BA1. . . . . . . . . .82 C2
Bourton SP8. . . . . . .137 D5
Bradford-on-Avon
BA15. . . . . . . . . . .100 E7
Bromham SN15 . . . . . .96 A5
Calne SN11 . . . . . . . .81 B2
Calne Without SN11. .79 F3
Chippenham SN15 . . . .78 D7
Chiseldon SN4. . . . . . .65 D3
Codford BA12. . . . . .195 A3
Donhead St Andrew
SP7. . . . . . . . . . . . .203 B8
22 Durrington/Bulford
SP4. . . . . . . . . . . . .198 B7
East Knoyle SP3. . . . .141 B3
Erlestoke BA13 . . . .179 A2
Kilmington BA12 . . . .123 D6
Landford SP5. . . . . .212 D5
Limpley Stoke BA2. . . .99 B5
Maiden Bradley with
Yarnfield BA11. . . .123 D8
Marlborough SN8. . . .213 D3
Melksham Without SN12 94 A7
Purton SN5. . . . . . . .33 C5
Rockbourne SP6. . . .210 A5
Royal Wootton Bassett
SN4. . . . . . . . . . . . .47 D1
2 Shaftesbury SP7. .202 B2
1 Trowbridge BA14. .105 D7
Zeale SP8. . . . . . . .138 A3

New Rd Ct BA15 . . . .100 E7
New Severalls The
SN9. . . . . . . . . . . . .182 E7
Newson Rd
8 Swindon SN25 . . . .34 C5
5 Swindon SN25 . . . .34 D5
New St
16 Market Lavington
SN10. . . . . . . . . . .179 F1
Salisbury SP1. . . . . .152 A8
Winterbourne Stoke
SP3. . . . . . . . . . . . .196 F3
Newstead Cl 1 SN25 .34 F6
New Terr BA14 . . . . .101 C7
New Terrace BA14. . .101 D6
Newth's La SN5. . . . . .19 D2
NEWTON. . . . . . . . . .161 B2
Newton Abbot Cl 6
BA14. . . . . . . . . . . . .77 F6
Newton Barrow★
SP2. . . . . . . . . . . . . .130 E3
Newton Cl SP5 . . . . .161 C3
NEWTON GROVE. . . . . .27 E4
Newton La SP5 . . . . .161 B3
Newton Rd SP2. . . . .145 D1
Newtons Wlk SN8 . . .170 B8
NEWTON TONY. . . . . .199 B3
Newton Tony CE Prim
Sch SP4. . . . . . . . . .199 B3
Newton Way SN2 . . . .35 C4
NEWTOWN
Shalbourne. . . . . . . .176 E2
West Tisbury . . . . . .203 B7
Newtown
Bradford-on-Avon
BA15. . . . . . . . . . .100 C6
Broad Chalke SP5 . .205 C4
Heytesbury BA12. . .194 C5
Hullavington SN14. . . .41 F1
Trowbridge BA14. . .105 C8
Westbury BA13 . . . .109 C3
NEW TOWN
Alton. . . . . . . . . . . .173 D3
Farnham. . . . . . . . . .207 C2
Ramsbury. . . . . . . . .170 C2
Sixpenny Handley. . .207 F6
Swindon . . . . . . . . . .50 D6
Newtown Com Prim Sch
BA14. . . . . . . . . . . .105 C8
Newtown La
Hinton Charterhouse
BA2. . . . . . . . . . . . . .98 F1
Hinton Charterhouse
BA2. . . . . . . . . . . . .103 A8
New Town La SN6. . .163 E6
Newtown Rd SN8 . . .170 C2
New Ward Rd SP4 . . .198 E7
New Zealand Ave
SP2. . . . . . . . . . . . . .145 D2
Niblett St BA15. . . . . .100 E2
Nicholas Ct SN1 . . . . .50 C2
Nicolson Cl 6 SP4 . .217 E3
Nicolson Vale SP4. . .132 B1
Niebull Cl SN1. . . . . . .28 A5
Nightingale Ave
Melksham SN12. . . . . .94 D4
8 West Wellow SO51 .212 F6
Nightingale Cl
Melksham SN12. . . . . .94 D4
8 West Wellow SO51. .212 F6
Nightingale Dr BA13. .109 B4
Nightingale La
South Marston SN3. . . .36 F4
Tisbury SP3 . . . . . . .203 C6
Nightingale Rd BA14. .105 A8
Nightingale Way
5 Calne SN11. . . . . . .81 B5
South Cerney GL7 . . . . .7 A6
Nightingale Wlk SP2. .145 E1
Nightjar Cl SN4 . . . . . .94 D4
Nightwood Copse 3
SN5. . . . . . . . . . . . . .34 A1
Nindum Rd SN3 . . . . .36 C1
Nine Acre Dr SN13 . . .76 D1
NINE ELMS. . . . . . . . . .49 A8
Nine Elms La SN5. . . . .48 F8
Nive Rd SN4. . . . . . . .168 E8
Noade St SP5. . . . . . .206 E4
Nobles Pl 5 SN13 . . . .76 C1
Noble St SN16. . . . . . .40 C8
Nocton Rd SN4 . . . . . .64 E3
Noctule Ave BA14. . .106 A8
Nolan Cl 1 SP5. . . . . .34 F8
Nolands Rd SN11 . . .166 D2
NOMANSLAND. . . . . .212 C4
Norbin
South Wraxall BA15. . .83 F1
South Wraxall BA15. . .91 F8
South Wraxall SN13. . .84 A2
Norborne Rd SN4. . . .167 C7
Norcliffe Rd SN3. . . . .51 B4
Noredown Way SN4 . .47 E1
Noremarsh Com Jun Sch
SN4. . . . . . . . . . . . . .47 E1
Nore Marsh Rd SN4. . .47 E1
Norfolk Cl 1 SN3. . . . .50 F6
Norfolk Rd SP2 . . . . .151 E7
NORLEAZE. . . . . . . . .108 F8
Norley La SN11. . . . . . .80 C3
Norman Cl SN15. . . . . .79 A4
Norman Dr
Old Sarum SP4. . . . . .146 C8
Winterbourne SP4. . .132 C1
Normandy Rd
Overtown SN4. . . . . . .64 D3
South Tidworth SP9. .216 D4
Normandy Way 14
SP6. . . . . . . . . . . . . .210 D1
Norman Rd SN2 . . . . .35 C1

NORMANTON . . . . . . .197 F3
Norney Rd BA13 . . . .179 A4
Norridge View 4
BA12. . . . . . . . . . . .116 E7
NORRINGTON
COMMON. . . . . . . . . .93 C6
Norrington Gate SN12 .93 C5
Norrington Green
SN12. . . . . . . . . . . . .93 C6
Norrington La SN12. . .93 C6
Norrington Manor★
SP5. . . . . . . . . . . . . .204 A2
Norris Cl SN4. . . . . . . .65 C3
Norris Rd BA14 . . . . .102 B3
Northacre Ind Est
BA13. . . . . . . . . . . .108 D5
Northampton St SN1. .50 D6
North Bank Rise SN4. .47 F2
Northbourne Rd SN25 .35 A7
NORTH BRADLEY. . . . .105 D4
North Bradley CE Prim
Sch BA14. . . . . . . . .105 D2
NORTH BREWHAM. . . .122 A6
NORTHBROOK. . . . . .179 E1
Northbrook. . . . . . . . .179 F1
Northbrook Cl 1
SN10. . . . . . . . . . . . .179 F1
Northbrook Rd
Melksham SN12. . . . . .93 F7
Swindon SN25 . . . . . .35 A1
North Cft SP3. . . . . . .188 B3
NORTH CHARFORD. . . .211 C6
North Charford Crossing
SP6. . . . . . . . . . . . . .210 F6
North Charford Dro
SP6. . . . . . . . . . . . . .210 C8
North Comm La SP5 .212 B7
North Cote SN11. . . . . .81 A4
Northcote Cres 7
BA11. . . . . . . . . . . . .110 A7
Northcroft Rd 1
SN13. . . . . . . . . . . . .76 B1
North Down
Hurstbourne Tarrant
SP11. . . . . . . . . . . .185 F1
Hurstbourne Tarrant
SP11. . . . . . . . . . . .185 F2
North Dr 4 SN3 . . . . .34 F8
Northen Cl GL7 . . . . . .10 E6
NORTHEND. . . . . . . . . .82 A5
Northend BA1. . . . . . . .82 A6
NORTH END. . . . . . . . . .6 E2
North End
Ashton Keynes SN6 . . . .6 C1
Calne SN11 . . . . . . . .81 A4
North End Gdns SN16. .25 C1
Northen Terr
Durrington SP4 . . . .197 F7
Larkhill SP4 . . . . . . .198 A7
Northern Rd SN2 . . . .35 A1
North Farm RG17. . . .165 B2
Northfield BA15 . . . . . .99 F7
Northfield La SN14 . . . .66 A2
Northfields
Bulkington SN10 . . . .178 E5
Calne SN11 . . . . . . . .81 A4
1 Lambourn RG17. . .165 A2
Northfield Way SN3. . .51 B7
Northgate Gdns
SN10. . . . . . . . . . . .214 A4
Northgate St SN10 . .214 A4
North La
Nomansland SP5 . . . .212 C4
Warminster BA12 . . .116 D6
West Tytherley SP5 . .149 F5
Northlands Ind Est
BA12. . . . . . . . . . . .117 B7
Northleaze SN13 . . . . .76 D1
North Leaze Cl SN2. . .34 F3
Northleigh BA15. . . . . .91 E1
Northleigh Terr SP2. .144 D3
North Mdw National
Nature Reseve★ SN6. .8 C1
North Mdw Rd SN6. . . .8 C1
Northmoor La GL7. . . . .6 F8
NORTH NEWNTON. . . .181 E4
North Rd
Amesbury SP4. . . . . .217 E2
Ashmore SP5 . . . . . .206 E5
Mere BA12. . . . . . . .139 A6
North Row BA12. . . . .117 A7
Northside SP4. . . . . .146 D8
North St
Broad Chalke SP5 . .205 B4
Calne SN11 . . . . . . . .81 B4
Mere BA12. . . . . . . .139 A5
Pewsey SN9. . . . . . .215 C5
Salisbury SP2. . . . . .145 F1
Swindon SN5 . . . . . . .50 C5
Wilton SP2. . . . . . . .144 D3
North Standen Rd
RG17. . . . . . . . . . . . .177 A6
North Star Ave SN2. . .50 B8
North Star Ind Est
SN2. . . . . . . . . . . . . .50 B7
NORTH STREET. . . . . .210 E5
NORTH TIDWORTH. . . .216 D8
Northview 20 RG17. .177 B7
North View
Berwick St James
SP3. . . . . . . . . . . . . .196 F2
Highworth SN6. . . . . .22 F5
North View Hts RG17. .177 C7
North View Pl SN8 . . .213 D4
Northview Prim Sch
SN6. . . . . . . . . . . . . .23 C1
North Wall SN6. . . . . .19 D8
Northway SP4 . . . . . .134 B7

North Way
Calne SN11 . . . . . . . .81 A4
Trowbridge BA14. . . .105 A7
North Wlk SP1. . . . . .152 A8
Northwood SN15 . . . . .70 E2
NORTH WRAXALL. . . . .67 B3
NORTH WROUGHTON. .64 B8
NORTON. . . . . . . . . . .41 D5
NORTON BAVANT. . . . .194 A6
Norton Dr SP4. . . . . .146 D6
NORTON FERRIS . . . . .124 C4
Norton Gr SN3. . . . . . .50 D5
Norton Rd
Sutton Veny BA12 . . .117 C1
Sutton Veny BA12 . . .194 A5
Norwood Castle (site
of)★ SN16 . . . . . . . . .4 F2
Norwood Cl 3 SN3. . .51 D4
NOTTON. . . . . . . . . . .86 B8
Notton House Sch
SN15. . . . . . . . . . . . .86 B8
Notton Pk
Lacock SN14. . . . . . . .78 A1
Notton SN15. . . . . . . .86 B8
Thingley SN14. . . . . . .77 F2
Nova Hroed Acad SN2 34 D2
Noyes Cl
Chippenham SN14 . . . .77 F8
Haydon Wick SN6. . . .34 C5
N Swindon District Ctr
SN2. . . . . . . . . . . . . .34 E6
Nuffield Cl SN5. . . . . . .49 B8
Nunns Pk SP5 . . . . . .161 D4
NUNTON. . . . . . . . . .152 D1
Nunton Dro SP5 . . . .152 D1
Nunwick Way 4 SN1 .50 A2
Nurseries The
Christian Malford
SN15. . . . . . . . . . . . .58 A2
Swindon SN1 . . . . . . .50 B4
Nursery Cl
4 Amesbury SP4. . . .217 B3
Atworth/Whitley SN12 .92 E8
Trowbridge BA14. . . .102 A3
Wroughton SN4 . . . . . .64 A5
Nursery Gdns
Corsham SN13. . . . . . .85 A8
Mere BA12. . . . . . . .139 A5
Nursery Rd
Colerne SN14. . . . . . .75 A3
Salisbury SP2. . . . . .145 E1
Siddington GL7. . . . . .6 B8
Nursery The SN16. . . . .27 F6
NURSTEED. . . . . . . . .214 E1
Nursteed Cl SN10. . . .214 D3
Nursteed Com Prim Sch
SN10. . . . . . . . . . . . .214 E3
Nursteed Pk SN10 . . .214 E2
Nursteed Rd SN10 . . .214 C2
Nursteed Rd Ind Est
SN10. . . . . . . . . . . . .214 C1
NUTBANE. . . . . . . . . .193 A4
Nutbane La SP11 . . . .193 A4
Nuthatch Cl 4 SN3. . .51 E6
Nuthatch Rd SN11. . . .81 B5
Nutley Ct 8 SN8. . . .183 D8
Nutmeg Cl 7 SN2 . . .34 D4
Nyland Rd SN3 . . . . . .51 C7
Nyland Rd SN3 . . . . . .51 B7
NYTHE. . . . . . . . . . . .51 C7
Nythe Rd SN3. . . . . . .36 B1

**O**

Oakapple Cl 4 SN4. .163 B6
Oak Ash Gn SP2 . . . .144 C2
Oak Ave GL8. . . . . . . .24 F7
Oakbournes The 5
SP1. . . . . . . . . . . . . .146 C5
Oak Cl
Bishops Cannings
SN10. . . . . . . . . . . .172 B2
Pitton & Farley SP5. .154 E7
South Newton SP2. . .130 B2
Tidworth SP9 . . . . . .216 E7
Oak Dr
Alderbury SP5 . . . . .153 C2
Highworth SN6. . . . . .22 F5
Trowbridge BA14. . . .105 C3
Oakes Cl SN4 . . . . . . .133 E7
Oakes Ct 9 RG17. . . .177 B7
Oakes La GL9. . . . . . . .52 B5
Oakford La SN14. . . . . .74 B2
Oakford Wlk SN3 . . . . .51 A6
Oak Gdns SN3 . . . . . . .36 A4
Oakham Cl SN5. . . . . .49 C5
Oak Hill SN8. . . . . . . .176 E6
Oakhurst Com Prim Sch
SN25. . . . . . . . . . . . .34 B7
Oakhurst Way
Swindon SN25 . . . . . .34 A7
Swindon SN25 . . . . . .34 C7
Oakie Cl SN25 . . . . . . .35 A5
Oak La
Easterton SN10 . . . .179 F2
Figheldean SP4 . . . .190 B2
Mere BA12. . . . . . . .139 B4
Oaklands SN13 . . . . . .76 B1
Oaklands Cl 12 SP6 .210 D1
Oaklea La SP5 . . . . . .153 E2
Oakleaze SN10 . . . . . .44 D1
Oakleigh Dr SP5 . . . .212 C5
Oakley Bsns Pk SP3. .201 E5
Oakley Flats GL7. . . . .10 D6
Oakley La
Farnham DT11. . . . . .207 D2

Oakley La continued
Sixpenny Handley SP5 .208 B4
Oakley Rd SP2. . . . . .144 F4
Oak Lodge Cl SN14 . . .78 C8
Oak Pk BA14. . . . . . .104 F5
Oak Pl SP4 . . . . . . . .217 C4
Oak Rd
Chippenham Without
SN14. . . . . . . . . . . .77 A8
Colerne SN14. . . . . . .74 F5
Down Ampney GL7. . . .8 E6
OAKSEY. . . . . . . . . . . .15 F7
Oaksey CE Prim Sch
SN16. . . . . . . . . . . . .16 A8
Oaksey Rd
Minety SN16. . . . . . . .16 C4
Somerford Keynes SN16 .5 E1
Swindon SN2 . . . . . . .35 C4
Oak St GL7. . . . . . . . . .2 C4
Oaks The
Chippenham SN15 . . . .70 D2
Coate SN1 . . . . . . . . .51 A2
Kemble GL7. . . . . . . . .4 F7
Warminster BA12 . . .117 A8
Oak Tree Ave SN2 . . . .35 D3
Oak Tree Bsns Pk SN3 .36 C7
Oak Tree Cl BA14 . . .101 B1
Oak Tree Prim Sch
SN3. . . . . . . . . . . . . .51 A4
Oak Way GL7. . . . . . . .6 F6
Oakwood Dr SN2. . . . .94 B4
Oakwood Gr SP5 . . . .153 D3
Oakwood Rd SN5 . . . .49 C7
Oamaru Way SN10. . .214 D3
OARE. . . . . . . . . . . . .174 B2
Oare Hill SN8. . . . . . .174 C2
Oare Prim Sch SN8 . .174 B2
Oasis Acad BA14. . . .105 D7
Oasis Leisure Ctr SN2 .50 B7
Oasthouse Cl 3 SN5. .49 A8
Oate Hill SN15. . . . . . .78 F6
Oatfields BA14. . . . . .101 D4
Oathill La GL7 . . . . . . .3 B8
Oathills SN13. . . . . . . .84 F8
Oatlands SN5. . . . . . . .48 F6
Oatmeal Row 5 SP1. .152 A8
Oat Rd 13 SP11 . . . . .193 F2
Oatway Rd SP9 . . . . .216 D8
Obelisk Terr 6 BA12. .116 F7
Oberon Way SP5 . . . . .35 A5
Ocotal Way SN1 . . . . .50 D8
Odcroft Cl SN15 . . . . .79 F4
Oddford Vale 17 SP3 .203 E8
O'Donnell Cl SN15 . . .70 E1
ODSTOCK. . . . . . . . .152 A1
Odstock Rd
Britford SP2. . . . . . .152 B4
Swindon SN2 . . . . . . .35 C6
Offerton Rd 8 SN1. . . .50 A2
Ogbourne Rd SN14. . . .75 B3
OGBOURNE MAIZEY. .213 C7
Ogbourne Rd SN8 . . .169 E6
OGBOURNE ST
ANDREW. . . . . . . . .168 F3
OGBOURNE ST
GEORGE. . . . . . . . . .169 A5
Ogbourne St George & St
Andrew CE (Controlled)
Prim Sch SN8 . . . . .168 F5
Ogbury Camp★ SP4 .198 A1
Ogilvie Sq SN11 . . . . .81 C3
Okebourne Pk SN3 . . .51 C3
Okeford Cl SN3. . . . . .51 C7
OKUS. . . . . . . . . . . . .50 A4
Okus Gr SN2. . . . . . . .35 D4
Okus Rd SN1. . . . . . . .49 F3
Okus Trad Est SN3 . . .50 A4
Olaf Cl 10 SP10 . . . .193 E2
Old Alexander Rd
SN16. . . . . . . . . . . . .27 F4
Old Bakery Cl SN16. . .28 E2
Old Barn GL8 . . . . . . . .3 C5
Old Batch The BA15. .100 B8
Old Bath Rd
Cherhill SN11. . . . . . .166 F1
Cherhill SN11. . . . . . .172 D8
Old Beasants SN8. . . .174 A6
Old Blandford Rd
SP2. . . . . . . . . . . . . .151 F4
Old Boundary Rd 5
SP7. . . . . . . . . . . . . .202 C1
Oldbrick Fields BA14. .105 A5
Old Brickyard Rd
SP6. . . . . . . . . . . . . .210 B1
Old Broughton Rd
SN12. . . . . . . . . . . . .94 A5
Oldbury Castle (Hill
Fort)★ SN11 . . . . . .172 C8
OLDBURY ON THE
HILL. . . . . . . . . . . . .24 B5
Oldbury Prior SN11. . .81 C1
Oldbury Way SN11. . . .81 B1
Old Castle Rd SP1. . .146 A5
Old Chapel Cl SP5 . . .153 D3
Old Chase Rd SN8 . . .169 A4
Old Coach Rd
Durrington/Bulford
SP4. . . . . . . . . . . . .217 D8
North Wraxall SN14. . .67 D2
Shipton Bellinger SP11 191 F1
Old Coach Works 19
RG17. . . . . . . . . . . .165 A1
Old Comm Way 13
SP11. . . . . . . . . . . . .192 A5
Old Cranborne Rd
BH21. . . . . . . . . . . .209 B3
Old Cranbourne Rd
SP6. . . . . . . . . . . . . .209 C5

**Old Ct** SN4 . . . . . . . . . . 47 D1
**Old Dairy Cl**
Bermerton Heath SP2 . 145 C3
Swindon SN2 . . . . . . . . . 35 E3
**Old Dairy Ct** SN12 . . . .94 C5
**Old Dairy Dr The** SN14 .68 B7
**Old Dairy La** SN4 . . . . 167 F2
**Old Dairy The**
Amesbury SP4 . . . . . . . 217 C3
Nunton SP5 . . . . . . . . . 152 D1
**Old Derry Hill** SN15 . . . 79 D2
**Old Dilton** BA13 . . . . . 112 D6
**Old Dilton Rd** BA13 . . 112 E7
**Old Down Rd** GL9 . . . . .52 C8
**Olde Fairfield** SP8 . . . 138 A2
**Oldenburgh Rd** 🔳
BA13 . . . . . . . . . . . . . 108 E1
**Old English Dr** 🔳
SP10 . . . . . . . . . . . . . 193 D2
**Old Estate Yd The** GL7 . .8 D7
**Old Farm Cl**
Hankerton SN16 . . . . . . 15 C2
Hullavington SN14 . . . . 41 F1
**Old Farmhouse /
Cotswold Community
The** SN6 . . . . . . . . . . . . .6 C4
**Old Farmhouse The**
SN10 . . . . . . . . . . . . . 214 C1
**Old Farm Rd** BA14 . . . 105 F7
**Oldfield Pk** BA13 . . . . 108 E3
**Oldfield Rd**
Salisbury SP1 . . . . . . . 146 C5
Westbury BA13 . . . . . . 108 E4
**Oldford Hill** BA11 . . . . 110 A8
**Old Forge Cl**
Brinkworth SN15 . . . . . . 45 E6
Heytesbury BA12 . . . . . 194 C5
**Old Granary La** SP4 . . 217 B3
**Old Hardenhuish La**
SN14 . . . . . . . . . . . . . . .70 B1
*Oldhat Barrow* ★
SN9 . . . . . . . . . . . . . . 183 A3
**Old Hayward La**
RG17 . . . . . . . . . . . . . 171 B1
**Old Hollow** BA12 . . . . 139 B6
**Old Hospl Rd** SN9 . . . . 215 B6
**Old Hungerford La**
SP11 . . . . . . . . . . . . . 185 C5
**Old Jockey** SN13 . . . . . .83 F3
*Old King Barrows* ★
SP4 . . . . . . . . . . . . . . 197 F5
**Old Lady La** SN26 . . . . . .21 E1
**Oldlands Wlk** SN3 . . . . .51 A3
**Old Malmesbury Rd**
SN4 . . . . . . . . . . . . . . . .47 E4
**Old Malthouse La**
SP4 . . . . . . . . . . . . . . 147 B7
*Old Manor House* ★
BA12 . . . . . . . . . . . . . 194 A4
**Old Mdws Wlk** SP2 . . . 151 E7
**Old Midford Rd** BA2 . . .98 A7
**Old Mill Gdns** SP2 . . . 151 E7
**Old Mill La** SN3 . . . . . . 50 D3
**Old Oak Cl** 🔳 SP11 . . . 193 F2
**Old Orch The** SN16 . . . .28 A6
**Old Post Office La** 🔳
SP4 . . . . . . . . . . . . . . .190 A3
**Old Pound Ct** SP8 . . . . 137 D1
**Old Railway Cl** GL7 . . . . .2 D5
**Old Rd**
Alderbury SP5 . . . . . . . 153 C4
Chippenham SN15 . . . . . 78 D8
Derry Hill/Studley
SN11 . . . . . . . . . . . . . . 80 B2
**Old Rly Cl** 🔳 SN16 . . . . .28 A4
*Old Ropeworks The* ★
SN8 . . . . . . . . . . . . . . 213 E2
*Old Sarum* ★ SP1 . . . . 145 F6
**Old Sarum Barracks**
SP4 . . . . . . . . . . . . . . 146 C8
**Old Sarum Bsns Pk**
SP4 . . . . . . . . . . . . . . 146 C8
**Old Sarum Pk** SP4 . . . 146 D8
**Old Sarum Prim Sch**
SP4 . . . . . . . . . . . . . . 146 C8
**Old Sawmills The**
RG17 . . . . . . . . . . . . . 177 F3
**Old Sawmill The**
BA12 . . . . . . . . . . . . . 123 F5
**Old Sch Cl** SN15 . . . . . .96 C7
**Old Sch Ct** SN3 . . . . . . .51 B6
**Old School Ct** SP4 . . . 190 A3
**Old School Ct** SN14 . . .74 A8
**Old School Dr** 🔳
SP11 . . . . . . . . . . . . . 192 A5
**Old Sch Yd** SN13 . . . . . .85 A8
**Old Severalls The**
SN9 . . . . . . . . . . . . . . 182 E7
**Old Shaftesbury
(Shaston) Dro**
Bishopstone SP2 . . . . . 150 A6
Harnham SP2 . . . . . . . 151 D5
Netherhampton SP2 . . 151 A5
**Old Shaftesbury
(Shaston) Drove**
SP5 . . . . . . . . . . . . . . 150 E5
**Old Shaw La** SN5 . . . . .48 F8
**Oldsodbury Rd** GL9 . . .52 F6
**Old Sodbury Rd** GL9 . .52 F6
**Old Sodom La** SN15 . . .59 B8
**Old St** SP2 . . . . . . . . . . 152 A6
**Old Sta Yd The** 🔳
RG17 . . . . . . . . . . . . . 165 A1
**Old Surgery Cl** SN5 . . .33 C4
**OLD TOWN** . . . . . . . . .50 D3
**Old Track** BA2 . . . . . . . .98 F7

**Old Vicarage La**
Alderbury SP5 . . . . . . . 153 C1
Kemble GL7 . . . . . . . . . . .4 F7
Swindon SN3 . . . . . . . . . 36 F4
**Old Vineries The** 🔟
SP6 . . . . . . . . . . . . . . . 210 C1
*Old Wardour Castle* ★
SP3 . . . . . . . . . . . . . . 203 D5
**Old Ward Rd** 🔳 SP4 . 198 E6
**Old Were Ct** 🔳 BA12 . 117 A7
**Old Yard** SN10 . . . . . . 187 D8
**Olive Gr** SN2 . . . . . . . . .35 B3
**Olivemead La** SN15 . . .45 C1
**Oliver Ave** SN13 . . . . . .76 F2
**Oliver Cl** SN5 . . . . . . . .48 F2
*Oliver's Castle (Fort)* ★
SN10 . . . . . . . . . . . . . . .97 C6
**Olivers Cl** SN11 . . . . . 166 B1
**Olivers Ct** SN11 . . . . . .89 C8
**Olivers Hill** SN11 . . . . 166 B1
**Oliver's La** 🔳 SN16 . . .28 A3
**Oliver Tomkins CE Jun &
Inf Sch** SN5 . . . . . . . .49 B5
**Olivier Cl** SP2 . . . . . . . 145 C5
**Olivier Rd**
Swindon SN25 . . . . . . . . 35 B6
Wilton SP2 . . . . . . . . . 144 B5
*Olympiad L Ctr* ★ SN15 78 E8
**Olympian Rd** SN9 . . . . 215 B5
**Olympia The** SN8 . . . . 168 E3
**Olympic Pk Rd** 🔟
SP11 . . . . . . . . . . . . . 193 E2
**Omar Rd** SN13 . . . . . . .84 F6
**Omdurman St** SN2 . . . .35 B1
**One Sch Global Salisbury
Campus** SP2 . . . . . . 144 B4
**Ontario Way** 🔳 SP4 . 217 F8
**Onyx Cl** SN2 . . . . . . . . .25 C4
**Opal Rd** SN26 . . . . . . . .21 A1
**Orange Cl** SN6 . . . . . . .23 A6
**Orbital Rd**
Wroughton SN4 . . . . . . .63 F3
Wroughton SN4 . . . . . . 167 F8
Wroughton SN4 . . . . . . 168 A8
**Orbital Sh Pk** SN25 . . .34 E6
**Ox Drove**
Alvediston SP5 . . . . . . . 207 F8
Chicklade SP3 . . . . . . . 200 B5
Dinton SP3 . . . . . . . . . 142 C7
Dinton SP3 . . . . . . . . . 201 E5
Homington SP5 . . . . . . 157 A3
**Oxencroft** 🔳 SP7 . . . . 202 C2
**Oxenden Cl** BA13 . . . . 109 B5
**Oxendene** BA12 . . . . . 113 F2
**OXENWOOD** . . . . . . . . 184 E6
**Oxford Cl** SN11 . . . . . . .81 B3
**Oxford Gdns** SN14 . . . 101 F1
**Oxford Mws** 🔳 BA13 . 109 A3
**Oxford Rd**
Calne SN11 . . . . . . . . . .81 B3
Swindon SN3 . . . . . . . . 36 A1
Upavon Down SN9 . . . 182 B2
**Oxford St**
Aldbourne SN8 . . . . . . 170 A6
Deanend SP5 . . . . . . . . 207 E5
Hungerford RG17 . . . . 177 C8
Lambourn RG17 . . . . . 165 A1
Malmesbury SN16 . . . . . 28 A3
Marlborough SN8 . . . . 213 D3
Ramsbury SN8 . . . . . . 170 B2
Swindon SN1 . . . . . . . . 50 B6
**Oxleaze La** SN16 . . . . .15 B2
**Oxon Pl** SN6 . . . . . . . . 163 E6
**Ox Path The** SN8 . . . . 174 B2
**Ox Row** 🔳 SP1 . . . . . . 152 A8
**Oxyard** BA12 . . . . . . . . 195 B2
**Ox Yd** GL7 . . . . . . . . . . . .3 C8

## P

**Pack Hill** SN4 . . . . . . . .51 F2
**Pack Horse** SN5 . . . . . .33 D8
*Packhorse Bridge* ★
SN15 . . . . . . . . . . . . . . .86 E5
**Pack Horse La** SN5 . . . .33 E8
**Pack Horse La** BA2 . . .98 A7
**Packington Cl** SN5 . . . .49 B7
**Packway The**
Durrington SP4 . . . . . . 197 D7
Shrewton SP3 . . . . . . . 197 A7
**Paddington Dr** SN5 . . .49 E5
**Paddock Cl**
Enford SN9 . . . . . . . . . 190 A6
Great Somerford SN15 . 44 A2
🔳 Shaftesbury SP7 . . . 202 D1
Sixpenny Handley SP5 . 208 A3
Swindon SN25 . . . . . . . 34 E5
Winterbourne SP4 . . . 133 B2
**Paddock End** SN14 . . . .70 A7
**Paddock La**
Chilmark SP3 . . . . . . . . 200 F2
Corsham SN13 . . . . . . . 84 D8
**Paddocks The**
🔟 Aldbourne SN8 . . . . 170 A6
Chippenham SN15 . . . . . 78 E6
Mere BA12 . . . . . . . . . 139 A5
🔳 Ramsbury SN8 . . . . 170 B2
🔳 Swindon SN3 . . . . . . 36 A2
Westbury BA13 . . . . . . 109 A4
**Paddock The**
🔳 Bradford-on-Avon
BA15 . . . . . . . . . . . . . 100 D6
Highworth SN6 . . . . . . . 23 A3
Market Lavington
SN10 . . . . . . . . . . . . . 180 A1
🔳 Tisbury SP3 . . . . . . 203 E8
**Paddock Way** SP1 . . . 146 E2
**Paddock Wood** 🔳
SP4 . . . . . . . . . . . . . . 198 B7
**Padfield Gdns** SN12 . . .93 F1

**Orwell Cl** *continued*
Swindon SN25 . . . . . . . 35 A5
**Osborne Rd** BA14 . . . 101 E3
**Osborne St** SN2 . . . . . .50 B8
**Oslings La** BA1 . . . . . . .82 B2
**Osprey Cl**
Bower Hill SN12 . . . . . . 94 D1
Swindon SN3 . . . . . . . . 51 E6
**Osprey Rd** BA12 . . . . . 116 D5
**Osterley Rd** SN25 . . . . .34 E6
**Otford Cl** SN5 . . . . . . . .48 F4
**Otter Row** 🔳 SN3 . . . .51 B8
**Otter Way** SN4 . . . . . . .47 F2
**OUTMARSH** . . . . . . . . 102 F7
**OUTWICK** . . . . . . . . . . 210 D4
**Overbrook** SN3 . . . . . . .51 C3
**Overhouse Dr** 🔳 SP3 . 203 E8
**Over St** SP3 . . . . . . . . . 129 D7
**Overton Gdns** SN3 . . . .36 B2
**OVERTOWN** . . . . . . . . .64 D4
**Overtown Hill** SN4 . . . .64 C5
**Overway La** SP7 . . . . . 203 D2
**Owen Cl** SN10 . . . . . . . 214 D3
**Owen Ct** SN3 . . . . . . . .36 A1
**Owl Cl**
Swindon SN3 . . . . . . . . 51 E6
Warminster BA12 . . . . 116 D5
**Owlets The** SN3 . . . . . .51 E6
**Owlswood** 🔳 SP2 . . . . 152 A5
**Ox Dro**
Ashmore SP5 . . . . . . . . 206 D7
Ashmore SP5 . . . . . . . . 206 E7
Barford St Martin SP3 . 143 A6
Berwick St John SP5 . . 207 B7
Bishopstone SP5 . . . . . 205 F2
Bower Chalke SP5 . . . . 208 A8
Broad Chalke SP5 . . . . 205 C1
Kimpton SP11 . . . . . . . 192 A1
Teffont SP3 . . . . . . . . . 201 C5
Wilton SP2 . . . . . . . . . 144 A5

**Padstow Rd** SN5 . . . . . .49 F5
**Page Cl**
Calne SN11 . . . . . . . . . .81 C3
Chippenham SN14 . . . . . 78 A7
**Paget Cl** SP9 . . . . . . . . 216 B8
**Pagnell La** SN3 . . . . . . 179 D1
**Pagoda Pk** SN5 . . . . . . .49 D7
**Pains Hill** SO51 . . . . . . 162 F7
**Pains Way** 🔳 SP4 . . . . 217 C2
**Painters Mead** BA14 . . 102 A2
**Pakenham Rd** SN3 . . . . .51 B4
**Palairet Cl** BA15 . . . . . 100 D4
**Palestine Rd** SP11 . . . 199 F3
**Palmer Dr** BA15 . . . . . 100 D8
**Palmer Gr** BA14 . . . . . 102 F6
**Palmer Rd**
Devizes SN10 . . . . . . . . 214 C5
Salisbury SP2 . . . . . . . 145 E2
Trowbridge BA14 . . . . 101 D2
**Palmer St** SN14 . . . . . . .78 C7
**Palmerston Meadow**
SN9 . . . . . . . . . . . . . . 190 A6
**Palmers Way** 🔳 SN4 . 163 A6
**Palm Rd** BA14 . . . . . . . .75 A5
**Palomino Pl**
Swindon SN5 . . . . . . . . 34 B2
🔳 Westbury Leigh
BA13 . . . . . . . . . . . . . 108 E1
**Pampas Ct** 🔳 BA12 . . 116 E6
**Pans La** SN10 . . . . . . . 214 B2
**Panters Rd** SP3 . . . . . . 204 C8
**Pantiles The** 🔳 SP6 . . 210 C1
**Pantry Bridge** BA14 . . 178 D5
**Parade The**
Marlborough SN8 . . . . 213 D3
Swindon SN1 . . . . . . . . 50 C6
**Paradise La**
Longbridge Deverill
BA12 . . . . . . . . . . . . . 116 E1
Rowde SN10 . . . . . . . . . 96 E2
**Parham La** SN10 . . . . . 179 E2
**Parhams Ct** SN4 . . . . . .47 E1
**Parhams Hill** SP7 . . . . 203 B1
**Parham Wlk** 🔳 SP5 . . .48 F5
**Park Ave**
Chippenham SN14 . . . . . 78 B8
Corsham SN13 . . . . . . . 84 A8
Highworth SN6 . . . . . . . 23 A5
**Park Cl**
Calne SN11 . . . . . . . . . .81 C2
Malmesbury SN16 . . . . . 27 F4
Salisbury SP1 . . . . . . . 146 A4
Trowbridge BA14 . . . . 105 D3
**PARK CORNER** . . . . . . .99 A4
**Park Dr** SP3 . . . . . . . . . 201 B3
**Park End** SN6 . . . . . . . . .17 F8
**Parkers Cl** SP5 . . . . . . 159 A1
**Parkers La** SN15 . . . . . .70 D6
**Park Field** SN10 . . . . . 214 C5
**Park Fields** SN15 . . . . .78 C8
**Parkhouse Cnr** SP4 . . 199 D6
**Parkhouse Rd** SP9 . . . 199 C8
**Park La**
Castle Combe SN14 . . . . 68 A7
Cherhill SN11 . . . . . . . 166 C1
Chippenham SN15 . . . . . 78 D8
Corsham SN13 . . . . . . . 76 D1
Great Somerford SN15 . 44 A2
Heytesbury BA12 . . . . 194 D5
Heywood BA13 . . . . . . 109 C7
Lea & Cleverton SN16 . . 29 D3
Lydiard Millicent SN5 . . 48 D7
Malmesbury SN16 . . . . . 27 E5
North Wraxall SN14 . . . 68 A2
Odstock SP5 . . . . . . . . 152 D4
Salisbury SP1 . . . . . . . 146 A3
Sutton Benger SN15 . . . 57 D2
Swindon SN1 . . . . . . . . 50 A6
West Dean SP5 . . . . . . 149 F1
**Parklands**
Malmesbury SN16 . . . . . 27 E4
Trowbridge BA14 . . . . 101 D2
**Parklands Rd** SN3 . . . .50 D5
**Parklands The** SN14 . . .55 E8
**Parkland Way** SP4 . . . 133 D6
**Park Mead** SN16 . . . . . .27 F4
**PARK NORTH** . . . . . . . .51 A5
**Park Pl** SN6 . . . . . . . . . . .6 F1
**Park Rd**
Fordingbridge SP6 . . . 210 D1
Malmesbury SN16 . . . . . 27 F4
Market Lavington
SN10 . . . . . . . . . . . . . 179 D1
Rushall SN9 . . . . . . . . 181 F3
Salisbury SP1 . . . . . . . 146 D2
Shrewton SP3 . . . . . . . 196 F6
Shrewton SP3 . . . . . . . 197 A6
Tidworth SP9 . . . . . . . 216 D5
Trowbridge BA14 . . . . 105 D8
Westbury BA13 . . . . . . 112 B8
**Parkside**
Chippenham SN15 . . . . . 78 D8
Swindon SN3 . . . . . . . . 36 A3
**PARK SOUTH** . . . . . . . .51 A4
**Park Springs** SN5 . . . . .49 C5
**Park St**
Charlton SN16 . . . . . . . 29 A6
Heytesbury BA12 . . . . 194 C5
Hungerford RG17 . . . . 177 B7
Salisbury SP1 . . . . . . . 146 B2
Swindon SN3 . . . . . . . . 36 C2
Trowbridge BA14 . . . . 105 C7
**Parkstone Wlk** SN3 . . .51 B3
**Park Terr** SN15 . . . . . . .78 C8
**Park The**
Erlestoke SN10 . . . . . . 179 A1
🔳 Lambourn RG17 . . . 165 A2

**Park View**
Chirton SN10 . . . . . . . 180 F4
Devizes SN10 . . . . . . . 179 D8
**Park View Dr**
Lydiard Millicent SN5 . . 48 D8
🔳 Westbury BA13 . . . 108 F1
**Park Vw Point** DT11 . . 207 A3
**Parkwater Rd** SP5 . . . 161 E1
**Park Way** RG17 . . . . . . 177 B6
**Parliament Row** SN16 . 28 A2
**Parliament St** SN14 . . .78 B7
**Parr Cl** SN5 . . . . . . . . . .49 A6
**Parsley Cl** SN2 . . . . . . . 34 D5
**Parsloes Cl** SN4 . . . . . .64 E3
**Parsonage Cl**
🔳 Fordingbridge
SP6 . . . . . . . . . . . . . . . 210 D1
Salisbury SP1 . . . . . . . 145 E5
*Parsonage Down
National Nature
Reserve* ★ SP3 . . . . . 196 D5
**Parsonage Gn** SP2 . . . 151 E6
**Parsonage Hill** SP5 . . 154 D7
**Parsonage La**
Charlton Musgrove
BA9 . . . . . . . . . . . . . . 136 C2
Hungerford RG17 . . . . 177 B7
🔳 Lamborn RG17 . . . . 165 A1
🔟 Market Lavington
SN10 . . . . . . . . . . . . . 179 F1
**Parsonage Pk Dr** 🔳
SP6 . . . . . . . . . . . . . . . 210 D1
**Parsonage Pl** 🔳
RG17 . . . . . . . . . . . . . 165 A2
**Parsonage Rd**
Amesbury SP4 . . . . . . . 217 B3
Swindon SN3 . . . . . . . . 36 A3
Trowbridge BA14 . . . . 102 A1
**Parsonage The** SP5 . . 208 B4
**Parsonage Vale** SN8 . 183 D2
**Parsonage Way** SN15 . .70 F1
**Parsons Cl** SP4 . . . . . . 133 D5
**Parsons Gn** 🔳 SP3 . . . 196 E6
**Parsons La** BA12 . . . . . 116 E2
**Parson's La** SN6 . . . . . .22 B7
**Parsons Pl** SN26 . . . . . .20 B1
**Parsons Pool** 🔟 SP7 . 202 C2
**Parsons Way** SN4 . . . . .47 E1
**Partridge Cl**
Chippenham SN14 . . . . . 70 B2
🔳 Corsham SN13 . . . . 76 E1
**Partridge Hill** SP5 . . . 212 E6
**Partridge Way** SP4 . . . 146 C8
**Passmore Cl** SN3 . . . . .51 E7
**Pasteur Dr** SN1 . . . . . . .50 A3
**Pasture Cl** SN2 . . . . . . .49 E7
**Pastures The** BA15 . . . .99 E3
**Pasture Wlk** 🔟 SP11 . 193 F2
**Patchway** SN14 . . . . . . .78 B8
**Patchway The** SN10 . . 214 D3
**Pathfinder Way**
Bowerhill SN12 . . . . . . .94 C2
🔳 Swindon SN25 . . . . 34 E6
**PATNEY** . . . . . . . . . . . . 180 F5
**Patney Rd** SN10 . . . . . 180 F5
**Paton Cl** GL7 . . . . . . . . . .1 E7
**Pat-yat** GL7 . . . . . . . . . .4 B5
**Paulet Cl** 🔳 SN5 . . . . .49 A4
**Pauls Croft** SN6 . . . . . .19 D7
**Paul's Dene Cres**
SP1 . . . . . . . . . . . . . . 146 A5
**Paul's Dene Rd** SP1 . . 146 A5
**Paul St** SN13 . . . . . . . . .76 F1
**Paveley Cl** BA13 . . . . . 108 E3
**Pavely Cl** SN15 . . . . . . .78 C6
**Pavely Gdns** BA14 . . . 102 A1
**Paven Cl** SN5 . . . . . . . . .33 A4
**Pavenhill** SN5 . . . . . . . .33 A4
**PAXCROFT** . . . . . . . . . 102 C3
**Paxcroft Prim Sch**
BA14 . . . . . . . . . . . . . 101 F1
**Paxcroft Way** BA14 . . 105 F8
**Paxmans Rd** BA13 . . . 108 E5
**Payne Cl** SN5 . . . . . . . . .78 E4
**Payne's Hill** 🔳 SP1 . . 152 B8
**Peacock Cl** SN8 . . . . . . 173 E6
**Peaks Down** SN5 . . . . . .34 B2
**Peak The** SN5 . . . . . . . .33 B3
**Pealsham Gdns** 🔳
SP6 . . . . . . . . . . . . . . . 210 D1
**PEAR ASH** . . . . . . . . . . 137 C4
**Pear Ash La**
Penselwood BA9 . . . . . 137 B4
Pen Selwood BA9 . . . . 137 C4
**Pearce Cl** SN2 . . . . . . . .35 E6
**Pearce Way** SP1 . . . . . 146 D5
**Pearl Cl** BA14 . . . . . . . . 101 D2
**Pearl Rd** SN5 . . . . . . . . .49 A7
**Pearson Rd** SN25 . . . . .20 C1
**Peartree Cl**
Atworth/Whitley SN12 . 85 C1
Purton SN5 . . . . . . . . . 33 C5
🔳 West Wellow SO51 . 212 F6
**Pear Tree Dr** SP5 . . . . 212 D8
**Pear Tree La** SN10 . . . 187 B8
**Pear Tree Orch** 🔳
BA13 . . . . . . . . . . . . . 186 B7
**PEATMOOR** . . . . . . . . . .34 B1
**Peatmoor Com Prim Sch**
SN5 . . . . . . . . . . . . . . .34 A1
**Peatmoor Way** SN5 . . .34 A1
**PECKINGELL** . . . . . . . . .71 B2
**Peel Cir** SN13 . . . . . . . . .84 D8
**Peel Cl** SN12 . . . . . . . . .94 A3
**Pegasus Way** SN12 . . .94 C1
**Peglars Way** SN1 . . . . .49 F3
**Pekin Way** SP9 . . . . . . 216 D4

**Pelch La** SN12 . . . . . . . 178 D8
**Pelham Ct**
Broad Chalke SP5 . . . . 205 B4
Marlborough SN8 . . . . 213 E3
**Pembridge Rd** SP6 . . . 210 E1
**Pembroke Cl** 🔳
BA14 . . . . . . . . . . . . . 105 D6
**Pembroke Ctr** SN2 . . . .34 E1
**Pembroke Gdns** SN25 . .34 E1
**Pembroke Gn** SN16 . . . .28 F1
**Pembroke Park Prim Sch**
SP2 . . . . . . . . . . . . . . 145 D4
**Pembroke Rd**
Chippenham SN15 . . . . . 79 A4
Melksham SN12 . . . . . . 94 B4
Salisbury SP2 . . . . . . . 145 C2
Upavon Down SN9 . . . 182 B2
**Pembroke St** SN1 . . . . .50 B4
**Pencarrow Cl** 🔳 SN25 .34 E6
**Pen Cl** SN25 . . . . . . . . . .35 A4
**Pendennis Rd** SN5 . . . .49 A3
**Penfold Gdns** SN1 . . . . .50 C4
**PENHILL** . . . . . . . . . . . .35 C5
**Pen Hill**
Brixton Deverill SP3 . . . 127 A5
Monkton Deverill BA12 126 E6
Stourton with Gasper
BA10 . . . . . . . . . . . . . 122 F1
**Penhill Dr** SN2 . . . . . . . .35 C4
**PENKNAP** . . . . . . . . . . 112 E8
**Penknap Rd** BA12 . . . . 112 D8
**PENLEIGH** . . . . . . . . . . 108 D2
**Penleigh Cl** SN13 . . . . .84 F3
**Penleigh Rd** BA13 . . . . 108 D2
**Pen Mill Hill** BA9 . . . . 137 E3
**Penn Comm Rd** SO51 212 E3
**Penn Ct** SN11 . . . . . . . .81 C3
**Penneys Piece** 🔳
BA11 . . . . . . . . . . . . . 110 C6
**Penn Hill Rd** SN11 . . . .81 C3
**Pennine Cl** SN12 . . . . . .94 D4
**Penning Rd** SP2 . . . . . 145 B4
**Pennings Dro**
Coombe Bissett SP5 . . 151 A1
Coombe Bissett SP5 . . 157 A8
**Pennings Rd**
North Tidworth SP9 . . . 191 D5
Tidworth SP9 . . . . . . . 216 C8
**Penn Marsh** SO51 . . . . 212 E3
**Pennycress Cl** SN25 . . .34 E4
**Pennycress Dr** SN12 . . .94 C3
**Penny Farthing Cl**
RG17 . . . . . . . . . . . . . 177 A7
**Pennyfarthing St**
SP1 . . . . . . . . . . . . . . 146 B1
**Penny Hill** SN8 . . . . . . 191 E8
**Penny La**
Amesbury SP4 . . . . . . . 217 D1
Chippenham SN15 . . . . . 78 F4
Swindon SN3 . . . . . . . . 50 F7
**Penny Royal Cl** SN11 . .80 F3
**Penny's Cl** SN13 . . . . . .84 D8
**Penny's Cres** 🔳 SP6 . 210 D2
**Pennys La** SP6 . . . . . . . 210 D2
**Penny's La**
Pitton & Farley SP5 . . . 154 E7
🔳 Wilton SP2 . . . . . . 144 D3
**Penrose Wlk** SN3 . . . . .51 A5
**Penruddock Cl** SP2 . . 145 C3
**PENSELWOOD** . . . . . . 137 B4
**Penselwood Loop**
BA9 . . . . . . . . . . . . . . 137 A3
**Pensford Way** BA11 . . 110 D6
**PENTON CORNER** . . . 193 A1
**PENTON GRAFTON** . . 193 A2
**Penton La** SP11 . . . . . . 193 A3
**PENTON MEWSEY** . . . 193 B2
**PENTRIDGE** . . . . . . . . . 208 E4
**Pentridge Cl** SN3 . . . . .51 C7
**Pentylands Cl** SN6 . . . .22 F7
**Penzance Dr**
Swindon SN5 . . . . . . . . 49 F5
Swindon SN5 . . . . . . . . 49 F5
**Pepperacre La** BA14 . . 101 F1
**Pepperbox Hill** SN5 . . .34 B2
**Pepperbox Rise** SP5 . . 153 E2
*Pepperbox The* ★
SP5 . . . . . . . . . . . . . . 160 C6
**Peppercombe Cl** 🔳
SN10 . . . . . . . . . . . . . 180 B4
*Peppercombe Wood
Nature Reserve* ★
SN10 . . . . . . . . . . . . . 180 B4
**Peppercorn Orch**
BA14 . . . . . . . . . . . . . 178 A6
**Pepper Pl** BA12 . . . . . . 117 D7
**Perch Cl** SN11 . . . . . . . .81 B5
**Percheron Cl** 🔳 SN5 . .49 A7
**Percheron Pl** BA13 . . . 108 D2
**Percy St** SN2 . . . . . . . . .49 F7
**Peregrine Cl** SN3 . . . . .51 D8
**Peregrine Ct** 🔳 SN11 . .81 B5
**Perham Cres** 🔳
SP11 . . . . . . . . . . . . . 192 B5
**PERHAM DOWN** . . . . . 191 F4
**Perhamdown Rd** SP9 216 E6
**Peridot Cl** SN25 . . . . . . .34 C3
**Periwinkle Cl** SN2 . . . .34 C3
**Perrinsfield** GL7 . . . . . . . .2 D5
**Perriwinkle Cl** BA12 . . 116 D6
**PERRY GREEN** . . . . . . .29 B7
**Perry's La**
Seend SN12 . . . . . . . . . 178 D8
Wroughton SN4 . . . . . . 64 A6

Perth Rd SP11 . . . . . . . **191** F4
Peshawar Cl SP9 . . . . . . **216** B7
Peter Furkins Ct SN1 . .**50** A5
Petersfield Green
  SP9. . . . . . . . . . . . . . . **216** C6
Petersfield Rd SN3 . . . .**51** B4
PETERSFINGER . . . . . . . **152** E7
Peters Finger Rd
  SP5. . . . . . . . . . . . . . . **152** E7
Peto Gdn The★ BA15 . .**99** E2
Petter Cl SN14 . . . . . . . .**64** B7
Petticoat La
  Redlynch SP5 . . . . . . **211** D8
  Westbury BA13 . . . . . **112** C8
Pettridge La BA12 . . . **139** A5
PETTY FRANCE. . . . . . . .**38** B8
Petty France Farm La
  GL9. . . . . . . . . . . . . . . .**38** B8
Petty La SN11 . . . . . . . . .**79** F3
Pevensey Way SN5 . . . .**49** C5
Pew Hill SN15 . . . . . . . .**70** E2
PEWSEY . . . . . . . . . . . . **215** D4
Pewsey Downs National
  Nature Reserve★
  SN8. . . . . . . . . . . . . . **173** C2
Pewsey Prim Sch
  SN9. . . . . . . . . . . . . . **215** B5
Pewsey Rd
  Marlborough SN8. . . . **213** D2
  Rushall SN9 . . . . . . . **181** E2
Pewsey Sports Ctr &
  Swimming Pool
  SN9. . . . . . . . . . . . . . **215** B5
Pewsey Sta SN9 . . . . . **215** B5
Pewsey Vale Sch
  SN9. . . . . . . . . . . . . . **215** B5
PEWSEY WHARF ★
  SN9. . . . . . . . . . . . . . **215** E1
Pewsey White Horse★
  SN9. . . . . . . . . . . . . . **173** C2
Pewsham Lock SN15 . . .**78** E5
Pewsham Rd SN2 . . . . . .**35** D5
Pewsham Way SN15 . . .**78** E4
Pheasant Bsns Pk
  SN14. . . . . . . . . . . . . .**78** B5
Pheasant Cl
  🔟 Chippenham Without
    SN14 . . . . . . . . . . . .**77** F6
  Swindon SN3 . . . . . . .**51** E5
Pheasant Dr
  Old Sarum SP4. . . . . . **146** B8
  Trowbridge BA14. . . . **105** E6
Pheasantry The GL7 . . . .**8** E7
Philip Cl SN12 . . . . . . . .**94** C6
Philip Ct SP2 . . . . . . . . **145** D3
Philips House & Dinton
  Pk★ SP3. . . . . . . . . . **201** E2
Philip Rd
  🔟 Durrington/Bulford
    SP4. . . . . . . . . . . . . **198** B7
  Wilton SP2 . . . . . . . . **144** B5
Phillip Cl SN10 . . . . . . **214** C4
Phillips Cl SN14 . . . . . . .**77** F7
Phillips Gr SN14 . . . . . . .**68** F6
Phillips La
  Salisbury SP4. . . . . . . **145** E6
  Swindon SN1 . . . . . . .**50** D4
Phillips Way BA14 . . . . **105** E2
Phipps Cl BA13 . . . . . . **108** F4
Phoebe Way SN25 . . . . .**34** B7
Phoenix Cl SN14 . . . . . .**78** F6
Phoenix Gdns 🔟 SN25 .**34** B7
Phoenix Rise BA13 . . . **108** E3
Phoenix Sq SN9 . . . . . . **215** C4
Piccadilly SN4 . . . . . . . **184** C8
Picked Mead 🔟 SN13 . .**84** E8
Pickernell Rd SP9 . . . . **216** D8
Picket Cl SP6 . . . . . . . . **210** D1
Picket Cnr SP6 . . . . . . . **211** F3
Picketleaze SN14 . . . . . .**78** A7
Picket Post
  Corsley BA12 . . . . . . **116** A3
  Longbridge Deverill
    BA12. . . . . . . . . . . . **115** E3
Picket Post Gate
  BA12. . . . . . . . . . . . . **116** A4
Pickford Way 🔟 SN25 .**34** B6
PICKWICK. . . . . . . . . . . .**76** E2
Pickwick SN13. . . . . . . . .**76** F2
Pickwick Cl SN2 . . . . . . .**35** E5
Pickwick Rd SN13 . . . . . .**76** F2
Picquet The 🔝 BA13. . . **186** B7
Picton Rd SN5. . . . . . . . .**49** A7
Pictor Cl SN13. . . . . . . . .**76** D1
Pierce Rd SP9 . . . . . . . **216** D8
Piernik Cl SN25 . . . . . . .**34** E6
Pigeon House La SN3 . .**36** A3
Pig La
  Bishops Cannings
    SN10 . . . . . . . . . . . **172** C1
  Hullavington SN16 . . . .**41** A3
Pigott Cl 🔟 SP4 . . . . . . **190** A4
Pigtrough La SP7 . . . . . **203** B4
Pike Cl BA14. . . . . . . . . **102** B1
Pike Cnr SN16 . . . . . . . .**17** D7
Pikefield Cres SN16 . . . .**29** A6
Pike House CI SN6 . . . . .**19** C8
Pilgrim Cl SN5. . . . . . . . .**49** A7
Pilgrims Ct SP1. . . . . . . **146** E2
Pilgrims Mead SP1 . . . . **146** C5
Pilgrims Way SP1. . . . . **146** E2
Pill Hill SP5 . . . . . . . . . **161** C4
Pilots View SP4 . . . . . . **217** D3
Pilton Cl SN5. . . . . . . . . .**49** A8
Pimperleaze Rd
  Charnage BA12 . . . . . **139** E5

Pimperleaze Rd continued
  Mere BA12. . . . . . . . . **139** F1
PINCKNEY GREEN. . . . . .**90** E5
Pinckneys Way 🔞
  SP4. . . . . . . . . . . . . . **198** B7
Pine Cl
  Corsham SN13. . . . . . .**76** A1
  Landford SP5 . . . . . . **212** C5
  Melksham SN12. . . . . .**94** A3
Pinecroft La SP5. . . . . . **149** C8
Pine Ct 🔟 BA11. . . . . . **110** B7
Pine Ct SN2 . . . . . . . . . .**35** E2
Pine Gr BA14 . . . . . . . . **105** C6
PINEHURST . . . . . . . . . .**35** D3
Pinehurst Rd SN2. . . . . .**35** C2
Pinehurst Sports Ctr
  SN2. . . . . . . . . . . . . . .**35** B3
Pines Rd SN10 . . . . . . . **214** C2
Pines The SN2 . . . . . . . **211** A1
Pinetree Rise SN2 . . . . .**35** B3
Pinetum Cl SN10. . . . . . **214** C2
Pineview Cl SP5 . . . . . . **211** C6
Pine Wlk
  Amesbury SP4 . . . . . . **217** D3
  Trowbridge BA14. . . . **105** C3
Pinewood Sch SN14 . . .**37** F2
Pinewoods Cl SP2 . . . . **145** B4
Pinewood Way
  Colerne SN14. . . . . . . .**74** F7
  Salisbury SP2. . . . . . . **145** B4
Pinfield La SN15. . . . . . .**78** F4
Pinhills SN11 . . . . . . . . .**81** A2
Pink La SN16 . . . . . . . . .**29** E5
Pinkney Pk★ SN16. . . . .**25** F1
Pinnegar Way SN3. . . . .**51** F6
Pinnocks Pl SN2. . . . . . .**35** F4
Pintail Ct SN15 . . . . . . . .**60** B1
Pintail Way BA13 . . . . . **109** B4
Pinto Cl SN2. . . . . . . . . .**34** C3
Pioneer Cl 🔞 SN5 . . . . .**49** A7
Pioneer Rd SN3 . . . . . . .**34** B7
Pipehouse BA2 . . . . . . . .**98** A4
Pipehouse La BA2 . . . . .**98** F4
Pipers Cl SN4. . . . . . . . .**61** D8
Pipers Way SN1 . . . . . . .**50** C4
Pipistrelle Cres BA14 **106** A8
Pipitdene SN3. . . . . . . . .**51** D7
Piplar Gd BA15 . . . . . . **100** D4
Pippins The 🔞 BA12 . **116** F7
Pippin The SN11. . . . . . .**81** B3
Pippit Pl 🔝 SN12 . . . . . .**94** D5
Pips Field Way GL7 . . . . .**1** F6
Pipsmore Rd
  🔟 Chippenham SN14 . .**70** A1
  Chippenham SN14 . . . .**78** A1
Pitchens End SN4. . . . . **167** C7
Pitchens The SN4 . . . . . .**64** B5
Pitch Pan La BA12 . . . . **139** B4
Pitman Ave BA14 . . . . . **105** B7
Pitman Ct BA14 . . . . . . **105** B6
Pit Head La BA12 . . . . . **117** E4
Pitt Cl 🔞 SN1. . . . . . . . .**50** E7
PITTON. . . . . . . . . . . . . **148** C3
Pitton CE (VA) Prim Sch
  SP5. . . . . . . . . . . . . . **148** B3
Pitton Rd
  Firsdown SP5 . . . . . . **148** E6
  Pitton & Farley SP5 . . **154** D8
  Winterslow SP5 . . . . **134** F1
Pitts Croft SN13 . . . . . . .**84** E5
Pittsfield SN6 . . . . . . . . .**19** D7
Pitts La
  Bishopstone SP5 . . . . **205** F4
  Chitterne BA12 . . . . . **195** D7
  Sedgehill & Semley
    SP7. . . . . . . . . . . . **202** B7
PITTS THE . . . . . . . . . . **205** F5
Pit Wlk SP4 . . . . . . . . . **199** C4
Pix Mead Gdns 🔟
  SP7. . . . . . . . . . . . . . **202** D1
Pk La
  Corsham SN13. . . . . . .**85** A3
  Neston SN13 . . . . . . . .**84** F4
Pk Rd GL9. . . . . . . . . . . .**38** E7
Place Rd SN12. . . . . . . . .**94** A4
PLAITFORD . . . . . . . . . **212** E6
PLAITFORD GREEN . . . **212** F8
Plane Tree Cl SN12 . . . . .**85** C1
Planks The SN3. . . . . . . .**50** D4
Plantation Rd
  Chippenham SN14 . . . .**78** C8
  Tidworth SP9 . . . . . . **216** D5
  Wellow SO51 . . . . . . **212** F4
Plantation The SP5 . . . **149** A5
Plants Gn SN12 . . . . . . **117** B6
Plassey Rd SP9 . . . . . . **216** C7
Platford St SN11. . . . . . .**81** B2
Platt Cl RG17 . . . . . . . . **177** C6
Plattes Cl SN5 . . . . . . . .**49** B8
Platt La RG17 . . . . . . . . **170** E7
Play Cl SN5. . . . . . . . . . .**33** C4
Player Ct 🔞 SP6. . . . . . **210** D2
Playhouse Salisbury★
  SP2. . . . . . . . . . . . . . **146** A1
Pleydell Rd SN1 . . . . . . .**50** C2
Pleydells 🔞 SN6. . . . . . .**19** D8
Plough La
  Kington Langley SN15 . .**70** C5
  Marston SN10 . . . . . . **179** A4
Plough Way 🔞 SP1 . . . **193** F2
Plume of Feathers La
  SN8. . . . . . . . . . . . . . **213** E3
Plum La SN10 . . . . . . . . **180** E4
Plummer Cl SN4. . . . . . . .**64** A6
Plumpton Cl SN14 . . . . . .**77** F6
Plymouth St SN1 . . . . . .**50** D6
Poachers Way SN25 . . . .**34** F7
Pochard Way GL7. . . . . . .**6** F6

Pockeredge Dr SN13. . . .**84** C7
Pockeridge Rd SN13. . . .**84** C7
Pointers Way SP4 . . . . . **217** D3
Polaris Way SN2 . . . . . . .**50** B7
Polden Rd SP1 . . . . . . . **152** C7
Polebarn Rd BA14 . . . . **105** D8
Pollen Cl SP4 . . . . . . . . **190** B2
Pollen La SP4 . . . . . . . . **190** B2
Polonez Ct SN25. . . . . . .**34** D6
Poltondale SN3. . . . . . . .**51** D7
Pomeroy La BA14. . . . . **104** B6
Pond House La SP11. . . **185** D3
Pond La
  Charlton SN16 . . . . . . .**29** F4
  Charlton SN16 . . . . . . .**30** A4
  Purton SN5. . . . . . . . . .**19** B1
Pond St SN5. . . . . . . . . .**34** F5
Pontefract Ave BA14. . **106** B7
Ponting's St SN26 . . . . .**21** C2
Ponting St SN1 . . . . . . . .**50** C7
POOLE KEYNES . . . . . . . .**5** C4
Poole Keynes House
  GL7. . . . . . . . . . . . . . . .**5** B4
Poole Rd
  Malmesbury SN16 . . . .**27** F5
  Malmesbury SN16 . . . .**28** A4
  Swindon SN25 . . . . . . .**34** E3
Pooles Mdw SN8 . . . . . **169** A5
Pool Gastons Rd SN16 .**27** F3
Pool Gn SN13. . . . . . . . .**84** E6
Pool Mdw SN4 . . . . . . . .**61** F8
Poores Rd 🔝 SP4. . . . . **198** B7
Poor St SN5. . . . . . . . . . .**33** A3
Pope Cl SN25 . . . . . . . . .**34** F5
Popham Ct SN15. . . . . . .**78** E6
Poplar Ave SN2 . . . . . . .**35** C2
Poplar Cl SP2 . . . . . . . . **151** C7
Poplar Coll SN15 . . . . . . .**78** E8
Poplar La BA14 . . . . . . . **101** C1
Poplars The
  Chippenham SN14 . . . .**70** A1
  Fovant SP3. . . . . . . . . **204** D8
  Trowbridge BA14. . . . **105** A5
Poplar Tree La BA14 . . **104** B3
Poplar Way
  Colerne SN14. . . . . . . .**74** F5
  Colerne SN14. . . . . . . .**75** A5
  Salisbury SP1. . . . . . . **146** C5
Popplechurch Dr 🔝
  SN3. . . . . . . . . . . . . . .**51** E7
Poppy Cl SN11. . . . . . . . .**80** F4
Poppy Fields SN25 . . . . .**35** E3
Porchester Cl 🔞
  SP10. . . . . . . . . . . . . **193** C2
Portal Ave SN13 . . . . . . .**84** B8
Portal Cl SN15. . . . . . . . .**70** C1
Portal Pl SN15. . . . . . . . .**60** A1
Portal Rd SN2 . . . . . . . . .**35** A2
PORTASH. . . . . . . . . . . **201** B2
Port Down RG17. . . . . . **177** C7
Porte Marsh Ind Est
  SN11. . . . . . . . . . . . . .**81** C5
Porte Marsh Rd SN11 .**81** C5
Porters Mead SN13 . . . .**76** F1
Portfield Rd SP5 . . . . . . **150** A4
Porth Cl 🔞 SN25 . . . . . .**34** C7
Port Hill SN8 . . . . . . . . **213** D5
Portland Ave
  Britford SP2 . . . . . . . **151** F5
  Swindon SN1 . . . . . . .**50** A4
Portland Pl BA13 . . . . . **109** B5
Portland Rise SN13 . . . .**84** E7
Portland Way SN11 . . . .**81** C2
Portman Rd SN12. . . . . .**94** A6
Portmore Cl SN5 . . . . . .**34** C2
Portnell's La BA12 . . . . **137** F4
PORTON. . . . . . . . . . . . **133** D4
Porton Rd
  Amesbury SP4 . . . . . . **217** D3
  Porton SP4 . . . . . . . . **132** E8
  Porton SP4. . . . . . . . . **133** B8
Port Regis Prep Sch
  SP7. . . . . . . . . . . . . . **202** A3
Portsmouth St SN1 . . . .**50** D6
Portway
  Chippenham SN14 . . . .**78** B6
  Frome BA11. . . . . . . . **110** A4
  Laverstock SP4 . . . . . **146** B7
  Warminster BA12 . . . **117** A7
Port Way BA13 . . . . . . . **186** A6
Portway Gdns 🔟
  BA11. . . . . . . . . . . . . **110** A4
Portway Ind Est SP10 **193** B1
Portway La BA12 . . . . . **117** A8
Portway The SP1 . . . . . **145** F4
Portwell 🔞 SN6 . . . . . . .**19** D7
Poseidon Cl SN25. . . . . .**34** B6
Postmill Dr SN4 . . . . . . .**47** F1
Postoffice La SN9 . . . . **215** C5
Post Office La
  Atworth/Whitley SN12 . .**92** F8
  Broad Hinton SN4 . . . **167** C7
  Corsham SN13 . . . . . . .**77** A1
  Culkerton GL8. . . . . . . .**3** A4
  Post Office Rd RG17 . . **177** F3
Poston Way BA15. . . . . .**99** D7
Pot La BA11 . . . . . . . . . **110** F8
Potley La SN13 . . . . . . . .**84** E7
Potterdown Rd 🔞
  SN2. . . . . . . . . . . . . . .**35** C5
POTTERNE . . . . . . . . . . **179** D5
Potterne Rd SN10. . . . . **214** A1
POTTERNE WICK . . . . . **179** E4
Potters Way SP1. . . . . . **152** D8
Pottery La RG17 . . . . . . **177** E3
Pottle St BA12. . . . . . . . **119** A6
Pottows Field SN11. . . **166** B1
Poulsen Cl BA12. . . . . . **117** A5

POULSHOT . . . . . . . . . **179** B6
Poulshot Rd SN10 . . . **179** A5
Poulton BA15. . . . . . . . **100** C5
Poulton Cl BA15. . . . . . **100** C5
Poulton La BA15 . . . . . **100** E5
Poulton St SN2. . . . . . . .**50** C8
Pouncette Cl SP4 . . . . **217** D1
Pound Cl
  Lyneham SN15 . . . . . . .**60** A3
  Semington BA14 . . . . **105** F4
Pound Farm Cl BA14. . **101** E4
Pound Hill
  Landford SP5 . . . . . . **212** C7
  Melchet Park & Plaitford
    SO51 . . . . . . . . . . . **212** F7
  St Paul Malmesbury Without
    SN16 . . . . . . . . . . . .**43** A3
Pound La
  Bradford-on-Avon
    BA15. . . . . . . . . . . **100** C5
  Damerham SP6 . . . . . **209** E3
  Melchet Park & Plaitford
    SO51 . . . . . . . . . . . **212** F7
  Semington BA14 . . . . **102** A6
  Shaftesbury SP7 . . . . **202** D2
  Swindon SN2 . . . . . . .**35** B2
  Wilcot SN8 . . . . . . . . **174** B2
Pound Mead 🔝 SN13 . .**84** F8
Pound Piece
  Ashbury SN6 . . . . . . . **164** A8
  🔝 Hungerford RG17. . **177** B7
Pound Pill SN13 . . . . . . .**77** A1
Pound Rd SN6. . . . . . . . .**22** F7
Pound Row BA12 . . . . . **116** F6
Pound St
  Ebbesborne Wake
    SP5. . . . . . . . . . . . **204** D3
  Warminster BA12 . . . **116** F6
Pound The
  Bromham SN15 . . . . . .**96** B7
  Mere BA12 . . . . . . . . **139** B5
Poveys Pl 🔟 SN6 . . . . . **163** E6
Powell Pl 🔞 SN2 . . . . . .**34** E2
Powell Rise SN16 . . . . . .**28** B5
Power Rd SP4 . . . . . . . . **197** E2
Pownall Rd SN4 . . . . . . **198** A6
Poynder Pl SN11. . . . . . **166** A6
Poynder Rd SN13 . . . . . .**76** E1
Poynings Way SN5. . . . .**48** F4
Pragnell Ct SN4 . . . . . . **133** E6
Prescombe Down
  National Nature
  Reserve★ SP5. . . . . . **204** C4
Preshute CE Prim Sch
  SN8. . . . . . . . . . . . . . **213** A1
Preshute La SN8. . . . . . **213** B2
Prestbury Dr BA12 . . . **117** C5
Prest Grove SN14. . . . . .**67** D2
Prestly Wood 🔞
  SN13. . . . . . . . . . . . . .**76** B1
PRESTON
  Aldbourne. . . . . . . . . **170** B4
  Lyneham and
    Bradenstoke . . . . . . .**60** D1
Preston La SN15 . . . . . . .**60** B1
Pretoria Rd 🔝 SP11. . . **192** B5
Priddy Cl BA11 . . . . . . . **110** C7
Prideaux Dr SP7 . . . . . . **202** A5
Priestley Gr SN11. . . . . .**81** C2
Priestley Prim Sch
  SN11. . . . . . . . . . . . . .**81** C2
Priestly Wood Rd 🔟
  SN13. . . . . . . . . . . . . .**76** B1
Primmers Pl BA13 . . . . **108** F5
Primrose Cl
  Calne SN11 . . . . . . . . .**81** B5
  Swindon SN2 . . . . . . .**34** D5
Primrose Dr BA14 . . . . **101** D4
Primrose Dr SN2 . . . . . .**94** C4
Primrose Hill
  Tockenham SN4. . . . . .**60** D6
  Wilton SP2 . . . . . . . . **144** D4
Primrose La
  Manningford SN9. . . . **181** F6
  Redlynch SP5. . . . . . . **211** C2
Primrose Pl 🔞 SP4 . . . **198** B7
Primrose Rd
  🔝 Ludgershall SP11. . **192** A5
  Salisbury SP2. . . . . . . **145** C4
Primrose Way SN14. . . .**70** B2
Primrose Wlk 🔟
  BA12. . . . . . . . . . . . . **116** F7
Prince Charles Cl 🔝
  SP11. . . . . . . . . . . . . **192** A5
Prince Charles Dr
  SN11. . . . . . . . . . . . . .**81** C3
Princecroft County Prim
  Sch BA12. . . . . . . . . . **116** E6
Princecroft La 🔞
  BA12. . . . . . . . . . . . . **116** E6
Princes Cl SN25. . . . . . **211** D8
Princes Hill SP5 . . . . . . **211** D8
Princess Anne Rd 🔞
  BA11. . . . . . . . . . . . . **110** A7
Princess Gdns
  Trowbridge BA14. . . . **101** E4
  Warminster BA12 . . . **117** D6
Princess Margaret Hospl
  SN3. . . . . . . . . . . . . . .**51** D1
Princess Mary Gdns 🔞
  SP11. . . . . . . . . . . . . **192** A5
Princes St SN1. . . . . . . .**50** C6
Priorsfield SN8. . . . . . . **213** E2
Prior's Hill SN4. . . . . . . .**64** B5
Priors Wlk GL7 . . . . . . . .**2** C2
Priory Ave RG17 . . . . . **177** B6
Priory Cl
  Alderbury SP5 . . . . . . **153** F2

Priory Cl continued
  Bradford-on-Avon
    BA15. . . . . . . . . . . **100** C7
  🔝 Hungerford RG17. . **177** B6
  🔝 Shrewton SP3. . . . **196** E6
  Wilton SP2. . . . . . . . **144** C2
  Wilton SP2. . . . . . . . **144** D2
Priory Coll SN1 . . . . . . .**50** C4
Priory Gn SN6 . . . . . . . .**23** A6
Priory La SN16. . . . . . . .**28** B2
Priory New Rd SN13 . .**76** F2
Priory Pk BA15 . . . . . . **100** D7
Priory Pl 🔝 RG17 . . . . **177** B6
Priory Rd
  Hungerford RG17. . . . **177** B6
  Swindon SN3 . . . . . . .**51** A4
Priory Sq 🔝 SP2 . . . . . **146** A1
Priory St SN13 . . . . . . . .**76** F2
PRIORY VALE . . . . . . . . .**34** C8
Priory Way 🔟 SN13 . . . .**84** E8
Pritchard Cl SN2. . . . . . .**35** F5
Privet La SP11 . . . . . . . **192** D2
Privet Way 🔝 SN13 . . . .**84** E8
Proby Pl BA14 . . . . . . . **102** A1
Professions Cnr SP5. . **206** D6
Pro Logis Pk SN3 . . . . . .**36** C6
Prospect
  Box SN13 . . . . . . . . . .**83** B4
  Corsham SN13. . . . . . .**85** A7
Prospect Fields SN12 . .**92** F8
Prospect Hill SN1. . . . . .**50** C5
Prospect Pl
  Bathford BA1. . . . . . . .**82** D2
  Mere BA12. . . . . . . . . **138** F5
  Swindon SN1 . . . . . . .**50** C4
Prospect Rd RG17 . . . . **177** B7
Prospect Sq 🔝 BA13. . **109** A3
Prospero Way
  🔟 Swindon SN25 . . . .**34** C6
  Swindon SN25 . . . . . . .**34** D6
Proud Cl SN5. . . . . . . . .**33** B3
Providence La SN13 . . .**76** F1
Providence Terr SN15 .**78** D7
Provis Mead SN15 . . . . .**79** A4
Provost St 🔞 SP6. . . . . **210** D1
Pub La SN10. . . . . . . . . **180** F8
Pucklands SN10 . . . . . . **180** E5
Puck Well Nature
  Reserve★ BA12 . . . . **140** C4
Pudding La SN14 . . . . . .**78** B5
Puddleslosh La SP6. . . **210** C2
Pugin Cl SN25 . . . . . . . .**34** B8
Pullman Dr SP2 . . . . . . **145** B3
Pulsar Rd 🔝 SN25 . . . . .**34** B7
Pump La
  Bathford BA1. . . . . . . .**82** B1
  Long Newnton GL8 . . .**13** C4
Purbeck Cl SN13. . . . . . .**51** C7
Purbeck Pl SN11. . . . . . .**81** D2
Purcell Rd SN25 . . . . . . .**34** E8
Purleigh Rd SN13 . . . . . .**76** E1
Purley Ave SN3 . . . . . . .**51** B3
Purley Rd SN4. . . . . . . . .**51** F1
Purley Way SO51 . . . . . **212** C4
PURLPIT. . . . . . . . . . . . .**93** A8
Purlpit SN12. . . . . . . . . .**85** A1
Purlyn Acre SN8 . . . . . . **213** D4
Purslane Cl SN2 . . . . . . .**34** C3
PURTON. . . . . . . . . . . . .**33** B4
PURTON COMMON. . . . .**33** A5
Purton Mus★ SN5. . . . . .**33** C4
Purton Rd
  Cricklade SN6 . . . . . . .**19** D7
  Haydon Wick SN2. . . . .**34** C3
  Swindon SN25 . . . . . . .**34** C3
PURTON STOKE . . . . . . .**19** C1
Purvis Cl 🔝 SP4 . . . . . **217** E3
Pyatts Cnr BA14 . . . . . **178** C4
Pye La SN4 . . . . . . . . . . **167** A8

Quadrangle The SN15 .**78** C6
Quakers La SN11 . . . . . .**73** E7
Quakers Rd SN10 . . . . . **214** C5
Quakers Wlk SN11. . . . .**73** F7
Quantock Cl
  Melksham Without
    SN12 . . . . . . . . . . . .**94** D4
  🔝 Warminster BA12. . **117** A8
Quarr Barton SN11. . . . .**81** B3
Quarries The SN11 . . . . .**50** C3
Quarrybrook Cl SN3 . . .**36** E5
Quarry Cl
  Corston SN16. . . . . . . .**42** E5
  Winsley BA2. . . . . . . . .**99** D6
Quarry Cres SN6. . . . . . .**22** F6
Quarrydale Cl SN11. . . .**81** B2
Quarry Field SN15 . . . . .**34** A3
Quarry Fields Ind Est
  BA12. . . . . . . . . . . . . **138** C5
Quarry Hill SN13. . . . . . .**83** E6
Quarry Ho SN16 . . . . . . .**42** F5
Quarry La
  Colerne SN14. . . . . . . .**75** B3
  Melbury Abbas SP7. . . **206** A7
Quarry Mews SN1 . . . . .**50** C3
Quarry Rd
  Bratton BA12. . . . . . . **186** B6
  Swindon SN1 . . . . . . .**50** C4
Quartermaster Rd
  BA13. . . . . . . . . . . . . **108** D6
Quarterway La BA14 . **101** E1
Quavey Rd SP5 . . . . . . **211** D7
Quebec Rd
  Bulford SP4 . . . . . . . . **217** F8

Quebec Rd continued
  Chiseldon SN4 . . . . . . **168** E8
Queen Alexandra Rd
  SP2. . . . . . . . . . . . . . **145** D3
Queenborough SN5. . . .**49** C4
Queen Elizabeth Dr
  SN2. . . . . . . . . . . . . . .**34** C4
Queen Manor Rd
  Clarendon Park SP5. . . **147** B1
  Clarendon Park SP5. . . **147** B2
  Laverstock SP5 . . . . . **152** E8
Queen Mary Rd SP2. . . **145** B3
QUEEN OAK . . . . . . . . . **138** A3
Queen Oak★ SN8. . . . . **175** C4
Queen Oak Rd SP8. . . . **138** A3
Queens Ave
  Corsham SN13. . . . . . .**76** F3
  Highworth SN6. . . . . . .**23** A6
Queen's Barrow★
  BA12. . . . . . . . . . . . . **201** A7
Queensberry Rd
  Amesbury SP4 . . . . . . **217** C4
  Salisbury SP1. . . . . . . **146** A3
Queens Chase BA12. . . **117** A8
Queens Cl
  🔝 Ludgershall SP11. . **192** A5
  Sutton Benger SN15 . . .**57** D2
Queens Club Gdns
  Sch SN14. . . . . . . . . . .**78** A6
Queen's Crescent Prim
  Sch SN14. . . . . . . . . . .**78** A6
Queens Dr SN3 . . . . . . .**51** B2
Queen's Dr SN3 . . . . . . .**50** E6
Queensfield SN2. . . . . . .**35** D5
Queens Gdns
  🔞 Fordingbridge
    SP6. . . . . . . . . . . . **210** D1
  Trowbridge BA14. . . . **101** E4
Queens Gr BA9 . . . . . . . **137** C3
Queens Rd
  Hannington SN6. . . . . .**21** F8
  Mere BA12. . . . . . . . . **139** B6
  Salisbury SP1. . . . . . . **146** B2
  🔝 Tisbury SP3. . . . . . **203** E8
  Trowbridge BA14. . . . **101** C2
Queen's Rd
  Devizes SN10. . . . . . . **214** A2
  Royal Wootton Bassett
    SN4 . . . . . . . . . . . . .**47** E2
  Westbury BA13 . . . . . **108** E3
  Westbury BA13 . . . . . **108** F2
Queens Sq
  Box SN13 . . . . . . . . . .**83** D5
  Chippenham SN15 . . . .**78** F6
  Westbury BA13 . . . . . **108** E3
Queen St
  Hale SP6 . . . . . . . . . . **211** B5
  Salisbury SP1. . . . . . . **146** A1
  Swindon SN1 . . . . . . .**50** B6
  Wilton SP2. . . . . . . . . **144** D4
QUEEN STREET . . . . . . .**31** B3
Queensway
  Andover SP10 . . . . . . **193** C2
  Melksham SN12. . . . . .**94** C4
  🔞 Netheravon SP4. . . **190** A3
  Warminster BA12 . . . **117** D6
Queens Way SN8 . . . . . **213** F2
Queintin Rd SN1 . . . . . .**50** D3
QUEMERFORD . . . . . . . .**89** D8
Quemerford
  Calne SN11 . . . . . . . . .**81** C1
  Quemerford SN11. . . . .**89** E8
QUEMERFORD GATE
  SN11. . . . . . . . . . . . . **172** A8
QUIDHAMPTON . . . . . . **145** A2
Quidham St SP5 . . . . . **204** F2
Quilling Cl BA14 . . . . . **105** E7
Quinton Pl BA12 . . . . . **195** A3

Rabley Wood View
  SN8. . . . . . . . . . . . . . **213** E4
Race Plain Rd SP2 . . . . **150** D7
Rackham Cl SN25. . . . . .**34** C8
Radcliffe Rd SP2. . . . . . **152** A6
Radcot Cl SN5. . . . . . . . .**34** A1
Radley Bottom
  Hungerford Newton
    RG17. . . . . . . . . . . **171** D2
  Hungerford Newtown
    RG17. . . . . . . . . . . **171** E1
  Kintbury RG17 . . . . . . **177** C7
Radley Cl SN3 . . . . . . . . .**51** C7
Radnor Cl SN10. . . . . . . **214** C2
Radnor Pk SN16 . . . . . . .**42** E4
Radnor Pl 🔞 SN12. . . . .**94** A2
Radnor Rd SP1 . . . . . . . **146** A3
Radnor St SN1 . . . . . . . .**50** A5
Radstock Ave SN3 . . . . .**51** B6
Radway Rd SN3 . . . . . . .**35** F3
Radways Cl GL7 . . . . . . . .**1** F6
Raffin La SN9. . . . . . . . . **215** C2
RAGGED
  APPLESHAW . . . . . . . **192** F3
Raggett St SN1 . . . . . . . .**50** C5
Raglan Cl SN3 . . . . . . . . .**50** E2
Ragleth Gr BA14 . . . . . **101** E2
Rag Ride SN8. . . . . . . . . **184** B2
Rail Road La SN4 . . . . . .**61** F4
Railway Dr BA13 . . . . . **108** F3
Railway Village Mus★
  SN1. . . . . . . . . . . . . . .**50** B6
Railway Wlk 🔟 BA11. **110** A4
Rainer Cl SN3 . . . . . . . . .**36** B3
Rainham Rd 🔞 SN25. . .**34** F7

Rake Way 10 SP11 ... 193 F2
Raleigh Ave SN3.......50 F6
Raleigh Cres SP4..... 217 E3
RAM ALLEY .........175 B2
Rambler Cl
  Trowbridge BA14..... 101 A1
  Trowbridge BA14..... 105 A8
Rambridge Cres SP2. 145 B5
Ramleaze Dr
  Salisbury SP2........145 C5
  Swindon SN5 ........ 49 A7
Ramnuggur Rd SP9.. 216 D3
Rampart Rd SP1..... 146 B1
Ramsay Rd SN11..... 81 D3
RAMSBURY ......... 170 A2
Ramsbury Ave SN2 ...35 B6
Ramsbury Dr
  Hungerford RG17.... 177 C7
  Old Sarum SP4...... 146 B7
Ramsbury Manor★
  SN8................ 169 F1
Ramsbury Prim Sch
  SN8................ 170 B2
Ramsbury Terr RG17.. 177 C7
Ramsbury Wlk BA14.. 105 D6
Ramscliff SN10 ...... 187 F7
Ramscombe La BA1 ...82 A6
Ramsden Rd SN1 .....48 F3
Ramshill Dro
  East Winterslow SP5.. 149 F8
  Winterslow SP5...... 134 F1
Ramsthorn Cl SN2.... 34 D4
Randall Cl SN13 ..... 76 D1
Randall's Croft Rd
  SP2................ 144 B2
Randolph Cl SN3..... 50 F5
Rank The BA14 ...... 105 C3
Rannoch Cl 4 SN5 ...34 B2
Ransome Cl SN5......49 B8
Ransome Terr BA13.. 108 E3
Raspberry La 8 SP7. 202 B1
Ratcliff's Gdn 15 SP7 202 C1
RATFORD...........80 E5
Ratford Hill SN11 .... 80 D5
RATFYN ........... 217 C5
Ratfyn Barrow★ SP4. 217 B4
Ratfyn Rd SP4 ...... 217 B4
Rat Hill SN14........54 E2
Raven Cl SP9 ....... 216 D6
Ravenglass Rd SN5 .. 49 C6
Ravenhurst SN16 .... 14 E6
Ravenscroft
  7 Salisbury SP2.... 152 A5
  Swindon SN3 ....... 51 C8
Ravenscroft Gdns
  BA14 ............. 101 F1
Ravensdale 7 SN1 ...50 A2
Ravensroost Wood &
Mdws Nature Reserve★
  SN16.............. 31 A5
Ravens Wlk SN4 ..... 48 A2
Rawlence Rd
  Salisbury SP2....... 145 B3
  Wilton SP2......... 144 C2
Rawlings Cl SN3......36 E4
Rawlings Ct SP11.... 192 A5
Rawlingswell La
  SN8............... 213 E3
Rawlinson Rd SP4 ... 198 E6
Rawlins Pk SN8...... 167 C1
Rawlins Rd SN9...... 215 C5
Rawston Cl SN3 ..... 51 C6
Raybrook Cres SN2...49 E6
Ray Cl
  Chippenham SN15.....78 F5
  Swindon SN25...... 34 A4
Rayfield Gr
  Swindon SN2 ....... 50 B8
  Swindon SN2........ 35 B1
Reading St 4 SN1...50 B6
Read St SN1.........50 A5
Rea Rd SN13.........84 F6
Recreation Rd
  10 Durrington/Bulford
  SP4............... 198 B2
  Ludgershall SP11.... 192 A6
Rectory Cl
  Alton SN8.......... 181 C8
  North Tidworth SP9... 216 C7
  Overtown SN4 ...... 64 E3
  Stanton St Quintin SN14 56 B4
  11 Warminster BA12.. 117 A8
Rectory Ct SP4...... 133 F7
Rectory Hill SP5..... 155 F3
Rectory La
  Alderbury SP5....... 153 E2
  Breamore SP6....... 210 E5
  Charlton Musgrove
  BA9 .............. 136 B1
  Cricklade SN6 ...... 19 E8
  Letcombe Bassett
  OX12 ............. 165 F8
Rectory Pl 4 SP11... 192 F1
Rectory Rd
  Alderbury SP5....... 153 E2
  Clarendon Park SP5... 153 D8
  Salisbury SP1....... 151 F8
  Sutton Mandeville SP3. 204 C7
Rectory Wood 1
  SN8............... 170 A6
Reculver Way 6
  SP10.............. 193 C2
Red Barn La SN4......63 E3
Redbridge Cl 1 SN1..49 F4
Redcap Gdns SN5.....49 A7
Redcliffe St SN2......49 F6

Red Cross House★
  SN10.............. 214 B4
REDENHAM ........ 192 E4
Redenham Dro SP11.. 192 E4
Redford Cl SP1...... 146 D3
Redgrave Cl BA14.... 105 D6
Redhill Cl SN11.......79 F2
Redhouse Gdns 2
  ................... 34 D7
Redhouse Way
  Swindon SN25....... 34 B7
  Swindon SN25....... 34 C7
  Swindon SN25....... 34 D7
Red La
  East Winterslow SP5.. 149 C7
  Mildenhall SN8...... 169 B2
  Sixpenny Handley SP5. 208 A3
Redland SN14 ....... 78 B8
Redland La BA13 .... 108 F2
Redland Prim Sch
  SN14.............. 78 B8
REDLANDS.......... 22 F3
Redlands 3 BA13.... 186 B7
Redlands Cl SN6...... 23 A4
Red Lion La SN6...... 19 E8
Red Lion Mews SN6... 23 A6
Red Lodge Cl SN4 .... 61 E8
REDLYNCH ......... 211 D8
Redlynch Cl SN2......35 C5
Redman Rd SN11 .....81 C6
Redmans La SP7..... 206 A7
Red Oaks Prim Sch
  SN25.............. 34 D7
Red Pit BA13 ....... 112 A8
Red Post La SP11.... 192 F1
Redposts Dr SN1 .....49 E4
Redruth Cl SN3.......51 B5
REDSTOCKS.........95 A2
Redstocks La SN12 ...95 A2
Red Way The BA12... 115 F3
Redwing Ave SN14.... 70 B2
Redwing Rd SN12.... 94 D5
Redwood Way SN14 ...75 A5
Redworth Dr SP4 .... 217 C2
Redworth Wlk SP4... 217 C2
Reed Cl SN3......... 36 C1
Reed Pl SN15........ 96 F1
Reeds SN6.......... 19 E8
Reeds Farm Rd SN16.. 28 A4
Reeds Gd SN8 ...... 213 F3
Red Wlk 10 SN4 .... 198 C7
Rees Dr SP4 ........ 132 B1
Reeves Cl 2 SN3.... 51 C4
Reeves Piece 14
  BA13.............. 186 B7
Reeves Rd SN10 .... 214 D1
Regal Ct
  3 Trowbridge BA14.. 105 C8
  Warminster BA12.... 117 A6
Regent Circus 6 SN1. 50 C5
Regent Cl
  15 Hungerford RG17.. 177 B7
  Swindon SN1....... 50 C6
Regents Pl
  Bradford-on-Avon
  BA15.............. 100 D5
  Studley Green BA14... 104 F6
Reid's Piece SN5 .....33 B3
Reith Way 2 SP10.... 193 B1
REME Museum★
  SN15.............. 60 A1
Rendall's Barn GL7 ....4 E5
Rendells Ct SN10 .... 214 B3
Renoir Cl 2 SN25.....35 A8
RESTROP...........33 A2
Restrop Rd SN5...... 33 A3
Restrop View SN5 .... 33 A4
Retingham Way SN2...36 A5
Reto Gr BA15........ 99 F3
Retreat The
  Frome BA11........ 110 B4
  Highworth SN6...... 22 F6
Revell Cl SN2........35 E4
REYBRIDGE .........86 D7
Reynolds Ct 4 SP10. 193 D1
Reynolds Rise 18
  SP7............... 202 D1
Reynolds Way SN25... 35 A8
Rhine Cl SN1........ 49 F4
Rhodes Moorhouse Way
  1 SP4............ 132 B1
Rhuddlan 5 SN3..... 49 B4
Rhymes La GL7 ....... 1 E3
Ricardo Rd SN15......78 D8
Richard Jefferies Mus★
  SN3............... 51 B2
Richards Cl SN4 ..... 47 D1
Richards Dr SN14.... 66 E1
Richardson Rd SN25... 35 A8
Richards Way SP2 ... 151 E7
Richard Webb Mews
  SN1............... 50 B3
Richborough Dr 3
  SP10.............. 193 C2
Richmond Cl 2
  BA14.............. 105 A7
Richmond Cres SP9... 216 E6
Richmond Ct SN6..... 6 F1
Richmond Rd
  Calne Without SN11... 81 A4
  2 Salisbury SP2.... 146 A1
Rickbarton 2 SN10.. 187 E7
Rickfield BA15....... 100 B6
Rickworth Pl BA12... 195 A3

Rickyard The 9 SP7. 202 D1
Riddell Way SP2..... 151 D7
RIDGE ............. 200 F2
Ridge SP3.......... 200 F4
Ridge Gn SN5 ....... 49 B7
Ridgemead SN11 .....81 B4
Ridge Nether Moor
  SN3............... 51 D2
Ridge The
  Broad Blunsdon SN26 .. 21 B2
  Redlynch SP5....... 211 C7
Ridgeway SP3....... 201 A3
Ridge Way SP7...... 202 C3
Ridgeway Cl SN2 .... 34 F2
Ridgeway Ct BA12 ... 117 B6
Ridgeway Farm CE Acad
  Sch SN25.......... 34 B3
Ridgeway La
  Dauntsey SN15 ..... 44 E1
  Latton SN6........ 9 D3
Ridgeway Rd
  Salisbury SP1....... 146 B2
  Swindon SN2 ....... 35 E5
Ridgeway Sch The
  SN4............... 64 B7
Ridgeway The
  Chiseldon SN4....... 65 D2
  Crudwell SN16....... 14 E6
  Liddington SN4...... 163 A2
  Warminster BA12 .... 117 B6
Ridgmount 6 SP4 ... 198 B7
Ridings Mead SN14... 70 C2
Ridings The SN14..... 70 A8
Rifles La SP7........ 202 D1
Rigel Cl SN25....... 34 C7
Rigsby's La
  Minety SN16........ 16 F5
  Upper Minety SN16... 16 A5
Rinsdale Cl SN5 ..... 34 B1
Ripley Rd SN1....... 50 C4
Ripon Cl SN14 ...... 78 A5
Ripon Way SN3...... 51 A3
Ripple Field SN5..... 49 B4
Rise Rd BA12....... 194 C4
Rise The SN11.......89 C8
Risingham Mead SN5. 49 C5
Ritter Cl GL7 ....... 1 F6
RIVAR ............. 184 F8
Rivar Rd
  Rivar SN8......... 184 F8
  Shalbourne SN8..... 176 F1
Rivenhall Rd SN5.....49 C5
Riverbourne Rd
  Laverstock SP1...... 146 D1
  Salisbury SP1....... 152 D8
Riverdale Cl 9
  Fordingbridge
  SP6............... 210 D1
  Swindon SN1....... 50 C2
Riverdale Wlk SN1....50 C2
Rivergate SN5....... 49 C8
Rivermead SN3...... 133 F8
Rivermead Dr SN5 ... 49 C7
Rivermead Ind Est
  SN5............... 49 C7
River Mead Sch SN12 .94 B5
River Par SN15 ...... 78 D7
River Pk SN8 ....... 213 D2
River Ray Ind Est SN2. 49 E7
Riverside
  Calne SN11 ........ 89 D8
  Wilton SP2......... 144 D3
Riverside Cl
  Salisbury SP1....... 146 D2
  South Newton SP2... 130 A4
Riverside Dr
  Chippenham SN15..... 79 A8
  Melksham SN12...... 94 A6
Riverside Pk SN15 ....44 A2
Riverside Pl SP6..... 210 E1
Riverside Rd SP1 .... 146 D2
Riverside Terr SP3... 129 E7
Rivers Reach 6
  BA11.............. 110 A4
River St
  Chippenham SN15..... 78 E7
  Pewsey SN9........ 215 C5
Rivers Way SN6...... 22 F6
River View SN25...... 34 B3
River Way
  5 Durrington/Bulford
  SP4............... 198 C7
  South Cerney GL7.... 6 F7
  Trowbridge BA14..... 101 C1
Rixon Gate
  Ashton Keynes SN16.. 17 F8
  Ashton Keynes SN6... 7 A1
  Ashton Keynes SN6... 18 A8
Roach's La GL9...... 38 C1
Robbers' Stone★
  SN10.............. 187 E6
Robbins Ridge SP4 .. 217 D1
Robert Franklin Way
  GL7................ 2 A7
Robert Le Kyng Prim Sch
  SN1............... 50 A5
Roberts Cl SN4 ...... 64 B5
Roberts of Kandahar Rd
  BA12.............. 113 F1

Roberts Rd
  North Tidworth SP11.. 192 A5
  Salisbury SP2....... 145 D3
Robin Cl BA12 ...... 117 C6
Robin Hill La SP4.... 217 C8
Robin Hood's Ball★
  SP4............... 189 C1
Robin Hood's Bower★
  BA12.............. 117 B1
Robinia Cl SN9 ..... 215 D5
Robin Rd SP4....... 132 C1
Robins Cl
  Chippenham SN14..... 70 B2
  Royal Wootton Bassett
  SN4............... 48 A2
Robinscroft SN26..... 21 A1
Robinsgreen SN3..... 51 D7
Robins Hill RG17.... 177 F3
Robinson Cl SN3..... 51 D6
Robinson Gr 2 SP4.. 132 B1
Rochdale Ave SN11...81 B4
Roche Cl SN3....... 51 D4
Rochelle Ct 19 SN10. 179 F1
Rocher Cl BA13..... 108 F3
Rochester Cl 5 SN5..49 B4
Rochford Cl
  East Winterslow SP5.. 149 D7
  Swindon SN5 ....... 49 A5
ROCKBOURNE ...... 210 A5
Rockbourne Rd SP5.. 156 E3
Rockbourne Mus★
  SP6............... 210 A3
Rockbourne Roman
  Villa★ SP6......... 210 A4
Rockdown Ct SN2.... 35 D4
Rocker Bench SN6.... 163 E6
Rockfel Rd RG17.... 165 A1
Rockfield SN14...... 75 B3
Rock La BA12....... 117 D6
ROCKLEY .......... 168 C2
Rockley SN8......... 168 D2
Rockley Rd SN8 .... 213 C7
Rockmoor La SP11... 185 C5
Rock Rd BA14....... 105 B7
RODBOURNE
  St Paul Malmesbury
  Without ........... 43 A3
  Swindon .......... 35 A1
RODBOURNE
  BOTTOM .......... 43 A2
RODBOURNE
  CHENEY .......... 35 B2
Rodbourne Cheney Prim
  Sch SN25.......... 35 A3
Rodbourne House
  SN16.............. 43 B4
Rodbourne Rd
  Corston SN16....... 42 F4
  Rodbourne SN15 .... 43 C3
  Rodbourne SN16 .... 43 A3
  St Paul Malmesbury Without
  SN16.............. 42 F4
  Swindon SN2....... 49 F7
Roddenbury Cl BA11. 110 B5
Roddenbury View
  BA12.............. 115 A8
Rodden Manor★
  BA11.............. 110 D4
Rode Rd BA11...... 110 A5
Rode Bridge★ BA11. 103 C1
Rode Comm BA11 ... 107 A8
Rode Common BA14.. 104 B1
RODE HILL ........ 103 F1
Rode Hill
  Box SN13.......... 82 F8
  Colerne SN14....... 74 D1
  Ditteridge SN13..... 83 A8
  Rode BA11......... 103 F1
RODMARTON .......3 C8
Rodmarton SN25..... 20 B1
Rodmarton La GL7.... 3 C8
Rodney Ct SP10..... 193 F1
Rodsleigh BA14..... 104 F6
Rodway 13 SN4..... 163 A6
Rodway Cl BA14 .... 101 E2
Rodwell Cl 3 SN3.... 51 A4
Rodwell Pk BA14 ... 101 E2
Roebuck Cl SN4..... 47 F7
Roger Penny Way
  SP6............... 211 C3
Rogers Cl
  Quidhampton SP2 ... 145 A3
  Swindon SN3....... 51 A7
Rogers Meadow SN8. 213 D5
Rogers's La RG17.... 171 D7
Roger Way
  Old Sarum SP4 ..... 146 C8
  8 Winterbourne SP4. 132 C1
ROLLESTONE ....... 196 F6
ROLLESTONE CAMP.. 197 B7
Rollestone Crossroads
  SP3............... 197 B8
Rollestone Rd SP3... 196 E6
Rollestone St 1 SN1. 146 B1
Rolleston St 1 SN1... 50 C5
Roman Cres SN3..... 50 B3
Roman Meadow SP5..
  ................... 211 A8
Roman Rd
  Salisbury SP2....... 145 D2
  West Tytherley SP5 .. 149 F6
Roman Way
  Andover SP10 ...... 193 E2
  Chippenham SN15.... 79 B5
  Highworth SN6...... 22 F5
  Lechlade GL7........ 2 D5

Roman Way continued
  15 Market Lavington
  SN10.............. 179 F1
  Warminster BA12 ... 112 F1
  Warminster BA12 ... 116 F8
Roman Way Prim Sch
  SP10.............. 193 E2
Romer Rd SP2....... 152 A6
Romney Cl BA12..... 116 D7
Romney Rd 2 SP11.. 193 F2
Romney Way SN5..... 49 A6
Romsey Rd
  Amesbury SP4 ...... 217 D2
  Cowesfield Gate SP5.. 162 C3
  Whiteparish SP5..... 162 B3
  Romsey Road SP5 ... 162 A3
Romsey St SN2...... 49 F7
Ron Golding Cl SN16..28 A5
ROOD ASHTON ..... 106 C8
Rood Ashton Pk
  BA14.............. 106 C8
Rookery Cottages
  SP5............... 155 F4
Rookery La
  Ansty SP3.......... 203 F6
  Breamore SP6....... 210 D5
  Swallowcliffe SP3 ... 204 A6
Rookery Meadow
  SN8............... 174 A6
Rookery Pk
  Calne SN11 ........ 89 C7
  Quemerford SN11 ... 89 B8
Rookes La SN10 .... 179 D5
Rooks La BA11...... 110 E6
Rooks Nest Cl SN15... 78 F4
Rooksnest La RG17 .. 185 F8
Rook St BA12....... 139 A4
ROOK STREET ...... 139 A4
Rookwood Gdns 9
  SP6............... 210 C1
Ropewind SN8 ...... 176 F1
Rope Wlk SN12...... 94 B3
Rope Yd SN4 ....... 47 E2
Rorkes Drift Dr SP9.. 216 D4
Rosary The SN4 .....47 F2
Rose Ave BA12 ..... 117 E6
Rosebery St SN1..... 50 D7
Rosebrock Gdns
  SN12.............. 94 C3
Rosedale Gdns BA14. 101 A1
Rosedale Rd SN3..... 51 B4
Rosefield Way BA13.. 108 F4
Rosehill Cl SN15..... 59 D3
Roseland Ave SN10.. 214 C3
Rosemary Cl
  Calne SN11 ........ 80 F4
  Great Bedwyn SN8 .. 176 B3
  Laverstock SP1...... 146 D1
  Swindon SN2....... 34 D5
Rosemary La
  Freshford BA2....... 99 B4
  Lacock SN15........ 86 B6
  2 Salisbury SP1.... 152 A8
  Rosemary Way GL7 .. 94 D4
Rosenheim Rise 1
  BA13.............. 186 B7
Rose St SN2........ 49 F7
Rosetta Cl 6 SN25...34 B7
Rosewood Ct SN3 ... 51 D3
Rossett Gdns BA14... 105 A8
Rossetti La SN25..... 34 D8
Ross Gdns SN2...... 36 A4
Ross Rd SP4........ 197 E2
Rother Cl SN25...... 34 F5
Rothe Rise BA13.... 108 F1
Rotherstone SN10 .. 214 A4
Rotten Row SN4 .... 163 A6
Rougemont Cl SP1 .. 146 B1
Roughmoor Farm Cl
  SN4............... 33 F1
Roughmoor Way SN5. 34 A1
Rough St SN13 ..... 83 A2
Roundaway La SP11. 193 A5
Round Barrow Cl
  SN14.............. 75 B3
Round Hill
  25 Fordingbridge
  SP6............... 210 D1
  Maiden Bradley BA12. 118 F3
  Maiden Bradley BA12. 118 F5
  Round Hill★ SN14 ...67 A7
Roundhills Mead SN6.. 23 B6
Round House La SN11. 81 D1
Round House La GL7...2 B3
Roundpond SN12 .... 93 F6
Roundponds SN12.... 93 F6
Roundstone St BA14. 101 D3
ROUNDWAY ........ 214 D7
Roundway Cl SN11... 89 B1
Roundway Down SN5. 49 B3
Roundway Gdns
  SN10.............. 214 B6
Roundway Ind Est
  SN10.............. 214 C6
Roundway Pk SN10.. 214 C5
Roundway Rise SN11. 89 C8
Roundwood View
  SN15.............. 58 A3
Roundwood Way
  SN13.............. 84 C2
Rovers Farm & Visitor
  Ctr★ SN6.......... 37 B6
Roves La SN6........ 23 B1
Rowan Cl
  Colerne SN14....... 75 A5
  5 Durrington/Bulford
  SP4............... 198 C7
  Salisbury SP2....... 145 B4

Rowan Ct
  Frome BA11........ 110 B7
  Melksham SN12...... 94 A3
Rowan Dr
  Bishops Cannings
  SN10.............. 214 F6
  Royal Wootton Bassett
  SN4............... 47 E1
Rowan La SN13......84 C5
Rowan Rd SN2....... 35 A3
Rowans The SN16.... 27 F4
Rowbarrow SP2 .... 152 B5
Rowbarrow Cl 3
  SP2............... 152 B5
Rowbarrow La 4
  SP2............... 152 B5
ROWDE ............ 96 D2
Rowde CE Prim Acad
  ................... 96 E2
Rowde Ct Rd SN10... 96 D1
Rowdeford Sch SN10 . 96 D3
Rowden Hill SN15 ....78 C6
Rowden La
  Bradford-on-Avon
  BA15.............. 100 D4
  Chippenham SN15.... 78 C5
Rowden Rd SN15..... 78 C6
Rowe Mead SN15.... 78 E5
Rowe's Hill BA12 ... 119 C8
Rowe's Hill BA12 ... 119 C8
Rowhill SO43....... 212 D2
Row La SN12........ 178 C7
Rowland Hill Cl SN3 .. 51 E4
Rowlands Cl BA1..... 82 B2
Rowley Medieval Village
  of★ BA15.......... 99 F1
Rowley Pl SN12..... 94 B4
Row The SP5 ....... 211 C8
Rowton Heath Way
  SN5............... 49 A4
Roxby Rd SN9....... 216 D7
Royal Cescent The
  SN4............... 64 B7
Royal Cl SN15...... 78 D6
Royal Field Cl SN15... 55 E8
Royal Oak Cl SN15 .. 78 F6
ROYAL WOOTTON
  BASSETT.......... 47 C2
Royal Wootton Bassett
  Acad SN4.......... 47 D3
Royal Wootton Bassett
  Inf Sch SN4........ 47 C1
Royal Wootton Bassett
  Mus★ SN4......... 47 D1
Royce Cl 5 SP10 ... 193 B1
Royston St SN3...... 51 A4
Rubens Cl SN25..... 34 F8
Ruby Cl SN26....... 20 F1
Ruckley Gdns SN3 ... 36 B2
Rudd Rd 6 SN11.....81 B5
RUDGE ............ 107 D5
Rudge Hill BA11 .... 107 D5
Rudge La
  Beckington BA11 .... 107 B6
  Lower Rudge BA11... 107 C5
  Wilcot SN8......... 174 B1
Rudge Rd BA11..... 107 B2
RUDLOE ............ 76 B1
Rudman Pk SN14.... 78 F2
Rumble Dene SN15... 78 E5
Rune Dr 4 SP10.... 193 D2
Runnymede Gdns 6
  BA14.............. 105 D6
RUSHALL .......... 181 E2
Rushall CE Prim Sch
  SN9............... 181 E3
Rushall Cl SN2....... 35 B5
Rushall Dro SN9..... 181 D1
Rushall Rd SN9..... 181 F3
Rushcroft Cl SN16.... 28 F1
Rushey La BA15...... 91 F3
Rushmead La
  Marshfield SN14 .... 66 A3
  South Wraxall BA15... 91 C5
Rushmere Path SN25. 34 C5
Rushmore Down La
  SP11.............. 185 C1
Rushmore Pk★ SP5. 207 D5
Rushton Rd SN3..... 51 A3
Rushworth Row SP4. 217 C2
Rushy Platt Ind Est
  SN5............... 49 E4
Rushy Platt Nature
  Reserve★ SN1 ..... 49 F4
Ruskin Ave
  Melksham SN12...... 94 B4
  Swindon SN2....... 35 F3
Ruskin County Jun Sch
  SN2............... 35 F4
Ruskin Dr
  Royal Wootton Bassett
  SN4............... 47 F3
  Warminster BA12 ... 116 D6
Russel Cl GL9....... 24 B3
Russell Mill La SN10. 179 D1
Russell Rd 1 SP2.... 145 E2
Russell St SP2...... 144 D3
Russell Wlk SN3..... 50 E6
Russet Ave GL7....... 2 E3
Russet Ct BA12 .... 116 F7
Russley Cl
  Swindon SN5........ 33 F1
Russley Gn 3 SN8... 164 C3
Russley Pk★ SN8.... 164 A3
Rusty La SN12...... 178 E8

Rutherford Cl SN11. . . 81 D3
Rutland Cl SN12. . . . .94 C3
Rutland Cres BA14. . . . 105 C6
Rutland Rd **1** SN3. . . . . .50 F5
Rutter Cl **16** SP7 . . . . 202 D1
Rutts La **3** SN10. . . . 187 E7
Ruxley Cl SN4 . . . . . . . 47 D1
Ryan Ave SN14 . . . . . . .78 A7
Ryan Cl SN5 . . . . . . . . .34 B2
Rybury Camp (Hill Fort)★
SN10. . . . . . . . . . . . 173 A2
Rycote Cl SN5 . . . . . . . .49 A6
Rydal Cl SN25 . . . . . . . .34 F5
Rye Cl SN5 . . . . . . . . . .49 A7
Rye Hill BA12. . . . . . . 120 B6
Ryeland Way
  **26** East Anton SP11 . . 193 F2
  Trowbridge BA14. . . . 105 E7
Ryeleaze SN10. . . . . . 179 D5
Rye Way **14** SP11 . . . 193 F2
Rylands Way SN4 . . . . .47 E2
Rylane SN1. . . . . . . . . .50 B1
Ryles La SN8 . . . . . . . 174 B6
Rymer's La SP11 . . . . 185 E4
Ryon Cl **11** SP10 . . . . 193 E2
Rysy Ct **3** SN25. . . . . .34 E6

## S

Sack Hill BA12. . . . . . 113 F1
Sackville Cl SN3 . . . . . .50 F7
Saddleback Cl SN11 . . .81 C2
Saddleback La SN10 . . 179 E5
Saddleback Rd SN5. . . .49 A7
Saddlers Mead SP2. . . 144 C3
Saddlers Mews SP11. 192 D1
Saddlers Way SN8 . . . 183 D7
Sadlers Field SN6. . . . . . 6 F1
Sadlers Mead SN15 . . . .78 E8
Sadlers Rd RG17. . . . . 177 C3
Sadler Wlk SN3. . . . . . .50 F5
Saffron Cl
  Royal Wootton Bassett
  SN4 . . . . . . . . . . . . . 47 E4
  **2** Swindon SN2 . . . . 34 E3
Saffron Meadows
  SN11. . . . . . . . . . . .80 F3
Sage Cl SN2 . . . . . . . . .34 D5
St Albans Cl
  Salisbury SP1. . . . . . 146 D5
  Swindon SN2 . . . . . . . 49 E7
St Aldhelm Rd BA15. . . 100 E5
St Aldhelms Cl SN16 . . .27 F4
St Aldhelms Rd SN16 . . .27 F4
St Alphege Gdns **7**
  SP10. . . . . . . . . . . . 193 D1
St Ambrose Cl SN3 . . .51 D6
ST ANDREW RIDGE . . .35 A8
St Andrews SP1 . . . . . 146 D2
St Andrew's CE VA Prim
  Sch SP1. . . . . . . . . 146 E3
St Andrews Cl SN4. . . .64 B7
St Andrew's Cl
  Wilton SP2. . . . . . . . 144 B2
  Wootton Rivers SN8. . 174 F1
St Andrews Gn SN3 . . .51 E7
St Andrews Rd
  Tidworth SP9. . . . . . 216 C6
  Warminster BA12 . . . 116 D6
St Andrew's Rd
  Melksham SN12. . . . . . 94 C5
  Salisbury SP2. . . . . . 145 C2
  South Newton SP2. . . 130 B2
St Andrews Ridge **4**
  SN25. . . . . . . . . . . . . 35 A8
St Annes Cl
  Amesbury SP4 . . . . . 217 C4
  Southwick BA14. . . . . 105 A4
St Ann Pl SP1. . . . . . . 152 B8
St Ann St SP1. . . . . . . 152 B8
St Arild's Rd SP1. . . . .24 B4
St Athan Cl BA14. . . . . 178 B8
St Augustine's RC Coll
  BA14. . . . . . . . . . . . 105 B8
St Augustine's Rd **5**
  BA14. . . . . . . . . . . . 105 B8
St Austell Way SN5 . . .49 F6
St Barbara's Rd SN3 . .84 D8
St Barnabas CE Sch
  SN10. . . . . . . . . . . . 179 F1
St Bartholomew's CE
  Prim Sch SN4 . . . . .47 E2
St Bartholomew's St
  SP7. . . . . . . . . . . . 203 B4
St Bedes Cl **5** SP1 . . 146 D5
St Birinus Ct GL7 . . . . . 2 C5
St Birinus Gdns SP10 193 D1
St Birinus Rd **4** SP5 . 211 C7
St Birstan Gdns **9**
  SP10. . . . . . . . . . . . 193 D1
St Brendans Cl SP1. . . 146 C5
St Catherine La
  St Catherine BA1. . . . . .74 A1
  St Catherine BA1. . . . . .82 A8
St Catherines Cl SN11. .81 C4
St Catherines RC Prim
  Sch SN2. . . . . . . . . . .35 F5
St Christophers Cl **4**
  SP1. . . . . . . . . . . . 146 D5
St Clair Rd SP2 . . . . . 152 B6
St Clements Ct SN3 . . .51 A4
St Clements Way
  SP1. . . . . . . . . . . . 146 C5
St Davids Cl SP1 . . . . 146 D5

St David's Way SN8. . 213 D3
St Dennis Rd **7** SN16. .28 A3
St Dunstan Cl SN11. . . .81 B5
ST EDITH'S . . . . . . . . .96 D5
St Edith's Cl SP2. . . . 144 C1
St Edith's Marsh SN15 96 D5
St Edmund's Church St **2**
  SP1. . . . . . . . . . . . 146 B1
St Edmund's Girls' Sch
  SP1. . . . . . . . . . . . 146 B1
St Edmund's RC Prim Sch
  SN11. . . . . . . . . . . . .81 C5
St Edwards **12** SP7. . 202 C2
St Edwards Meadow
  SP4. . . . . . . . . . . . 133 B2
St Edwards Sch
  SO51. . . . . . . . . . . . 162 B2
Saintes Cl **1** SP1 . . . 146 D5
St Francis Ave SN15 . .78 C6
St Francis CE Prim Sch
  SN25. . . . . . . . . . . . . .34 C5
St Francis Cl SN9 . . . 215 D5
St Francis Rd SP1 . . . 146 A4
St Francis Sch SN9 . . 215 E6
St George's CE Prim Schl
  BA14. . . . . . . . . . . . 102 E6
St Georges CE Sch
  SP8. . . . . . . . . . . . 137 E1
St George's Cl
  Ogbourne St George
  SN8 . . . . . . . . . . . . 169 A5
  Warminster BA12 . . . 117 E5
St Georges Ct BA14. . . 102 E5
St Georges Pl BA14. . . 102 E5
St Georges RC Prim Sch
  BA12. . . . . . . . . . . . 117 D5
St Georges Rd
  **35** Fordingbridge
  SP6. . . . . . . . . . . . 210 D1
  Tidworth SP9. . . . . . 216 C6
St George's Rd
  Salisbury SP2. . . . . . 151 D7
  Semington BA14 . . . . 102 E5
  **11** Shaftesbury SP7. . 202 C1
St Giles Cl SN16 . . . . .29 A2
St Gregory's Ave SP2 145 D2
St Helens Gdns SN4. . . .64 B5
St Helens View SN1. . . .49 F4
St Ives Cl SN3 . . . . . . .51 B7
ST JAMES . . . . . . . . . 202 C1
St James Cl SN15 . . . . .59 A7
St James Cl SN3 . . . . . .35 D5
St James Dr **5** SN13. .84 B8
St James St SP11 . . . 192 A5
St John Rd SN4. . . . . . .64 A4
St Johns Alley SN10. . . 214 A3
St John's Catholic Prim
  Sch BA14. . . . . . . . 105 B8
St John's CE Prim Sch
  SP3. . . . . . . . . . . . 203 D8
St John's CE Sch
  BA12. . . . . . . . . . . . 117 C6
St Johns Churchyard
  SN10. . . . . . . . . . . . 214 A3
St Johns Cl
  Pewsey SN9. . . . . . . 215 D5
  **19** Tisbury SP3. . . . 203 E8
St John's Cl
  Donhead St Mary SP7. 203 A1
  Marlborough SN8. . . . 213 D4
  **2** Salisbury SP1. . . . 152 D8
St John's Cres BA14. . 104 F6
St John's Ct SN10 . . . 214 A3
St John's Ct SP2. . . . . 144 C3
St John's Hill **7** SP7. . 202 B1
St John's Marlborough
  SN8. . . . . . . . . . . . 213 D1
St John's Priory Pk
  GL7. . . . . . . . . . . . . . 2 E3
St John's RC (Aided)
  Prim Sch BA14 . . . . 105 A8
St John's Rd
  Frome BA11. . . . . . . 110 B5
  Warminster BA12 . . . 117 C5
St Johns Sq SP2 . . . . 144 C3
St John's St
  Devizes SN10. . . . . . 214 A3
  Lechlade GL7. . . . . . . .2 C4
  Malmesbury SN16 . . . .28 B2
  Salisbury SP1. . . . . . 152 B8
St John's Way SN16. . . .29 A6
St Joseph's Catholic
  College SN3. . . . . . . .50 E7
St Joseph's Catholic Prim
  Sch SN10. . . . . . . . 179 D8
St Joseph's Catholic Sch
  SP1. . . . . . . . . . . . 146 E3
St Josephs Cl SP1 . . . 146 C4
St Joseph's Dr SN15 . .78 C6
St Josephs RC Prim Sch
  SN16. . . . . . . . . . . . .28 B3
St Josephs Way SN15 . .60 B2
St Judes Cl SP1. . . . . 146 D4
St Julians Cl SN3 . . . . .36 E4
St Just Cl SP4 . . . . . . 199 B3
ST KATHARINES. . . . . 175 F4
St Katharine's CE (VC)
  Prim Sch SN8 . . . . . 170 A6
St Katherine Gn **2**
  SN3. . . . . . . . . . . . . .51 E7
St Katherines SN4 . . . 167 C6
St Katherine's Pl **17**
  SN4. . . . . . . . . . . . 163 A6

St Laurence CE Prim Sch
  GL7. . . . . . . . . . . . . .2 D3
St Laurence Rd BA15. . 100 E5
St Laurence Sch
  BA15. . . . . . . . . . . . 100 C7
St Lawrence Cl SP1. . . 145 E5
St Lawrence Cres **6**
  SP7. . . . . . . . . . . . 202 C2
St Lawrence Rd GL7 . . . 2 C4
St Lawrence Sq **8**
  RG17. . . . . . . . . . . . 177 B7
St Leonard's CE Prim
  Acad SN26 . . . . . . . .21 C1
St Leonard's Church★
  BA12. . . . . . . . . . . . 194 A4
St Leonards Cl SN16 . . 16 D3
St Leonard's Cl SP4. . . 217 D8
St Leonard's Row
  SN16. . . . . . . . . . . . . 16 D3
St Lukes Cl **8** SP1. . . 146 D5
St Lukes Dr SN15 . . . .78 C6
St Luke's Sch SN2 . . . .35 D5
St Margarets Cl SN11. .81 A4
St Margaret's Cl **2**
  SP1. . . . . . . . . . . . 152 C8
St Margarets Gdns
  SN15. . . . . . . . . . . . .78 C6
St Margaret's Gdns
  SN12. . . . . . . . . . . . .94 C5
St Margaret's Gn **1**
  SN3. . . . . . . . . . . . . .36 B2
St Margaret's Hill **1**
  BA15. . . . . . . . . . . . 100 D6
St Margarets Hospl
  SN3. . . . . . . . . . . . . .36 B4
St Margaret's Mead
  SN8. . . . . . . . . . . . 213 F2
St Margaret's Pl **2**
  BA15. . . . . . . . . . . . 100 D6
St Margaret's Rd SN1. 50 D3
St Margarets Ret Pk
  SN4. . . . . . . . . . . . . .36 D2
St Margaret's St
  BA15. . . . . . . . . . . . 100 D6
St Margaret's Villas **3**
  BA15. . . . . . . . . . . . 100 D6
St Mark's Ave SP1 . . . 146 B3
St Marks CE Jun Sch
  SP1. . . . . . . . . . . . 146 B3
St Mark's Rd SP1 . . . 146 B2
St Martins SN8 . . . . . 213 E3
St Martin's CE VA Prim
  Sch SP1. . . . . . . . . 152 C8
St Martins Cl SP3 . . . 143 A4
St Martin's Cl SP3 . . . 143 A4
St Mary's BA14 . . . . . 178 A3
St Mary's Broughton
  Gifford (VC) CE Prim
  Sch SN12. . . . . . . . . .93 B3
St Mary's CE Inf Sch
  SN8. . . . . . . . . . . . 213 E2
St Marys CE Prim Sch
  SN5. . . . . . . . . . . . . .33 C4
St Mary's Church
  (remains of)★ SP7. 206 A5
St Mary's Cl
  Chitterne BA12 . . . . 195 D6
  Dinton SP3. . . . . . . 201 E2
  Kempsford GL7 . . . . . 10 E6
  Lyneham SN15 . . . . . .59 C3
  Potterne SN10. . . . . 179 D5
  Redlynch SP5. . . . . . 211 D7
  Sixpenny Handley SP5. 208 A4
  Trowbridge BA14. . . . 101 E4
  Wilton SP2. . . . . . . . 144 C1
  **1** Wylye BA12. . . . . 201 E8
St Mary's Ct BA12. . . . 112 E4
St Marys Field GL7. . . . .1 A5
St Marys Gdns SN10 . 214 B4
St Mary's Gdns BA14. 101 E4
St Mary's Gn SN2 . . . .35 B1
St Marys La
  Dilton Marsh BA13. . . 108 B1
  Westbury BA13 . . . . . 112 C8
St Mary's La **2** SN16. .28 A3
St Mary's Pl SN15. . . .78 D8
St Mary's RC Prim Sch
  SN16. . . . . . . . . . . . .78 C6
St Mary's Rd
  Dinton SP3. . . . . . . 201 E2
  Frome BA11. . . . . . . 110 B5
  **12** Market Lavington
  SN10. . . . . . . . . . . . 179 F1
  Salisbury SP2. . . . . . 151 F7
St Mary's Roman Catholic
  Prim Sch SN2. . . . . .35 A1
St Mary's Sch
  Calne SN11. . . . . . . . .81 B3
  Coombe SP7. . . . . . . 202 C2
St Mary's St **1** SN16. .28 A3
St Mary St SN15 . . . . .78 E7
St Matthews Cl
  Rowde SN10. . . . . . . .96 D2
  **6** Salisbury SP1. . . . 146 D5
St Mellion Cl SN15. . . .78 F7
St Michaels Ave SP9 . 216 C6
St Michael's Ave SN6 . .22 E6
St Michael's CE Aided
  Prim Sch SN8 . . . . . 170 A6
St Michael's CE Prim Sch
  SP4. . . . . . . . . . . . 190 B4
St Michaels Cl SN15 . .59 F4
St Michael's Cl
  **8** Aldbourne SN8. . . 170 A6

St Michael's Cl continued
  Brinkworth SN15. . . . . 45 E6
  **3** Lambourn RG17 . . 165 A1
  Trowbridge BA14. . . . 102 A3
  Wilton SP2. . . . . . . . 144 B1
St Michael's Ct BA2. . .98 E8
St Michael's Rd
  Melksham SN12. . . . . . 94 A3
  Salisbury SP2. . . . . . 145 C4
St Michael's View
  SP9. . . . . . . . . . . . 216 E7
St Michaels Vw BA12 138 F5
St Nicholas CE Prim Sch
  SP4. . . . . . . . . . . . 133 E6
St Nicholas CE VC Prim
  Sch SN15. . . . . . . . .96 A7
St Nicholas Cl
  Calne SN11. . . . . . . . .81 C4
  **11** Ludgershall SP11. . 192 B5
  Porton SP4. . . . . . . 133 D6
  Trowbridge BA14. . . . 105 D3
  Wilton SP2. . . . . . . . 144 B1
  Winsley BA15. . . . . . .99 D7
St Nicholas' Rd SP1. . 152 A7
St Nicholas Sch SN14 .70 C2
St Osmund's Catholic
  Prim Sch SP1 . . . . . 152 A7
St Osmund's Cl SP1. . 146 A5
St Patricks Ave SP9 . . 216 B5
St Patrick's Catholic Prim
  Sch SN13. . . . . . . . .77 A1
St Paul's Dr SN3 . . . . .51 E6
St Paul's Prim Sch
  SN15. . . . . . . . . . . . .70 D2
St Paul's Rd SP2 . . . . 145 F1
St Paul's St SN2 . . . . .35 C1
St Paul St SN15 . . . . .78 D8
St Peter's CE Academy
  SN14. . . . . . . . . . . . .78 A8
St Peter's CE Prim Sch
  SP11. . . . . . . . . . . . 192 E4
St Peter's Church★
  SP3. . . . . . . . . . . . 127 D4
St Peters Cl
  Chippenham SN15 . . . .78 C6
  **5** Shipton Bellinger
  SP9. . . . . . . . . . . . 199 D8
St Peter's Cl
  Wilton SP2. . . . . . . . 144 B2
  Winterbourne Stoke
  SP3. . . . . . . . . . . . 196 F3
St Peter's Pump★
  BA12. . . . . . . . . . . . 123 C3
St Peters Rd SP1 . . . . 146 C5
St Philip's Rd SN2 . . . .35 E3
St Philip St **3** SN13. .84 B8
St Quentin Cl SN3 . . . .36 B4
St Rumbold's Rd **9**
  SP7. . . . . . . . . . . . 202 C1
St Sampson's CE Prim
  Sch SN6. . . . . . . . . . 19 D8
St Stephen's Pl BA14. 105 D8
St Swithin Way **8**
  SP10. . . . . . . . . . . . 193 D1
St Teresas Cl **7** SP1 . 146 C5
St Teresa's Dr SN15. . .78 C7
St Thomas à Becket C of
  E (Aided) Prim Sch
  SP3. . . . . . . . . . . . 188 B3
St Thomas Cl **14**
  SP10. . . . . . . . . . . . 193 D2
St Thomas' Rd BA14 . 101 D1
St Thomas's Sq SP1. . 146 A1
St Thomas's Way
  SP1. . . . . . . . . . . . 146 C5
St Ursula's Cl **9** SP1 . 146 D5
Salamanca Dr SP9. . . 216 D3
Salamander Ct SP7. . . 216 D7
Salcombe Gr SN3. . . . .50 E5
SALISBURY. . . . . . . . . 152 C7
Salisbury Arts Ctr★
  SP1. . . . . . . . . . . . 146 B1
Salisbury Bsns Pk
  SP1. . . . . . . . . . . . 152 D7
Salisbury Cath★ SP1 152 A8
Salisbury Cath Sch
  SP1. . . . . . . . . . . . 152 A7
Salisbury Cl
  **1** Chippenham SN14 . .78 A6
  **8** Westbury Leigh
  BA13. . . . . . . . . . . . 108 E1
Salisbury District Hospl
  SP5. . . . . . . . . . . . 152 B3
Salisbury Hill SN8 . . . 213 E1
Salisbury Hollow
  BA13. . . . . . . . . . . . 186 D8
Salisbury Medieval Hall★
  SP1. . . . . . . . . . . . 152 A8
Salisbury Mus &
  Stonehenge Gallery★
  SP1. . . . . . . . . . . . 152 A7
Salisbury Racecourse
  SP2. . . . . . . . . . . . 150 E5
Salisbury Rd
  Amesbury SP4 . . . . . 217 B3
  Breamore SP6 . . . . . 210 F5
  Cobley SP5. . . . . . . 208 E7
  Codford St Mary BA12. 195 B2
  Coombe Bissett SP5 . 150 F1
  Coombe Bissett SP5 . 151 A2
  Coombe Bissett SP5 . 151 B4
  Downton SP5. . . . . . 211 A8
  Fordingbridge SP6. . . 210 E1
  Hungerford RG17. . . . 177 B6
  Lopcombe Corner SP5. 134 B5
  Marlborough SN8. . . . 213 E2
  Netheravon SP4. . . . . 190 A3
  Pewsey SN9. . . . . . . 215 B3

Salisbury Rd continued
  Pewsey SN9. . . . . . . 215 C3
  Plaitford/Landford
  SO51. . . . . . . . . . . . 212 E6
  **14** Shaftesbury SP7. . 202 C1
  Sherfield English SO51 162 E2
  Shipton Bellinger SP9. 199 D7
  **9** Shrewton SP3. . . . 196 E6
  South Tedworth SP9. . 216 C3
  Steeple Langford SP3 . 128 C8
  Steeple Langford SP3 . 128 D8
  Steeple Langford SP3 . 196 C1
  Upton Lovell BA12. . . 194 F3
  Wilton SP2. . . . . . . . 144 E3
Salisbury Rd Ind Est
  SN9. . . . . . . . . . . . 215 B3
Salisbury Sch of English
  SP1. . . . . . . . . . . . 152 B8
Salisbury Sixth Form Coll
  SP1. . . . . . . . . . . . 152 B8
Salisbury St
  Amesbury SP4 . . . . . 217 A3
  Devizes SN10. . . . . . 179 D8
  **26** Fordingbridge SP6 210 D1
  Mere BA12. . . . . . . . 139 A5
  **3** Shaftesbury SP7. . 202 C1
  Swindon SN1 . . . . . . . 50 D7
Salisbury Sta SP2. . . . 145 F1
Salisbury Swimming
  Baths SP1. . . . . . . . 146 B2
Sally In the Wood BA1 .90 C6
Sally Kings La **5**
  SP7. . . . . . . . . . . . 202 B2
Salmons Leap SN11. . . .81 A5
Saltash Rd SN5 . . . . . .49 F5
Salter Cl BA14 . . . . . . 105 E7
Saltersford La SN14. . . .78 A5
Salters Hill BA9. . . . . . 137 A1
SALTERTON . . . . . . . . 131 D4
Salt La
  Salisbury SP1. . . . . . 146 B1
  Winterbourne SP4. . . 133 C3
Saltram Cl SN3 . . . . . .51 C6
Salt Spring Dr SN4. . . .47 C1
Salzgitter Dr SN25. . . .35 A8
SAMBOURNE. . . . . . . 116 F5
Sambourne Chase
  BA12. . . . . . . . . . . . 117 A7
Sambourne Gdns
  BA12. . . . . . . . . . . . 117 A6
Sambourne Rd
  BA12. . . . . . . . . . . . 117 A7
Sambre Rd
  Chiseldon SN4 . . . . . .65 D1
  Draycot Foliat SN4. . . 168 E8
Sams La SN26 . . . . . . .21 C1
Samson St SP9. . . . . . 216 D4
Sandacre Rd
  **1** Swindon SN5 . . . . 34 A1
  **2** Swindon SN5 . . . . .48 F8
Sandalwood Rd **1**
  BA13. . . . . . . . . . . . 108 E1
Sandbourne Rd **7**
  SN25. . . . . . . . . . . . .34 D5
Sanden Cl RG17 . . . . . 177 B7
Sanders Cl SN2. . . . . . .35 F4
Sanders Rd BA14 . . . . 101 C2
Sandes Cl SN15. . . . . .78 C7
Sandfield
  Littleton Panell SN10. . 187 E8
  Sutton Veny BA12 . . . 194 A5
Sandford Pk BA14 . . . 104 F7
Sandgate SN3 . . . . . . . .36 B1
Sandhills Rd SP3 . . . . 142 A4
Sandland Drove SP5. . 160 F4
Sandlea Cl SN14. . . . . .68 F5
Sandleaze SN10 . . . . 179 C4
Sandle Copse SP6 . . . 210 B1
SANDLEHEATH. . . . . . 210 B2
Sandleheath Rd SP6. . 210 A1
Sandown Ave SN3 . . . .50 E3
Sandown Cres **9**
  SN13. . . . . . . . . . . . .76 C1
Sandown Ctr BA14. . . 105 E4
Sandown Dr SN14 . . . .77 F6
Sandown Pl **7** SP2 . . 145 F1
Sandpiper Bridge SN3 .51 E7
Sandpiper Gdns SN14 .70 A2
Sandpit Hill SP3 . . . . 141 A2
Sandpit La BA12. . . . . 112 D5
Sandpit Rd SN11. . . . . .81 D4
Sandpits La
  Sherston SN16. . . . . . 25 C1
  Steeple Ashton BA14. . 106 E6
Sandpitts La
  Gastard SN13. . . . . . .85 F5
  Lacock SN15 . . . . . . .86 A5
Sandquarry La BA9 . . . 137 B1
Sandridge Comm
  SN12. . . . . . . . . . . . .94 D5
Sandridge Hill SN12 . . .95 A6
Sandridge La SN15 . . . .95 C7
Sandridge Pk★ SN12 . .95 B6
Sandridge Rd SN12. . . .94 B5
Sandringham Rd
  Swindon SN3 . . . . . . .50 F3
  Trowbridge BA14. . . . 105 D3
Sandringhams The
  SP5. . . . . . . . . . . . 153 E1
Sandroyd Sch SP5 . . . 207 C5

Sands Cl SN10 . . . . . . .96 D1
Sands' La SP7 . . . . . . 203 C3
Sands La SN10 . . . . . . .96 D2
Sand St
  Longbridge Deverill
  BA12 . . . . . . . . . . . 121 A6
  Longbridge Deverill
  BA12 . . . . . . . . . . . 121 A6
  Longbridge Deverill
  BA12 . . . . . . . . . . . 121 B7
Sands The SN9 . . . . . 181 C7
Sandstone Rd SN25. . . .34 F7
Sandwood Cl SN5 . . . .34 B2
Sandy La
  Edington BA13 . . . . . 186 C7
  Marten SN8 . . . . . . . 184 D8
  Redlynch SP5. . . . . . 211 D8
  Swindon SN1 . . . . . . . 50 B4
SANDY LANE. . . . . . . .88 B4
Sandy Lea Ave **5**
  SN13. . . . . . . . . . . . .76 B1
Sandy Leaze BA15 . . . 100 C6
Sandy Ridge SN11 . . . .81 C1
Sanford St **3** SN1. . . .50 C6
Sangster Ave SN12 . . .94 B4
SANHAM GREEN . . . . 177 B5
Sapphire Rd SN26 . . . .21 A1
Sarsen Cl SN1 . . . . . . .49 F4
Sarson La SP11 . . . . . 192 E1
Sarum Ave SN12. . . . . .94 B2
Sarum Cl
  Salisbury SP2. . . . . . 145 E3
  Shipton Bellinger SP9. 199 C8
Sarum Gdns BA13 . . . 109 A4
Sarum Rd BA14 . . . . . . .78 A6
Sarum St Paul's CE Prim
  Sch SP2. . . . . . . . . 145 F2
Sarum Way
  Calne SN11. . . . . . . . .81 A3
  **2** Hungerford RG17. . 177 B6
Sasson Ct SN2 . . . . . . 145 C3
Sassoon Cl BA12. . . . . 116 D6
Saunders Ave SP4 . . . 146 C6
Saunders Gr SN13 . . . 76 D1
Saunders Meadow
  SN8. . . . . . . . . . . . 183 E1
Savernake Ave SN12. . .94 C6
Savernake Cl **4**
  BA12. . . . . . . . . . . . 117 A7
Savernake Cres SN8 . 213 F2
Savernake Ct SN8 . . . 213 E2
Savernake Hospl
  SN8. . . . . . . . . . . . 175 A7
Savernake Rd
  Burbage SN8. . . . . . . 175 D1
  Corsham SN13. . . . . . .84 D8
  Hudswell SN13. . . . . . .84 D8
Savernake St SN1. . . . .50 B5
Savill Cres SN4 . . . . . .63 F7
Sawpit Dr SN8. . . . . . 175 C6
Sawpit Hill BA12. . . . . 140 B4
Sawyer Cl SP9 . . . . . . 216 D8
Sawyer Rd SN25 . . . . .35 B6
Sawyers Cres **3** SN13 76 D1
Sawyers Cl SN16. . . . . .17 A2
SAWYERS HILL . . . . . .17 A2
Sawyers Hill SN16 . . . .17 A2
Saxby Rd SN15 . . . . . .70 F2
Saxifrage Bank SN12. .94 C3
Saxon Cl
  Cricklade SN6 . . . . . . 19 D7
  **14** Market Lavington
  SN10. . . . . . . . . . . . 179 F1
  Sherston SN16. . . . . . 25 C1
  Westbury BA13 . . . . . 109 A4
Saxon Ct
  North Tidworth SP9. . . 216 D7
  **8** Swindon SN3 . . . . 50 D4
Saxon Dr BA14. . . . . . 101 E4
Saxonhurst **4** SP5. . . 211 B8
Saxon Leas SP5. . . . . 149 C6
Saxon Meadow SP5. . . 211 A8
Saxon Mill
  Chiseldown SN4. . . . . .65 D5
  Swindon SN25. . . . . . .34 B2
Saxon Rd SP2 . . . . . . 151 F6
Saxon Rise SN8. . . . . 183 E1
Saxons Acre BA12 . . . 116 D6
Saxon Spur **10** SP7. . 202 C2
Saxon St SN14 . . . . . . .78 B8
Saxon Way
  Andover SP10 . . . . . 193 A2
  Fairford GL7. . . . . . . . .1 F7
  Winsley BA15. . . . . . .99 F7
Saxton Wlk SN5 . . . . . .49 B8
Scallows La SO51. . . . 212 F7
Scamblers Mead
  SP11. . . . . . . . . . . . 193 A2
Scamell's Rd SP2. . . . 146 A2
Scarborough Rd SN2 . .49 F8
Scarlet Cl **8** SN25. . . .34 F7
Scholard's La **16** SN8 170 B2
Scholars Cl **34** SN11. . 192 A5
Scholars Pk SN10. . . . .96 E2
Scholars Way SN12 . . .93 F6
School Cl
  Chiseldown SN4. . . . . .65 E4
  Keevil BA14. . . . . . . 178 B5
  St Paul Malmesbury Without
  SN16. . . . . . . . . . . . .28 A1
  Vernhams Dean SP11 . 185 C3
School Dr **2** SP4 . . . 198 B7
School Hill
  Alderbury SP5 . . . . . 153 C2
  Brinkworth SN15. . . . . 45 E1
School La
  All Cannings SN10. . . 180 F8

**School La** continued
1 Amesbury SP4 . . . . **217** B3
Badminton GL9 . . . . . . . **38** E2
Bromham SN15 . . . . . . . **96** A1
Castle Combe SN14 . . . **68** A7
Castle Eaton SN6 . . . . . . **10** B4
East Garston RG17 . . . **171** E8
Grittleton SN14 . . . . . . . **54** E5
Hindon SP3 . . . . . . . . . **200** B3
Lea SN16 . . . . . . . . . . . **29** A2
Little Bedwyn SN8 . . . . **176** C5
Marlborough SN8. . . . . **213** A4
Melbury Abbas SP7 . . **206** B7
Melksham Without
  SN12 . . . . . . . . . . . . . **93** D8
Meysey Hampton GL7 . . **1** A4
South Cerney GL7 . . . . . . **6** F7
Staverton BA14 . . . . . . **101** D5
Westbury BA13 . . . . . **108** E1
Wroughton SN4 . . . . . . . **64** A6
**School Rd**
Calne SN11 . . . . . . . . . . **81** A4
1 Durrington/Bulford
  SP4 . . . . . . . . . . . . . **198** C7
Kemble GL7 . . . . . . . . . . . **4** F7
Nomansland SP5 . . . . . **212** C4
Redlynch SP5 . . . . . . . . **211** E6
Seend SN12 . . . . . . . . . **178** D8
**School Wlk** SN14 . . . . **78** A7
**Scimitar Way** SN3 . . . . **36** B5
**Scorhill La** SN1 . . . . . . . **50** A2
**Scotby Ave** SN3. . . . . . . **50** E2
**Scotchel Gn** SN9. . . . . **215** D5
**Scotland** BA14. . . . . . . **105** B2
**Scotland Hill**
  Clanville SN15 . . . . . . . **56** F5
  Seagry SN15 . . . . . . . . **57** A5
**Scotland La**
  Beckington BA11 . . . . **107** C4
  Landford SP5 . . . . . . . **212** B8
**Scotland Rd** SN12. . . . . **94** A6
**Scotney Cres** 2 SN25. . **34** F6
**Scots La** SP1 . . . . . . . **146** A1
**Scott Cl**
  Burbage SN8 . . . . . . . **183** C8
  Swindon SN25 . . . . . . . **34** C8
**Scott's Cl** SP5 . . . . . . **211** A8
**Scott's Hill** SP7. . . . . . **203** C4
**Scott Thomlinson Rd**
  GL7. . . . . . . . . . . . . . . . **1** F6
**Scott Way** SN1. . . . . . . **49** E3
**Scouts La** SP5 . . . . . . **149** F4
**Scratchbury Camp** ★
  BA12. . . . . . . . . . . . . **194** B7
**Scrubbity Barrows** ★
  SP5. . . . . . . . . . . . . . **207** E4
**Scythe Cl** 12 SP11. . . . **193** F2
**Seacole Cres** SN1. . . . . **50** A3
**Seaford Cl** SN5 . . . . . . . **49** A6
**Seagrim Rd** SP2 . . . . . **144** C2
**Seagry CE Prim Sch**
  SN15. . . . . . . . . . . . . . **57** D6
**Seagry Ct** SN2 . . . . . . . **35** B5
**Seagry Heath**
  Great Somerford SN15 . **43** F1
  Great Somerford SN15 . **44** A1
  Lower Seagry SN15. . . . **57** F7
**Seagry Hill** SN15. . . . . . **57** D3
**Seagry Rd**
  Hullavington SN14 . . . . **56** D6
  Sutton Benger SN15 . . . **57** D2
**Seaton** Cl SN25 . . . . . . **34** F5
**Second Broad Dr**
  SP3. . . . . . . . . . . . . . **128** C2
**Secret Gdn The** GL7 . . . **6** F7
**Sedgebrook** SN3 . . . . . **51** D2
**Sedgefield Gdns**
  SN10. . . . . . . . . . . . . **214** B4
**Sedgefield Way** SN14 . . **77** F6
**SEDGEHILL** . . . . . . . . . **202** C2
**Sedge Rd** 29 SP11 . . . **193** F2
**SEEND** . . . . . . . . . . . . . **178** E7
**Seend CE Prim Sch**
  SN12. . . . . . . . . . . . . **178** D8
**SEEND CLEEVE** . . . . . . **178** C7
**Seend Hill** SN12 . . . . . **178** F8
**Sefton La** SN8 . . . . . . **168** B1
**Sefton Rd** 4 SN25. . . . . **34** C7
**Sefton Way** SN25 . . . . . **34** C7
**Selby Cres** SN5 . . . . . . . **49** B4
**Seldon Cl** 4 SN3. . . . . . **50** E6
**Selions Cl** SN14. . . . . . . **70** B2
**SELLS GREEN** . . . . . . . . **93** E1
**Selwood Acad** BA11 . . **110** B6
**Selwood Cl** 1 SN1. . . . . **50** E7
**Selwood Cres** 1
  BA11. . . . . . . . . . . . . **110** A7
**Selwyn Rd** SN25 . . . . . . **20** C1
**SEM HILL** . . . . . . . . . . . **202** E5
**SEMINGTON** . . . . . . . . **102** E5
**Semington Bypass**
  BA14. . . . . . . . . . . . . **102** F4
**Semington Rd**
  Berryfield SN12. . . . . . . **94** A1
  Melksham Without
  BA14 . . . . . . . . . . . . **178** A8
**Semington Strand**
  SN1. . . . . . . . . . . . . . . **49** F3
**Semington Turnpike**
  BA14. . . . . . . . . . . . . **102** F5
**SEMLEY** . . . . . . . . . . . **202** F5
**Semley Cofa Prim Sch**
  SP7. . . . . . . . . . . . . . **202** F5
**Semley Wlk** SN2 . . . . . . **35** C4
**Senior Dr** SP2 . . . . . . . **152** A5
**Sergeant Rogers Way**
  Devizes SN10. . . . . . . **172** A2

**Sergeant Rogers Way**
continued
  Roundway SN10. . . . . . **214** E7
**Serotine Cres** BA14. . . **106** A7
**SERRINGTON** . . . . . . . **129** D7
**Seth Ward Dr** SP1 . . . . **146** D4
**Seven Barrows** ★
  Lambourn RG17. . . . . . **165** A5
  South Tedworth SP9. . . **191** B3
**Sevenfields** SN6. . . . . . **23** A7
**Seven Fields Nature**
  **Reserve** ★ SN25. . . . . **35** B5
**Seven Fields Prim Sch**
  SN2. . . . . . . . . . . . . . . **35** B4
**SEVENHAMPTON**. . . . . . **23** B2
**Severn Ave** SN25 . . . . . **35** A4
**Severn Cl** SN11. . . . . . . **81** A5
**Severn Rd** SN12 . . . . . . **94** A6
**SEVINGTON**. . . . . . . . . **55** A2
**Sexton** Cl SN25 . . . . . . **20** B1
**Seymour Ct** BA14 . . . . **101** C1
**Seymour Gdns** SP4 . . . **217** A3
**Seymour Rd**
  Chippenham SN15 . . . . . **78** F8
  Swindon SN3 . . . . . . . . **50** F6
  Trowbridge BA14. . . . . **101** C2
**Seymours Ct** ★ BA11 . . . **107** C4
**Shackleton Cl** SN12. . . . **94** D1
**Shackleton Rd** SN10 . . **214** D2
**Shackleton Sq** SP10 . . **193** F2
**Shady Bower** SP1. . . . . **152** C8
**Shady Bower Cl** SP1 . . **152** C8
**SHAFTESBURY** . . . . . . . **202** A1
**Shaftesbury Ave** SN3 . . **51** A4
**Shaftesbury CE Prim Sch**
  SP7. . . . . . . . . . . . . . **202** D2
**Shaftesbury Ct** BA14 . . **105** A4
**Shaftesbury Dro** SP2. **151** E5
**Shaftesbury Leisure Ctr**
  SP7. . . . . . . . . . . . . . **202** C1
**Shaftesbury Mus** ★
  SP7. . . . . . . . . . . . . . **202** C1
**Shaftesbury Rd**
  Barford St Martin
  SP3. . . . . . . . . . . . . . **143** B3
  Compton Chamberlayne
  SP3. . . . . . . . . . . . . . **205** A8
  East Knoyle SP3. . . . . . **141** C1
  Fovant SP3. . . . . . . . . **204** F8
  Mere BA12. . . . . . . . . **139** B4
  Mere BA12. . . . . . . . . **139** C2
  Motcombe SP7. . . . . . . **202** A3
  Wilton SP2 . . . . . . . . . **144** B3
**Shaftesbury Sch** SP7. **202** C1
**Shaftesbury St** 19
  SP6. . . . . . . . . . . . . . **210** D1
**Shaftsbury Cl** SN5 . . . . **33** C5
**Shails La**
  Melksham Without
  SN12 . . . . . . . . . . . . **178** A8
  Trowbridge BA14. . . . . **101** C1
**Shakespeare Ave**
  SP10. . . . . . . . . . . . . **193** C1
**Shakespeare Dr** SN8. **213** C2
**Shakespeare Path**
  SN3. . . . . . . . . . . . . . . **35** F3
**Shakespeare Rd**
  Royal Wootton Bassett
  SN4 . . . . . . . . . . . . . . **47** F3
  Salisbury SP1. . . . . . . **145** F4
**SHALBOURNE** . . . . . . . **176** F2
**Shalbourne CE Prim Sch**
  SN8. . . . . . . . . . . . . . **176** F2
**Shalbourne Cl**
  Hungerford RG17. . . . . **177** A7
  Swindon SN2 . . . . . . . . **35** B5
**Shalford La** BA9 . . . . . **136** A3
**Shallowbrooks La**
  Luckington SN14 . . . . . **39** F7
  Sherston SN14. . . . . . . **39** F8
  Sherston SN14. . . . . . . **40** A6
**Shallows The** SP6 . . . . **210** F4
**Shallow Wagon La**
  BA13. . . . . . . . . . . . . **108** F6
**Shambles The** BA15. . **100** D7
**Shanklin Rd** SN2. . . . . . **34** E4
**Shapland** SN25 . . . . . . **20** C1
**Shaplands** 4 SN3 . . . . . **36** A2
**Shapwick Cl** SN3 . . . . . **51** C7
**SHARCOTT**. . . . . . . . . **182** A6
**Sharcott Dro** SN9. . . . **215** A4
**Share La** SP3. . . . . . . . **203** C6
**Sharp Cl** SN5. . . . . . . . . **49** B7
**Sharplands**
  Sutton Benger SN15 . . . **57** D2
  Sutton Benger SN15 . . . **57** E1
**Sharpley Cl** SP6 . . . . . **210** D2
**SHARPSTONE**. . . . . . . . **99** A4
**Sharpstone La** BA2 . . . . **99** A4
**Sharratt Ave** 4 SP1. . . **146** C5
**Shaston Ct** SP2 . . . . . . **144** C3
**Shave La** BA10. . . . . . . **122** A4
**SHAW**
  Melksham Without . . . . . **93** D7
  Swindon . . . . . . . . . . . **49** B7
**Shaw CE(VC) Prim Sch**
  SN12. . . . . . . . . . . . . . **93** D8
**Shawgrove** SN8 . . . . . **176** B3
**Shaw Hill**
  Collingbourne Ducis
  SN8 . . . . . . . . . . . . . **191** F7
  Melksham Without
  SN12. . . . . . . . . . . . . . **93** D7
**Shaw Rd** SN5. . . . . . . . . **49** B7
**Shaw Ridge Leisure Pk** ★
  SN5. . . . . . . . . . . . . . . **49** B6
**Shaw Ridge Prim Sch**
  SN5. . . . . . . . . . . . . . . **49** B7

**Shaw Village** ★ SN8 . . **173** F4
**Shear Cross** BA12. . . . **116** E1
**Shearings The** SN1 . . . . **50** C4
**Shearman St** BA14. . . . **105** D7
**Shears Dr**
  Amesbury SP4 . . . . . . . **217** C1
  Amesbury SP4 . . . . . . . **217** D1
**Shearwater**
  Horningsham BA12 . . . **119** F6
  Longbridge Deverill
  BA12. . . . . . . . . . . . . **120** A7
**Shearwater Way** SN13 **84** D7
**Shearwood Rd** SN5 . . . **34** A1
**Sheasby Cl** SP5. . . . . . **208** A3
**Sheen Cl**
  Salisbury SP2. . . . . . . **145** B5
  4 Swindon SN5 . . . . . . **49** A4
**Sheepbridge Rd** SP4. **198** E7
**Sheepcote Barton** 3
  BA14. . . . . . . . . . . . . **105** E7
**SHEEPDROVE** . . . . . . . **165** B2
**Sheepdrove Rd**
  RG17. . . . . . . . . . . . . . **165** B2
**Sheep Fair Way** 13
  RG17. . . . . . . . . . . . . **165** A1
**Sheepridge** SN8 . . . . . **168** E3
**Sheepscroft** SN14 . . . . **70** B2
**Sheep St**
  Devizes SN10. . . . . . . **214** B3
  Highworth SN6. . . . . . . . **23** A6
**Sheepwash La** 2
  BA12. . . . . . . . . . . . . **201** E8
**Sheerwold Cl** SN3 . . . . **36** B3
**Sheffield La** SN13. . . . . **76** D1
**SHEFFORD**
  **WOODLANDS** . . . . . . **171** E4
**Shelburne Rd** SN11. . . . **81** C1
**Shelburne Way** SN11 . . **79** F2
**Sheld Dr** SN15. . . . . . . . **60** A1
**Sheldon Bsns Pk**
  SN14. . . . . . . . . . . . . . **77** D8
**Sheldon Manor & Gdns** ★
  SN14. . . . . . . . . . . . . . **69** D1
**Sheldon Rd** SN14 . . . . . **78** B7
**Sheldon Sch** SN14 . . . . **70** B1
**Shelfinch** SN5. . . . . . . . **49** D4
**Shelley Ave** 2 SN4 . . . . **47** F3
**Shelley Dr** SP1 . . . . . . **145** F4
**Shelley Gdns** SN12. . . . **94** B4
**Shelley St** SN1. . . . . . . . **50** B5
**Shelley Way** BA12 . . . . **116** D6
**Shelly's Wlk** GL7. . . . . . . **2** D4
**Shenton Cl** SN3. . . . . . . **36** B3
**Shepherds** SN13. . . . . . **84** D6
**Shepherds Breach** 1
  SN4. . . . . . . . . . . . . . . **47** E2
**Shepherds Cl**
  Coombe Bissett SP5 . . **151** A1
  Odstock SP5 . . . . . . . . **152** A1
  Odstock SP5 . . . . . . . . **158** A8
**Shepherds Croft** SP5 **204** F1
**Shepherds Dro** BA14. **106** C3
**Shepherd's La**
  Donhead St Andrew
  SP7. . . . . . . . . . . . . . **203** B2
  Selwood BA11 . . . . . . . **114** D6
**Shepherds Mead**
  BA13. . . . . . . . . . . . . **112** A8
**Shepherd Spring Jun &
  Inf Sch** 33 SP10. . . . **193** E2
**Shepherds Rise** SP11 **185** C3
**Sheppard Cl** SN15 . . . . **78** F5
**Sheppard's Acre** SN16 **29** A6
**Sheppards Rise** SN15 . **46** B7
**Sheppard St** SN1 . . . . . **50** B7
**Shepperd St** SP9 . . . . **216** D8
**Shepperton Way** SN25 . **34** F6
**Sherborne Pl** SN3 . . . . . **51** B7
**Sherborne Rd** BA14. . . **101** A1
**Sherborne St** GL7. . . . . . **2** C4
**Sherbourne Dr**
  Old Sarum SP4. . . . . . . **146** B8
  Winterbourne SP4. . . . **132** C1
**Sherfield** SP4 . . . . . . . **133** A2
**Sherfield English La**
  SO51. . . . . . . . . . . . . **212** F7
**Sherfield English Rd**
  SP5. . . . . . . . . . . . . . **212** E6
**Sherfields** SN4 . . . . . . . **47** E1
**Sherford Rd** SN25 . . . . **34** E4
**Sheridan Dr** SN4. . . . . . **47** F3
**Sheringham Ct** SN3. . . **51** D3
**Sherington Mead**
  SN15. . . . . . . . . . . . . . **79** B4
**Sherrer La** SN26 . . . . . . **20** C2
**SHERRINGTON** . . . . . . **194** F1
**Sherrington La** BA12. **195** A2
**Sherrington Mead**
  SN15. . . . . . . . . . . . . . **79** B4
**SHERSTON**. . . . . . . . . . . **25** B1
**Sherston Ave** SN2 . . . . **35** C5
**Sherston CE Prim Sch**
  SN16. . . . . . . . . . . . . . **25** C1
**SHERSTON PARVA
  OR PINKNEY**. . . . . . . . **25** E2
**Sherston Rd**
  Brokenborough SN16 . . **27** E4
  Luckington SN14 . . . . . **39** E5
  Sherston SN14. . . . . . . **40** A6
**Sherwood Ave** SN12 . . **94** C6
**Sherwood Cl** 3
  BA12. . . . . . . . . . . . . **117** A8
**Sherwood Rd** SN3 . . . . **51** B4
**Shetland Cl**
  Swindon SN5 . . . . . . . . **49** B7
  Westbury BA13 . . . . . . **108** D2
**Shetland Gdns** SN5 . . . **49** A7
**Shipley Dr** SN25 . . . . . . **34** F6

**SHIPTON
  BELLINGER** . . . . . . . . **199** D8
**Shipton Bellinger Prim
  Sch** SP9. . . . . . . . . . **199** C8
**Shipton Gr** SN3. . . . . . . **50** E5
**Shipton Hill** 3 SN16 . . **28** A4
**SHIPTON MOYNE** . . . . . . **26** E8
**Shiptons La** SN15. . . . . **43** F2
**Shire Cl** SN5. . . . . . . . . . **49** A7
**Shire Ct** 2 SN1. . . . . . . . **50** A5
**Shire Hill** SN14 . . . . . . . **66** A7
**Shires Sh Ctr The**
  BA14. . . . . . . . . . . . . **105** C8
**Shire Way** BA13 . . . . . **108** E2
**Shirley Cl** SN3. . . . . . . . **50** F7
**SHOCKERWICK** . . . . . . . **82** E5
**Shockerwick Farm La**
  BA1. . . . . . . . . . . . . . . **82** E6
**Shockerwick La** BA1. . **82** D4
**Shoddesden La** SP11. **192** B4
**Shoemaker La** SN15 . . **45** F6
**SHOE THE** . . . . . . . . . . . **66** F1
**Shop La**
  Badminton GL9 . . . . . . **38** E2
  Wingfield BA14 . . . . . . **104** C6
**Shoreland Cl** BA13. . . . **108** F3
**Shore Pl** BA14 . . . . . . . **100** F1
**SHORNCOTE** . . . . . . . . . . **6** A6
**Short Dro** SN4. . . . . . . . **163** C6
**Short La**
  Andover SP11 . . . . . . . **193** B1
  Barford St Martin SP3. **143** A4
**Shortlands** SP2 . . . . . . **144** B3
**Short River Rd** BA14 . . **109** D2
**Shorts Gn La** SP7 . . . . **202** A4
**Short St**
  Dilton Marsh BA13. . . . **112** A6
  Ludgershall SP11. . . . . **192** A5
  Melksham SN12 . . . . . . **94** C6
**Shoscombe Gdns** 3
  BA11. . . . . . . . . . . . . **110** C7
**Shoscombe Gn** SN3. . . **51** B6
**Showfield** SN4 . . . . . . . **47** D3
**Shrapnel Rd** 1 SP4. . **197** E7
**Shrewsbury Rd** SN3. . . **50** F6
**SHREWTON** . . . . . . . . . **196** E6
**Shrewton CE(VC) Prim
  Sch** SP3. . . . . . . . . . **196** E7
**Shrewton Cl** BA14 . . . . **105** D6
**Shrewton Rd** BA12. . . . **195** E6
**Shrewton Wlk** SN25. . . **35** C5
**Shripple La** SP5 . . . . . . **149** D6
**Shrivenham Rd**
  Highworth SN6. . . . . . . . **23** B4
  South Marston SN4 . . . **37** C3
  Swindon SN1 . . . . . . . . **50** F2
  Swindon SN3 . . . . . . . . **36** E2
**Shropshire Cl**
  Salisbury SP2. . . . . . . **145** C5
  1 Swindon SN5 . . . . . . **49** B7
**Shurnhold** SN12 . . . . . . **93** F5
**Shute End** SP5. . . . . . . **153** B2
**Shute End Rd** SP5 . . . . **153** B4
**Shuter Gr** SN25. . . . . . . **35** B8
**Shutts La**
  Coombe Bissett SP5 . . **151** A1
  Coombe Bissett SP5 . . **157** A8
**Sidbury Circular Rd**
  SP9. . . . . . . . . . . . . . **216** B7
**Sidbury Hill Ave** SP9 **216** C8
**Siddal St**
  Swindon SN25 . . . . . . . **34** D8
  Swindon SN26 . . . . . . . **20** D1
**Sidings The** 2 SP5 . . . **211** B8
**Sidmouth Par** SN10. . . **214** B3
**Sidney Cl**
  3 Swindon SN3 . . . . . . **50** E6
  Swindon SN5 . . . . . . . . **48** F4
**Sidney St** SP2 . . . . . . . **145** F1
**Sidney Wood Ct** SN14 . **78** C7
**Sigerson Rd** 2 SN25. . **34** C5
**Signal St** SP4. . . . . . . . **198** E6
**Signal Way**
  Chippenham SN14 . . . . . **78** B8
  Swindon SN1 . . . . . . . . **50** D3
**Silbury Cl**
  Chippenham SN14 . . . . . **78** A6
  Westbury BA13 . . . . . . **108** F4
**Silbury Hill** ★ SN8. . . . **173** C7
**Silbury Mews** SN25 . . . **34** E3
**Silbury Rd** SN11 . . . . . . **81** A3
**Silchester Way** SN5. . . **49** C6
**Silk Houses** BA12 . . . . **123** E4
**Sillars Green** SN16. . . . **27** F6
**Sillen La** SP6 . . . . . . . . **209** B6
**Sillington La** SN10 . . . **179** B7
**Silman Cl** SN13 . . . . . . **76** D1
**Silton Rd**
  Bourton SP8. . . . . . . . . **138** A2
  Zeale SP8. . . . . . . . . . **137** F2
**Silver Barrow** ★
  SP3. . . . . . . . . . . . . . **188** D2
**Silver Birch Rd** BA14. **105** B5
**Silver Cl** SN16 . . . . . . . **17** B2
**Silver La**
  Compton Bassett
  SN11 . . . . . . . . . . . . **166** B4
  Selwood BA11 . . . . . . . **114** C6
**Silverless St** SN8 . . . . **213** D3
**Silver Meadows**
  BA14. . . . . . . . . . . . . **105** A5
**Silver Rd** SN9. . . . . . . . **215** B5
**Silver St La**
  Brokenwood BA13 . . . . **107** E6
  Bromham SN15 . . . . . . . **87** D1
  Trowbridge BA14. . . . . **105** B5
**Silver St**
  Alderbury SP5 . . . . . . **153** B2

**Silver St** continued
  Bradford-on-Avon
  BA15. . . . . . . . . . . . . **100** D5
  Calne SN11 . . . . . . . . . **81** B1
  Calne Without SN11. . . **89** B8
  Colerne SN14. . . . . . . . **75** B3
  Corsham SN13. . . . . . . **85** C6
  Kington Langley SN15 . . **70** F7
  Malmesbury SN16 . . . . . **28** A3
  Minety SN16 . . . . . . . . . **17** B2
  Potterne SN10 . . . . . . **179** D5
  Salisbury SP1. . . . . . . **152** A8
  Sherston SN16. . . . . . . **40** C8
  South Cerney GL7 . . . . . . **6** C7
  Steeple Ashton BA14. . **178** A3
  Trowbridge BA14. . . . . **105** D8
  Warminster BA12 . . . . **117** A7
  Westbury BA13 . . . . . . **112** C8
  Wilton SP2 . . . . . . . . . **144** D3
**Silverton Rd** SN3 . . . . . **51** B6
**Silver Wood** SP5. . . . . **153** C3
**Silverwood Dr** SP1. . . . **146** E2
**Silverwood Sch** BA14 . **101** C1
**Silveston Way** SN16. . **27** A4
**Simmance Way** SP4 . . **217** C2
**Simnel Cl** SN5 . . . . . . . . **48** F5
**Simonds Rd** 17 SP11. . **192** A5
**Sir Bernard Lovell Rd**
  SN16. . . . . . . . . . . . . . **28** C1
**Siren Cl** 8 SN3. . . . . . . **51** B8
**Six Acre La**
  Charnage BA12 . . . . . . **139** F5
  Shalbourne RG17. . . . . **176** F3
  West Knoyle BA12. . . . **140** A4
**SIXPENNY
  HANDLEY** . . . . . . . . . . **208** A3
**Sixpenny Handley Fst Sch**
  SP5. . . . . . . . . . . . . . **208** A4
**Skew Bridge Cl** SN4 . . **47** C1
**Skew Bridge Rd** SP2 . **145** D2
**Skew Rd** SP2 . . . . . . . . **145** B2
**Skinner's Cl** SN6. . . . . . **22** B7
**Skye** Cl SN6 . . . . . . . . . . **22** F7
**Skylark** SN26 . . . . . . . . **21** B1
**Skylark Rd** 6 SN12 . . . **94** D5
**Skylark Rise** 11 SN6. . . **19** D8
**Skynet Dr** SN13. . . . . . . **84** B8
**Slab La** SP5 . . . . . . . . . **211** C7
**Slade Dr** SN3. . . . . . . . . **36** B1
**Sladesbrook** BA15. . . . **100** E8
**Sladesbrook** BA15. . . . **100** D8
**Slade St** SN2 . . . . . . . . . **34** E2
**Slades The** SN11. . . . . . . **81** C3
**Slag La** BA13 . . . . . . . . **108** F5
**Slaite La** SN14 . . . . . . . **66** C5
**Slater Rd** SN9 . . . . . . . **215** C5
**Slate Way** SN25 . . . . . . **34** C8
**SLAUGHTERFORD** . . . . . . **76** A4
**Slaughterford Rd**
  SN14. . . . . . . . . . . . . . **68** C1
**Slay Barrow** ★ SP4. . . **189** A6
**Sleightholme Ct** 2
  BA14. . . . . . . . . . . . . **105** C7
**Sleight La** SN10. . . . . . **179** F6
**Sleight Rd** SN10 . . . . . **214** E1
**Slessor Rd**
  Lyneham SN15. . . . . . . **60** A1
  Lyneham & Bradenstoke
  SN15 . . . . . . . . . . . . **166** A8
**Slim Rd** BA12. . . . . . . . **113** E1
**Sling Orch** SP3 . . . . . . **204** E7
**Sling Rd** SP4 . . . . . . . . **198** E7
**Slipper La** SN4 . . . . . . . **65** D4
**Slipway The** BA14. . . . **101** D4
**Slodbrook La** SP8. . . . **138** D1
**Slowgrove Cl** BA14 . . . **105** F8
**Smallbrook Gdns** 3
  BA14. . . . . . . . . . . . . **101** D5
**Smallbrook La** BA12 . . **117** D5
**Smallbrook Mdws Nature
  Reserve** ★ BA12 . . . . **117** C5
**Smallbrook Rd** BA12. . **117** B5
**Small St** SN10 . . . . . . . **180** F4
**Smannell Rd** SP11 . . . **193** F2
**Smart Cl** SN25 . . . . . . . . **34** E8
**Smay Down La** SN8 . . **184** E6
**Smeaton Rd**
  1 Andover SP10. . . . . . **193** B1
  Salisbury SP2. . . . . . . **145** E1
**Smithem Brook** SN3 . . **51** D6
**Smitham Bridge Rd**
  RG17. . . . . . . . . . . . . . **177** B7
**Smithfield St** 2 SP4. **217** B3
**Smithmead** SN14. . . . . **33** F6
**Smiths Cl** SN9 . . . . . . . **215** B5
**Smith's Cl** SN5 . . . . . . . **33** C5
**Smith's Hill** OX12 . . . . **165** F7
**Smith St**
  Nettleton SN14 . . . . . . **67** A6
  West Kington SN14 . . . . **66** F7
**Smiths Yd** SN13 . . . . . . **77** A2
**Smithy La** SN9 . . . . . . . **181** C6
**Smithys La** SN8 . . . . . . **183** C8
**Smithywell Cl** BA14 . . **105** F8
**Snail-Creep Hanging** ★
  SP3. . . . . . . . . . . . . . **200** E7
**Snails' La** SN10. . . . . . **214** A3
**Snappersnipes** BA13. **109** A4
**Snapps Cl** SN4. . . . . . . . **64** B5
**Snap Village** ★ SN8 . . **169** C7
**Snarlton La** SN12. . . . . . **94** D5
**Snell Ave** SN16 . . . . . . . **28** A5
**Snoddington Rd**
  Fyfield SP11. . . . . . . . **192** D1
  Shipton Bellinger SP9 . **199** E2
**Snowberry La** SN12. . . **94** C3
**Snowdon Pl** SN2. . . . . . **35** E4
**Snowdrop Cl** 2 SN25. . **34** D5

**Sch–Sou** **241**

**Snow Hill**
  Dinton SP3. . . . . . . . . **201** F2
  Hilmarton SN11. . . . . . . **73** F5
**Snowshill Cl** SN25. . . . . **34** F5
**Snowswick La** SN7. . . . **12** E7
**Snuff St** SN10. . . . . . . **214** A4
**Sobers Sq** SP11. . . . . . **193** F2
**Sodbury Rd** GL9. . . . . . . **52** F7
**SODOM**. . . . . . . . . . . . . . **59** C7
**Sodom La** SN15. . . . . . . **59** C7
**Solar Way** SP4. . . . . . . **217** F4
**Soldier's Ring** ★ SP6. **209** D4
**Solstice Pk Ave** SP4. . **217** D4
**Solstice Pk Bsns Park**
  SP4. . . . . . . . . . . . . . **217** D4
**Solstice Rise** SP4 . . . . **217** B3
**Somerbrook** SN11. . . . . **44** B2
**Somerdale** 6 SN5 . . . . **49** C6
**Somerford Cl** SN2 . . . . . **35** C4
**SOMERFORD KEYNES**. . **5** F3
**Somerford Lakes
  Reserve** ★ GL7. . . . . . . **5** D2
**Somerleyton Cl**
  SN10. . . . . . . . . . . . . **187** D8
**Somerset Cl** 1 RG17. **177** B7
**Somerset Cres** SN12. . **94** B3
**Somerset Ct** 11 SN4. . **163** B6
**Somerset Dr** BA13 . . . **109** A5
**Somerset Rd**
  Salisbury SP1. . . . . . . **146** B3
  Swindon SN2 . . . . . . . . **34** F1
**Somerset Way** BA14 . . **102** F6
**Somerton Gdns**
  BA11. . . . . . . . . . . . . **110** C7
**Somerville Ct** 2
  SN3. . . . . . . . . . . . . . **193** F1
**Somerville Rd** SN3. . . . . **50** F6
**Somme Rd** SP11. . . . . . **191** F4
**Soprano Way** SN14 . . . **48** B8
**Sopwith Pk** 7 SP10. . . **193** C1
**SOPWORTH**. . . . . . . . . . **24** D1
**Sopworth La** SN14 . . . . **39** E6
**Sopworth Rd** SN14. . . . **39** E5
**Sorley Cl** SN8. . . . . . . . **213** B3
**Sorrel Cl**
  Melksham SN12 . . . . . . **94** B3
  Royal Wootton Bassett
  SN4 . . . . . . . . . . . . . . **47** E4
**Sorrel Dr** SN14 . . . . . . . **70** B2
**Sorrel St** SN11. . . . . . . . **81** D5
**Sound Copse** SN5 . . . . **34** B2
**Southall** Cl SN25 . . . . . **20** C1
**Southampton Rd**
  Alderbury SP5 . . . . . . **153** A5
  Alderbury SP5 . . . . . . **153** D3
  Fordingbridge SP6. . . . **210** E1
  Landford SP5 . . . . . . . **212** C7
  Landford SP5 . . . . . . . **212** D6
  Salisbury SP1. . . . . . . **152** C7
**Southampton St** SN1 . **50** D6
**Southay** BA13. . . . . . . . **186** B7
**South Bank** SN8 . . . . . **174** F2
**Southbank Gdns**
  RG17. . . . . . . . . . . . . . **165** B1
**Southbank Glen** SN4. . **47** F2
**Southbourne Way**
  SP4. . . . . . . . . . . . . . **133** D6
**Southbourne Way**
  SP4. . . . . . . . . . . . . . **133** D6
**SOUTH BREWHAM** . . . **122** A4
**SOUTHBROOK** . . . . . . . **139** B4
**Southbrook** BA12. . . . . **139** C4
**Southbrook Gdns**
  BA12. . . . . . . . . . . . . **139** B4
**Southbrook La** BA13 . **178** B1
**Southbrook Rd** SN12. . **93** F6
**Southbrook St** SN2 . . . . **35** B1
**Southbroom Infs Sch**
  SN10. . . . . . . . . . . . . **214** C2
**Southbroom Rd**
  SN10. . . . . . . . . . . . . **214** B3
**Southbroom St James
  Church Academy**
  SN10. . . . . . . . . . . . . **214** C2
**SOUTH CERNEY**. . . . . . . . **7** A6
**South Charford Dro**
  SP6. . . . . . . . . . . . . . **210** D6
**South Cliffe Rd** 6
  SN10. . . . . . . . . . . . . **179** F1
**SOUTHCOTT** . . . . . . . . **215** D3
**Southcott Rd**
  Pewsey SN9. . . . . . . . . **215** D4
  Pewsey SN9. . . . . . . . . **215** F2
**Southcroft Dr** BA13. . . **111** D4
**Southcroft Rd** 2
  SN13. . . . . . . . . . . . . . **76** E1
**South Cross La** SN10. **179** C3
**Southdown** 3 SN4 . . . **163** A5
**South Down Way**
  BA12. . . . . . . . . . . . . **116** D7
**South End**
  South Tedworth SP9. . . **216** C4
  Swindon SN25 . . . . . . . **34** F8
**SOUTHEND** . . . . . . . . . **168** F4
**Southernwood Dr**
  SN4. . . . . . . . . . . . . . . **47** E4
**Southerwicks** SN13. . . **84** D7
**Southey Cl** 3 SN25 . . . **34** F7
**Southfield**
  2 Aldbourne SN8. . . . . **170** A6
  Southwick BA14. . . . . . **104** F2

**Southfield** continued
West Overton SN8.... 173 F6
**Southfield Jun Sch**
SN6.................23 A5
**Southfields** BA11.... 110 A3
**Southfield Way** BA11 110 A3
**Southgate**
Devizes SN10........214 B2
Stonebridge BA11... 110 D7
**Southgate Cl** SN10.... 214 B2
**South La**
Downton SP5........211 A8
Nomansland SP5.....212 C4
**Southleigh** BA15...... 100 C5
**Southleigh View**
BA12..............117 C5
**SOUTH MARSTON**....36 F5
**South Marston CE Prim**
**Sch** SN3............36 E4
**South Marston Park**
SN3................36 C7
**South Mdw La** SN5....19 F3
**Southmead** SN14......78 B6
**South Mill Cl** SP4.... 217 B2
**South Mill Hill** SP4... 217 B1
**South Mill Rd** SP4.... 217 B2
**SOUTH NEWTON**..... 130 B2
**South Newton Hospital**
SP2...............130 B2
**South Pk**★ SP11..... 192 B4
**South Pl**
Calne SN11..........81 B2
Corsham SN13........77 A1
**Southside**
Laverstock SP4......146 D8
Shipton Moyne GL8.... 26 E7
**Southside Cl** SN16......42 E4
**South St**
Aldbourne SN8.......170 A6
Avebury SN8.........173 B8
Broad Chalke SP5....205 B4
Corsham SN13........77 A1
Great Wishford SP2.. 130 A3
Salisbury SP2.......145 F1
Swindon SN1..........50 C4
Warminster BA12.....116 E5
Wilton SP2..........144 C1
**SOUTH TIDWORTH**... 216 D4
**South Ugford Medieval**
**Village of**★ SP2..... 144 A2
**South View** RG17..... 177 B7
**South View Ave** SN8....50 E5
**South View Pl** SN8.... 213 E3
**Southview Rd** BA14... 105 D6
**Southville Cl** BA15... 100 E5
**Southville Rd** BA15... 100 E5
**Southward La** SN8.... 170 A6
**Southwark Cl** SP9.... 216 E6
**Southway** SP4........134 B7
**South Way**
Alderbury SP5.......153 E2
Trowbridge BA14.....105 D7
**Southway Rd** BA15... 100 D4
**Southwell Cl** SN14....78 A1
**South Western Rd**
SP2...............145 F1
**SOUTHWICK**........ 104 F3
**Southwick Ave** SN14...35 B5
**Southwick CE Prim Sch**
BA14...............104 F3
**Southwick Ctry Pk**★
BA14...............104 F5
**Southwick Mws** SN...
BA14...............105 C5
**Southwick Rd** BA14... 105 C4
**South Wilts Grammar**
**School for Girls**
SP1...............146 A3
**Southwold Cl** SN25....34 B6
**Southwood Rd** BA14... 105 F8
**SOUTH WRAXALL**.... 91 D6
**Sovereign Ct** SP2..... 145 F1
**Soyuz Cres** SN25......34 B7
**Spackman La** SN13....84 E8
**Spa Cl** SN6...........23 B6
**Spa Ct** SN10..........94 B3
**Spanbourn Ave** SN14..78 D7
**Spaniels Bridge Rd**
SN10...............172 C1
**Sparcells Dr** SN5......34 B2
**Spa Rd** SN12..........94 B3
**Sparkes Dr** SP5...... 153 F1
**Sparrow St** BA14..... 105 E6
**SPA THE**............94 C2
**Spa The** BA14........92 E1
**Speedwell Cl**
Melksham SN12......94 C2
Swindon SN25........34 E5
Trowbridge BA14..... 105 D6
**Spencer Cl**
Melksham SN12......94 A6
Swindon SN5..........48 F7
**Spencers Orch**
Bradford-on-Avon
BA15..............100 D5
Wroughton SN4.......64 B6
**Spenser Cl** SN3........51 A7
**Speresholt** SN5.......49 D4
**Spey Ct** SP10........193 F1
**Spiders Island** SP5... 153 F2
**Spiers Piece** BA14.... 178 B3
**Spindle Tree Ct**
Swindon SN2..........35 B2
Swindon SN25.......35 B2
**Spine Rd** GL7..........7 E7

**Spine Rd (East)** GL7....7 C4
**Spine Rd W** GL7........6 A2
**Spine Rd West** GL7.....5 F2
**Spine Road (East)** SN6...6 F3
**Spingfield Rd** BA12... 139 B5
**Spin Hill** SN10.......179 E1
**Spinners Croft**
BA14...............105 D7
**Spinners Way** BA12... 139 B6
**Spinney Cl**
Chippenham SN14......78 A6
Liddington SN4......163 A4
**Spinney Rd** SP11..... 192 A5
**Spinney The**
Lechlade GL7..........2 C4
Littleton Panell
SN10..............187 E8
Trowbridge BA14.....105 F8
**SPIRTHILL**...........73 B4
**Spitalcroft Rd** SN10.. 214 C4
**Spital La** SN6.........19 E7
**Spitfire Rd**
Calne SN11..........81 D3
Laverstock SP4......146 D8
**Spitfire Way** SN3......36 C7
**Spode La** SN25........34 D7
**Spout La** SN1........178 F8
**Spouts La** SO51.......212 F7
**Spracklands** SP3..... 201 F2
**Sprats Barn Cres** SN4. 47 D3
**Spratsgate La** GL7......6 B4
**Spray Leaze** SP11.... 192 B5
**Spray Rd** RG17.......177 C2
**Sprays** SN8..........183 D8
**Spread Eagle Hill**
SP7...............206 B6
**Spreckley Rd**
SN11..............166 A1
**Spring Bottom** SP4... 197 E2
**Spring Cl** SN1.........50 C6
**Springers Cl** SN10... 214 D4
**Springfield** BA15..... 100 E6
**Springfield Bldgs**
SN15................78 D8
**Springfield Cl**
Corsham SN13........84 A8
Shaftesbury SP7.....202 C2
Trowbridge BA14.....101 E2
**Springfield Cres**
Redlynch SP5.......211 C7
Royal Wootton Bassett
SN4................47 D2
**Springfield Dr** SN11...81 A3
**Springfield Gdns**
SN12................85 C1
**Springfield Pk**
Tisbury SP3.........203 E8
Trowbridge BA14.....101 E1
**Springfield Rd**
Rowde SN10..........96 D1
Swindon SN1..........50 C3
Westbury BA13.......108 F2
**Springfields Acad The**
SN11...............81 A3
**Springfield Sports Ctr**
SN13................76 F1
**Spring Gdns**
Corsham SN13........77 A2
Lechlade GL7..........2 C4
Swindon SN1..........50 C6
**Springhead** BA12.....194 A4
**Springhill Cl** SN5.....49 C5
**Spring La** SN13........84 C7
**Springlines** SN4......163 B6
**Spring Meadow** SN8.. 191 D8
**Spring Meadows**
BA14...............105 A5
**Spring Rd** BA11......110 A6
**Spring The** SN10..... 187 E8
**Spring Tining** SN13....76 F1
**Spruce Ct** SN25.......35 B2
**Spur Of Maury's La**
SO51..............212 F6
**Spur The** BA13.......112 D8
**Spur Way** SN2.........35 E3
**Spye Pk** SN12.........87 E2
**Squalls La** SP3.......203 F6
**Square The**
Calne SN11..........81 B3
Mere BA12..........139 A5
Pewsey SN9.........215 C5
Swindon SN3.........50 D4
**Squarey Cl** SP5......211 A7
**Squires Copse** SN5....34 A1
**Squires Hill Cl**
Royal Wootton Bassett
SN4................47 F2
Royal Wootton Bassett
SN4................48 A2
**Squirrel Cres** SN4.....47 F2
**Squirrel's Cnr** BH21..208 D1
**Stable Cl** SN11......192 A5
**Stables Rd** SP9.......216 C4
**Stacey's La** SN4......163 B5
**Stackpole Cres**
SN25...............34 C8
**Stadium View** SN25....35 B8
**Stafford St** SN1.......50 B5
**Stag Hill** RG17.......171 A1
**Stainers Mead** SP7...202 A5
**Staldon Rd** SN1.......50 B2
**Stallard St** BA14.....105 C8
**Stalls The** BA12......114 F5
**Stambrook Pk** BA1.....82 A5
**Stamford Cl** SN5......49 B5
**Stanbridge Pk** SN5...49 E4
**Stanbury Rd** SP11....192 C1
**Stancomb Ave** BA14.. 101 E1

**Stancombe Pk** SN5..49 D5
**Standen Way** SN25.....35 A7
**STANDERWICK**.......107 B2
**Standerwick** BA13... 107 E3
**Standings Cl** SN5.....49 A8
**Stanford Rd** SN25.....34 C7
**Stanier Cl** BA11.....110 D6
**Stanier Rd** SN11......81 C6
**Stanier St** SN1........50 B5
**STANLEY**............80 A6
**Stanley Cl** SN4......163 B6
**Stanley Ct** SP2......151 E8
**Stanley Honey Ct**
SN3................50 F6
**Stanley La** SN15......79 D6
**Stanley Little Rd** SP2. 145 B3
**Stanley St** SN1........50 C5
**Stanley Terr** SN10... 214 B2
**Stanmore St** SN1......50 A5
**Stannon La** SN1.......50 B2
**Stansfield Cl** SN5....49 D4
**Stanton Cl** BA11.....110 D6
**Stanton Ctry Pk**★ SN6.36 B8
**STANTON**
**FITZWARREN**.......22 B1
**Stanton La** SN14......56 A1
**Stanton Pk Farm**★
SN6................36 B8
**Stanton Pk Nature**
**Reserve**★ SN6......36 B8
**STANTON ST**
**BERNARD**..........173 A1
**STANTON ST**
**QUINTIN**...........56 B4
**Stanton St Quintin Com**
**Prim Sch** SN14.....56 B4
**Stanway Cl** SN3.......51 A4
**Staplefoot Rd** SP5... 207 E6
**STAPLEFORD**........129 E7
**Stapleford Castle Ring &**
**Bailey**★ SP3.......129 D8
**Stapleford Cl** SN15....78 E4
**Stapleford Rd**
Stapleford SP3......129 C8
Stapleford SP3......196 D1
**Stapleford Way** SN2....35 B6
**Stapler's La** SN6......22 B5
**Staples Hill** BA2......99 C3
**Stapleton Cl** SN6......22 F5
**Stardust Cres** SN25.. 34 B7
**Star Ground** BA14.... 101 F8
**Staring Cl** SN5........48 F8
**Star La** SN4...........74 D8
**Star The** BA14.......101 E7
**STARTLEY**...........43 D1
**Station App**
Bradford-on-Avon
BA15..............100 D6
Frome BA11.........110 A4
Ludgershall SP11....192 A5
Melksham SN12.......94 A6
Minety SN16..........17 C2
Swindon SN1.........50 D3
Trowbridge BA14.....105 C8
Westbury BA13......108 E4
**Station Ind** SN15......78 D8
**Station Ind Est** SN1...50 B6
**Station Rd**
Ashbury SN6.........164 A8
Badminton GL9.......38 F1
Calne SN11..........81 B2
Chiseldown SN4......65 D4
Christian Malford SN15. 58 A2
Codford BA12........194 F3
Corsham SN13........77 A1
Devizes SN10.......214 A3
East Garston RG17...171 E7
Great Wishford SP2.. 129 F3
Great Wishford SP2.. 130 A2
Heytesbury BA12....194 C4
Highworth SN6.......22 F6
Holt BA14............92 E1
Hungerford RG17....177 B7
Kemble GL7...........4 F7
Lambourn RG17......165 A1
Lechlade GL7..........2 D5
Limpley Stoke BA2....99 C5
Minety SN16..........17 C1
Purton SN5...........33 C5
Royal Wootton Bassett
SN4................47 D1
Sandleheath SP6....210 C1
Sedgehill & Semley
SP7...............202 D5
South Cerney GL7.....7 B7
Swindon SN1..........50 B7
Tidworth SP9........216 D5
Warminster BA12....117 B7
Westbury BA13......108 E5
**Station Road** SN15....58 A3
**Station Terr** SP2......145 F1
**Station Way** SN11..... 105 C8
**STAVERTON**..........101 C6
**Staverton CE (VC) Prim**
**Sch** BA14...........101 C5
**Staverton Way** SN2....35 C6
**Stavordale Priory**★
BA9...............136 D5
**Stavordale Priory La**
BA9...............136 C4
**Steadings The**
Royal Wootton Bassett
SN4................47 F1
Salisbury SP4.......146 D6
**STEAM Mus of the Great**
**Western Railway**★
SN2................50 A6
**Stedham Wlk** SN3......51 B4

**Steele Cl** SN10......214 D4
**Steels Dro** SP6.......211 A4
**Steels La** SP6........209 F2
**Steel's La**
Penselwood BA9.....136 F3
Pen Selwood BA9....137 A3
**Steepe Way** SN8......175 C1
**Steep Hollow** SP3.... 201 E3
**STEEPLE ASHTON**....178 B3
**Steeple Ashton Rd**
BA13..............186 C8
**STEEPLE**
**LANGFORD**.........128 D8
**Steeple Vw** SN1........50 A6
**Steep St** BA12........139 A6
**Steiner Academy Frome**
BA12..............111 D2
**Steinlen Cl** SN25......20 D1
**Stenbury Cl** SN25.....35 A7
**Stenness Cl** SN5......34 C2
**Stephen Martin Gdns**
SP6...............210 D1
**Stephens Cl**
Lechlade-on-Thames
GL7.................2 A1
Salisbury SP2......151 E4
**Stephenson Dr** BA11. 110 C6
**Stephenson Rd**
Salisbury SP2.......145 E1
Swindon SN25........35 C7
The Ham BA13.......108 D5
**Stephens Rd** SN3......36 A1
**Stephens Way** BA12.. 116 F8
**Steplake La**
Sherfield English
SO51..............162 E1
Sherfield English SO51 212 F8
**Steplake Rd** SO51....212 F8
**Step Stones** SN25.....34 A3
**Sterling Pk** SP10.... 193 C1
**STERT**..............180 B6
**Stert Valley La** SN10. 180 A6
**Stevenson Rd** SN2.....34 C5
**Stewart Cl**
Chippenham SN15.....78 F4
Swindon SN25........35 B6
**Steway La** BA1.........82 B6
**STIBB GREEN**.......175 D1
**Stibb Hill** SN10......187 F7
**Stickleback Rd** SN11..81 B6
**Stickley Cl** SN26......20 B1
**Stickway** SP5........206 F3
**Still Man Cl** BA14.... 101 E8
**Stirling Cl**
Bower Hill SN12.....178 B8
Wroughton SN4.......64 A7
**Stirling Rd**
Market Lavington
SN10..............180 A1
South Marston Park SN3 36 C6
**Stirling Way** BA11... 110 C6
**STITCHCOMBE**.......175 D8
**Stitching's La** SN9... 181 D5
**Stobberts Pl** SN10...179 F1
**Stobberts Rd**
SN10..............179 F1
**Stockbridge Copse**
SN5................34 A2
**Stockbridge Rd** SP5.. 135 F3
**Stockham Cl** SN6......19 F8
**Stockham Gdns** SN6...19 F8
**Stock La**
Aldbourne SN8......169 D4
Landford SP5.......212 C1
**STOCKLEY**............89 C4
**Stockley Hollow** SN11..89 C4
**Stockley La**
Calne Without SN11...89 C6
Quemerford SN11.....89 C6
**Stockley Rd** SN11.....89 C2
**Stockport Rd** SP4....217 D1
**Stocks Bridge La**
SP5...............151 A1
**Stock's Cross** SO43.. 212 D2
**Stock St** BA12........139 B4
**STOCKS THE**.........178 C7
**STOCKTON**..........195 B1
**Stockton Earthworks**★
BA12..............201 A6
**Stockton House**★
BA12..............195 B1
**Stockton Rd** SN2......35 C4
**Stockwell Rd** SN10...214 C4
**Stockwood Cl** SN1....146 C3
**Stockwood Rd** SN14...78 B6
**STOFORD**.............130 A3
**Stoford Bottom** SP2..130 A4
**Stoke Comm La** SN5...19 A2
**Stoke Common La**
SN6................18 E1
**Stoke Common Mdws**
**Nature Reserve**★
SN6................18 E1
**STOKE FARTHING**....205 D4
**Stokehill** BA14.......106 A8
**Stoke Mdw** SN11.......81 B1
**Stoke Mead** BA2.......98 F7
**Stokesay Dr** SN5......49 C4
**Stokes Rd** SN13.......85 A8
**Stonar Sch** SN12......92 B8
**Stone Ave**★ SN8.....173 C8
**STONEBRIDGE**.......110 C7
**Stonebridge Cl** SN8..213 F3
**Stonebridge Dr** BA11 110 B7
**Stone Cl**
Half Way Firs SN13...76 C1
The Common SP5....149 C6

**Stonecrop Way** SN25..34 E5
**Stonefield Cl** SN5.....49 C7
**Stonefield Dr** SN6.....23 A5
**Stonehenge**★ SP4... 197 C5
**Stonehenge Cursus**★
SP4...............197 C6
**Stonehenge Rd**
Amesbury SP4......198 A4
Swindon SN1..........50 A2
West Amesbury SP4..197 F4
**Stonehenge Sch The**
SP4...............217 B4
**Stonehenge Visitor Ctr**★
SP4...............197 C5
**Stonehill** SN16........30 B7
**Stonehill Barn** GL8.....3 C6
**Stonehill Gn** SN5.....49 D6
**Stonehill La** GL8.......3 C6
**Stone La**
Lydiard Millicent SN5... 33 E1
Ramsbury SN8......175 D8
**Stonelea Cl** SN14......78 B7
**Stoneleigh Rise**
BA11..............110 A6
**Stoneover La**
Lydiard Tregoze SN4.. 48 A3
Royal Wootton Bassett
SN4................47 F2
**Stone (site of King's**
**Elm)**★ SP3........142 B1
**Stones La** SN6..........8 B1
**Stonewall Terr** BA11. 110 A3
**Stoneworks The** SN13..84 C6
**Stoney Bridge** BA12.. 140 D5
**Stoney Cross**
BA11..............192 A5
**Stoney Dro** SP11......185 D4
**Stoney La**
Bromham SN15........88 A1
Bromham SN15........96 A8
**Stoneywell** SN25......20 B1
**Stonybeck Cl** SN5......49 D6
**Stony Gutter** BA14....102 D1
**Stony La**
Damerham SP6.......209 E2
Lambourn RG17.....171 B6
St Catherine BA1.....82 A8
**Stoppers Hill** SN15...46 B7
**Stops Hill** SP3.......200 B3
**Stop St** SP3..........200 C2
**Storey Mws** SN16......28 A1
**Stork House Dr**
RG17..............165 A1
**STORMORE**...........112 A8
**Stormore** BA13.......111 F8
**Storms Farm Rd**
SO51..............212 F1
**Storridge Rd** BA13....108 C6
**Stour La** SN11........110 A4
**Stour Cl** SO51........212 F6
**Stourhead House &**
**Gdns**★ BA12.......123 F1
**STOURTON**..........123 F1
**Stourton Bushes**
BA12..............107 E4
**Stourton House Flower**
**Gdn**★ BA12.......123 F1
**Stourton La** BA12.....123 E3
**Stourton Pk** BA14.....102 B3
**Stour Wlk** SN25.......35 B4
**Stowell Pk**★ SN8.....182 A8
**Stradbrook** BA13.....186 B7
**Straight La**
Dean SP5...........207 E3
Lambourn RG17.....171 A3
**STRAIGHT SOLEY**....171 A3
**STRAND THE**.........178 B6
**Strand The**
Calne SN11..........81 B3
Steeple Ashton BA14..178 A3
**STRANGWAYS**........198 A6
**Strangways** SP4......197 F6
**Stranks Cl** SN6........23 A4
**Strap La** BA10........122 C8
**Stratford Cl** SN5......49 D5
**Stratford Rd** SN1.....146 A3
**STRATFORD SUB**
**CASTLE**............145 F5
**Stratford Sub Castle CE**
**Prim Sch** SP1......145 D5
**STRATFORD TONY**... 150 C2
**Stratford Tony Rd**
SP5...............150 E2
**Stratton Orch** SN3....36 A2
**Stratton Rd**
Pewsey SN9.........215 C4
Swindon SN1..........50 F8
Swindon SN25........35 F1
**Stratton Rd & Marshgate**
**Ind Est** SN1........50 F8
**STRATTON ST**
**MARGARET**..........36 A3
**Strattons Wlk** SN12...94 B4
**Strawberry Hill** SN10.187 E7
**Strawberry La** GL7.....1 A4
**Street La**
Brewham BA10......122 A4
Sedgehill & Semley
SP7...............202 C5
**Street The**
All Cannings SN10...172 F1
Alvediston SP5......204 D3
Bishops Cannings
SN10..............172 B3
Brinkworth SN15.....45 F6
Broughton Gifford SN12 93 B4
Castle Combe SN14...68 A7
Castle Eaton SN6....10 B4
Charlton SN16........29 B6

Cherhill SN11........166 B1
Chilmark SP3.......201 A3
Chirton SN10........180 F4
Crudwell SN16.......14 E5
Didmarton GL9........24 C3
East Knoyle SP3....141 C1
Holt BA14............101 D8
Hullavington SN14....41 F1
Kilmington BA12.....123 F4
Latton SN6............8 C4
Lea SN16............28 F1
Liddington SN4......158 C4
Little Somerford SN15.. 44 C5
Luckington SN14......39 E4
Lydiard Millicent SN5...48 D8
Marden SN10........179 A5
Marston Maisey SN6....9 D6
Milton Lilbourne SN9..182 E7
Motcombe SP7.......202 A5
Nettleton SN14.......53 B4
Oaksey SN16.........15 F8
Pitton & Farley SP5..154 E7
Shipton Moyne GL8...26 E8
Swindon SN25.........34 E3
West Knoyle BA12...140 D5
Winterslow SP5......149 A5
Yatton Keynell SN14..68 F6
**Stroma Way** SN6.......22 E7
**Strongrove Hill** RG17 177 A7
**Strongs Cl**
Sherston SN16........25 C1
Steeple Ashton BA14..178 C4
**Stroud La** SN10......179 F5
**Stroud's Hill** SN4.....65 D4
**Stuart Cl**
Swindon SN3.........50 F6
Trowbridge BA14.....101 E4
**Stuart Gn** BA12......117 A6
**Stubbs Ct** SP10......193 D1
**Stubbs La** SN14.......70 A7
**Stubhampton Bottom**
DT11..............206 C3
**Stubsmead** SN3........51 C5
**Stuckton Rd** SP6......210 E1
**Studd St** SP9.........216 D8
**Studio Theatre**★
SP2...............146 A2
**Studland Cl** SN3......51 B3
**Studland Pk** BA13....109 B2
**STUDLEY**.............80 B3
**Studley Castle**★ SP6. 211 F3
**Studley Cnr** SN11......80 B4
**Studley Gdns** SN11....80 A3
**Studley Gn Prim Sch**
BA14..............105 A6
**STUDLEY GREEN**..... 104 F7
**Studley Hill** SN11......80 A4
**Studley La** SN11.......80 A3
**Studley Rise** BA14.... 105 D6
**STURFORD**...........115 E6
**Sturford La** BA12.....115 D6
**Styles Ave** BA11.....110 C4
**Styles Cl**
Frome BA11.........110 B4
Porton SP4.........133 D5
**Styles Hill** BA11......110 B4
**Styles Way** SN5.......49 A5
**Styles The** SP5......205 F4
**Sudeley Dr** GL7........6 F6
**Sudeley Way** SN5.....48 F5
**Sudley Way** SN5.......48 F5
**Suffolk Cl** SN16.......29 A7
**Suffolk Pl** GL7........8 D7
**Suffolk Rd**
Salisbury SP2.......151 E6
Westbury BA13......112 D8
**Suffolk St** SN2........50 C8
**Sully** BA15...........100 D6
**Sumbler Dr** SN11......81 D3
**Summerdown Ct**
BA13..............109 A4
**Summer Down Wlk**
BA14..............105 C5
**Summerhouse Rd** SN4 63 F7
**Summer La**
Castle Combe SN14...53 F3
Castle Combe SN14...54 A3
Monkton Combe BA2...98 D8
**Summerleaze**
Corsham SN13........76 D1
Trowbridge BA14.....105 A6
**Summerlock App**
SP2...............146 A1
**Summerlug** SN4......133 A1
**Summer Oaks** SP7....202 A5
**Summer Rd** BA13.....108 F4
**Summers La** SN4......167 C7
**Summers St** SN2......49 F7
**Sumsions Dr** SN13....76 D1
**Sunbeam Dr** SN14......78 B3
**Sundays Hill**
Brinkworth SN15......30 B1
Brinkworth SN15......30 D1
Brinkworth SN15......45 C8
**Sunderland Cl**
SN12..............178 B8
**Sunflower Way**
SP11..............193 F2
**Sunhill Cl** GL7.........1 E7
**Sun La** BA13..........108 E4
**Sunningdale Cl** SN15..78 F7
**Sunnybank Rd** BA13..109 A5
**Sunnyhill** SN8........191 D8
**Sunnyhill La** SN8.....174 C1

Sunnyhill Rd SP1 . . . . 146 A4
Sunnyside SN10 . . . . . 187 E8
Sunnyside Ave SN1 . . . .50 A4
Sunnyside Cl SP10. . . 193 C1
Sunrise Way SP4 . . . . 217 D4
SUNTON . . . . . . . . . . . 183 E1
Surrendell Cottage
SN14. . . . . . . . . . . . . . .55 B8
Surrey Pl
Trowbridge BA14. . . . 105 B7
1 Trowbridge BA14. . 105 C7
Surrey Rd SN2. . . . . . . .35 A1
Sussex Rd SP2. . . . . . 151 E6
Sussex Sq SN3 . . . . . . .50 E6
Sussex Wlk 2 BA14. . 101 F1
Sutherland Cresent
SN14. . . . . . . . . . . . . . .70 B3
Sutherland Ct 5
SP10. . . . . . . . . . . . . 193 D1
Suthmere Dr SN8. . . . 183 D8
SUTTON BENGER. . . . . .57 C2
Sutton Benger CE Prim
Sch SN15. . . . . . . . . . .57 D2
Sutton Bottom SP3 . . 141 B5
Sutton Gdns SN15 . . . .57 E1
Sutton Hill
Sherrington BA12 . . . 195 A4
Sutton Mandeville SP3. 204 C7
Sutton Waldron SP7. . . 206 A3
Sutton La
Langley Burrell Without
SN15 . . . . . . . . . . . . .71 C5
Sutton Benger SN15 . . 57 D1
SUTTON
MANDEVILLE . . . . . . 204 C8
Sutton Parva BA12. . . 194 A4
Sutton Pk SN26. . . . . . .21 C1
Sutton Rd
Fovant SP3. . . . . . . . . 204 D7
Kington Langley SN15 . . .70 F7
Swindon SN3 . . . . . . . .51 C4
SUTTON ROW . . . . . . 204 B7
SUTTON VENY . . . . . . 117 F1
Sutton Veny CE Sch
BA12. . . . . . . . . . . . . 194 A4
Suvla La 6 SP4. . . . . . 198 E6
Swaddon St SN11. . . . .81 B4
Swainsford BA12 . . . . 139 A1
Swaledale Rd BA12 . . 116 D6
Swallet House SN1 . . . .58 D5
SWALLETT GATE . . . . . .59 A6
Swallow Cl
Tidworth SP9 . . . . . . 216 D6
2 Warminster BA12. . 116 E5
SWALLOWCLIFFE . . . . 204 A6
Swallowdale SN3. . . . .51 D7
Swallow Dr
Frome BA11. . . . . . . . 110 B6
4 Trowbridge BA14 . . 105 B8
Swallowfield Ave SN3. .50 F5
Swallowmead 1
SP2. . . . . . . . . . . . . . 152 A5
Swallows Mead 9
SN4. . . . . . . . . . . . . . .48 A2
Swallows Rise BA13 . . 108 E4
Swanage Wlk SN25 . . .34 E3
Swan Barton SN16. . . .40 C8
SWANBOROUGH . . . . . .22 C4
Swanborough Cl 6
SN15. . . . . . . . . . . . . .78 F4
Swanborough Tump *
SN9. . . . . . . . . . . . . . 181 F6
Swanbrook SN3 . . . . . 51 D8
Swan Cl
9 Durrington/Bulford
SP4. . . . . . . . . . . . . 198 C2
Lechlade GL7 . . . . . . . .2 C4
Salisbury SP2. . . . . . 152 A6
South Cerney GL7 . . . . .7 A6
1 Swindon SN3 . . . . .51 C8
Swan Ct BA14 . . . . . . 104 F3
Swan Dr BA14 . . . . . . 101 D5
Swangate RG17. . . . . 177 B8
Swangrove La GL9 . . . .38 D8
Swan La SN6 . . . . . . . .17 F5
Swan Meadow SN9 . . 215 D3
Swan Rd
Corsham SN13. . . . . . .76 C1
Pewsey SN9. . . . . . . . 215 C4
Swan's Bottom 7
SN8. . . . . . . . . . . . . . 170 B2
Swan's Cl 9 SN8 . . . . 170 B2
Swansfield GL7. . . . . . . .2 D6
Swans Mdw GL7 . . . . . .2 D7
Swattons Cl SP4. . . . . 217 E8
Swayne Cl 6 SN5. . . . .75 F5
Swayne Rd SP2. . . . . . 144 C2
Swaynes Cl 1 SP1. . . 146 B2
Sweetapplecl SP9 . . . 216 D8
Sweet Briar Rd SN12. .94 C3
Sweetmans Rd SP7 . . 202 C2
Swift Ave SN25 . . . . . . .35 A7
Swiftdown 5 SP2. . . . 152 A5
Swift Dr BA14 . . . . . . 105 E6
Swift Link GL7. . . . . . . .7 A6
Swift Mead BA12 . . . . 116 E5
Swillbrook Lakes Nature
Reserve * SN16 . . . . .16 F8
SWINDON. . . . . . . . . . . .50 E4
Swindon Acad SN25 . . .35 C5
Swindon Academy
SN2. . . . . . . . . . . . . . .35 B2
Swindon Arts Ctr *
SN1. . . . . . . . . . . . . . .50 C4
Swindon Coll
Marlborough SN8. . . . 213 D3
Swindon SN2 . . . . . . . 50 B8

Swindon & Cricklade
Rly * SN25. . . . . . . . . .33 F8
Swindon Mus & Art Gall *
SN1. . . . . . . . . . . . . . .50 D4
Swindon Rd
Avebury SN8. . . . . . . 167 C1
Cricklade SN6 . . . . . . .19 F7
Cricklade SN6 . . . . . . .20 A8
Highworth SN6. . . . . . .22 F3
Highworth SN6. . . . . . .23 A4
Hilmarton SN11. . . . . .73 F3
Kington Langley SN15 . .70 F5
Lea SN16 . . . . . . . . . . 43 E8
Lydiard Tregoze SN4 . . 48 C2
Lydiard Tregoze SN4 . . 48 D2
Malmesbury SN16 . . . . 28 C1
Royal Wootton Bassett
SN4 . . . . . . . . . . . . . .47 F3
Swindon SN1 . . . . . . . .36 A1
Wroughton SN4 . . . . . .64 C7
Swindon St SN6 . . . . . .23 A5
Swindon Sta SN2 . . . . .50 B7
Swindon Town Football
Club SN1. . . . . . . . . . 50 D7
Swinford Paddocks
SN16. . . . . . . . . . . . . .27 E2
Swinley Dr SN5. . . . . . .34 A1
Sword Gdns 5 SN1. . . .49 F4
Swynford Cl GL7. . . . . .10 D6
Sycamore Cl
Long Newnton GL8 . . . . 13 B4
Lyneham & Bradenstoke
SN15 . . . . . . . . . . . . .60 C2
North Tidworth SP9 . . 216 E6
Sixpenny Handley SP5. 208 A3
Sycamore Dr
Calne SN11 . . . . . . . . .81 D5
8 Frome BA11. . . . . . 110 B7
Salisbury SP1. . . . . . . 146 C5
Sycamore Gr
Swindon SN2 . . . . . . . .35 C2
Trowbridge BA14 . . . . 105 C5
Westbury BA13 . . . . . 108 F3
Sydnalls La BA12 . . . . 115 D6
Sylvester Dr 4 BA14. 101 F1
Symonds SN5 . . . . . . . .49 B3
Symons Cl SP9 . . . . . . 216 D8
Syon Cl
Corsham SN13. . . . . . .84 E8
4 Swindon SN25 . . . . .34 F6
Syringa Ct SP2 . . . . . . 145 D1
Sywell Rd SN3 . . . . . . .51 C8

T

Tadpole Farm CE Prim
Acad SN26 . . . . . . . . .20 C1
Tadpole Farm CE Prim
Sch SN25. . . . . . . . . . 20 C1
Tadpole La
Blunsdon St Andrew
SN25 . . . . . . . . . . . . .34 C8
Purton SN5. . . . . . . . . 33 F8
Swindon SN25 . . . . . . . 34 A8
Talavera Rd SN4 . . . . . 168 E8
Talavera Way SP9 . . . 216 D3
Talbot Cl
Melksham SN12. . . . . .94 D5
Salisbury SP1. . . . . . . 146 C4
Talbot Rd BA14 . . . . . 105 A7
Talboys (Medieval Hall
House) * BA14 . . . . 178 B4
Tallis Wlk SN5. . . . . . . .49 A5
Tallow La 5 SN4 . . . . 163 A6
Tall Trees SN14. . . . . . .78 D7
Tallys La BA9 . . . . . . . 136 E1
Tamar Cl SN25. . . . . . . .35 A4
Tamar Rd SN12. . . . . . .94 A6
Tamesis Dr GL7. . . . . . . .4 F7
Tame Way GL7 . . . . . . . .1 E6
Tamworth Dr SN5 . . . . .49 A7
Tanarisk Cl SN11 . . . . .81 C1
Tangier Cl BA12 . . . . . 117 A8
TANGLEY . . . . . . . . . . . 193 A7
Tangley Bottom Rd
SP11. . . . . . . . . . . . . 185 A1
Tangmere Cl 13
SN12. . . . . . . . . . . . . 178 B8
TANIS . . . . . . . . . . . . . . .96 C2
Tankard La 15 SN8. . . 170 B2
Tankey's Cl 6 BA11 . . 110 A7
Tank La SP5 . . . . . . . . 205 B4
Tan La
Bourton SP8. . . . . . . . 137 C2
Bourton SP8. . . . . . . . 138 A2
Tanner Cl SN15. . . . . . .78 F5
Tanners Cl
Royal Wootton Bassett
SN4 . . . . . . . . . . . . . .47 D2
Winterbourne SP4 . . . 133 A1
Tanners Field SP4 . . . 217 D3
Tanners Hill SN16 . . . .40 C8
Tanners La
Sandleheath SP6 . . . . 210 A1
Shrewton SP3 . . . . . . 196 E7
Winterbourne SP4 . . . 133 A1
Tansley Moor SN3. . . . 51 E3
Tanyard La 6 SP7. . . . 202 B1
Tanyard Way BA13. . . 112 D0
Taplow Wlk SN3. . . . . .51 A4
Taramah Gdns 10
SP3. . . . . . . . . . . . . . 203 E8
Targetts Mead SP3 . . 203 E8
Tarka Cl SN5. . . . . . . . .34 F7
Tarragon Cl SN2. . . . . .34 C4
Tarrant's Hill 24
RG17. . . . . . . . . . . . . 177 B7

Tarters The SN16 . . . . . 40 D8
Tascroft BA12 . . . . . . 116 B5
Taskers La SN8 . . . . . 183 D8
Tatry Rd 10 SN25 . . . . 34 D6
Taunton Cl 2 SN14. . . .77 F5
Taunton St SN1. . . . . . .50 A6
Tavinor Dr SN15 . . . . . .78 E4
Tavistock Rd SN3. . . . . 51 B5
Tawny Cl SN13. . . . . . . 84 C6
Tawny Owl Cl SN3 . . . .51 C8
Taylor Cres SN3 . . . . . .36 A4
Taylors Cl SN16. . . . . . .17 B1
Taylors Gn SN8 . . . . . 174 A7
Taylors La SN8 . . . . . . 168 B1
Taylors View BA14. . . 101 D1
Teal Ave SN15 . . . . . . . 60 A1
Teal Cl BA13. . . . . . . . 109 B4
Tealgate RG17. . . . . . . 177 B8
Tealsbrook SN3 . . . . . .51 D7
Teal Way GL7. . . . . . . . . .7 A6
Teapot St BA12 . . . . . 201 E8
Teasel Cl
Devizes SN10 . . . . . . 214 D8
28 Ludgershall SP11. . 192 A5
Teasels The BA12. . . . 116 F6
Techno Ind Est SN2 . . .35 E1
Tedder Ave SN13 . . . . .84 A8
Tedder Cl SN2. . . . . . . .35 B2
Tees Cl SN3 . . . . . . . . . 35 A4
Teeswater Cl SN5. . . . .49 A6
TEFFONT EVIAS . . . . . 201 C2
Teffont Field Bldgs *
SP3. . . . . . . . . . . . . . 201 D4
TEFFONT MAGNA . . . 201 C3
Teffont Manor * SP3. 201 D2
Teichman Cl BA12 . . . 117 C6
Telegraph SP5 . . . . . . 212 A4
Telford Pool SN2 . . . . .49 F8
Telford Rd SP2 . . . . . . 151 E8
Tellcroft Cl SN13 . . . . .84 F8
Tellings Orch SN16 . . . 16 D3
TELLISFORD . . . . . . . . 103 E4
Tellisford La BA2 . . . . 103 C4
Tellisford Rd BA2. . . . 103 E7
Tempest Rd 9 SP4. . . 217 D3
Templar's Firs SN4 . . . .61 E8
Templars Way Ind Est
SN4. . . . . . . . . . . . . . .61 D7
TEMPLE . . . . . . . . . . . 115 C6
Temple St SN1 . . . . . . .50 C5
TEMPLETON . . . . . . . 177 D5
Ten Acres SP7. . . . . . . 202 C2
Tenby Cl SN3 . . . . . . . .50 F3
Tench Rd SN11. . . . . . .81 B5
Tennis Cnr Dro BA11. 187 D2
Tennyson Rd SN4. . . . .47 F3
Tennyson St SN1. . . . . .50 B5
Tenzing Gdns SN25 . . .35 C3
Teo Cl SN25. . . . . . . . . 35 B8
Tern Cl SN11 . . . . . . . . 81 D2
Terncliff SN3. . . . . . . . 51 D7
Tetbury Hill SN16. . . . .27 F6
Tetbury Hill Gdns
Malmesbury SN16 . . . .27 F5
10 Malmesbury SN16 . . 28 A5
Tetbury La
Charlton SN16 . . . . . . .14 F1
Charlton SN16 . . . . . . .29 A7
Crudwell SN16. . . . . . 14 D6
Tetbury Rd
Brokenborough SN16 . . 27 E7
Culkerton GL8 . . . . . . . .3 A5
Didmarton GL9. . . . . . .24 A3
Sherston SN16. . . . . . .25 D2
Tethering Dro SP6. . . 211 C6
Tewkesbury Way
Lydiard Millicent SN5. . 48 E7
Swindon SN5 . . . . . . . 49 A6
Thackeray Cl SN3. . . . .51 D4
Thackeray Cres SN12 . .94 B4
Thames Ave SN25. . . . .34 E5
Thames Cl
South Cerney GL7 . . . . .6 F6
Warminster BA12 . . . 117 A8
Thames Cres SN12. . . .94 A6
Thamesdown Dr
Haydon Wick SN25. . . . 34 B7
Swindon SN25 . . . . . . 35 A7
Swindon SN25 . . . . . . 35 B8
Thames La SN6 . . . . . . .19 E8
Thames St GL7 . . . . . . . .2 C3
Thames View
Ashton Keynes SN6. . . .17 F8
Broad Blunsdon SN26 . . 21 A2
Ewen GL7. . . . . . . . . . .5 C8
Thatcham Cl SN11. . . .81 A4
Thatchers The SN25 . . .35 C7
The Arc 6 SN25 . . . . . .35 A8
Theatre Sq SN1. . . . . . .50 C6
The Ave
Odstock SP5. . . . . . . . 158 B7
Swindon SN3 . . . . . . . 36 C8
The Bank SN4. . . . . . . 133 B2
The Banks SN15 . . . . . .59 E4
The Belt SP3 . . . . . . . 142 D3
The Brook SN25 . . . . . .34 A3
The Buffer SN25. . . . . .34 B2
The Causeway BA12. . 194 A4
The Chase Pk SN14 . . . 55 D4
The City BA13 . . . . . . 186 C7
The Cl
Hilmarton SN11 . . . . . .73 F3
South Cerney GL7 . . . . .7 A7

The Cl continued
Winterbourne Bassett
SN4 . . . . . . . . . . . . . 167 C5
The Clay SN10. . . . . . 188 A8
The Comm
Damerham SP6 . . . . . 209 F2
Heddington Wick SN11 . . 88 E3
The Common SN15 . . . .96 A2
The Copse
Batheaston BA1. . . . . . 82 A3
Broad Blunsdon SN26 . . 21 B2
The Cres
Dilton Marsh BA13. . . . 112 B8
Lea SN16 . . . . . . . . . . 43 E8
Swindon SN25 . . . . . . 34 A2
The Crossing SN16. . . .16 F4
The Deanery CE Acad
SN1. . . . . . . . . . . . . . .49 E3
The Drive S051. . . . . 162 C1
The Drove
Coulston BA13 . . . . . . 186 E8
Stourton with Gasper
BA12 . . . . . . . . . . . 124 B2
Upton Scudamore
BA12 . . . . . . . . . . . 112 B4
The Druck BA12 . . . . . 116 E1
The Elms SP3. . . . . . . 204 D8
The Farm SN25 . . . . . .34 A3
The Folly SN11. . . . . . .80 A2
The Forum 5 SN1. . . . .49 C5
The Garretts GL7 . . . . .1 E7
The Gdns SN11 . . . . . . .81 B4
The General's Ave
SP5. . . . . . . . . . . . . . 207 D6
The Gibb SN14. . . . . . . 54 A2
The Gn BA12 . . . . . . . 116 F2
The Green
Broughton Gifford
SN12 . . . . . . . . . . . . 93 B2
Christian Malford SN15. 58 A2
Goatacre SN11. . . . . . .73 F6
Luckington SN14 . . . . . 39 E4
The Halve BA12. . . . . . 116 D6
The Hollows SP4 . . . . 131 C3
The Island BA12 . . . . 119 B7
The Kennels BA12 . . . 117 F1
The La SP4 . . . . . . . . . 133 D6
The Landings GL7 . . . . .7 B6
The Laurels
Castle Eaton SN6. . . . . 10 B4
Midford BA2. . . . . . . . . 98 C5
The Leasowes SN25. . . .20 B1
The Link GL8 . . . . . . . . 25 B7
The Lotts SN6 . . . . . . . .6 F1
The Lynch BA12 . . . . . 139 B5
The Marsh
Longbridge Deverill
BA12 . . . . . . . . . . . 120 F6
Longbridge Deverill
BA12 . . . . . . . . . . . 121 A6
Mount Sorrel SP5 . . . . 205 A3
The Matravers Sch
BA13. . . . . . . . . . . . . 108 F8
The Mdws
Bourton SN4. . . . . . . . .37 F3
Luckington SN14 . . . . . 39 F4
The Mead Com Prim Sch
BA14. . . . . . . . . . . . . 104 C6
The Moor
Leigh SN16. . . . . . . . . .17 F3
Minety SN16. . . . . . . . 17 A3
The New Forest CE Prim
Sch SP5. . . . . . . . . . . 149 A5
THEOBALD'S GREEN. 172 A8
Theobald St SN1. . . . . .50 B6
The Old Barnyard
BA12. . . . . . . . . . . . . 112 F4
The Old Orch BA15. . . 100 E7
The Old Turnpike
SN11. . . . . . . . . . . . . .88 E1
The Orch
Bradford Leigh BA15. . .91 F1
Cherhill SN11. . . . . . . 166 B1
Lydiard Millicent SN5. . 48 D8
Swindon SN3 . . . . . . . 36 C8
The Paddock BA12. . . 117 C6
The Philip Green
Memorial Sch BH21 209 B1
The Plantation SP5 . . 149 A5
The Portway
Winterbourne SP4 . . . 132 F2
Winterbourne SP4 . . . 133 A3
The Pry SN5. . . . . . . . . 33 F5
The Pyghtell SN14 . . . .39 E5
The Quarry SN11 . . . . .81 B1
The Race Plain SP2. . . 150 D6
The Reeds SP3 . . . . . . 201 B3
The Ridge SN9 . . . . . . 215 C5
The Ridgeway SN4. . . 168 C8
The Row Service Rd
SN25. . . . . . . . . . . . . 35 D1
The Royal Cres SP9 . . 216 D7
The Sidings SN5 . . . . . 33 D5
The Spinney
Malmesbury SN16 . . . . 28 C1
Trowbridge BA14 . . . . 106 A8
The Spitfire Retail Pk
BA14. . . . . . . . . . . . . 105 D5
The Springs SN14. . . . .70 F6
The St
Acton Turville GL9 . . . . .52 F6
Alderton SN14 . . . . . . .39 F2
Alderton SN14 . . . . . . .40 A3
Castle Combe SN14. . . .67 F5
The Stables SP3 . . . . . .50 F4
Thestfield Dr BA14. . . 101 D4
The Stones SN25 . . . . . 34 A2
The Street SP5 . . . . . . 148 F5

The Sunflowers SN25 . .35 F3
The Tannery BA14 . . . .92 E1
Thetford Way SN25 . . .34 E1
The Turnpike SN11. . . .88 D2
The Village Gn BA13 . 109 A8
The Wern GL7. . . . . . . . .2 B4
The Wharf SN15 . . . . . .86 E5
Thicketts Rd SN8 . . . . 169 C1
THICKWOOD . . . . . . . . 75 D6
Thickwood La SN14. . . 75 C6
THINGLEY . . . . . . . . . . .77 F1
Thingley Top SN13. . . . 85 D8
Thirsk Cl SN14. . . . . . . 78 A5
Thirsk Dr BA14 . . . . . . 106 B8
Thistlebarrow Rd
SP1. . . . . . . . . . . . . . 146 A4
Thistledown 6 SN4 . . 163 A6
Thomas Bunn Cl
BA11. . . . . . . . . . . . . 110 A7
Thomas Byron Rd
SN10. . . . . . . . . . . . . 214 C1
Thomas Cl SN11. . . . . .81 C1
Thomas Hardy Dr 8
SP7. . . . . . . . . . . . . . 202 D2
Thomas Mead SN15. . .78 E5
Thomas St SN2. . . . . . .49 F7
Thomas Wyatt Rd
SN10. . . . . . . . . . . . . 214 B1
Thompson Cl SP2. . . . 151 F5
Thompson St SN5 . . . .33 A3
Thompson Rd SP9 . . . 216 C7
Thompsons Hill SN16 . .40 C7
Thomson Way SN8. . . 213 B2
Thorley St SN25 . . . . . .35 A6
Thornbank SN12. . . . . .94 A3
Thornbridge Ave SN3. .51 A4
Thornbury Rd BA13 . . 108 F4
Thorne Cl SP5 . . . . . . 150 F1
THORNEND . . . . . . . . . .58 C1
Thorne Rd
2 Netheravon SP4. . . 190 A4
Swindon SN3 . . . . . . . 51 C4
Thorneydown Rd
SP4. . . . . . . . . . . . . . 133 E1
Thorney Pk SN3 . . . . . .64 B3
Thornford Dr SN5 . . . . .49 C5
THORNHILL. . . . . . . . . .61 F1
Thornhill Dr SN25 . . . .35 A8
Thornhill Ind Est SN2 . .35 E1
Thornhill Mews SN16 . .27 E2
Thornhill Rd
Swindon SN3 . . . . . . . 36 D4
Swindon SN3 . . . . . . . 36 D4
Warminster BA12 . . . 116 D5
Thorns The SN8 . . . . . 213 D5
Thornton Cres SP2 . . . 144 F4
Thornycroft La SN10. . 172 C1
Thoulstone La BA12 . . 112 A4
Threadgill Way 6
SP9. . . . . . . . . . . . . . 199 C8
Threadneedle St SN14.78 C5
Three Barrows *
SN8. . . . . . . . . . . . . . 164 B3
Three Cuppes La 4
SP1. . . . . . . . . . . . . . 146 B1
Three Horseshoes Wlk 4
BA12. . . . . . . . . . . . . 117 A7
Three Oak Hill Dr
SN8. . . . . . . . . . . . . . 175 D4
Three Post La 15
RG17. . . . . . . . . . . . . 165 A2
Three Shire Stones *
SN14. . . . . . . . . . . . . .74 D1
Three Sisters Rd 1
SN4. . . . . . . . . . . . . . 163 B6
Thresher Dr SN25. . . . .35 C6
Thrushel Cl SN25. . . . .34 E4
Thruxton Motor Racing
Circuit * SP11. . . . . 192 C1
Thurlestone Rd SN3 . . 50 E5
Thurlow Cl 10 SP4 . . . 217 E3
Thursday St SN25. . . . 34 D6
Thyme Cl SN2 . . . . . . . 34 C3
Thyme Rd SN12. . . . . . .94 D3
Tibb's Meadow SP11. 192 D8
Tiberius Rd 24 SP10. . 193 E2
TIDCOMBE . . . . . . . . . 184 C5
Tidcombe (Long
Barrow) * SN8 . . . . 184 D4
TIDDLEYWINK . . . . . . .69 A4
Tidford Cts GL7. . . . . . . .2 C3
Tidling Cnr SN16 . . . . .16 C5
TIDPIT. . . . . . . . . . . . . 209 C6
TIDWORTH . . . . . . . . . 216 E7
Tidworth Cl 3 SN1. . . .49 F4
Tidworth Coll SP9 . . . 216 D6
Tidworth Leisure Ctr
SP9. . . . . . . . . . . . . . 216 D6
Tidworth Oval * SP9. 216 C5
Tidworth Rd
Bulford SP4. . . . . . . . . 199 A7
Collingbourne Ducis
SN8 . . . . . . . . . . . . 191 D7
Idmiston SP4. . . . . . . 133 E8
Ludgershall SP11. . . . 191 F5
Milston SP4 . . . . . . . . 191 B1
Porton SP4. . . . . . . . . 133 E7
Tiffany Cl SN25 . . . . . . 20 D1
Tile Hill BA10 . . . . . . . 122 A5
Till Cl 15 SP11. . . . . . 193 F2
Tilley's La SN3. . . . . . . .36 A2
TILSHEAD . . . . . . . . . . 188 B3
Tilshead Wlk SN2. . . . .35 B5
Timandra Cl 1 SN25. . .35 A4
Timberley La SP5 . . . . 211 E2
Timbers Hill BA12 . . . 114 D5
Timber St SN15. . . . . . .78 E2
Timbrells Cl GL7. . . . . . .6 F7

Timbrells Pl SN14. . . . .78 C6
Timbrell St BA14. . . . . 101 D1
Timbrells The GL7. . . . . .5 C8
Timoney Pl 3 SN1. . . . 50 B1
Timor Rd BA13 . . . . . . 108 E2
Tinhead Hill BA12. . . . 186 D6
Tinhead Rd BA13 . . . . 186 C8
Tinings The SN15 . . . . .79 A8
Tinkers Field SN4. . . . .47 D2
Tinkers Mead SN9 . . . 215 D4
Tinney Cl SP5 . . . . . . . 211 C6
Tin Pit SN8 . . . . . . . . . 213 E4
Tintagel Cl
18 Andover SP10. . . . 193 E2
Swindon SN5 . . . . . . . 49 B4
Tintern Rd SN10 . . . . 214 B1
Tippett Ave 3 SN25 . . .34 E7
TISBURY . . . . . . . . . . . 203 D8
Tisbury Cl 1 SN2. . . . .35 C6
Tisbury & District Sports
Ctr SP3 . . . . . . . . . . 203 D8
Tisbury Rd SP3. . . . . . 204 D8
Tisbury Row SP3 . . . . 203 F8
Tisbury Sta SP3. . . . . 203 D8
Tismeads Cres SN1 . . . 50 C2
Titchfield Cl 5 SN5. . . 48 F5
Tithe Barn Cres SN1 . . 49 F3
Tittymouse La SP11. . 192 F1
Tiverton Rd SN2 . . . . . .35 C1
Tobruk Cl 6 SP11. . . . 193 E4
Tobruk Rd SP11. . . . . 191 F3
Tobys Ct 25 SP7 . . . . 202 C2
TOCKENHAM. . . . . . . . .60 E3
Tockenham Cnr SN4. . 60 D6
Tockenham Way SN2. .35 B6
TOCKENHAM WICK. . . 60 D7
Toghill Cres SN3. . . . . .76 B1
Tokes La SP7. . . . . . . . 202 E6
Tollard Cl SN3. . . . . . . .51 C6
TOLLARD FARNHAM. 207 B2
TOLLARD ROYAL . . . . 207 B4
Toll Down Way SN14. . . 53 A4
Tollgate Cl SP4 . . . . . 217 A5
Tollgate Pk SP7 . . . . . 202 C3
Tollgate Rd
Andover SP10. . . . . . 193 C1
Salisbury SP1. . . . . . . 152 B8
Tombs Rd SP4 . . . . . . 198 A6
Tomlinson Cl GL7. . . . . .1 E7
TOOTHILL. . . . . . . . . . . .49 C4
Topaz Cl SN25. . . . . . . .34 F8
Topcliffe Rd BA14 . . . 106 B8
Top Farm GL7 . . . . . . . .4 F7
Top La
Atworth/Whitley SN12 . .85 C1
Stourton with Gasper
BA12 . . . . . . . . . . . 137 D7
Toppers Cl SN25. . . . . .35 A3
Top Rd
Ebbesbourne Wake
SP5. . . . . . . . . . . . . 204 C3
Kempsford GL7 . . . . . . 10 C7
Top St SN15 . . . . . . . . .44 A2
Tor House 3 BA13. . . 109 A3
Tormarton Rd
Acton Turville GL9 . . . . 52 E6
Marshfield SN14 . . . . . 66 A2
Tornado Cl SN11. . . . . .81 D3
Tornio Cl SN10 . . . . . . 214 D4
Toronto Rd SP4 . . . . . 217 F8
Torr Cl SN14. . . . . . . . .70 B2
Torridge Cl SN25 . . . . .34 F4
Torrington Ct SN3 . . . .51 A5
Torun Way SN25. . . . . . 34 D6
Tottenham Ho * SN8. 175 D4
Tottenham Pk * SN8. . 175 C4
Totterdown Cl 3 SN3. .51 E7
Totterdown La GL7 . . . .1 F3
Totts La SN14. . . . . . . .75 D7
Totworth Rd SN25 . . . .34 C8
Toucan St BA14. . . . . . 105 E6
Touchorne La SP3. . . . 141 A4
Tournament Rd SP2 . . 145 C3
Tout Hill SP7 . . . . . . . 202 B2
Tovey Cl 3 SP10 . . . . 193 F1
Tovey Rd SN2 . . . . . . . .35 B2
Tow Barrow (Long
Barrow) * SN8 . . . . 184 B4
Towcester Cl SN14. . . .77 F5
Towcester Pl 1 SN14. .77 F5
Towcester Rd
North Bradley BA14. . . 105 E4
Swindon SN3 . . . . . . . 51 C8
Towell Rd 5 SP4 . . . . 198 A6
Tower Cl
Andover SP10. . . . . . 193 C2
Trowbridge BA14. . . . 105 A7
Tower Hill
Dilton Marsh BA13. . . . 112 D7
Iwerne Minster DT11 . 206 A1
Tower Mews SP1. . . . . 146 B2
Tower Rd
Melksham SN12. . . . . .94 C5
Stourton with Gasper
BA10 . . . . . . . . . . . 122 F3
Swindon SN5 . . . . . . . 34 B2
Tower View SN10. . . . . 96 D2
Town Bridge BA14. . . 101 C1
Town Bridge Bradford-
on-Avon * BA15. . . 100 C6
Town Cl SN14 . . . . . . . .69 F8
Town Farm Pl SP5. . . . 208 B4
Townfield 10 SN8. . . . 170 B2
Town Gdns * SN1. . . . .50 C4

Town Mill SN8. . . . . . . 213 D2
Town Path SP2 . . . . . . 151 E7
TOWNSEND
  Poulshot. . . . . . . . . . 179 A6
  Urchfont. . . . . . . . . . 180 C3
Townsend
  Allington SN10. . . . . . 172 F1
  Chitterne BA12 . . . . . 195 D7
  Great Cheverell SN10 . 187 C8
  Pitton & Farley SP5. . . 148 C4
Town's End BA12. . . . . 138 F5
Townsend Cl BA12. . . . 138 F5
Townsend La
  Martin SP5. . . . . . . . 208 F6
  Martin SP6. . . . . . . . 209 A6
Townsend Pl SN14. . . . 77 F8
Townsend Rd SN4 . . . . 37 F5
Towpath Rd BA14. . . . 101 D4
Toyd Down SP6. . . . . . 209 C6
Toynbee Ave
  Swindon SN25 . . . . . . 20 D1
  Swindon SN25. . . . . . 34 C8
Tozer Way SP5 . . . . . . 153 F1
Tracy Cl SN25. . . . . . . . 35 A6
Trafalgar Cl **11** SN13 . . 76 C1
Trafalgar Ho ★ SP5 . 159 D4
Trafalgar Sch at Downton
  The SP5. . . . . . . . . . 211 A8
Trafalgar Sq SP4 . . . . 133 B2
Trajan Rd SN3. . . . . . . . 36 C1
Tramways SN13. . . . . . .84 F8
Transfer Bridges Ind Est
  SN1. . . . . . . . . . . . . . 50 D8
Travellers Rest SN13. . 76 C1
Travers Cl SN4 . . . . . . . 81 D3
Trecastle Rd **11** SN1 . . 50 A2
Tree Courts Rd **3**
  SN25. . . . . . . . . . . . . .35 B2
Treforest Cl **11** SN25. .34 C7
Tregantle Wlk SN3. . . 51 C6
Tregoze Prim Sch
  SN5. . . . . . . . . . . . . . 49 A6
Tregoze Way SN5. . . . 48 F6
Trellis St SN25. . . . . . . 20 C1
Trenchard Ave
  Box SN13 . . . . . . . . . 84 A8
  Calne Without SN11. . .81 F1
  **4** Corsham SN13 . . . 76 B1
  Winterbourne SN4 . . . 33 A1
Trenchard Cl **5** SN14. .78 A6
Trenchard Rd
  Lyneham SN15. . . . . . 60 A1
  Stanton Fitzwarren SN6 22 B2
Trent Cres SN4 . . . . . . .94 A6
Trentham Cl SN3 . . . . . 51 A4
Trent Rd SN25. . . . . . . 35 A4
Trevello Rd SN1. . . . . . 50 B2
Trevithick Cl **5**
  BA11. . . . . . . . . . . . 110 C6
Triangle The SP5. . . . 161 D4
Trigg Cres SP4 . . . . . . 132 B1
Trimm's Dro SP6 . . . . 211 A4
Trimnells SN14 . . . . . . 75 B3
Trinity Cl SN3. . . . . . . . 51 A3
Trinity Pk SN11. . . . . . .81 C1
Trinity Rd
  **14** Shaftesbury SP7. .202 D1
  Shrewton SP3 . . . . . . 196 F7
Trinity Rise SP11 . . . . 193 A2
Trinity St SP3. . . . . . . . 132 B8
Trinity VA CE Prim Sch
  SN10. . . . . . . . . . . . 214 C5
Trinity View Rd SP9. . 216 C7
Trollope's Hill BA2. . . .90 A1
Tropenell Cl **2** SN13. .76 E1
Trout La SN13. . . . . . . .84 B7
TROWBRIDGE . . . . . . 101 E3
Trowbridge Cl SN2 . . 35 D4
Trowbridge Com Hospl
  BA14. . . . . . . . . . . . 101 D2
Trowbridge Lodge Pk
  BA14. . . . . . . . . . . . 105 F8
Trowbridge Mus ★
  BA14. . . . . . . . . . . . 105 D8
Trowbridge Rd
  Bradford-on-Avon
    BA15 . . . . . . . . . . 100 E5
  Bratton BA13. . . . . . 186 A8
  Farleigh Hungerford
    BA2. . . . . . . . . . . 103 D7
  Seend SN12. . . . . . . 178 C7
  Trowbridge BA14. . . . 102 A2
  Westbury BA13. . . . . 109 B5
Trowbridge Sports Ctr
  BA14. . . . . . . . . . . . 105 B6
Trowbridge Sta
  BA14. . . . . . . . . . . . 105 C8
Trow La
  Brinkworth SN15 . . . . .59 F8
  Maiden Bradley with
    Yarnfield BA12. . . . 118 E4
Trowle BA14. . . . . . . . 101 A2
TROWLE COMMON . . 100 F2
Truman Cl SN3 . . . . . . 51 C4
Truro Wlk SN14. . . . . . .77 F6
Truscott Ave SN25. . . .34 E8
Trusloe Cotts SN8 . . . 173 B8
Tryhorn Dr SP1. . . . . . 146 C5
Tryon Cl SN3 . . . . . . . . 51 D2
Tubbs Farm Cl **6**
  RG17. . . . . . . . . . . . 165 A1
Tucker Cl **6** SP4 . . . . 217 C2
Tuckers La SN4. . . . . . 163 D6
TUCKINGMILL. . . . . . 203 D8
TUCKING MILL . . . . . . 98 D8

Tucking Mill Cotts
  BA2. . . . . . . . . . . . . . 98 D8
Tucking Mill La BA2 . .98 C7
Tuckwell Rd GL7. . . . . . .10 E6
Tudor Cl SN15. . . . . . . .79 A4
Tudor Dr BA14. . . . . . 101 E4
Tudor Wlk SN3. . . . . . 50 F6
Tugela Rd SN15. . . . . . .70 E1
Tuggy's La BA2. . . . . . .98 E1
Tulip Tree Cl SN2. . . . 35 C2
Tulse Hill
  Zeale BA12. . . . . . . . 138 A4
  Zennor BA12. . . . . . . 137 F3
Tumlins SN10 . . . . . . . 180 F8
Tunball La SN8. . . . . . 184 F4
Tuners La SN16. . . . . . .14 E6
Tunnel Hill SP5. . . . . . 153 C2
Tunnicliffe Cl SN3 . . . 50 E2
Tupman Rd SN13. . . . . .76 E2
Turf Ho La SN11. . . . . . 72 D1
Turin Cl **17** SP10. . . . 193 E2
TURLEIGH . . . . . . . . . .99 F6
Turleigh Hill BA15 . . . .99 F6
Turl St SN1. . . . . . . . . . 50 C6
Turnball La SN4 . . . . . 65 D4
Turnberry Cl SN15. . . .78 F7
Turner Cl **2** SP1. . . . 151 E7
Turner Ct SP10. . . . . . 193 D1
Turner St SN1. . . . . . . 50 A5
Turnham Gn SN5. . . . . .49 A4
Turnpike Cl **4** SN8. . . 170 A6
Turnpike Ct BA14. . . . 102 F5
Turnpike Ct **5** BA12. . 117 A7
Turnpike Rd
  Blunsdon St Andrew
    SN26 . . . . . . . . . . 35 C8
  Broad Blunsdon SN26 . 21 B1
  Highworth SN6. . . . . . 23 A6
Turnpike The
  Chippenham SN15 . . . 79 B5
  East Knoyle SP3. . . . . 202 D8
Turnstile Wlk **3**
  BA14. . . . . . . . . . . . 105 C7
Turntable Pl BA13 . . . 108 F5
Turpin Way SN14 . . . . .77 F7
Tuscan Rd SN25 . . . . . 34 D7
Tutton Hill
  Colerne SN14. . . . . . . 75 B3
  Colerne SN14. . . . . . . 75 C1
  Ditteridge SN13. . . . . 83 C8
Twatley Cotts SN16 . . .27 C4
Tweed St SN25 . . . . . . 34 F4
Twickenham Cl SN3 . .51 B8
Twickenham Way
  SN15. . . . . . . . . . . . . 70 E1
Twineham Gdns SP5. . 153 F2
Twineham Rd SN25. . . 34 C8
Twyford Cl SN3. . . . . . 51 A6
Twynham Cl SP5. . . . . 211 A4
Twynnoy Cl SN16. . . . . .28 A5
Tyburn Cl SN5. . . . . . . 49 B5
Tydeman St SN2. . . . . 35 D1
Tye Gdns SN5 . . . . . . . 48 F5
Tylees Ct SN10 . . . . . . 214 B3
Tylers Cl SP2. . . . . . . . 151 D7
Tyndale Gdns SN3 . . . 51 C6
Tyndales Meadow
  SP3. . . . . . . . . . . . . 201 F2
Tyneham Rd SN3 . . . . 51 B6
Tyning Cl **1** BA14 . . . 105 A7
Tyning La **9** BA13 . . . 186 B7
Tyning Pk SN11. . . . . . .81 C1
Tyning Rd
  Bathampton BA2 . . . . 82 A2
  Winsley BA15. . . . . . . 99 E7
Tynings La BA1. . . . . . .82 A7
Tynings The
  Biddestone SN14. . . . 76 D7
  Westbury BA13 . . . . . 108 F2
Tynings Way BA15 . . . 99 F3
Tyning The BA2. . . . . . .99 B4
Tyrone Ave SP4. . . . . . 198 E2
Tythe Cl **17** SP11. . . . 193 F2
TYTHERINGTON . . . . 194 B4
Tytherington Rd
  Corton BA12. . . . . . . 194 C3
  Heytesbury BA12. . . . 194 C5
Tytherley Rd SP5. . . . 149 E6
Tytherly La BA2. . . . . . .98 E1
TYTHERTON LUCAS . . 71 D1

**U**

Uddens Rd SP5. . . . . . 207 C4
UFFCOTT . . . . . . . . . . 167 E8
Uffington Pl BA13. . . . 109 A5
UGFORD. . . . . . . . . . . 144 A3
Ugford SP2. . . . . . . . . 144 A3
Ullswater Cl SN3 . . . . 51 E3
Ulysses Rd **2** SN25. . .34 B7
Umbers Hill **2** SP7 . . 202 B1
Uncles La BA15. . . . . . 100 E6
Underacre Cl **1**
  BA14. . . . . . . . . . . . 106 B8
Underdown Cl **12**
  SN4. . . . . . . . . . . . . 163 A6
UNDERHILL . . . . . . . . 140 F2
Underhill
  East Knoyle SP3. . . . . 141 A2
  Mere BA12. . . . . . . . 138 F5
  Pen Selwood BA9 . . . 137 B2
Underwood Dr SP4 . . 217 D2
Union Rd
  Chippenham SN15 . . . 78 D8
  Tisbury SP3 . . . . . . . 203 E7
Union Row SN1. . . . . . 50 D4

Union St
  Melksham SN12. . . . . 94 A4
  Ramsbury SN8 . . . . . 170 B2
  Swindon SN1 . . . . . . . 50 C5
  Trowbridge BA14. . . . 101 D1
Unity St SN14. . . . . . . .78 C7
UPAVON . . . . . . . . . . . 181 F2
Upavon Airfield SN9 . 182 B1
Upavon Ct SN2 . . . . . . 35 C5
Upcott SN6. . . . . . . . . . .8 C4
Upcott Ct SN6. . . . . . . 8 D4
Upfield SN3 . . . . . . . . . 51 D3
Upham Rd SN3 . . . . . . 50 E5
Upham Village ★
  SN8. . . . . . . . . . . . . 169 C8
Upland Rise BA13. . . . 109 B2
Uplands BA13. . . . . . . 187 B7
Uplands Cl BA2. . . . . . .98 F7
Uplands Sch SN25 . . . 34 D8
Uplands The BA12. . . 117 C7
Upnor Cl SP11. . . . . . . 191 F4
Upper Backway SP3. . 196 F7
Upper Broad St BA14 101 C1
UPPER BURGATE . . . . 210 E3
UPPER CASTLE
  COMBE. . . . . . . . . . . .68 B8
UPPER
  CHICKSGROVE . . . . 201 A1
Upper Church Fields
  SN8. . . . . . . . . . . . . 213 E1
UPPER CHUTE . . . . . . 192 D8
Upper Cocklebury La
  SN14. . . . . . . . . . . . .78 F8
Upper Dro SP10 . . . . . 193 C1
Upper Eddington
  RG17. . . . . . . . . . . . 177 C8
UPPER ENHAM . . . . . 193 F4
Upper Folly SP2 . . . . . 144 B1
Upper Garston La **8**
  BA13. . . . . . . . . . . . 186 B7
UPPER GREEN . . . . . . 177 E2
UPPER INGLESHAM . . .12 B5
Upper Isbury SN8 . . . 213 E2
Upper La SN13. . . . . . . 84 D7
UPPER LAMBOURN. . . 164 F3
Upper Lambourn Rd
  RG17. . . . . . . . . . . . 165 A2
Upper Ley SN13. . . . . . 83 D5
Upper Marsh La
  BA12. . . . . . . . . . . . 117 A5
Upper Marsh Rd
  BA12. . . . . . . . . . . . 117 A6
Upper Mill SN25. . . . . .34 A2
UPPER MINETY . . . . . 16 D3
Upper Mount Pleasant
  BA2. . . . . . . . . . . . . . 99 A4
Upper Noremarsh SN4 47 F1
Upper North Rd SP5 . . 207 C5
Upper Ox Hill SN15. . . 34 A3
Upper Pavenhill SN5. . .32 F4
UPPER PICKWICK . . . . 76 C3
Upper Potley SN13. . . .84 E7
Upper Regents Pk
  BA15. . . . . . . . . . . . 100 D6
UPPER SEAGRY . . . . . 57 D6
Upper St SP2. . . . . . . . 151 D7
UPPER STRATTON. . . .35 E4
UPPER STREET. . . . . . 210 D5
UPPER STUDLEY . . . . 105 A5
Upper Studley BA14 . 105 A6
UPPER TOWN . . . . . . . 58 D4
UPPER UP . . . . . . . . . . 6 E6
UPPER UPHAM. . . . . . 169 C8
Upper Waterhay Nature
  Reserve ★ SN6 . . . . 18 D7
Upper Water St SP4 139 B5
Upper Westwood Rd
  Westwood BA15. . . . . .99 F4
  Westwood BA15. . . . 100 A3
UPPER WOODFORD . 131 C7
UPPER WRAXALL. . . . .66 E2
Uppington La SP3 . . . 129 E8
Up St BA12 . . . . . . . . . 194 E4
UPTON
  East Knoyle . . . . . . . 141 A5
  Vernhams Dean . . . . 185 D2
Upton Cl
  Swindon SN25 . . . . . . .34 F5
  **5** Warminster BA12. . 116 E7
Upton Folly BA12 . . . . 194 E4
Upton Great Barrow ★
  BA12. . . . . . . . . . . . 194 F5
UPTON LOVELL. . . . . . 194 E3
Upton Rd
  Linkenholt SP11. . . . . 185 E4
  Upton SP11 . . . . . . . 185 D2
  Upton SP11 . . . . . . . 185 E1
UPTON
  SCUDAMORE . . . . . 112 E5
URCHFONT . . . . . . . . . 180 C4
Urchfont CE Prim Sch
  SN10. . . . . . . . . . . . 180 B4
Urchfont Way SN2. . . .35 C4
Ursa Way **16** SN25 . . 34 B7
Utah Cl SN1 . . . . . . . . . 49 F4
Utah Ct SN6 . . . . . . . . . 23 A4
UTC Swindon SN1. . . . 50 A6
Utterson View SN15 . .78 C7
Uxbridge Rd SN5 . . . . 49 A3

**V**

Vaggs Hill BA2 . . . . . . 103 F4
Vale Leaze SN15. . . . . .44 C5
Valens Terr SN13 . . . . .83 C6
Valentia Ct **19** SN12. . 178 B8
Vale Rd SP5. . . . . . . . . 211 C7

Vale View SN4. . . . . . . 47 D1
Vale View Rd SP2. . . . 130 B2
Valiant Cl SN12 . . . . . 178 B8
Valletta Gdns SN14 . . .56 B5
Valley Cl SP5. . . . . . . . 211 C7
Valley Rd SN13 . . . . . . .76 E1
Valleyside SN1. . . . . . . .50 A4
Valley The SP2 . . . . . . 145 C5
Valley View SN11. . . . . .81 A2
Valley Vw **18** SN8 . . . 170 A6
Valley Way SN14. . . . . .75 C6
Vanbrugh Gate SN1. . .50 E5
Vancouver Dr **9** SP4 217 F8
Van Diemen's Cl SN8 213 E2
Van Erp Cl SN25 . . . . . .20 B1
Vanessa Ave SP1 . . . . 146 D1
Vasterne. . . . . . . . . . . .60 F8
Vasterne Cl SN5 . . . . . 33 B5
Vasterne Hill SN5. . . . 33 B5
Vastern Wharf SN4 . . .61 A7
Vaughan Williams Way
  SN25. . . . . . . . . . . . . 34 D7
Vega Cl **10** SN25 . . . . 34 B7
Velley Hill SN13 . . . . . 85 C5
Venice Cl **30** SP11 . . . 193 D1
Venn The **11** SP7. . . . 202 C2
Ventnor Cl SN2. . . . . . 34 E4
Ventry Cl **3** SP1. . . . . 146 B2
Ventry The **4** SP1 . . . 146 B2
Verden Way **19** SP10 . 193 D2
Verney Cl SN3. . . . . . . .51 D6
Vernham Bank SP11. . 185 B3
VERNHAM DEAN . . . . 185 C3
Vernham Dean Gullum's
  Prim Sch SP11 . . . . 185 C3
VERNHAM ROW . . . . . 185 B4
Vernham Row La
  SN8. . . . . . . . . . . . . 185 A4
Vernham St SP11 . . . . 185 B4
VERNHAM STREET . . . 185 B4
Vernon Cl **2** SP4 . . . . 217 E3
Verona Rd SP1 . . . . . . 145 F4
Verulam Cl SN3. . . . . . 51 D8
Verwood Cl SN3. . . . . .51 B4
Vespasian Cl SN3 . . . . 51 C8
Vespasian Rd
  **19** Andover SP10. . . 193 E2
  Forest Hill SN8. . . . . . 175 A7
Vesta Cl SN26 . . . . . . . .21 A1
Vetch Way **27** SP11 . . 193 F2
Vicarage Cl
  Calne SN11 . . . . . . . . .81 B3
  Marlborough SN8. . . . 213 B3
Vicarage Cotts SN15 . .57 F6
Vicarage Gdns
  Dilton Marsh BA13. . . 112 B8
  Malmesbury SN16 . . . 28 B2
  **3** Netheravon SP4. . . 190 A3
Vicarage La
  Charlton SN16 . . . . . . 29 B7
  Colerne SN14. . . . . . . 75 C3
  Easterton SN10 . . . . . 179 F2
  Hankerton SN16 . . . . 15 B1
  Highworth SN6. . . . . . 23 A6
  Steeple Ashton BA14. 178 A3
  Upavon SN9 . . . . . . . 181 F2
Vicarage Mews BA12 116 F7
Vicarage Pk **1** SP5 . . 211 C7
Vicarage Rd
  Redlynch SP5. . . . . . . 211 E7
  Swindon SN2 . . . . . . . 34 F1
  Tisbury SP3 . . . . . . . 203 E8
Vicarage St BA12. . . . 116 F7
Vice La SO51 . . . . . . . 212 E2
Victoria Cl
  Lyneham SN11. . . . . . 73 E8
  Wilton SP2. . . . . . . . 144 C4
Victoria Cross Rd
  SN4. . . . . . . . . . . . . .63 F7
Victoria Ct SP1 . . . . . . 146 A3
Victoria Dr
  **10** Bulford SP4 . . . . 217 F8
  Lyneham SN15. . . . . . 60 B1
Victoria Gdns
  **14** Sandleheath SP6 . 210 C1
  Trowbridge BA14. . . . 101 E2
Victoria Mws BA12. . . 116 E6
Victoria Pk SN10. . . . . 187 B8
Victoria Rd
  Devizes SN10. . . . . . 214 B4
  Frome BA11. . . . . . . 110 A4
  Salisbury SP1. . . . . . 146 A2
  Sandleheath SP6 . . . 210 C1
  Swindon SN1 . . . . . . . 50 C5
  Trowbridge BA14. . . . 101 E3
  Warminster BA12 . . . 116 C6
  Wilton SP2. . . . . . . . 144 C3
Victoria St **21** SP7 . . 202 C2
Victoria Terr SN11. . . . .81 B3
Victory Rd BA13 . . . . . 108 C6
Viking Cl SN25. . . . . . . .34 F7
Viking Way
  Andover SP10 . . . . . . 193 E2
  Salisbury SP2. . . . . . 152 B5
Vilett St SN1. . . . . . . . .50 B6
Village Mus the Castle
  Combe ★ SN14 . . . . .68 A7
Village St
  Alton SN8. . . . . . . . . 173 D1
  Upton SP11 . . . . . . . 185 D2
Villiers Cl
  Chippenham SN15 . . . .78 F7
  Lydiard Tregoze SN5. . .48 F7
Vimoutiers Ct **18**
  SP6. . . . . . . . . . . . . 210 D1
Vimy Cres
  Bulford SP4 . . . . . . . 217 F8

Vimy Cres continued
  **8** Durrington/Bulford
    SP4. . . . . . . . . . . . 198 E6
Vincent Cl SN12 . . . . . .94 C4
Vincients Rd SN14. . . .69 F1
Vincients Wood Nature
  Reserve ★ SN14 . . . .77 F7
Viner's La SN14. . . . . . .77 F7
Viner's Lo **13** SP5 . . . . .53 B5
Vinescroft **4** BA14 . . 101 D5
Vines Cl **3** SN12. . . . . 94 D5
Virginia Cl **11** SP4 . . 217 E3
Virginia Dr BA12. . . . . 116 E7
Virginia Way SP4 . . . . 132 C1
Viscount Way SN3. . . . 36 C6
Vista Ct **4** BA13 . . . . 109 A3
Vistula Cres **2** SN25. .34 E6
Vize La SN4 . . . . . . . . 167 B7
Vockins Cl SP9. . . . . . 216 C8
Volpe Cl SN5. . . . . . . . 48 F4
Volta Rd SN1. . . . . . . . 50 C6
Vorda Rd SN6 . . . . . . . 23 A7
Vowley View SN4. . . . 47 F1
Voyager Dr SN25 . . . . 34 B7

**W**

Wade Hill SN6. . . . . . . .22 F5
Wade Mews SN5. . . . . 70 E1
Wade Rd **3** SN25. . . . 34 D7
Wadleys Drove BH21. 209 B1
WADSWICK . . . . . . . . .84 B4
Wadswick La SN13. . . .84 B3
Wadworth Rd SN10. . 214 C4
Waggoner Cl SN25. . . . 35 B6
Wagtail Cl SN3 . . . . . . 51 C8
Waiblingen Way
  SN10. . . . . . . . . . . . 214 A4
Wain-a-Long Rd
  SP1. . . . . . . . . . . . . 146 C1
Wains Way SP4 . . . . . 190 A3
Wainwright Cl **4** SN3. 51 D4
Wainwright Dr **5**
  BA11. . . . . . . . . . . . 110 C7
Wainwright Mews
  SN4. . . . . . . . . . . . . .64 B4
Waite Meads Cl SN5 . .33 C4
Wakefield Cl
  Kempsford GL7 . . . . . 10 E6
  Swindon SN5 . . . . . . . 49 A4
Walbury Hill (Fort) ★
  RG17. . . . . . . . . . . . 185 F8
WALCOT EAST . . . . . . .50 F6
Walcot Rd SN3 . . . . . . 50 E5
WALCOT WEST. . . . . . 50 E5
Walden Lodge Cl
  SN10. . . . . . . . . . . . 214 B2
Waldron Cl **3** SN3. . . .51 C4
Waleran Cl SP5. . . . . . 153 E2
Walker Rd BA11. . . . . 110 A4
Walker's La **3** RG17 . 165 A2
Walkinshaw Rd **5**
  SN2. . . . . . . . . . . . . .34 E2
Wallbridge Ave **2**
  BA11. . . . . . . . . . . . 110 A4
Wallbridge Gdns **1**
  BA11. . . . . . . . . . . . 110 A4
Wallbridge Mills
  BA11. . . . . . . . . . . . 110 B4
Waller Rd SN10. . . . . . 214 E7
Wallingford Cl SN5 . . .49 C3
Wallingtons Rd RG17 177 F4
Wallis Dr SN25 . . . . . . .35 A8
Wallsworth Rd **4** SN3 .51 A4
Walmesley Chase
  **1** Trowbridge BA14. . 101 F1
  Trowbridge BA14. . . . 102 A1
Walnut Cl
  Harnham SP2. . . . . . 151 D7
  **3** Netheravon SP4. . . 190 A4
  Pewsey SN9. . . . . . . 215 D5
  Rowde SN10 . . . . . . . 96 D1
  Sutton Veny BA12 . . . 121 F8
Walnut Dr SN14 . . . . . .74 F6
Walnut Gr BA14 . . . . . 105 B6
Walnut Rd BA12 . . . . . 139 B4
Walnut Tree Cl SN3. . . 36 B2
Walnut Tree Gdns
  SN5. . . . . . . . . . . . . . 48 D8
Walnut Trees Hill
  SN6. . . . . . . . . . . . . 164 A8
Walnut Wlk **1** BA11 . 110 B7
Walronds Cl SN8 . . . . 170 C8
Walsingham Rd SN3. . 50 F6
Walter Cl SN5. . . . . . . .49 A6
Walter Sutton Cl SN11 .80 F3
Walter Way **2** SP4 . . 132 C1
Walton Cl **5** SN1. . . . .50 F4
Walwayne Ct Prim Sch
  BA14. . . . . . . . . . . . 105 B8
Walwayne Ct Sch
  BA14. . . . . . . . . . . . 101 B1
Walwayne Field SN2. . .36 A5
Walworth Rd SP10. . . 193 F1
WANBOROUGH. . . . . 163 A5
Wanborough Prim Sch
  SN4. . . . . . . . . . . . . 163 A6
Wanborough Rd
  Swindon SN3 . . . . . . 36 C1
  Wanborough SN4. . . .51 F6
Wansdyke ★ SN11. . . 172 C5
Wansdyke Com Sch
  SN10. . . . . . . . . . . . 214 B1
Wansdyke Rd SN8 . . . 176 B4
Wantage Rd RG17 . . . 165 B2
Waram Ct RG17. . . . . 177 C8

Warbeck Gate **11** SN5. .48 F5
Warbler Cl **1** BA14 . . 105 B8
Warburton Cl BA14 . . 105 A6
Ward Cl SN5. . . . . . . . . 33 A3
Wardley Cl SN3. . . . . . .51 A4
WARDOUR . . . . . . . . . 203 D6
Wardour Cl SN3. . . . . . 50 E3
Wardour Pl **4** SN12 . .94 A2
Wardour RC Prim Sch
  SP3. . . . . . . . . . . . . 203 C6
Wardour Rd **3** SN14. . .78 A6
Wardrobe Mus ★
  SP1. . . . . . . . . . . . . 152 A8
Wareham Cl SN5 . . . . .49 B5
WARLEIGH. . . . . . . . . . 90 D5
Warleigh Dr BA1. . . . . .82 A3
Warleigh La BA1. . . . . .82 B1
War Meml Ave **13**
  RG17. . . . . . . . . . . . 177 B6
Warmer's Inn La **16** 27 D8
WARMINSTER. . . . . . . 116 E7
Warminster Ave **2**
  SN2. . . . . . . . . . . . . . 35 C5
Warminster Bypass
  Norton Bavant BA12 . 194 A5
  Sutton Veny BA12 . . . 117 F3
Upton Scudamore
  BA12. . . . . . . . . . . . 112 E2
  BA12. . . . . . . . . . . . 116 D5
Warminster Coll
  BA12. . . . . . . . . . . . 117 A7
Warminster Com Hospl
  BA12. . . . . . . . . . . . 117 A7
WARMINSTER
  COMMON. . . . . . . . 116 E5
Warminster La
  Upton Scudamore
    BA12. . . . . . . . . . . 112 F2
  Warminster BA12 . . . 113 A2
Warminster La N
  BA12. . . . . . . . . . . . 112 F3
Warminster Mus ★
  BA12. . . . . . . . . . . . 117 B7
Warminster Old Rd
  Upton Scudamore
    BA12. . . . . . . . . . . 112 A4
  Upton Scudamore
    BA12. . . . . . . . . . . 112 F5
  Upton Scudamore
    BA12. . . . . . . . . . . 113 A3
Warminster Rd
  Claverton BA2 . . . . . . 90 B4
  Edington BA2 . . . . . . 186 E3
  Frome BA11. . . . . . . 110 B4
  Heytesbury BA12. . . . 187 B3
  Hinton Charterhouse
    BA2. . . . . . . . . . . . .98 C5
  Hinton Charterhouse
    BA2. . . . . . . . . . . . .99 A2
  Norton Bavant BA12 . 194 A6
  South Newton SP2. . . 130 B1
  Stapleford SP3. . . . . . 129 C6
  Upton Scudamore
    BA12. . . . . . . . . . . 112 F3
  Westbury BA13. . . . . 108 F5
  Wilton SP2. . . . . . . . 144 D5
Warminster Sambourne
  CE Prim Sch BA12 . . 116 F6
Warminster Sch
  BA12. . . . . . . . . . . . 116 F7
Warminster Sports Ctr
  BA12. . . . . . . . . . . . 117 D6
Warminster Sta
  BA12. . . . . . . . . . . . 117 B7
Warneage Gn **2**
  SN4. . . . . . . . . . . . . 163 A5
Warneford Cl **4** SN5 . 49 C4
Warneford Cres **4**
  SP4. . . . . . . . . . . . . 132 B2
Warner Cl **2** SN3. . . . 36 B3
Warren Bsns Pk GL8 . .24 F5
Warren Cres SN11. . . . .81 C4
Warrener Cl SN25 . . . . 35 B7
Warren Rd BA14. . . . . 101 D5
Warrens La SP5 . . . . . 159 A4
Warwick Cl
  Chippenham SN14 . . . .77 F5
  Salisbury SP1. . . . . . 145 F3
Warwick Cres SN12. . .94 B3
Warwick Rd SN1. . . . . .50 C5
Washbourne Rd SN4. . .47 B6
Washern Cl SP2 . . . . . 144 C1
Washers Pit ★ DT11.. 206 D3
Washington Rd BA13 108 C6
Washmeres SN14. . . . .75 B2
Washpool
  Lydiard Millicent SN5. .33 F1
  Swindon SN5 . . . . . . .48 F8
Washpool La
  Kemble GL7 . . . . . . . . .5 B7
  Kempsford GL7 . . . . . 10 E8
  Kempsford GL7 . . . . . 11 A7
Wason Rd **5** SP4 . . . 197 E6
Waste Dr GL8. . . . . . . . 25 A8
Wastfield SN13. . . . . . .84 F8
Watercrook Mews **2**
  SN5. . . . . . . . . . . . . . 49 D5
Water Ditchampton
  SP2. . . . . . . . . . . . . 144 C4
Waterdown Cl **2** SN2. .34 C4
Water Field SN5 . . . . . 33 A3
Waterford Beck
  BA14. . . . . . . . . . . . 104 F6
Water Furlongs **2**
  SN6. . . . . . . . . . . . . 175 C8
Watergate La SP4 . . . 217 C2
Watergates SN14. . . . .75 C3
WATERHAY. . . . . . . . . .18 C7

Waterhole Ave **1**
SN13 . . . . . . . . . . . . . .76 C1
Waterhouse La BA2. . . .98 F8
Water La
Collingbourne Ducis
SN8 . . . . . . . . . . . . .184 B1
Enford SN9 . . . . . . . . .190 B6
Horningsham BA12 . . .119 A8
Salisbury SP1 . . . . . . .152 A8
Somerford Keynes GL7 . .6 A3
Water Lily Cl BA14 . . . 101 D4
Waterloo Rd SP1 . . . .152 C7
Watermead SN3 . . . . . .36 C2
Watermeadow La
BA12 . . . . . . . . . . . .195 C1
Water Meadows SN16 .28 A2
Watermint Way SN11 . .80 F4
Waters Bank Rd
Box SN13 . . . . . . . . . .84 B8
**1** Rudloe SN13 . . . . . .84 B8
Waters Edge SN15 . . . .78 E5
Watersmeet Rd SP2 . .152 A6
Waters Rd SP1 . . . . . .146 A4
Water St
Berwick St John SP7 . . 203 E1
Durrington/Bulford
SP4 . . . . . . . . . . . . .217 D8
Mere BA12 . . . . . . . . .139 B5
Upton Lovell BA12 . . . .194 E3
Waters View GL7 . . . . . .6 F6
Waterworks Rd BA14 105 B7
Watery La
Corsham SN15 . . . . . . .85 A3
Donhead St Mary SP7 . 203 A3
Shaftesbury SP7 . . . . .202 C1
Shipton Bellinger SP9 . 216 C1
Sutton Veny BA12 . . . .117 F4
Swindon SN5 . . . . . . . .48 F7
Watling Cl SN2 . . . . . . .49 E6
Watson Rd SP4 . . . . . 197 E7
Watson's Ct **2** SN12 . .94 B4
Watt Cl **4** SP10 . . . . .193 C1
Watt Rd SP2 . . . . . . . .151 D8
Watts La SN14 . . . . . . .41 F1
Watt's Way **22** SN10. .179 F1
Wavell Rd
Salisbury SP2 . . . . . . .152 A6
Swindon SN2 . . . . . . . .35 B2
Tidworth SP9 . . . . . . .216 B8
Warminster BA12 . . . .113 D1
Waverley Cl
**7** Fordingbridge
SP6 . . . . . . . . . . . . .210 D2
Frome BA11 . . . . . . . .110 C6
Waverley Ct
**4** Corsham SN13 . . . . .84 F8
Corsham SN13 . . . . . . .85 A8
Waverley Gdns SN12 . .94 A3
Waverley Rd
Fordingbridge SP6 . . .210 D2
Swindon SN3 . . . . . . . .36 C1
Waylands
Cricklade SN6 . . . . . . .19 E7
Devizes SN10 . . . . . . .214 D3
Wayne Cl SN25 . . . . . . .35 A5
Wayside Cl
Frome BA11 . . . . . . . .110 C6
Kington Langley SN15 . .70 E7
Swindon SN2 . . . . . . . .49 E7
Wayte St **5** SN25 . . . . .34 E3
Weaveland Rd **2**
SP3 . . . . . . . . . . . . .203 E8
Weavern Cl SN14 . . . . .78 A7
Weavern La SN13 . . . . .76 A5
Weavers Cl
Chippenham SN14 . . . .77 F7
**3** Malmesbury SN16 . . 28 A5
Weavers Crofts SN12 . .94 A5
Weavers Dr BA14 . . . .105 D7
Weavers La RG17 . . . .177 E3
Weavers Mead SN10 . 179 C1
Weavers The SN3 . . . . .50 D4
Webb Cl SN15 . . . . . . .78 E5
Webbers Ct BA14 . . . .105 A6
Webbington Rd SN15 . .78 E5
Webb La SN25 . . . . . . .34 D8
Webbs Ct SN15 . . . . . .60 A3
Webb's La SN10 . . . . .179 D8
Webbs Pl SN25 . . . . . . .34 A5
Webbs Way
Burbage SN8 . . . . . . .183 D8
Malmesbury SN16 . . . .28 A5
Webbs Wood SN5 . . . . .34 A2
Wedgewood Cl SN2 . . .50 A7
WEDHAMPTON . . . . . 180 E4
Wedmore Ave SN15 . . .70 C1
Wedmore Cl BA11 . . . .110 C7
Wedmore Dr BA13 . . . .109 A5
Weedon Rd SN3 . . . . . .51 B8
Weeke Cl **1** SP5 . . . . .210 F8
Weir Heyes Ave **7**
SN13 . . . . . . . . . . . . .76 B1
Weir La SN14 . . . . . . . .74 A8
Weirside Ave SN4 . . . . .64 B8
Weir The BA13 . . . . . .186 C8
Welbeck Cl SN14 . . . . .50 F5
Welby Cl SN25 . . . . . . .34 B8
Welcombe Ave SN3 . . .51 A5
Welford Cl SN3 . . . . . . .51 C8
WELL BOTTOM . . . . . 206 E3
Well Cl SN4 . . . . . . . . .65 D4
Weller Rd SN13 . . . . . .76 C1
Welle Sley Cl **18**
SN12 . . . . . . . . . . . . 178 B8

Wellhead BA12 . . . . . .139 A6
Wellhead Dro BA13 . . .109 A1
Wellhead La BA13 . . . .109 A1
Well House Cl SP6 . . . .210 B6
Wellington Academy The
SN11 . . . . . . . . . . . . .191 F5
Wellington Dr
Bishops Cannings
SN10 . . . . . . . . . . . .214 F7
Bower Hill SN12 . . . . . .94 C1
Wellington Lions Prim
Acad SP9 . . . . . . . . .216 D8
Wellington Pl SN14 . . . .55 F8
Wellington Rd
**5** Durrington/Bulford
SP4 . . . . . . . . . . . . .198 F7
South Marston SN3 . . . .36 C6
Wellington Sq SN12 . . .94 C1
Wellington St SN1 . . . . .50 C7
Wellington Way SP2 . .145 D3
Well La
Godshill SP6 . . . . . . . .211 A1
Hawkesbury GL9 . . . . . .38 E5
**4** Shaftesbury SP7 . . .202 B2
Wellow Dr BA11 . . . . .110 C7
Wellow La BA2 . . . . . . .98 D1
Wellow Wood Rd
SO51 . . . . . . . . . . . .212 F8
Wells Cl
Chippenham SN14 . . . .78 A5
Durrington SP4 . . . . . .198 A6
Wellscote Gdns **7**
BA14 . . . . . . . . . . . .105 D6
Wells Rd SP4 . . . . . . .198 A6
Wells St SN1 . . . . . . . . .50 C6
Wellsted Cl SP5 . . . . .149 F4
Welsh Way GL7 . . . . . .1 D8
Welton Rd SN5 . . . . . . .49 D6
Wembley St SN1 . . . . . .49 F8
Wenhill Hts SN11 . . . . .81 B2
Wenhill La SN11 . . . . . .81 A1
Wensleydale Cl SN5 . . .49 B6
Wentworth Cl SN15 . . . .78 F7
Wentworth Pk **1** SN5. .49 A4
Were Cl **3** BA12 . . . . .116 F7
Werg SN8 . . . . . . . . . .175 B8
Wesley Cl BA14 . . . . . .104 E2
Wesley La BA14 . . . . . .104 E2
Wesley Rd BA14 . . . . .105 C7
Wesley St SN1 . . . . . . .50 C4
Wessex Cl
Calne SN11 . . . . . . . . .81 C3
Chippenham SN14 . . . .78 B8
**2** Hungerford RG17 . .177 B7
Melksham SN12 . . . . . .94 B3
Semington BA14 . . . . .102 E5
Wessex Pl **29** RG17 . .177 B7
Wessex Rd
Chippenham SN14 . . . .78 B8
Salisbury SP1 . . . . . . .146 C1
Wilton SP2 . . . . . . . . .144 C1
Wessex Way SN6 . . . . .23 D7
Wessex Wlk BA13 . . . .109 A4
Wessington Ave SN11 .81 C1
Wessington Ct SN11 . . .81 C1
Wessington Pk SN11 . .81 C1
West Allcourt GL7 . . . . .2 C4
WEST AMESBURY . . . .198 A4
WEST ASHTON . . . . . .106 B3
West Ashton CE (VA)
Prim Sch BA14 . . . . .106 B4
West Ashton Rd
BA14 . . . . . . . . . . . .105 E8
Westbourne Cl SP1 . . .152 C8
Westbourne Gdns **6**
BA14 . . . . . . . . . . . .105 B8
Westbourne Mws
BA14 . . . . . . . . . . . .105 B8
Westbourne Rd
Trowbridge BA14 . . . .105 B8
Westbury BA13 . . . . . .109 A3
West Bourton Rd
SP8 . . . . . . . . . . . . .137 D1
WESTBROOK . . . . . . . .95 E8
Westbrook SN15 . . . . . .96 A8
Westbrook Cl
Chippenham SN14 . . . .78 A7
**14** Hungerford RG17 . .177 B7
Westbrook Gn SN15 . . .95 E8
Westbrook Rd
Bromham SN15 . . . . . .88 A1
Swindon SN2 . . . . . . . .35 A1
WESTBURY . . . . . . . .109 B2
Westbury CE Jun Sch
BA13 . . . . . . . . . . . .108 F3
Westbury Ind Est
BA13 . . . . . . . . . . . .108 F3
Westbury Infants' Sch
BA13 . . . . . . . . . . . .108 F3
WESTBURY LEIGH . . . .108 E1
Westbury Leigh
BA13 . . . . . . . . . . . .108 E1
Westbury Leigh CE Prim
Sch BA13 . . . . . . . . .108 E1
Westbury Pk SN4 . . . . .47 D1
Westbury Rd
Bratton BA13 . . . . . . .186 A7
Cheverell Magna
SN10 . . . . . . . . . . . .179 C1
Great Hinton BA14 . . . .102 F3
Heywood BA13 . . . . . .109 A8
North Bradley BA14 . . .105 E3
Semington BA14 . . . . .102 F3
Swindon SN2 . . . . . . . .35 B2
Warminster BA12 . . . .113 A2
Westbury Sta BA13 . . .108 E5
Westbury View SN12 . .94 C4

Westbury Visitor Ctr★
BA13 . . . . . . . . . . . .109 A3
Westbury White Horse★
BA13 . . . . . . . . . . . .109 A1
West Cepenway SN14. .69 F1
West Cepen Way
Chippenham SN14 . . . .70 B3
Chippenham Without
SN14 . . . . . . . . . . . . .77 F5
WEST CHISENBURY . 189 F7
Westcombe La BA12 . .195 E1
Westcott Cl **9** BA11 . .110 C6
Westcott Pl SN1 . . . . . .50 A5
Westcott St SN1 . . . . . .50 A5
Westcroft SN14 . . . . . . .78 A5
Westcroft St BA14 . . . .101 C1
WEST CRUDWELL . . . . 14 D7
WEST DEAN . . . . . . . .155 F3
West Dean Rd SP5 . . .149 F5
West Ditch La
West Ashton BA14 . . . .106 E3
West Ashton BA14 . . . .106 E4
West End
Bishops Cannings
SN10 . . . . . . . . . . . .172 B3
Ebbesbourne Wake
SP5 . . . . . . . . . . . . .204 C3
Foxham SN15 . . . . . . .72 B7
Melksham SN12 . . . . . .94 A3
Westbury BA13 . . . . . .109 A3
West End Cl SN14 . . . . .78 C8
West End Gdns GL7 . . . .1 E7
West End Hill BA11 . . .123 C8
West End La
Bishopstone SN6 . . . .163 E6
Donhead St Andrew
SP7 . . . . . . . . . . . . .203 B3
West End Rd
Salisbury SP2 . . . . . . .145 E2
Swindon SN3 . . . . . . . .36 A1
West Ennox La SN13 . .84 A6
Westerham Wlk SN11 . .81 C2
Westerleigh Cl SN14 . . .78 B6
Western Downland CE
Aided Prim Sch
SP6 . . . . . . . . . . . . .210 A5
Western Downland CE
(VA) Prim Sch (Infant
Site) SP6 . . . . . . . . .209 F2
Westerngate SN5 . . . . .34 B1
Western St SN1 . . . . . .50 C5
Western Way
Melksham SN12 . . . . . .93 F3
Salisbury SP2 . . . . . . .145 B3
Westfield BA15 . . . . . .100 B7
Westfield Chase **13**
SN8 . . . . . . . . . . . . .170 A6
Westfield Cl
**15** Durrington/Bulford
SP4 . . . . . . . . . . . . .198 B7
Laverstock SP1 . . . . . .146 D2
Trowbridge BA14 . . . .105 A6
Westfield Rd BA14 . . . .105 A7
Westfields BA12 . . . . .137 F4
Westfield Way SN2 . . . .34 D4
WEST GRAFTON . . . . .183 E7
WEST GRIMSTEAD . . .154 C2
Westgrove **17** SP6 . . .210 D1
West Hay Gr GL7 . . . . . .4 F7
West Highland Rd
SN25 . . . . . . . . . . . . .34 F7
WEST HILL . . . . . . . . . .85 B1
West Hill
Broad Blunsdon SN26 . .21 B2
Heytesbury BA12 . . . . .194 D7
Melksham Without SN12 85 B1
Westhill Cl SN16 . . . . . .22 F5
West Hill La
Bishopstone SN4 . . . . .163 D5
Donhead St Andrew
SP7 . . . . . . . . . . . . .203 B3
West End Rd

Westminster Meml Hospl
SP7 . . . . . . . . . . . . .202 B1
Westminster Rd
Salisbury SP2 . . . . . . .145 F2
Swindon SN5 . . . . . . . .49 B4
Westmorland Rd SN1 . .50 D5
WESTONBIRT . . . . . . . 25 D8
Westonbirt Arboretum★
GL8 . . . . . . . . . . . . . .25 B8
Westonbirt Rd
Westonbirt GL8 . . . . . .25 E6
Westonbirt GL8 . . . . . .26 A8
Westonbirt Sch GL8. . . .25 E8
Weston Cl SN11 . . . . . .81 D6
Weston Cl **9** SP11 . . .193 E4
Weston La SP5 . . . . . .149 B5
WEST OVERTON . . . . .173 F6
West Par BA12 . . . . . .116 F6
West Pk SP7 . . . . . . . .192 E3
West Pk★ SP6 . . . . . . .210 A3
West Pk Dr SP6 . . . . . .209 F3
West Pk La SP6 . . . . . .209 F3
West Pk Rd SN13 . . . . .76 E1
Westpoint Bsns Pk
SN14 . . . . . . . . . . . . .70 A1
West Portway SP10 . . .193 C1
WESTROP . . . . . . . . . .77 C1
Westrop SN6 . . . . . . . .23 A6
Westrop Prim Sch
SN6 . . . . . . . . . . . . . .22 F6
West St Pl BA12 . . . . .116 E6
Westside SP4 . . . . . . .199 A2
Westside Cl SP4 . . . . .146 C8
West St
Aldbourne SN8 . . . . . .169 F6
Aldbourne SN8 . . . . . .170 A6
Barford St Martin SP3 . 143 A4
Castle Combe SN14 . . .67 F7
Castle Combe SN14 . . .68 A7
**22** Fordingbridge SP6 210 D1
Great Somerford SN15 . .43 F7
Great Wishford SP2 . . .129 F4
Lacock SN15 . . . . . . . .86 D5
**1** Malmesbury SN16 . . 28 A3
Salisbury SP2 . . . . . . .145 F1
Trowbridge BA14 . . . .105 C8
Warminster BA12 . . . .116 E6
Wilton SP2 . . . . . . . . .144 C3
WEST STOWELL . . . . .173 F1
West Swindon Sh Ctr
SN5 . . . . . . . . . . . . . .49 B5
West View SN3 . . . . . . .51 B7
West View Cotts
SP11 . . . . . . . . . . . . .185 D5
West View Cres
SN10 . . . . . . . . . . . .214 A3
Westview Orch BA2. . . .99 B5
West View Rd BA1 . . . .82 A3
West Vw Rd SN8 . . . . .191 A8
West Way GL7 . . . . . . . .2 C5
Westway Cl SN14 . . . . .68 B7
WESTWELLS . . . . . . . .84 C6
Westwells SN13 . . . . . .84 C6
Westwells Rd SN13 . . . .84 B7
West Wick **6** SP5 . . . .210 F8
West Wiltshire Craft Ctr★
BA13 . . . . . . . . . . . .108 D6
West Wilts Trading Est
BA13 . . . . . . . . . . . .108 D7
WEST
WINTERSLOW . . . . .148 F5
West Wlk SP1 . . . . . . .152 A7
WESTWOOD
Salisbury . . . . . . . . . .145 B5
Westwood . . . . . . . . . .99 F2
Westwood Manor
House★ BA15 . . . . . .100 A3
Westwood Rd
Corsham SN13 . . . . . . .84 B8
Farleigh Hungerford
BA2 . . . . . . . . . . . . .103 E8
Salisbury SP2 . . . . . . .145 B4
Swindon SN2 . . . . . . . .35 C6
Trowbridge BA14 . . . .101 A1
Westwood BA15 . . . . . .99 F1
Wingfield BA15 . . . . . .100 D2
Westwoods BA1 . . . . . .82 B3
Westwood St Thomas
Sch SP2 . . . . . . . . . .145 A4
Westwood-with-Iford
Prim Sch BA15 . . . . . .99 F3
WEST YATTON . . . . . . .68 D3
West Yatton Rd SN14 . .68 E5
Wetherby Cl **1** SN14. .78 A5
Wetherby Gdns **24**
SP10 . . . . . . . . . . . .193 D2
Wet La BA12 . . . . . . . .139 D2
Wet Pits La SN8 . . . . .168 E3
WEXCOMBE . . . . . . . .184 B6
Wexland Ave SP4 . . . .189 F3
Wey Cl SN25 . . . . . . . . .35 A4
WEYHILL . . . . . . . . . .192 F1
Weyhill Cl SN3 . . . . . . .51 B5
Weyhill Gdns **7**
SP11 . . . . . . . . . . . . .192 F1
Weyhill Rd SP11 . . . . .193 A1
Weymouth St BA12 . . .117 A6
WHADDON
Alderbury . . . . . . . . . .153 A1
Hilperton . . . . . . . . . .102 C7
Whaddon Bsns Pk
SP5 . . . . . . . . . . . . .153 F1
Whaddon La
Hilperton BA14 . . . . . .102 B5
Trowbridge BA14 . . . .102 A3
Whall Cl SN26 . . . . . . .20 B1
Whalley Cres SN4 . . . .63 F6
Wharf Ct SN12 . . . . . . .93 B7

Wharf Ctr The★
SN10 . . . . . . . . . . . .214 A4
Wharfings The GL7 . . . .10 D6
Wharf La
Kempsford GL7 . . . . . .10 D6
Lechlade GL7 . . . . . . . .2 D3
Wharf Rd SN4 . . . . . . .49 C1
Wharf St SN10 . . . . . . .214 A4
Wharf The SN13 . . . . . .83 D6
Wharf Theatre & Ctr The
SN10 . . . . . . . . . . . .214 A4
Wharncliffe St **3**
SN25 . . . . . . . . . . . . .34 D8
Whatcombe Brow
SP3 . . . . . . . . . . . . .196 D8
Whatley Dr SN9 . . . . . .215 C5
Whatleys Cl SN10 . . . .214 A3
Whatleys Orch SN6 . . .163 E6
Wheat Cl BA14 . . . . . .102 A4
Wheatcroft Way SN1. . .50 E7
Wheatfield Ave SN14 . .78 A4
Wheatlands SN25 . . . . .34 E4
Wheatley Cl SP9 . . . . .216 D8
Wheatsheaf Gdns
SN25 . . . . . . . . . . . . .35 E3
Wheatsheaf La SN16 . .16 A8
Wheatstone Rd SN3 . . .51 E4
Wheeler Ave SN2 . . . . .35 D2
Wheeler Cl SN9 . . . . . .215 B5
Wheeler Pl SN10 . . . . . .96 E1
Wheelers La BA12 . . . .117 B5
Wheeler Way SN16 . . . .28 A5
Wheelwright's Cl
SP5 . . . . . . . . . . . . .208 A4
Whelford Rd GL7 . . . . .10 D7
Whilestone Way SN3 . .36 C1
Whinyates Rd **2** SP4 197 E7
Whistley Rd SN10 . . . .179 C8
Whitbourne Ave SN3. . .50 F5
WHITBOURNE
MOOR . . . . . . . . . . .115 C7
WHITBOURNE
SPRINGS . . . . . . . . .115 E5
Whitbred Cl **2** SN5. . . .49 B7
Whitbred Rd SP2 . . . . .145 C5
Whitby Gr SN2. . . . . . . .34 F1
Whitchers Meadow
SP5 . . . . . . . . . . . . .153 D4
Whitcombe Cl SN15. . . .73 F8
White Barrow (Long
Barrow)★ SP3 . . . . .188 B1
White Beam Ct SN2 . . .35 B2
Whitebridge Rd SP1 . .146 D1
White Castle SN5 . . . . .49 C3
White Cliff★ BA13 . . . .186 B6
Whitecroft BA13 . . . . .112 C8
White Eagle Rd SN25 . 34 D5
White Edge Moor
SN3 . . . . . . . . . . . . . .51 D2
White Ennox La SN13 . .83 F7
White Farm La SN8 . . .185 C7
Whitefield Cl BA1 . . . . .82 B4
Whitefield Cres SN4 . . .34 A1
Whitefriars La SN6 . . . . .6 E3
Whitefriars Rd **1**
SP1 . . . . . . . . . . . . .152 B7
Whitegates SN14 . . . . .68 A8
White Hart La **12**
SP7 . . . . . . . . . . . . .202 C1
Whiteheads La SN16 . .100 D7
Whitehead St SN1 . . . . .50 B5
Whitehill
Bradford-on-Avon
BA15 . . . . . . . . . . . .100 D7
Hindon SP3 . . . . . . . .200 B3
WHITE HILL . . . . . . . .139 C2
White Hill
Bishopstone SN4 . . . . .163 D5
Farley SP5 . . . . . . . . .154 D8
Pitton SP5 . . . . . . . . .148 C2
Pitton & Farley SP5 . . .148 C3
Whitehill Cl **11** SN8. . .170 B2
Whitehill Ind Pk SN4. . .47 B1
Whitehill La SN4 . . . . . .47 B2
Whitehill Way SN5 . . . .48 F3
Whitehorn Cl SN4 . . . . .47 E4
Whitehorn Dr SP5 . . . .212 C5
White Horse Bsns Pk
BA14 . . . . . . . . . . . .105 D4
White Horse Cl BA14 . .105 E6
Whitehorse Dr SN9 . . .215 B4
White Horse Dr **8**
BA11 . . . . . . . . . . . .110 C6
White Horse Rd
Cricklade SN6 . . . . . . .19 D8
Forest Hill SN8 . . . . . .175 A7
Winsley BA15 . . . . . . . .99 E7
Wroughton SN4 . . . . . .167 F8
White Horse Sports Ctr
SN11 . . . . . . . . . . . . .81 C1
White Horse Way
Calne SN11 . . . . . . . . .81 B1
Devizes SN10 . . . . . . .214 C5
Devizes SN10 . . . . . . .214 D6
Westbury BA13 . . . . . .109 A4
Whitehouse La GL8 . . . .26 D8
Whitehouse Rd SN2 . . .50 A8
White La SN8 . . . . . . . .184 B1
Whiteland Rise BA13 . .109 B2
Whitelands Rd SN3 . . . .36 A1
Whitelawn La BA14 . . .106 F4
White Lion Pk SN16 . . .27 C4
Whitelocks Piece
RG17 . . . . . . . . . . . .171 A1
Whiteman St SN2. . . . . .50 C6
Whitemarsh BA12 . . . .139 B4
WHITEPARISH . . . . . . .161 D4

Whiteparish All Saints CE
Prim Sch SP5 . . . . . .161 D3
White Pit La SP7 . . . . .206 B6
WHITEPITS . . . . . . . . .126 A7
White Rd
Mere BA12 . . . . . . . . .139 B6
Savernake SN8 . . . . . .175 A6
White Row Hill BA14 . .105 A5
Whiterow Rd BA14 . . . .105 A6
Whitesbury Rd SP5 . . .152 B1
Whites Cnr SN12 . . . . .85 D1
White Sheet Castle★
BA12 . . . . . . . . . . . .124 E1
Whitesheet CE(VA) Prim
Acad BA12 . . . . . . . .138 C4
Whitesheet CE (VA) Prim
Sch BA12 . . . . . . . . .123 B8
White Sheet Hill Nature
Reserve★ BA12 . . . . .124 E2
White Sheet La BA12 . 124 C3
White's Hill SN8 . . . . . .169 F2
Whitesheet SP5 . . . . . .211 D6
Whitesheet Hill SP5 . . .211 D6
White Shute RG17 . . . .171 A8
White St
Easterton SN10 . . . . . .180 A1
Horningsham BA12 . . .119 B8
**21** Market Lavington
SN10 . . . . . . . . . . . .179 F1
Whitestone Rd BA11 . .110 B6
Whites Way SN15 . . . . .57 C2
Whiteway SP5 . . . . . . .147 F6
White Way
Broad Town SN4 . . . . .167 A8
Pitton SP5 . . . . . . . . .148 B4
Pitton & Farley SP5 . . .148 C3
Whitgift Cl SN5 . . . . . . .48 F5
WHITLEY . . . . . . . . . . .85 C1
Whitley Rd **14** SN8 . . .170 A6
Whitlock Rise SP5 . . . .205 F5
Whitmarsh Cl **7** SP4 190 A4
Whitmore Cl SN5 . . . . .48 F6
Whitney St SN1 . . . . . . .50 C5
WHITSBURY . . . . . . . .210 B5
Whitsbury Rd
Fordingbridge SP6 . . .210 D2
Odstock SP5 . . . . . . . .158 A7
Whittingham Dr SN4. . . .64 E3
Whittington Rd SN5 . . .49 C6
Whittle Ave SN11 . . . .166 A1
Whittle Cl SN14 . . . . . .78 A7
Whittle Rd
**4** Andover SP10 . . . .193 B1
Salisbury SP2 . . . . . . .145 D1
Whittle Ride SN8 . . . . .184 B1
Whittocks La BA12 . . .116 C5
WHITTONDITCH . . . . .170 D3
Whittonditch Rd SN8 . .170 E3
Whitworth Rd SN25 . . . .35 A3
Wichelstone Cl SN1. . . .50 C3
Wichel Way
Swindon SN1 . . . . . . . .49 B2
Swindon SN1 . . . . . . . .49 E2
WICK . . . . . . . . . . . . .210 F8
Wick Ball Camp★
SP3 . . . . . . . . . . . . .201 D3
Wickdown Ave SN25. . . .34 F3
Wicker Hill **2** BA14. . .105 C8
Wickfield SN10 . . . . . .214 B2
Wickhill SN11 . . . . . . . .80 C8
Wick Hill SN15. . . . . . . .72 B1
Wick La
Devizes SN10 . . . . . . .214 B1
Downton SP5 . . . . . . .210 E8
Lacock SN15 . . . . . . . .85 F4
Manningford SN9. . . . .181 F5
Wanborough SN4. . . . . .51 F6
Wick Rd
Oaksey GL7 . . . . . . . . .4 B3
Oaksey SN16 . . . . . . . . .5 A1
Oaksey SN16 . . . . . . . .16 A8
Wicks Cl SN15 . . . . . . .34 E5
Wicks Dr SN15 . . . . . . .78 F5
Wickwater La GL7 . . . . .7 C4
WIDBROOK . . . . . . . .100 E4
Widbrook Meadow
BA14 . . . . . . . . . . . .105 A8
Widbrook View BA15 100 E5
Widdenham SN14 . . . . .75 D2
WIDHAM . . . . . . . . . . .33 C5
Widham SN5 . . . . . . . . .33 C6
Widhill La SN26. . . . . . .21 A1
Wigmore Ave SN3 . . . . .50 F3
WILCOT . . . . . . . . . . .182 A7
Wilcot Ave SN2 . . . . . . .35 D5
Wilcot Cl
Amesbury SP4 . . . . . .217 D2
Trowbridge BA14 . . . .105 C6
Wilcot Rd
Pewsey SN9 . . . . . . . .215 B5
Pewsey SN9 . . . . . . . .215 C5
Wilcox Cl SN2 . . . . . . . .35 C2
Wild Acre **9** SN4 . . . .163 A6
Wild Cross
Little Chalfield BA15 . . .92 B6
South Wraxall SN12. . . .91 F6
Wilderness The
BA15 . . . . . . . . . . . .100 C7
Wildern Sq SN3 . . . . . .36 A4
WILDHERN . . . . . . . . .193 D5
Wildmoorway La GL7 . . .7 B7
Wiley Terr SP2 . . . . . . .144 D4
Wilkins Cl SN2. . . . . . . .35 F5
Wilkinson Cl SN12 . . . .94 C5
WILLESLEY . . . . . . . . .25 C6

**Willesley Dr** GL8 . . . . . . **25** B7
**William Cl** SP1 . . . . . . **146** D1
**William Morris Prim Sch**
SN26 . . . . . . . . . . . . . . . . **20** E2
**William Morris Way**
Swindon SN25 . . . . . . **34** D8
Swindon SN26 . . . . . . **20** D2
**William Rd** SN10 . . . . . **214** D2
**William Robbins Ct**
SN25 . . . . . . . . . . . . . . . . **34** F3
**Williams Cl** 6 SN12 . . **94** B4
**Williams Gr** SN13 . . . . **85** A8
**Williamson Cl** 3
SP11 . . . . . . . . . . . . . . **192** A5
**William St**
Calne SN11 . . . . . . . . . **81** C4
Swindon SN1 . . . . . . . . **50** A5
**William Stumpes Cl** 7
SN16 . . . . . . . . . . . . . . . **28** A5
**Willington Rd** SN25 . . . **34** E7
**Willis Cl**
5 Chippenham SN15 . . **78** F4
Great Bedwyn SN8 . . . **176** C3
**Willis Way** SN5 . . . . . . . **33** B3
**Willoughby Cl** BA13 . . **108** E2
**Willoughby Rd** SP4 . . **197** E6
**Willow Ave** 5 SP6 . . **210** D1
**Willowbank** SN4 . . . . . **70** A2
**Willowbrook** SN5 . . . . . **33** C4
**Willowbrook End**
SN15 . . . . . . . . . . . . . . . . **57** D2
**Willow Cl**
Laverstock SP1 . . . . . **146** D2
Melksham SN12 . . . . . . **94** A3
**Willow Cres**
Broughton Gifford
SN12 . . . . . . . . . . . . . . **93** A5
Warminster BA12 . . . . **117** C5
**Willow Dr**
Devizes SN10 . . . . . . **214** E5
4 Durrington SP4 . . . **198** B7
**Willow Gr**
Chippenham SN15 . . . . **70** E2
South Cerney SN5 . . . . . . **7** A6
Trowbridge BA14 . . . . **105** B5
Westbury BA13 . . . . . **108** E3
**Willow Gro** 9 SN6 . . . . **19** D8
**Willowherb Cl** SN25 . . . **34** E5
**Willowmead Cl** SP5 . . **150** F2
**Willows Ave** SN2 . . . . . **35** C3
**Willows The**
Calne SN11 . . . . . . . . . **89** E8
Highworth SN6 . . . . . . . **23** A5
Swindon SN5 . . . . . . . . **34** A2
**Willow View** BA14 . . . **105** C3
**Willow View Cl** SN16 . . **27** F4
**Willow Way** SP7 . . . . . **202** A4
**Willow Wlk** SN4 . . . . . . **64** B6
**Wills Ave** SN1 . . . . . . . **50** E8
**Wilman Way** SP2 . . . . **151** F5
**Wilmot Cl** SN5 . . . . . . . **48** F6
**WILSFORD**
Wilsford . . . . . . . . . . . **181** B4
Wilsford cum Lake . . . **197** F2
**Wilsford Group**
(Tumuli) ★
SP4 . . . . . . . . . . . . . . **197** D2
**Wilsford Rd** SN9 . . . . . **181** C5
**Wilson Rd**
Larkhill SP4 . . . . . . . . **197** E6
Swindon SN25 . . . . . . . **34** F6
**Wilson Sq** BA12 . . . . . **117** C7
**WILTON**
Grafton . . . . . . . . . . . . **184** A8
Wilton . . . . . . . . . . . . . **144** C2
**Wilton and Barford CE**
**Prim Sch** SP2 . . . . . **144** B2
**Wilton Carpet Factory** ★
SP2 . . . . . . . . . . . . . . **144** D4
**Wilton Dr** BA14 . . . . . **105** D6
**Wilton Ho** ★ SP2 . . . . **144** D2
**Wilton Pk** ★ SP2 . . . . **144** D1
**Wilton Rd**
Barford St Martin
SP3 . . . . . . . . . . . . . . **143** C3
East Grafton SN8 . . . . **184** A7
Quidhampton SP2 . . . **144** F3
Wylye BA12 . . . . . . . . **201** F8
**Wilton Windmill** ★
SN8 . . . . . . . . . . . . . . **184** B8
**Wilton Wlk** SN6 . . . . . . **35** C6
**Wiltshire Ave** SN2 . . . . **50** A8
**Wiltshire Cl**
Bulford SP4 . . . . . . . . **217** D4
3 Hungerford RG17 . . **177** B7
**Wiltshire Coll**
Chippenham SN15 . . . . **78** E1
Chippenham SN15 . . . . **78** E8
Devizes SN10 . . . . . . **214** B3
Trowbridge BA14 . . . . **105** C8
Westbury BA13 . . . . . **109** A3
**Wiltshire Coll & Univ Ctr**
BA14 . . . . . . . . . . . . . **105** B6
**Wiltshire Cres**
Melksham SN12 . . . . . . **94** C3
Royal Wootton Bassett
SN4 . . . . . . . . . . . . . . . **61** A7
**Wiltshire Dr** BA14 . . . **105** D5
**Wiltshire Gall The** ★
SP1 . . . . . . . . . . . . . . **145** F1
**Wiltshire Heritage Mus** ★
SN10 . . . . . . . . . . . . . **214** A3
**Wiltshire Music Ctr**
BA15 . . . . . . . . . . . . . **100** B8

**Wiltshire Path** SN14 . . . **24** C2
**Wiltshire Rd** SP2 . . . . **151** E6
**Wiltshire Way** BA13 . . **109** A4
**Wimpole Cl** SN3 . . . . . . **51** B4
**Winchcombe Ave**
SN10 . . . . . . . . . . . . . . . **97** D1
**Winchcombe Cl** SN5 . . . **48** F7
**Winchcombe Gdns** GL7 . **6** F6
**Winchester Cl**
Amesbury SP4 . . . . . . **217** D2
2 Chippenham SN14 . . **78** A6
North Bradley BA14 . . **105** C2
Swindon SN3 . . . . . . . . **36** B1
**Winchester St** SP1 . . . **146** B1
**Wincombe Bsns Pk**
SP7 . . . . . . . . . . . . . . **202** C3
**Wincombe La** SP7 . . . **202** D2
**Wincombe Pk** ★ SP7 . . **202** D3
**Windbrook Meadow**
SN2 . . . . . . . . . . . . . . . . **36** A4
**Windermere** SN3 . . . . . **51** D3
**Windermere Rd**
BA14 . . . . . . . . . . . . . **101** E6
**Windflower Rd** SN25 . . **34** E5
**Winding Way** SP2 . . . . **145** B3
**Windlass Way** SN15 . . . **78** E5
**Windlesham Rd** SP1 . . **146** B4
**Windmill Cl**
1 Aldbourne SN8 . . . . **170** A7
Alderbury SP5 . . . . . . **153** E2
4 Shaftesbury SP7 . . **202** C2
**Windmill Dr** SP9 . . . . . **216** D8
**Windmill Hill Bsns Pk**
SN5 . . . . . . . . . . . . . . . . **48** F3
**Windmill Hill**
(Causewayed
Enclosure) ★
SN4 . . . . . . . . . . . . . . **167** A2
**Windmill La**
Hurstbourne Tarrant
SP11 . . . . . . . . . . . . . **193** F8
Kemble GL7 . . . . . . . . . . **4** F8
Winterbourne SP4 . . . **133** B4
**Windmill Piece** SN4 . . . **65** D4
**Windmill Rd**
Kemble GL7 . . . . . . . . . . **4** F8
Royal Wootton Bassett
SN4 . . . . . . . . . . . . . . . **47** F1
**WINDMILLS** . . . . . . . . **193** F7
**Windmill Tump (Long
Barrow)** ★ GL7 . . . . . **3** A7
**Windrush** SN16 . . . . . . . **22** E5
**Windrush Rd** SN25 . . . . **35** A3
**Windsor Ave** SN12 . . . . **94** B3
**Windsor Cl**
Chippenham SN14 . . . . **78** A6
Lydiard Tregoze SN4 . . . **47** F6
**Windsor Cres** BA11 . . **110** A5
**Windsor Dr**
Devizes SN10 . . . . . . **214** D3
1 Trowbridge BA14 . . **105** B5
Westbury BA13 . . . . . **109** B4
**Windsor Mews** 8
SP4 . . . . . . . . . . . . . . **198** B7
**Windsor Rd**
Calne Without SN11 . . . **81** F1
9 Durrington/Bulford
SP4 . . . . . . . . . . . . . . **198** B7
North Bradley BA14 . . **105** E4
9 Salisbury SP2 . . . . **145** F1
Swindon SN3 . . . . . . . . **50** F2
**Windsor St** 10 SP2 . . . **145** F1
**Windwhistle Cnr**
SP7 . . . . . . . . . . . . . . **202** E2
**Windwhistle La**
Alderbury SP5 . . . . . . **160** B7
Grimstead SP5 . . . . . . **154** B1
**Windwhistle Way**
SP5 . . . . . . . . . . . . . . **153** F2
**Windyridge** BA15 . . . . . **99** F3
**Wine St**
Bradford-on-Avon
BA15 . . . . . . . . . . . . . **100** C6
Devizes SN10 . . . . . . **214** B3
**Wingate Par** SN2 . . . . . **35** A2
**WINGFIELD** . . . . . . . . **104** C6
**Wingfield** SN2 . . . . . . . . **36** A5
**Wingfield Ave** SN2 . . . . **35** C6
**Wingfield Rd** BA14 . . . **105** A7
**Win Gn View** 7 SP7 . . **202** B2
**Wing Rd** SP4 . . . . . . . . **198** E6
**Winifred St** SN1 . . . . . . **50** D3
**Winkelbury Hill (Hill
Fort)** ★ SP7 . . . . . . . **207** C8
**Winkins La** SN15 . . . . . . **44** A2
**Winkworth Cottage**
SN16 . . . . . . . . . . . . . . . **29** C2
**Winlaw Cl** SN5 . . . . . . . **49** C7
**Winnipeg Rd** 1 SP4 . **217** F8
**Winscombe Ct** BA11 . . **110** B5
**WINSLEY** . . . . . . . . . . . . **99** E7
**Winsley Bypass** BA15 . . **99** E7
**Winsley CE VC Prim Sch**
BA15 . . . . . . . . . . . . . . **99** E7
**Winsley Cl** SN2 . . . . . . . **35** C4
**Winsley Hill** BA2 . . . . . . **99** B6
**Winsley Rd** BA15 . . . . **100** B7
**Winstanley Cl** 8 SN5 . **49** A4
**Winston Rd** SN12 . . . . . **93** F1
**WINTERBOURNE
BASSETT** . . . . . . . . **167** B5
**WINTERBOURNE
DAUNTSEY** . . . . . . **133** B2
**WINTERBOURNE
EARLS** . . . . . . . . . . **133** A1
**Winterbourne Earls CE
Prim Sch** SP4 . . . . **133** A1

**WINTERBOURNE
GUNNER** . . . . . . . . **133** D3
**WINTERBOURNE
MONKTON** . . . . . . . **167** B3
**Winterbourne Rd** 9
SN25 . . . . . . . . . . . . . . . **34** D5
**WINTERBOURNE
STOKE** . . . . . . . . . . **196** F4
**Winterbourne Stoke
Group (Tumuli)** ★
SP4 . . . . . . . . . . . . . . **197** C4
**Winter Gn** SN10 . . . . . . **80** F3
**Winter's Dro** SN9 . . . . . **215** E2
**Winterslow CE (Aided)
Prim Sch** SP5 . . . . . **149** B6
**Winterslow Rd**
Idmiston SP4 . . . . . . **198** C1
Porton SP4 . . . . . . . . **133** D6
Swindon SN2 . . . . . . . . **35** B5
2 Trowbridge BA14 . . **105** B5
**Winton Cl** SP9 . . . . . . . **216** D4
**Winton Rd** SN3 . . . . . . . **36** B4
**Winwick Rd** SN5 . . . . . . **49** B4
**Wirral Way** SN25 . . . . . **34** F7
**Wirr The** SP3 . . . . . . . . **128** D7
**Wise Cl** SN2 . . . . . . . . . **35** E3
**Wise La** SP3 . . . . . . . . **141** A2
**Wiseman Cl** 2 SN3 . . . . **51** E6
**Wishart Way** SN15 . . . . **78** F5
**Wishford Rd**
Great Wishford SP2 . . **130** A1
Middle Wishford SP4 . **130** A6
Wilton SP2 . . . . . . . . **144** B5
Woodford SP4 . . . . . . **131** A5
**Witan Cl** 8 SP10 . . . . . **193** E2
**Witchcombe Cl** 1
SN10 . . . . . . . . . . . . . **187** B8
**Witchcombe La** SN10 **179** B1
**Witchell La** SN10 . . . . **180** B3
**Witfield Cl** SN5 . . . . . . . **33** B5
**Witham Way** SN2 . . . . . **35** F4
**Withering Rd** SN1 . . . . . **50** A3
**Witherington Rd**
Alderbury SP5 . . . . . . **153** C2
Downton SP5 . . . . . . **159** C5
**Witherington Ring (Field
System)** ★ SP5 . . . . **159** D7
**Witheys The** 10 SN4 . . **163** A6
**Withies The** SN8 . . . . . **175** D1
**Withy Bed**
Bushton SN4 . . . . . . . **166** E8
Clyffe Pypard SN4 . . . . **61** C1
**Withybed La** RG17 . . . **177** F5
**Withy Cl**
Royal Wootton Bassett
SN4 . . . . . . . . . . . . . . . **47** D3
Trowbridge BA14 . . . . **105** A8
**Withymead Rd** SN14 . . . **74** A8
**Wittenham View** 7
SP4 . . . . . . . . . . . . . . **217** C2
**Wittensford La** SO51 . **212** F1
**Witt Rd** SP5 . . . . . . . . **149** D5
**Witts La** SN5 . . . . . . . . . **33** B5
**Wivenhoe Ct** 7
BA11 . . . . . . . . . . . . . **110** C6
**Wizard Education** SN1 . **50** C5
**Woburn Cl**
Swindon SN5 . . . . . . . . **34** F6
Trowbridge BA14 . . . . **105** A8
**Wolferstan Dr** SP1 . . . **146** D5
**Wolfhall Rd** SN8 . . . . . **183** D8
**Wolsely Ave** SN3 . . . . . **51** A4
**WOLVERTON** . . . . . . . **138** B4
**Wolverton Cl** SN14 . . . . **77** F6
**WOODBOROUGH** . . . . **181** D6
**Woodborough CE Aided
Prim Sch** SN9 . . . . . **181** C6
**Woodborough Cl**
BA14 . . . . . . . . . . . . . **105** D5
**Woodborough Rd**
Beechingstoke SN9 . . **181** B6
Corsham SN13 . . . . . . . **85** B7
Pewsey SN9 . . . . . . . . **215** A5
**Woodbridge Rd**
BA13 . . . . . . . . . . . . . **186** B8
**Woodbury** RG17 . . . . . **165** B1
**Woodbury Cl** 2 SN5 . . . **49** A8
**Woodbury Gdns** SP2 . . **152** A5
**Woodbury La** SP2 . . . . **152** B5
**Woodbury Rise** SP2 . . **152** B5
**Woodbury Yd** 5 SP2 . **152** B5
**Woodchester** SN5 . . . . . **49** C5
**WOODCOCK** . . . . . . . . **117** C6
**Woodcock Cl** SP9 . . . . **216** D6
**Woodcock Gdns**
BA12 . . . . . . . . . . . . . **117** C6
**Woodcock Ind Est**
BA12 . . . . . . . . . . . . . **117** D7
**Woodcock La** BA12 . . **117** B7
**Woodcock Pk**
Warminster BA12 . . . . **117** C6
Warminster BA12 . . . . **117** C7
**Woodcock Rd** BA12 . . **117** C6
**Woodcock Ride** GL8 . . . **25** B7
**Woodcombe** SN12 . . . . . **94** C6
**Woodcote Rd** SN8 . . . . **185** B8
**Woodcutters Mews**
SN25 . . . . . . . . . . . . . . . **35** C6
**WOODCUTTS** . . . . . . . **207** D4
**WOODFALLS** . . . . . . . **211** D7
**Woodfern** SP6 . . . . . . . **210** F1
**Woodfolds** SN16 . . . . . . **15** F7
**Woodford Cl**
Devizes SN10 . . . . . . **214** C1
3 Swindon SN2 . . . . . **35** C6
**Woodford Valley CE
Primary Acad** SP4 . **131** C5

**WOODGREEN** . . . . . . **211** A4
**Wood Hall Dr** SN2 . . . . **34** D3
**+ + Woodhayes Rd** BA11 **110**
C6
**Woodhenge** ★ SP4 . . . **217** A7
**Woodhill Ave** SN11 . . . . **81** C3
**Woodhill Pk** ★ SN4 . . **166** E7
**Woodhill Rise** SN11 . . . **81** C4
**Woodhill Village** ★
SN4 . . . . . . . . . . . . . . **166** D8
**WOODHOUSE** . . . . . . **193** F3
**Woodhouse Castle (rems
of)** ★ BA12 . . . . . . . **114** E1
**Woodhouse Gdns**
BA14 . . . . . . . . . . . . . **102** B2
**Woodhouse La** DT11 . **206** F1
**Woodhouse Rd** 3
SN3 . . . . . . . . . . . . . . . **50** F5
**Wood La**
Brinkworth SN15 . . . . . **46** D7
Chapmanslade BA13 . **111** D4
Chippenham SN15 . . . **111** A7
Fonthill Gifford SP3 . . **200** C2
Lydiard Millicent SN5 . . **32** A1
Nettleton SN14 . . . . . . . **67** B8
Purton SN5 . . . . . . . . . **31** E1
Sherston GL8 . . . . . . . . **25** B5
**Woodland Cl** SN3 . . . . . **36** A6
**Woodland Dr** SP5 . . . . **149** B6
**Woodland Heritage Ctr
The** ★ BA13 . . . . . . . **107** F5
**Woodland Ind Est**
BA13 . . . . . . . . . . . . . **108** F2
**Woodland Pk** SN11 . . . . **81** B2
**Woodland Rd**
Patney SN10 . . . . . . . **180** F5
2 Warminster BA12 . . **116** E6
**Woodlands** SN13 . . . . . . **76** C2
**Woodlands Cl** SN15 . . . . **58** A3
**Woodlands Dr** BA2 . . . . **99** B6
**Woodlands Edge**
BA14 . . . . . . . . . . . . . **105** F7
**Woodlands La** SP5 . . . **203** E1
**Woodlands Manor** ★
BA12 . . . . . . . . . . . . . **139** A3
**Woodlands Prim Sch**
SP2 . . . . . . . . . . . . . . **145** B4
**Woodlands Rd**
Chippenham SN14 . . . . **78** C8
Gillingham SP8 . . . . . . **138** F1
Mere BA12 . . . . . . . . **139** B2
Mildenhall SN8 . . . . . . **169** A1
Pewsey SN9 . . . . . . . . **215** A4
**Woodlands Rd Ind Est**
BA12 . . . . . . . . . . . . . **139** B4
**WOODLANDS ST
MARY** . . . . . . . . . . . **171** B6
**Woodlands The**
BA12 . . . . . . . . . . . . . **113** A1
**Woodland View**
Calne SN11 . . . . . . . . . **81** B1
South Newton SP2 . . . **130** B2
Westbury BA13 . . . . . **112** B8
Wroughton SN4 . . . . . . **50** B1
**Woodland Way**
Devizes SN10 . . . . . . **214** A1
Salisbury SP1 . . . . . . **146** E2
Stonebridge BA11 . . . **110** D7
**Woodlea** SN14 . . . . . . . . **75** C6
**Woodlea Grange**
SP5 . . . . . . . . . . . . . . **153** E2
**Wood Leaze** SN10 . . . . **214** F6
**Woodley La** SP5 . . . . . **206** E5
**Woodling Cres** SP6 . . **210** F1
**Woodman Mead** 5
BA12 . . . . . . . . . . . . . **116** F7
**Woodmarsh** BA14 . . . . **105** D4
**WOODMINTON** . . . . . **204** E1
**Woodpecker Cl** SN12 . . **93** C4
**Woodpecker Dr**
BA14 . . . . . . . . . . . . . **105** E6
**Woodpecker Mews**
SN14 . . . . . . . . . . . . . . . **70** B2
**Wood Rd** SP4 . . . . . . . **198** A6
**Woodroffe Sq** SN11 . . **81** C2
**Woodrow**
Durnford SP4 . . . . . . **132** C8
Great Durnford SP4 . . **197** F1
Melksham Without
SN12 . . . . . . . . . . . . . . **94** D7
**Woodrow Rd** SN12 . . . . **94** C6
**Woodsage Way** SN11 . . **80** F3
**Woods Cl** SN16 . . . . . . . **25** C1
**WOODSEND** . . . . . . . . **169** C7
**WOODSHAW** . . . . . . . . . **48** A2
**Woodshaw Mead** 8
SN4 . . . . . . . . . . . . . . . **48** A2
**Woods Hill** BA2 . . . . . . . **99** A6
**Woodside Ave** SN3 . . . . **50** B5
**Woodside Bottom Rd**
SP5 . . . . . . . . . . . . . . **212** C4
**Woodside Rd**
Salisbury SP2 . . . . . . **145** C3
South Marston Park SN3 **36** C7
**Woodsman Rd** SN25 . . . **35** B6
**Woods's La** SP3 . . . . . **200** F2
**Wood St**
Calne SN11 . . . . . . . . . **81** B4
Clyffe Pypard SN4 . . . . **61** D1
Royal Wootton Bassett
SN4 . . . . . . . . . . . . . . . **47** D2
Swindon SN1 . . . . . . . . **50** D4
**Woodstock Ct** SN8 . . . **213** F2
**Woodstock Gdns**
SN12 . . . . . . . . . . . . . . **94** B3

**Woodstock Rd** SP1 . . **146** B2
**Woodvill Rd** SP1 . . . . . **146** D4
**Woodward's Way**
SP5 . . . . . . . . . . . . . . **207** A2
**Woodway Cotts** GL9 . . . **24** E5
**WOODYATES** . . . . . . . **208** D6
**Woolands La** 1 SP7 . . **202** B2
**Woolcott La** SP8 . . . . . **137** D1
**Wooley Dr** BA15 . . . . . **100** E7
**Woolford Grange** 2
SN4 . . . . . . . . . . . . . . . **48** A2
**Wool House Gdns**
BA12 . . . . . . . . . . . . . **195** A2
**Woollaton Cl** SN5 . . . . . **49** A5
**WOOLLEY** . . . . . . . . . . **100** E7
**Woolley Cl** BA15 . . . . . **100** E7
**Woolley Dr** BA15 . . . . . **100** E7
**Woolley GREEN** . . . . . **100** F8
**Woolley Orch** BA15 . . . **100** E7
**Woolley Pk** BA15 . . . . . **101** A7
**Woolley St** BA15 . . . . . **100** E7
**Woolley Terr** BA15 . . . . **100** E7
**Woolmer Dro** SN8 . . . . **168** F6
**Woolner Rd**
Swindon SN25 . . . . . . . **20** C1
Swindon SN25 . . . . . . . **34** C8
**Woolpack Meadows**
BA14 . . . . . . . . . . . . . **105** E7
**WOOLSINGTON** . . . . . . **49** E5
**Wootton Bassett Rd**
SN5 . . . . . . . . . . . . . . . **49** E5
**WOOTTON RIVERS** . . **174** E2
**Wor Barrow (Long
Barrow)** ★ SP5 . . . . **208** C4
**Worcester Lodge** ★
GL9 . . . . . . . . . . . . . . . **24** A3
**Wordsworth Cl** 1 SN4 **47** F3
**Wordsworth Dr** SN2 . . . **35** F4
**Wordsworth Rd** SP1 . . **146** B2
**Workway Dro** SN8 . . . . **173** E2
**Worlidge Dr** SN5 . . . . . . **49** B8
**Wormcliff La** SN13 . . . . **83** A4
**Wormwell La** BA16 . . . . **26** C8
**Wormwood** SN13 . . . . . **84** B3
**Worsley Rd** SN5 . . . . . . **49** A4
**Worsted Cl** BA14 . . . . . **105** E7
**Wortheys Cl** SN16 . . . . . **28** A5
**Worthies La** SN16 . . . . . **28** A4
**Worthington Cl** 2
SN3 . . . . . . . . . . . . . . . **51** B7
**WORTON** . . . . . . . . . . . **179** B4
**Worton & Marston Prim
Sch** SN10 . . . . . . . . **179** B4
**Worton Rd** SN10 . . . . . **179** C4
**Wouldham Cl** SP11 . . . **191** F4
**Wrag View** SN6 . . . . . . . **23** A4
**Wren Cl**
Frome BA11 . . . . . . . . **110** B7
3 Warminster BA12 . . **116** E5
**Wren Ct**
Calne SN11 . . . . . . . . . **89** E8
Trowbridge BA14 . . . . **105** B6
**Wrenscroft** 8 SP2 . . . **152** A5
**Wrenswood** SN3 . . . . . . **51** D8
**Wright Cl** 9 SN25 . . . . . **35** A8
**Wright's La** RG17 . . . . **185** E8
**WROUGHTON** . . . . . . . . **64** A5
**Wroughton Airfield**
SN4 . . . . . . . . . . . . . . . **63** B7
**Wroughton Inf Sch**
SN4 . . . . . . . . . . . . . . . **64** A6
**Wroughton Jun Sch**
SN4 . . . . . . . . . . . . . . . **64** A7
**Wroughton Science
Museum** ★ SN3 . . . . **64** B1
**Wych Elm Rd** BA11 . . **110** C6
**Wych Gn** SO51 . . . . . . **212** D3
**Wychurch Rd** 4 SN16 . **28** A5
**Wyck Village** ★ SP3 . . **203** E7
**Wycombe Cl** SN11 . . . . . **79** F2
**Wycombe La** SN10 . . . **172** F1
**Wyke Rd** BA14 . . . . . . . **101** E4
**Wyld Ct** SN25 . . . . . . . . **34** E8
**Wyle Down National
Nature Reserve** ★
BA12 . . . . . . . . . . . . . **201** E7
**WYLYE** . . . . . . . . . . . . **201** F8
**Wylye Cl**
Quidhampton SP2 . . . **144** F2
Swindon SN25 . . . . . . . **34** F4
Warminster BA12 . . . . **116** F5
**Wylye Rd**
Steeple Langford SP3 . **128** B2
Tidworth SP9 . . . . . . . **216** D7
Warminster BA12 . . . . **117** A5
Wylye BA12 . . . . . . . . **201** F8
**Wylye Valley CE VA Prim
Sch** BA12 . . . . . . . . **195** B3
**Wymans Field** SN8 . . . **173** F6
**Wyncies The** 2 SN6 . . **163** E6
**Wyndham Cl** SN15 . . . . **79** A8
**Wyndham La** SP4 . . . . **199** A2
**Wyndham Pk** SP1 . . . . **146** B2
**Wyndham Pk Inf Sch**
SP1 . . . . . . . . . . . . . . **146** B3
**Wyndham Rd**
Salisbury SP1 . . . . . . **146** A2
Swindon SN2 . . . . . . . . **50** A7
**Wyndhams Pl** SP3 . . . **200** E1
**Wyndham Terr** SP1 . . **146** B2
**Wynd The** SN11 . . . . . . . **81** B4
**Wynford Rd** BA11 . . . . **110** B6
**Wynndale Cl** SN3 . . . . . **36** A4
**Wynsome St** BA14 . . . **104** F3
**Wynwards Rd** SN25 . . . **35** A5
**Wythburn Rd** BA11 . . . **110** C5

**Wyvern Cl** SN1 . . . . . . . **50** C2
**Wyvern Coll** SP1 . . . . . **146** E3
**Wyvern Rd**
Bowerhill SN12 . . . . . . **94** D1
Bulford SP4 . . . . . . . . **198** E6
**Wyvern Theatre & Arts
Ctr** ★ SN1 . . . . . . . . . **50** C6
**Wyvern Wlk** BA13 . . . . **108** E3
**Wyville Rd** BA11 . . . . . **110** C6

**Y**

**Yard Ct** BA12 . . . . . . . **117** B6
**Yard La** SN15 . . . . . . . . **96** D7
**Yardlee Wlk** 2 SN1 . . . **50** A2
**Yardley Cl** SN2 . . . . . . . **34** F2
**Yard's La** SN9 . . . . . . . **181** C5
**Yarmley La** SP5 . . . . . . **149** B6
**Yarmouth Cl** SN5 . . . . . **49** B4
**YARNBROOK** . . . . . . . . **105** F3
**Yarnbrook Gdns** 4
BA14 . . . . . . . . . . . . . **105** C5
**Yarnbrook Rd**
Steeple Ashton BA14 . **102** E1
West Ashton BA14 . . . **105** F3
**Yarnbrook Road**
BA14 . . . . . . . . . . . . . **106** C7
**Yarnbury Castle (Fort)** ★
BA12 . . . . . . . . . . . . . **196** B3
**Yarnton Cl** SN5 . . . . . . . **49** A8
**Yarrow Cl**
East Anton SP11 . . . . . **193** F2
Swindon SN2 . . . . . . . . **34** C3
**YATESBURY** . . . . . . . . **166** E2
**Yatesbury La**
Winterbourne Bassett
SN11 . . . . . . . . . . . . . **167** A5
Yatesbury SN11 . . . . . **166** E4
**YATTON KEYNELL** . . . . **68** E6
**Yatton Rd** SN14 . . . . . . . **68** E1
**Yeates Field Vw**
BA12 . . . . . . . . . . . . . **117** C6
**Yeatmans Cl** 6 SP7 . . **202** B2
**Yeatmans La** 3 SP7 . . **202** B2
**Yeats Cl** SN25 . . . . . . . . **35** A8
**Yelland Wlk** 4 SN1 . . . . **50** B1
**Yellowhammer Cl** 2
SN3 . . . . . . . . . . . . . . . **51** C8
**Yellow Way Rd** BA11 . . **118** A5
**Yells Way** GL7 . . . . . . . . . **1** F6
**Yeoman Cl**
5 Market Lavington
SN10 . . . . . . . . . . . . . **179** F1
Swindon SN5 . . . . . . . . **49** A7
**Yeoman Way** BA14 . . . **105** C7
**Yeovil Cl** SN3 . . . . . . . . . **51** B5
**Yerbury St** 1 BA14 . . . **105** E8
**Yew Bank Cott Triangle**
BA9 . . . . . . . . . . . . . . . **137** A4
**Yews The** BA12 . . . . . . **139** A6
**Yewstock Cres W**
SN15 . . . . . . . . . . . . . . . **70** C1
**Yewtree Cl** 8 SP4 . . . . **198** C7
**Yew Tree Cl**
Calne SN11 . . . . . . . . . **81** A3
Chirton SN10 . . . . . . . **180** F4
The Common SP5 . . . . **149** B6
**Yew Tree Dr** SN4 . . . . . **167** B8
**Yew Tree Gdns** SN3 . . . **36** E4
**Yew Tree La** SN4 . . . . . **167** C7
**Yew Way** SN13 . . . . . . . **84** E8
**Yiewsley Cres** SN3 . . . . **36** B2
**Yockney Cl** SN13 . . . . . . **76** E1
**Yonder Way** 7 SN4 . . **163** A6
**York Bldgs** BA11 . . . . . **101** D1
**York Cl**
Chippenham SN14 . . . . **78** A6
Corsham SN13 . . . . . . . **76** F7
**York Dro** SP5 . . . . . . . . **212** C4
**York La** SN15 . . . . . . . . . **46** F7
**York Rd**
Calne SN11 . . . . . . . . . **81** D4
7 Hungerford RG17 . . **177** B6
Lyneham SN15 . . . . . . . **60** B2
Salisbury SP2 . . . . . . **145** F1
Stapleford SP3 . . . . . . **197** B1
Swindon SN1 . . . . . . . . **50** D6
Upavon Down SN9 . . . **182** B1
**Youngs Ct** BA13 . . . . . **109** A4
**Youngs Paddock**
SP5 . . . . . . . . . . . . . . **149** C6
**Ypres Rd** SN4 . . . . . . . **168** F3
**Yule Hill** SP3 . . . . . . . . **203** F6

**Z**

**Zakopane Rd** 4 SN25 . **34** D6
**Zander Rd**
Calne SN11 . . . . . . . . . **81** A5
Calne SN11 . . . . . . . . . **81** B5
**ZEALS** . . . . . . . . . . . . . **137** F4
**Zeals Bypass** BA12 . . **138** B5
**Zeals Gn Dr** BA12 . . . . **138** A4
**Zeals Rise** BA12 . . . . . **137** F4
**Zig Zag Hill** SP7 . . . . . **206** D9
**Zion Rd** SP11 . . . . . . . . **199** F3
**Zoar Cl** SN4 . . . . . . . . . . **64** A6
**Zouch Ave** SP9 . . . . . . **216** C7
**Zouch Cl** SP9 . . . . . . . . **216** C7
**Zouch Farm Rd**
North Tidworth SP9 . . **216** C7
Tidworth SP9 . . . . . . . **216** C7
**Zouch Prim Sch** SP9 . **216** B8